I0644572

"There is a long history of Christians wondering if miracles are to continue. These wonderings are complicated by the reality that even most of those who do embrace the continuation of such Spirit-empowered actions do not themselves participate in such miracles and have not witnessed them. Stories of others bolster their sagging belief. In this book we have a full disclosure of the reality that God has continued to work marvelous deeds. Accompanying that history is a dismantling of the arguments for cessationism. This book will be a gold mine for class discussions and pastoral care."

—**Scot McKnight**, Houston Theological Seminary

"Craig Keener continues to amaze. Anyone who can write a four-volume technical commentary on a single book of the Bible (Acts) and have it all worth reading is already astonishing, but Keener carries on a vibrant charismatic spiritual life on top of that. He has already provided the most comprehensive collection of documented contemporary miracles in his two volumes on that topic. Now he and coauthor Daniel Kolenda expand the scope to include numerous examples of prophecy, tongues, and the like, in service of a detailed rebuttal of John MacArthur's *Strange Fire*, all based on careful exegesis of Scripture and a study of Christian history. The charismatic gifts, like all the others, are still with us today, and will be until Christ returns. Keener and Kolenda have surely written the definitive disproof of the view that these gifts were only for Bible times. From this point onward, cessationism really needs to cease!"

—**Craig L. Blomberg**, Denver Seminary (emeritus)

"Craig Keener and Daniel Kolenda's *Spiritual Gifts Are for Today* offers readers a most-welcome and much-needed treatment of a controversial topic. In place of dogmatic and dubious assertions, readers will find carefully thought-out, exegetically defended study of the relevant passages of Scripture that make their case. Recommended reading!"

—**Craig A. Evans**, The Bible Seminary, Katy, Texas

"Quite frequently, when I finish a book, I'm left asking questions that it did not address. This applies not only to books defending the contemporary validity of all spiritual gifts but also to those that affirm what is known as cessationism. I'm happy to say that this book by Keener and Kolenda is as comprehensive as any I've read on the subject. They closely examine every relevant biblical text. They explore and unpack every theological issue that comes up in the debate between continuationists and cessationists. They respond to every question that cessationists are inclined to ask and provide cogent answers to the objections that are often raised. And they do all of this and more in a charitable and Christ-like spirit. In addition, their treatment of the issue in church history is superb, and the many verifiable healings they describe are remarkably effective in building one's faith and stirring us all to pray fervently for the sick. This is now the go-to text on this subject. I've never been inclined to say that a book is so thorough that nothing more can be said on the topic, but I can't imagine anyone adding to the exhaustive contribution that Craig and Daniel provide us in this volume."

—**Sam Storms**, founder, Enjoying God Ministries; founder and executive director, Convergence Church Network

# Spiritual Gifts Are for Today

## A Biblical Case for the Continuing Work of the Spirit

Craig S. Keener
and Daniel Kolenda

Baker Academic
*a division of Baker Publishing Group*
Grand Rapids, Michigan

Published by Baker Academic
a division of Baker Publishing Group
Grand Rapids, Michigan
BakerAcademic.com

Printed in the United States of America



Library of Congress Cataloging-in-Publication Data
Names: Keener, Craig S., 1960– author | Kolenda, Daniel author
Title: Spiritual gifts are for today : a biblical case for the continuing work of the Spirit / Craig S. Keener and Daniel Kolenda.
Description: Grand Rapids, Michigan : Baker Academic, a division of Baker Publishing Group, [2026] | Includes bibliographical references and index.
Identifiers: LCCN 2026013582 | ISBN 9781540970770 cloth | ISBN 9781493456123 ebook | ISBN 9781493456130 pdf
Subjects: LCSH: Gifts, Spiritual | Gifts, Spiritual—Biblical teaching
Classification: LCC BT767.3 .K44 2026
LC record available at https://lccn.loc.gov/2026013582

Unless otherwise indicated, Scripture quotations are the authors' own translation.



Italics in Scripture quotations have been added by the authors for emphasis. Italics in the NASB and LEB have been preserved from the original unless otherwise noted.



Baker Publishing Group publications use paper produced from sustainable forestry practices and postconsumer waste whenever possible.

26 27 28 29 30 31 32 7 6 5 4 3 2 1

To our cessationist friends,
who welcome us charismatics and Pentecostals
as brothers and sisters in Christ despite our differences

# Contents

# Detailed Contents

# Preface

## Teaming Up

This book represents the partnership of a New Testament scholar and a global evangelist. Daniel Kolenda is the appointed successor of Reinhard Bonnke, leading a ministry that over several decades has seen some hundred million professions of faith in Christ. Continuing signs and wonders have often been God's means of bringing attention to the gospel in these settings. Craig Keener has written more than forty books totaling more than twenty thousand pages, with more than a million copies in circulation. Most of his research relates directly to the New Testament and its world, but he has also researched and written extensively on subsequent miracles and the work of the Spirit. Daniel contributed more of the initial material engaging and evaluating popular cessationist arguments, but we both worked on the biblical case for continuationism. At some points it will be clear which of us is writing; at other times, we have gone over the material so many times that it is too intertwined for us to remember ourselves who contributed which words. We hope that our work together offers a helpful model of different members of Christ's body working together (1 Cor. 12:14–27)—in contrast to the approach to which we are responding, one that effectively amputates some gifts from the body.

## How We Each Got Involved

I (Craig) was trying to mind my academic business and ignore popular-level cessationism (the extrabiblical idea that, by God's will, some spiritual gifts are no longer for today). It didn't seem to me that a book like this one should even be needed today. Scripture identifies the final era before Jesus's return, already starting at Pentecost, as the era of the Spirit and prophetic empowerment; it offers no solace to those who want to explain this promise away as if it were supposed to end in antiquity.

Scholars have their own forums for discussing differences (normally) charitably, such as the Counterpoints book *Are Miraculous Gifts for Today?*[1] Moreover, I felt that I already had said everything I needed to say on this subject in *Gift & Giver* (2001; repackaged with a new afterword in 2020). On rereading sections of that book for this one, I have noticed that little has changed in the biblically weak arguments used for popular-level cessationism except that they have now been amplified by social media. Meanwhile, there are enough problems in popular-level charismatic teaching to keep us charismatic (and other) scholars busy trying to protect and teach our own churches.

Finally, however, the abysmal lack of accurate biblical interpretation in the Strange Fire and Cessationism conferences, followed by the equally tendentious *Cessationist* movie,[2] pushed me to respond. John MacArthur and his colleagues undoubtedly make many valuable contributions to the church, but in this case it was a negative contribution that pulled me away from my normal full-time work. As miracles often get people's attention for the gospel, the spectacular antimiracle claims in these anticharismatic circles got my attention by reminding me of cessationism's continuation.

I was backlogged on academic projects, and my response remained on the back burner, during which time Daniel Kolenda began responding to popular cessationism in a series of well-prepared, persuasive YouTube videos.[3] (Of course many other competent YouTubers have appropriately challenged cessationism, from Michael Brown and Sam Storms to John Piper and Mike Winger.) I found Daniel's response thorough and I agreed with most of his points, so I began abandoning the idea of writing a book.

Meanwhile, I joked with Daniel (with whom I was in contact for other reasons) that his excellent teaching had made my book superfluous and saved me a lot of time. But even though he regularly sees miracles on the front line of global evangelism, he saw value in cowriting a book with a scholar who especially studies miracles in Scripture and secondarily has interviewed many contemporary eyewitnesses. Much of the work involved in the following collaboration was trimming out redundancies because our respective notes so often independently advanced the same ideas.

1. Grudem, *Gifts*. For some common ground, see esp. Grudem, "Preface," 18–19.

2. Lanphere, *Cessationist*.

3. See, e.g., the series of videos Kolenda, "Cessationism 1" through "Cessationism 12"; Kolenda, "Cessationist Movie"; Kolenda, "Cessationists Disobeying"; Kolenda, "Embarrassing Story"; Kolenda, "False Prophecies."

# Acknowledgments

Steve Alt edited some of Daniel's material, much of which Daniel presented in a series of YouTube videos. Craig also occasionally draws from his earlier material used in blog posts and, requiring more formal acknowledgment, his *Gift & Giver*, including the 2020 afterword. We necessarily cite a wider range of sources in later chapters where postbiblical history diverges more from our personal expertise. Some of our historical insights in this book reflect the research of our friend, historical theologian Jon Ruthven, whom we surely would have consulted for our historical sections but for his passing in 2022. We also express gratitude to our careful and very patient editor on this volume, James Korsmo, and to our ever-supportive acquisitions editor, Jim Kinney. Thanks also to Blake Jurgens for his great work on the indexes.

We should also mention that we wrote this book (minus edits) before John MacArthur's passing. We respect his emphasis on expository preaching and agree with some of his criticisms of popular charismatic errors, while lamenting his cessationism. We had hoped that our vigorous, biblically based challenges to some of his claims about spiritual gifts might have led to fruitful dialogue in the future. As it is, when we see Christ face-to-face all of us will know fully. Whether in death or when Jesus returns, a day will come for each of us when we won't need partial gifts anyway, and ultimately all of Jesus's true followers will celebrate together before his throne.

# Abbreviations

## General

| | |
|---|---|
| AT | author's translation |
| BCE | before the Common Era |
| ca. | *circa*, about |
| CE | Common Era |
| cf. | *confer*, compare |
| chap(s). | chapter(s) |
| d. | died |
| DSS | Dead Sea Scrolls |
| e.g. | *exempli gratia*, for example |
| esp. | especially |
| i.e. | *id est*, that is |
| n.s. | new series |
| NT | New Testament |
| OT | Old Testament |
| p(p). | page(s) |
| trans. | translator, translated by |
| v(v). | verse(s) |

## Old Testament

| | |
|---|---|
| Gen. | Genesis |
| Exod. | Exodus |
| Lev. | Leviticus |
| Num. | Numbers |
| Deut. | Deuteronomy |
| Josh. | Joshua |
| Judg. | Judges |
| Ruth | Ruth |
| 1–2 Sam. | 1–2 Samuel |
| 1–2 Kings | 1–2 Kings |
| 1–2 Chron. | 1–2 Chronicles |
| Ezra | Ezra |
| Neh. | Nehemiah |
| Esther | Esther |
| Job | Job |
| Ps(s). | Psalm(s) |
| Prov. | Proverbs |
| Eccles. | Ecclesiastes |
| Song | Song of Songs / Song of Solomon |
| Isa. | Isaiah |
| Jer. | Jeremiah |
| Lam. | Lamentations |
| Ezek. | Ezekiel |
| Dan. | Daniel |
| Hosea | Hosea |
| Joel | Joel |
| Amos | Amos |
| Obad. | Obadiah |
| Jon. | Jonah |
| Mic. | Micah |
| Nah. | Nahum |
| Hab. | Habakkuk |
| Zeph. | Zephaniah |
| Hag. | Haggai |
| Zech. | Zechariah |
| Mal. | Malachi |

### New Testament

| | |
|---|---|
| Matt. | Matthew |
| Mark | Mark |
| Luke | Luke |
| John | John |
| Acts | Acts |
| Rom. | Romans |
| 1–2 Cor. | 1–2 Corinthians |
| Gal. | Galatians |
| Eph. | Ephesians |
| Phil. | Philippians |
| Col. | Colossians |
| 1–2 Thess. | 1–2 Thessalonians |
| 1–2 Tim. | 1–2 Timothy |
| Titus | Titus |
| Philem. | Philemon |
| Heb. | Hebrews |
| James | James |
| 1–2 Pet. | 1–2 Peter |
| 1–3 John | 1–3 John |
| Jude | Jude |
| Rev. | Revelation |

### Ancient Texts, Text Types, and Versions

| | |
|---|---|
| LXX | Septuagint |
| MT | Masoretic Text |

### Modern Versions

| | |
|---|---|
| ASV | American Standard Version |
| CSB | Christian Standard Bible |
| ESV | English Standard Version |
| KJV | King James Version |
| LEB | Lexham English Bible |
| NASB | New American Standard Bible |
| NCV | New Century Version |
| NET | New English Translation |
| NIV | New International Version |
| NJB | New Jerusalem Bible |
| NKJV | New King James Version |
| NRSV | New Revised Standard Version |
| WEB | World English Bible |

### Apocrypha and Septuagint

| | |
|---|---|
| 1–2 Esd. | 1–2 Esdras |
| 1–4 Macc. | 1–4 Maccabees |
| Wis. | Wisdom of Solomon |

### Old Testament Pseudepigrapha

| | |
|---|---|
| *2 Bar.* | *2 Baruch* |
| *1 En.* | *1 Enoch (Ethiopic Apocalypse)* |
| *Let. Aris.* | *Letter of Aristeas* |
| *Sib. Or.* | *Sibylline Oracles* |
| *T. Mos.* | *Testament of Moses* |

### Josephus and Philo

#### *Josephus*

| | |
|---|---|
| *Ag. Ap.* | *Against Apion* |
| *Ant.* | *Jewish Antiquities* |
| *War* | *Jewish War* |

#### *Philo*

| | |
|---|---|
| *Conf.* | *On the Confusion of Tongues* |
| *Heir* | *Who Is the Heir?* |
| *Moses* | *On the Life of Moses (1–2)* |

### Mishnah, Talmud, and Related Literature

| | |
|---|---|
| *b.* | Babylonian Talmud |
| *t.* | Tosefta |
| *y.* | Jerusalem Talmud |
| bar. | Baraita |
| *ʿAbod. Zar.* | *ʿAbodah Zarah* |
| *B. Meṣ.* | *Baba Meṣiʿa* |
| *Ber.* | *Berakot* |
| *Hor.* | *Horayot* |
| *Ḥul.* | *Ḥullin* |
| *Moʿed Qat.* | *Moʿed Qatan* |
| *Šabb.* | *Šabbat* |
| *Sanh.* | *Sanhedrin* |
| *Soṭah* | *Soṭah* |
| *Sukkah* | *Sukkah* |
| *Yebam.* | *Yebamot* |
| *Yoma* | *Yoma* (= *Kippurim*) |

### Other Rabbinic Works

| | |
|---|---|
| *Abot R. Nat.* | *Abot de Rabbi Nathan* |
| *Mek.* | *Mekilta* (ed. Jacob Z. Lauterbach) |
| *Pesiq. Rab Kah.* | *Pesiqta de Rab Kahana* |
| *Pesiq. Rab Kah. Sup.* | *Pesiqta de Rab Kahana Supplement* |
| *Rab.* | *Rabbah* (+ biblical book) |

### Apostolic Fathers

| | |
|---|---|
| *Barn.* | *Barnabas* |
| *1–2 Clem.* | *1–2 Clement* |
| *Did.* | *Didache* |
| Ignatius, *Phld.* | *To the Philadelphians* |
| Ignatius, *Smyrn.* | *To the Smyrnaeans* |
| *Mart. Pol.* | *Martyrdom of Polycarp* |

### Ancient Christian Works

#### *Athanasius*

| | |
|---|---|
| *Inc.* | *On the Incarnation* |

#### *Augustine*

| | |
|---|---|
| *Conf.* | *Confessions* |
| *Ennar. Ps.* | *Ennarations on the Psalms* |
| *Ep.* | *Epistles* |
| *Trin.* | *On the Trinity* |

#### *Clement of Alexandria*

| | |
|---|---|
| *Quis div.* | *Quis dives salvetur* |
| *Strom.* | *Stromateis* |

#### *Cyprian of Carthage*

| | |
|---|---|
| *Ep.* | *Epistles* |
| *Laps.* | *On the Lapsed* |

#### *Didymus of Alexandria*

| | |
|---|---|
| *Triad.* | *On the Trinity* |

#### *Dionysius of Alexandria*

| | |
|---|---|
| *Ep.* | *Epistle* |

#### *Epiphanius*

| | |
|---|---|
| *Pan.* | *Panarion (Adversus haereses)* |

#### *Eusebius*

| | |
|---|---|
| *Comm. Isa.* | *Commentary on Isaiah* |
| *Comm. Ps.* | *Commentary on the Psalms* |
| *Hist. eccl.* | *Historia ecclesiastica* |

#### *Gregory the Great*

| | |
|---|---|
| *Dial.* | *Dialogues* |

**Hippolytus**

| | |
|---|---|
| *Ref.* | *Refutation of All Heresies* |

***Irenaeus***

| | |
|---|---|
| *Haer.* | *Adversus haereses* |

***Jerome***

| | |
|---|---|
| *Ep. Gal.* | *Epistle to the Galatians* |
| *Epist.* | *Epistles* |

***John Chrysostom***

| | |
|---|---|
| *Hom. Acts* | *Homilies on the Acts of the Apostles* |
| *Hom. Cor.* | *Homilies on the Epistles of Paul to the Corinthians* |
| *Hom. 1 Cor.* | *Homilies on the First Epistle to the Corinthians* |
| *Hom. Rom.* | *Homilies on the Epistle of Paul to the Romans* |

***Justin Martyr***

| | |
|---|---|
| *1 Apol.* | *First Apology* |
| *2 Apol.* | *Second Apology* |
| *Dial.* | *Dialogue with Trypho* |

***Origen***

| | |
|---|---|
| *Cels.* | *Contra Celsum* |
| *Comm. Matt.* | *Commentary on Matthew* |
| *Comm. Rom.* | *Commentary on Romans* |
| *Hom. Jos.* | *Homilies on Joshua* |

***Quadratus***

| | |
|---|---|
| *Apol.* | *Apology* |

***Tertullian***

| | |
|---|---|
| *An.* | *De anima* |
| *Apol.* | *Apologeticus* |
| *Marc.* | *Adversus Marcionem* |
| *Prax.* | *Adversus Praxean* |
| *Scap.* | *Ad Scapulam* |
| *Spect.* | *De Spectaculis* |

***Theodoret of Cyrrhus***

| | |
|---|---|
| *Comm. 1 Cor.* | *Commentary on 1 Corinthians* |
| *Comm. Rom.* | *Commentary on Romans* |

## Other Greek and Latin Works[1]

### *Aelius Aristides*

*Def. Or.* *In Defense of Oratory*

### *Appian*

*Bell. civ.* *Bella civilia*
*Hist. rom.* *Historia romana*

### *Arrian*

*Alex.* *Anabasis of Alexander*

### *Chariton*

*Chaer.* *Chaereas and Callirhoe*

### *Cicero*

*Nat. d.* *De natura deorum*
*Sest.* *Pro Sestio*

### *Dio Chrysostom*

*Or.* *Orations*

### *Diodorus Siculus*

*Libr. Hist.* *Library of History*

### *Dionysius of Halicarnassus*

*Rhet. Alex.* *Rhetorica ad Alexandrum*
*Rom. Ant.* *Roman Antiquities*

### *Epictetus*

*Diatr.* *Diatribai (Dissertationes)*

### *Euripides*

*Alex.* *Alexandros*
*Elec.* *Electra*

### *Heliodorus*

*Aeth.* *Aethiopica*

### *Heraclitus*

*Hom. Prob.* *Homeric Problems*

### *Hermogenes (of Tarsus)*

*Issues* *On Issues*

### *Herodian*

*Hist.* *History*

### *Herodotus*

*Hist.* *Histories*

### *Homer*

*Il.* *Iliad*
*Od.* *Odyssey*

### *Justinus*

*Epit.* *Epitome of the Philippic History of Pompeius Trogus*

### *Libanius*

*Declam.* *Declamations*

### *Lucan*

*Civ. W.* *On the Civil War*

### *Lucian*

*Alex.* *Alexander the False Prophet*
*Dem.* *Demonax*
*Hist.* *How to Write History*
*Z. Rants* *Zeus Rants*

### *Macrobius*

*Sat.* *Saturnalia*

### *Maximus of Tyre*

*Or.* *Orations*

### *Minucius Felix*

*Oct.* *Octavius*

### *Ovid*

*Metam.* *Metamorphoses*

### *Plato*

*Crat.* *Cratylus*

1. Note that we have normally classified works under the name of their putative author without necessarily implying authenticity. This is because too many cases are disputed to make this distinction useful, and readers will normally find works in collections of the putative author.

***Pliny the Younger (Pliny Y.)***

| | |
|---|---|
| *Ep.* | *Epistles* |

***Plutarch***

| | |
|---|---|
| *Aem. Paul.* | *Aemilius Paulus* |
| *Alex.* | *Alexander* |
| *Arat.* | *Aratus* |
| *Cam.* | *Camillus* |
| *Demosth.* | *Demosthenes* |
| *Dial. L.* | *Dialogue on Love* |
| *Educ.* | *On the Education of Children* |
| *Is. Os.* | *Isis and Osiris* |
| *Lect.* | *On Lectures* |
| *Mor.* | *Moralia* |

***Polybius***

| | |
|---|---|
| *Hist.* | *History of the Roman Republic* |

***Proclus***

| | |
|---|---|
| *Poet.* | *On Poetics* |

***Quintilian***

| | |
|---|---|
| *Decl.* | *Declamations* |
| *Inst.* | *Institutes of Oratory* |

***Seneca the Elder (Seneca E.)***

| | |
|---|---|
| *Controv.* | *Controversiae* |

***Seneca the Younger (Seneca)***

| | |
|---|---|
| *Lucil.* | *Ad Lucilium* |

***Sextus Empiricus***

| | |
|---|---|
| *Pyr.* | *Outlines of Pyrrhonism* |

***Statius***

| | |
|---|---|
| *Silv.* | *Silvae* |

***Suetonius***

| | |
|---|---|
| *Aug.* | *Divus Augustus* |
| *Cal.* | *Gaius Caligula* |
| *Nero* | *Nero* |

***Tacitus***

| | |
|---|---|
| *Agr.* | *Agricola* |
| *Ann.* | *Annales* |

***Valerius Maximus***

| | |
|---|---|
| *Mem.* | *Memorable Deeds and Sayings* |

***Velleius Paterculus***

| | |
|---|---|
| *Comp.* | *Compendium of Roman History* |

***Virgil***

| | |
|---|---|
| *Aen.* | *Aeneid* |

***Xenophon***

| | |
|---|---|
| *Ages.* | *Agesilaus* |

***Xenophon of Ephesus***

| | |
|---|---|
| *Eph. Tale* | *Ephesian Tale* |

## Later Christian Writers

***Bede***

| | |
|---|---|
| *Comm. Acts* | *Commentary on the Acts of the Apostles* |
| *HEGA* | *Historia Ecclesiastica Gentis Anglorum (Ecclesiastical History of the English People)* |

***John Calvin***

| | |
|---|---|
| *Inst.* | *Institutes of the Christian Religion* |

***Martin Luther***

| | |
|---|---|
| *Gal.* | *Commentary on Galatians* |
| LW | Luther, Martin. Luther's Works. American Edition. Edited by Jaroslav Pelikan, Helmut Lehmann, Christopher Boyd Brown, and Benjamin T. G. Mayes. Concordia; Fortress, 1955–86; 2008–. |
| WA | *D. Martin Luthers Werke*. Complete critical ed. 60 vols. Herman Böhlaus Nachfolger, 1883–1980 |

## Modern Editions

*ANET* *Ancient Near Eastern Texts Relating to the Old Testament*. Edited by J. B. Pritchard. Princeton University Press, 1950.

*ANET*[2] *Ancient Near Eastern Texts Relating to the Old Testament*. Edited by J. B. Pritchard. 2nd ed. Princeton University Press, 1955.

*ANF* *Ante-Nicene Fathers*. Edited by Alexander Roberts and James Donaldson. 10 vols. Reprint, Hendrickson, 1994.

*NPNF*[1] *The Nicene and Post-Nicene Fathers*. Series 1. Edited by Philip Schaff. 14 vols. Reprint, Hendrickson, 1994.

*NPNF*[2] *Nicene and Post-Nicene Fathers*. Series 2. Edited by Philip Schaff and Henry Wace. 14 vols. Reprint, Hendrickson, 1994.

PG Patrologia Graeca [= Patrologiae Cursus Completus: Series Graeca]. Edited by J.-P. Migne. 161 vols. Paris, 1857–86.

PL Patrologia Latina [= Patrologiae Cursus Completus: Series Latina]. Edited by J.-P. Migne. 217 vols. Paris, 1844–55.

# Introduction

This book is not meant to defend every charismatic practice or figure; there are plenty of these with which one or both of us take issue, and a number against which we have even spoken out. Likewise, so long as one grants the biblical teaching that God can speak prophetically today, we are right to test particular prophetic claims and even err on the side of caution. But that is not this book's subject. Here our point is not to defend the faulty thesis that everything done in the name of the Spirit is correct (clearly it is not). Rather, it is that Scripture presents the full range of spiritual gifts as valid for the entire course of this age. Even if everyone were doing them wrong (which we do not believe is the case), that would not mean that these gifts *cannot* be done right.

In short, Old Testament prophets promised an end-time outpouring of the prophetic Spirit, which the New Testament declares vindicates the exalted Christ (Acts 2:17–18). To deny that we are in the era of the prophetic Spirit, therefore, is to deny that the promised new-covenant era has dawned and that the kingdom's messiah has truly entered history. Nowhere does Scripture teach the cessation of any gifts before Christ's return. Thus, to claim that particular spiritual gifts have ceased is to impose a postbiblical theological grid on the Bible. This is the very offense of which cessationism typically accuses practitioners of such gifts of doing: risking postbiblical doctrine that contradicts Scripture. In the name of supporting "Scripture alone," it subordinates Scripture to a particular church tradition. Cessationism creates a special era, nowhere envisioned in Scripture, to explain why we do not live in the era of the prophetic Spirit biblically envisioned for God's children in the New Testament.

## This Book's Three C's

We should start by defining three *c* words that appear multiple times in this book.

The first *c* word is *cessationism*. "Cessationism" refers to the idea that certain spiritual gifts, including prophecy, tongues, healing, and miracles, have, by God's will, "ceased" (hence, "cessationism"). Usually these are said to be "signs" or "supernatural" gifts. A standard definition runs like this: "The cessationist position argues that there are no miraculous gifts of the Holy Spirit today. Gifts such as prophecy, tongues, and healing were confined to the first century, and were used at the time the apostles were establishing the churches and the New Testament was not yet complete."[1] From our perspective, this is like saying that God has stopped doing through us anything we would absolutely need him to do, leaving us only with natural gifts (which even unsaved people may have) that God simply blesses.[2] There are different kinds of cessationists. As noted below, this book is written to counter the more feisty ones who denounce continuationists.

The second *c* word is *continuationism*. "Continuationism" refers to the idea that all spiritual gifts mentioned in the Bible may continue beyond the early church (hence, "continuationism"), since their ministry reflects the biblical pattern and the Bible offers no indication that God would change that pattern.

The third *c* word is *charismatic*. Unlike "continuationism," the term "charismatic" carries all sorts of baggage today. Many of us who practice the more disputed spiritual gifts today disavow many beliefs and practices associated with some contemporary charismatic figures. But we use the term in its original, biblical sense simply to mean "continuationist in *practice*." That is, charismatics believe that all the gifts (in Greek, *charismata*) that Paul says God gave to Christ's body continue to be given. We therefore welcome and seek to cultivate them to the extent that God grants in our spheres within the body of Christ. Naturally, charismatics are all continuationists, and a significant proportion of continuationists (but not all) are also charismatic. Statisticians often prefer the term "renewalist," which contains less baggage, but because "charismatic" is familiar to more readers, we use it here, yet in the manner that we have specified.

For practical purposes, the biblical and theological parts of this book simply contrast cessationists and continuationists in general. The difference between charismatics and other continuationists is more important later in the book where some harsh cessationist charges are leveled specifically against

1. Grudem, "Preface," 10. Cf. Pennington, *Cessationism*, 3: "Cessationists believe the Holy Spirit no longer sovereignly gives individual Christians the temporary sign gifts, also known as the miraculous gifts, described in the New Testament." Reformed continuationists might wonder how "sovereignly" figures into such a statement, but Pennington, *Cessationism*, 18–19, actually does allow in principle that God could endow someone with miraculous abilities, so long as we distinguish that from the NT gift.

2. Not coincidentally, the gifts that cessationists normally reject tend to be those rejected by deists and skeptics in recent centuries because these gifts would require special divine action.

charismatics, practitioners of the debated spiritual gifts (as if all such practitioners share the same beliefs and practices). But since the book is about the continuation (the continuing rather than ceasing) of spiritual gifts, continuationism is the primary issue (charismatics by definition are all continuationists).

Some of the more critical cessationists of the sort this book addresses have highlighted genuine errors among charismatics, errors that a number of charismatics themselves have also pointed out.[3] Charismatic Bible scholar and apologist Michael Brown, for example, already challenged what he considered "strange fire" among errant charismatics over two decades before the Strange Fire conference.[4] Not everything labeled "charismatic" or "Spirit-filled" today is genuine—but then, neither are all alleged Bible expositions. Other books deal appropriately with such debates, but the focus of this one is whether Scripture teaches that God intended these gifts to stop before our day or continue in it. If the Bible teaches that all spiritual gifts are for today, then we should seek them for edifying God's people even if *no one* else has the real thing (though we believe that in reality many do have it).

## Over-the-Top Cessationism

Lest those familiar only with friendly cessationists suppose that our concern is an overreaction, let's take a few moments to hear virulent charges from a sensationalistically cessationist pastor, many of whose YouTube videos have hundreds of thousands and sometimes millions of views. John MacArthur's understanding of charismatics seems largely drawn from watching particular televangelists rather than attending services in mainstream continuationist congregations.[5] Here are some examples:

- "Charismatic theology has made no contribution to true biblical theology or interpretation; rather, it represents a deviant mutation of the truth. Like a deadly virus, . . . [and] like a doctrinal version of Frankenstein's monster, [charismatic theology is] a hideous hybrid of heresy, ecstasy, and blasphemy."[6]

3. See, e.g., Brown, *End*; Brown, *Holy Fire*; King, *Guidebook*; King, *Applying Principles*.

4. Brown, *Power of God*, 17. Reformed charismatic R. T. Kendall's 2014 book *Holy Fire* also includes a chapter called "Strange Fire," denouncing charismatic errors.

5. One also witnesses many strident misrepresentations of regular charismatics, based on a few televangelists, in the movie *Cessationist* (Lanphere, *Cessationist*). In my (Craig's) opinion, the production quality, including the ominous music, vastly exceeds the quality of the theology articulated. I do agree with some claims in the movie (not least the focus of the Spirit on mission), but some of its caricatures proved so extreme that they provoked me to (not "holy") laughter.

6. MacArthur, *Strange Fire*, xvi. MacArthur's comparison of charismatic theology to "a deadly virus" seems to echo atheist Richard Dawkins's critique of religion generally.

- "The religious leaders of Israel blasphemously attributed the work of the Spirit to Satan (Matt. 12:24). The modern Charismatic Movement does the inverse, attributing the work of the devil to the Holy Spirit."[7]
- Charismatics are "an enemy" and "a Trojan horse of subjectivism, experientialism, ecumenical compromise, and heresy. Those who compromise in this way are playing with strange fire."[8]
- "In recent years, no other movement has done more to damage the cause of the gospel, to distort the truth, and to smother the articulation of sound doctrine. Charismatic theology has turned the evangelical church into a cesspool of error and a breeding ground for false teachers."[9]
- "In earlier generations, the Pentecostal-Charismatic Movement would have been labeled heresy. Instead, it is now the most dominant . . . strain of so-called Christianity."[10]
- "Yet the gospel that is driving those surging numbers is not the true gospel, and the spirit behind them is not the Holy Spirit. What we are seeing is *in reality* the explosive growth of a false church, as dangerous as any cult or heresy that has ever assaulted Christianity."[11]
- After generously acknowledging that "there are sincere people within the Charismatic Movement," MacArthur warns that "by continually exposing themselves to the false teaching and counterfeit spirituality of the Charismatic Movement, they have placed themselves (and anyone under their spiritual care) in eternal jeopardy."[12]

### No Theological or Evangelistic Contributions?

This seems rather a broad brush that condemns a movement that is bringing millions of people to Christ around the world. As for contributing nothing to "true biblical theology or interpretation," I (Craig) can attest that Pastor MacArthur was displaying his lack of acquaintance with (or at least appreciation for) a significant range of biblical scholarship and exposition today, not least the Pentecostal scholar Gordon Fee's work as at one time editor of the New International Commentary on the New Testament series. In another book I devote several pages to listing some of the many charismatic scholars teaching outside specifically charismatic institutions.[13] Baker Academic has

7. MacArthur, *Strange Fire*, xiii.

8. MacArthur, *Strange Fire*, xiv.

9. MacArthur, *Strange Fire*, xv.

10. MacArthur, *Strange Fire*, xvi. Note particularly "so-called."

11. MacArthur, *Strange Fire*, xvii. Resistance to Pentecostals among some of their fellow evangelicals has a long history (Worthen, *Apostles*, 36–37, 141).

12. MacArthur, *Strange Fire*, 81–82. He acknowledges that the people he warns "embrace substitutionary atonement," the Trinity, "the unique authority of the Bible," the reality of hell, and the like. Craig responded to MacArthur more briefly in Keener, "Review."

13. Keener, *Spirit Hermeneutics*, 297–303.

undertaken a Word and Spirit Commentary on the New Testament series, written by scholars in Pentecostal and charismatic traditions. The academic publisher Brill also has a series of Global Pentecostal and Charismatic Studies, many of whose contributors are charismatic scholars, and a Pentecostal commentary series. Others of us maintained or grew in our evangelical faith during secular academic training partly due to our charismatic experience and formation.

As for conversions due to the true gospel, even our own ministry challenges such claims. I (Daniel) am carrying on the ministry of Reinhard Bonnke through Christ for All Nations. Together our ministry has registered some one hundred million conversions. The gospel we preach is that Jesus Christ, God's Son, died for our sins and arose according to the Scriptures, and we trust wholly in his finished work that puts us right with God and empowers us to live a new life in Christ. If a critic denies that this is the true gospel, what gospel does the critic preach? Many other Pentecostal and charismatic ministries around the world devote themselves tirelessly to proclaiming Christ.

### *No Social Benefit?*

MacArthur, who is theologically opposed to Roman Catholicism,[14] admits that Catholics achieve at least some social good with hospitals and social services, but he then uses this concession to lambast charismatics: "There is essentially zero social benefit to the world from the charismatic movement. Where's the charismatic hospital? Social services? Poverty relief?"[15]

Based perhaps on impressions from some US televangelists, MacArthur inaccurately slanders an entire movement of hundreds of millions of people.[16] That the accusation is inaccurate is beyond dispute among those who are better informed. Here are just a few examples:

- Non-Pentecostal sociologists have found massive social engagement among the poor by global Pentecostals.[17] Indeed, when they consulted

14. See Grace to You, "Roman Catholicism": "a false and deceptive form of Christianity." Cf., e.g., also the claim that it is a "false gospel," in MacArthur, "Roman Catholics"; Grace to You, "Explaining 1"; Grace to You, "Explaining 2."

15. Cripplegate, "Q&A 2"; cited in Brown, *Authentic Fire*, 64.

16. The figure of hundreds of millions readily fits recent estimates; see, e.g., Cox, *Fire*, xv; Cox, "Foreword," xxi; Sanneh, *Disciples*, 275; Johnson, Barrett, and Crossing, "Christianity 2010," 36; Johnson and Ross, *Atlas*, 102; Noll, *Shape*, 22. Note the dialogue between Michael Brown and MacArthur's colleague Philip Johnson recorded in Brown, *Authentic Fire*, 80–81n41; counterexamples to Johnson in Brown, *Authentic Fire*, 64–70.

17. Miller and Yamamori, *Pentecostalism*; see further Shaull, "Reconstruction," 132–33, 150–59, 174–78, 194, 207, esp. 211–12; Petersen, *Might*, passim; Abraham, "Spirit," 88, 97, 100–102; César, "Life," 25, 31; Hong, "Mission," 300; Hollenweger, "Azusa Street," 7–8; Westmeier, *Pentecostalism*, 84–85, 88; Satyavrata, *Pentecostals and Poor*, 9–18; cf. Harris and Palmer, *Spirit*.

four hundred experts on which rapidly growing, indigenous global churches were most involved in helping the poor, the sociologists were surprised to find that close to 85 percent of those churches were Pentecostal or charismatic.[18]

- The chief center of early Indian Pentecostalism was Pandita Ramabai's Mukti Mission, a refuge for orphan brides; Ramabai was also an early leader for justice for women in India.[19]
- In 1910 Pentecostal missionary Lillian Trasher sailed to Egypt, where she founded a major orphanage that continues to minister to the needy today.[20]
- Teen Challenge is an addiction recovery ministry with more than 1,400 programs in 140 nations; with a remarkable 70 to 80 percent cure rate, it is explicitly grounded in classical Pentecostal experience.[21]
- Church of God in Christ, the largest Pentecostal denomination in the United States and one of the largest predominantly African American denominations, has a social justice ministry and has long been deeply involved in transforming local urban communities.[22]
- During apartheid, Pentecostal churches in Soweto were working to meet physical and educational needs;[23] unlike most of the South African Reformed churches at that time, various charismatic and Pentecostal churches there were involved in interracial ministry.[24]
- In 1963, Pentecostals John and Lois Bueno in El Salvador founded what became Latin America Childcare (now ChildHope); it was advanced further in 1978 by Douglas and Myrna Petersen and now serves nearly one hundred thousand children in Latin America.[25]
- The Assemblies of God Relief and Development Services meets needs in rural Ghana, including by working with the United Nations High Commisioner for Refugees to serve the Egyeikrom refugee camp.[26]

18. Miller and Yamamori, *Pentecostalism*, 42–43, highlighted in Satyavrata, *Pentecostals and Poor*, 15–16.

19. Anderson, *Ends of the Earth*, 32–33; Burgess, "Pandita Ramabai," 194–95.

20. See, e.g., Hammond, "Heroes."

21. See Global Teen Challenge, "Home Page."

22. On Black Pentecostalism in the US, see esp. Alexander, *Fire*, passim. Cf., e.g., Church of God in Christ, "Office."

23. Anderson, *Ends of the Earth*, 140.

24. See, e.g., the testimony of Vineyard leader Alexander Venter in Venter, *Reconciliation*. Cf. also Assemblies of God Zulu evangelist Nicholas Bhengu (Bhengu, "South Africa"; Hollenweger, *Pentecostals*, 126–39, esp. 129, 131; Poewe, "Nature," 6).

25. See ChildHope, "Home Page."

26. See the profile at https://acdep.org/new/index.php/regions/upper-east-region?id=125:implementing-1&catid=85:in-the-tables, accessed September 7, 2025.

- Despite some outsiders' criticism on other points, the Korean Yoido Full Gospel Church once led by David Yonggi Cho has engaged in extensive relief work.[27]
- In Hong Kong, Jackie Pullinger and St. Stephen's Society have spent decades serving among the urban poor and addicts there.[28]
- In Mozambique, Rolland and Heidi Baker, with colleagues in Iris Global, sacrificially care for thousands of orphans, feed tens of thousands of displaced persons, and start schools, all the while sharing the message of Christ.[29]
- In the Democratic Republic of Congo, the hospital founded by Nobel Peace Prize recipient Dr. Denis Mukwege, who is both a surgeon and Pentecostal preacher, has treated more than seventy thousand rape victims.[30]
- Convoy of Hope, a significant Christian humanitarian organization,[31] serves the needy globally and is affiliated with the Assemblies of God, the largest Pentecostal denomination globally.[32]

I (Craig) have a long-standing involvement with some renewalist social ministries myself. For example:

- My mentors included retired Pentecostal church planters Everett and Esther Cook, who used their retirement income to run a street mission where I and other Bible college students helped in feeding the homeless as well as preaching the gospel; this followed a model common in the early Pentecostal movement, which hosted hundreds, or likelier thousands, of street missions.[33]
- For nearly four decades, I have sponsored a child through OneChild (originally Calcutta Mission of Mercy), an Assemblies of God child sponsorship organization. It was once affiliated with an Assemblies of God–founded hospital (Mercy Hospital) in Calcutta. We also sponsor a child through another largely charismatic ministry in a higher-security nation (as well as periodically helping some other charismatic and noncharismatic ministries in high-security nations).

27. Anderson, *Ends of the Earth*, 232.

28. See St. Stephen's Society, "About Us"; cf. also Pullinger, *Dragon*; Miller and Yamamori, *Pentecostalism*, 99–105.

29. See, e.g., Iris Global, "What We Do"; also Baker and Baker, *Enough*; Stafford, "Miracles."

30. Belz, "Crimes," 75–76, 80–81; see also Mukwege, *Power*.

31. See Convoy of Hope, "Home Page."

32. See Wikipedia, "Convoy of Hope."

33. Such work developed from the nineteenth century social ministry of radical evangelicals; see, e.g., Magnuson, *Salvation*; Smith, *Revivalism*.

- I, along with a vast number of others, have long been involved in ethnic reconciliation ministry.[34]

### *Different Kinds of Cessationists*

Cessationists haven't ceased yet, but some kinds are getting much rarer than they used to be.

I (Daniel) recognize that apprehensions still linger in many people's minds that prevent them from fully embracing many kinds of experiences in the Spirit. Many wonder whether these experiences are even available to us today. Such doubts may persist in your own heart. Maybe you have never seen an authentic miracle. Or perhaps your denomination rejects the modern exercise of particular gifts. Or maybe a pastor or theologian you respect teaches that these phenomena belonged only to the "apostolic age." Through this book we will seek to deal with these objections head-on, and by God's grace, remove them from your thinking once and for all.

Certain doctrinal debates endlessly stalemate because both sides seem to have such powerful biblical arguments. This debate does not need to be like those. As far as we're concerned, this should be an open-and-shut case. It is one of the few doctrinal hills we are willing to die on. For any relatively objective seeker of truth, the Scriptures are clear on this issue. For us, Scripture is *so* authoritative that we should privilege its message over any subsequent theological constructs.

Obviously the Bible touches on many topics beyond spiritual gifts, so the differences between cessationists and charismatics do not preclude vast areas of potential agreement between the two sides on other matters. Cessationists and charismatics often work together in mission, in scholarship, and in other venues. This is the experience of both authors of this book, and we are grateful to our cessationist brothers and sisters for partnership in the gospel. I (Craig) am relatively sure that the two Baptist Bible college students who first brought me the gospel on the street were cessationists, and I will be eternally grateful for their witness that led to my conversion. I also served together with some very close cessationist friends for a number of years on the executive committee of the Evangelical Theological Society.

Moreover, just as there is a great variety of charismatics (ranging from some whom almost everyone appreciates to others whom almost everyone

34. Craig's work is noted in, e.g., White, "Calling"; Johnston, "Ordination"; Mitchell, "Scholar"; also Keener, "Gospel and Reconciliation"; Keener, "Gospel"; Keener, "Invitations"; Keener, "Reconciliation"; Keener, "Invitations to Reconciliation"; for Craig's relevant work with Glenn Usry, see, e.g., Usry and Keener, *Religion*; Keener and Usry, *Faith*; and for Craig's relevant work with his African wife, Médine, see, e.g., Keener and Keener, *Reconciliation*; Keener and Keener, "Temple." For other charismatics, see, e.g., Dawson, *Wounds*; Dawson, *Reconciliation*.

thinks are beyond the pale), there is a great range of types of cessationist. One website, for example, divides cessationists into four categories:

- Concentric cessationists allow miracles to occur in regions of the world where the gospel goes for the first time.
- Classical cessationists allow for occasional miracles.
- Full cessationists say there are virtually no miracles today.
- Consistent cessationists deny the entire fivefold ministry of Ephesians 4:11, including pastors and teachers.[35]

Although I (Craig) would not define their position as cessationist, I have "cessationist" friends who acknowledge that God performs miracles today but simply insist that no one today has an automatic *gift* of healing through which healing always happens. This form of "cessationism" has such a large tent that it includes most of us *continuationists*! I do not personally know any charismatics who claim that *everyone* is healed when they pray. I also would expect the cure rate to be higher in places where the kingdom is breaking new ground, as it was in the Gospels and Acts, and I would expect Jesus to have the most perfect cure rate (with those directly mentored by him also ahead of the rest of us).

Yet I wouldn't see this as a change in God's way of working, apart from Jesus's own special role (on which we all agree). Daniel and I don't believe that everybody got healed immediately even during the ministries of the first apostles (see Gal. 4:13; Phil. 2:26–27; 2 Tim. 4:20). God was sovereign in the first century too. In practice, these moderate cessationist friends and I—a full-fledged charismatic—are close on a majority of points![36] If that were the only kind of cessationist I knew, I wouldn't be taking the time to write this book. My beef is with the harder cessationists who vocally assault charismatics' experiences, not with the ones with whom I share so much common spiritual and biblical ground.

Likewise, most of the cessationists I (Daniel) have known are fine Christians who love Jesus and value the Scriptures. Many cessationists simply believe in good faith what they've been taught from childhood and have not thought to reexamine this position in light of Scripture. And though some of the more prominent popular cessationist teachers are condescending, even downright nasty, toward those outside their camp, the majority in that camp are sincere brothers and sisters in Christ. So our response to the harsh cessationists does not apply to all, or even most, within the cessationist community. Moreover, most cessationists today are not full cessationists in the style of B. B. Warfield,

35. Monergism, "Cessationists View."
36. See Keener, "Ongoing Evidence," 338–39.

denying all postbiblical miracles.[37] In biblical context, the main point of Paul's discussions of spiritual gifts is their service to Christ's body; the topic of gifts should not be used to promote division, whether from the cessationist or continuationist side.

### *Nonexperience Versus Biblical Argument*

When healing doesn't happen, someone prophesies falsely, or positive spiritual gifts are not part of our experience, one way to address an apparent disconnect between these things and some biblical passages is to say that real gifts aren't for today. But that's not the only solution, and it's not a biblical one (see instead, e.g., 1 Cor. 14:29; 1 Thess. 5:19–22; 2 Tim. 4:20). And some who are partly cessationist are in practice too honest with what they find in the text of Scripture to embrace that approach theologically.

Many cessationists today belong to a category that I (Daniel) would call observational cessationists. They do not argue for cessationism from a theological perspective. They might even know the Scriptures well enough to realize that it is impossible to make a cogent biblical argument for cessationism. Yet they are still cessationists in practice because they lack the confidence to explore further. Maybe they've never seen someone operating genuinely in one of the Spirit's debated gifts. So while theologically they believe miracles may be possible, their observations determine their practice. For example, Southern Baptist evangelist Paul Washer might fit this category.

In a video online, someone asked Washer if he believes speaking in tongues is for today. He replied,

> Even though men godlier than I would disagree with me, theologically or doctrinally I do not say that tongues have ceased. Alright, so everybody thinks, "Oh man, he believes in tongues." No, hold it. I just don't think that's the issue. When I go to the text, . . . I see the arguments and stuff, but I can't say that I can say in my conscience that these things have ceased. . . . I kind of call myself a practical cessationist in that I do not say those things have ceased. I've seen God heal people. But have I seen a man that had the gift of healing? No. . . . I believe tongues in the book of Acts; every time it occurs, it is a real, phonetic language. . . . And when they occurred, everybody knew something supernatural was going on.[38]

37. See, e.g., Gaffin, "View," 41–42. Tim Challies: "As a pastor I see miracles often. . . . Cessationism [simply] means the Spirit no longer gives believers miraculous spiritual gifts as a normative Christian experience as it was for the apostles" (Challies, "Strange Fire Conference").

38. "Paul Washer on Tongues: Are They for Today?," YouTube video, accessed September 5, 2024, https://www.youtube.com/watch?v=zWOGm8TiWJ8, (the quote runs from 2:48–5:03; this video has since been made private).

He goes on to concede that he's heard from godly Baptist and Presbyterian missionaries that "strange things" have occurred "on the fringe of missions." He seems to indicate that he believes such reports.

Putting aside for the moment potential questions regarding part of Washer's rationale, his statement perfectly exemplifies what I am calling observational cessationism. Quite commendably, he acknowledges honestly that he cannot in good conscience make a biblical case for cessationism, but neither has he seen what he believes are authentic expressions of particular gifts. His cessationism is not based on Scripture, but he remains largely cessationist in practice. In my view, Washer's stance is inconsistent. He admits he cannot deny those gifts on scriptural grounds, and that alone should motivate him to seek and find such gifts for the body of Christ. But at least he seems to acknowledge that the Bible, taken by itself, would support continuationism. Put the other way, Washer is too genuinely loyal to Scripture to try to fabricate a false argument from Scripture against the gifts for today.

### *Responding to the Hypercritics*

In this book we challenge classical cessationists, who make theological arguments to justify the lack of certain spiritual gifts in their circle. But even classical cessationists are not all of a kind. Some (such as Richard Gaffin and Thomas Schreiner) are even genuine biblical scholars with whom I (Craig) as a fellow biblical scholar share much in common. Both are charitable; I thanked Richard Gaffin for how charitable his plenary lecture on the Spirit was at the Evangelical Theological Society, and I sought to be equally charitable in mine on the Spirit in Acts.[39] I regularly learn valuable insights from scholars associated with generally cessationist institutions, including some at the Master's University, of which John MacArthur was long president, and from good friends who teach at other traditionally cessationist institutions including Dallas Theological Seminary and Westminster.

Schreiner in one book affirms and argues for classical cessationism but graciously declares at key points, "I could be mistaken in arguing for cessationism."[40] He also nuances his cessationism. He even allows that some good may exist in the experiences practiced by charismatics, such as what they believe are tongues, though he doubts that these represent the biblical gift.[41] Likewise, before challenging continuationists, Sam Waldron expresses his appreciation that they at least take "the New Testament seriously" and that they are "unabashedly supernaturalist in [their] understanding of Christianity."[42]

39. These are available in print as Gaffin, "Spirit"; Keener, "Spirit and Mission."
40. Schreiner, *Spiritual Gifts*, 1, 153, 171.
41. Schreiner, *Spiritual Gifts*, 130–31.
42. Waldron, *Continued*, 21.

Our book is, as we said, especially a response to "harder" cessationists who treat continuationism and charismatic experience as a dangerous error that must be publicly opposed, and often even a dividing line of orthodoxy. Unfortunately, their arguments are so widely circulated as to require a response. Some in fact denounce virtually all charismatics and even dismiss the genuineness of our faith. Given their misrepresentation of various charismatics, this book may well put us on their radar to misrepresent us as well (to the degree they acknowledge us at all). But it's no surprise that God's servants sometimes do get misrepresented (Matt. 5:11–12 // Luke 6:22–23; 2 Cor. 6:8).[43]

Because critics have brought considerable confusion to Christ's body in certain parts of the world, we have seen the need to respond. The targets of this book and reason for its tone, then, are not the claims of all cessationists but those of the particularly provocative ones. Since they sometimes denounce charismatic teachers for not always naming names when we challenge charismatic errors, we will name some cessationist teachers to show that we are not simply inventing the arguments we criticize.

Because this is an especially intraevangelical debate, we take for granted in the book that we share premises, such as conservative attributions of authorship, that might require defense themselves in an academic work for a different kind of audience. Those who do not share those assumptions, of course, remain welcome to listen in if they are curious about the debate.

Cessationists may complain that we do not treat their doctrine respectfully in this book. That may well be true: When the common basis of our discussion is Scripture, it is difficult to respect a system that we believe so blatantly defies Scripture. But we do hope that all cessationists, including those named, will recognize that we do not disrespect them personally as fellow believers. Even when Saul hounded David out of the land of Israel, David honored Saul and defended Israel, and Christians with even the strongest of disagreements or wounds need to stand together for the gospel we share. Despite pushing back forcefully based on what we believe Scripture says, we work from the assumption that most cessationists, including the vocal critics, are our genuine brothers and sisters in Christ. We should also note that we are responding to published positions, not permanently identifying their advocates with such positions. After all, we do believe in miracles!

43. Even by fellow believers; see, e.g., Acts 21:21; Rom. 3:8. Calvin also experienced this, though he valued unity in Christ over differences in doctrine that he deemed minor (Parker, *Calvin*, 171; cf. more fully Rankin, "Spirit"; Park, "Calvin").

# I

# Cessationism

Reading the Bible on its own does not lead ordinary readers to doubt that spiritual gifts are for today. That doubt normally arises either from failing to experience or witness such gifts, or more commonly from being taught that they do not continue. For that reason, we wouldn't need to argue much for the continuation of such gifts without there being prior arguments for those gifts' cessation. Here we challenge up front the position we are engaging.

# 1

# Cessationism as Heresy

The title of this chapter is entirely clickbait. But for those who read at least chapter introductions (and not just tables of contents), we don't really believe that most cessationists are heretics. We just want to illustrate why they would be if we held them to the standards to which their harshest voices hold charismatics.

Although no Christian cessationists take cessationism as far as this chapter addresses, this chapter is an attempt to show what cessationism would have to look like if it were more consistent (grateful as we are that it is not). This chapter is tongue-in-cheek, and we parallel it in our book's conclusion with an (admittedly much shorter) tongue-in-cheek denunciation of what hyper-continuationism might look like. Still, the consistency problem is serious for most forms of cessationism, and we introduce here some points that we will develop in later chapters. Yet we're not pulling our punches. If it sounds like we are reducing cessationism to the absurd, welcome to our world: That is how cessationism genuinely sounds from our reading of Scripture as well as our experience of the Spirit.

## Why Cessationists Can Blow Off Applying Scripture for Today

If what Paul says about new-covenant church practice and the many-membered body of Christ is not for today, surely nothing in the New Testament is. It's all for the first century only! A cessationist may respond that it's only *particular* spiritual gifts that aren't for today. But why those in particular when no biblical text distinguishes those from the others (see chap. 6 below)? Because they weren't in evidence at the time and place of cessationism's origin? If so, the effective canon requires not merely the New Testament itself (in its setting), but the theological setting that birthed cessationism. Or must we exclude these gifts because they require something more "supernatural" than other gifts? If so, the effective canon requires the philosophical skepticism of David Hume.

Cessationism leaves us either with a hermeneutic that rejects embracing Scripture for today or (far more often, for believers) with a postcanonical philosophical "canon" that allows us to sift what is or isn't for today. In its most radical form, this canon coincidentally may offer a Christianity acceptable to the world: God acts, but never in ways that secularists cannot explain away fairly easily.

## Why Salvation Is Not for Today

In the New Testament, salvation and prophecy belong to the same era of promise. See Acts 2:17–21: "In the last days, . . . your sons and daughters shall prophesy. . . . And everyone who calls on the Lord's name will be saved." On the cessationist rejection of continuing prophecy, therefore, consistency would require them to reject also salvation. Joel prophesied that prophetic experience would characterize the promised coming era (Joel 2:28–29), the era of salvation by calling on the Lord (2:32). When Jesus's followers began worshiping in tongues on the day of Pentecost, Peter declared that the promised era had arrived. Based on what the crowd themselves was witnessing and hearing (Acts 2:33: "what you see and hear"), Peter makes his argument.

- The worship in tongues fulfills Joel's prophecy (Acts 2:16).
- It is therefore now the promised "last days" (2:17).
- Prophecy, prophetic visions, and dreams characterize this promised last-days era (2:17–18).
- In this period *all* God's people (*pasan sarka*, "all flesh"), of whatever gender or age, may prophesy (2:17–18).
- This period will close with cosmic end-time signs and the day of the Lord (2:19–20).
- In this period whoever calls on the Lord's name will be saved (2:21).[1]
- This outpouring demonstrates that Jesus is the exalted Lord at God's right hand (2:33–35), both Lord and Messiah (2:36).

In short, if tongues and prophecy, which Peter explicitly associates with the Spirit's outpouring, aren't for today, it's not the last-days era of Christ's

1. The rest of the content of Acts also shows the gifts of prophecy and salvation by calling on Christ occurring in the same era.

exaltation and salvation. And, by contrast, if it was already the "last days" when Peter preached, and the ultimate day of the Lord has not yet come, then we remain in the promised end-time era before Jesus's return.

Where would rejection of prophecy for today lead us? If we are not in the promised eschatological era characterized by prophecy, prophetic visions, and dreams, then neither was it that era when Peter preached. After all, Peter characterized his time as the "last days," and it is clearly later in history now than it was back then.

So if this is not the era of prophecy that Joel envisioned, Peter's argument falls apart. In this case, we cannot claim to be in the messianic era or the period in which we can be saved by calling on the Lord's name. Worse yet, Peter's particular argument for Jesus as exalted Lord fails. How could he be exalted as Lord and Messiah without the promised experience of his messianic era?

To be consistent, those who argue that prophecy is not for today should argue that salvation by calling on the Lord's name is not yet for today. To be even more consistent, they should argue either that God never poured out the Spirit in attestation of Jesus's enthronement, or at least that he took the Spirit back along with that evidence of Jesus's enthronement. If the latter is the case, the "last days" got interrupted or terminated without explicit biblical warrant. Happily, we personally know no cessationists who are truly *this* consistent. But cessationism undercuts the chief *biblical* evidence God has provided for Christ's enthronement.

## Why We No Longer Need Teaching

Paul says that we will not need limited gifts such as knowledge or prophecy once perfection comes. Some cessationists say that the "complete" or "perfect" of 1 Corinthians 13:10 has already come, so we no longer need some gifts. In 1 Corinthians 13, love clearly matters more than the gifts, in context inviting us to use gifts to build up the body *in love* (1 Cor. 14:1; Eph. 4:11–16). But if love makes gifts even *superfluous*, a consistent approach would apply that superfluity to all the gifts, including teaching (see chap. 5 below). By contrast, continuationists believe these gifts become superfluous only when Christ is revealed in glory, when we shall have something far more complete than these gifts.

Paul is clear in 1 Corinthians 13:8–12 that the present forms of knowledge, tongues, and prophecy will no longer be needed when we see God face-to-face and know as we are known. If (with some cessationists) this has already happened, then we should now know God perfectly and there is nothing more for us to learn. Elsewhere in 1 Corinthians knowledge (*gnōsis*) includes recognition of true information (1 Cor. 1:5; 8:1, 7, 10–11; 13:2; 14:6),[2] but 13:12 indicates a time when God will supplant our limited horizon of information with full knowledge of him.

Today most cessationists do grant that this passage refers to the future, while still contending (without using this passage) that tongues and prophecy have passed away. Yet this passage does in fact seem explicit as to when these gifts will pass—when we see Jesus face-to-face. Let's follow consistently the logic of saying tongues and prophecy have already passed.

- If tongues and prophecy have passed, so has knowledge (specified in the same line in 13:8).
- If we have perfect knowledge only when partial knowledge has passed away, then such perfect knowledge has already supplanted partial knowledge (13:9–10).
- In that case we know fully now and we already see Jesus face-to-face (13:12).

But if we aren't currently seeing Jesus face-to-face, then we aren't yet at the time when partial knowledge, prophecy, and tongues have passed away. If the present, partial knowledge *has* passed, yet without being supplanted by perfect knowledge, then we don't know anything. Unfortunately, if we don't know *anything*, we don't even *know* that we don't know anything. If that doesn't make sense (and it doesn't), then, in light of this passage, neither does a cessationist reading of this passage.

A minority of cessationists still contend that the passage refers to a completed Bible. Do they insist that we see God face-to-face there? Or that we know fully, or even know fully the content of the Bible? Few have memorized the entire Bible in Greek and Hebrew, and it is doubtful that even they would claim to understand *everything* there fully.

Cessationists divide gifts of the Spirit, retaining some, such as teaching, for today while relegating others, such as tongues, to past eras. As we shall see (chap. 6), none of the many *biblical* lists of gifts offer such a distinction.

2. Because the meaning of "word of knowledge" (1 Cor. 12:8) is debated, we exclude it here. Many charismatics treat this gift as revelatory knowledge; but revelatory knowledge is a form of prophecy (e.g., 1 Sam. 9:20; 10:2; 1 Cor. 14:24–25) so Paul's expression "word/speaking of knowledge" might equate—given Paul's usage of both *logos* and *gnōsis* elsewhere (1 Cor. 1:5; cf. also, e.g., Rom. 15:14; 1 Cor. 1:17; 2:1, 4, 13)—with the gift of *teaching* in other lists (Rom. 12:7; 1 Cor. 12:28–29; Eph. 4:11; see, e.g., Augustine, *Trin.* 14 [Bray, *Corinthians*, 121]; Gee, *Gifts*, 27–34, 110–19 (as cited in Lim, "Gifts," 465n14); Cullmann, *Worship*, 20; Horton, *Spirit*, 272–73; Dunn, *Jesus and Spirit*, 217–22; Keener, *Gift & Giver*, 116; Williams, *Renewal Theology*, 2:355–57; Pogoloff, *Logos*, 110–11; Belleville, "Live," 137). This is how ordinary ancient hearers would understand such a phrase (cf., e.g., Dio Chrysostom, *Or.* 49.10; *1 En.* 14:3; 37:2; 99:10). On this view, as "revelation" parallels "prophecy" in 14:6, so "knowledge" parallels "teaching."

Not rooted in Scripture, such a distinction rests on a postbiblical doctrinal tradition. It is too bad that the very people who warn against postbiblical prophecy, lest it compete with Scripture, have to base this very view on a postbiblical doctrinal tradition that no biblical text explicitly supports.

Cessationists could become more consistent by simply jettisoning *all* gifts of the Spirit, including leadership or administration, teaching, helping, giving, evangelism, and the like. We are very glad that we have never met a cessationist who is consistent in this regard.

## The Messiah Hasn't Really Come Yet

Under the above rubric, "Why salvation is not for today," we pointed out that a consistent cessationism would reject a chief biblical evidence for Christ's enthronement. We revisit that point here.

In the Gospels, Jesus inaugurates the kingdom (Mark 1:15; Matt. 11:4–6 // Luke 7:22–23; Matt. 12:28 // Luke 11:20; Luke 17:21; see chap. 3 below). All Christians acknowledge that the King has come yet will come again. That is why we speak of God's kingdom as already and not yet—already inaugurated by Jesus's first coming and to be consummated at his second. At Jesus's first coming, not only did he preach God's kingship, but he demonstrated it by healing and casting out demons (Matt. 4:23; 9:35; 10:7–8; 12:28; Luke 9:2, 11; 10:9).

But wait! Granted that Jesus inaugurated his reign at his first coming, isn't he *still* reigning at the Father's right hand? We readily grant that his kingdom is not yet consummated, raising all the righteous dead and emptying all the hospital beds. But if it has begun in the world, should not signs of the kingdom remain among us? That is, Jesus did not just introduce his reign; he established it and still reigns (Matt. 28:18; Acts 2:33–36).

Moreover, Jesus did not merely proclaim and demonstrate the kingdom himself; he authorized his followers to do likewise. This applied not merely to the Twelve (Matt. 10:7–8; Luke 9:2) but also to the Seventy or Seventy-Two (Luke 10:9, 19). And aren't we supposed to keep preaching the good news of his reign until the end of the age (Matt. 24:14; 28:18–20; Acts 20:25; 28:23, 31; 1 Thess. 2:12)? If not, do we believe that instead of being already/not yet, the kingdom *used to be* on earth and won't be again until Jesus returns? This sounds tantamount to denying that Jesus currently reigns as Lord at the Father's right hand. Continuationists believe that his reign continues to work among us, continuing to be expressed in healings and deliverance, especially where his kingdom continues to expand into new areas. Happily, many cessationists at least admit that signs occur where the gospel breaks new ground (albeit usually leaving such activity in practice to charismatics, whose converts then can be properly reeducated by cessationist academics).

## Why the Spirit Does Not Live Inside Christians

In John 16:13–15, the Spirit reveals Jesus to his followers. Whatever the Spirit hears from the Father or Jesus, he shares with us (16:13), just as Jesus shared whatever he heard from the Father (15:15). The Spirit comes to teach us all things and remind us of what Jesus said (14:26). Some of the stricter cessationists, however, deny that Christians today can hear the voice of the Spirit.[3] They contend that this experience was limited to Jesus's first disciples so they could write Scripture; thus Jesus's sheep no longer hear his voice (contrast 10:3–5, 16, 27). To be consistent, the promise in John's context that the Spirit would be with us forever and dwell in us (14:16–17, 23) must also have been only for the first disciples.

Against this reasoning, 1 John clearly addresses a group wider than the first disciples (1:3), and 1 John speaks of the Spirit within all believers teaching us (2:27), remaining in us (3:24; 4:13), and testifying to us (5:6). Has the Spirit stopped teaching us or testifying to us? Does anything in the text itself suggest that the Spirit may do so only when we read Scripture?

Paul is also clear that if we are Jesus's followers, the Spirit testifies to our spirits that we are God's children (Rom. 8:16). If God no longer speaks to our spirits, then Paul's expectation of the Spirit's testimony is no longer for today, and correspondingly we do not have the Spirit of Christ or belong to him (8:9).

Happily, we know no cessationists who take resistance to hearing God's voice this far. (If they only mean that our experience of the Spirit should be *consistent* with Scripture, we agree fully; so do most other charismatics.)

## God Speaks Only Through Professors

Despite Peter's proclamation that "your sons and daughters will prophesy" (Acts 2:17), most cessationists relegate prophetic gifts to a bygone era, along with Paul's suggestion that "you may all prophesy one by one" (1 Cor. 14:31).

The gift of teaching, however, remains, and for the strictest cessationists appears to be the only gift we have that now provides access to God's voice. As charismatic theologian Jon Ruthven pointed out, most ancient scribes believed that only the Torah and the Pharisaic stream of interpretation surrounding it were normative. The scribal movement thereby effectively limited control of interpretation to itself, disallowing prophecy and minimizing the authority of even a voice speaking from heaven.[4]

3. See, e.g., Pennington, *Cessationism*, 19.

4. See, e.g., Greenspahn, "Prophecy"; Keener, *Acts*, 1:892; for subordination of the *bat qol*, the heavenly voice, see, e.g., *b. B. Mes.* 59b; *Song Rab.* 8:9, §3.

By contrast, the new covenant promised that God would write his law in his people's hearts. Under the new covenant, all God's people would know him, and they would no longer need anyone to *teach* them to know him, because he would forgive them (Jer. 31:31–34). Paul explains that God made him and his colleagues agents of this new covenant, not by the letter but by the Spirit (2 Cor. 3:6).

Since, on cessationist terms, we lack apostles like Paul, who was an agent of the new covenant, do we know whether new-covenant agents remain? Perhaps the new-covenant pattern of believers knowing God for themselves more directly is no longer for today?[5] On the strictest cessationist approach, we now hear God only through Scripture, and especially through its most elite agents—namely, (cessationist) Bible teachers.[6]

While I (Craig) would be happy if more people actually *listened* to us Bible teachers, I rather doubt that many people, cessationist or not, are ready to relegate God's voice today only to Bible teachers. Happily, most of us believers are ready to testify, "I know Jesus personally." In the new-covenant era, Jeremiah 31:34 says, "they will all know me," but it also says, "they will no longer teach each other" to know God. Thus, it might be easier to argue that what is not for this era is *teaching* rather than prophecy, which Joel 2:28–29 explicitly situates in the last-days era of salvation.[7] First John 2:27 even says, "You don't need anyone to teach you." Happily, the context in 1 John includes authoritative teaching, and Scripture includes teaching among spiritual gifts.

## Forget Missions

Historically, many early Protestants were uncomfortably consistent. They believed that certain commands—including the Great Commission—were only for the first, apostolic generation. Just as God empowered the first apostles by the Spirit to lay the foundation for the church, so the mission to the nations was only for the first witnesses (Acts 1:8), not for subsequent ones.

Most of us today would question whether Acts really teaches that. It is true that Jesus originally addressed Acts 1:8 to the apostles (1:2; cf. 2:32; 3:15; 5:32; 10:39, 41) or to the Eleven and those with them (see Luke 24:33), and that the commission in the first place belonged to witnesses who had been present for Jesus's ministry (Acts 1:21–22). Nevertheless, subsequent converts can join in this role of witness (22:15, 20; 26:16), testifying of what they see and hear (2:33; 22:14–15). Just as power for the mission to the "ends of the

5. Ruthven, *Cessation*, xx, xxiii.

6. Highlighting the continuance of teachers (as opposed to many other gifts; Pennington, *Cessationism*, 94) can be self-serving for teachers, leaving us on top.

7. In fact, the point of both passages is that all believers will know and hear God for themselves.

earth" (1:8) continues (2:39), so does the mission itself. Luke didn't record the book merely for those with antiquarian interest as if it belonged in a sort of Christian antique shop. Luke wrote to inspire a continued Spirit-led mission to the nations, which is the way that most of us preach Acts today.

But this was a hard sell to many early heirs of the magisterial Reformers. Unlike the early Moravians,[8] many mainstream Protestants left missions especially to Catholics (though partly because German and Swiss Protestants lacked the naval access afforded to Spain and Portugal during this period).[9] Although Luther's views on specifics may have varied over his lifetime, at one point he declares that miracles ceased once the gospel was preached throughout the world—that is, in the apostolic era.[10] Following Martin Luther's perspective,[11] Lutheran theologian Johann Gerhard (1582–1637) believed that the Great Commission was only for the apostles; God had already offered the gospel to all peoples once for all in the first century, and he would not do so again.[12]

John Calvin found other grounds to support individuals evangelizing,[13] and he did commission some followers to reach France and indigenous peoples in Brazil.[14] Nevertheless, Calvin himself applied the biblical Great Commission only to the apostles, to whom it was specifically addressed.[15] In this he contrasts to some degree with Anabaptists, who insisted that all Christians were responsible for the Great Commission.[16] Reformed theologian Gijsbert Voetius (1589–1676) was among the earliest Reformed thinkers to develop a theology of evangelizing the unreached,[17] but some Calvinists insisted that if God wanted to convert people, he would do it without Christians' help.[18] Against some of their peers, Calvinist Baptists Andrew Fuller (1754–1815)

8. Neill, *History of Missions*, 237–38; Tucker, *Jerusalem*, 69–74.

9. Neill, *History of Missions*, 221–22; Tucker, *Jerusalem*, 67.

10. Eire, *Flew*, 60–61. Wittenberg's divinity faculty treated supporters of missions as false prophets (Billman, *Thread*, 34).

11. Tucker, *Jerusalem*, 67.

12. Neill, *History of Missions*, 222.

13. Cf. also Calvin's concern for foreigners (Ames, "Calvin and Foreigner"); missional seventeenth-century Puritans in Haykin and Robinson, *Ends of the Earth*, 75–90.

14. Tucker, *Jerusalem*, 67–68. This was, however, through the church's collective preaching (cf. Stevens, "Idea of Mission"; on the Reformers and global preaching through the church, ca. 1555–1654, see the argument of Medeiros, "Commitment").

15. Mauldin, *Fullerism*, 41–48; Stevens, "Idea of Mission." For Calvin, magistrates now exercise this role (Mauldin, *Fullerism*, 45). For some themes in Calvin relevant to the church's mission, however, see Wilson, "Missional Church."

16. Mauldin, *Fullerism*, 43; Sunshine, "Missions," 13. Even Anabaptists at the time went only to Europeans who spoke their language (Sunshine, "Missions," 13).

17. Irvin and Sunquist, *History*, 284.

18. Galli, "Wouldn't Give Up." For their appeal to election, see also Tucker, *Jerusalem*, 67, 115.

and William Carey (1761–1834) had to defend the view that the Great Commission was still for today.[19]

Happily, most of us today recognize that the Great Commission remains in effect until the end of the age (Matt. 10:23; 24:14; 28:19–20; see chap. 3 below)—even though Jesus addressed it *directly* only to the first disciples. Moreover, if the commission remains, so does the power of God's presence by the Spirit for accomplishing that mission (Matt. 28:20; Mark 13:10–11; Luke 24:49; John 20:21–22; Acts 1:8; 2:39). Likewise, if biblical precedent counts for anything (certainly it should count more than extrabiblical theological ideas), that power should continue to be expressed at times in signs and wonders.

Indeed, historically, those who denied that the Great Commission applied to their times were normally also the voices that denied that signs would continue; they believed that the original apostles completely fulfilled the commission and its attendant signs. Those who expected the mission to continue generally expected signs to accompany the evangelization of yet-unreached regions.[20]

## Don't Bother the Demons

Jesus called an exorcism a miracle, an act of power (Mark 9:38–39). If miracles are not for today (as the most extreme cessationists maintain), then exorcism must not be for today.[21] This means either that demons ceased (or at least that they ceased to bother anyone) with the completion of the canon or that God has left us without the recourse of deliverance in dealing with them.[22]

19. George, "Revival," 50–51. See Carey, *Enquiry*. In the US, however, predestinarian justification for Baptist antimissionism apparently developed later than other justifications (McCall, "Reassessing," 326).

20. Boys, *Evidence*, 35, 93–96, 106, 145, 207, 210–11; see further our chap. 21. Most cited Mark 16:15–18 (e.g., Boys, *Evidence*, 105), but the connection is already clear elsewhere (e.g., Acts 14:3; Rom. 15:18–19). Some early Protestant examples of accepting both miracles and mission include Hugo Grotius, Heinrich Bullinger, John Foxe, and Johann Albrecht Bengel (Boys, *Evidence*, 96, 151–52, 236, 255–57). Some sound like they denied both yet elsewhere testify to some miracles (241–43)!

21. Warfield apparently believed that Jesus's resurrection banished all demons, denying authentic exorcism after the apostolic era (Billman, *Thread*, 34), which required rejecting massive testimony from antiquity, including a primary source of new converts in the third century (MacMullen, *Christianizing*, 61–62), and massive evidence today (see, e.g., Keener and Vaughan, *Demons*).

22. Like many others in church history, Calvin believed that demonic miracles still occurred (Boys, *Evidence*, 122); he was not, however, as opposed to Christian ones as he has sometimes been portrayed. Martin Bucer (Boys, *Evidence*, 136), Luther (162–70, though without the medieval frills), and others did believe that demons could be expelled. Still, Luther's resistance to traditional Catholic exorcistic rites left Catholic exorcists dominant in the sphere of exorcism for more than a century (Midelfort, *History*, 97).

In practice, the ceasing of divine miracles would mean that any superhuman works through individuals today will not be divine miracles, but rather (as some of the harshest cessationists have suggested) the devil's miracles. In other words, the devil is free to show his power, and Christians just have to put up with it until Jesus comes back. In practice, the devil can display his power through individuals in ways that (given full cessationism) God will not. New Testament texts that would suggest otherwise are not (on full cessationist terms) for today.[23]

Yet Christians' success at exorcism was, along with healing, a major reason for conversion to Christianity well into the 300s.[24] The North African theologian Tertullian even insisted that any Christian who could not cast out demons was a fake Christian.[25] Those who believe that such activity ceased with the close of the canon have to reject the basis for many conversions in antiquity (never mind today), as well as the testimony of many church fathers.[26] Those who believe that such activity ceased only gradually can allow the testimony of the earliest church fathers but not later testimonies. Either way, they're probably stuck with quite a lot of demons on their hands today.

Happily, we know no cessationist who doubts that demons still exist and that we might need to confront them at times. Nevertheless, we also have met cessationists who have encountered demons, recognized their own inconsistency during the process of having to cast them out, and then become continuationists.

This chapter has been largely tongue-in-cheek,[27] but we hope that it highlights some potential inconsistencies in cessationism. In the next chapter, we address potential problems with cessationism in a more literal way.

23. Catholics and various historians sometimes highlight the inconsistency: "How does one account for the fact that Protestants left the devil in full control of his preternatural powers while they stripped God of his supernatural powers on earth?" (Eire, *Flew*, 22). "While they rejected the possibility of divine miracles, Protestants continued to believe that the devil could perform 'impossible' feats" (Eire, *Flew*, 290; cf. also 291).

24. MacMullen, *Christianizing*, 61–62; Frend, *Rise*, 566–67.

25. Tertullian, *Apol.* 23.4–6.

26. See sources in, e.g., MacMullen, *Christianizing*, 27–28, 40–41, 60–61; Lampe, "Miracles," 215–17; Hillgarth, *Paganism*, 11–12, 183; Young, "Miracles in History," 107–8; Martin, "Resisting," 49–50, 58–59; Sears, "View," 103–4.

27. As well as being a trap to expose the sort of critics who review books or chapters based on titles without reading their content.

# 2

# Some *Real* Problems with Cessationism

Serious problems with extreme cessationism include its hermeneutic (its way of understanding Scripture), its treatment of Christ's body, its relation to the church's mission, and its relation toward God. Some cessationist circles have meanwhile painted all charismatics with a wide brush based on the worst examples among charismatics, even as they avoid confronting the serious biblical and logical weaknesses of their own arguments.

## Problems Affecting Bible Interpretation

While *lists* of spiritual gifts consume only a small portion of Scripture, mostly in Paul's letters, activities that characterize controversial gifts, such as prophecy and healing, consume considerable space in Scripture, not least in the Gospels and Acts. Cessationism shifts how we should read such passages. If these passages do not model anything for our continuing collective mission, how do they provide teaching (as all Scripture should, according to 2 Tim. 3:16)? The cessationist approach renders these passages less relevant for us than normal biblical texts should be (contrast how Paul reads Scripture in 1 Cor. 10:6, 11).

A serious problem with cessationism is thus what it does to our actual embrace of the Bible. Hermeneutics is the study of how we interpret texts; consciously or unconsciously, our hermeneutic guides how we appropriate biblical passages for today. Normally, when we apply Scripture, we look for continuity between the message of the text and circumstances today. This process is not limited to, and is much simpler for, those whose theology *allows* a greater degree of continuity.

### *Continuity or Discontinuity?*

Most Christians allow some continuity and some discontinuity (such as promise and fulfillment) between the Old Testament and the New Testament. But how much discontinuity should we expect between the New Testament and today, without any clear biblical warning? If we expect any, how *biblical* is that approach? And how would we decide what to follow and what has changed? Culture has changed, and this must be taken into account. (I, Craig, not only agree but have also devoted decades of research to that quest.) But what about more theological matters? The harder the cessationist, the more they must posit radical discontinuity with certain patterns of God's working in Scripture, even in New Testament letters.[1] Most churches hold services bearing little resemblance to the clearest biblical model we have for them, in 1 Corinthians 14:26. It is too bad that the main biblical passage revealing what a church meeting was like focuses on particular gifts that, according to cessationists, were going to pass away in a few years or decades, and Scripture does not even explicitly warn us about that.

When I (Craig) was a young Christian I attended some Bible studies taught by what even many traditional dispensationalists would have regarded as a hyperdispensationalist (a far cry from today's much more balanced "progressive dispensationalists"). Despite many edifying features of the Bible studies, this teacher's group believed that not even baptism or the Lord's Supper was for this dispensation, accepting as for today only what was taught in Paul's prison epistles (especially Ephesians, Philippians, and Colossians). Although I always disagreed with them regarding spiritual gifts, I appreciated their love for the parts of the Bible that they did apply. For several months I accepted their basic premise of radical discontinuity between the testaments, until my continued study of Scripture made that premise unworkable.

Reading Paul, I soon realized that he grounded his arguments for salvation by faith in Christ in Old Testament models. If he was wrong, the most I could salvage of my young faith was Jesus plus the Old Testament, and I would need to observe the stipulations of ancient Israelite law. As I worked through Deuteronomy, however, I discovered that it was full of grace. God had *always* saved people by grace through faith; the change or discontinuity between testaments had to do not with grace but with fuller revelations and subsequent revelatory and saving events in history. The ultimate saving event, of course, was God becoming flesh and dying and rising for us. But reading

1. This section draws on Keener, *Spirit Hermeneutics*, 54–56: "Noncessationist, or continuationist, reading."

the Bible for continuity wherever possible helped me to welcome its message for my own life today.[2]

Hermeneutical consistency becomes an important issue for our debate. When the biblical canon was limited to the Old Testament, no one had reason to expect that prophecy would cease. Biblical narratives would promote the expectation that it would continue, and promises of the outpoured Spirit, as in Joel 2:28–29, would lead to greater anticipation for the future. Yet the rabbinic movement eventually declared that true prophecy had long ceased and that they—the theologians who interpreted the Torah—were God's only spokesmen.[3] Who was closer to the spirit of Scripture, the rabbis or the early Christians?

After the New Testament fulfills the Old Testament pattern and widens its scope further, with the Spirit of prophecy now available to all believers (Acts 2:17–18), an unannounced cessation of prophecy would mark an even starker rupture with Scripture. The thesis of such a cessation posits a *post*–New Testament church dispensation not expressly mentioned in Scripture. It follows the rabbinic rather than the early Christian pattern, essentially denying in practice that we have entered the era of the outpoured prophetic Spirit.

### Canon Within a Canon?

Many have accused Martin Luther of having a canon within a canon. He used his emphasis on justification by faith to value some biblical texts above others (John above the Synoptics, Paul and 1 Peter above James, and so forth).[4] While some passages are indeed more central or theologically packed than others, many feel that Luther took this emphasis too far. John Calvin's Reformed tradition emphasized greater balance in this regard, and Calvin himself wrote commentaries on much of the Old Testament and all the New Testament except 2 John, 3 John, and Revelation.

In practice, however, even many who affirm the entire canon work with a functional canon within the canon. When it comes to spiritual gifts, cessationism effectively establishes such a canon within the canon. While most

2. Our historic language of "testaments" is really a misnomer, since most of the material in both sections is narrative not directly part of the covenants per se. For one survey of approaches to the relationship between the "testaments," see Baker, *Testaments*, 34–176.

3. After the death of Malachi, *t. Sotah* 13:3; *b. Sanh.* 11a, bar.; *b. Sotah* 48b, bar.; *b. Yoma* 9b; *Song Rab.* 8:9, §3; at some other time but before their own, *t. Sotah* 12:5; *Pesiq. Rab Kah.* 13:14; *Num. Rab.* 15:10; *Song Rab.* 8:9, §3; see further Davies, *Paul*, 208–15; Bamberger, "Prophet," 306; Leivestad, "Dogma"; Hill, *Prophecy*, 33–35. On this teaching conveniently reducing competition with their own role as interpreters of past revelation, see Greenspahn, "Prophecy." For the analogy with (and perhaps influence on) Reformed cessationism, see Löfstedt, "Silence."

4. On Luther's "critical statements about certain biblical books," alongside "his commitment to the unity of Scripture," Chester, *Reading Paul*, 22, cites Thompson, *Sure Ground*, chaps. 2–4; Kolb, *Luther and Word*, chaps. 2–4. Many comment that he had a functional canon within a canon (though the analogy with Marcion, as in Scheck, "Introduction," 21, 23–24, is overstated).

cessationists in practice try to understand how we should live out the Bible today, cessationism can restrict what it requires of us to its direct statements or commands. Cessationists tend to adhere especially to those commands in the New Testament or sometimes even just to those in the epistles—*except* for those very epistles' commands to pursue spiritual gifts. Cessationism ceases to read the Bible as being for today precisely where its words relate to certain conspicuous features of God's action, as in spiritual gifts—even though God is the *least* changing and culturally bound figure in the Bible (Num. 23:19; 1 Sam. 15:29; Mal. 3:6; James 1:17). By insisting that God no longer performs the kinds of works through believers that he did in Bible days, cessationism separates the Bible world from the "real," practical world in which we live, the opposite of the sort of hermeneutic that New Testament authors used with the Old Testament.

God inspired prophecy and spoke to his people in many times and places throughout the Bible, and the Bible nowhere declares that this activity would stop. Indeed, the last we hear in the Bible, this age between Jesus's comings is *characterized* by prophecy (Acts 2:17–18; see chap. 4 below) and Paul gives instructions for spiritual gifts in church (1 Cor. 12–14; see chap. 6 below). How is it biblical to depend on a postbiblical theological explanation in lieu of any clear biblical teaching and consequently expect God not to act the way he often acts throughout the Bible?

Some may also reduce the amount of Scripture they need to obey in practice by minimizing biblical narratives as sources for learning God's message—thus excluding much of the Gospels and Acts from consideration. Not only does this contradict the way Paul taught from biblical narratives in his letters—for example, in Romans 4:22–24, where Paul argues for our justification by faith by applying the model of Abram's justification; or 1 Corinthians 10:11, where Paul applies judgments on unfaithful Israelites to unfaithful Christians. It also risks undercutting the explicit claim of 2 Timothy 3:16 that *all* Scripture is profitable for teaching. This approach is concerning, especially when it comes from critics who claim that continuationists are the ones who do not respect Scripture. Granted, we must learn theology from narratives in ways that differ from the ways we learn it in proverbs, oracles, letters, and the like. But, as we shall see, cessationism limits the amount of Scripture it "allows" to speak to this subject to such a narrow range of texts that it effectively rules out much of the voice of Scripture before letting it address the question. In the case of spiritual gifts, cessationism excludes not only biblical narratives, but even direct commands in a Pauline letter to a key church.

When people today challenge biblical sexual ethics, we biblically conservative Christians consider them too liberal. When people challenge dimensions of the Spirit's empowerment for fellow members of Christ's body, however, they claim to be conservative defenders of the canon. They may have a longer pedigree in tradition than those who revise sexual ethics, but we believe that in practice the approaches of both similarly undermine the authority of Scripture. The elements that they discard are not mere cultural accommodations in Scripture but matters involving God's own activity and explicit biblical promises.

### *Who Bears the Burden of Proof?*

Respect for Scripture should invite us to welcome its models and teaching, though we may need to recontextualize the principles behind its cultural expressions for different cultural settings. Some hard cessationists have argued that although no clear text announces that the gifts would pass away after the close of the canon, neither do any texts argue the opposite.[5] This is truly a curious way of arguing, since one would expect such a dramatic shift away from both Old and New Testament prophetic models to be announced explicitly in Scripture. It is a tacit admission that Scripture does not teach their position. Instead, Paul seems to assume that prophecy and tongues remain until we see Jesus face-to-face, partial knowledge being valuable until it is supplanted by perfect knowledge (1 Cor. 13:8–12; see chap. 5 below).

This cessationist argument also appears a curious tactic when we consider the selective nature of the reasoning. Would someone argue that the unity of Christ's multigifted body would pass away with the completion of the canon unless there is explicit evidence to the contrary (cf. Eph. 4:11–13)? Or more analogously, would someone argue that since the canon is complete, we no longer need the gift of teaching? Why some gifts and not others? (Teaching seems to run more risk of competing with the canon than tongues would.) Or perhaps the Spirit no longer bears witness with our spirit that we're God's children, since the New Testament nowhere *explicitly* declares that this divine assurance must continue? Some people argue that we should not use instrumental music because it is not mentioned in the New Testament; others could respond that they might well then exclude cars and electric lights.[6]

But the cessationist does not simply argue from silence against something not stated in Scripture. He or she actively excludes something that *is* in the Bible (such as the model of prophecy throughout biblical history and the biblical command to pursue it in 1 Cor. 14:1, 39), without any explicit biblical evidence that it was supposed to stop. The basis for this is not Scripture but a theological inference

5. Cf. even Saucy, "View," 123–24 (quote from 124): "If the New Testament does not explicitly teach that certain miraculous gifts will cease, neither does it explicitly teach that they will continue throughout this entire age."

6. Admittedly, our brothers and sisters who are instrumental-music cessationists do produce many of the best a capella singers. And if the power grid ever goes down, no one will be better prepared than the Old Order Amish.

about Scripture.[7] Ironically, cessationism is a postbiblical doctrine—the very thing that cessationists claim most to fear from allowing postbiblical prophecies!

In contrast to such an approach, it seems to us more biblically faithful to read the biblical narrative as a model for understanding how God works in our world, and to live in the light of that narrative. This is the way that most Christians of any stripe seek to read most of the New Testament. Such a reading takes faith, inviting an entirely new worldview or approach to reality around us. It introduces the expectation of a God who works actively and sometimes visibly (as well as regularly invisibly) in the world around us. We thus trust his providence in our lives and expect his Spirit to guide us and to perform unusual works where he finds them appropriate to further his purposes. Such a reading invites today's church to experience God's activity in the way that many early Christians did, provided we are willing to engage in the same wholehearted commitment and mission that they did.

### *What Happens When Believers Read the Bible for Themselves?*

What if new believers read the Bible for themselves without the doctrinal lens of cessationism? Former cessationist biblical scholar Jack Deere insists, "If you were to lock a brand-new Christian in a room with a Bible and tell him to study what the Scriptures have to say about healing and miracles, he would never come out of the room a cessationist."[8] Inductive study can even sway some of those schooled in cessationism. Like Deere and trained at the same institution, Sam Storms taught cessationism until Scripture turned him charismatic.[9]

The issue may arise most often for new believers. It must be an interesting conversation when new believers within cessationist congregations are first told by their pastors, "Don't worry about all that supernatural stuff you're reading about in that book; most of that's not for you." The Reformers fought long and hard to get the Word of God into the hands of ordinary people so they could read it and understand it for themselves. Now that we are able to do so, and everyone can clearly see what the Scriptures say, some of those who follow in the tradition of those same Reformers insist that we cannot trust the plain sense of the text. We need their special, extrabiblical paradigm through which to interpret the Scriptures.[10]

7. Astonishingly, Tom Pennington's book titled *A Biblical Case for Cessationism* is anything but (though admittedly, authors do not usually get to name their books); like other cessationist arguments, it is theological inference rather than an examination from *biblical* theology. As John Carpenter, a Reformed pastor, notes, "Even responsible cessationists will concede, the Bible doesn't teach cessationism" (Carpenter, "Recovering"; cited in Brown, *Authentic Fire*, 171).

8. Deere, *Surprised*, 54.

9. Cf. Storms, "View," 175.

10. There can be no question that the cessationist paradigm is extrabiblical. It proposes a new way God interacts with people that began after the canon closed. That new way is based

One could multiply examples of what happens when believers read Scripture for themselves without being handed a Western sieve. The late Peruvian missiologist Samuel Escobar, who was my (Craig's) close friend and colleague, reports a conversation with an indigenous teacher from the Peruvian jungle. When local people noticed demons in the Western linguist's translation of Mark, the Western linguist explained that such spirits were only a first-century concern. While the local teacher respected the linguist, he insisted that their local environment matched what they found in Mark: "We know that there really are demons and spirits; they're around here."[11]

One anthropologist recounts the experience of a fellow anthropologist named Jacob Loewen, who was doing Bible translation among the Choco people in Panama.[12] The wife of Loewen's host, Aureliano, was dying from what was obviously pneumonia; Loewen sent to a nearby town for medicine, only to discover that none was available. While Loewen had translated the promise of healing in James 5:14–15, he knew that he did not have faith to pray. Nevertheless, reading this passage, the local believers prayed with him for her healing, and she rallied slightly. By the next morning, however, she was dying again, so the local believers anointed her with oil, without inviting Loewen, and this time she rose from the bed completely well, returning immediately to her household labors (cf. Mark 1:31). When Aureliano declared happily that God's Spirit had chased away the fever spirits, Loewen observed that they had not invited him and his Western colleague to pray this time. Aureliano apologized but noted, "It doesn't work when you and David are in the circle. You and David don't really believe." The writer remarks that he knew few Christians more consistent than Loewen, yet even Loewen found "himself unable to transcend the secular assumptions and understandings of his particular birth society."[13]

## Rightly Discerning the Body of Christ

What if new believers read the Bible for themselves without the doctrinal lens of cessationism? That is essentially what happened around the world as interdenominational Bible societies and missions provided Christians with Bibles in their own languages. Reading the Bible for themselves, most of the global church went charismatic. Or to put it more precisely, inductive study of the Bible itself did not lead anyone to come up with cessationism. The

---

not on Scripture itself but on tradition and especially the rationalism developed by postbiblical theologians.

11. Escobar, *Tides*, 86. This paragraph and the next come from Keener, *Miracles*, 1:230; 2:835–36.

12. Wilson, "Seeing," 202–4 (citing Loewen's account from 1974).

13. Wilson, "Seeing," 204.

Reformation emphasis on *sola scriptura*, the Bible alone, does not support the cessationism of some who claim the Reformers' mantle.

### Going Global

Some cessationists complain that even in the West, including among many Reformed Christians, continuationism has become the dominant view.[14] Even though hard cessationist teachers are increasingly proliferating anticharismatic ideology in East Asia and elsewhere, continuationism remains even more dominant outside the West. Western scholar of global Christianity Philip Jenkins notes that in general Christianity in the Global South is quite interested in "the immediate workings of the supernatural, through prophecy, visions, ecstatic utterances, and healing."[15] Such an approach, closer to the early Christian worldview than modern Western culture is, appeals to many traditional non-Western cultures.[16] Hwa Yung, retired bishop of the Methodist church in Malaysia, notes that the charismatic, Pentecostal character of Majority World churches reflects not so much direct influence by Pentecostals or charismatics as simply the worldview of the majority of humanity. Most cultures have never embraced the Western, mechanistic, naturalistic Enlightenment worldview that rejects the supernatural.[17]

14. MacArthur, "Foreword," v (he may qualify the expression with "confessedly" Reformed, but other Reformed Christians could challenge his selectivity in appropriating Reformed tradition in view of his decidedly non-Reformed eschatology). Waldron, *Continued*, 14, laments that continuationists have won "the propaganda battle." But while we might regard some charismatic broadcasts (no less than the Strange Fire conference) as "propaganda," propaganda has little to do with cessationism being absent from Scripture, the average Bible-reading Christian's base starting point.

15. Jenkins, *Next Christendom*, 107, who also complains that Westerners too often contest the legitimacy of such perspectives (on p. 121 offering the specific example of liberal Episcopal bishop John Spong's ethnocentric complaints about African Anglican bishops' "superstitious" and "Pentecostal" "extremism"). Admittedly, this observation is a generalization, since many in the West also report such experiences (cf. Kang, "World," 38).

16. See, e.g., Pocock, Van Rheenen, and McConnell, *Face*, 136–37; cf. Keener, "Spirit," 170. For Pentecostal relevance to indigenous healing traditions as well as offering a connection to the Gospels and Acts, see also, e.g., Porterfield, *Healing*, 126; Yong, "Independent Pentecostalism," 401. Cultural receptivity to spiritual realities does not necessarily lead to embracing the same spirits as before. Lehmann, *Struggle*, 145, compares Latin American Pentecostal healings with earlier possession cults but underlines significant differences (the former demonizing the latter's spirits, and Pentecostals having followers whereas possession cults have clients). Scholars argue that in Africa as well, Pentecostals have demonized the old spirits and have grown at the expense of the older "Spirit churches" that accommodated them (Van Dijk, "Technologies," 221; for an example, see Kalu, "Mission," 13–14); the fast-growing charismatic churches are often displacing both traditional mission churches and independent churches (Mwaura, "Integrity," 198). Turaki, "Missiology," 281, also notes that they are often evangelizing "nominal second generation Christians."

17. Yung, "Integrity," 173. Cf. also Yung, *Quest*, 238–39; Poewe, "Rethinking," 248.

"Signs and wonders" are among the most prominent factors drawing people to faith in Christ in the Majority World today,[18] with healings and exorcisms proving particularly effective,[19] regardless how much some vocal Western cessationists might wish to put the brakes on this activity. Addressing the future of global Christianity, Moonjang Lee notes, "The growing churches in the non-Western world are mostly Pentecostal-Charismatic, as seen in the Pentecostal movements in Latin America, Independent Churches in Africa, and Charismatic movements in Asia." Observing that Christianity is losing its traditional Western forms, Lee warns that it will need to fully recover its early charismatic character to survive and flourish.[20]

Estimates of global figures for charismatic and Pentecostal Christians are in the hundreds of millions.[21] As of the year 2000, some estimated that there were 126 million Pentecostal or charismatic Christians in Africa, 134.9 million in Asia, and 141.4 million in Latin America, with 79.6 million in North America, whereas there were almost none a century earlier.[22] By 2010, the estimate was more than 600 million Pentecostals, charismatics, and neocharismatics (out of roughly two billion church members, or 1.5 billion church attenders, in the world).[23] The comparable figures for evangelicals more traditionally defined are about 263 million for 2010 and 348 million for 2025.[24]

Charismatics broadly defined thus comprise roughly 28 percent of global church membership, and perhaps closer to 40 percent of regular church attenders. Several years ago, Pentecostals proper accounted for an estimated 94,383,000; charismatics for 206,579,000; and Third Wave adherents for 313,048,000.[25] Numbers are surely higher today; one Pentecostal denomination alone, the Assemblies of God, estimates more than 88 million adherents globally today.[26]

18. Yung, "Integrity," 173–75.

19. Yung, "Integrity," 174. For the correlation of church growth with healing campaigns, see already McGavran, "Healing and Growth," in 1979 (cited in more recent format in McGee, *Miracles*, 174).

20. Lee, "Future," 105.

21. Defining "charismatic" broadly, David Barrett in the late 1980s estimated there would be more than 600 million by 2000, or nearly 30 percent of world Christianity ("Statistics," 813), though he estimated downward closer to 2000 (roughly 524 million in Barrett, "Renewal," 388; cf. 460 million in Synan, *Tradition*, ix, 281, for 1995; 530 million in Synan, "Streams," 372, for 1999); Sanneh estimates almost 590 million for 2005 (and a projected nearly 800 million by 2025; *Disciples*, 275); in 1994, Harvey Cox already accepted an estimate of 410 million (Cox, *Fire*, xv) and a few years later suggested that "Pentecostals" could "equal Catholics in number by" 2030 (Cox, "Miracles," 88); cf. the breakdown of figures in Synan, *Grow*, 5–11 (though note the many inactive "postcharismatics").

22. Noll, *Shape*, 22, cites these figures (as "best estimates," 23) from Barrett, *Encyclopedia*.

23. Johnson, Barrett, and Crossing, "Christianity 2010," 36.

24. Johnson, Barrett, and Crossing, "Christianity 2010," 36.

25. Johnson and Ross, *Atlas*, 102.

26. Assemblies of God, "About."

Some estimate that Pentecostal and charismatic Christians multiplied by more than 600 percent from 1970 to 2000; by such estimates they thus constituted 27.4 percent of world Christianity by 2006.[27] By this estimate, they may constitute roughly one twelfth of the world's population.[28] Sociologist Peter Berger contends that Pentecostalism, presumably in the broad sense, "accounts for something like 80 percent of its [evangelical Protestantism's] worldwide growth."[29] It has also functioned as a brake on radical secularization.[30]

Emphasizing Pentecostalism's growth in the Global South, where it is especially flourishing and culturally relevant,[31] historian Robert Bruce Mullin observes that already by the end of the twentieth century there were "more Pentecostals worldwide" than mainline Protestants.[32] Catholic theologian Ralph Martin concludes, "In all of human history, no other non-political, non-militaristic, voluntary human movement has grown as rapidly as the Pentecostal-charismatic movement."[33] While miracle claims also proliferate

27. Hanciles, *Beyond Christendom*, 121; on Pentecostal and charismatic Christianity leading Christian expansion today, see also Noll, *Shape*, 115 (citing Martin, *Tongues*; Martin, *Pentecostalism*). By mid-2006, these movements had grown more than eight times since 1970 (Barrett, Johnson, and Crossing, "Missiometrics 2006," 28). These projections may require adjustment; these authors estimate 588,502,000 by mid-2005 (Barrett, Johnson, and Crossing, "Missiometrics 2005," 29), thus a 7,594,000 increase by 2006; 602,792,000 by mid-2007 (Barrett, Johnson, and Crossing, "Missiometrics 2007," 32), with a 6,696,000 annual increase; but 601,682,000 for 2008 (Barrett, Johnson, and Crossing, "Missiometrics 2008"), thus an adjustment of 1,110,000 lower (though 1970 figures also appear nearly four million lower). By 2007 Pentecostals broadly defined may have represented 29 percent of world church attenders (Barrett, Johnson, and Crossing, "Missiometrics 2007," 32); Cox, "Foreword," xxi, similarly ranks them at a quarter of global Christendom. Tomkins, *History*, 245, notes figures between one-sixth and a quarter of global Christendom but notes that even such figures underestimate.

28. Satyavrata, "Globalization," 3.

29. Berger, "Faces," 425. Cf. Tomkins, *History*, 220: "the fastest-growing form of Christianity ever."

30. Anderson, *Ends of the Earth*, 8.

31. For Pentecostalism in the Majority World, see, e.g., Yong, *Spirit Poured*, 33–80 (in Africa and the African diaspora, see 59–80; in Asia, 45–58; in Latin America, 33–45); Anderson, *Pentecostalism*, passim, including on Brazil (72–73), Congo (111), Kenya (112, 113), West Africa (116), the United States (117), Indonesia (130); Jenkins, *Next Christendom*, 122–31; various essays in Dempster, Klaus, and Petersen, *Globalization of Pentecostalism*, including the section overview; Klaus, "Global Culture"; Robeck, "Charismatic Movements," 150–54. For its growth in much of Asia, see, e.g., Ma, "Challenges," 195–96; Ma, "Theology"; Yung, "Pentecostalism"; Anderson, "Face"; in Latin America, e.g., Petersen, "Latin American Pentecostalism"; in Africa, e.g., Maxwell, *African Gifts*, 6–7. For the rapid expansion of Pentecostal missionaries from the Majority World, see, e.g., Pate, "Missions," 244–46; for one favorable perspective on the movement's growth, see Wagner, "Perspective," 266–68.

32. Mullin, *History*, 211 (cf. 276); cf. similarly Noll, *Shape*, 32. Sweeney, *Story*, 153, calls "Holiness-Pentecostalism" (encompassing also charismatics) "perhaps the fastest-growing movement that the church has ever seen." They constitute a significant proportion of world Christianity (see figures in Noll, *Shape*, 22, citing Barrett, *Encyclopedia*).

33. Martin, *Catholic Church*, 87.

far beyond Pentecostal and charismatic circles,[34] especially in the Majority World, Pentecostals and charismatics alone offer sufficient numbers of eyewitness miracle claims to illustrate that the sorts of eyewitness claims that some skeptics have doubted possible are in fact widespread. (A large proportion of mainline Christians in the Majority World fit the broad Western definition of charismatic.)[35] Signs and wonders eventually contributed to the young Anglican Province of South East Asia being "one of the fastest growing parts of the Anglican Communion."[36] My (Craig's) wife Médine comes from the mainstream but continuationist Evangelical Church of Congo; she does not speak in tongues, but half of her siblings do, and she reports many prophecies and healings from her church circles, including her sister being raised from the dead after three hours.

### *More Sober Figures?*

Because of fluid definitions, estimates of global charismatics include an assortment of groups that would not all endorse one another's orthodoxy.[37] Certainly some cessationists question their orthodoxy. Explicitly rejecting charismatic Catholics and alleged adherents to prosperity teaching, cessationist pastor and teacher Tom Pennington complains that "well over 50% of those in a movement that claims to be a true work of the Holy Spirit have instead embraced false gospels."[38]

Perhaps the Spirit moves by grace among those who welcome him and not only among those whose theology is acceptable to conservative cessationists. I (Craig) share serious concerns about "wealth" teachings;[39] yet I believe that many have artificially inflated the figures of "prosperity" adherents by misreading the definitions used in some surveys. Again, my wife Médine is from

34. See examples in Keener, *Miracles*.

35. Noll, *Shape*, 34 (claiming "almost all" but admitting "some hyperbole").

36. Noll, *Shape*, 1. Bishop Chiu sought to keep the local charismatic movement in biblical bounds and also welcomed the Lambeth Conference resolution that affirmed healing the sick (11).

37. Most Trinitarian Pentecostals, for example, reject the orthodoxy of the roughly 25 million Oneness Pentecostals (who, incidentally, return the favor); sociologists also classify global Pentecostalism more by style than theology. For a nuanced and cautious discussion of the figures, see Anderson, *Pentecostalism*, 11; even the lowest estimates, however, attest remarkable growth (Davies and Conway, *Christianity*, 76). The highest statistics normally include indigenous independent churches (see, e.g., Burgess, *Revolution*, 5–6). For the diversity of movements that most social scientists classify as Pentecostals, see, e.g., Droogers, "Globalisation," 46–48, 57–59; cf. Anderson, "Varieties"; Bergunder, "Turn," 52–56.

38. Pennington, *Cessationism*, 13.

39. See, e.g., Keener, *Suffering*, chap. 8. As stated elsewhere, I live as simply as I can and, when single, lived as close to subsistence as possible (Keener, "Ongoing Evidence," 368–69). For concerns with genuine prosperity teaching's proliferation in Africa, see, e.g., Phiri and Maxwell, "Riches."

the Evangelical Church of the Republic of Congo. When I read to her the definition used to determine numbers of prosperity advocates, she said that from an African perspective this wording simply means depending on God (sometimes for dear life) for provision, not becoming wealthy in a Western sense.

Others have also pointed out that definitions of "prosperity" employed in an African context are fluid, some focusing simply on needed provision.[40] In fact, when the survey is examined more closely, the figures for charismatics do not differ significantly from those for Christians in general in the comparable regions![41] The Strange Fire conference neglected to point out that the same survey shows (in contrast to MacArthur parading the worst charismatic examples) that Pentecostals and charismatics on average have higher commitment to evangelism, the authority of Scripture, and prayer than do other groups of Christians—all features that MacArthur could have applauded![42]

Nevertheless, even if one halved the usual estimates of charismatics to some three hundred million, the movement's growth since its recognition in the early twentieth century is phenomenal. If one speaks more broadly of continuationists—that is, noncessationists—one easily speaks of the majority of global Christianity, including the majority of global evangelicalism.

### Dismembering Christ's Body

One serious practical problem with any strident form of cessationism is thus what it does to the body of Christ. First, it reduces the biblical, God-designed diversity of gifts in Christ's body. Second, it cuts off fellowship and unity with those who follow explicit biblical teachings regarding God's gifts to the church. Paul says that the body needs all its members, and he speaks of those diverse members in terms of their varied gifts to Christ's body (Rom.

40. See Alexander, *Signs*, 65–66; Smith, *Thinking*, 43n70; cf. Gifford, "Healing," 251–52; see also the nuanced indigenous understanding in Kalu, *African Pentecostalism*, 255–63; Byaruhanga-Akiiki and Kealotswe, *Healing*, 100–102; the contextual motivational factor noted in Gifford, "Miracles," 24; Born, "Churches," 128; a balanced African approach to the issues in Ndyabahika, "Attitude"; Asamoah-Gyadu, "Leadership," 152–54; Folarin, "State," 89–90); Asian observations in Ma, "Theology," 66, 70–72 (cited by Brown, "Introduction," 11); for complexity and local variation, see Brown, "Introduction," 17–18. Some "prosperity" churches actually focus on economic empowerment for the poor; yet others also exploit their followers to prosper the teachers (cf. Newell, "Witchcraft," 477–84); for a mixture of Western and African influences in prosperity teachings, see Gifford, "Healing"; Gifford, "Developments," 516; Gifford, "Healing," 256–57, 262–63; cf. Gifford, *Pentecostalism*. Elsewhere in the world, cf. studies in, e.g., Bowler, "Bodies"; Coleman, "Wealth"; Walsh, "Santidad"; Währisch-Oblau, "Healing in Migrant Churches," 68–69.

41. See the analysis in Brown, *Authentic Fire*, 137–40, who also points out that while many of the Christians surveyed simply would have hoped for a roof that didn't leak, most of their Western critics are well endowed financially.

42. See the analysis in Brown, *Authentic Fire*, 141–42.

12:4–8; 1 Cor. 12–14; Eph. 4:11–13). Nowhere does he distinguish "temporary" gifts from "permanent" ones. So when, in line with Scripture, God equips some members of the body with particular gifts that some churches refuse to allow, the refusal is like tying one's hands or feet or other members so they cannot function in the way God designed. That is not healthy for the body as a whole, much less for those members.

Third, pushing away fellow believers in the name of evangelicalism polarizes Christ's body. Most early Pentecostals and many early charismatics understood themselves as evangelical (gospel-focused) in faith even before their experiences with the debated spiritual gifts. Most recognized their spiritual kinship with fellow believers in Scripture and responded to abuse or marginalization graciously by continuing to acknowledge respectfully other Bible believers. As younger generations have grown up in more socially respected circles, however, they often have less patience with abuse. Imbibing a stereotype of evangelicals based on those who most easily command their online attention—namely, their most vocal critics—some have shifted to studying in more theologically liberal institutions. Today charismatics are welcomed in most seminaries, from evangelical to mainline, but the harsh cessationist voices have hardened lines and increased polarization.

When most Protestants were cessationists and did not dialogue with non-Protestants anyway, their cessationism was at least not as divisive (they were dividing more over other issues). Today, when most Christians around the world see no biblical reason to believe that gifts have ceased, cessationism can be divisive when cessationists make an issue out of it. Pinning division on cessationists rather than charismatics takes for granted what we will argue as obvious later in the book—namely, that the Bible is clear in its support of spiritual gifts. Nevertheless, we charismatics, too, can act proud and divisive if we do not embrace cessationists as brothers and sisters, or if we pressure others to always share the same gifts we experience and value. Not all cessationists break fellowship with charismatics, but this book is written especially in response to the kinds of cessationists who do.

Some cessationists accuse charismatics of being divisive for splitting congregations. Sadly, this has sometimes been the case when immature charismatics have valued their personal experience above the unity of the church. But it is also often true that cessationists (or anticharismatics without articulating *any* theological justification) have driven charismatics out of their churches. Because of rapid charismatic expansion through evangelism globally, in most of the world today it is strident cessationists who are denouncing charismatic churches rather than the reverse.

Those of us with the gift of teaching (such as Craig) won't usually be on the forefront of global evangelism working signs. Those on the forefront of global evangelism (such as Daniel) don't need to be Hebrew scholars. No one has all the gifts. But those of us called to be teachers will face a strict accounting (James 3:1), and we need to teach about the other gifts rightly for the sake of the rest of Christ's body whom we are called to teach. What if our teaching discourages those through whom God *would* perform signs to support evangelism? Granted that not everyone gets healed in this life, what if someone doesn't get healed from something painful or difficult because we have discouraged someone else from growing in gifts of healing? What if someone doesn't get warned or encouraged because we have discouraged someone else from cultivating the gift of prophecy? Discouraging gifts that would build up the church harms the health of Christ's body (Eph. 4:16).

## Hindering Rather Than Stretching Faith

The biggest spiritual problem with cessationism is that it limits God's activity through his agents in the world. Paul says that we will not need gifts such as prophecy or knowledge when we see Jesus face-to-face; but he thereby implies that we *do* need such gifts to help us out until then.

Luke's emphasis in Acts on the Spirit's prophetic empowerment (Acts 2:17–18) especially involves speaking as witnesses for Christ (1:8). In Acts, healing and other signs were the most common means of drawing attention to the gospel. This issue is probably larger in theory than in practice; cessationists today almost never deny the importance of evangelism, and most cessationists today are willing to pray for God to heal people and recognize that God still does some miracles. But in breaking new ground for the kingdom, healing and the Spirit's direct leading often play a larger role than many cessationists feel comfortable with.

Cessationism risks stunting faith. Saying that all "supernatural" or "miraculous" gifts have ceased—anything that we could not possibly appear to do on our own with "natural" gifts—leaves less responsibility for us to trust God for what we couldn't even pretend to do on our own. The gifts that have supposedly ceased are "coincidentally" the ones that only countercultural faith can embrace. Essentially cessationism leaves Bible teachers, administrators, and theologians—cessationism's main purveyors—exclusively in charge of the church, because teaching is considered a "natural" gift and the "supernatural" ones are not for today.[43] Again, such a distinction is not biblical, and many cessationists in practice do exercise faith for areas that their theology allows. (I, Craig, as a Bible scholar, *do* want to depend on God's Spirit for the gift of

43. Local church leaders *should* be able to teach (Gal. 6:6; 1 Tim. 3:2; 5:17; 2 Tim. 2:24; Titus 1:9), but other gifts may also make important leadership contributions in their respective spheres (Acts 11:28–30; 13:1; 15:2; 21:8; Eph. 4:11; 2 Tim. 4:5).

teaching. And for an absent-minded professor like me, administration would definitely not be a *natural* gift!)

But the doctrine itself, especially in its strictest form, can leave us dependent on purely intellectual resources at the expense of depending on God to work beyond what is humanly possible. It leaves our faith passive in areas where God may invite us to be active. Contrast Jesus's most notable petitioners in the Gospels. Such a danger might appear in 2 Timothy 3:5: "Having a semblance of reverence but denying its power." Of course, this failing is even more true for those who neglect attention to even *biblical* miracles. When Israel forgot God's acts of power in the past, they failed to attend properly to his power in the present (Ps. 78:42–43).

## Internal Inconsistency

In my (Daniel's) view, there are good reasons why vocal cessationists focus more on denouncing errant charismatics than on presenting their own position systematically. Cessationism is self-contradictory, theologically untenable, and rationally inconsistent. This is why we must lay it out in this book—so it can be seen for what it is. In 2013, a group of vocal cessationists devoted an entire conference (called Strange Fire) to attacking charismatics. When they weren't busy portraying many charismatics as demonized heretics, they painted the rest of us as biblically illiterate and theologically ignorant. While making outrageous claims about those in the continuationist camp, they did not take the time to present the biblical arguments to which we continuationists appeal. But that was unnecessary; by articulating their own perspective, even if ever so briefly, they actually supported ours.

Even though the conference leaders devoted one session to articulating the case for cessationism, overall they shied away from emphasizing their position. Instead, most of their energy seemed devoted to slandering charismatics. Paul condemns slander as a deathworthy sin (Rom. 1:30–32; cf. Ps. 101:5), and it appears in many biblical sin lists (Mark 7:22; 2 Cor. 12:20; Eph. 4:31; Col. 3:8; 1 Pet. 2:1; cf. Titus 3:2). The broad-brush condemnation of charismatics at the conference, however, was surely slanderous, with some accusations demonstrably false (as we illustrate elsewhere in this book).[44] Still, the session that did explain the cessationist position was a gift to charismatics everywhere. Nothing can undermine cessationism like cessationist doctrine itself.

44. John MacArthur's Strange Fire conference misrepresented charismatics with many quotes and videos taken out of context. At this writing the messages that made such statements are still publicly posted (e.g., https://www.youtube.com/results?search_query=strange+fire+conference+john+macarthur, accessed Sept. 5, 2024), without apology.

That is why we will address some of the arguments presented in that session by Pennington in the following chapters.

We will take certain of these more extreme cessationist theologians and teachers to task, highlighting their own quotes and arguments. We hate calling people out by name. Our contention is with these teachers' ideas, not with them as brothers in Christ. Still, in order to represent their cessationist position accurately, and in order to have something concrete to interact with, we believe we must be specific and honest about their ideas.[45]

Cessationism is unbiblical not only in its particular hermeneutic but in its entire worldview. In cessationism's most dogmatic form, articulated by the otherwise normally quite orthodox B. B. Warfield, its roots descend into the same soil of unbelief from which sprout naturalism and deism. These doctrines have robbed many of our brothers and sisters of some of the most precious experiences God has to offer this side of eternity. So if our words do offend you, please take them as the faithful "wounds of a friend" (Prov. 27:6).

## Conclusion

Cessationism imposes on the Bible a grid that prevents embracing some of what the Bible teaches—even in the very sections, such as Paul's letters—that cessationists otherwise apply most often to our present era. Cessationism also imposes division on Christ's body by excluding some members and their gifts (though this does not justify continuationists' returning the favor at times). Cessationism can be used to justify allowing our faith to atrophy in some areas that, biblically, may need to be stretched.

45. Many of our charismatic colleagues have written polite rebuttals to cessationism with the utmost courtesy. At times they have treated the cessationist view as a respectable and valid doctrinal position, worthy of a conciliatory response. They have often, out of respect for their opponents' seniority, and perhaps concerned about their own academic credibility, conceded the theological high ground, offering a careful continuationist defense with apologies. But though we write out of love and respect for cessationists as fellow Christians, we do not respect the doctrine of cessationism. It is biblically indefensible and has led people to reject gifts from the Lord himself. And it often does so while communicating a self-assured air of loyalty to the Bible that it actually denies. Hard cessationism stirs us with a spiritual indignation that would be disingenuous to conceal.

# II

# Continuationism

In chapters 1–2, we introduced the discussion of cessationism. In chapters 3–8, we offer arguments for the continuation of gifts and challenge key cessationist arguments. After that, we turn to more specific cessationist arguments surrounding miracles, prophecy, and tongues. The final sections of the book address the less authoritative and more debatable arguments from experience and history.

# 3

# The Gospels and God's Kingdom

This chapter focuses on Matthew's teaching about God's kingdom and John's teaching about the work of the Spirit. Although 2 Timothy 3:16 is clear that all Scripture is profitable for teaching, those who will accept only arguments based on teaching in the epistles can fast-forward to chapter 5. (Still, you might want to take a long look at Acts 2:17–18 in chap. 4 along the way, since it clearly describes biblical expectations for the present age between Jesus's first and second comings. Meanwhile, appendix 1 responds to questions about theology in narrative.)

In the Gospels, Jesus inaugurates the kingdom. Jesus announces that the promised time has arrived and God's reign is about to burst on the scene (Mark 1:15). The kingdom's consummation remains future, but there is a real sense in which it has begun in the world—for the King has come!

All Christians acknowledge that the King has come yet will come again; that is why we speak of God's kingdom as both "already" and "not yet." God already inaugurated Jesus's reign at his first coming and will consummate it at his second. In Jesus's ministry, the kingdom entered the world like a tiny seed easily overlooked (Mark 4:31), but its future is too massive to miss (4:32). That seed remains planted and is still bearing fruit (cf. 4:26–29). The kingdom that Jesus inaugurated *remains* inaugurated. Because Jesus reigns at God's right hand (Mark 12:36; Acts 2:34–35), his kingship has continued to be at work in the world since his first coming. Indeed, he currently holds all authority in heaven and on earth (Matt. 28:18).

Some detractors speak of his kingdom being "postponed."[1] Although all of us agree that it is not yet consummated, Jesus has clearly not become unenthroned. While not physically present on earth, Jesus remains present and fully active in the church through the Spirit: "For where two or three have come together in my name, I am there in their midst" (Matt. 18:20); "I am with you all the days till the end of the age" (28:20).[2] Some early Protestant cessationists, who believed that the Great Commission no longer applies, explained "the end of the age" in 28:20 as the completion of the apostles' commission. These cessationists contended that the age ended when the apostles died out[3]—even though the same Greek term in 24:3 seems to apply to Jesus's future coming and, in 13:39–40, 49, plainly applies to the day of judgment.

All that to say, Jesus still reigns, so his kingdom is present now even if it will be more fully so in the future.

## Demonstrating God's Reign

At Jesus's first coming, he not only preached God's kingship, but he also demonstrated it by healing and casting out demons (Matt. 4:23; 9:35; 10:7–8; 12:28; Luke 9:2, 11; 10:9). When critics blamed his exorcisms on Satan (Matt. 12:24 // Luke 11:15), he pointed out that Satan casting out Satan would mean that Satan's kingdom was divided (Matt. 12:25–26 // Luke 11:17–18); on the contrary, Jesus embodied the kingdom to which Satan's was hostile—namely, God's kingdom. Jesus thus warns his skeptical critics that since he casts out demons by the Spirit or finger of God, God's kingdom has come upon them (Matt. 12:28 // Luke 11:20). In other words, Jesus was already demonstrating God's reign.

Likewise, when John the Baptist's messengers ask whether Jesus is really the coming Spirit- and fire-baptizer that John supposed, Jesus sends John's messengers back to him with this message:

> Go tell John the things you've heard and seen:
>
> > Blind people see.
> > Disabled people walk.
> > Those with skin diseases are cleansed and deaf people hear.

1. Many of us believe that one aspect of this makes sense, in that the Jewish people as a whole have yet to acknowledge him (Rom. 11:12, 15, 25–27); but the kingdom message (e.g., Acts 8:12; 14:22; 28:31; Gal. 5:21; 1 Thess. 2:12) and signs (e.g., Acts 8:6–7; 14:3, 10; Rom. 15:18–19) were also essential among non-Jews.
2. This continues a Matthean idea introduced with Jesus's incarnation as God "with us" in Matt. 1:23.
3. See Musculus in Boys, *Evidence*, 210–11.

> Dead people are raised.
> Good news is preached to poor people.
> And it will be well with whoever does not stumble over me. (Matt. 11:4–6 // Luke 7:22–23)

Without publicly revealing his secret identity at this point, Jesus appeals to John's knowledge of Scripture. Jesus may not be drowning the world in fire yet, but he appropriates Isaiah's wording to show that he is inaugurating his kingdom:

> Then the eyes of blind people will be opened
> And the ears of deaf people will be opened.
> Then disabled people will leap like a deer. (Isa. 35:5–6a)

> . . . because the LORD anointed me to herald good news to the lowly. (Isa. 61:1bc)

Likewise, when Pharisaic critics demand when the kingdom will come, Jesus retorts, "God's kingdom is in your midst" (Luke 17:21)—true precisely because Jesus, the true King, stands among them. And Jesus still reigns, now more openly than before (Matt. 28:18).

### *Has the Kingdom Ceased, Too?*

> Truly I tell you, among those born of women there has not risen anyone greater than John the Baptist; yet whoever is least in the kingdom of heaven is greater than he.
>
> Matthew 11:11 NIV

Those who come after John the Baptist belong to the kingdom (Matt. 11:11–13; 13:38, 52; Luke 16:16).

Responding to cessationism, Robert Graves asks, "Has the kingdom ceased, too?"[4] Jesus did not merely proclaim and demonstrate the kingdom himself; he authorized his followers to do so as well. This applied not merely to the Twelve (Matt. 10:7–8; Luke 9:2) but also to the Seventy or Seventy-Two (Luke 10:9, 19).

The New Testament's already/not yet theology is not an exclusively charismatic idea. Reformed scholar Geerhardus Vos articulated it more than 120 years ago in a clear and particularly helpful form,[5] and the concept has become widespread, even in progressive dispensationalism, especially through

4. Graves, "Cessationism," 50.
5. Vos, *Teaching*.

the influence of George Eldon Ladd.[6] It was Ladd's scholarship that directly shaped the kingdom theology of John Wimber and the Vineyard Movement.[7]

Kingdom preaching and demonstration did not end with the ministry of Jesus or those he commissioned during his earthly ministry. Jesus speaks about his kingdom at the beginning of Acts (1:3; cf. 1:6), and Philip the evangelist (8:12), Paul and Barnabas (14:22), and Paul on his own (19:8; 20:25) continue preaching the kingdom message, right up to the final scenes of Acts (28:23, 31).[8] Paul, Barnabas, and almost certainly Philip were Hellenists living in Judea, and they were not among the original Twelve or Seventy (cf. Acts 4:36–37; 6:5; 22:3). Meanwhile, kingdom signs continue at the end of Acts (28:8–9); Paul notes that dramatic signs continued to be part of his bringing good news (Rom. 15:19). They seem to persist at whatever time is envisaged in Revelation 11:5–6. Less dramatic but more connected with charismata, gifts such as healings and miracles (1 Cor. 12:9–10) also continue beyond Jesus's earthly ministry and among a range of Jesus's followers, not just "apostles." As many cessationists also allow, James assures elders of healing in answer to prayer (James 5:14–16).

For Paul as for Jesus, the kingdom remains present (Rom. 14:17; 1 Cor. 4:20; Col. 1:13) as well as future (1 Cor. 6:9–10; 15:24, 50; Gal. 5:21). Contrasting his spiritual authority with that of the Corinthians, Paul insists, "God's kingdom is not expressed by mere speaking, but by power" (1 Cor. 4:20). Charismatic biblical scholar Michael Brown asks, "When and where did this change? When and where did the nature of this kingdom power become diminished? Where does the New Testament even hint at the idea that the kingdom of God that Jesus inaugurated only paid a visit and then departed? And surely no one would argue that the kingdom of God left the earth when the New Testament canon was closed!"[9]

### *Signs Embodying the Kingdom*

John MacArthur rightly emphasizes that the gospel message must include the cross and a call to repentance. He then, however, condemns charismatic evangelical movements such as Wimber's Vineyard for emphasizing signs and wonders for evangelism, as if the second emphasis contradicts the first.[10] MacArthur is surely right that the good news of Jesus is not *mere* signs; yet MacArthur seems to ignore the biblical value of signs for drawing attention to that good news: "The Lord was bearing witness to the

6. See Ladd, *Gospel of Kingdom*, here esp. 47. For some seminal works from progressive dispensationalism, see Saucy, *Case*; Blaising and Bock, *Progressive Dispensationalism*.

7. See, e.g., Vineyard USA, "History."

8. Morphew, "Cessationism," 6; see further discussion in Keener, *Acts*, 1:670–71.

9. Brown, "Miracles and Kingdom," 30.

10. MacArthur, *Chaos*, 139. In ministry contexts, signs and wonders belong to the same semantic field as "miracles" (Greig, "Purpose," 319–27).

message about his grace, giving signs and wonders to occur through their hands" (Acts 14:3). Indeed, the model, Spirit-empowered church prayed for signs specifically for this purpose, and God answered: "Grant that your servants may speak your message with boldness, by stretching out your hand to heal and to cause signs and wonders through the name of your holy servant Jesus" (4:29–30).

Indeed, insofar as signs demonstrate the kingdom, they point to key aspects of its character. They are not the consummation of the kingdom, but they do offer a foretaste. They reveal God's care for some kinds of needs: provision for people's health (e.g., Mark 1:31–34), food (8:2–8), safety (4:38–39), and the like, the sorts of blessings that God frequently offers those who seek his kingdom first (Matt. 6:33 // Luke 12:31). Thus, like Jesus's teaching, they reveal God's character, his heart. As many scholars note, Jesus's works as well as his words communicated the message about the kingdom.[11] New Testament scholar James D. G. Dunn argues that God's kingdom proclaimed in the Gospels is effected through the Spirit there;[12] others also show that, in Paul's letters, the Spirit continues to effect God's reign in believers.[13]

Consistent with Paul's claim that the kingdom is expressed not only in word but in power (1 Cor. 4:20), Paul speaks of heralding good news (Rom. 15:20) in terms of the saving work Christ effected through him by both word and action (15:18), "in the power of signs and wonders, in the power of the Spirit" (15:19a). This was how, he explains, he "fulfilled the good news" (15:19c). The Greek terminology here is not simply "proclaimed good news" but rather "fulfilled good news" (using the verb *plēroō*).[14] As New Testament scholar E. P. Sanders recognizes, Paul not only preached but attracted attention through miracles.[15]

## Matthew, God's Kingdom, and Narrative Models

Contrary to earlier cessationist Protestants who argued that the Great Commission was not for today, most Christians of all stripes now affirm that the commission to the first apostles (Matt. 28:19–20) remains relevant for the church throughout this age.

11. Brown, "Miracles and Kingdom," 32–33 (citing Raymond Brown); Williams, "Following Christ's Example," 63–64 (citing Fuller, *Mission*, 40; Jeremias, *Theology*, 85); Morphew, "Calvin and Kingdom," 127 (citing Twelftree, *Miracle Worker*, 271, 347; Twelftree, *Name*, 128).

12. Dunn, "Kingdom," emphasized in Ruthven, "Charismata 2," 166–67; cf. Matt. 12:28.

13. E.g., Cho, "Spirit and Kingdom"; Cho, *Spirit and Kingdom*.

14. See also Twelftree, "Ministry and Miraculous," 138–39; Ruthven, "Charismata 3," 187.

15. Sanders, *Paul: Life*, 122–23. He cites not only the clear 2 Cor. 12:12 but also 1 Thess. 1:5 (121, 177) and charismata in the churches (1 Cor. 1:7; 12:1–29; Gal. 3:5).

### *Kingdom Authority*

But we should note that this commission begins with Jesus's notice of the basis for his authorization: "All authority has been given me [by the Father] in heaven and on earth" (Matt. 28:18). This statement revisits Jesus's earlier claim that he has authority on earth, an authority demonstrated by healing the sick (9:6). With his exaltation, Jesus now rules over not only earth but even heaven itself. The kingdom *remains* inaugurated; it is for today.

This statement climaxes the motif of Jesus's authority in this Gospel (7:29; 21:27), sometimes expressed in miracles (9:6, 8). Jesus explicitly delegates this miracle authority to his twelve disciples (10:1) in a discourse that, as we shall see, has implications for subsequent ministry as well. Moreover, the motif of Jesus's authority is inseparably intertwined with the theme of God's *kingdom* (*basileia*, which often means "rule" or "reign")—a central issue in this Gospel (e.g., 3:2; 4:17; 5:3, 10; 6:10; 24:14). (Matthew uses the term more than fifty times, close to one-third of the New Testament uses, and these are often strategically located.)

Jesus has been proclaiming God's authority or reign verbally and also demonstrating it by healing and exorcism (4:23; 9:35; 12:28), and he also commissions his disciples to do the same (10:7–8). Matthew's emphasis on the continuity of preaching the kingdom by John (3:2), Jesus (4:17), and his disciples (10:7) climaxes in the Great Commission proclamation (the church's message) of *Jesus's* kingdom authority (28:18–19).

When we come to the Great Commission, therefore, it reflects Jesus's authorization to expand the same kingdom mission he has exemplified by preaching and demonstrating God's reign earlier in this Gospel. This commission also evokes and draws on the model mission in Matthew 10, which, like the Great Commission, continues till the end of the age (10:23; 24:14; 28:20). Jesus commands his disciples to teach others to obey all that he has taught them (28:20)—which in Matthew necessarily includes chapter 10. Of the lengthy instructions and warnings in chapter 10, only the limitation to the house of Israel (10:5–6) is specifically revoked (28:19), while the scope of the mission is expanded rather than revoked.

In other words, so long as the Great Commission is for today, so also is the work of God's kingdom, which includes preaching and demonstrating Jesus's authority.

### *Jesus's Mission Discourse (Matt. 10)*[16]

The Gospels are not meant to be brag sheets for the apostles, as their honest depiction of the disciples' failures makes clear. The Gospels are meant to reveal to us Jesus's ministry and teaching, so we, too, can learn from Jesus.

16. Most of this section comes from Keener, *Gift & Giver*, 100–101.

We have four Gospels instead of one so we can hear the special emphases they each preached to their respective target audiences.

Before each of his Gospel's first two discourse sections, Matthew includes a summary of Jesus's kingdom works (4:23–25; 9:35).[17] There Jesus not only proclaimed and explained the kingdom; he demonstrated God's authority by healing the sick and expelling demons.[18]

God has been confirming Jesus's message about his kingdom with healing (Matt. 9:35), but now, because of his compassion (9:36), Jesus wants to extend the mission further. When Jesus came in the flesh, he could be in only one place at a time; hence, he was limited in how many people he could heal until he trained others to help with the work (9:37). So he instructs his disciples to pray for more workers (9:38). He then commissions the same disciples as workers (10:10, using the same Greek term for "worker" as in 9:38). They, too, will preach the kingdom (10:7), live by its values (10:9–10), and heal the sick (10:8). Thus Jesus multiplies his compassionate mission by means of his followers. Jesus's compassion, of course, continues today (cf. Heb. 13:8).

Matthew does not report their commission only in order to recount a past considered irrelevant to the present. Instead, he uses their past commission also as an important model for his continuing mission. Ancient historians and biographers narrated accounts about the past partly to provide models for their own audiences.[19] The Gospel does later specifically revoke this first mission's limitation to Israel (10:5–6; 28:19). But for the most part, Matthew includes the mission discourse in chapter 10 not least as a model to teach the church how to continue to evangelize. The following points suggest this:

1. The commission to "go" makes this passage a model for the Great Commission in 28:19 (although the emphasis there is on disciple-making through baptizing and instructing).
2. The disciples here perpetuate the kingdom message of John the Baptist and Jesus (3:2; 4:17; 9:35; 10:7), and this message about Jesus's divine authority is also ours today (28:18–19).
3. At least some of Jesus's agents will continue to *demonstrate* God's reign the way Jesus did, through healings and exorcisms (9:35; 10:8), a commission Matthew nowhere revokes (in contrast to his subsequent revoking of 10:5–6).

17. With slight modification, I borrow this sentence and the next from Keener, *Matthew*, 155; cf. 308. On summary reports in ancient literature, see Aune, *Environment*, 54; in the biblical Kings narratives, see, e.g., 1 Kings 14:19–20, 31; 15:8, 24.

18. Ladd, *Gospel of Kingdom*, 47.

19. See comment in chap. 4 below under "Acts as Mere History or Also a Model?"

4. These signs fulfill Scripture and attest not simply to Jesus's earthly ministry but also to his message of the new era, God's kingdom (11:4–6; see again Isa. 35:5–6).
5. The compassion that motivated Jesus (Matt. 9:36) remains operative, as does the principle of agency for those who remain Christ's representatives by the gospel (10:40–42).[20]
6. Acts and Paul's writings (cf. also James 5:13–18) suggest that Jesus's commission to heal and to live simply remained the standard for early Christian missionaries.
7. Most tellingly, Matthew here includes material about the end time that appears in a different location in Mark; obviously the end time stretches beyond the first disciples' short-term mission (cf. Matt. 11:1).[21] (Ancient biographers had the freedom to rearrange their material.)[22] Some of Jesus's teachings that Matthew includes here would not have been relevant to the first mission; he borrows these from a discourse by Jesus about the disciples' future (see especially Mark 13:9).[23] Thus Matthew 10:17–18 warns about prosecution before synagogues and pagan courts. That Matthew 10:18–20 speaks of Roman governors in the plural (Judea had only one governor) indicates that Matthew again points beyond the immediate mission of the Twelve to the continuing mission of the church among the nations.
8. Still more clearly, Jesus explicitly declares that their mission to Israel will continue until Jesus's return (10:23). It thus looks beyond the immediate occasion into the future.

Especially in view of points 7 and 8, Matthew does not just tell us about the first disciples' commission (though he does that); he also tells us that this mission must continue until the Son of Man returns (10:23). Thus, these missionary instructions remain relevant for his own audience, not just apostles

20. The principle in Matt. 10:40–42 does apply to first-century apostles (cf. 2 Cor. 5:19–20), but it also applies to all of Christ's agents (Matt. 25:40, 45; see discussion below) and his body more generally (Acts 9:4).

21. Most scholars believe that Mark wrote before our current version of Matthew's Gospel. Most evangelical scholars accept Papias's report that in the first century Papias learned from an eyewitness of Jesus's ministry that Mark provides, esp. the memoirs of Peter (Papias frg. 3.14–15; slightly later, Justin, *Dial.* 106). (Papias writes much earlier than Augustine, who insisted on Matthean priority.) Matthew and Luke also elevated the literary level beyond that of Mark.

22. Keener, *Christobiography*, 138–42; note, e.g., Philo, *Moses* 2; Xenophon, *Ages.* 3–11; Suetonius, *Aug.* 9; *Cal.* 22.1; *Nero* 19.3; see further Momigliano, *Development*, 13–14, 86; Ytterbrink, *Gospel*, 94; Bosworth, *Arrian*, 60; Licona, *Differences*, 185–96, esp. 191–96. Anyone who doubts this practice in Matthew need only compare, for example, Matt. 8–9 with the parallel material in Mark, or even Matt. 21:12–13, 18–22 with Mark 11:12–25.

23. See Bruce, *Message*, 68; Morosco, "Matthew 10."

of the past. Each of the above points could be explained and defended in greater detail, but together they suggest that the kingdom mission, which includes kingdom signs, continues. By systematically excluding enough of the biblical evidence from consideration (say, all narrative, or even more radically, all biblical evidence before the death of the apostles—i.e., all biblical evidence), one can prove almost anything. But if the entire New Testament speaks to us, we should continue to anticipate signs on the cutting edge of evangelism.

### *A Mission to the End*

That all nations will be judged by how they have received Jesus's agents (Matt. 25:31–46) also suggests that the mission Matthew envisions in Matthew 10 continues to the end. The nations will be judged by how they have received Jesus's brothers and sisters (25:40)—whom Jesus has already defined as his own followers (12:48–50; 23:8; cf. 28:10). Against the common interpretation that this passage refers to caring for the needy generally, most scholars think it refers to the church's continuing mission until the end. (Scripture *does* command us to care for the needy,[24] but the present question is what this particular passage means.) Parallels with Matthew 10 suggest that Matthew 10 does anticipate this continuing mission (see table 3.1).

**Table 3.1. Parallels with Matthew 25**

| Matthew 10 and elsewhere before Matt. 25 | Matthew 25 |
|---|---|
| Good news about the kingdom must be preached among all nations before the end comes (24:14) | The nations are judged at the end (25:32) |
| If they give you even a cup of cold water (10:42) | The righteous fed and gave drink to Jesus's representatives (25:35) |
| Whatever house takes you in (10:11–13) | The righteous took in Jesus's representatives, though they were strangers (25:35) |
| Courts, beatings, persecution (10:16–22) | The righteous visited Jesus's representatives when they were sick or in prison (25:36) |
| Whoever receives you receives me (10:40) | Whatever you did for my representatives, you did for me (25:40) |
| Jesus's followers are his brothers and sisters (12:48–50) | My representatives are my brothers and sisters (25:40) |
| The wicked who do not receive Jesus's representatives will be judged (10:14–15) | The wicked who did not receive Jesus's representatives will be judged (25:41–46) |

24. See discussion in Keener, *Suffering*, chap. 8.

## Excursus: Jesus as Role Model in Matthew[25]

Besides Matthew's explicit passages about mission, Jesus's narrative model teaches us about his character and concern, which remain the same today. In chapters 8 and 9, Matthew provides ten specific examples of Jesus's healing power in nine accounts, interweaving these practical demonstrations of Jesus's authority with a recurring summons to submit to that authority (8:18–22; 9:9–17, 35–38). In view of Matthew 9:37–38, Jesus seeks to expand this ministry of proclamation and healing through his followers in 10:7–8.

> Matthew 9:37–38: "The harvest is great, but there aren't many workers. So ask the harvest's master to send out workers into his harvest!"

> Matthew 10:5, 10: "Jesus sent these twelve. . . . 'The worker merits their food.'"

Although the Gospel writers draw spiritual points from these accounts, most of these stories teach us something about physical healing as well. The gospel is not just about God transforming our spirits; his action on our bodies offers a sign that supports Jesus's bodily resurrection and prefigures our own. By allegorizing the application of healing stories exclusively to symbols of what God does with the soul, interpreters can strip them of what they consider nonessentials—whether in skeptical approaches to Scripture or, to a lesser extent, in cessationism.[26]

The healing of the man with a skin disease in Matthew 8:1–4 teaches us about the nature of faith and about the Lord's heart toward the infirm. The diseased man approaches Jesus with complete trust in his authority. Though his situation is desperate, he likewise humbly acknowledges that the choice of whether or not he is healed belongs to Jesus (8:2). Meanwhile, Matthew also shows us something about Jesus's character: He wants to heal the man (8:3). Jesus is so concerned with the man's desperate condition that he touches the untouchable, thereby sharing the man's ritual impurity in the eyes of his culture (8:3). Whatever God's purposes may be in a specific situation, none of us should doubt that Jesus's character and compassion remain the same today. Is this not among the lessons Matthew offers in this narrative?

Another healing narrative includes two miracles: the healing of a woman who has been bleeding for years and the raising of a dead girl. Jesus again appears ready to heal and even to restore to life, as his response to Jairus shows (9:18–19). The bleeding woman adds a new element of teaching to the story, however. She displays scandalous faith (9:20–21). Under biblical and Jewish law, this woman communicated ritual impurity to anyone she touched (Lev. 15:21–22, 25–27). For her to press her way to Jesus in a crowd, and then further to intentionally touch Jesus's cloak, was scandalous. Yet she was desperate. She lived in a society in which most women could not earn adequate money to survive on their own, and her condition virtually guaranteed that she could never marry.

25. I borrow here from Keener, *Gift & Giver*, 99–100; with overlap from Keener, *Matthew* (1997), 196, 198–99; and a few changes.

26. So Morphew, "Calvin and Kingdom," 129.

So convinced was she of Jesus's power that she acted scandalously, desperately staking everything on his ability to heal her. The narrative concludes not with Jesus rejecting her or concealing her touch but with him publicly acknowledging her condition so that he could publicly pronounce her healed (Matt. 9:22). Jesus accepted her desperation as an act of faith (9:22). That our Lord Jesus shows such mercy should not surprise us: He is the one who bore our infirmities, suffering in our place so we might go free (8:17). Matthew offers many other examples, but these should suffice here.

Matthew emphasizes that compassion was Jesus's primary motivation for ministry to people (9:36). If his character remains the same today, we may be confident that Jesus still wishes to heal and deliver many people, as he did long ago. (Again, most cessationists today recognize that God does heal, even miraculously, though full cessationists do not.)

### *Jesus's Commands in Matthew 10 Apply to the Church's Mission*

Some logistical circumstances differ between the original Galilean mission and subsequent ministry, such as some additional means of mission support exemplified at times in Acts and Paul's letters (Acts 18:3; 20:34; 1 Cor. 4:12; 9:6, 12, 18; Phil. 4:15–16; 2 Thess. 3:7–8). Likewise, Jesus's followers today do not ordinarily expect beatings in Jewish synagogues (I, Craig, have always experienced gracious hospitality there). The principles, however, remain relevant for continuing mission.

Part of Jesus's commission to the church to make disciples of all peoples (Matt. 28:19) is to teach them to obey all that Jesus has commanded (28:20a). This mission continues until the end of the age (28:20b; cf. 24:14). What has Jesus commanded? One of Matthew's five major discourse sections in Matthew 10 suggests that at least some of Jesus's followers, supported logistically by his other followers, will carry on the groundbreaking evangelism described in Matthew 10. The "going" in Matthew 28:19 in light of Jesus's authority (28:18) may well play on the going in 10:5–7, revoking one element: Whereas in 10:5–6, the going was exclusively to Jewish people, in 28:19 the recipients will be all peoples. One element that is not revoked and thus apparently remains part of the mission is continuing Jesus's ministry of healing, demonstrating the kingdom as well as proclaiming it in words (9:35; 10:8). This does not, of course, mean that each individual Christian will do everything in Matthew 10. It does mean that Jesus's movement as a whole must continue the mission as a whole.

That Paul follows Jesus's instructions in shaking off dust (Acts 13:51) and (less dramatically) in accepting hospitality in homes (Acts 16:15) suggests that Jesus's followers understood the instructions as relevant for their own day even though Jesus addressed them originally to his first disciples.[27] Indeed, Mark

27. Williams, "Following Christ's Example," 73; Graves and Greig, "Cessationism," 90–91.

16:9–20 shows that the early second-century church (on the usual scholarly view, recognized in the NIV and most other translations, that this section is a later addition) continued to understand Jesus's final commission as including both preaching and healing.[28]

## Jesus's Commission in John's Gospel

John's Gospel speaks less often about God's "kingdom" in explicit terms, but because it also reports Jesus's teaching to his disciples, we include it in this kingdom chapter. Most cessationists do not seem to restrict to the first apostles the promises about the Spirit in John's Gospel,[29] but in case anyone does, it is worth reiterating some of these promises.

### *The Spirit Empowers, Teaches, and Indwells*

As in Acts 1:8, so in John 20:21–23, Jesus empowers the disciples with the Spirit to enable their commission. The sending explicitly parallels his own mission ("Just as the Father sent me, I send you"). Jesus has already provided salvation in John's Gospel, a role that no one else can fulfill (John 14:6). His followers *are*, however, sent to bring that message to the world (17:18). Although this mission applies in the first place to Jesus's original disciples, his concerns look beyond them (10:16; 17:20–21).

Jesus's discourse in John 14–16 in the first case also directly addresses his original disciples. Consider John 15:27: "You will testify too, since you have been with me from the beginning."[30] We weren't there "from the beginning," yet John writes all of his Gospel also to teach us who are not firsthand witnesses, based on what the original disciples witnessed (20:29–31). Thus the theme of "witness" applies also to Jesus's forerunner John (1:7–8, 15, 34; 3:26; 5:33), a Samaritan woman (4:39), witnesses of Lazarus's raising (12:17), and most relevantly in this context, the Spirit (15:26). The Spirit comes to believers (16:7) to convict the world (16:8–11) and to reveal Jesus to believers (16:13–15).[31] As with the Great Commission to Jesus's first disciples in Matthew 28:18–20 or Acts 1:8, the first disciples serve as a narrative model here for all believers to come.

Likewise, Jesus's promise that he and the Spirit would dwell in them (John 14:23; 15:4–5) surely extends beyond the original apostles. That is also true

28. Graves and Greig, "Cessationism," 91. Those who, by contrast, believe the section an original part of Mark's Gospel have even more reason to attend consistently to its promises.

29. See, e.g., MacArthur, *Chaos*, 99, 176–77.

30. Correctly noted by Waldron, *Continued*, 23. Some other examples would be no less obvious (e.g., John 14:9; 16:5–6, 19, 31).

31. See discussion in Keener, *John*, 2:1029–32, 1035–43.

about the Spirit teaching Jesus's followers (John 14:26; 16:13). Someone might argue that John records this promise for simply historical interest about, or to confirm the teaching only of, the first-century apostles. Yet 1 John emphasizes that this gift of the Spirit teaches *all* believers: "As for you, the anointing that you received from him dwells in you. . . . His anointing teaches you about all things" (1 John 2:27). Clearly John allows that the Spirit teaches believers generally. "This is how we know that he dwells in us, by the Spirit that he has given us" (1 John 3:24; cf. 4:13). Not all spirits are the Spirit of God; but rather than rejecting all prophecies, John instructs believers how to recognize which prophecies are from God's Spirit and which are from the spirit of antichrist (1 John 4:1–3, 6).

Everyone accepts as for today Jesus's instruction to love one another (John 13:34–35; 15:12, 17), a teaching that recurs abundantly in 1 John (2:7–11; 3:11, 23; 4:21). This is another example that illustrates that the message of Jesus's final discourse in John's Gospel applies beyond the first disciples.

#### *Hearing the Spirit*

Jesus's sheep know him and his voice (John 10:4). Applied to a healed man in the context (9:35–38), these words cannot be limited to the apostles. Indeed, because Jesus has established the relationship with us, he can declare, "I know my own and my own know me, *just as* the Father knows me and I know the Father" (10:14–15). He even calls his first followers "friends, because I have made known to you everything that I have heard from my Father" (15:15). This relationship would not end after Jesus's ascension, for "the Spirit of truth . . . will speak whatever he hears. . . . He will take what is mine and declare it to you" (16:13–14). Just as Jesus made known what he heard from the Father, so the Spirit would continue to make known what he hears.[32]

Some cessationists believe that God speaks *only* through Scripture; he does not even prompt "believers through inward impressions and feelings."[33] This is a problem not just for reading John's Gospel. Believers in general, not just apostles, experience God's voice to us personally. Perhaps some define God's voice more narrowly, but Paul is explicit that all believers should experience the Spirit's assurance of God's love for us (Rom. 5:5, 8; Eph. 3:16, 19), his reminder that we are his children (Rom. 8:16), and his encouragement that a special inheritance awaits us (1 Cor. 2:9–10; Eph. 1:17–18). The Spirit reveals to us deeply God's heart (1 Cor. 2:9–16). While he certainly does this often

32. See discussion in Keener, *John*, 1:805–8; 2:1011–14, 1038–39.

33. Pennington, *Cessationism*, 19. Pennington further warns (p. 172) that believers should "reject all forms of supposed continuing revelation, including subjective impressions of God's will." Contrast more moderately Schreiner, *Spiritual Gifts*, 90–92, who rightly allows that God may lead through impressions so long as we do not depend on them as if they were always accurate. Contrast also rightly Saucy, "View," 143.

through Scripture, the Spirit who lives in us is hardly limited to speaking when we have our Bibles open in front of us.[34]

### Greater Works

More often debated by cessationists is John 14:12. Because Jesus says "the one who trusts in me," it is difficult to limit the promise to only the first apostles (historically, however, some Protestant interpreters did just that).[35] The debate centers more around the question of the "works" that Jesus means.[36] "Whoever trusts in me will do the works that I do, and will do even greater works because I am going to the Father." By going to the Father, Jesus will no longer do the works in the same way directly on earth, but he will multiply them even more through his followers. (This might be the sense of "greater" works—surely not that each individual will do greater works, but that Jesus's widespread movement as a whole will.) Because he goes to the Father, he can send the Spirit (16:7).

What does he mean by doing his works? The previous verses seem to describe Jesus's works in terms of his signs (14:10–11), which is also the typical use of this noun in the plural form with Jesus or the Father as its subject (5:20, 36; 9:3–4; 10:25, 32, 37–38; 15:24).[37] Meanwhile, the following verses refer to making requests to God in Jesus's name (14:13–14; cf. 15:7, 16; 16:23–26). Most of us are undoubtedly just scratching the surface of these promises for prayer.

As we have noted, there are other similar promises in the Gospels (e.g., Matt. 7:7–11; Mark 11:23–24). We don't ordinarily need to move *literal* mountains, and mountain moving was a Jewish hyperbole for doing what seemed virtually impossible.[38] The point of hyperbole, however, is to get our attention, in this case that nothing is impossible for God.

It presumably went without saying that there are unstated limits. Jesus did not have to say, "Don't ask for selfish things," for example (cf. Mark 10:35–40). John does not need to make "according to God's will" explicit in 1 John 5:15, for example, because he has already made it clear in 5:14–15: "This is the

34. Cf. also Saucy, "View," 143.

35. See, e.g., Bucer's comment on John 14:12 (in Boys, *Evidence*, 115; though cf. Boys, *Evidence*, 134–36); and Musculus (p. 206; but contrast Cartwright on p. 250). Why defend the Bible as uniquely authoritative for believers and then make so much of it inapplicable for their lives? Luther's approach was better (see Burgess, *Peoples*, 141, citing Luther's sermon on Ascension Day, 1523).

36. MacArthur, *Chaos*, 126: "Nothing in the context of John 14 speaks of supernatural signs and wonders."

37. Emphasized in Graves and Greig, "Cessationism," 93–94, with detailed attention to the grammar. See discussion in Keener, *John*, 2:945–50.

38. E.g., *b. Ber.* 63b–64a; *Sanh.* 24a; *'Abot R. Nat.* 6A; 12, §29B. Bengel allows that it may yet happen literally (Boys, *Evidence*, 255).

confidence we have in approaching God: that if we ask anything according to his will, he hears us. And if we know that he hears us—whatever we ask—we know that we have what we asked of him" (NIV).

Insofar as asking in Jesus's name (John 14:13–14) means something like asking as Jesus's representatives, it also assumes that we pray as Jesus would. Similarly, the promise of answered prayer in Mark 11:23–24 rests on the instruction in 11:22 to trust in God, which implies speaking and acting in accordance with his character. Nevertheless, if there is hyperbole in the simple, unadorned promises such as "Ask and receive," it is to invite us to trust God more, not to make us shake our heads and skip the verses. Cessationist or continuationist, we are still invited to depend on God for what lies beyond our human abilities. And for cessationist or continuationist, stretching that spiritual muscle always initially involves some pain.

## Conclusion: The Kingdom Continues, Because Jesus Still Reigns

The good news about God's kingdom must be proclaimed among all nations before the end comes (Matt. 24:14). If we look at what Scripture says rather than at what it doesn't, it's more consistent with biblical patterns to expect that God continues to demonstrate his reign through signs attesting the message as he did in Scripture rather than to expect that he would stop doing so. Indeed, those interpreters who historically relegated such signs only to Jesus and the apostles were often the same interpreters who relegated the Great Commission only to them as well.

But if some do not find Matthew or John sufficiently persuasive on this point, Acts 2:17 and 1 Corinthians 13 offer more explicit biblical evidence.

# 4

# Acts

## *Prophesying in the Last Days*

Moses wished for all God's people to be prophets (Num. 11:29), and Joel shows that this desire would become a reality in the promised new era (Joel 2:28–29): "I will pour out my Spirit on all people, and your sons and daughters will prophesy." Even before Jesus came, the key sign promised for the new, messianic era was that God would pour out his Spirit (e.g., Isa. 32:15; 44:3; 59:21; 61:1; Ezek. 39:29; Zech. 12:10). Often in the Old Testament (Num. 11:25–29; 1 Sam. 10:6; 19:20; Neh. 9:30; Zech. 7:12), God's servants would express this experience of the Spirit in part by prophesying. Joel predicts a major advance beyond the common Old Testament model, however: Now *all* God's people would prophesy, rather than just a few prophets (Joel 2:28–29; cf. Jer. 31:34). Starting at Pentecost, this Spirit-moved speech could be expressed (at least often) in tongues or direct prophecy:

> Acts 2:4: "And they were all filled with the Holy Spirit and began to speak in other tongues just as the Spirit was giving them utterance."
>
> Acts 10:46: "For they heard them speaking in tongues and magnifying God."
>
> Acts 19:6: "And when Paul laid hands on them, the Holy Spirit came on them, and they started both speaking in tongues and prophesying." (Cf. Luke 1:67.)

For Luke, the outpoured Spirit of prophecy (Acts 2:17–18) demonstrates that the messianic era has begun and Jesus is thus the Christ (2:33). Cessationism undercuts New Testament evidence of Jesus's kingship and a major promise-fulfillment motif in biblical theology. As British New Testament scholar Max Turner observes, cessation of the prophetic Spirit "would inevitably have seemed" to Luke "like a failure at the very heart of what Joel's promise of the Spirit was all about."[1]

## The Last-Days Outpouring Has Begun

Acts narrates the outpouring of the Spirit that equips the church for its mission to the ends of the earth (Acts 1:8). In the foundational, programmatic passage of Acts, the filling of believers (2:4) reveals that the last-days outpouring of God's Spirit has begun (2:17–18). God did not pour out the Spirit only to pour the Spirit back; throughout the New Testament, the "last days" represents the present era, inaugurated by Jesus's exaltation and stretching until the second coming (so also 1 Tim. 4:1; 2 Tim. 3:1; Heb. 1:2; 1 Pet. 1:20; 2 Pet. 3:3; 1 John 2:18). If it was the "last days" when Peter spoke in Acts 2:17, then if anything, now it would be even *laster* days (if we may coin a term).

Moreover, this era of the outpoured Spirit and empowerment for mission explicitly continues beyond Pentecost: "The promise is for you, your children, and all who are far away" (2:39; cf. Eph. 2:13, 17). Nor is this the last time in Acts that God's people experience a special, renewed empowerment by the Spirit (see already Acts 4:31).[2]

What did this outpouring entail? The occasion that demonstrated Peter's point was the believers' worship in tongues (2:4). The list of expressions that Peter provides from Joel specifies prophecy, visions, and dreams. In light of Peter's addition to Joel of "and they will prophesy" in 2:18, Peter apparently takes divinely sent visions and dreams as examples of the broader category of prophetic experience.

Peter appeals to this outpouring as proof of Jesus's exaltation to the Father's right hand (2:33). That the promised outpouring marks specifically Jesus's exaltation demonstrates that Jesus is both Lord and Christ (2:36).[3] Thus one might argue that "to deny the Spirit (of prophecy) is, by implication, to deny Christ's exaltation . . . (Matt. 12:28–32)."[4]

How then can some Christians deny that prophetic enablement is for today?

1. Turner, *Gifts*, 298.

2. Nor is the language of the Spirit being poured out limited to the day of Pentecost; see Acts 10:45 (also other fluid images regarding the Spirit such as baptism in 1:5; 11:16; filling in 2:4; 4:8, 31; 9:17; 13:9, 52).

3. See Carson, *Showing Spirit*, 154–55.

4. Rightly, Ruthven, *Cessation*, 157, although he is commenting on 1 Thess. 5:20.

### *When Are the Last Days?*

Peter's mention of "last days" is no accident. Based on the context in Joel (Joel 3:1), Peter changes Joel's "afterward" (2:28) to "in the last days" (Acts 2:17).[5] This deliberate adaptation leaves no doubt that he refers to the era between Jesus's exaltation and return—that is, Christ's enthronement until his enemies are subjugated (2:34–35, citing Ps. 110:1).

As Southern Baptist scholars Gregg Allison and Andreas Köstenberger emphasize regarding the last days of Acts 2, "This [present] period—all of it—is the age of the Spirit, the time of the new covenant, the era of the church. And it is characterized from beginning to end by Spirit-given prophetic and visionary activity—the continuation of the sign gifts—as illustrated by the ongoing narrative of Acts in which Luke recounts healings, miracles, speaking in tongues, prophecies, and the like."[6] Likewise, the careful New Testament scholar D. A. Carson criticizes Warfield's insistence that miracles ceased after Jesus's apostles, pointing out that Jesus's signs were to identify not only his or his first delegates' immediate ministries but the new age that bears witness to his exaltation.[7]

Here are other New Testament passages that identify the last days using that or equivalent terminology (using the ESV):

> 1 Timothy 4:1: "Now the Spirit expressly says that in later times some will depart from the faith by devoting themselves to deceitful spirits and teachings of demons." (Paul applies this warning to those forbidding marriage and particular foods in his own day [4:3–5].)
>
> 2 Timothy 3:1: "But understand this, that in the last days there will come times of difficulty." (Paul applies this warning to wicked people [3:2–9] such as already flourished in his own day [3:13].)
>
> 2 Peter 3:3: ". . . knowing this first of all, that scoffers will come in the last days with scoffing, following their own sinful desires." (Peter applies this warning to the scoffers of his own day [3:3–5].)
>
> Hebrews 1:2: "But in these last days he has spoken to us by his Son, whom he appointed the heir of all things, through whom also he created the world." (This

5. As also Brown, "Miracles and Kingdom," 40; also Brown, *Authentic Fire*, 195. In Joel, some English chapter divisions, though used here, differ from those in the Hebrew and Greek versions.

6. Allison and Köstenberger, *Holy Spirit*, 433; see also Wilson, *Spirit and Sacrament*, 115; Morphew, "Cessationism," 5. Earlier, rightly Bosworth, *Healer*, 189 (cf. Perkins, *Bosworth*, 209): The only biblically promised age of the Spirit and new covenant, apart from the age to come, is the one between the first and second comings.

7. Carson, *Showing Spirit*, 156–57.

and the following passages that mention the last days include the first century so clearly that we do not even need to explain their context.)

1 Peter 1:20: "He was foreknown before the foundation of the world but was made manifest in the last times for the sake of you."

1 John 2:18: "Children, it is the last hour, and as you have heard that antichrist is coming, so now many antichrists have come. Therefore we know that it is the last hour."

#### *It's* Still *the Last Days*

It's *still* the last days, rather than (somehow!) earlier than it used to be. As David Briones, professor at Westminster Seminary California, notes, "The age to come has come upon this age. . . . Christ's first coming marks the beginning of the last days. Christ's second coming will mark the end of the last days."[8] So also Reformed premillennialist George Eldon Ladd: "The presence of Christ—and therefore the blessings of the new age—were now available to all believers, regardless of the limitations of time and space."[9] Or Pentecostal scholar Douglas Oss: "There is not a scrap of biblical evidence that the last days are subdivided, postponed, or changed prior to the day of the Lord."[10]

Specifically, these days conclude with "the great and glorious day of the Lord" (Acts 2:20). This terminus coincides with what one might gather from Paul's view of the termination of this age's gifts such as tongues and prophecy: "what we should expect given Paul's words in 1 Corinthians 13:8–13."[11] The agreement of Luke and Paul on this point is undoubtedly no accident. As Robert Graves notes, "There is not one verse of Scripture that explicitly or implicitly states that signs and wonders and the gifts of the Spirit will cease before the Parousia, that is, before the revealing of Christ at the end of the ages. There are, however, many that state or imply that the gifts will continue until the Parousia."[12]

Michael Brown similarly argues the following:

1. It requires hermeneutical gymnastics to suppose that God shifted from Joel's and Peter's description of the outpouring of the Spirit to a new, nonprophetic kind of outpouring not promised in Scripture.

8. Briones, "Already, Not Yet."

9. Ladd, *Presence of Future*, 272, cited in Graves and Greig, "Cessationism," 89.

10. Oss, "View," 267. Storms, "Statement," 318, meanwhile, suggests that Gaffin's postbiblical distinction between the apostolic period and "church history" ironically (Gaffin is, like Storms, amillennial) draws on dispensational rather than biblical categories.

11. Graves, "Cessationism," 49.

12. Graves, "Cessationism," 50; Graves points to Ruthven's list of *nineteen* passages (in his *Cessation*, 107) that he takes to at least imply continuationism.

2. It requires the same to deny that we remain in the "last" days that were already in effect in the first century.
3. Why should we substitute a nonbiblical understanding of this outpouring for the explicit biblical promise of prophesying, visions, dreams, and the like?[13]

The exalted Christ, whose testimony is the very Spirit of prophecy, initiated a new era in which the Spirit of God would be poured out on all flesh and remain until the end of the age (1 Cor. 1:7; Eph. 1:8–10; 4:13; 1 Pet. 1:5; 1 John 2:27–28).[14] As Carson observes, "For Luke the Spirit does not simply inaugurate the new age and then disappear; rather, he *characterizes* the new age";[15] and, "It has been shown in some detail that for Luke the coming of the Spirit is not associated merely with the dawning of the new age but with its presence, not merely with Pentecost but with the entire period from Pentecost to the return of Jesus the Messiah."[16] This also means that, against full cessationists,[17] healing and miracles characterize not just Jesus's Galilean ministry "but also . . . the new age he is inaugurating."[18]

#### *A Promise Not Limited to the First Disciples*

As already noted, this era of the outpoured Spirit and empowerment for mission explicitly continues beyond the disciples at Pentecost: "The promise is for . . . all who are far away" (Acts 2:39). In Acts, this "promise" refers to being baptized in the Holy Spirit (1:4–5: "Wait for the Father's promise. . . . You'll be baptized in the Holy Spirit"). This is the promise of the Spirit that Jesus received and poured out in ways witnessed by Peter's audience (2:33: "The promise of the Holy Spirit . . . you both see and hear"). This promise was clearly not meant to be limited to the Twelve only (cf. Luke 3:16), and the Spirit had probably fallen on the 120 as early as in Acts 2 (see 1:15).

The promise is also specifically called the *gift* of the Holy Spirit (Acts 2:38), identical to the gift in 10:45 and 11:17 (cf. also the *giving* of the Spirit

13. Brown, *Authentic Fire*, 198–99.

14. See, for example, Keener, *Acts*, 1:877–82, regarding the outpouring of the Spirit in Acts 2:17: "No one could read Luke's 'last days' as a temporary event in Jerusalem that had given way to a cessation of signs and revelations in Luke's own day, unless they viewed the 'last days' as a failed experiment" (880–81). See also Brown, *Authentic Fire*, 194–99.

15. Carson, *Showing Spirit*, 151. Carson does not take Acts's comments about tongues as paradigmatic for individuals.

16. Carson, *Showing Spirit*, 155, citing Turner, "Luke and Spirit"; Turner, "Spiritual Gifts," esp. 41ff. For a similar reading of the Old Testament evidence, see Dumbrell, *Covenant*.

17. Carson notes here Warfield, *Counterfeit Miracles*; similarly MacArthur, *Charismatics*, 73; Walvoord, *Holy Spirit*, 173.

18. Carson, *Showing Spirit*, 156–57, noting also Turner, "Spiritual Gifts," 24–26; Richardson, *Miracle Stories*; Kallas, *Significance*; Loos, *Miracles*.

in 5:32; 8:18; 15:8). In both Acts 2 and 10–11, the gift of the Spirit was expressed in tongues (as the Spirit *gave* them utterance in 2:4), although this is not the only expression of the Spirit's outpouring in Acts. The passage also tells us that they *received* the Spirit (2:38), as in 1:8, and as happened to others in 8:15, 17; 10:47; 19:2. This is not a gift for the Twelve (2:23) or for the 120 (1:15) alone. Indeed, it is explicitly for all who repent and confess Jesus in baptism (2:38).[19]

Scholars debate how to reconcile the promise in 2:38 with the apparent delay in 8:14–16 and, to a much lesser extent, in 9:17 and possibly 19:2, 5–6. Calvin suggested that the Samaritans in Acts 8 lacked not the Spirit per se but the external signs of the Spirit, such as in 10:46 and 19:6,[20] "not that they were altogether destitute of the Spirit, seeing that they had from the same both faith, and a godly desire to follow Christ; but because they were not furnished with those excellent gifts, wherein appeared afterwards greater glory of Christ's kingdom."[21] This suggestion seems reasonable in view of Luke's emphasis on prophetic signs (2:17–18), which Luke highlights in many of his accounts of initial outpourings of the Spirit (2:4; 10:45–46; 19:6; cf. 8:18, where Simon witnessed something).

Whatever one's approach to 8:14–16, however, the point remains that the gift of the Spirit is for all believers and that what Luke describes is not limited to the Twelve. In several passages (Luke 1:67; Acts 2:4, 17–18; 10:44–46; 19:6; 28:25; cf. 4:8, 31; 6:10), Luke associates with this gift prophetic speech or Spirit-given words for prayer. That does not mean that those who lack such expressions lack the Spirit. It does remind us that Luke considers prophetic empowerment a corollary of the gift not just in Acts 2:17–18 but as a normal expression of it.

### *Prophecy for All Believers*

When God put his Spirit on the elders of Israel in Numbers 11:25–26, they prophesied. When Joshua protested two elders continuing to prophesy even in the camp (11:27–28), Moses replied that he wished that all God's people were prophets (11:29). Although one would not expect any normal prophet to assume Moses's own stature (Num. 12:6–8; Deut. 18:15–19), Moses's more generic wish for all God's people to be prophets would come to pass.[22]

19. For Luke's emphasis on the Spirit's empowerment being for all believers, underlined by his examples of corporate outpourings, see also Menzies, "Luke-Acts," 104.

20. Calvin, *Acts*, 236 (as cited in Hertig, "Mystery Tour," 110).

21. Calvin, *Acts* comment on 8:16 (https://ccel.org/ccel/calvin/calcom36/calcom36.xv.iii.html). Calvin, however, went on to associate these gifts only with the apostolic era (see discussion in chap. 21).

22. With also Ruthven, *Cessation*, xx, 185; Oss, "View," 247–48, 263; Cotton, "Spirit in Numbers 11."

At the promised time of restoration (Joel 3:1), God would pour out his Spirit on all his people and they would prophesy (2:28–29).[23] Joel is emphatic that this promise is for *all* God's people; he leaves no doubt that it is for both genders, all ages, all classes, and indeed "all flesh."[24] As Carson points out, in light of Numbers 11,

> Joel's concern is not simply with a picky point—more people will prophesy some day—but with a massive, eschatological worldview. What was anticipated was an entirely new age, a new relationship between God and his people, a new covenant; and experientially this turns on the gift of the Spirit. Put more generically, what the prophets foresaw was what some have labeled "the prophetic Spirit." All who live under this new covenant enjoy the gift of this prophetic Spirit; and this is no mere creedal datum, but a lived, transforming, charismatic (in the broad, New Testament sense of that word . . . ), vital experience.[25]

The promised experience for God's end-time people marks the church, including its gentile members, as the locus of God's saving action in this age. In both Acts and Paul's letters, it is this bestowal of the gift on gentile believers that demonstrates that they have been grafted into God's people as heirs of the last-days Spirit promise of Joel and the other prophets (Acts 10:47; 15:8–9; Gal. 3:2–5, 14).

So while Paul acknowledges that not all are prophets in any specialized sense (1 Cor. 12:29; Acts 11:27; 13:1; 21:9–10),[26] he, like Moses, would like all God's people to prophesy (1 Cor. 14:5), and even suggests that in local house congregations they *could* all prophesy, provided they did so one at a time (14:31).[27]

Despite important notes of continuity between the Old Testament and the New Testament, the new covenant does introduce some elements of discontinuity (or, perhaps better, climax, fulfillment, and amplification), as is evident regarding the Spirit and inner transformation.[28] While the New Testament gift has significant continuity with Old Testament prophecy (in the senses

23. Joel 3:1–2 in the MT and LXX, but here and throughout we cite just the English versification for the sake of our wider readership.

24. Peter's quotation adapts "servants" to *God's* servants, flattening the class distinction further.

25. Carson, *Showing Spirit*, 153–54; cf. Thiselton, *Spirit*, 104; Oss, "View," 248.

26. Here I (Craig) would have some partial affinity with Gaffin, "Response to Storms and Oss," 291, in that I recognize more diversity in expressions of prophetic empowerment than exclusively prophecy in the narrowest sense (see Keener, *Acts*, 1:523–24, 909–11; see also Menzies, *Development*, 205–77).

27. House congregations probably averaged fifteen to fifty persons. The particular instruction here would present much greater logistical problems in a megachurch setting such as the meetings in the Jerusalem temple.

28. Carson, *Showing Spirit*, 152–53, highlights Jer. 31:29–34; Ezek. 36:25–27; Isa. 44:3–5.

addressed later in this book), Jesus's exaltation introduces one conspicuous difference highighted by Joel 2: Prophecy (hearing and speaking for God) is no longer the domain of a few but is now available to all. It is to be in fact a primary marker of God's people in the interim period between Jesus's first and second comings.

The biblical picture is not of a few medieval-type supersaints but of all God's people being gifted in hearing from and speaking for God in various ways. Just as many of us forget our full identity as new creations in Christ, many of us are living short of the privileges God has made available to us in Christ, privileges that bring honor to the exalted Jesus.

## Surveying Signs in Acts

In Acts, as Don Williams points out, "it is the Risen Lord who continues his kingdom ministry" in the church.[29] Note the following (here using the ESV):

> Acts 1:1: "In the first book, O Theophilus, I have dealt with all that Jesus began to do and teach."

> Acts 3:16: "And his name—by faith in his name—has made this man strong whom you see and know, and the faith that is through Jesus has given the man this perfect health in the presence of you all."

> Acts 9:4: "And falling to the ground, he heard a voice saying to him, 'Saul, Saul, why are you persecuting me?'"

> Acts 9:34: "And Peter said to him, 'Aeneas, Jesus Christ heals you; rise and make your bed.' And immediately he rose."

### *Drawing Attention to the Gospel*

When as a fairly new believer I (Craig) pondered how to be more effective in discerning opportunities to share Christ, I studied patterns in Acts. God is not obligated to do things the same way all the time, but where can a genuinely Bible-based believer at least look for default expectations better than the New Testament? God employs various means and venues to draw people's attention to the gospel in Acts, including synagogue expositions (Acts 13:16–47), something like academic debate forums (18:28; 19:9), and legal cases (7:1–53; 26:4–29). Easily the most common means in Acts, however, is through signs. Once I noticed this pattern, I began praying for people's needs, and (especially when God answered in surprising ways) this opened

29. Williams, "Following Christ's Example," 72.

the door for a fuller witness of the gospel. Note, for example, the following cases in Acts:

> Acts 2:4–5, 12, 16 (NASB): "And they were all filled with the Holy Spirit and began to speak with different tongues, as the Spirit was giving them *the ability* to speak out. Now there were Jews residing in Jerusalem, devout men from every nation under heaven. . . . They all continued in amazement and great perplexity, saying to one another, 'What does this mean?' . . . [Peter said,] 'This is what has been spoken through the prophet Joel.'"

> Acts 3:11–13 (NASB): "While he was clinging to Peter and John, all the people ran together to them at the portico named Solomon's, completely astonished. But when Peter saw *this*, he replied to the people, 'Men of Israel, why are you amazed at this, or why are you staring at us, as though by our own power or godliness we had made him walk? The God of Abraham, Isaac, and Jacob, the God of our fathers, has glorified His servant Jesus.'"

> Acts 4:8–10 (NASB): "Then Peter, filled with the Holy Spirit, said to them, 'Rulers and elders of the people, if we are on trial today for a benefit done to a sick man, as to how this man has been made well, let it be known to all of you and to all the people of Israel, that by the name of Jesus Christ the Nazarene, whom you crucified, whom God raised from the dead . . ."

> Acts 5:12, 14 (NIV): "The apostles performed many signs and wonders among the people. . . . More and more men and women believed in the Lord and were added to their number."

> Acts 6:8–10 (NIV): "Now Stephen, a man full of God's grace and power, performed great wonders and signs among the people. Opposition arose, however, from members of the Synagogue of the Freedmen . . . who began to argue with Stephen. But they could not stand up against the wisdom the Spirit gave him as he spoke."

> Acts 8:6–7, 13 (NIV): "When the crowds heard Philip and saw the signs he performed, they all paid close attention to what he said. For with shrieks, impure spirits came out of many, and many who were paralyzed or lame were healed. . . . Simon himself believed and was baptized."

> Acts 9:34–35 (ESV): "And Peter said to him, 'Aeneas, Jesus Christ heals you; rise and make your bed.' And immediately he rose. And all the residents of Lydda and Sharon saw him, and they turned to the Lord."

> Acts 9:40–42 (ESV): "But Peter put them all outside, and knelt down and prayed; and turning to the body he said, 'Tabitha, arise.' And she opened her eyes, and when she saw Peter she sat up. And he gave her his hand and raised her up. Then,

calling the saints and widows, he presented her alive. And it became known throughout all Joppa, and many believed in the Lord."

Acts 13:9–12 (ESV): "But Saul, who was also called Paul, filled with the Holy Spirit, looked intently at him and said, '. . . The hand of the Lord is upon you, and you will be blind and unable to see the sun for a time.' Immediately mist and darkness fell upon him, and he went about seeking people to lead him by the hand. Then the proconsul believed, when he saw what had occurred, for he was astonished at the teaching of the Lord."

Acts 15:12 (ESV): "And all the assembly fell silent, and they listened to Barnabas and Paul as they related what signs and wonders God had done through them among the Gentiles."

Acts 16:25–26, 30 (NET): "About midnight Paul and Silas were praying and singing hymns to God, and the rest of the prisoners were listening to them. Suddenly a great earthquake occurred, so that the foundations of the prison were shaken. Immediately all the doors flew open, and the bonds of all the prisoners came loose. . . . Then [the jailer] brought them outside and asked, "Sirs, what must I do to be saved?"

Acts 19:11–13, 16–17 (NRSV): "God did extraordinary miracles through Paul, so that when the handkerchiefs or aprons that had touched his skin were brought to the sick, their diseases left them, and the evil spirits came out of them. Then some itinerant Jewish exorcists tried to use the name of the Lord Jesus over those who had evil spirits. . . . Then the man with the evil spirit leaped on them, mastered them all, and so overpowered them that they fled out of the house naked and wounded. When this became known to all residents of Ephesus, both Jews and Greeks, everyone was awestruck; and the name of the Lord Jesus was praised."

### *Has God Changed Methods?*

Granted that God uses various means, throughout Acts God often attested the gospel and drew attention to it through signs. Why would a Bible-based Christian expect this approach to change without any biblical warning? One might wish that those who offer theological justifications for such a change could at least offer a single explicit text in support, but to our knowledge they have never yet done so.

Contrary to what some have suggested, in Acts signs are not limited to the twelve apostles who knew Jesus, nor to apostles at all. Acts focuses especially on particular figures, especially Peter and Paul, but provides us sufficient information about others to recognize that signs extended beyond these figures. Note explicit signs through Stephen (6:8), Philip (8:6–7), and both healing and empowerment of the Spirit through Ananias (9:17–18). If we consider signs more broadly, there are the 120 at Pentecost (1:15; 2:1–4); Cornelius's household (10:46); the disciples at Ephesus (19:6), and, in Luke's Gospel, the Seventy-Two (or Seventy; Luke 10:9, 17). Aren't these examples enough to suggest a biblical pattern of God doing such signs through anyone he wishes and not just the Twelve?

Signs that look like those earlier in Acts continue at the end of Acts (28:8–9). The cessationist claim that they stop after the narrative ends appeals not to the pattern in Acts but deliberately appeals to a point after the biblical text ends—that is, where there is no concrete biblical evidence to argue from. It reminds me (Craig) of a dispute I once had with someone who claimed that the church would become the fourth member of the Trinity. After I pointed out that we remain God's servants as far in the future as the Bible depicts (Rev. 22:3), she insisted, "It's further in the future than that." One can argue anything by taking verses out of context; one can argue anything even more eloquently by sidestepping the need for verses altogether, insisting that the only evidence we have is in the biblical accounts. Then one can argue, as conventional cessationism in essence does, that the opposite of the biblical pattern is what we should really believe.

### *Summarizing the Case Again*[30]

Luke presents the empowerment of the church at Pentecost as a desirable or even normative experience for Christians (Acts 2:38–39).[31] As is clear in Acts 1:8, this experience includes empowerment to speak by the Spirit's inspiration, especially for witness. Acts at least sometimes associates this empowerment also with (or attests it by) "inspired" utterances such as prophecy or tongues (see 2:4; 10:45–46; 19:6; especially 2:17–18).

Referring to the "gift of the Spirit" earlier promised to all believers (Acts 1:4–5), Peter explicitly says that "this promise" is not only for all his hearers who turn to Christ but for their descendants and "all who are far off," all whom the Lord calls (2:38–39). Here Peter also finishes the line from Joel 2:32: "all that the Lord calls" (Acts 2:39). The gift of the Spirit rightly belongs to all who turn from sin and accept Jesus Christ as Lord. Acts assumes that the gift made available at Pentecost remains in force.

30. I (Craig) urged the following arguments some three decades ago in Keener, *Gift & Giver*, 95–98, edited only slightly here; much of it effectively summarizes the observations now offered above.

31. This is not the place to discuss the relationship among Luke's pneumatology, soteriology, and missiology; on that see, e.g., Keener, *Gift & Giver*, 137–69; Keener, *Acts*, 1:500–505, 520–23, 920. Suffice it here merely to clarify, in the unlikely event anyone assumes otherwise, that we do not deem Spirit-led speech necessary for salvation, except for the essential, "Jesus is Lord!" (1 Cor. 12:3).

Further, Peter's opening quote from Joel indicates that the gift must remain today. Peter correctly interprets Joel's prophecy as referring to "the last days" (2:17), indicated by Joel's context (Joel 3:1) and by that of other prophets (e.g., Isa. 32:15; 44:3; Ezek. 39:29) that God would pour out his Spirit in the end time. "Last days" was a biblical expression for that period (Isa. 2:2; Mic. 4:1). The outpoured Spirit signals that Christ has taken his seat at the Father's right hand (Ps. 110:1; Acts 2:33–35) and that his reign has in one sense been inaugurated. Unless God allowed the last days to begin and then retracted them—pouring out his Spirit and then taking his Spirit back, attesting Christ's reign and then concealing it—we must still be in the era of the outpoured Spirit. If it was the last days in Acts 2, it is hardly earlier than the last days now.

More to the point, the very structure of Peter's argument requires that this gift be available throughout this present age as people are saved through trusting in Christ. When foreigners are amazed to hear disciples speaking in other languages under the Spirit's inspiration, Peter insists that this experience fulfills Joel's prophecy about the Spirit of prophecy being poured out in the last days. This being the case, Peter argues, the rest of the prophecy is also in effect: Whoever calls on the name of the Lord will be saved (2:21). Salvation and the gift of the Spirit belong to the same era; indeed, it is conversion that provides access to the gift of the Spirit (2:38).

Of course, not all aspects of Pentecost are normative for all of this age. Some aspects of the first Pentecost—such as the wind and fire—were not repeated after Acts 2. But while some narratives in Acts may leave room for debate as to how frequently tongues accompanied the gift of the Spirit, in practice, tongues and prophecy often marked reception of the Spirit's prophetic empowerment (ability to speak for God) in Acts 2:4; 10:44–47; and 19:6 (cf. Luke 1:67). And why not, if a key point of this empowerment is prophetic (Acts 2:17–18: "Your sons and daughters will prophesy. . . . And they will prophesy")? In fact, when Peter hears the gentiles speaking in tongues, he marvels that they "received the Spirit in the very same way that we did" (Acts 10:47).

Acts provides a pattern that suggests that such prophetic phenomena often accompany the gift of the Spirit in the sense Luke emphasizes without ever suggesting that the pattern should change. Since (1) the gift is permanent (2:39), (2) Luke three times uses tongues-speaking to attest the reception of the gift, (3) he depicts this response as an experience arising from the Spirit's inspiration rather than from human culture (2:4), and, finally, (4) he nowhere implies that this phenomenon is to cease, a heavy burden of proof lies on anyone who would argue that tongues and prophetic speech are no longer for today. Luke presents a model of the Spirit's working in his narratives, and if he had wished to restrict aspects of the model that were not relevant to his audience, we would expect him to make such a restriction clear. And if we do not learn from biblical models, why do we claim that all Scripture is useful for teaching?

### *Luke Links Ministry Models*

Besides such explicit teaching (2:17–18), Luke provides other clues concerning the church's continuing empowerment for mission. He selects and arranges his account to link ministry figures and indicate a degree of continuity in his models of ministry.[32] This is similar to how Matthew repeats the shared message of John (Matt. 3:2), Jesus (4:17), the Twelve (10:7), and Jesus's movement (28:18–20). It suggests that many of the sort of ministry works that Jesus did in the Gospel continued in both the Jerusalem church, exemplified especially in the ministry of Peter (Acts 1–12), and the diaspora mission, exemplified especially in the ministry of Paul (Acts 13–28; cf. Gal. 2:7–8).[33] Acts likewise emphasizes the miracle-working ministries practiced by the original apostles (5:12), later apostles (14:3), and other Spirit-empowered witnesses (6:8). As already noted, in Acts signs and wonders remain the most frequent method of drawing people's attention to the gospel.

In antiquity, a particular volume in a multivolume work sometimes begins by revisiting the conclusion of the previous volume, but most volumes do not do so. That Acts 1–2 recapitulates key themes of the Gospel of Luke's conclusion suggests that Luke wants to draw attention to this key transition, as Jesus commissions his church to carry on his ministry work (Luke 24:47–49; Acts 1:8). Those so commissioned in the first place were the apostles (Acts 1:2) and those who were with them (Luke 24:33; Acts 1:22; 10:41). The Great Commission, however, is ultimately for the entire church, who can also testify of what we have seen and heard (2:33; 8:6; 22:14–15; cf. Luke 2:20; 7:22). The first witnesses become a model for the church's continuing witness. Thus others converted after Jesus's resurrection also became witnesses (Acts 22:15, 20; 23:11; 26:16), and all of us certainly can testify about God's kingdom (cf. 28:23). The mission to the ends of the earth does not conclude at the end of Acts, the death of the apostles, or the Council of Nicaea.

The transition from Jesus's earthly ministry to that of his church is particularly obvious in the church being empowered by the prophetic Spirit in connection with Jesus's ascension (Luke 24:49–51; Acts 1:8–11). The one earlier ascension narrative with which Jesus's first disciples and Luke's original audience would be most familiar was that of Elijah. When God took Elijah to heaven, Elisha received a double portion of the Spirit that was on Elijah (2 Kings 2:9–14). As Elisha continued the mission of Elijah, so the empowered church carries on much of the mission of Jesus. Acts 2:39 ("This promise is for . . . all who are far away, for whoever the Lord our God will call") reveals that the empowerment is for all the church, not just the first witnesses (Acts 2:39).

32. With also Ruthven, "Charismata 3," 186.

33. For detailed explanation and charts, see Talbert, *Patterns*; Tannehill, *Unity*; more briefly, O'Toole, "Parallels"; Keener, *Acts*, 1:556–62.

### *Acts as Mere History or Also a Model?*

Consistency with the authority of Scripture leads us to recognize that Acts offers us models. Certainly Paul reads Old Testament narratives as precedents and models, positive or negative (e.g., Rom. 4:22–24; 15:4; 1 Cor. 10:11), as did Jesus (e.g., Mark 2:25–26) and other New Testament writers (e.g., Heb. 11:4–40; 12:16). And if they did so regarding human behavior, how much more would they expect to learn from God's behavior (John 6:31; Rom. 11:4; 1 Cor. 10:5–6)? New Testament writers also draw on the model of Jesus (e.g., Rom. 15:3; Heb. 12:1–3; 1 Pet. 2:21; 1 John 2:6), and so presumably would do so from other models once these were available (cf. Acts 20:31; 1 Cor. 4:16; 11:1; 2 Tim. 3:10–11). (See further this book's appendix on theology from narrative.)

Those who doubt that an ancient history or biography would be meant to provide examples to follow reveal their complete unfamiliarity with how ancient historians and biographers (as opposed to annalists or novelists) wrote.[34] If the biblical models above do not suffice, the following two paragraphs briefly summarize some of the other ancient evidence for those who feel that they need it.

Most ancient historians sought to communicate lessons through the events they chose to recount.[35] History, ancients opined, preserves the memory of honorable or shameful acts for posterity and moral instruction.[36] For example, Tacitus, one of our most reliable historical sources for the early Roman Empire, viewed exposing vice and praising virtue as his historical obligation.[37] Historians generally believed that not merely themselves but also statesmen[38] and orators[39] could use these events and actions as precedents and guides for future decisions.[40] Jewish writers in this period worked with the same

34. Here we draw from esp. Keener, *Christobiography*, 132–33, 193–200, which condenses but also augments and develops material from Keener, *Acts*, 1:149–58.

35. Cf., e.g., Chaplin, "Conversations"; Bosworth, *Arrian*, 155; McInerney, "Arrian and Romance"; Galinsky, "Introduction," 4, 21; Gowing, "Memory," 43–48, esp. 46–47; Becker, *Birth*, 23.

36. E.g., Herodotus, *Hist.* 1.1 pref.; Polybius, *Hist.* 1.1.1; 1.57; 7.12; Diodorus Siculus, *Libr. Hist.* 10.3.1; 11.11.2, 6; 11.38.6; 15.1.1; 17.38.4; Dionysius of Halicarnassus, *Rom. Ant.* 1.2.1; 1.6.3–5; Justinus, *Epit.* pref. 4; Valerius Maximus, *Mem.* 2.pref.; Lucian, *Hist.* 59; Maximus of Tyre, *Or.* 22.5. See also Fornara, *Nature*, 113–16; Judge, *First Christians*, 249–51; Rüpke, "Knowledge," 93–94.

37. Tacitus, *Agr.* 1; *Ann.* 3.65; 4.33; Laistner, *Historians*, 113–14; Williams, "Germanicus" (addressing Tacitus's perspective in one work).

38. Dionysius of Halicarnassus, *Rom. Ant.* 5.56.1; Polybius, *Hist.* 3.31.11–13.

39. See, e.g., Dionysius of Halicarnassus, *Rom. Ant.* 6.80.1; *Rhet. Alex.* 8.1429a.21–1430a.13; Cicero, *Sest.* 48.102; cf. also Kennedy, "Survey," 21.

40. On such historical "paradigms" see also Diodorus Siculus, *Libr. Hist.* 37.4.1; Herodian, *Hist.* 3.13.3; on both past and present paradigms, cf. Velleius Paterculus, *Comp.* 2.92.5.

expectations.[41] Most ancient historians also sought to interpret the divine will in some patterns in history.[42]

Most scholars find the Gospels closer to ancient biographies than to histories more narrowly defined. But as did other kinds of historical writers, biographers frequently sought to teach moral lessons from their accounts.[43] Readers could ask, "What's the *moral* of this story?" (Whereas today we often use fictitious stories to convey lessons, in antiquity it was historians and biographers, far more than novelists, who sought to convey lessons in their writing.) Biographic information was meant to be used to instruct learners in virtue through the process of imitation.[44]

Had Luke intended to show that miracles had started to wane in the early church, why would he have nearly closed his narrative by telling about all the miracles and healings that Paul performed on Malta (Acts 28:1–10)? Isn't this meant to give the opposite impression? Moreover, most narrative specialists on Acts believe that Luke uses an ancient kind of narrative conclusion that leaves the ending "open" in order to invite us into the continuing mission.[45] This appears to be evidence that, from a biblical perspective, the signs-attested, Spirit-empowered mission is ongoing.

As Marquette professor William Kurz explains, "The open ending of Acts . . . provides a ready invitation to treat Acts from the perspective of canonical readers. The lack of closure invites continuation. The same kind of open-endedness . . . can also invite later generations of 'us' Christian readers into Paul's mission of 'preaching the kingdom of God and teaching about the Lord Jesus Christ quite openly and unhindered' (Acts 28:31 RSV). . . . The tension between 'already and not yet' in fulfillment of the narrative's promises provides a natural invitation to actualize the narrative and apply it to the canonical readers' situation."[46]

So long as the mission remains to be completed, we continue to need the Spirit's power to fulfill it (Acts 1:8), and that same power is promised to us (2:39, evoking also God's promise in 1:4).[47] Likewise, we who continue this

41. See Philo *Abraham* 4; Josephus, *Ag. Ap.* 2.204; 4 Macc 1:7–8; Kelhoffer, "Maccabees at Prayer"; Keener, *Acts*, 1:154–55.

42. See, e.g., Justinus, *Epit.* 24.3.10; Appian, *Hist. rom.* 7.8.53; esp. Squires, *Plan*; Squires, "Plan"; Shauf, *Divine*.

43. Pelling, "Adaptation," 135; Burridge, *Gospels*, 145–46, 181; Hägg, *Biography*, 239–81, esp. 274; cf. Dihle, "Biography," 367–74. Plutarch expressly notes that his interest in moral lessons fits historiographic practice (Plutarch, *Aem. Paul.*1.1–3).

44. Plutarch, *Arat.* 1.4. Cf. Kurz, "Models," 182–83, on biography and narrative models for imitation.

45. See, e.g., Marguerat, *Histoire*, 333; Marguerat, *Historian*, 152–54, 230; Rosner, "Progress," 232–33; Keener, *Acts*, 4:3758–63.

46. Kurz, "Nature," 293–94.

47. This paragraph follows Keener, *Spirit Hermeneutics*, 167.

mission remain part of God's continuing work in history, a narrative to which Acts points.

## Conclusion

The point of this chapter may be aptly summarized the way that I (Craig) summarized evidence from Acts in a recent article:

> Rightly understanding Joel to be speaking eschatologically, Peter paraphrases Joel: "In the *last days*," God says, "I will pour out my Spirit on all flesh" (Acts 2:17). Luke does not want his audience to miss the point that this message is for us. If it was already the last days on [Peter's] Pentecost, then it surely remains "last days" throughout Acts and indeed until Jesus returns; this is how the rest of the NT uses the phrase (1 Tim. 4:1; 2 Tim. 3:1; Heb. 1:2; 1 Pet. 1:20; 2 Pet. 3:3; 1 John 2:18). (It can hardly have been "last days" then and become *earlier* than "last days" afterward.)
>
> God did not pour out the Spirit only to pour the Spirit back, to empower the church only to disempower it afterward (cf. Acts 2:39). Peter cites the experience of the outpoured Spirit to verify that God had inaugurated the messianic era; the Messiah is enthroned at the Father's right hand (2:33, 36). This is the era of the Messiah reigning until his enemies are fully subjected (2:34–35), the era of prophetic empowerment (2:17–18), the era when whoever calls on the Lord's name will be saved (2:21).[48]

48. From Keener, "Power for Mission," 236, here slightly edited.

# 5

# Until We See Face-to-Face (1 Cor. 13:8–12)

> Love never ends. But if there are prophecies, they will be set aside; if there are tongues, they will cease; if there is knowledge, it will be set aside. For we know in part, and we prophesy in part, but when what is perfect comes, the partial will be set aside. When I was a child, I talked like a child, I thought like a child, I reasoned like a child. But when I became an adult, I set aside childish ways. For now we see in a mirror indirectly, but then we will see face to face. Now I know in part, but then I will know fully, just as I have been fully known.
>
> 1 Corinthians 13:8–12 NET

## Gifts Until Jesus's Return in 1 Corinthians 1:7–8

Paul raises the topic of spiritual gifts toward the beginning of 1 Corinthians, preparing for his fuller treatment later in the letter. In 1 Corinthians 1:7–8, Paul expects spiritual gifts (*charismata*) to continue to strengthen the Corinthians until Jesus is revealed on the day of the Lord Jesus: "So you don't lack in any grace-gift at all while you wait eagerly for our Lord Jesus the Messiah to be revealed. He will also fortify you to the end, so that you'll be blameless in the day of our Lord Jesus the Messiah." As God's gifts, spiritual gifts are inherently good; God does not give bad grace-gifts. This is not to suggest that all is well with the Corinthians' *use* of spiritual gifts; Paul will address problems in detail in 1 Corinthians 12–14. But it was customary to build rapport at the beginning of a communication, so Paul acknowledges the benefits of these gifts up front.

When Paul introduces the grace given to them (1:4), he specifies some of their favorite gifts. They were enriched in all speech (*logos*) and knowledge (*gnōsis*; 1:5). Even non-Christian Corinthians valued speech and knowledge, sponsoring oratorical competitions and praising those able to speak extemporaneously on various topics. The Greek world's two major advanced disciplines were rhetoric (public speaking) and philosophy, and students of rival teachers in Corinth sometimes came to blows. This attitude had also spilled over into the church, with Corinthians evaluating Paul and Apollos by their culture's standards of public speaking (1 Cor. 2:13–3:4; cf. 1:17; 2:1, 4). The Corinthians valued the wrong kind of wisdom (1:17–24, 30; 2:1–7, 13; 3:19), and exalted knowledge above love (8:1, 7, 10–11). It is no wonder that Paul opens his first list of gifts with a "word [*logos*] of wisdom" and a "word [*logos*] of knowledge" (12:8). Although Paul will also address at length the abuse of God's gift of tongues (1 Cor. 14), it is clear that the Corinthians are abusing not only tongues but also God's gift of knowledge; it has become a source of arrogance (8:1). Not only tongues speakers but also we Bible teachers are at risk.

The gifts themselves remain good, however. Paul says that Christ's testimony was confirmed among them (1:6), "so that (*hōste*) you don't lack any spiritual gift as you wait eagerly for the revelation of Jesus" (1:7). Jesus's "revelation" (*apokalypsis*) refers to the time of his future coming (cf. also Rom. 2:5; 8:19; 2 Thess. 1:7; 1 Pet. 1:7, 13; 4:13). While we await Jesus's coming, then, we can expect Christ to *continue* to confirm us to the end, so we may be blameless on the day of Christ (1 Cor. 1:8). The end (*telos*) also refers to the time of his coming (1 Cor. 15:24), the day of the Lord (3:13; 5:5; Rom. 2:5, 16; 13:12; 2 Cor. 1:14; Phil. 1:6, 10). The period of gifts here thus coincides with the period when Christ continues to strengthen us, until his return. This pattern becomes even more explicit later in 1 Corinthians, in 13:8–12.

## Until We See Face-to-Face (1 Cor. 13:12)

The New Testament is consistent in its picture of when the gifts will pass away. They will pass when we no longer need them because we have such a complete experience of God in Christ that the gifts will no longer serve any benefit. Here are examples of this:

- The kingdom-preaching (Matt. 10:7), signs-working (10:8) mission of bringing good news to the Jewish people continues until the Son of Man comes (10:23).

- God will pour out his Spirit on all people, who will prophesy and have visions and dreams, and people will be saved, in the last days (already effective when Peter preached on Pentecost) until the day of the Lord (Acts 2:17–18, 20).
- 1 Corinthians 1:7 (NIV): "Therefore you do not lack any spiritual gift as you eagerly wait for our Lord Jesus Christ to be revealed."
- 1 Corinthians 13:8–10, 12 (NRSV): "Love never ends. But as for prophecies, they will come to an end; as for tongues, they will cease; as for knowledge, it will come to an end. For we know only in part, and we prophesy only in part; but when the complete comes, the partial will come to an end. . . . For now we see . . . dimly, but then we will see face to face. Now I know only in part; then I will know fully, even as I have been fully known."
- Ephesians 4:11–13 (NRSV): "The gifts he gave were that some would be apostles, some prophets, some evangelists, some pastors and teachers, to equip the saints for the work of ministry, for building up the body of Christ, until all of us come to the unity of the faith and of the knowledge of the Son of God, to maturity, to the measure of the full stature of Christ."
- One might also consider the continuation of prophets, sometimes accompanied by miracles, who appear in the book of Revelation (Rev. 11:5–6, 10, 18; 16:6; 18:20, 24), which some interpreters apply to the present and others to the future, but none only to the past.[1]

### *Cessationist Arguments from 1 Corinthians 13*

Although today very few scholars try to argue cessationism from 1 Corinthians 13, some voices do in the wider, nonscholarly church world. Some claim that the "perfect" (13:10) refers to the completion of the New Testament.[2] So let's read the passage and address it briefly. Based on 1 Corinthians 13:10, some cessationists assert the following:

1. The "perfect" is the closed canon of Scripture.
2. The "perfect" will render obsolete spiritual gifts like prophecy and tongues (if these critics mention knowledge, they usually assign it a special, supernatural meaning).
3. Therefore, the closed canon of Scripture has rendered such spiritual gifts obsolete.

1. MacArthur, *Strange Fire*, 300–301n34, applies it to the future, but (as a pretribulationalist) "after the church age is over."

2. E.g., Toussaint, "Tongues"; Houghton, "Reexamination"; cf. Hodges, "Tongues"; Johnson, "Tongues."

One cessationist author expresses this popular view in a commentary on 1 Corinthians: "Miraculous gifts were given by the power of the Holy Spirit (1 Cor. 12:8–11) and they were given for a limited period of time. Paul said these special abilities would last 'till' the perfect (the completed New Testament) came. . . . The gift of tongues would 'cease' (v. 8) and other gifts such as prophecy and supernatural knowledge would be replaced by the 'perfect' (God's completed word)."[3]

The glaring problem with this view is that the passage does not say, nor remotely imply, that the "perfect" is the closed canon of Scripture. Such a reading is in fact exegetically impossible. Consider two reasons:

- The "perfect" will render not only prophecy and tongues obsolete, but also knowledge. If the latter has not happened, there is no reason to assume the former has. Knowledge in 1 Corinthians includes theological and moral knowledge (1 Cor. 8:1, 7, 10–11).
- The coming of the "perfect" (13:10) means we should know fully, completely and "face to face" (13:12). This cannot refer to a closed canon. The closed canon itself—in this very passage!—claims that our knowledge in this age is partial. If our present knowledge were perfect and full, we would hardly be engaged in this cessationist-continuationist debate. Even with Scripture in our hands, though the knowledge it affords us is abundant and authoritative, we still "know only in part" and "see in a mirror, dimly" compared to our knowledge in the coming age.

Some contend that whatever the "perfect" is, knowledge, prophecy, and tongues passed away in the church's infancy.[4] The arrival of maturity in 1 Corinthians 13:11–12, however, corresponds to seeing Christ face-to-face (cf. perhaps also Eph. 4:13).

Michael Brown rightly complains that the appeal to 1 Corinthians 13 as support for cessationism is "one of the most impossible interpretations put on a biblical text in the history of interpretation—and a relatively recent one at that."[5] One Pentecostal scholar lists samples of eighty "non-Pentecostal" (though by no means all cessationist) commentators who view "the perfect" in verse 10 as still future.[6]

3. Price, *First Corinthians*, 614.

4. Thomas, "Tongues." Contrast rightly Garland, *1 Corinthians*, 622; Ruthven, *Cessation*, 125–26. On the use of child-mature contrasts in antiquity, see esp. Elbert, "Exegesis," 506–7.

5. Brown, *Authentic Fire*, 204.

6. Graves, *Praying in the Spirit*, 200–201.

### *When Do We See Him Face-to-Face?*

> Whether *there are* prophecies, they will fail; whether *there are* tongues, they will cease; whether *there is* knowledge, it will vanish away. For we know in part and we prophesy in part. . . . For now we see in a mirror, dimly, but then face to face. Now I know in part, but then I shall know just as I also am known. (1 Cor. 13:8–9, 12 NKJV)

The vast majority of New Testament scholars today recognize that applying 1 Corinthians 13:10 to the completion of the New Testament makes no sense of the context.[7]

- Do we see face-to-face (13:12)? This wording, like seeing "dimly," alludes to the ancient Greek rendering of Numbers 12:6–8, in which God reveals himself to prophets in visions or dreams, but speaks with Moses face-to-face and not dimly.
- Do we know as we are known? The context contrasts the present knowing in part (13:9) with our full knowledge at Jesus's return, when our present partial knowledge will be done away with (13:8, 10).[8] Who knows Jesus already to the degree that he knows us?
- Since the gift of teaching involves communicating knowledge, when knowledge passes, the gift of teaching passes. Knowledge passes at the same time as prophecy, when we know as we are known (13:8–10).
- Another problem with the idea that Paul refers here to the completion of the New Testament is that there is no way he could expect the Corinthians to know that a New Testament canon was coming unless he explained that to them.[9] (After all, the Greek neuter *to teleion* does not mean this anywhere else in Scripture.) But they should already know that *Jesus* is coming (1 Cor. 1:7–8; 4:5; 11:26; 15:23; 16:22), including from Paul's two most recent uses of this specific form for "comes," *elthē* (4:5; 11:26).

7. Application to the canon "is simply nonsense" (Hays, *First Corinthians*, 229) and "impossible" (Fee, *Gospel*, 7–8). See, e.g., Thrall, *First and Second Corinthians*, 94; Grudem, *Prophecy*, 210–19; Collins, *Corinthians*, 486; Martens, "First Corinthians 13:10"; Garland, *1 Corinthians*, 622; Forbes, *Prophecy*, 85–91.

8. For what it might be worth, later Jewish teachers understood Jer. 31:31–34 as promising the fullness of knowledge in the age to come (Davies, *Paul*, 224; cf. *b. Šabb*. 63b, in Davies, *Torah*, 82). Irenaeus attributes to Gnosticism the view that one can have perfect knowledge in this age (*Haer*. 2.28).

9. Paul was presumably aware that God's Spirit was guiding his writing (1 Cor. 5:4; 7:40; 14:37), but guidance by the Spirit does not entail canonicity (see chaps. 12–13 below).

- Since Paul expected that Jesus could possibly return in his own lifetime (1 Thess. 4:15–16; 1 Cor. 15:51), how certain can we be that he *himself* expected a New Testament canon?[10]
- Finally, if at some point in this age "knowledge" passes, how would we *know* it (or anything else)?

The availability of Scripture can hardly ensure perfect knowledge, given the many different interpretations of Scripture that exist. Second Peter warns that the unstable twist the Scriptures (3:16) but nevertheless urges us to pay close attention to the Scriptures, which, it apparently says, are "like a lamp shining in a dark place." We should heed them "until the day dawns and the morning star rises in your hearts" (1:19). That is, the Bible carries us through the darkness of this present age, but we will experience the fullest revelation when Jesus comes back.[11] His return will end all our interpretive debates.[12] While we already experience the foretaste of the new covenant in Christ, inaugurated well before the completion of the New Testament (Luke 22:20; 1 Cor. 11:25; 2 Cor. 3:6), in its ultimate fulfillment teaching will be superfluous, for we shall all know the Lord fully (Jer. 31:31, 34).

The passage as a whole (1 Cor. 13:8–12) reinforces this contrast between the present era and the second coming *repeatedly*, making it clear that incomplete prophecy, tongues, and knowledge belong to this present era and are superseded *when Christ returns* (see table 5.1).

**Table 5.1. Contrasts in 1 Corinthians 13:8–12**

| Now | Then |
|---|---|
| Prophecies, tongues, knowledge (13:8) | Prophecies, tongues, knowledge will end (13:8) |
| We know in part, we prophesy in part (13:9) | When the complete comes, the partial will end (13:10) |
| Speaking, thinking like a child (13:11) | Full maturity (13:11; cf. Eph. 4:13) |
| Now we see dimly (13:12a) | Then we shall see face-to-face (13:12b) |
| Now I know in part (13:12c) | Then I shall know fully, *just as* I have been known (13:12de) |

10. Turner, *Gifts*, 294.

11. For this understanding, see briefly Keener, *1–2 Peter, Jude*, 81–82.

12. Perhaps 1 Cor. 13–cessationists merely insist that we have *Scripture* perfectly. Still, the many textual variants (the different ways that it was copied over the centuries) show that it was not *preserved* completely perfectly (though I would argue that for most ordinary purposes it was preserved adequately). That is, God inspiring the Bible is no guarantee that everybody who copied it would do so infallibly. So if the perfect was the Bible, did its perfection pass away when copyists made mistakes copying it?

Those who treat the completion of the canon as if it were Jesus's second coming risk being like those who claimed that the day of the Lord had come (2 Thess. 2:2) or that the general resurrection was already past (2 Tim. 2:18)!

### *Most Cessationists Treat the Passage as Ambiguous*

Most scholars, including cessationist scholars, now reject the view that 1 Corinthians 13 refers to the completion of the canon.[13] Thus, for example, Richard Gaffin, a prominent cessationist, concedes that "the view that they describe the point at which the New Testament canon is completed cannot be made credible exegetically."[14]

Earlier cessationist theologian Donald W. Burdick likewise recognized that 1 Corinthians 13:8–10 "does not say that tongues were to cease at the end of the apostolic age. In fact, it allows for the existence of tongues until . . . we see Christ 'as he is' (1 John 3:2). Then there will be no more place for tongues or prophecy for knowledge will be complete. To make 1 Corinthians 13:8 prove that God intended glossolalia to cease at the end of the apostolic age is to violate the valid rules of biblical interpretation in the interest of a previously determined position."[15] Not only does this passage fail to prove that tongues have passed away, but it actually indicates quite the opposite. As Burdick admits, "[This passage] allows for the existence of tongues until 'that which is perfect' has come."

Is knowledge still with us? Is the imperfect still here? Do we still know in part? Then according to this passage there is no way to separate tongues and prophecy from this age. Moreover, to claim that the "perfect" has already come is to imply that our present level of knowledge, perception, and maturity is as good as it will ever get! If that were the case, I (Daniel), for one, would be terribly disappointed. If our current condition is what Paul calls "perfect," the word would seem to be meaningless.

John MacArthur and his circle also agree that the "perfect" refers to the end time,[16] though MacArthur adds inconsistently that based on Ephesians 2:20 (addressed in chap. 7 below), such gifts have passed away anyway.[17]

13. For continuationist rejections of the view, see, e.g., Dollar, "Theology of Healing," 48; Carson, *Showing Spirit*, 66–76; Grudem, *Prophecy*, 210–19; Fee, *Corinthians*[2], 714–15n381; Fee, *Presence*, 204–14; Fee, *Gospel*, 7–8; Forbes, *Prophecy*, 85–91; also Fee and Stuart, *How to Read*, 60. See esp. Elbert, "Face to Face," taking into account hundreds of Koine Greek examples to show that this passage refers to the second coming.

14. Gaffin, *Perspectives*, 109.

15. Burdick, *Tongues*, 36. Burdick wrongly supposes that Pentecostals seek to evangelize for tongues rather than for Christ (*Tongues*, 88, as cited in Graves, "Focus," 94).

16. MacArthur, *Chaos*, 231n20 ("the eternal state"); MacArthur, *Strange Fire*, 301n34 (while suggesting a resurgence of prophecy in the "Tribulation and Millennial Kingdom," fitting his decidedly non-Reformed dispensational eschatology).

17. MacArthur, *Strange Fire*, 301n34.

To evade the text's clear implications, cessationists often treat it as ambiguous. Sam Waldron suggests that Paul in 1 Corinthians 13:10 "says nothing about when the gifts of prophecy and tongues pass away. He only refers to the passing of the present partial knowledge that was conveyed through those gifts."[18] Yet Paul *explicitly* does refer to both knowing and prophesying as partial in 13:9, indicating that the supplanting of the partial with the perfect in 13:10 refers to both.

Cessationist Pauline scholar Thomas Schreiner likewise dismisses a cessationist case built on this text,[19] even suggesting that the passage offers the best case for continuationism.[20] To evade such a continuationist case, however, he suggests that the Lord simply "didn't reveal clearly to Paul that the gifts would end because he didn't want the Corinthians or Paul to know" that he wouldn't return in the first century; "if Paul taught that some of the gifts would slowly cease, then it would be evident to both Paul and the Corinthians that Jesus would not and could not come during their lifetime."[21] To us this sounds like saying Paul was mistaken about the timing (though Schreiner would likely explain it instead as ambiguous) but that God allowed this error in Scripture for that generation's own good.

Other knowledgeable cessationists also prefer to view 1 Corinthians 13 as ambiguous rather than admit it into the cessationist-continuationism debate. Cessationist theologian Richard Gaffin says, "Paul is not intending to specify the time when any particular mode will cease."[22]

### *Clearly the End of the Age*

By contrast, D. A. Carson challenges the claim that the passage is ambiguous about the time of cessation: "Gaffin recognizes that this passage cannot be used to teach that prophecy and tongues ceased in the first or second century, so he tries to neutralize the connection with the parousia by saying that the exact time of cessation is not specified at all, which can then be dealt with on dogmatic rather than exegetical grounds. But Paul specifies that prophecy and other gifts will cease *when* perfection comes."[23]

Some argue that the passage supports the passing away of tongues before knowledge and prophecy, noting that Paul uses different verbs. But the verse's parallelism (noted earlier) undercuts such a claim, and Paul uses different verbs

18. Waldron, *Continued*, 64.
19. Schreiner, *Spiritual Gifts*, 147–53.
20. Schreiner, *Spiritual Gifts*, 153.
21. Schreiner, *Spiritual Gifts*, 156, conceding that his suggestion "is speculative and could be off-center."
22. Gaffin, *Perspectives*, 111. Cf. Saucy, "View," 123.
23. Carson, *Showing Spirit*, 69n57. See similarly Grudem, *Prophecy Today*, 235, cited in Graves, "Cessationism," 50.

here for the sake of variation, as he often does (e.g., 1 Cor. 12:4–6). Moreover, even if one were tempted to make the verbs mean something different, nothing would make one verb suggest that tongues had passed away earlier—nothing, that is, except the need of an interpreter to make the passage say that.[24] Against some cessationist arguments,[25] Carson has shown that the Greek middle form of "cease" (1 Cor. 13:8) does not here mean "cease of themselves" and that New Testament usage does not support such a supposed distinction.[26]

Church fathers who discussed the question of gifts' cessation in 1 Corinthians 13:8–12 were unanimous that it referred to the end of the age.[27] Irenaeus regarded knowing and prophesying "in part" as our state "on the earth," in this age.[28] For Augustine, the coming of the "perfect" corresponds to the eschatological resurrection of our bodies.[29] Reacting against the Montanists, early church fathers unanimously insisted that "the perfect" in 1 Corinthians 13:10 refers to the time of Jesus's future return.[30] In this connection Eusebius insists that "it is necessary that the prophetic charisma be in all the Church until the final coming."[31] John Calvin apparently viewed a noneschatological understanding of 13:12 as "stupid."[32]

## The Era of the Spirit

Like Luke in Acts, Paul regards the present era as the era of the Spirit. Jewish people disagreed among themselves on whether prophets continued in their day (the elites generally said no; what later became the rabbinic movement thus rejected contemporary prophecy). Many people believed in prophets, but no non-Christian movement in antiquity resembled anything like what Paul describes in his churches: prophecies and other charismatic experiences pervading an entire movement and displayed as normal in its congregations.

24. Here I adapt Keener, *Gift & Giver*, 106.

25. MacArthur, *Chaos*, 231n20.

26. Carson, *Fallacies*², 76–77 (in the 1984 ed., the critique is 77–78); see also Carson, *Showing Spirit*, 66–67; Fee, *Presence*, 206n467; esp. Elbert, "Exegesis," 509–10; note also sources cited in Ruthven, *Cessation*, 119–20. On the imperfection of our present knowledge, see also John Chrysostom, *Hom. Cor.* 20.3; Origen, *Comm. Rom.* 3.10–11 (on Rom. 3:30–31).

27. See most thoroughly Shogren, "Perfect Would Come"; Shogren, "Prophecy and Canon" (noted in Ruthven, *Cessation*, 123); Shogren, "Gift of Tongues," 409.

28. Irenaeus, *Haer.* 2.28.7, in Ruthven, *Cessation*, 122, and noting also *Haer.* 4.9.2.

29. Augustine, *City of God* 22.29 (LCL 7:368–70; Kovacs, *1 Corinthians*, 223); Augustine, *Spirit and Letter* 38, 41, 49, 64.

30. See Ruthven, *Cessation*, 122, noting esp. Epiphanius, *Pan.* 48.5.4 (PG 41:855); Didymus of Alexandria, *Triad.* 3.41 (PG 39:984); Origen, *Cels.* 6.20; and others further, Shogren, "Gift of Tongues," 409. Paul himself did not yet know fully (Origen, *Comm. Rom.* 3.3.14 on Rom. 3:10).

31. Ruthven, *Cessation*, 122, citing *Against Alcibiades* in Eusebius, *Hist. eccl.* 5.17.4.

32. Turner, *Gifts*, 295.

Sometimes this novel, countercultural experience became messy, as in Corinth, but it was part of the distinctive fabric of early Christianity. In Paul's churches, as in Acts, such experience testified that Jesus's movement distinctively believed that it had entered the messianic era of the Spirit. The charismata belong to the eschatological era of the Spirit between Jesus's first and second comings.[33]

Why is prophecy so sparse in many churches today? Why is this testimony of Christ's exaltation and the messianic era more silent than it was in the first century? Surely it is not because Christ has become unexalted or because the perfect has already come. Perhaps it is because much of Christendom has forgotten God's gift. Perhaps, as Paul suggested to Christians in Corinth, we should collectively seek for God to send the true gift among us (1 Cor. 14:1, 39).

33. Cf. also Graves, "Cessationism," 51; Hernando, "Continuationism," 115; Twelftree, "Ministry and Miraculous," 132.

# 6

# Gift Lists, Gift Commands

Cessationists do not exclude all gifts for today—only the "supernatural," "miraculous," "extraordinary," or "revelatory" ones.[1] But where does this distinction come from in the biblical text? Or did human beings merely invent it to make some gifts seem obsolete?

John MacArthur says that Scripture distinguishes "the *permanent edifying gifts*, including knowledge, wisdom, prophecy (authoritative preaching), teaching, exhortation, faith (or prayer), discernment, showing mercy, giving, administration, and helps (see Rom. 12:3–8; 1 Cor. 12:8–10, 28)" from "the *temporary sign gifts*."[2] Really? Where does Scripture distinguish them? "We can legitimately divide the spiritual gifts in the New Testament into two basic categories," declares Tom Pennington, "the non-miraculous, permanent gifts and the miraculous temporary gifts."[3] If "we can legitimately divide" them, what is the passage of *Scripture* that establishes such a division as legitimate?

Conversely, a Reformed critic of this approach rightly counters, "'Revelatory gifts' is a term made up by cessationists to get us to the conclusion that they have ceased. Calling them 'ceased gifts' and then concluding from that name that they have ceased, would be no more circular in reasoning [than

1. For the modern history of the distinction, see Ruthven, *Cessation*, 49, 83; Deere, *Still Surprised*, 97, 224.

2. MacArthur, *Chaos*, 199. His mention of "edifying" with the "permanent" gifts is intriguing, since "knowledge" sometimes can be deployed in unedifying ways (explicit in 1 Cor. 8:1, 10), tongues edifies the worshiper (1 Cor. 14:4), and prophecy, which MacArthur deems temporary, explicitly edifies the church (14:3–5), as all charismata in the assembly should do (14:12, 26; Eph. 4:12, 16). For such a distinction, without opposition to other gifts, cf. Kruger, *Introduction*, 222.

3. Pennington, *Cessationism*, 90.

that]. . . . And so cessationism is a self-contradictory doctrine that claims the Bible is sufficient so we don't need spiritual gifts (that the Bible tells us we need) but we do need the doctrine of cessationism (that the Bible doesn't teach)."[4]

We continuationists regard such distinctions as postbiblical, arbitrary, and inconsistent. A natural-supernatural distinction owes more to the skeptical philosopher David Hume than to Scripture, where terms such as "supernatural" do not appear.[5] Such a distinction violates biblical thought, because *everything* is God's creation, including the food on our tables (cf. 1 Tim. 4:3–5). Excluding "supernatural" grace-gifts would leave only those gifts that would require that God work through us in a way that we could accept yet explain naturally—that is, only gifts that would not challenge the assumptions of someone with no faith. These would be gifts that any deist or atheist would find unobjectionable on principle. Indeed, the distinction ultimately demeans even the supposedly "natural" or "ordinary" *charisma* of teaching. May it never be simply an intellectual exercise devoid of reliance on God's Spirit—a non-Christian might then possess the same "gift."

## Examining Biblical Gift Lists

Does inductive study of the biblical lists of *charismata*, or "freely given gifts,"[6] support the cessationist distinction between permanent gifts and temporary ones? Or is the distinction an entirely postbiblical one imposed on the biblical text?

The biblical lists in fact reveal that the cessationist distinction is arbitrary and entirely postbiblical. It is evident in none of the many lists in the epistles. The Bible makes no distinction between miraculous gifts (such as prophecy and healing) and those gifts often considered nonmiraculous (such as mercy and giving). Paul, unlike cessationists, consistently lists these gifts together. He mentions "prophecy" in the same breath as "teaching" (Rom. 12:6–7); "apostles" in the same breath as "administrating" (1 Cor. 12:28); and a "tongue" in the same breath as a "psalm" (1 Cor. 14:26). Dividing *charismata* into categories like "miraculous" and "nonmiraculous" is precisely what Paul does *not* do. The Bible groups them together because each gift is equally animated by the grace and power of the Holy Spirit. Each gift is a *charisma*, and each member of the body is "charismatic."

4. Carpenter, "Recovering," noted in Brown, *Authentic Fire*, 204.

5. Cf. the phrase "supernatural gifts" in, e.g., Saucy, "View," 121, 131n57; Schreiner, *Spiritual Gifts*, 148; Pennington, *Cessationism*, 168 (quoting favorably William Shedd).

6. For academic studies on the *charismata* in Paul, see, e.g., Turner, *Gifts*, 182–302 (esp. 262–67); Schatzmann, *Charismata*, passim (esp. 1–13); Fee, *Presence*, 146–261 (and esp. 32–35, 886–95); Carson, *Showing Spirit*, passim; Keener, *Gift & Giver*, 89–136; very briefly, Keener, "Gifts."

To maintain the cessationist distinction, one would have to divide the following gift lists something like what we see below. Granted, some differ regarding the category to which some gifts belong, depending on how these gifts are defined. So, for example, we, unlike some others, construe "knowledge" in its usual sense in 1 Corinthians (1 Cor. 1:5; 8:1, 7, 10–11) rather than as direct revelation. In keeping with 1 Corinthians 14:2, 14, discussed further in chapter 16, we construe tongues, whether as genuine foreign languages or not, as those naturally unknown to the speaker. But the following is our best effort to attempt to distinguish clearly "supernatural" from potentially "natural" gifts.

### *The Lists*

**List 1. Romans 12:6–8:**
**We have gifts that differ according to the *grace* given to us . . .**

| Gift | Potentially natural? |
|---|---|
| prophesying . . . in accordance with your faith | no |
| serving | yes |
| teaching | yes |
| to encourage | yes |
| giving | yes |
| to lead | yes |
| to show mercy [charity] | yes |

*Note:* Translations from the NIV.

**List 2. 1 Corinthians 12:8–10:**
**To one there is given through the Spirit . . .**

| Gift | Potentially natural? |
|---|---|
| a message of wisdom | yes |
| to another, a message of knowledge by means of the same Spirit | yes |
| to another, faith by the same Spirit | maybe |
| to another gifts of healings by that one Spirit | no |
| to another miraculous powers | no |
| to another prophecy | no |
| to another distinguishing between spirits | no |
| to another speaking in different kinds of tongues | no |
| and to still another the interpretation of tongues | no |

*Note:* Translations from the NIV.

### List 3. 1 Corinthians 12:28: And God has appointed in the church . . .

| Gift | Potentially natural? |
|---|---|
| first apostles | no |
| second prophets | no |
| third teachers | yes |
| then miracles | no |
| then gifts of healing | no |
| helping | yes |
| administrating | yes |
| various kinds of tongues | no |

*Note:* Translations from the ESV. Differences between 12:28–30 and 12:8–10 suggest that Paul does not treat any of these lists as exhaustive (Adewuya, "Spirit in 1 Corinthians," 156).

### List 4. 1 Corinthians 12:29–30: Are all / Do all . . . ?

| Gift | Potentially natural? |
|---|---|
| Are all apostles? | no |
| Are all prophets? | no |
| Are all teachers? | yes |
| Do all work miracles? | no |
| Do all possess gifts of healing? | no |
| Do all speak in tongues? | no |
| Do all interpret? | no |

*Note:* Translations from the NRSV.

### List 5. 1 Corinthians 13:1–2: If I have . . .

| Gift | Potentially natural? |
|---|---|
| tongues | no |
| prophecy | no |
| knowledge | yes (if it is given its usual meaning in 1 Corinthians—1:5; 8:1, 7, 10–11) |
| faith | maybe |

### List 6. 1 Corinthians 13:8–9: Gifts that pass at Christ's return

| Gift | Potentially natural? |
|---|---|
| prophecies | no |
| tongues | no |
| knowledge | yes (if given its usual meaning in 1 Corinthians—1:5; 8:1, 7, 10–11) |

### List 7. 1 Corinthians 14:6: What good shall I do you if I speak in tongues but not the other gifts?

| Gift | Potentially natural? |
|---|---|
| tongues | no |
| revelation | no |
| knowledge | yes |
| prophecy (related to revelation) | no |
| instruction (related to knowledge) | yes |

*Note:* Translations from the NJB.

### List 8. 1 Corinthians 14:26: When you come together, each one has . . .

| Gift | Potentially natural? |
|---|---|
| a hymn (leading in worship)[7] | yes |
| a lesson [teaching] | yes |
| a revelation | no |
| a tongue | no |
| or an interpretation | no |

*Note:* Translations from the NIV.

7. Worship often includes singing (2 Chron. 29:28, 30; Ps. 66:4). Whereas the Levites led this in the OT, all believers constitute priests in the NT (1 Pet. 2:5, 9; Rev. 1:6; 5:10; 20:6; cf. Exod. 19:6; Rev. 22:3), and continue to sing (Eph. 5:19; Col. 3:16; cf. Rev. 5:9; 14:3; 15:3).

**List 9. Ephesians 4:11:**
**And He [God] gave . . .**

| Gift | Potentially natural? |
|---|---|
| some *as* apostles | no |
| some *as* prophets | no |
| some *as* evangelists | yes |
| some *as* pastors (or pastor-teachers) | yes |
| some *as* teachers (or pastor-teachers) | yes |

*Note:* Translations from the NASB.

**List 10. 1 Peter 4:11**

| Gift | Potentially natural? |
|---|---|
| Whoever speaks must do so as one speaking the very words of God | yes for speaking, but no for God's very words |
| Whoever serves must do so with the strength that God supplies | yes for serving, but no for special empowerment? |

### *Where Does the Natural-Supernatural Distinction Come From?*

While frequently focusing on the body of Christ, New Testament writers treat these gift lists in contexts that suggest they belong to the same sort of expectations for Christian living "as having sanctified attitudes ([Rom. 12:]9–21), being good citizens (13:1–7), living righteously (13:8–14), and so on."[8]

Out of ten lists, none of them offer the distinction that cessationists wish to make, even though Paul or Peter could have made such a distinction easily. The distinction is based instead on a cessationist theological presupposition imposed onto the text. It is *not itself biblical.* The bases for such distinctions are all from *outside* Scripture—extrabiblical philosophy or the gifts observed or not observed (arguments from experience) in certain circles in certain periods of history. The only New Testament list that might present only a single category would be Acts 2:17–18, if we take as separate expressions prophecy, dreams, and visions. All these would be understood in their context as God's special (what gets called supernatural) activity (as opposed to, say, pizza-digestion dreams).

As Michael Brown notes, surveying the list in 1 Corinthians 12:27–28: "Where is the slightest hint in the text—sola Scriptura!—that we can somehow extract teachers, helpers, and administrators from this list, claiming that only

8. Oss, "View," 275.

these giftings and callings continue until today, while eliminating miracles, gifts of healing, and tongues?" Turning to Paul's questions in 12:29–30, Brown then observes, "Based on cessationist interpretation, the only thing that remains in the Body today from this list is teachers. What?"[9]

Cessationists lack a method or warrant intrinsic to the biblical text for retaining some gifts and relegating others to the past.[10] Yet most of them would eagerly condemn such an arbitrary interpretive approach if applied to other doctrinal issues (or perhaps to selective fruits of the Spirit or NT lists of vices).

The one pattern noteworthy in the cessationist distinctions is that the only supernatural gifts or experiences they embrace (from regeneration to administrative gifts) are those that are also fundamentally internal—invisible to the naked eye. Everything that could be seen, tested, verified, or experienced in any objective way—anything that would carry a burden of proof or subject their claims to some kind of scrutiny—has been relegated to an arbitrary category of gifts belonging to another era. Their interpretation is thus not only arbitrary but also unfalsifiable.

### *Consistent Features: Grace, Prophecy*

The epistles have several gift lists. They each use some similar terminology, especially regarding "grace" (*charis*, Rom. 12:6; Eph. 4:7; 1 Pet. 4:10) or "graciously given gift" (*charisma*, Rom. 12:6; 1 Cor. 12:4, 9, 28–31; 1 Pet. 4:10). Such *charismata* for ministry also appear in 1 Timothy 4:14; 2 Timothy 1:6; and possibly Romans 1:11.

Together, these lists include ministries such as

- giving,
- teaching,
- prophesying,
- speaking wisely,
- healings,
- worship leading, and
- evangelism.

9. Brown, *Authentic Fire*, 201.

10. The most Gaffin can do is to claim that there is inadequate representation of the gifts of healing and miracles in the NT and that the NT gives no clear statement that they will continue beyond the apostolic era ("View," 42). In response, first, the NT church assumed the continuation of the gifts. The burden of proof is on cessationists to provide any NT evidence that the gifts would cease. Second, the NT does say the gifts would continue. Paul, in 1 Cor. 13:10, states that the gifts will continue until the perfect comes.

The New Testament consistently shows that we must not boast or be arrogant about our gifts. They are God's *gifts*, benefits of his unmerited favor toward us. Thus, all are empowered by God's *grace* (*charis*) and God's Spirit (we use the NRSV in the following passages):

> Romans 12:6: "We have gifts that differ according to the *grace* [*charis*] given to us."
>
> 1 Corinthians 12:4: "Now there are varieties of gifts [*charismata*], but the same Spirit."
>
> 1 Corinthians 12:9: "to another faith by the same Spirit, to another gifts [*charismata*] of healing by the one Spirit."
>
> Ephesians 4:7: "But each of us was given grace [*charis*] according to the measure of Christ's gift."
>
> 1 Timothy 4:14: "Do not neglect the gift [*charisma*] that is in you, which was given to you through prophecy with the laying on of hands by the council of elders."
>
> 2 Timothy 1:6: "For this reason I remind you to rekindle the gift [*charisma*] of God that is within you through the laying on of my hands."
>
> 1 Peter 4:10: "Like good stewards of the manifold grace [*charis*] of God, serve one another with whatever gift [*charisma*] each of you has received."

B. B. Warfield regarded "the greater gifts" as the nonmiraculous ones, which he claimed that Scripture prefers.[11] Yet after 1 Corinthians 12:31 urges[12] believers to seek the "greater gifts," Paul then specifies the gift of prophecy (which Warfield believed had ended) as a greater gift (14:1, 5). Did Warfield bother to read the context? Although the greatest gift in any given setting is whatever gift will build up Christ's body in love, it seems noteworthy that Warfield took his cues about the relative importance of gifts from earlier theologians, not from Scripture itself.

Prophecy also appears in nearly all the gift lists (Rom. 12:6; 1 Cor. 12:10; 13:2, 8; 14:6; cf. also 1 Tim. 1:18; 4:14; Rev. 11:6; 19:10). The most prominent ministry of God's message in the Old Testament, it often appears near the top of lists in the epistles (Rom. 12:6; 1 Cor. 12:28; Eph. 4:11). Because it is particularly valuable for building up Christ's body (1 Cor. 14:3–4), Paul urges

11. See the criticism in Ruthven, *Cessation*, 49.

12. The verb is undoubtedly imperative, given its recurrence in 14:1 in parallel with the imperative to pursue love.

with special insistence that believers seek the gift (1 Cor. 14:1, 39; cf. 12:31); indeed, it was apparently ideal to have multiple persons prophesying in each house gathering (14:5, 24, 29, 31), and potentially anyone could receive the gift (14:31). Although in 1 Corinthians Paul applies the title "prophet" functionally to anyone who prophesies (14:29, 32), he recognizes that not all are gifted to the same degree (Rom. 12:6) and that in practice not all believers fill this role (1 Cor. 12:29). Prophets also appear in Acts (Acts 11:27–28; 21:9–11; cf. 19:6), where they could also function as local church leaders (13:1).

Even if we did not know of any true prophecies today, following Paul's teaching about prophecy's usefulness and his exhortation to seek it should lead us to pray for that gift for the church. "Pursue love, and passionately desire the works of the Spirit, especially that you may prophesy" (1 Cor. 14:1).

New Testament scholar Douglas Oss rightly finds in 1 Corinthians 12–14, as in Acts, teaching about what is meant to be "characteristic and normal during the last days. . . . One should search the New Testament with a view toward determining what is normal in the church during the period from Pentecost to the return of the Lord."[13]

## The Value of Charismata

So long as the body of Christ remains, we need all its members. Paul treats the charismata as expressions of various members of Christ's body (Rom. 12:4–8; 1 Cor. 12:4–30).[14] Is Christ's body for today? If we believe that we are Christ's body, organically connected to the head, why should Christ not often continue to work through us as he worked in the past, not least in Paul's letters? Or to put it differently, is it not more biblical to expect the New Testament pattern than to expect the opposite?

Jack Deere, a former cessationist professor who was forced to reexamine his position when he encountered modern miracles, provides several reasons from 1 Corinthians 12–14 alone to refute cessationism. In his popular—and also biblically and theologically informed—response to cessationism, *Surprised by the Power of the Spirit*, he points out these things:[15]

- The gifts are for the common good (12:7).
- God commands us to zealously pursue spiritual gifts (12:31; 14:1).
- Paul warns us not to prohibit speaking in tongues (14:39).
- Paul valued tongues (14:5, 18).

13. Oss, "Response to Saucy," 171, also cited in Graves, "Cessationism," 51.

14. Cf. Williams, "Following Christ's Example," 72.

15. Here I am repurposing Keener, *Gift & Giver*, 106–7, which summarizes Deere, *Surprised*, 134–43.

- Spiritual gifts are necessary for the health of the body of Christ (12:12–27).
- Would God place such commands in Scripture if they were relevant for only four decades, especially since during most of that time the majority of ancient Christians would not yet have had access to Paul's letter?
- Finally, Paul is explicit that these gifts will not cease until Christ's return (13:8–12).

A shared feature in the context of all Paul's lists is the analogy of parts of the body (quoting from the NIV):

> Romans 12:4–6: "For just as each of us has one body with many members, and these members do not all have the same function, so in Christ we, though many, form one body, and each member belongs to all the others. We have different gifts, according to the grace given to each of us. If your gift is prophesying, then prophesy in accordance with your faith."

> 1 Corinthians 12:12: "Just as a body, though one, has many parts, but all its many parts form one body, so it is with Christ."

> Ephesians 4:11–12, 16: "So Christ himself gave the apostles, the prophets, the evangelists, the pastors and teachers, to equip his people for works of service, so that the body of Christ may be built up. . . . From him the whole body, joined and held together by every supporting ligament, grows and builds itself up in love, as each part does its work."

It impairs the ideal function of the body if any parts are missing. You can live without an eye or even two eyes. You can live without a hand or even two hands. But those are not ideal situations that we would normally seek. Most of us do not go around voluntarily amputating our hands or eyes.[16] Regarding the gifts, Paul insists (still NIV),

> 1 Corinthians 12:19: "If they were all one part, where would the body be?"

> 1 Corinthians 12:26: "If one part suffers, every part suffers with it; if one part is honored, every part rejoices with it."

Has the body of Christ ceased? We are still one body, and we still need all the members. If in fact all biblical gifts remain today, some churches amputate or at least atrophy certain members, which is healthy neither for the members nor for the churches. Some other churches may just pile up or fasten together

16. Keener, *Gift & Giver*, 213.

the members amputated by other churches. But ideally, we all need one another as fellow members of Christ's body.

Theologian Jon Ruthven rightly warned, "In a statement particularly relevant to the cessationist polemic, Paul stresses that no member can disqualify or denigrate his or her own gift in preference for another (12:14–20), neither can any member refuse to recognize the validity and expression of any other gift of the Spirit working in the Christian community, be it the gift of miracles, prophecy, or any other so-called 'ordinary' or 'extraordinary' gift (12:21–27). Those expressing a particular spiritual gift simply 'cannot say' about any other spiritual gift, 'I don't need you!' (12:21)."[17]

People everywhere in antiquity understood that the proper and necessary response to any sort of gifts was *gratitude*.[18] The harsh response of some cessationists to others' gifts to Christ's body does not meet this criterion.

## Commands for Charismata: Our Most Recent Biblical Marching Orders

MacArthur insists, "In all the New Testament epistles, there are only five commands related to the believer and the Holy Spirit"—namely, Galatians 5:25; Ephesians 4:30; 5:18; 1 Thessalonians 5:19; and Jude 20.[19] His concordance approach unfortunately leaves out direct commands about spiritual gifts, including some in the very contexts he cites, such as not despising prophecy in 1 Thessalonians 5:20 (in the context of 5:19) or the invitation to worship in Ephesians 5:19 (in the context of 5:18), where "spiritual songs" may refer to songs from the Holy Spirit.

What characterizes the new covenant is worship by God's Spirit, as opposed to mere dependence on earthly temples or fleshly circumcision (John 4:23–24; Phil. 3:3). Presumably this worship by the Spirit includes spiritual songs (Eph. 5:19; Col. 3:16; in the NT, the adjective "spiritual" usually refers to God's Spirit, not something like New Age ideas). Spiritual songs might be sometimes related to singing with one's spirit in 1 Corinthians 14:15, which refers in context to singing in a tongue (14:14). Since, according to cessationists, tongues have ceased and only knowledge remains, they might need to avoid some of the "spiritual" worship such passages address.

17. Ruthven, "Charismata 3," 179.
18. See Barclay, *Gift*.
19. MacArthur, *Chaos*, 116.

### *Direct Commands*

Following are some direct commands, as continuationists often point out (here quoting the NRSV):

> 1 Corinthians 12:31: "But *strive* for the greater gifts. And I will show you a still more excellent way."
>
> 1 Corinthians 14:1: "Pursue love and *strive* for the spiritual gifts, and especially that you may *prophesy*."
>
> 1 Corinthians 14:12: "So with yourselves; since you are eager for spiritual gifts, *strive* to excel in them for building up the church."
>
> 1 Corinthians 14:29: "Let two or three prophets speak, and let the others weigh what is said."
>
> 1 Corinthians 14:39: "So, my friends, be *eager to prophesy*, and do not forbid speaking in tongues."
>
> 1 Thessalonians 5:20: "Do *not despise* the words of prophets."[20]

Do any circles today disobey these passages—for example, by despising the gift of prophecy?[21] Do they do so based not on Scripture but on their extrabiblical theological assumptions? What about forbidding believers to speak in tongues? As Brown notes, "Paul tells us not to, and there's not a sentence in the Bible reversing" the admonition.[22] Or as I (Craig) wrote elsewhere, "The rule Paul gives us is not to despise prophecies but to test them (1 Thess. 5:20–21). We may find that many prophecies fail the test (I would agree); but to discard all prophecies wholesale is despising them, is it not?"[23]

Some object that the commands are in the plural, and therefore, they suppose, not relevant for individuals. But Paul's other commands to churches are also plural, such as commands to love and forgive one another.[24] These are invitations to all to participate. Paul thus invites everyone in these churches to participate in seeking for gifts for building up the church, even though not every individual will receive every gift.

20. Although the verse lacks an imperative, the idea is probably implicit also in Rom. 12:6 (Allison and Köstenberger, *Holy Spirit*, 432).

21. Pennington, *Cessationism*, 172, warns that believers should "reject all forms of supposed continuing revelation, including subjective impressions of God's will." How much more "prophecies"?

22. Brown, *Authentic Fire*, 202.

23. Keener, "Ongoing Evidence," 353.

24. Storms, "Response to Saucy," 163.

The context of the famous love chapter, 1 Corinthians 13, tells us which gifts to seek most. The two verses that *frame* 1 Corinthians 13 are these:

> 12:31: "But be zealous for the greater gifts."
>
> 14:1: "Pursue love and be zealous for the bestowals of the Spirit, *especially* the gift of prophecy."

Prophecy is more edifying to the body than uninterpreted tongues because it is intelligible. It was also more available to the Corinthian churches than teaching because these churches were only two to three years old and would not yet have had many teachers.

### *Obeying the Commands*

We should follow our most recent biblical marching orders. Some minimize the portions of Scripture we need to obey directly today, limiting that range of passages to the epistles. Paul's gift instructions are, incidentally, in such epistles. Of course, the epistles address particular, concrete situations, but the pervasiveness of prophetic gifts in congregations was both radically countercultural and encouraged by Paul too much to merely reflect a local situation.

Continuationists say that the New Testament doesn't claim that gifts will cease, and cessationists say it doesn't claim they won't. Some therefore conclude that the evidence is unclear either way. "But," as Andrew Wilson points out, "in light of the hermeneutical principle we would normally use, . . . the reality is different. Our default setting, if you like, should be one of obeying these passages, . . . unless a clear case to the contrary can be made from the text."[25] This is what we do with other commands that are not based on merely the culture or the situation, such as loving one another or avoiding murmuring. Thus, "the burden of proof should always be on the person who says we don't have to obey an apostolic instruction, rather than on the person who says we do."[26] Each side may accuse the other of an argument from silence,[27] but continuationism is "*anything but*" such an argument, since "it is difficult to imagine how the New Testament authors could have said any more clearly than this what new covenant Christianity was supposed to look like."[28]

25. Wilson, *Spirit and Sacrament*, 109, citing Rom. 12:6; 1 Cor. 12:31; 14:1, 39; 1 Thess. 5:19–21. Wilson's larger case for continuationism is on pp. 89–120.

26. Wilson, *Spirit and Sacrament*, 108, also noted in Allison and Köstenberger, *Holy Spirit*, 432.

27. Noted by, e.g., Saucy, "Response to Storms," 228.

28. Storms, "View," 205. Gaffin, "Response to Storms and Oss," 286, dismisses Storms's statement while missing his point.

In 1 Thessalonians 5:20–22, that means,

> Don't despise prophecies,
> but test all things:
> hold onto what is good,
> avoid everything that appears evil.

Charismatics should pay close attention to the testing of all things (cf. also 1 Cor. 14:29; Rev. 2:2)—much closer than we usually do. But why would we need to discern among prophecies if we could simply discard them all? That would be far neater. Yet Paul's instruction is to separate the baby from the bathwater rather than to discard both; he clearly expects that there are babies available. Meanwhile, are there any circles today that, instead of testing the particulars, simply despise all prophecies? Is this not direct disobedience to Paul's teaching?

Whatever other reasons many of us do not experience any particular gifts, one reason may be because we do not pursue them as Paul commands (1 Cor. 12:31; 14:1). Occasionally an interpreter insists that the command to "strive for the greater gifts" in 1 Corinthians 12:31 is a complaint (i.e., you strive for gifts but shouldn't) rather than a command,[29] but the same term in the same form is clearly imperative (a command) in 14:39 and in 14:1, which, with 12:31, frames 1 Corinthians 13.[30] Against Paul's command to seek gifts such as prophecy (12:31; 14:1, 39), MacArthur insists that it is wrong "to selfishly seek any spiritual gift when we've been told that spiritual gifts are sovereignly chosen and distributed by the Holy Spirit."[31] As continuationists we respond: Should not God's sovereignty in bestowing gifts (12:11) bless us with confidence rather than reluctance to pray as he invites us to?[32] Granted, God is not obligated to give particular gifts to individuals; moreover, Paul surely does not imply that all Christians should exercise all gifts (12:28–30). Yet Paul certainly suggests that God *desires* to give gifts such as prophecy to the body of Christ. Discouraging believers from trusting God's invitation

29. MacArthur, *Strange Fire*, 146.

30. See in greater detail Fee, *Presence*, 196; esp. Carson, *Showing Spirit*, 53–57.

31. MacArthur, *Strange Fire*, 147. My (Craig's) uncorrected advance reader's copy lacks the qualification "selfishly," apparently added by MacArthur or someone else during final editing.

32. When the psalmist declares that God does what he pleases (Pss. 115:3, 16a; 135:6), it is not to discourage trust in him, as if God's will is arbitrary (as in Islam); rather, it contrasts him with other gods (115:2–8; 135:5) who can do nothing (135:15–18). Instead of trusting in idols (115:8), it urges us, we should trust in the Lord our help (115:8–11; 135:18). In the Gospels, Jesus both wills (Mark 1:40–41) and is able (9:22–23) to bless. We trust that when God says no, it is for our good, but we pray with the expectation that he may well often say yes (Matt. 7:11 // Luke 11:13) or invite us to persist in prayer (cf., e.g., Gen. 18:23–32; Exod. 32:10–14; Mark 7:27–29; 10:48).

runs counter to new-covenant ministry. Such discouragement urges us not to trust God's promise or obey his invitation.

On occasion, a cessationist responds by arguing that these commands address only an early stage of the new covenant rather than our current stage, but where in the New Testament is the new covenant divided in such stages? The *only* new-covenant era revealed in the New Testament is the age of the Spirit described there; this cessationist adds a new era that the Bible nowhere mentions. Is this discovered by an inference that functions something like a new revelation? In the name of defending the authority of Scripture, such a claim actually undermines the canonical integrity of the New Testament. On such an approach, even Paul's epistles are no longer binding where they challenge our theology![33] The New Testament often contrasts the present age with the coming one (e.g., 1 Cor. 2:6–8; 2 Cor. 4:4; Gal. 1:4; 1 Tim. 6:17); it nowhere adds an interim between them.

If apostles and prophets have ceased, and numerous commands to pursue spiritual gifts are no longer relevant, is the New Testament now a special canon intended only for believers in the first century? The Scriptures that continue to apply to us would then constitute a canon significantly different from the body of divine teachings that believers in the first century followed—a new canon within (or even outside) a canon, determined by an extrabiblical doctrine.

Cessationism simultaneously expands, neglects, and nullifies Scripture—all in the name of protecting it from the very threat that cessationism represents. In 2 Samuel 6:6–7, Uzzah reached out and touched the ark to protect it. But in the process he disobeyed what the Lord actually said in the law, and God punished him. A desire to protect the Scriptures is not a warrant to disobey them.

### *Building Up the Church*

It is true that we do not need to lay again the original foundation of the universal church. No charismatic we know argues for that. But how do we build on that foundation? Ephesians 2:20 speaks of the foundation, but the next verse speaks of the entire building (*oikodomē*) growing into a holy temple in the Lord. What helps us build? Paul returns to that thought later in Ephesians. Ephesians 4:11 lists apostles and prophets among those who in 4:12 "equip the saints for the work of ministry, for *building up* the body of Christ." He is further explicit that we need all the members working together for *building up* (*oikodomē*) the church in love (4:16). (We will say more on this subject in chap. 7.)

So how do we build up the body? *Building up* (*oikodomē*) here is a construction image suitable to the image of foundations also in 1 Corinthians 3:9–10; later in 1 Corinthians Paul speaks of building up (*oikodomē*) the

33. See the complaint in Ruthven, *Cessation*, xixn18, calling the approach "heterodox."

church through spiritual gifts, especially prophecy (14:3, 5, 12, 26). The church was not founded in supernatural power only to continue by the works of the flesh (cf. Gal. 3:3, 5). Paul is explicit that spiritual gifts—including so-called revelatory ones—constitute a key way that the church is built up. Hindering the proper exercise of such gifts dishonors rather than honors the purpose of the foundation.

Unless perhaps one wishes to argue that the need for the church and for building it up are no longer for today?[34] A cessationist might instead suggest that God changed the explicit biblical rules without telling us, but again, how "biblical" is this solution? Isn't it a postbiblical doctrine read back into the Bible?

## Conclusion

Biblical lists of gifts are arranged in various ways, but none offer the postbiblical distinction that cessationists insist on. Moreover, the most recent biblical commands we have regarding spiritual gifts, including the particularly debated gift of prophecy, urge us to seek them and not to suppress them. No subsequent biblical commands revoke these invitations, nor does the New Testament anywhere warn us that they might be revoked before the second coming of Jesus.

The evidence here thus matches the evidence of Acts 2:17–18 and 1 Corinthians 13:9–12 and the models in many other passages. Is it cessationists or continuationists who take biblical teaching regarding spiritual gifts more seriously? Which group is really upholding Scripture itself, and which group is upholding instead a postbiblical theological construct?

34. One might argue that the New Testament does not narrate such activity after the New Testament narration stops—an argument similar to one sometimes arrayed against the continuation of gifts.

# 7

# Ephesians

## *A Weak Foundation for Cessationism*

In Ephesians, the debate between continuationists and cessationists has focused especially on two passages. Cessationists often cite Ephesians 2:20:[1] ". . . built upon the foundation of the apostles and prophets, with Christ Jesus himself as the cornerstone" (NRSV). Continuationists, by contrast, often cite Ephesians 4:11–13:

- And He gave
  - some *as* apostles,
  - some *as* prophets,
  - some *as* evangelists,
  - some *as* pastors and teachers,
- for the equipping of the saints
  - for the work of ministry,
  - for the building up of the body of Christ;
- until we all attain
  - to the unity
    - of the faith,
    - and of the knowledge of the Son of God,
  - to a mature man,
  - to the measure of the stature which belongs to the fullness of Christ. (NASB, formatting added)

1. "The key verse" (Schreiner, *Spiritual Gifts*, 171).

In contrast to Ephesians 2:20, Ephesians 4:11–13 seems more analogous to the gift passages in Romans and 1 Corinthians, noting the involvement of giving by grace (Eph. 4:7; cf. Rom. 12:6), a measure (Eph. 4:7; cf. Rom. 12:3, 6), the body of Christ's many members (Eph. 4:4, 12, 16; cf. Rom. 12:4–5; 1 Cor. 12:12–27), and a list of more than two gifts (Eph. 4:11; cf. Rom. 12:6–8; 1 Cor. 12:8–10). I (Craig) remember noticing the relevance of Ephesians 4:11–13 for continuationism from my own reading of Ephesians by 1978, before being exposed to any teaching about the passage.

## Cessationism in Ephesians 2:20?

Whereas a majority of cessationist teachers recognize that 1 Corinthians 13:8–12 does not support their case, most now root their case especially in the theological implications that they draw from Ephesians 2:20. Since apostles and prophets no longer exist, they argue, neither do all the other gifts—or, more specifically, the other ones that cessationists reject as being for today.

John MacArthur argues that Ephesians 2:20 "clearly teaches that the apostles were appointed to be the foundation of the church. . . . They were the church's founders. That role was fulfilled by them and by definition can never be repeated."[2] Because apostles were the church's foundation, he insists, there cannot be apostles afterward.[3]

Nancy Almodovar notes that "apostles and prophets are the foundation. No builder ever places a foundation a second time in a building. Foundations are once for all tasks."[4]

Tom Schreiner warns that "if prophecy still exists today, it is hard to resist the conclusion that the foundation established by the apostles and prophets hasn't been completed, and that the New Testament prophets are still adding to the foundation of apostolic teaching."[5]

MacArthur rightly observes that "the earliest church fathers did not view themselves as apostles,"[6] although we should note that they were generally church leaders or scholars rather than people laying new foundations in unevangelized areas. One of the earliest sources from that period, the *Didache* (possibly composed by the end of the first century), does in fact mention continuing apostles and prophets and how to distinguish true from false ones:

> Let every apostle who comes to you be welcomed as if he were the Lord. . . . But if he asks for money, he is a false prophet. . . . Also, do not test or evaluate

2. MacArthur, *Chaos*, 123.
3. MacArthur, *Strange Fire*, 96–97, 101.
4. Almodovar, *Questions*, 16.
5. Schreiner, *Spiritual Gifts*, 107–8; cf. 171–72.
6. MacArthur, *Strange Fire*, 102.

> any prophet who speaks in the spirit, for every sin will be forgiven, but this sin will not be forgiven. However, not everyone who speaks in the spirit is a prophet, but only if he exhibits the Lord's ways. By his conduct, therefore, will the false prophet and the prophet be recognized. . . . But if anyone should say in the spirit, "Give me money" or anything else, do not listen to him. But if he tells you to give on behalf of others who are in need, let no one judge him. (*Did.* 11.3–12, trans. M. Holmes)

### *Apostles Here*

Although we deal with New Testament definitions of apostles and prophets in subsequent chapters (chaps. 8 and 12), we must mention the conclusions of those studies here before proceeding, since the issue arises here. Schreiner, for example, contends that "we don't have apostles like Paul and Peter and John anymore. They gave us the authoritative teaching by which the church continues to live to this day, and that is the only teaching we will need until Jesus returns. . . . The apostles were uniquely appointed for the early days of the church to establish orthodox doctrine."[7]

We recognize that the Twelve were a special group close to Jesus in the flesh, and (by definition, given their death) they do not continue. But while the Gospels and (usually) Acts limit the title "apostle" to the Twelve, Paul plainly applies the title more broadly, and not only to the Twelve and himself (Rom. 16:7; 1 Cor. 9:5–6; 15:5–7; Gal. 1:19; 1 Thess. 2:6–7 [with 1:1]). After the New Testament, various church traditions apply the expression "apostolic" in various ways—some for bishops, some for missionary church planters, and so forth.[8]

If we examine Paul's own use of the expression, apostles seem to be especially involved in establishing (ideally self-propagating) churches in new regions. Their role is not writing Scripture; of the original Twelve apostles, at most *three* wrote Scripture. While Paul was a non-Twelve apostle and wrote Scripture, much of the New Testament was written by non-apostles (notably Mark, Luke, and Jude). Continuationists and cessationists agree that nobody is founding the universal church or writing Scripture today. What we agree *does* continue (whatever we call it) is reaching new spheres with the gospel. This role seems to characterize what Paul and his fellow non-Twelve apostolic laborers were all doing. So whether we believe apostolic ministry ceased or continues depends on which sort of biblical apostolic ministries we are talking about. This observation does not immediately dictate what sort of apostles

7. Schreiner, "Cessationist."

8. Nor need one exclude overlap among these categories. Craig's friend Benjamin Kwashi, for example, has been both the Anglican archbishop of Jos, Nigeria, and a leader in a church planting movement in that region of Nigeria; see Boyd, *Bomb*; Sanusi, *Gloria*.

Ephesians 2:20 addresses, but it does warn us to explore the language with openness to other options.

### Gaffin's Foundation for Cessationism Here

Many cessationists follow the case laid out by New Testament scholar Richard Gaffin here. He rests his biblical case for the cessation of particular spiritual gifts almost entirely on Ephesians 2:20.[9]

Yet Gaffin's argument at this critical point, though using exegesis (Bible interpretation), is not strictly exegetical.[10] He starts with a rational argument, to which he then adds the exegesis of texts that would not by themselves support his argument. While any "logical argument" may look consistent from within the system that supports it, it will ordinarily fail to persuade those outside the system when it cannot make sense without other elements of the system to support it. Our objection here is the sort of objection that biblical scholars often raise against some systematic theologians or against other biblical scholars whom they feel are more beholden to particular theological or philosophical presuppositions than to the inspired text of Scripture.

As fellow New Testament scholar Gordon Fee, former editor of the New International Commentary on the New Testament series, observes concerning the heart of Gaffin's argument for cessation:

> The logic precedes the exegesis. . . . Gaffin's overruling question is, When will tongues cease? The one text that addresses this question at all . . . is 1 Corinthians 13:10, which almost certainly intends, "at the Eschaton," as its answer. But since the answer is the one Gaffin is uncomfortable with, he sets up his logical circles to answer his own question with, "at the end of the first century." But in no case does he, nor can he, show that the answer to that question is a part of the biblical author's intent in the texts that are examined.[11]

### Ephesians 2:20 a Weak Foundation for Cessationism

Others demur from finding cessationism in Ephesians 2:20, questioning the overreach and the logic of the argument. The foundational role of apostles and prophets here says nothing about whether apostles and prophets might have *other* roles besides the "foundational" one (as we shall see clearly later in the book, they did). As former cessationist teacher Jack Deere explains, "The founding director of a company or corporation will always be unique in

9. Gaffin, *Perspectives*.
10. Here I am adapting my response in Keener, *Gift & Giver*, 109–10.
11. Fee, *Gospel*, 77.

the sense that he or she was the founder, but that does not mean the company would not have future directors or presidents."[12]

Saying that the Twelve have passed away says nothing about whether gifts they shared with others also passed. The Twelve's obviously unique gift that cannot be repeated is their personal experience with Jesus during his earthly ministry. Likewise, to say that Paul has passed away no more requires gifts he shared with others to pass away (gifts that incidentally include the role of teacher; 1 Tim. 2:7; 2 Tim. 1:11) than to insist that compassion passed away with the death of Barnabas (Acts 4:36).

Further, that some prophets laid foundations does not automatically entail the same for all prophets. Certainly prophecy as described in Romans 12:6 and 1 Corinthians 12–14 does not require any foundational role.[13] The anonymous disciples who prophesied noncanonically in Acts 19:6 were hardly laying foundations for the universal church.[14] D. A. Carson, noting the wider use of "prophets" in the New Testament, regards use of Ephesians 2:20 to rule out subsequent prophecy as analogous to concluding "from Titus 1:12 ('Even one of their own prophets has said, "Cretans are always liars, evil brutes, lazy gluttons"') that New Testament prophets were [all] pagan poets from Crete."[15]

Ephesians 2:20 cannot refer to the closed canon. If in this verse Paul were speaking about the closed canon, then he would be implying that it was already closed at the time of his writing. That would mean not only that Ephesians and other later writings were not canonical but that we have no reason to accept Paul's statement that the canon was closed!

The foundation refers to people whose deaths some associate with the cessation of their gifts. The "cornerstone," which has already been set, does not refer to Christ's doctrine or teaching. It refers to Christ himself. So when we apply the metaphor consistently, the "foundation" must refer to the apostles and prophets themselves, not their writings. Likewise, by implication, the building is made up of the saints as living stones (see also 1 Pet. 2:5).[16] The passage talks only about people (albeit in the role here of bringing a message), not a closed canon. But cessationists would then argue that this means their ministry gifts died with them.

12. Deere, *Still Surprised*, 267n9; also noted by Storms, "Ephesians 2:20," 70.

13. With, e.g., Storms, "Response to Gaffin," 81; Storms, "Ephesians 2:20," 70–71; Alt, "Cease," 399. How would revealing the secrets of people's hearts (1 Cor. 14:24–25) become part of the church's foundation (Storms, "Ephesians 2:20," 71)? See further Ruthven, "Gifts."

14. Storms, "Response to Gaffin," 79–81.

15. Carson, *Showing Spirit*, 97; cf. Saucy, "Response to Gaffin," 69.

16. Moderate cessationist commentator (and one of the best Ephesians commentators) Harold W. Hoehner says, "First, the imagery depicted in the present context is that Christ, as a person (αὐτοῦ Χριστοῦ Ἰησοῦ = Christ Jesus himself and not Christ's own teaching), is the cornerstone, the apostles and prophets, as persons, are the foundation, and the saints, as persons, are the building. Second, this coincides with 4:11 and more specifically 1 Cor 12:28 which states, 'God placed or appointed (ἔθετο) in the church first apostles, second prophets, . . . ' as foundations for ministry." Hoehner, *Ephesians*, 399.

### *Old Testament Prophets or New Testament Prophets?*

When Paul speaks here of prophets, is he thinking of Old Testament prophets such as Isaiah or New Testament prophets such as Agabus? Insofar as he is distinguishing them, he must refer to New Testament prophets, as most cessationists would agree.[17] This message about the gentiles had "*now* been revealed to . . . prophets" (Eph. 3:5). When he speaks further of prophets in Ephesians, he includes their role in continuing to build up Christ's body, alongside evangelists and teachers (4:11).

Correspondingly, in context, their foundational role here is also very specific: their function as bringers of the message welcoming the gentiles (as we shall elaborate further below). We have only limited New Testament *examples* of prophecy, but some New Testament revelations do support the outreach to gentiles (Acts 9:15; 22:15), as do some revelations to members of the Twelve (Acts 10:19, 28; 11:12, 17). Still, apostles and prophets could also draw on the Old Testament prophets; that the message was only now revealed did not mean that it had never been provided before in ways unrecognized.[18] Thus Paul declares that his "gospel, . . . the revelation of the mystery long kept secret," was "now revealed *through the writings of the prophets*" (Rom. 16:25–26), who did sometimes speak of gentiles being grafted into the people of God. For example:

- Isaiah 19:23–25: God makes Egypt and Assyria his people along with Israel.
- Isaiah 56:3–8: Foreigners are joined to God's people.
- Zechariah 2:11: "Many nations shall join themselves to the Lord on that day, and shall be my people."

Ephesians 2:20 does teach us about a foundational message that need not be relaid. In the context of Paul's letters and Ephesians itself, however, it does not make obsolete the need for apostles or prophets in any *other* roles they may have had. (More on this point soon.)

### *A Universal Foundation*

Cessationists often argue that since apostles and prophets in Ephesians 2:20 are the "foundation," and foundations are on the bottom of a building, later generations cannot add any more apostles or prophets.[19] Aside from whether

17. So rightly also Schreiner, *Spiritual Gifts*, 107–8; Pennington, *Cessationism*, 79.

18. Regarding the message about Jesus, cf. 2 Cor. 3:14–15.

19. E.g., Gaffin, "View," 43 ("In any construction project (ancient or modern), the foundation comes at the beginning and does not have to be relaid repeatedly"); Waldron, *Continued*, 38; Almodovar, *Questions*, 16.

this argument reads too much into an architectural metaphor,[20] it does not address the passage's context or Paul's usage of "foundation" language. Should we rest an entire doctrine on an inference from a metaphor?

Nevertheless, we would actually agree that the apostolic and prophetic foundation in Ephesians 2:20 is universal for the church (cf. Matt. 16:18), and that Paul refers to the apostles and prophets of his own era. But the cessationist interpretation fails for multiple reasons. First, Paul nowhere claims that this is the *only* role for all apostles and prophets; in fact, just two chapters later he seems to expect them to be needed until the church reaches full maturity—the full image of Christ (Eph. 4:11–13). Christians today don't rewrite the gospel or Scripture; we do evangelize new regions and spheres. We therefore do not need apostles or prophets today to do the former; we may need apostolic missionaries to complete the latter. Likewise, we need to continue to build up the church to minister to one another, as apostles and others do in Ephesians 4:11–13.

Moreover, even the apostolic task of foundation-laying has not ceased. Although the foundation *here* is universal, Paul's letters do not limit the language of laying foundations *only* to the universal church. He elsewhere speaks of laying *local* foundations. Paul (a non-Twelve apostle) lays the true foundation (*Christ* himself) in Corinth (1 Cor. 3:10–11) and is committed to laying new foundations in new regions (Rom. 15:20).[21] Paul denounces "false apostles" (2 Cor. 11:13) who, instead of breaking new ground for the kingdom themselves, try to take over churches founded by Paul (10:13–16). If we need to break ground in new regions or spheres today, presumably we still need foundation-layers. It seems evident (at least to most of us) that the good news about God's kingdom has not yet been fully preached among all peoples, since the end has not yet come (Matt. 24:14). Apostles in the New Testament lay foundations in regions or spheres. The idea that the good news has *already* been established *throughout* the whole world (held by some cessationists in church history) may be a vestigial legacy of the church of the Roman Empire imagining that it encompassed most of the world.

In Ephesians 2, however, we agree that Paul is referring to a universal foundation, one that has already been laid and need not be laid again. (Often unheeded, its implications for racial, ethnic, and cultural unity in Christ's body need to be reinforced. But the foundation is already there.) In context,

20. The Dead Sea Scrolls already depicted God's people as a temple; for comment on the New Testament image and its background, see discussion in Keener, *Peter*, 129.

21. Cf. the Assemblies of God position paper "Apostles and Prophets" (released August 6, 2001), prudently discouraging use of the title today but also recognizing, "The function of apostle occurs whenever the church of Jesus Christ is being established among the unevangelized" (conclusion 5). It later explains, "Apostolic functions usually occur within the context of breaking new ground in unevangelized areas or among unreached people."

however, the universal foundation in this passage is probably not what cessationism's supporters suppose.

### A Particular *Revelation* Here

Scripture clearly is foundational, and God used many Old Testament prophets and some New Testament apostles to provide it. The apostles who knew Jesus personally laid the foundation of communicating his teaching, which we have in the Gospels. Old Testament prophets laid part of the rest of the foundation of Scripture. Scripture is a solid foundation for us, and all books of Scripture had been written by the time that John, the last of the original twelve apostles, died.

In this context, however, Paul is not referring to writing Scripture. So far as we know, Mark and Luke, who wrote two of the four Gospels (plus Luke wrote Acts), were not called apostles; nor did the original Twelve who knew Jesus in the flesh write most of the rest of the New Testament (Paul was not one of the Twelve). Not all Old Testament books are books of prophecy.[22] Most apostles and prophets never wrote Scripture.

While the *principle* articulated in Ephesians 2:20 may apply by analogy to Scripture, Paul's gospel focus in this context is not addressing all Scripture per se. (After all, the writing of Scripture was not even finished yet when Paul wrote Ephesians!) In context, the revelation that came through apostles and prophets here seems to be a more specific message now available within Scripture: the revelation that gentiles are welcome among God's people (see the context of Eph. 2:11–3:13). What is newly revealed is the mystery of Christ (3:3–4), unrevealed in other generations but "now revealed to his holy apostles and prophets by the Spirit" (3:5). Paul then specifies the content of this mystery of Christ that is now revealed to these apostles and prophets: "Gentiles are fellow heirs and fellow members" of God's people (3:6), the same point that Paul was expounding in 2:11–22 (cf. Acts 15:2, 8, 28, 32).

These early apostles and prophets laid a theological and missiological foundation corresponding to the practical foundations of many of the apostles establishing churches in new regions. Paul explicitly counts himself as one of these apostles (Eph. 3:1–4, 7–8), so his use of "apostles" includes (as usually in Paul's letters) a circle wider than the Twelve. Because of their work, the welcome of gentiles is already revealed; now we just rearticulate, explain, and obey it.

Again, however, this is not all that apostles and prophets do (1 Cor. 12:28; Eph. 4:11–13), so it need not entail that Christians should stop edifying one another with prophecy (1 Cor. 14:3–5) or that we should stop reaching new

22. Here virtually all cessationists and continuationists agree; it is the canon by which we test anything else (with MacArthur, *Chaos*, 62).

spheres. Calvinist Baptist missionary William Carey in his day had to debate narrower Calvinists who thought that the Great Commission was only for the apostles and had ceased. Today most of us agree with Carey against the Great Commission cessationists of his day. Many of us could even regard him as an apostle in the broader Pauline sense of breaking ground for the kingdom.

Early Christian apostles and prophets performed a revelatory function (Eph. 3:5). But Paul's apostolic ministry seems to extend beyond this initial revelation of the gospel to making it known as widely as possible (see 3:8–13). Paul's apostolic mission did not end when he made his gospel known to *someone*; the mission was to make it known to everyone (3:8–9), a mission not yet completed.[23]

## Gifts of God's Message to Equip the Church (Eph. 4:11–13)

In Ephesians 4:11–13, apostles, prophets, evangelists, and pastors and teachers continue to be needed to bring the church to full maturity.

MacArthur argues that Paul had no need to emphasize the cessation of apostles and prophets in Ephesians 4:11, since Paul already made that clear in Ephesians 2:20.[24] As we have seen, however, 2:20 says no such thing. Further, the two verses refer to separate events. In Ephesians 2:20 Paul speaks about the historical foundation of the church or, more likely in our view, specifically the welcome of gentiles as part of God's people. The laying of that foundation is indeed a past event (or process), just like the ascension.

In Ephesians 4:11, Paul also speaks of a past bestowal of ministry gifts on the church, in this case through Christ's ascension (4:8, 10).[25] The bestowal, however, is not a gift that Christ takes back from his church after one generation. Paul lists these gifts in parallel construction, so that all the gifts listed function together for edifying the church. If we read the text by itself without importing foreign assumptions, it appears that if we still need pastoring and teaching, we still need prophesying too.

### *Past Gift, Continuing Use*

Some object by emphasizing the aorist tense of the verb "gave" in Ephesians 4:11, since aorist indicative verbs are usually past tense (but not always, as explained below). As one cessationist author writes, "It does not say that

23. Repurposing Keener, *Gift & Giver*, 109. The gospel was *proleptically* proclaimed in all regions (Col. 1:23), but the completion remains (Rom. 11:25; 2 Pet. 3:9; see Keener, *1–2 Peter, Jude*, 114; Keener, *Matthew*, 572; Keener, *Matthew* [1997], 346–47).

24. MacArthur, *Strange Fire*, 101.

25. Ancient interpreters also connected Ps. 68 and gifts for the church here with Jesus's ascension; see Justin, *Dial.* 39; Augustine, *Trin.* 15.19.34.

God continually gives, but that He 'gave,' which is past tense."[26] So is this passage saying the ministry gifts are limited to the past? If that is what the aorist tense means here, then it covers all its direct objects—all the listed gifts—as past. The verb and the list do not separate the gifts that supposedly continue (pastors, teachers, and evangelists) from those that are supposedly obsolete (apostles and prophets). The same act of giving includes pastors alongside prophets, with no indication that Jesus would take one or two gifts back.

Paul is clear that the purpose of all the gifts in 4:11 is to equip the saints until the church reaches full maturity (Eph. 4:12–13), not merely until the foundation is once laid. So unless cessationists are willing to part with pastors, teachers, and evangelists, they cannot reject apostles and prophets and remain consistent.

More to the present point, the verb tense does not invite rejecting any of the gifts. Carson points out that the past tense of this Greek verb does not necessarily indicate something happened in the past "once for all."[27] We cannot interpret the way an aorist verb is used without context. To use it as evidence that any gifts in Ephesians 4:11 were both given and discontinued in the past is to reveal a misunderstanding of biblical Greek. That is exactly why Carson includes this misconception in his book about exegetical *fallacies*.

Indeed, the context of Ephesians 4:11 defines the meaning of Paul's aorist-tense "gave." The Greek verb *didōmi* here is in the aorist tense (in the form *edōken*) because it refers to the once-given grace given (*edothē*, also from *didōmi*) according to the measure of the gift (*dōrean*, a noun cognate) of Christ in 4:7. That is, it corresponds to the once-for-all exaltation of Christ, through which all these gifts were given to the church. Yet postascension apostles such as Paul and Silvanus, as well as all modern pastors and teachers, were called *after* that exaltation. (Paul was not even yet a believer when Jesus ascended.)

So the context affirms the ongoing, continuous nature of gifts already given by the ascended Jesus Christ to his church. If I give my wife a present for her birthday, I do not plan to take it back later. Christ's gift to his church may be past, but it is permanent until we reach full Christlikeness. The past tense of "gave" does not imply that the gifts provided by Jesus's victory would need to die out!

The God-given purpose of apostles continues. Cessationists usually claim that the role and function of apostles was to write Scripture, endorse the Scripture-writing of others, or bring foundational revelation in the first century until the canon was completed. If these were indeed the exclusive purposes for apostles, then we could safely assume the gift is now obsolete. But Paul explicitly names a purpose for apostles in Ephesians 4:11–13, and it is not

26. Almodovar, *Questions*, 16; cf. also Pennington, *Cessationism*, 61n1.
27. Carson, *Fallacies*$^2$, 68–73.

to "write Scripture" or carry out the other related reasons these cessationists list. Paul's stated purpose for the Lord's giving apostles is "for the equipping of the saints for the work of service, to the building up of the body of Christ" (Eph. 4:12). That function is still necessary, so the gift remains relevant.

### *Until We Reach Full Christlikeness*

As in 1 Corinthians 13, Ephesians explicitly tells us how long these gifts will last and exactly when they will become obsolete: "until we all reach unity in the faith and in the knowledge of the Son of God and become mature, attaining to the whole measure of the fullness of Christ" (Eph. 4:13 NIV). The Bible here gives us the one terminus for apostolic ministry: when the church has fully conformed to Christ's image in unity and maturity. Insofar as cessationists are concerned about an expiration date for apostolic ministry, they should take more seriously the date actually provided by the closed, authoritative canon itself.

Against a continuationist reading of Ephesians 4:13, MacArthur denies that the church's full conformity to Christ here refers to Jesus's return.[28] Yet the verse sounds very much like 1 Corinthians 13:11, which in context does speak of full knowledge at Jesus's return (13:10–12). Gaffin recognizes this point: "Almost certainly the 'unity/fullness' of verse 13 has in view the same state of affairs as the 'perfection' in 1 Corinthians 13:10 (echoed perhaps as well in the use of *teleios*, 'perfect' or 'mature,' in Eph. 4:13), namely, the situation brought by Christ's return."[29] Admittedly, it could simply be a status toward which we are called to grow (Eph. 4:14–15), so it might represent a continuous goal rather than an eschatological terminus. Even this observation would not, however, change the point that we continue to *need* to mature toward that goal. On either interpretation of 4:13, the gifts by which Paul says Christ achieves this goal thus remain relevant.

MacArthur also argues that 4:13 does not mean that all the roles cited in 4:11 must remain active until Jesus's return; they could have jump-started the church, which then continues to build itself up afterward.[30] But Paul's language seems curious if he thought only some of these gifts would persist till the achieving of the goal. Christ's *gift* to the church (Eph. 4:7, 11)[31] must *continue* to equip the church. It includes prophets no less than teachers, and it is inconsistent to accept our need for the one in this passage while denying the other. After all, Paul elsewhere explicitly associates "building up" Christ's

28. MacArthur, *Strange Fire*, 100–101.

29. Gaffin, "View," 55. He nevertheless denies that the passage tells us when certain gifts will pass, warning that if it did it would allow the continuance of apostles (56).

30. MacArthur, *Strange Fire*, 100–101.

31. These gifts, as in 1 Cor. 12:28, are associated not with an "apostolic period" but with the church (Ruthven, "Charismata 3," 179).

body (4:12) specifically with prophecy (1 Cor. 14:3–5), though this purpose is relevant for all the gifts (14:26; Eph. 4:16).

So even if one were to exclude the current relevance of apostles and prophets in Ephesians 4:11, the evangelists and pastor-teachers are meant to equip the rest of Christ's body to build one another up through their gifts. As pastors and/or teachers, we need to help the rest of the body mature in using their other biblical gifts to serve one another.

We highlight the grammatical structure of Ephesians 4:11–13 below:

- And He gave
  - some *as* apostles,
  - some *as* prophets,
  - some *as* evangelists,
  - some *as* pastors and teachers,
- for [*pros*] the equipping of the saints
  - for [*eis*] the work of ministry,
  - for [*eis*] the building up of the body of Christ;
- until we all attain
  - to [*eis*] the unity
    - of the faith
    - and of the knowledge of the Son of God,
  - to [*eis*] a mature man,
  - to [*eis*] the measure of the stature which belongs to the fullness of Christ. (NASB, formatting adapted)

Continuationists and cessationists alike presumably agree that Christ's body has room to grow in representing more fully his heart.

### *Gifts Among Gifts*

As in Romans 12 and 1 Corinthians 12, so in Ephesians 4 Paul addresses the unity of Christ's body (4:3–5).[32] Although Paul approaches gifts and Christ's body from a different angle than he did in Romans and 1 Corinthians (here the gifts are some members given to other members), he has not completely changed the subject. In this context, he still applies language familiar to us from Romans 12 and 1 Corinthians 12 ("measure," "grace"). He declares that God has distributed "grace" (*charis*, as in "graciously given gifts" or "grace-gifts," charismata) to each member of the body, providing each one a special portion of the gift of Christ. Paul might mean that the members of Christ's

32. This paragraph and the next adapt Keener, *Gift & Giver*, 110.

body carry on the non-atoning aspects of Jesus's own ministry ("the gift of Christ" in 4:7);[33] or he might mean simply the gift "from Christ" ("as Christ apportioned," NIV).

Explaining the gracious gift of Christ, Paul paraphrases a psalm that speaks of a triumphant ruler receiving and distributing plunder to his followers (Ps. 68:18 in Eph. 4:8). In Romans and 1 Corinthians, Paul writes that God has endowed each believer with special grace. However, in this passage Paul emphasizes another kind of gift first. Here the first gifts the exalted Christ gives to his body are a special group of persons who will in turn mobilize the other members of Christ's body for their ministries. This is clear from the grammar that distinguishes the role of these leaders ("for [*pros*] equipping the saints") from the role for which they equip the saints ("for [*eis*] the work of ministry, for [*eis*] the building up of the body of Christ").

When Paul refers to apostles here, he is not primarily thinking of the Twelve. The witnesses of Acts 1:21–22 from which the Twelve were drawn are explicitly witnesses from John's baptism to Jesus's ascension. Ephesians 4, by contrast, speaks of apostles that Jesus gave when he ascended and gave the gift of the Spirit.[34] So if Paul distinguishes apostles by time at all, he would be referring here to postresurrection ones, as he does often in his letters (e.g., Rom. 1:1; 1 Cor. 15:5–7; Gal. 1:19).

They are gifts to the body of Christ, given by Jesus when he "ascended on high, . . . took many captives and gave gifts to his people" (Eph. 4:8). In other words, through his death, resurrection, and ascension, Jesus conquered and plundered his enemies, then redistributed the spoils to his people. They thus represent the ascended Lord, who converted and called them, and the spoils of his hard-fought, sacrificial victory. To eliminate any of these gifts is to blunt Jesus's victory and compromise the church's capacity to be fully equipped.

## Hebrews and Gifts

Although nearly all scholars agree that Hebrews is not by Paul, because it is among the New Testament epistles it seems best to treat it in this chapter before moving on to examining less textually based cessationist arguments.

The fullest revelation of God until Jesus's second coming is his first coming: "Long ago, at many times and in many ways, God spoke to our fathers by the prophets, but in these last days he has spoken to us by his Son" (Heb. 1:1–2 ESV). This does not mean that God stopped speaking once Jesus came; after all, the author himself was still writing inspired Scripture. But God coming

33. The whole church does so as Christ's body (Eph. 4:16), but it is not clear whether that is the point here.

34. Morphew, "Cessationism," 11.

in the flesh was the ultimate revelation, and we expect nothing comparable until his return in glory. Jesus is the heart of our teaching, preaching, praying, and prophesying.

Some have nevertheless argued for cessationism on the basis of Hebrews 2:3–4. Tom Pennington writes, "The writer of Hebrews is teaching that God testified to the truthfulness and authenticity of the apostles' teaching by giving them the ability to perform supernatural signs and wonders. . . . So, the miraculous gifts entrusted to the apostles were intended to confirm that they were God's genuine instruments of revelation."[35]

Yet this is far from what the text actually *says*, which we believe supports instead continuationism. Jesus preached the saving message, confirmed by those who heard him (2:3)—a much larger group than the Twelve (cf. Luke 1:2): "This salvation, which was first announced by the Lord, was confirmed to us by those who heard him" (Heb. 2:3 NIV).

More critically for the matter at hand, in Hebrews 2:4, God attests not *apostles* with signs and wonders (though apostles are among those through whom God worked them, as with Paul in 2 Cor. 12:12) but God's *message* of salvation that they and other witnesses communicated. This is the message that we still preach, so we should expect God to continue to confirm it if the New Testament pattern holds: "God also testified to it by signs, wonders and various miracles, and by gifts of the Holy Spirit distributed according to his will" (Heb. 2:4 NIV). By signs here, God attests not the apostles but the message of his grace (Acts 14:3), his gospel (Heb. 2:3–4). That is what the apostles and their colleagues preached, and that is what we still preach. The NIV correctly adds "to it"—that is, God testified to the message of salvation, an understanding securely based on the context (i.e., 2:3).

Most translations include the term "gifts" here (e.g., ASV, ESV, KJV, NASB, NET, NIV, NJB) because the author speaks in Greek of the *merismois* of the Holy Spirit (2:4). This Greek term applies elsewhere to "gifts" of the Spirit that God distributes among believers generally (cf. 1 Cor. 12:4–6, 11).

Pennington objects, "The writer of Hebrews, writing just before AD 70, refers to the miraculous gifts in the past tense."[36] Pennington's objection based on the verb tense here misunderstands the nature of the way the aorist functions in Greek.[37] Aside from that complication, however, God surely did confirm the message with signs in the past, when the author's generation received the gospel (2:4; cf. also 13:7). For some to suggest that this indicates that God had stopped working signs, however, makes no more sense of the passage than to suggest from it that the gospel was no longer being preached because they received it in the past. The issue is simply that God attested the

35. Pennington, *Cessationism*, 56, 57.
36. Pennington, *Cessationism*, 161.
37. See Turner, *Gifts*, 293n25.

message when they originally heard and received it, which was naturally in the past (see, e.g., 10:32).[38] Hebrews gives us reason to believe that God *continues* to attest the message, not least since Jesus Christ is the same yesterday, today, and forever (13:8).[39]

Returning to a significant point of this chapter, Paul's use of the term *apostolos* is much broader than the use of some other New Testament writers, and reading other writers' usage into Paul has created various interpretive problems we must address in this book. It is therefore time to turn more deliberately to the question of the meaning of apostles and in what senses they might or might not continue.

38. Analogously, mentioning past persecution in 10:32–34 does not imply that persecution had stopped; see 12:4. Reference to the past also allows comparison to the inauguration of the older covenant in Heb. 2:1–2 (Alt, "Cease," 406).

39. Cf. the understanding of Lane, *Hebrews 1–8*, 39–40, pointed out in Storms, "View," 191n21; Alt, "Cease," 406. See further Kolenda, "Hebrews"; Grudem, "Expect," 235–36.

# 8

# Comparing Apostles and Oranges

## *What* Kind *of Apostles Ceased?*

A key basis for the theological argument of cessationism is that since apostles have passed away, therefore other gifts might have passed away too.

Cessationist theologian Thomas Edgar explains, "The fact that the gift of apostle ceased with the apostolic age is a devastating blow to the basic assumption underlying the entire charismatic perspective, namely, the assumption that all gifts are to be operative throughout the church age. We know that at least one gift ceased; therefore, their foundational assumption is incorrect."[1]

Tom Pennington reasons that since "the gift of Apostleship ceased without a crystal-clear New Testament statement that it would," "other significant changes" may have "happened with the passing of the Apostles as well. You see, once you agree that there are no Apostles today at the same level as Peter and Paul, then you have admitted that there was a major change in the gifting of the Spirit between the Apostolic and the post-apostolic age."[2]

Sam Waldron articulates the same argument: "The New Testament makes clear that Apostles of Christ are not given to the church today; they lived only in the first century. We know for sure, therefore, that one gift, and that the greatest gift, has ceased to be given. This clear New Testament teaching provides a vital premise for the argument against Continuationism. Unless it wishes to contradict the plainest evidence, Continuationism cannot claim that there is no difference in the gifts given to the church today and the gifts given to the church in the first century."[3]

1. Edgar, *Satisfied*, 232.
2. Pennington, "Case."
3. Waldron, *Continued*, 15. See also Saucy, "View," 102, 125.

Interestingly, these writers seem to use this argument to justify a view about spiritual gifts generally that they themselves admit is not specified in the New Testament itself. Their argument is that since one gift (that of apostleship) passed away without the Bible saying so, the same could or should be true of (particular) other gifts. If, however, the Bible does not specifically say that even the one gift has passed, do we really know biblically that it has?

## *Did* Apostles Cease?

As a twenty-first-century American Christian, I (Craig) would be happy to dispense with calling anyone "apostle" or "prophet" today. It's not part of my past or current church background, whether as a minister in the Assemblies of God, as a Baptist minister, or as a professor in Baptist and Wesleyan seminaries. Most people who call themselves apostles seem to me to be something other than that (Rev. 2:2). But the issue in this chapter is not what titles we give people; it's what the biblical data says. Scripture does not readily accommodate the disappearance of the functions to which such titles allude: foundation-layers in new spheres (often meaning church planting movements among unreached peoples) and people who hear from God and communicate to others what he's saying.

The passing of apostles would not *necessitate* the passing of other gifts.[4] If it did, why not those gifts specifically listed alongside apostles in Ephesians 4:11, such as evangelists, pastors, and teachers? But even if we accept the passing of apostles and particular other gifts along with them, we have another problem. Many cessationists simply take for *granted* the premise that apostles have passed rather than arguing it (though we will address later those who do argue for it): "Actually, many continuationists are cessationists when it comes to apostleship, for they also believe that the gift of apostleship in the technical sense has passed away."[5] But how do we know that apostles have passed? As Tom Pennington admitted in the quote above, Scripture nowhere actually says this. Yet he insists that we know that it is true anyway.[6]

### *Foundations Versus Apostles*

The passing of apostles itself depends on another theological inference not explicitly stated in Scripture. A key basis for the theological argument that apostles have passed away is that they existed only for the universal

4. See Storms, "Response to Gaffin," 77–78, noting that nonapostolic Christians still need, e.g., "edifying, encouraging, consoling" (i.e., the ministry of prophecy in 1 Cor. 14:3).

5. Schreiner, *Spiritual Gifts*, 157. Cf. earlier Gaffin, "View," 45: "Many continuationists are in fact cessationists, in that they recognize there are no apostles today."

6. Pennington, "Case." See also Saucy, "View," 123; Saucy, "Response to Storms," 228.

church's foundation, so once that foundation was laid there is no more need for apostles.

Schreiner reasons: "The basis for cessationism is the claim that the church was 'built on the foundation of the apostles and prophets' (Eph. 2:20)."[7] He concludes, "Now that the foundation of the church has been laid, we no longer have authoritative apostles like the Twelve, Paul, James, etc."[8]

We already addressed this argument briefly in chapter 7. But to summarize still more briefly: The foundation referred to in the context in Ephesians 2 is probably the revelation that God accepted gentiles as equal members of Christ's body. Meanwhile, more importantly, Ephesians 2:20 does not *limit* the role of apostles and prophets to this foundation; Paul mentions other purposes for these ministries in other passages, including in Ephesians itself. Nor does Ephesians 2:20 claim that the mentioned prophets' foundational role is their only role.[9] Prophets can build up Christ's body with prophecies (1 Cor. 14:3–5), and apostles also could lay foundations in new areas (Rom. 15:20; 1 Cor. 3:10).

Before proceeding, however, we should emphasize again that we are not arguing that anyone speaks with the authority of Jesus's own eyewitness companions or that anyone today can write Scripture. We ourselves are cessationists regarding completed events of the past that need never happen again—for example, no more virgin births, crucifixions of Jesus, or eyewitnesses of Jesus's earthly ministry. Nor are we condoning leaders or movements gathering followers for themselves by calling themselves apostles or apostolic. We are merely arguing that the apostolic gift in the New Testament had much wider connotations, such as those who break ground for God's kingdom and lay fresh foundations in unreached areas.

The monkey wrench in defining apostles in Paul's letters in too exclusive a manner is that these letters don't limit the title to the Twelve, or even to the Twelve plus Paul.[10]

### *Other Apostles: Big Versus Little Apostles?*

Thus one cessationist acknowledges, "We must make a distinction in the New Testament between those who were Apostles of Christ (big-A apostles) and those who were simply apostles of the churches (small-A apostles)."[11]

7. Schreiner, *Spiritual Gifts*, 157.
8. Schreiner, *Spiritual Gifts*, 158.
9. Storms, "Response to Gaffin," 79.
10. Many church fathers treated the Twelve plus Paul as the group, but this is not the earliest approach (see *Did.* 11.3–6). To illustrate the problem, cf. Gaffin, "View," 45n47: "those appointed by Christ and invested with his authority . . . : the twelve, Paul, and perhaps others."
11. Waldron, *Continued*, 24.

Nearly everyone agrees that we need to make some distinction; the debate involves who belongs to which group.

The original Twelve held a unique role and function and hold a special place (cf. Matt. 19:28 // Luke 22:30; Rev. 21:14).[12] Since the first century, the *Twelve* have "ceased." They died and, like all other believers, await the resurrection. The problem arises when a cessationist uses the Twelve's uniqueness and "cessation" as a premise to claim that the spiritual *gift* of apostleship passed away when they died. The New Testament is explicit that they were not the only apostles. That the Twelve who knew Jesus have passed away says nothing about gifts having passed—except the gift of having been with Jesus during his earthly ministry.

In the New Testament, in those instances when there is a clear distinction among apostles, Scripture almost always identifies only "the twelve."[13] Neither Paul nor anyone else is ever mentioned in this group. Paul is not part of any demarcated group of apostles, and yet he is clearly an apostle in the fullest sense of the word. So creating any special group of apostles that includes the Twelve plus Paul (or James) but excludes, say, Barnabas and Silas, has no genuinely biblical basis. Exegetically, it is purely arbitrary.

Some insist on the cessation of apostles because the church did not replace James, son of Zebedee, after his martyrdom.[14] But since the New Testament shows that there were other apostles besides the Twelve, James's nonreplacement merely shows that the *Twelve* did not keep getting replaced. And why would they? *These* particular apostles had to be witnesses of the period from John the Baptist to Jesus's resurrection (Acts 1:21–22). Even Paul, then, could not have replaced anyone among the Twelve. The nonreplacement of James shows only that no other apostle would join the Twelve. Yet Paul, who was not one of the Twelve, was nevertheless an apostle—as were other "apostles of Christ" called after Jesus's ascension.

Consider the logic that the death of the first generation of apostles entails the end of apostleship. Try applying that to gifts like teaching: Did the death of the first generation of teachers make teachers obsolete? Or as Jack Deere argues, "Paul is the only truly significant church planter in the New Testament, and most of the apostles seem to stay in Jerusalem rather than go out to plant churches. Does that mean only the few were intended to plant churches, and that when Paul died, church planting also died?"[15]

12. Though Revelation also seems to assume the continuing possibility of other apostles (Rev. 2:2; 18:20).

13. Matt. 10:2; 20:17; 26:14, 20, 47; Mark 3:14–16; 4:10; 6:7; 9:35; 10:32; 11:11; 14:10, 17, 20, 43; Luke 6:13; 8:1; 9:1, 12; 18:31; 22:3, 30, 47; John 6:67, 70, 71; 20:24; Acts 6:2; Rev. 21:14.

14. Schreiner, *Spiritual Gifts*, 158.

15. Deere, *Still Surprised*, 284.

### *Who Were the Other Apostles?*

The Gospels and usually Acts restrict the label "apostle" to the first apostles commissioned directly by Jesus during his earthly ministry, so it seems legitimate to restrict that kind of apostleship to that original group. But Paul, who also writes under the Spirit's inspiration, uses the term much more broadly, and Luke in at least one passage shares Paul's broader usage. These broader apostles include:

1. Barnabas, as an apostolic coworker with Paul (using the NIV in this section):

    Acts 14:4: "The people of the city were divided; some sided with the Jews, others with the apostles."

    Acts 14:14: "But when the apostles Barnabas and Paul heard of this, they tore their clothes and rushed out into the crowd, shouting."

    1 Corinthians 9:5–6: "Don't we have the right to take a believing wife along with us, as do the other apostles and the Lord's brothers and Cephas? Or is it only I and Barnabas who lack the right to not work for a living?"

    When Paul speaks of Barnabas and himself having the right to abstain from supporting themselves, he speaks in this context of a right that pertains to apostles (9:1–4). He uses the singular to refer to his defense to the Corinthians but shifts to plural in 9:4 because he is including Barnabas. Paul offers no distinction between his own kind of apostleship and that of Barnabas. The top apostles in Jerusalem recognized Barnabas as Paul's colleague in the gentile mission (Gal. 2:6–10).

2. James the Lord's brother, a leader in the Jerusalem church converted after Jesus's public ministry (1 Cor. 15:7):

    Galatians 1:19: "I saw none of the other apostles—only [*ei mē*, except] James, the Lord's brother."

3. Andronicus and Junia, probably a husband-wife ministry team (Rom. 16:7):[16]

16. With, e.g., Morris, *Romans*, 534; Belleville, "Re-examination," 232; Kruse, *Romans*, 562; Hultgren, *Romans*, 582–84; Schnabel, *Jesus in Jerusalem*, 56; Heim, "Women," 122–23. Cf. John Chrysostom, *Hom. Rom.* 31; Theodoret of Cyrrhus, *Comm. Rom.* on Rom. 16:7 (Bray, *Romans*, 372); Nicholas of Lyra (1270–1349) on Rom. 16:7 (in Levy, Krey, and Ryan, *Romans*, 294); for historical survey, Fitzmyer, *Romans*, 737–39; Jewett, *Romans*, 961. For a different and well-argued, albeit grammatically less likely, minority approach, see Burer and

> Rom. 16:7: "Greet Andronicus and Junia, my fellow Jews who have been in prison with me. They are outstanding among the apostles, and they were in Christ before I was."

4. Silas and Timothy (1 Thess. 2:6 or 7),[17] in light of 1 Thessalonians 1:1 (identifying the "we" as Paul, Silas, and Timothy):

> 1 Thessalonians 2:6 or 7: "We were not looking for praise from people, not from you or anyone else, even though as apostles of Christ we could have asserted our authority."

5. Various apostles beyond the Twelve (1 Cor. 15:5–7), perhaps including the Seventy or Seventy-Two (cf. Luke 10:1, 17):

> 1 Corinthians 15:5–7: "He appeared to Cephas, and then to the Twelve. After that, he appeared to more than five hundred of the brothers and sisters at the same time, most of whom are still living, though some have fallen asleep. Then he appeared to James then to *all the apostles*."

"*All the apostles*" clearly extends beyond the Twelve. That the church had to distinguish true from false apostles (on which see further comment below) also indicates that they could not simply begin with the assumption that the number of apostles was limited to those of whom they already knew:[18]

> 2 Corinthians 11:13: "For such people are false apostles, deceitful workers, masquerading as apostles of Christ."

> Revelation 2:2: "I know your deeds, your hard work and your perseverance. I know that you cannot tolerate wicked people, that you have tested those who claim to be apostles but are not, and have found them false."

This need for discerning true from false apostles remained true in one of the earliest documents from the apostolic fathers (*Did.* 11.3–8), although later church fathers often used the title in an extrabiblical way for the Twelve plus Paul, from which many today have, in contrast to New Testament usage, inherited this formula.[19]

---

Wallace, "Junia." Although Calvin, *Romans*, on 16:7, wrongly supposed that Paul normally "confines this title" to the order of the Twelve (even a simple concordance search shows this premise to be mistaken), he applies the term to the pair here as those "who planted Churches."

17. We include both 1 Thess. 2:6 and 2:7 because translations diverge in their versification here.

18. For this point see also Robertson and Plummer, *Corinthians*, 279; Deere, *Still Surprised*, 267.

19. In the second century, Paul became "the apostle" par excellence; see Thomas, *Works*, 11–12.

### *False Apostles*

Suggesting that apostleship may continue does not entail that all or most or even any so-called apostles today are necessarily genuine. Scripture summons us to discern true apostolic ministry from that which is false (Rev. 2:2), and there is no question that, by biblical standards, false apostles do abound today.[20] An Assemblies of God position paper states it well: "In the Early Church, false apostles did not pioneer ministries; they preyed on ministries established by others."[21]

Leaders who seek for the sheep to follow them rather than nurturing the sheep for Christ are wolves (Acts 20:29–30). If self-proclaimed apostles are not breaking ground for the kingdom in new spheres but are instead boasting in others' labors, Scripture calls them false apostles, servants of Satan (2 Cor. 10:13–18; 11:13–15). True apostles do not demand or seek honor in this life; characteristically, they suffer in order to advance the gospel in their spheres (1 Cor. 4:9–13; 2 Cor. 11:23–33). Those who want to be first in the kingdom must be last of all (Mark 10:44; cf. 1 Cor. 12:28 with 4:9).

Today there are people who simply seek to gather other leaders under them, as if having people under them makes them apostles. They value the title "apostle" as a promotion in ministry, employing a spiritual pyramid scheme that is the inverse of Jesus's model of servanthood. Competing among themselves and with others (2 Cor. 10:12), they try to lure people away from churches with older leadership structures, urging them to catch up with the spiritual times.[22] (Traditional denominations vary among themselves regarding appropriate leadership structures, from hierarchical to congregational models;

20. Some have even been arrested by the FBI, but false apostles obviously go far beyond those subject to government prosecution. Several paragraphs here rework Keener, *Gift & Giver*, 216–18 (the 2020 afterword). For discerning apostles, see again Rev. 2:2; *Did.* 11.

21. This appears among the conclusions in the Assemblies of God position paper "Apostles and Prophets."

22. Such movements do exist. Geivett and Pivec rightly note a number of abuses (e.g., Geivett and Pivec, *Reformation*), though their broad net picks up more circles than I (Craig) would deem problematic (and certainly more than I, and perhaps they, would label "false apostles"). Some represent simply a sort of relational "network Christianity" that extends the logic of Protestantism and independent, nondenominational churches. As independent church structure fits global democratization, so the rise of informal networks partly reflects a cultural shift toward digital connections; see Christerson and Flory, *Rise of Network Christianity*, 45, 102, 122–23, 150. Nor are such networks currently a political threat (136–37). See fuller discussion of various networks generally in Christerson and Flory, *Rise of Network Christianity*. To my knowledge, however, no one draws the lines in the same place or includes precisely the same figures, and outsiders to the movements almost inevitably miscategorize some members of relational networks. Working together on shared objectives does not entail unanimity on theological details or organization. Certainly not everyone who speaks of apostles or apostolic ministry today shares the same political views.

the problem we address here is self-serving leaders lacking accountability to God's movement and mission.)[23]

We have listened to the anguish of Spirit-filled believers in locations as diverse as Cuba, Ethiopia, and India regarding these false apostles and prophets who are dividing the church.[24] False apostles poach converts others labored for. (Some cessationists do the same, though without using any apostolic titles: In some parts of the world Pentecostals are winning the most unbelievers to the faith, and cessationists then labor to recruit the converts for cessationism.)

We wish we could be cessationists regarding false apostles (and false prophets and false pastor-teachers), but they continue today—and we continue to need the gift of discernment today. We don't ordinarily reject money because counterfeits exist, or doctors or scholars because quacks exist. Counterfeits derive their semblance of plausibility precisely by thriving parasitically on what they counterfeit. It takes little discernment to be a cessationist: One can simply discard them all, as well as all prophecies and the like. While I (Craig) find myself attracted to the simplicity of that approach, Paul explicitly warns against treating prophecies with contempt (1 Thess. 5:20). Yet those of us who believe that God continues to empower his church in a range of ways have a much greater responsibility to exercise discernment, especially with the sorts of prophecies that can do the most harm when they are mistaken. (Meanwhile, believers also have the same responsibility to evaluate *teaching* on the basis of Scripture. We believe that cessationism, no less than some unbiblical charismatic fashions, fails the biblical test.)

## Narrowing the Criteria for "Real" Apostles

If one narrows one's search criteria sufficiently, one can remove the relevance of enough evidence to argue almost any point from the silence that remains. When it comes to deciding which gifs are defunct, cessationists have become experts at narrowing criteria.

They try to account for Paul's apostleship while excluding others by creating a special standard for "apostles of Christ." Sam Waldron's book outlines three requirements:

1. Apostles of Christ had to be eyewitnesses of the resurrected Christ.
2. Apostles of Christ had to be appointed directly by Jesus himself.

23. Horizontal networks (on which see Christerson and Flory, *Rise of Network Christianity*, 60–65) have less risk of top-down abuse than vertical networks (on which see 54–60), but lack of accountability can remain a risk anywhere.

24. Cf. more fully my comments in Keener, "False Apostles"; Keener, "Recognizing False Apostles."

3. Apostles of Christ needed to have miraculous signs.[25]

"Only someone with *each* of these characteristics could claim to be an Apostle of Christ. Two out of the three were not sufficient. Every Apostle of Christ must, first, have physically seen the resurrected Lord; second, must have been appointed directly by Christ; and third, must have performed miraculous signs to vindicate himself as an Apostle of Christ."[26]

Nowhere does Scripture list these criteria explicitly as requirements for "apostles of Christ," but even if we accept them for the sake of argument, it is difficult to see why a person from any era cannot meet these requirements—at least in the way Paul met them. So it is worth examining where cessationists get these three apostolic prerequisites. We will look at each one and see how it holds up under scrutiny.

### *All Apostles Saw the Lord?*

Biblically, John MacArthur insists, "an apostle had to be a physical eyewitness of the resurrected Christ."[27] "No living person has seen the risen Christ with his or her own eyes; no one is able to perform miraculous signs like those done by the apostles in the book of Acts." Visions don't count, he says; they are unverifiable and not experienced with physical sight.[28] Thus Paul was the last person to see the risen Christ (1 Cor. 15:8), an observation that "would preclude anyone after Paul from having a legitimate claim to apostleship."[29]

Tom Schreiner concurs: "To qualify as an apostle, one had to be commissioned as an apostle and to see the risen Lord. Jesus Christ appeared to Paul on the Damascus Road and summoned him to apostolic service (Acts 9:1–19; 1 Cor. 9:1–2; Gal. 1:13–17)."[30]

Like others, Waldron uses especially three passages of Scripture to prove that being an eyewitness of the risen Christ is an apostolic requirement.[31] We quote these passages here so you can read them yourself and see whether *you* think they really support cessationists' conclusions (NASB):

25. Waldron, *Continued*, 25–29; cf. Pennington, *Cessationism*, 63–66. These three requirements for apostles are not unique to cessationist doctrine. I (Daniel) was also taught this as a classic Pentecostal, and many Pentecostals still accept and teach this today. But it goes well beyond the biblical text.

26. Waldron, *Continued*, 29–30.

27. MacArthur, *Strange Fire*, 92. He cites Acts 1:22; 10:39–41; 1 Cor. 9:1; 15:7–8, most of which we examine below. Cf. also Waldron, *Continued*, 25–26, 30.

28. MacArthur, *Strange Fire*, 92. Interestingly, MacArthur's criteria of verifiability vary considerably depending on the subject at hand.

29. MacArthur, *Strange Fire*, 94.

30. Schreiner, *Spiritual Gifts*, 158. "No one since apostolic times fits" the criterion of having seen the risen Christ (Schreiner, "Cessationist").

31. Waldron, *Continued*, 25–26.

> Acts 1:22: ". . . beginning with the baptism of John until the day that He was taken up from us—one of these *must* become a witness with us of His resurrection."
>
> Acts 10:39–41: "We are witnesses of all the things He did both in the land of the Jews and in Jerusalem. They also put Him to death by hanging Him on a cross. God raised Him up on the third day and granted that He be revealed, not to all the people, but to witnesses who had been chosen beforehand by God, *that is*, to us who ate and drank with Him after He arose from the dead."
>
> 1 Corinthians 9:1: "Am I not free? Am I not an apostle? Have I not seen Jesus our Lord? Are you not my work in the Lord?"

Remember, these verses should assert that one requirement to be an "apostle of Christ" is to see the resurrected Christ. But as you may have already wondered, how Paul satisfies these requirements is not clear. He is the wrench in the cessationist machine. Consider the following points.

Paul did not know Christ "according to the flesh" (2 Cor. 5:16). He did not know him during Jesus's time on earth (what Heb. 5:7 calls, lit., "the days of his flesh"), or at least did not understand him from the right vantage point until after his Damascus-road encounter.

- Paul thus could not fulfill the qualification of the first verse cited (Acts 1:22), given its context. Waldron fails to quote the previous verse, which is bound to the one he quotes: "Therefore it is necessary that *of the men who have accompanied us all the time that the Lord Jesus went in and out among us*—beginning with the baptism of John until the day that He was taken up from us—*one of these* must become a witness with us of His resurrection" (Acts 1:21–22 NASB, our emphasis). Paul did not even become a believer until after the ascension. He was not with the Twelve at the *end* of Christ's ministry, let alone at the beginning. Acts 1:21–22 is not about apostles of every kind, but only about the Twelve—regarding the man who would replace Judas Iscariot. In answer to prayer, Matthias is chosen. No others of the Twelve are replaced afterward. If we take this passage in Acts as a universal apostolic requirement, while also holding on to Waldron's requirements, Paul completely misses the cut; he is not an apostle. Waldron cannot have it both ways. He cannot extract the part about being a physical eyewitness, while leaving the other explicit requirement—being with Jesus from the beginning!—on the table.
- Likewise, Paul has nothing to do with the next passage (Acts 10:39–41). The same principles apply here as with Acts 1:21–22. Peter talks about those who, yes, witnessed Jesus after his resurrection, but also

"witnessed all the things" Jesus did before his death and who then "ate and drank with Him after His resurrection." Nor does the passage claim a universal requirement for apostleship.

- The third passage of course does apply to Paul (1 Cor. 9:1). The idea that to be an apostle one must "see" the Lord thus rests on 1 Corinthians 9:1. But while both seeing Christ and being an apostle underline Paul's authority, the verse does not explain their relationship. It is one of *four* rhetorical questions, not all of which exclusively describe apostleship, and which do not constitute a list of apostolic qualifications:
    - Am I not free?
    - Am I not an apostle?
    - Have I not seen Jesus our Lord?
    - Are you not my work in the Lord?

  Paul's apostleship may leave him "free" (9:19), but apostles are not the only people who are free, nor is freedom a prior criterion for apostleship. Neither does seeing Jesus automatically make one an apostle (Mark 5:6; Luke 23:8; 1 Cor. 15:6). The one question that likely *does* indicate Paul's apostleship in this context is the final one, which Paul states as the *seal* of his apostleship in 9:2: the Corinthian church. His apostolic ministry of breaking new ground for the kingdom, rather than seeing Jesus (a separate claim in his favor), demonstrates his apostleship. He appeals only to what others can see in him (2 Cor. 12:6).

Continuationists and cessationists agree at least that seeing the risen Christ by itself would not be enough to qualify one for apostleship. Some who saw him were apostles (1 Cor. 15:5, 7), but presumably most of the five hundred witnesses on one occasion were not (1 Cor. 15:6). People continue to have visions of the resurrected Christ today. It happens frequently in the Muslim world,[32] and I (Daniel) am aware of several credible cases in other places. This experience does not make all its recipients apostles.

### *Last of the Apostles?*

Schreiner argues that "we know that new apostles won't appear since Paul specifically says he was the last apostle (1 Cor. 15:8)."[33] MacArthur and Waldron agree.[34] The problem is that the text cited in support of this says nothing of the sort. Paul says he received the last resurrection appearance on the list of witnesses he provides in 15:5–8. Yet not all these witnesses were apostles, and

32. See, e.g., Trousdale, *Movements*; Doyle, *Dreams*. Doyle is a graduate of Dallas Theological Seminary.

33. Schreiner, "Cessationist"; Schreiner, *Spiritual Gifts*, 158.

34. MacArthur, *Strange Fire*, 94; Waldron, *Continued*, 39.

it is being a witness of the resurrection, not the gift of apostleship, that Paul addresses here. Notice 15:6: "After that He appeared to more than five hundred brothers *and sisters* at one time, most of whom remain until now, but some have fallen asleep" (NASB). Were they *all* apostles? Nor did all apostles see Jesus. Timothy certainly did not witness the risen Christ before Paul, if at all (see Acts 16:1), yet, as noted above, he appears to be an apostle in 1 Thessalonians 2:6–7.

Paul simply does not claim to be the last apostle here. He claims to be the last witness of the risen Christ, but even here he might mean simply last in this list of witnesses, an earlier list to which he appends his own testimony. That is, Paul says he was "last" among those witnesses, not among all "apostles of Christ" in history. Paul's point in context is to list witnesses, not all apostles (though all the prior apostles are *among* the witnesses). Again, earlier in the list, surely the five hundred witnesses (15:6) were not all apostles?

If Paul was the last person to witness the risen Christ altogether, then what about John in Revelation 1:13–20? If one objects that John was an apostle (though this would not help support Paul's supposed claim to see Jesus last),[35] the non-apostle Ananias saw Jesus in a vision after Paul's Damascus-road encounter with Jesus (Acts 9:10). MacArthur rules out the relevance of visions[36] so as to rule out apostles after the earthly ministry of Jesus and Paul's Damascus-road encounter, which he does not consider visionary. Yet MacArthur lacks evidence that the other non-Twelve apostles of Christ whom Paul mentions saw Jesus in the flesh—or for that matter, even in visions. Again, if one narrows criteria sufficiently (and cites a few verses that do not actually say what one claims), one can argue for almost anything.

As Douglas Oss notes, the "distinction between apostolic and subapostolic eras is foreign in the Bible and is only useful for describing the role of persons who founded the church (e.g., Eph. 2:20ff.)."[37]

## Scripture Is Complete

For cessationists, "The fact of the closed character of the canon . . . assumes and implies the closed character of the apostolate."[38]

35. Pennington, *Cessationism*, 63, says he doesn't count because he had already seen Jesus after the resurrection; "Paul was the last, . . . and there is no biblical precedent for Christ appearing to people today."

36. MacArthur, *Strange Fire*, 92. This might also rule out John's experience (Rev. 9:17), though Jesus's glory in Rev. 1:13–16 seems analogous to Paul's experience of the risen Christ (Acts 9:3).

37. Oss, "Response to Saucy," 171, cited in Graves, "Cessationism," 51.

38. Waldron, *Continued*, 40–41 (quote from 41). Deere, *Still Surprised*, 290, cites MacArthur, *Chaos*, 136–37, as claiming that "the apostles wrote nearly all of the New Testament," but I have not been able to locate this claim in the 1992 edition that I have.

### *Do All Apostles Write Scripture?*

Thus many cessationists object to apostles continuing because they think that apostles write Scripture—though most biblical apostles didn't. We may commend our cessationist brothers and sisters for rightly emphasizing that the canon of Scripture is complete; we agree, virtually by definition. The Greek word *kanōn* refers to a standard for measurement; the ancient church adopted this title for the collection of writings on which Christians largely agreed as all divinely inspired, sufficient, and authoritative. In other words, the biblical "canon" refers to those books that belong in the Bible as opposed to those that do not (a process Jewish thinkers had already been undertaking for our Old Testament). Jesus's coming climaxed biblical revelation, and only the circle that knew him and his first followers who learned directly from those followers were in the right place historically to finish Scripture.

Cessationists' argument from completed Scripture to the end of apostleship, however, is a non sequitur. Some cessationists demand, "If there are apostles today, why can't they write Scripture?" Several first-century apostles—and other leaders closely aligned with them—did indeed have a unique role in history to write Scripture. But we hold their writings as inspired because of who they were personally and because of their proximity to Jesus—not simply because they had the status of apostle. A rough analogy might be the founding fathers of the United States. They authored the Constitution and signed the Declaration of Independence. They founded the nation. They are not like other presidents, generals, diplomats, or representatives that followed them in history. They were special because of the role they played in the founding of the nation. That doesn't mean that there can be no more presidents, generals, or diplomats. Nor does it mean that America's leaders today are able to add to the Declaration of Independence, for example. These are distinct issues. Likewise, the gift of apostleship and writing Scripture are two separate issues.

Waldron graciously recognizes that charismatics are not out to change the canon: "The entire Christian church acknowledges that no new book has been added to the canon of the New Testament for almost twenty centuries. There is no debate about this."[39] Historically, there actually have been debates about the New Testament canon, not least during the Reformation, when Martin Luther treated Hebrews, James, Jude, and Revelation as much less certain than better-attested books.[40] But charismatics recognize the same New Testament canon as noncharismatics. (Indeed, we even try to obey its

39. Waldron, *Continued*, 40.

40. Still, Luther's comment about one of Melanchthon's works being *worthy* of inclusion in the Bible (Adams, "Introduction," xlviii) was not meant literally as an argument that it should actually be included.

precepts about spiritual gifts—1 Cor. 12:31; 14:1, 5, 12, 26, 39; 1 Thess. 5:20. Technically, the New Testament actually says more about apostles, prophets, and miracles than about evangelists and pastors.)

The canon is closed, since *by definition* the "canon" is the body of Scripture that the entire church (including charismatics) claims to accept as the measuring stick for any other revelation. That does not, however, mean that God has stopped speaking to individuals, much less that we should assume that God did not speak through the many prophets mentioned in Scripture whose words are not recorded there (see under "Extracanonical Revelation Recognized by Scripture" in chap. 13 below). At the very least, all Christians should hear God's Spirit reminding us that we are God's children (Rom. 8:16) and pointing to his love revealed in the cross (Rom. 5:5–9).[41]

No one is suggesting that these postbiblical experiences of hearing God should be added to Scripture. There is a good reason that Jeremiah's book is in the Bible rather than any from the rival prophets of his day: Jeremiah's message stood the test of time. Scripture is tested, the consensus basis we use to evaluate any other claim—including (in this book) the doctrinal claim of cessationism.

### *Scripture Is Complete Only If Apostles Ceased?*

Cessationists often contend that apostles have ceased because—as we all agree—Scripture is complete. But Scripture itself does not connect apostleship with a closed canon. In fact, apostleship was not even a qualification for writing Scripture. As Jon Ruthven points out, "The cessationist model of apostles and prophets as essentially serving as repositories of unwritten Scripture is a caricature."[42] Even using "the most conservative attribution of New Testament authorship," "when one actually adds up the number of words in the New Testament written by apostles, as opposed to non-apostles, the ratio is 59%–41% respectively!" If one further limits it to the original Twelve (thus excluding Paul as later than the earliest witnesses), apostles wrote less than half.[43]

Further, not only does no passage list the writing of Scripture as one of the duties of apostles, but very few of the apostles actually wrote Scripture. Again, "by the most conservative attribution of New Testament authorship," of the Twelve only three—Matthew, John, and Peter—actually wrote any of the New Testament. Of the many other apostles (cf. again, e.g., 1 Cor. 15:7), only two (Paul and James) wrote any other parts. Non-apostles such as Mark (more than 8 percent of the verses) and Luke (some 27 percent)

41. Most of this paragraph recites Keener, *Gift & Giver*, 216.
42. Ruthven, *Cessation*, 216.
43. Ruthven, *Cessation*, 216–17, noting that Paul "wrote 43% of the 'apostolic' 59%."

wrote significant parts of it; if we add in Hebrews and Jude, we are looking at close to 40 percent.[44]

On examination, the requirement that apostleship must pass away before the canon may be closed proves ephemeral—another postbiblical imposition onto the biblical text. This is unfortunately by necessity a pattern frequent in cessationist arguments. The Roman Catholic tradition allows for subsequent church tradition to augment or develop the teachings of Scripture, but it does not exclude continuing gifts of the Spirit, visions, and miracles. Ironically, the church traditions generally most opposed to the continuing of some gifts of the Spirit are churches in the Reformation tradition most adamant about *sola scriptura* (the Bible alone). Yet a genuinely *sola scriptura* approach exposes how beholden these cessationists are to their own extrabiblical tradition.

Cessationists reject all modern apostles, miracle-workers, and prophecy because they perceive these gifts as threats to the closed canon of Scripture. But isn't the precedent they set—rejecting clear New Testament teaching on the basis of counterbiblical inferences—the real threat to the integrity of Scripture? This is the sort of reasoning for which faithful biblical scholars challenge the more careless systematic theologians. Although we are by no means calling cessationist churches cults, it is also the sort of reasoning for which apologists challenge cults: forcing Scripture into prior theological molds while claiming unique loyalty to the Bible. Put another way, if deductions this tenuous constitute a valid hermeneutic, Scripture's *effective* canon becomes pretty subjective. Doesn't that do what cessationist critics complain that charismatics do?

## Apostles of Christ Versus Apostles of Churches

Two New Testament passages use the Greek term *apostolos* in the generic sense found in secular Greek. These refer to agents delegated by their churches for a mission other than preaching salvation (2 Cor. 8:23; Phil. 2:25). Even though Paul's other passages regarding apostles do not include this specification ("of the churches"), some cessationists wish to include most or all apostles beyond the Twelve and Paul in this category.

### *Who Are the "Apostles of Christ"?*

Waldron proposes

> a distinction in the New Testament between those who were Apostles of Christ (big-A apostles) and those who were simply apostles of the churches (small-A

44. If someone objects, "Well, maybe Mark, Luke, Jude, and the author of Hebrews were actually apostles even though Scripture does not call them this," they must be willing to concede the title to others beyond the Twelve plus Paul.

> apostles). Apostles of Christ are Christ's direct, legal representatives. Apostles of the churches are the churches' legal representatives and only indirectly, and in a lesser sense, the representatives of Christ. You can see apostles of the churches mentioned in Philippians 2:25 and 2 Corinthians 8:23. In the sense of apostles of churches, apostles do exist today. A missionary sent out by a local church would be an apostle of that church. A representative sent to a meeting of an association of churches is another example of an apostle of that church. . . . They are not, however, official apostles in the sense of being an Apostle of Christ.[45]

There are a number of problems with this position, but we'll focus on the issues most relevant to the present argument. The line that Waldron draws between the two apostolic categories—Apostles of Christ and apostles of the churches—is arbitrary. He assigns the Twelve plus Paul and James to the former category and then relegates the others to the second. He argues that since the Twelve plus Paul and James have died—and no one else can be part of that original group—the true apostolate has therefore ceased. But recognizing Paul's apostleship is the "crack in the wall" that interrupts the faulty logic in what Waldron calls his "cascade" argument.[46]

Paul often identifies himself as one of Christ's apostles, using phrases similar to "apostle of Christ" in his letter greetings (1 Cor. 1:1). Most of Paul's letters begin with similar references to his calling.[47] When Paul identifies himself as an "apostle of Christ Jesus" (or the like), Waldron suggests that this terminology distinguishes Paul from the other, "lesser" apostles.[48]

Yet this is not how Paul uses the label "apostles of Christ." He tells the Thessalonians, "We could have made demands as apostles of Christ" (1 Thess. 2:6 ESV). When Paul refers here to "apostles of Christ"—one of only two times that exact phrase appears in Scripture—context demands that he means "apostles" in its strongest sense: as Christ's representatives and gifts to the church. Paul, after all, counts himself among this group ("we") and treats their message as God's own efficacious word (2:13). And he is no mere church delegate or legal representative. He is an "apostle" in the fullest sense of the word. No one doubts this.

Therefore, "we . . . apostles of Christ" must refer to Paul and apostles like him. Everything Paul describes about himself and his companions points to their apostolic authority (not their "church delegate" authority). They

45. Waldron, *Continued*, 24. Southern Baptist readers will find familiar his description of churches' messengers.

46. See, e.g., Waldron, *Continued*, 16. Waldron writes, "The cessation of the apostolate is, therefore, the crack in the foundation of Continuationism, the fatal flaw in their thinking. . . . It is often assumed that the presumption must be in favor of the continuation of the miraculous gifts. If, however, they admit the apostolate does not continue, why should we share this presumption?" (Waldron, *Continued*, 42).

47. See 2 Cor. 1:1; Gal. 1:1; Eph. 1:1; Col. 1:1; 1 Tim. 1:1; Titus 1:1.

48. Waldron, *Continued*, 24–25.

preached the gospel with the Spirit's miraculous power (1 Thess. 1:5), endured severe persecution (1:6), acted as examples for the new believers (1:7), founded the church (1:1, 7–10), and chose not to use their apostolic authority to put pressure on their new converts (2:6–7). Mere delegates from other churches could not assume financial or other official "rights" over another congregation. The contrast Paul draws between being a burden or offering gentle service thus makes little sense unless Paul *and his companions* carry direct authority from Christ himself.

Yet by Waldron's definition of "apostles of Christ," these other apostles need to be from the Twelve (or James)—and that's not the case in this passage. Paul's letter plainly tells us who they were: Silvanus and Timothy (1 Thess. 1:1).[49] Neither 1 Thessalonians nor Acts mentions James or any of the twelve apostles bringing the gospel to Thessalonica. The Bible identifies only these three men—Paul, Silvanus, and Timothy—as the workers who founded the church in that city. Therefore they are the only candidates for Paul's reference to "we . . . apostles of Christ" (1 Thess. 2:6). This passage applies the phrase "apostles of Christ" specifically to apostles like Paul who were *not* from the Twelve or James.[50] Ironically, then, the only time Scripture uses Waldron's precise plural phrase ("apostles of Christ"), it refers in context to Paul and two other "apostles" outside the Twelve and James.

As noted earlier, the New Testament identifies a number of "apostles" who demonstrate that this group was much wider than such cessationists believe. They do not belong to the Twelve, or the Twelve-plus-Paul (or Twelve-plus-Paul-plus-James) group, nor do they belong to a lesser group of church representatives. Paul actually counts himself among this broader group of apostles. That means they ministered as apostles of Christ the way Paul did. So instead of forcing this group of apostles into the lesser category, we must scrap the categories as cessationists define them and allow the Scriptures to lead us. Let's consider some further relevant points.

### *Paul as a "Regular" Apostle*

Some suppose a category of "big-A" apostles besides the Twelve that nevertheless included Paul as distinct from other apostles such as Barnabas, Silas,

49. See also Acts 17:1–9 in light of 16:1–5 for the narrative explaining the identity of those traveling with Paul to Thessalonica—the only ones who could be included in the "we . . . apostles of Christ." Careful New Testament scholar Gene Green makes similar observations (Green, *Thessalonians*, 125–26).

50. Some argue against Timothy's inclusion among Paul's "We . . . apostles of Christ" in this passage. We do not believe there is any good reason to exclude him. But even if we were to exclude Timothy, Paul still must be referring to at least Silvanus/Silas as an "apostle" who (1) is not from the Twelve, (2) is explicitly numbered among the "apostles of Christ," and (3) functions on Paul's level of apostleship. Silvanus functions much like Barnabas in Paul's earlier mission, whom even Luke calls an apostle (Acts 14:4, 14).

and Timothy. Yet even when Paul's apostolic calling is a matter of intense debate (1 Cor. 4:3; 2 Cor. 11:1–11; cf. 2 Cor. 3:1–3), Paul fails to trot out any special "big-A" terminology as part of his credentials. He does not mention such a category even when his enemies compared him unfavorably with other so-called apostles (2 Cor. 11:5; 12:11)! He contrasts himself with false "apostles of Christ" (2 Cor. 11:13), a title that (when not false) he elsewhere shares not with the Twelve but with Silas and Timothy (1 Thess. 2:6–7).

What Paul does cite as proof of his apostolic credentials is this: his suffering. In five passages between both Corinthian letters, Paul catalogs his hardships specifically to demonstrate that he is an apostle of Christ.[51] At other times, Paul confirms his apostolic calling by referring to churches he planted and signs and wonders.[52] So when Paul defends his calling as an apostle of Christ, he does not mention, nor does he even indicate awareness, that he belongs to a group separate from other, lesser apostles. Yet his other "credentials" show that he is fully aware of a true apostolic calling outside of any connection to the Twelve.

#### *From Whom Does "Apostles of Christ" Distinguish Them?*

The phrase "apostles of Christ" does not distinguish Paul from apostles like Silvanus or Timothy. The designation "of Christ" may simply show that he is a true apostle (as opposed to a false one) or that he is Christ's emissary rather than that of someone else. It might specify and honor his sender without having in mind a distinction at all.

Many scholars today argue that in 1 Thessalonians 2:3–8, Paul draws on conventional language of sages who needed to distinguish themselves from greedy and immoral preachers that risked discrediting the entire profession.[53] What is most explicit is a distinction between apostles "sent" as agents from human institutions and those "sent" by Christ himself.

This is even clearer in another of Paul's early letters. In Galatians 1:1, Paul emphasizes that he is an apostle not through the agency of people but through the agency of Christ. His rivals in Galatia apparently were suggesting otherwise (Gal. 1:1);[54] Paul responds to a related charge about his message in 1:11–12. Some scholars suggest that his opponents in Galatia envision his pre-Christian agency for the chief priests (Acts 9:2; 22:5; 26:10) or the

51. 1 Cor. 4:8–13; 2 Cor. 4:7–13; 6:4–10; 11:21–33; 12:7–10. On suffering as one key feature of apostleship, see Keener, *Suffering*, chap. 2.

52. 1 Cor. 9:1–2; 2 Cor. 12:12.

53. See esp. Malherbe, "Gentle as Nurse," often followed (e.g., Best, *Thessalonians*, 94–95; Meeks, *Urban Christians*, 114); though cf. the qualifications in Malherbe, "Gentle as Nurse," 217; Marshall, *Thessalonians*, 61.

54. With, e.g., Jerome, *Ep. Gal.* 1.1.1; Dunn, *Galatians*, 25–26; Schreiner, *Galatians*, 74; Ngewa, *Galatians*, 6; Sanders, *Paul: Life*, 477–78.

mediation of Ananias (9:17).[55] More likely, they view him as a mere emissary of the Antioch church (11:30);[56] likeliest of all, they view him as having gotten his message secondhand from the Jerusalem apostles (cf. Gal. 1:17–20; 2:1–2, 6). In any case, they charge that he has at best a derivative, rather than direct, apostolic authority.[57] Perhaps gently sidestepping some debates, even Luke, one of Paul's most loyal traveling companions, titles him an apostle only rarely—specifically, in Acts 14:4, 14.

In my (Daniel's) travels, when I enter a foreign country, the immigration officer will often ask me what I do for a living. I will reply that I am a "minister." The follow-up question will then be: "Minister of what?" This is an appropriate question. "Minister" is not solely a religious word. Governments have "ministers" of education, finance, transportation, defense, and other departments. So I add the qualifier, "I am a minister of the gospel." But I say this not to distinguish myself from, or make myself superior to, other preachers. I say this to distinguish myself from ministers of secular institutions. Likewise, Paul identifies himself as an apostle of Jesus Christ as opposed to an apostle (*apostolos*, agent) of Rome, the Sanhedrin, or some other earthly establishment. In other contexts, however, "minister" may suffice because everyone there understands that I preach the gospel. Paul can often simply identify himself or others as "apostles" without qualification.

### Apostles of Churches

The other "apostolic" phrase that provided Waldron's labels is "apostles of the churches." There are only two passages in the New Testament that specify "apostles" in this generic sense (here NIV):

> 2 Corinthians 8:23: "As for Titus, he is my partner and co-worker among you; as for our brothers, they are representatives [Greek plural: *apostoloi*] of the churches and an honor to Christ."
>
> Philippians 2:25: "But I think it is necessary to send back to you Epaphroditus, my brother, co-worker and fellow soldier, who is also your messenger [Greek singular: *apostolos*], whom you sent to take care of my needs."

In both cases, translators choose English words other than "apostle" to translate the Greek word *apostolos*. Virtually every translation uses words like

55. Bruno the Carthusian, prologue (Levy, *Galatians*, 133); Martin Luther, *Gal.*, 1535 lectures, on 1:12. Even in Acts, however, Paul comprehends Jesus's identity before Ananias's arrival (Acts 9:4–5; 22:7–8).

56. Early Christians sometimes used "apostle" for simply commissioned agents of churches, as in 2 Cor. 8:23; Phil. 2:25.

57. Much of this paragraph derives from Keener, *Galatians*, 49–50.

"messenger" and "representative." Both contexts seem to indicate that Paul uses the word "apostle" in these passages to refer to generic messengers, rather than apostles as gifts to the church according to Ephesians 4:11. This pattern does not fit the context of passages that lack the "of the churches" qualification, where context suggests special authority (as with James; Gal. 1:19) or groundbreaking mission (as with Barnabas, Silas, and Timothy).

Therefore, Waldron's distinction between the allegedly narrow and obsolete "Apostles of Christ" and continuing "apostles of the churches" fails to fit the biblical evidence. He forces these categories onto the text to affirm cessationist theology, rather than allowing the text to make its own argument. This arbitrary categorization—and therefore elimination—of apostles is unbiblical.

### *A Postascension Yet Leading Apostle*

Paul was a postascension apostle who did not follow Jesus during his earthly ministry. Because of this, Paul's ministry actually *set a precedent for all future postascension apostles of Christ*. Cessationists must either relegate Paul to an exclusive and obsolete group such as the Twelve, or let him speak to a wider group that remains relevant so long as its mission of foundation-laying in areas continues.

Life would be much easier for cessationists if Paul were in fact one of the twelve apostles. Then they would not have to fabricate any awkward, extrabiblical categories of apostles. But Paul was not one of the Twelve. Though some have weakly argued Paul should have replaced Judas, that is simply not the case.[58] The need to fill Judas's place among the apostles was urgent, and Paul was not even a believer yet. Further, as is clear from Acts 1:21–22, Paul did not meet the explicit criteria for joining the Twelve. Paul was not—nor ever intended to be—one of the Twelve.

If the Twelve were a special group of apostles without Paul, and then Paul was *also* called to be an apostle of Christ, then Jesus can call others besides the Twelve. Jesus Christ has the right to appoint his own apostles. He did so with the Twelve. He did so with Paul. He also did so with James, Barnabas, Silvanus, and Timothy. We do not know what their appointments looked like, but we know that somehow Jesus must have made it clear. Perhaps we have a hint about Barnabas. He and Saul—later called Paul—were listed as "prophets and teachers" in Antioch. There was no mention of any apostles. But then the Holy Spirit spoke and sent them on a mission. Shortly after that, Luke calls them "apostles" (Acts 14:4, 14).

58. See rightly Schreiner, *Spiritual Gifts*, 157n1 (following Schnabel, *Acts*, 90–107); but contrast Schreiner, *Spiritual Gifts*, 158, regarding the nonreplacement of James. For further detail on replacing Judas, see Keener, *Acts*, 1:756–79.

In light of these things, I (Daniel) would like to present a "cascade argument" of my own, in contrast to that advocated by Waldron. We believe it more accurately reflects what we find in Scripture:

1. In the Bible, "apostles of Christ" include the original twelve apostles, but also a broader group consisting of Paul and several others on the same level. There is no biblical support to rank Paul (and perhaps James) with the Twelve and restrict the only true "apostles of Christ" to that group. The Twelve are special among apostles, but they are not the end of apostles of Christ. They are the beginning.
2. The apostles of Ephesians 4:11 consist of the broader group of apostles of Christ, which means the apostolic gift did not die with the twelve apostles (or Paul and James); apostles can still exist today.
3. The gift of apostles still exists, and the other gifts, including the miraculous ones, can still exist as well.

## Extra Credit: So What Are Apostles?

Rather than simply deconstructing extrabiblical classifications meant to support a questionable theological premise, we offer some comments here about what we think the New Testament suggests about apostleship. We extrapolate these from New Testament uses but recognize that limitations of the New Testament evidence may not answer all of everyone's questions; it certainly does not answer all our own.

Paul never provides a definition of apostleship, so one must survey his and other New Testament usage to see what characteristics apostles shared in common. Paul's use of the term *apostolos* is not restricted to the Twelve, but it includes them. Their passing on of Jesus's direct message provided foundations for the universal church (though for nuances see chap. 7 above), but they also established the church in Jerusalem, from which churches in other regions spread. Paul and his coworkers likewise established—laying foundations for—local or regional churches among those previously unreached. Although not all the other apostles Paul mentions laid foundations for the whole church through history, they laid foundations for churches or ministries in new regions or spheres (cf. Rom. 15:20; 2 Cor. 10:14–16).[59]

After examining every use of the term "apostle" in the New Testament, I (Craig) concluded that some features regularly characterized apostles, though apostles were otherwise diverse (Paul and the Twelve, for example, were very different in many respects).

59. In following paragraphs we repurpose Keener, *Gift & Giver*, 128–29.

First, apostles seem to have broken new ground, originating a God-initiated ministry. Beyond this, they diverge on the kind of new ground: The Twelve founded the church in Jerusalem by passing on Jesus's message, then remained there for many years. Paul, eager not to build on another's foundation (2 Cor. 10:15–18; 11:5–6; compare Rom. 15:17–20), planted small home groups across the Mediterranean world that gradually multiplied. He remained in contact with his converts but could not be with them most of the time; still, they were the proof of his ministry (1 Cor. 9:1–2; 2 Cor. 3:1–3).[60] Paul and his colleagues broke more new geographic ground than the Twelve.

Second, apostles apparently exercised an authority generated by their ministry role and foundation-laying, not by the church's institutional structure. The Twelve in Jerusalem exercised a special authority as the appointed overseers of Jesus's message (Acts 4:35–37; 5:2). This authority, however, was not a purely administrative authority. Rather, the Twelve willingly shared various aspects of institutional authority with the seven (6:6) and especially with local "elders" in the Jerusalem church (15:2, 4, 6, 22–23; 16:4). They were willing to recognize God's work in others' leadership (8:14) and listen to other Christians (9:27). My (Craig's) students come to class and do my assignments because they are registered at my seminary; that is, I am backed by my institution. It is my institution's authority rather than my personal authority that undergirds my role as professor. But those within apostles' spheres respect them because of their roles as founders and groundbreakers. God could call apostles to specialties (or peoples; Rom. 11:13; Gal. 2:8–9; 1 Tim. 2:7). Some compare apostles in general to imperial legates, in that they represent the authority of the one who sent them.

True apostles must be servants, not people who pull rank (compare Acts 15:22; 1 Cor. 4:9–16; 2 Cor. 11:5–15; Col. 1:24–25). Paul occasionally—though only when necessary—pulls rank and commands his churches (1 Cor. 4:18–21; 5:3–5; 2 Cor. 2:9; 13:1–3, 10; as a prophet, 1 Cor. 14:36–38). More often, though, he reasons with them (2 Cor. 1:24; 8:8) and provides an example of humble service (Acts 20:18–27, 33–35; 2 Cor. 1:3–7; 4:15). He continually reaffirms his love for his church people, even when he needs to reprove them (e.g., 2 Cor. 4:15; 5:13; 6:11–13; 7:3; 11:2, 11; 12:14–15, 19).

Third, both signs and sacrificial, simple living characterized apostolic ministry. Paul notes the signs God worked through him (2 Cor. 12:12) but highlights especially his sufferings. It is the commitment demonstrated in the latter that most fully distinguishes him from the false apostles (2 Cor. 11:13, 23–33).

60. Those with families may have often traveled less, at least until their children were grown and their spouses could travel with them; cf. Acts 8:40; 21:8–9; 1 Cor. 9:5. But this cannot be the whole story (cf. Mark 1:30).

## "Apostolic" Movements Today

Today many churches speak of "apostolic" missions or "apostolic" church planting.[61] They normally mean "apostolic" in the wider, Pauline sense of the term. For example, the Filadelfia movement in Rajasthan in North India has planted many churches, even growing 3,000 percent in one two-year period.[62]

The same is true for many who think of apostles as having special authorization to lead. Many older church traditions speak of apostolic succession, an unbroken chain of appointed leaders going back to the first-century apostles. Churches have used the language in other ways as well. Concerning Gregory Thaumaturgos, Basil of Caesarea asks, "Shall we not place among Apostles and Prophets a man who walked by the same Spirit as they?"[63] Theodore Beza regarded John Knox as "a sort of Apostle of the Scots."[64] An early Anabaptist leader sent out others to evangelize as "apostles."[65]

From Francis Asbury's arrival in the United States until his death, the number of Methodists by some estimates grew one thousand times over.[66] Near the end of his life, Asbury warned that the Reformation removed only some of the corruption that had quenched the spirit of the first-century church. The 1784 church conference in which he became the church's leader formed "an apostolic form of Church government."[67] Some, he warned, questioned whether the church of today could, "as in former apostolical days, have such doctrines, such discipline, such convictions, such conversions, such witnesses of sanctification, and such holy men. But I say that we can; I say we must; yea, I say we have."[68] Rejecting "the Catholic doctrine of the historic episcopacy,"

61. Again, I adapt paragraphs from Keener, *Gift & Giver*, 216–18.

62. Pothen, "Missions," 187. Nonbelievers have become open to the gospel especially as they have witnessed healings and other signs (Thollander, *Mathews*, 84, 87–90; Pothen, "Missions," 189–90). One leader in that movement is my (Craig's) friend Finny Philip, an Indian NT scholar who affirms the veracity of the works I have cited here (personal correspondence, August 14, 2008).

63. Basil of Caesarea, *On the Spirit* 29.74 (*NPNF*$^2$, 8:46–47; see McGee, *Miracles*, 5; Doles, *Miracles*, 32; Oliver, *Movements*, 78). The same passage mentions his nature miracles and prophetic gift.

64. Boys, *Evidence*, 214.

65. Hyatt, *Years*, 188.

66. See Noll, *Rise*, 190; less dramatically, see Mullin, *History*, 182–83; Sweeney, *Story*, 64; cf. other early Methodist figures in Bebbington, *Dominance*, 51; Wolffe, *Expansion*, 57–62, 70; Kidd, *Awakening*, 322; cf. also Baptists (eighty times over in seventy-two years, in Kidd and Hankins, *Baptists*, 77). Such figures characterize other periods of revival as well (see the sources cited in Keener, *Acts*, 1:998nn64–66), such as the Korean revival of 1907 (Lee, "Korean Pentecost," 81).

67. Asbury was not a politically driven or financially endowed bishop; he rode thousands of miles a year to serve all the churches, for very small pay, for Christ.

68. From Francis Asbury's valedictory address of 1813, reproduced in "Patriarch Broods."

Asbury sought to return to the New Testament's "true primitive order," "an apostolic order of poverty and itinerancy."[69]

Hudson Taylor, spearheading indigenous mission in the interior of China, certainly did apostolic-type work in the Pauline sense.[70] Likewise, leaders in the Azusa Street Revival and much of early Pentecostalism considered themselves part of an apostolic faith movement. The idea was not that everyone involved was an apostle but that they were restoring New Testament–style Christianity as in "apostolic" times. In that sense, they were continuing the heritage of other restorationist movements, going back to various earlier awakenings and revivals, the Reformation, some earlier monastic movements celebrating "apostolic poverty," and some ideals even of the Renaissance. Today, the E. Stanley Jones School of Mission and Ministry at Asbury Theological Seminary speaks of the church's "apostolic mission."[71] In Taiwan, some regard the Canadian Presbyterian missionary George Leslie Mackay (1844–1901) as "the apostle of Taiwan."[72]

So before we evaluate movements claiming to be apostolic today, it is important to distinguish what various movements and individuals mean by this label. Most churches actually do agree that "apostolic" in some broader sense continues, without suggesting that these ministries rival the *foundational* influence or impact of the first generation of Jesus's followers.

69. Cracknell and White, *Methodism*, 48. Outsiders accused Methodists of "laying claim to almost every apostolic gift" (Oliver, *Reformations*, 120, citing Warburton, *Doctrine of Grace*; Green, *Works*, 123).

70. For his story, see Taylor and Taylor, *Early Years*; Taylor and Taylor, *Secret*.

71. Asbury Seminary, "Jones School." Asbury church planters also speak of "apostolic vision and leadership" at Asbury Seminary, "Equips."

72. Fish, *Road*, 130–32.

# III

# Miracles

Traditionally, cessationism challenged the continuance of miracles. Today, usually it simply challenges continuing *gifts* of miracles and healings. For charismatics, this distinction may sound extremely fine, but this newer position is certainly an improvement over the older, more thoroughgoing cessationism that merits a hardier refutation. But is the supposed biblical foundation for either argument authentic? In chapter 9, we examine the question of miracle-working. In chapter 10, we examine biblical purposes for miracles, which go far beyond the traditional cessationist limitation of their purpose to attesting authors of Scripture. In chapter 11, we respond to some cessationists' challenge that modern miracle claims are not good enough to match the sort of miracles God did when New Testament apostles were alive.

# 9

# Don't Expect a Wonder-Worker

Full cessationists deny that God has done miracles since the completion of the New Testament (see chap. 21).

A strong majority of cessationists today, however, are now continuationist regarding miracles. They allow that God does perform miracles at times. They simply deny that anyone has a gift of miracles (in charismatic terms, this would mean someone through whom God often performs miracles).[1] They usually also deny that miracles are common.[2] See, for example, New Testament scholar Tom Schreiner: "Now that the church has the authoritative guidance for faith and practice in the Scriptures, the gifts and miracles which were needed to build up the early church are no longer needed, and they are not common."[3]

We might think that their distinction between miracles and miracle workers slices the data too thin (as one friend facetiously puts it, slicing the bread so thin that only one side is left),[4] but there is a theological reason for their distinction. Many believe that miracles were tied to the apostles (or Old Testament prophets), and that the end of apostles (and prophets) means the end of God performing miracles through individuals. We have already argued that

1. E.g., Gaffin, "View," 41; MacArthur, *Chaos*, 109, 210; Waldron, *Continued*, 12, 98; Schreiner, *Spiritual Gifts*, 164, 166; Pennington, *Cessationism*, 17.

2. MacArthur, *Chaos*, 210; Schreiner, *Spiritual Gifts*, 166–67. "Common" is, of course, a matter of degree; the New Testament narratives naturally focus on high points on the cutting edge of evangelism, not the everyday experience of "ordinary" disciples.

3. Schreiner, *Spiritual Gifts*, 167. More balanced is his preceding argument (166): Miracles' "primary purpose" (but not necessarily their sole one) "was to accredit divine revelation in Christ." We would argue that signs *still* bear witness to the good news of Christ.

4. We adapt the image, albeit knowingly out of context, from Avner Boskey.

the thesis that apostolic ministry ended is arbitrary, a postbiblical construct serving a theological end. But, for the sake of argument, let's say that apostolic ministry of all sorts ended. Were miracles tied exclusively to apostles?

## Miracles and "Sign Gifts" Merely to Authenticate Apostles?

Since Paul declares that "the signs of a true apostle were performed among you with utmost patience, with signs and wonders and mighty works" (2 Cor. 12:12), some tie them to the apostles in a unique sense. Otherwise anyone could claim to be an apostle, right? The verse itself, however, nowhere claims that miracles were *limited* to apostles, and as we shall see, Scripture is clear that they weren't.

### *Signs Only of Apostles?*

Cessationist teacher Kurt Jurgensmeier says, "It is obvious that Paul's appeal to miracle working is worthless, if in fact, many 'non apostolic' Christians were also performing miracles as super-supernaturalists claim."[5]

John MacArthur argues that "miracles were unique to the apostles, and those who worked most closely with them. The average Christian had no ability to perform signs and wonders."[6] "One never reads in the New Testament about miracles occurring at random among the Christian believers."[7]

With somewhat more careful wording, Tom Pennington writes: "In fact, the one New Testament gift most frequently connected to miracles, the gift of Apostleship, ceased."[8]

In its strictest form, the approach follows B. B. Warfield's example: "The power of working miracles was not extended beyond the disciples upon whom the Apostles conferred it by the imposition of their hands. As the number of these disciples gradually diminished, the instances of the exercise of miraculous powers became continually less frequent and ceased entirely at the death of the last individual on whom the hands of the Apostles had been laid."[9] Their purpose was "distinctively the authentication of the Apostles,"[10] and

5. Jurgensmeier, *Miracle Working*, 39. His "many" might sufficiently qualify the claim (cf. 1 Cor. 12:29).

6. MacArthur, *Chaos*, 120–21.

7. MacArthur, *Chaos*, 121.

8. Pennington, "Case."

9. Warfield, *Counterfeit Miracles*, 22–24, 245n51, cited and critiqued in Ruthven, *Cessation*, 58. Calvin was less rigid (Ruthven, *Cessation*, 22, cites *Inst*. 4.3.4; and Hejzlar, "Calvin and Cessation").

10. Warfield, *Counterfeit Miracles*, 3, 6, cited and critiqued in Ruthven, *Cessation*, 58. Cf. Pennington, *Cessationism*, 92: "The purpose of these gifts was to authenticate the apostles," so they were no longer needed once John finished the book of Revelation.

extraordinary gifts really "belonged, in a true sense to the Apostles."[11] "Their function thus confined them distinctively to the Apostolic Church, and they necessarily passed away with it."[12]

For Waldron, others who had "miraculous gifts" had them because the apostles "imparted" them to them, making gifts obsolete once apostles no longer existed to impart such gifts. He cites 2 Corinthians 12:12, which merely shows that true apostles work signs, not that *only* apostles work signs. He also cites Acts 8:14–20, where the Spirit was conferred when Peter and John laid hands on the Samaritans.[13] Yet God conferred the Spirit without apostolic intervention in Acts 2:4 and 10:44–46, and God conferred the Spirit on the apostle Paul through a *non*-apostle's ministry (Acts 9:17). Meanwhile, there is *no* text that speaks of miraculous gifts in the church (Rom. 12:6; 1 Cor. 12:10, 28–29; 14:24, 31; Gal. 3:5) that mentions them being conferred by apostles! People could seek for "supernatural" gifts without an apostle's presence (1 Cor. 14:1, 39). Timothy did receive a spiritual gift through Paul laying hands on him (2 Tim. 1:6)—though alongside the elders, who also laid hands on him and apparently prophesied to him (1 Tim. 4:14). This cessationist argument, then, is another extrabiblical claim simply designed to support the doctrine!

### *Miracles Just to Confirm Apostles?*

We examine in greater detail the biblical purposes of miracles in chapter 10 but note here the limited purpose many cessationists assign to miracles: "To confirm apostolic authority."[14] MacArthur offers a circular argument to this effect, insisting,

> Apostles were authenticated by miraculous signs.[15]

Then he reasons,

> But God has not placed spokesmen with miracle-working power in the church today.

And his evidence for this?

> Why would God authenticate bad theology? Why would He give miracle power to people who preach heresy?[16]

11. Warfield, *Counterfeit Miracles*, 21, cited and critiqued in Ruthven, *Cessation*, 84.
12. Warfield, *Counterfeit Miracles*, 6.
13. Waldron, *Continued*, 42.
14. MacArthur, *Chaos*, 116, 124.
15. MacArthur, *Chaos*, 124.
16. MacArthur, *Chaos*, 127.

Aside from the question of whether all miracle workers are also supposed to be teachers, and whether all miracle-working spokespeople preach heresy, there is a circularity in MacArthur's argument. Do the miracles authenticate the apostles and their message or do the apostles and their message authenticate the genuineness of the miracles?

### *Only Apostles Did Miracles?*

Any one purpose of biblical miracles need not be their only purpose. While the Bible states other purposes for miracles, however, it *never* states that their purpose (much less their sole or even primary purpose) was to authenticate apostles (much less to authenticate them as the sole authors of Scripture). So how would their death require the end of miracles (for full cessationists) or miracle workers (for more nuanced ones)? As Jack Deere points out, "If God only healed to show that the apostles were trustworthy teachers of doctrine, why didn't he just say that? Why did he let anyone else heal and do miracles? There is not a single unambiguous text teaching that miracles authenticated the apostles."[17]

That apostles worked signs (2 Cor. 12:12) does not mean that signs are limited to the ministries of apostles. In logic, *A* may be a member of set *B* without *A* encompassing all of *B*. (I, Craig, first learned that principle in high school geometry, reinforced in a later homiletics course addressing the difference between ethical and unethical forms of persuasion.) In this case, apostles may be among those through whom God works miracles without their being the only people through whom God may work miracles. All race car drivers must drive cars, but not all who drive cars must be race car drivers.

Signs can also accompany prophets (1 Kings 18:37–38) and evangelists (Acts 8:6–7). And miracles do not necessarily authenticate their workers in any case. Jesus will say to some miracle workers, "I never knew you" (Matt. 7:22; cf. 1 Sam. 19:20–24). False prophets also can often produce signs and wonders (Exod. 7:11, 22; 8:7; Deut. 13:1–2; Matt. 24:24; Mark 13:22; Acts 8:9–11; 13:6; 2 Thess. 2:9; Rev. 13:13). Didn't Judas perform miracles (Luke 9:1)? Miracles attest not apostles but the Lord himself and his gospel. Peter declares that God validated *Jesus* through miracles (Acts 2:22)—not Peter himself (3:12, 16; cf. 14:15). Describing the ministry of the apostles Paul and Barnabas, Luke says that the Lord "testified to the message of his grace" through signs and wonders (Acts 14:3; see also Heb. 2:3–4). Jesus is still Lord, and grace is the message that we still preach.

Paul himself lists apostleship, healing, and miracles as distinct gifts (1 Cor. 12:28). They are not inextricably linked. Christians can perform miracles and still not be apostles (e.g., Ananias in Acts 9:17–18). Paul himself affirms

17. Deere, *Still Surprised*, 284.

that various "normal" church members in Corinth healed, spoke in tongues, prophesied, and performed miracles (1 Cor. 1:7; 12:7–11). Although apostles are among those who work miracles (2 Cor. 12:12), Paul is explicit that the gift remains distinct from apostleship (1 Cor. 12:28–29).

Even Warfield acknowledges this fact: "This does not mean, of course, that only the Apostles appear in the New Testament as working miracles, or that they alone are represented as recipients of the charismata."[18] Yet Warfield continues to argue that miracles were still somehow apostolic by extension, due to the laying on of the apostles' hands. This allows him to exclude all other New Testament evidence as really apostolic and therefore to claim that no New Testament evidence contradicts his claim. Not only is this stretch of Scripture and logic tortuous; it is also simply wrong. The apostles did not lay their hands on the 120 at Pentecost. They did not lay their hands on Cornelius. Warfield acknowledges these facts yet still maintains his extrabiblical theory.[19]

### *Other Explicit Agents of Miracles in the New Testament*

Granted that not every Christian could perform miracles in the narrower sense, performing miracles was clearly not limited to apostles (NIV):[20]

> Mark 9:38–39: "'Teacher,' said John, 'we saw someone driving out demons in your name and we told him to stop, because he was not one of us.' 'Do not stop him,' Jesus said. 'For no one who does a miracle in my name can in the next moment say anything bad about me.'"

> Luke 10:1, 9, 17: "After this the Lord appointed seventy-two others. . . . 'Heal the sick who are there and tell them, "The kingdom of God has come near to you."' . . . The seventy-two returned with joy and said, 'Lord, even the demons submit to us in your name.'"[21]

> Acts 6:8: "Now Stephen, a man full of God's grace and power, performed great wonders and signs among the people."

> Acts 8:6–7: "When the crowds heard Philip and saw the signs he performed, they all paid close attention to what he said. For with shrieks, impure spirits came out of many, and many who were paralyzed or lame were healed."

18. Warfield, *Counterfeit Miracles*, 21.
19. Warfield, *Counterfeit Miracles*, 21–22.
20. See also, e.g., Wilson, *Spirit and Sacrament*, 92–93; Graves and Greig, "Cessationism," 91; Ruthven, "Charismata 3," 164.
21. One may exclude this passage from consideration here if one counts the Seventy-Two (or Seventy) as apostles, which I think likely; but if so, one is already acknowledging that miracle-working apostles extended far beyond the Twelve and Paul.

Nor was it limited in Acts to the seven on whom the apostles laid their hands, such as Stephen and Philip (Acts 6:5–6). Luke's biographic focus is more on a few select figures than on the church as a whole, so Peter and Paul are particularly prominent, but Luke and Paul both recognize the ministries of others. Here is what the New Testament says:

> Acts 9:17 (NIV): "Then Ananias went to the house. . . . Placing his hands on Saul, he said, 'Brother Saul, the Lord—Jesus, who appeared to you on the road as you were coming here—has sent me so that you may see again and be filled with the Holy Spirit.'"
>
> 1 Corinthians 12:7, 9–10 (NASB): "But to each one is given the manifestation of the Spirit for the common good. . . . To another [is given] faith by the same Spirit, and to another gifts of healing by the one Spirit, and to another the effecting of miracles."
>
> 1 Corinthians 12:28 (NASB): "And God has appointed in the church, first apostles, second prophets, third teachers, then miracles, then gifts of healings."
>
> 1 Corinthians 12:29–30 (NASB): "All are not apostles, are they? All are not prophets, are they? All are not teachers, are they? All are not *workers of* miracles, are they? All do not have gifts of healings, do they?"
>
> Galatians 3:5 (NASB): "So then, does He who provides you with the Spirit and works miracles among you, do it by works of the Law, or by hearing with faith?"

The miracles God works among the Galatians in Galatians 3:5 are not said to be through the hands of Paul.[22] Nor is there any hint that Paul was the entire body of Christ in Corinth, constituting by himself all the other members of Christ's body and their gifts (such as healings, miracles, or prophecy) in 1 Corinthians 12:7–10, 28–30. That Luke details key, leading figures in Acts is no surprise, but neither does it suggest that God was using only such key figures. Despite Luke's focus on such key figures, for example, we learn incidentally that many believers were spreading the word (8:4; 11:19). If we draw the net of "extraordinary" (allegedly terminated) gifts more widely, we might add, even in Acts, the 120, Agabus, and others (NASB):

> Acts 2:4: "And they were all filled with the Holy Spirit and began to speak with different tongues, as the Spirit was giving them *the ability* to speak out."
>
> Acts 10:45–46: "All the Jewish believers who came with Peter were amazed, because the gift of the Holy Spirit had also been poured out on the Gentiles. For they were hearing them speaking with tongues and exalting God."

22. See Twelftree, "Ministry and Miraculous," 135. They do indicate concrete manifestations of the Spirit's work (George, "Spirit in Galatians," 164).

Acts 11:28: "One of them, named Agabus, stood up and indicated by the Spirit that there would definitely be a severe famine all over the world. And this took place in the *reign* of Claudius."

Acts 13:1–2: "Now there were prophets and teachers at Antioch, in the church that was *there*. . . . While they were serving the Lord and fasting, the Holy Spirit said, 'Set Barnabas and Saul apart for Me for the work to which I have called them.'"

Acts 19:6: "And when Paul had laid hands upon them, the Holy Spirit came on them and they *began* speaking with tongues and prophesying."

Acts 21:9: "Now this man had four virgin daughters who were prophetesses."

Acts 21:10: "As we were staying there for some days, a prophet named Agabus came down from Judea."

Outside Acts, we may note other individuals such as local church elders (NIV):

1 Timothy 4:14: "Do not neglect your gift, which was given you through prophecy when the body of elders laid their hands on you" (cf. 1 Tim. 1:18).

James 5:14–15: "Is anyone among you sick? Let them call the elders of the church to pray over them and anoint them with oil in the name of the Lord. And the prayer offered in faith will make the sick person well; the Lord will raise them up."

Nor was healing prayer limited to apostles or elders (NIV):

1 Corinthians 12:9: ". . . to another faith by the same Spirit, to another gifts of healing by that one Spirit."

1 Corinthians 12:28: "And God has placed in the church first of all apostles, second prophets, third teachers, then miracles, then gifts of healing, of helping, of guidance, and of different kinds of tongues."

1 Corinthians 12:30: "Do all have gifts of healing? Do all speak in tongues? Do all interpret?"

James 5:16: "Therefore confess your sins to each other and pray for each other so that you may be healed. The prayer of a righteous person is powerful and effective."

If anybody should have been unqualified for spiritual gifts, we would expect it to be the messed-up church in Corinth—yet they flourished in the gifts

(1 Cor. 1:7). The gifts were available for ordinary people.[23] (By "ordinary" in this context, we mean non-apostles. God's sons and daughters are never merely "ordinary"!)

For some cessationists to respond to such evidence by simply denying that it is sufficient[24] is to show themselves impervious in this instance to evidence that contradicts their theory.

## Miracles Confirm Three Parts of Scripture?

### *Only Those on Whom the Apostles Laid Hands?*

As for miracles dying out as those on whom the apostles laid hands died out (Warfield's position), two major problems emerge. First, as even Warfield is aware, the evidence does not all fit his claim. He dismisses as exceptions the Spirit falling at Pentecost and on Cornelius's house, and while Warfield concedes that Paul was healed through Ananias in Acts 9:17, he treats this observation as irrelevant.[25] To sustain his thesis, he further insists that Paul's miraculous power came directly rather than mediated through anyone else[26]—even though Acts mentions that Paul was filled with the Spirit neither directly nor through another apostle laying hands on him but through Ananias laying hands on him![27] Moreover, not only apostles (2 Tim. 1:6) but elders (1 Tim. 4:14) conferred gifts by laying on hands. Warfield simply excludes from ultimate consideration any evidence so rudely inconvenient as to contradict his thesis.

Second, protesting that New Testament historical accounts recount true miracles happening only in the time of the apostles and their successors merely restates the obvious: Historical documents from the first century fail to narrate events that happened after their writing. Excluding the possibility of later events because documents before those events fail to narrate them is simply a way of dismissing all inconvenient evidence! Shall we analogously exclude teaching, singing, or traveling on foot because the New Testament does not narrate their occurrence after the events that it does narrate?

Some cessationists claim that miracles were so rare even in the Bible that they occurred only during three periods totaling roughly two hundred years.[28]

23. Wilson, *Spirit and Sacrament*, 93–94.

24. Gaffin, "Response to Storms and Oss," 292.

25. Warfield, *Counterfeit Miracles*, 22, 245n48.

26. Warfield, *Counterfeit Miracles*, 245n48.

27. See the critique in Ruthven, *Cessation*, 84–85, drawing further on Bruce, "Holy Spirit in Acts," 175.

28. MacArthur, *Chaos*, 112–17; also Pennington, *Cessationism*, 25–31; Pennington, "Case"; cf. also Saucy, "View," 103–4. For periods of revelation, see earlier Warfield, *Counterfeit Miracles*, 25–26.

They narrow this time frame by limiting miracles to just three short time periods—sixty-five to seventy years each. Pennington, for example, summarizes these as follows:

1. The period of Moses and Joshua, which he traces from 1445 through 1380 BC
2. The period of Elijah and Elisha, from about 860 through 795 BC
3. The period of Christ and the apostles

He thus concludes that "there were only three primary periods in which God worked miracles through uniquely gifted men."[29] "In about 4,000 years of Old Testament history, there were only 130 years in which God empowered men to work miracles."[30]

### *Ad Hoc Definitions*

As British New Testament scholar Max Turner remarks, this argument is "demonstrably false."[31] To make the argument work, its proponents have to design such a narrow definition of "miracle" for the purpose that it fails to correspond with normal historic definitions of the term, how the New Testament uses the term translated "miracles" (Mark 9:38–39; cf. 1 Cor. 12:10, 28–29), or most of Jesus's miracles, since the majority are healings (in the OT, cf. Gen. 20:17; 2 Kings 20:4–7; Isa. 38:21), and exorcisms (cf. 1 Sam. 16:23; Zech. 3:2) rather than parting the sea or fire from heaven. Thus MacArthur defines a "miracle" as "an extraordinary event wrought by God through human agency, an event that cannot be explained by natural forces."[32] After noting the common English definition of "miracle," Sam Waldron, like MacArthur, adds to it, "done by a miracle worker."[33] So what about the creation or the flood? These "are not miracles by the definition we have given."[34] Neither does it include Jesus's resurrection, although Jesus calls it a "sign" in Matthew 12:39–40 and John 2:18–19.[35] Although our use of the term "miracle" today often corresponds to biblical "signs," a "sign" in Scripture cannot be limited to MacArthur's narrow definition.[36]

29. Pennington, "Case."
30. Pennington, *Cessationism*, 31.
31. Turner, *Gifts*, 290.
32. MacArthur, *Chaos*, 106.
33. Waldron, *Continued*, 100.
34. MacArthur, *Chaos*, 107.
35. Storms, "View," 188, notes that miracles so defined also exclude the virgin birth and numerous other events we otherwise classify as miraculous.
36. See Deere, *Still Surprised*, 302, noting, e.g., Dan. 6:27; Acts 2:19–20.

The point may be to isolate what could be associated with a *gift* of miracles, even though God may do "signs" through prophetic pronouncements of judgment rather than directly through individuals in other ways (e.g., Exod. 8:21–23; 10:2). Yet even though the cessationist effort is supposedly to remove competition for extrabiblical revelation, the definition also excludes God extraordinarily *speaking* through human agency (i.e., prophecy). Cessationists do so in this case despite some cessationists treating revelation as "miraculous" in a broader sense or speaking of all the allegedly defunct gifts as "miraculous."[37] Otherwise the three periods of revelation would span most of biblical history, undermining what this cessationist argument was designed to prove.

### *Miracles Versus Prophesying?*

Pennington insists that God acted this way in these few time periods because "the primary purpose of miracles has always been to confirm the credentials of a divinely appointed messenger to establish the credibility of one who speaks for God, not one who teaches or explains the Word of God . . . but one in whose mouth God has put His very words."[38]

So if the focus is verifying God's messengers, why did miracles not occur at other major times of prophesying, and particularly in conjunction with the direct authoring of Scripture?

Cessationists who want to exclude miracles and prophecy together elsewhere have to separate these gifts here. It is hard enough to try to fit all miracles into three or four periods, but it is simply impossible to do so for prophecy, so they must define "miracles" much more narrowly here than as "miraculous or revelatory gifts." Yet cessationists who call New Testament prophecy a "miraculous gift" and identify it with Old Testament prophecy cannot consistently restrict "miracles" in the Old Testament nearly so narrowly.[39]

### *Square Pegs and Round Holes: Periods and Canon*

One problem with the argument is that even if miracles could be limited only to several periods, this would merely set a pattern of miracles clustering

37. Warfield, *Counterfeit Miracles*, 5: "miracles of knowledge, whether in the form of prophecy or of the discerning of spirits, miracles of speech, whether of the gift of tongues or of their interpretation." The subtitle of Pennington, *Cessationism*, is "Why the Miraculous Gifts of the Spirit Have Ended"; cf. Pennington, *Cessationism*, 3, 91: "the temporary sign gifts, also known as the miraculous gifts."

38. Pennington, "Case." As Alt, "Cease," 394–95, points out, various Old Testament miracles (Josh. 10:14; Isa. 38) might fit Pennington's definition of "miracle" yet "do not seem to serve the primary purpose of authenticating the prophet." Again, 396: "Pennington is guilty of a category error, arguing for the cessation of validation miracles, when the continuation miracles that charismatics believe in and practice are of a different type and serve a different purpose."

39. Storms, "View," 190.

in certain periods, not preclude such periods from recurring later. Various factors could account for the decline in some periods, whether God's direct purposes or the resistance of his people.[40] But the argument is constructed so that these periods coincide with periods of *canonical* revelation: the Torah, the Prophets, and the New Testament.

This construction has its own problems: For example, Elijah and Elisha (the second miracle cluster) were not writing prophets, and they ministered roughly a century *before* the first major writing prophets, Isaiah, Micah, Amos, and Hosea.[41] Nor can cessationists even claim that Elijah introduced the prophetic era; the New Testament begins the prophetic era with Samuel (Acts 3:24; 13:20; cf. Heb. 11:32).

For the more common three-period model today, miracles from Daniel's day come a couple centuries too late, so these critics arbitrarily exclude them from the schema.[42] And then there is the problem that when the definition of "miracles" is narrowed so as to exclude mere prophesying, the alleged periods of canonical revelation do not cover the much longer periods of delivering prophecies that came to be included in Scripture. In other words, the entire argument is so contrived and requires so much special pleading that any inductive approach to Scripture would require its immediate dismissal.

### *Other Periods of Divine Activity More Broadly*

If we allow for special divine action generally, or for God working through humans prophetically, God continued to act throughout the Old Testament. Granted, this activity was more prominent in some times and places than in others, which is also the case today. But the activity by no means fits conveniently into a narrow range of a few periods.

Deere, a former Old Testament professor (as well as former cessationist), provides an extensive list of more than one hundred "supernatural" phenomena in other periods of the Old Testament.[43] I mention here only a few of the nonprophetic examples:

- The plague afflicts Pharaoh's house (Gen. 12:17).
- Angels blind Sodom's men (Gen. 19:11).
- God heals Abimelech's household through Abraham's prayers (Gen. 20:17).

40. Storms, "View," 187, cites Pss. 74:9–11; 77:7–14; Mark 6:5. Cf. also Isa. 29:10; 30:10. A true prophet could also exist at the same time that false prophets flourished (Jer. 23:28).

41. Deere, *Still Surprised*, 290. See also Deere, "Periods."

42. Warfield guarded against this criticism by having four periods, one during Daniel's day (Ruthven, *Cessation*, 59). The weakness of this argument is that it does not correspond as well to periods of distinct revelation; Jeremiah and Ezekiel were already prophesying before much of Daniel's ministry (Dan. 9:2).

43. Deere, *Still Surprised*, 293–98.

- Sarah conceives Isaac (Gen. 21:1–8).
- God answers Isaac's prayer for Rebekah to bear a child (Gen. 25:21).
- Gideon's fleece is a sign (Judg. 6:36–40).
- Glory fills the temple (1 Kings 8:10–13).
- God withers and, through the prophet's prayer, heals Jeroboam's hand (1 Kings 13:1–6).
- God adds years to Hezekiah's life and heals him through Isaiah (2 Kings 20:5–6; Isa. 38:21).
- Sunlight goes back ten steps (2 Kings 20:10–11).
- Fire falls on Solomon's sacrifice (2 Chron. 7:1).
- God delivers Daniel's three friends in the fiery furnace (Dan. 3:25–27).
- God protects Daniel in the lions' den (Dan. 6:22).

Perhaps a detractor could protest that only healings through individuals count. Such did in fact occur, and they did so outside the three eras that these cessationists prescribe: through Abraham (Gen. 20:17), Isaac (25:21), an anonymous prophet (1 Kings 13:6), or Isaiah (2 Kings 20:5–6; Isa. 38:21). But then the detractor might choose to eliminate those exceptions by arguing that these cases resulted from prayer rather than a direct command. Yet that elimination would require correspondingly excluding cases where people received the Spirit through apostles' prayers (Acts 8:15) or Paul prayed for Publius's father's healing (28:8). It also renders more challenging "miracle" passages that combine prayer with command (Josh. 10:12–14; 1 Kings 18:36–38; Mark 11:23–24; Acts 9:40). That is, by always narrowing criteria a bit further, or dismissing counterexamples as mere exceptions, one can always achieve one's desired outcome. By narrowing criteria sufficiently, one could exclude any miracles in the Bible from counting. One may pursue this method, however, only at the expense of interpretive consistency.

It is appropriate to note the ebb and flow of miracles through history.[44] Some of us can sympathize with those who recognize God's past works (Ps. 22:5) while wondering whether we are somehow different (22:6; God does deliver—22:22–31). In the period of the judges, there was no Genesis 22–type intervention for Jephthah's daughter (Judg. 11:35–39), nor Genesis 19–type intervention for the Levite's concubine (Judg. 19:22–28). It is not without reason that Gideon wonders where all the miracles of the exodus are (Judg. 6:13)—although he utters this objection during what turns out to be an angelic revelation! Indeed, God gives Gideon a great victory, but without any pillar of fire or parted waters. Even the remarkable return from Babylon lacked the signs of the first exodus. The magnitude of miracles varied, but they do not

44. See, e.g., 1 Sam. 3:1. For the language of "ebbed and flowed," see also Oliver, *Movements*, xxv; Oliver, *Revivals*, 285.

correspond to periods of giving Scripture, as if this was their sole or even primary function. Finding precedent in God's earlier work (Pss. 44:1–3; 77:5–6, 11–20) enables trust (44:4–8, 26; 77:7–9) and protest when the current state of affairs seems comparatively deficient (44:9–25; 77:10). Lack of prophets can reflect a setting of judgment (Ps. 74:9; Isa. 29:10) or rejection of God's truth (Isa. 30:10; Jer. 11:21; Amos 2:11–12; 7:16) rather than always God's ideal plan. Lamenting the current dearth of miracles in contrast to the past expressed yearning for a *renewal* of God's actions (e.g., Pss. 74:9; 77:10–11), not a denial that they could ever recur.

### *Why Such a Narrow Definition?*

If one can produce sufficiently narrow definitions, one can achieve whatever predetermined outcomes one wishes. This is a sort of theological sleight of hand. Let's say you have a database containing the personal profiles of hundreds of thousands of people. And maybe you want to isolate a select group, say, many of the men going through a midlife crisis. With the right data, you could perform a query and narrow the constraints to all middle-aged men who have worked the same job for twenty years or more and have recently purchased a red sports car. By narrowing the criteria of your search sufficiently, you can force the system to produce your desired outcome. This is essentially what this argument does with Scripture.

One might compare some ancient rabbis, who insisted that God does not speak outside the Holy Land. What happened when God spoke to Ezekiel in Babylonia? That was in a pure place near water.[45] So what happened when God gave the Torah not in the Holy Land nor near water but on a mountain in the Sinai desert? The Torah had to be given where no one already lived, so no other nation could claim it.[46] If you limit the evidence sufficiently and define away the exceptions, you can support almost any thesis.

This "rare miracle" argument has taken the entire body of supernatural phenomena in Scripture, narrowed the search constraints to "miracle workers" and then further limited the criteria to a specific, subjective definition of "miracle": It applies only to people like Moses and Elijah who parted the sea and called fire down from heaven. Note Pennington: "Although God directly performed miracles during the ministries of several prophets (e.g., Samuel, David, Isaiah, and Daniel), there is no biblical evidence that warrants labeling those men as miracle-working prophets like Moses and Elijah."[47] That other evidence doesn't count. So long as one creates a sieve designed to exclude inconvenient examples, such events were indeed rare. Therefore, the

45. *Mek. Pisḥa* 1.63–64 (in Lauterbach, *Mekhilta*, 1:6).

46. *Mek. Baḥodesh* 5.97–98 (in Lauterbach, *Mekhilta*, 2:236–37).

47. Pennington, *Cessationism*, 26. MacArthur, *Chaos*, 109, cites esp. Moses, Elijah, and Jesus.

search concludes that a nonmiraculous environment is the biblical norm and cessationism represents a biblical position.

But all this would enable us to conclude is that miracles on the dramatic level of Moses and Elijah have ceased—since the existence of too many other miracles has forced this "rare miracle" argument to redefine miracles that narrowly. This argument conveniently leaves out the vast—indeed overwhelming—amount of biblical information that disproves its position. What about the patriarchs' dreams and visions or the matriarchs' miraculous healings to have children (potentially related to faith—Gen. 25:21; Rom. 4:19; Heb. 11:11)? What about the supernatural empowerment of judges like Samson or Gideon? What about the manifestations of God's glory, angelic appearances, and theophanies (God's physical appearance to people) throughout the Old Testament? And what about the prophets? What about their words, dreams, interpretations, visions, revelations, trances, and various other supernatural experiences? Aren't these events throughout Scripture relevant to the debate at hand?

As it pertains to revelatory miracles (like prophecy, dreams, and visions) we would argue that they are at least as relevant as calling fire from heaven or parting the sea—if not, in some cases, more relevant. For these are the very signs Joel said would increase in the "last days" (Joel 2:28). You may remember that Richard Gaffin said, "My main concern is the cessation of all revelatory or word gifts" (which he specifies as prophecy, tongues, interpretation of tongues, words of wisdom, and word of knowledge).[48]

But if these "word gifts" specifically represent the main point of contention, it seems all the more disingenuous that cessationists who use this argument have omitted from their discussion all the examples of "word gifts" in the Old Testament with their arbitrary constraints. In other words, these cessationists do not treat the "word gifts" as real miracles in the Old Testament, yet these are the main gifts that are supposed to be rejected as such in the New? This certainly looks like a sleight-of-hand argument.

This argument might help you understand what Jesus himself experienced. He had provided more than enough signs to prove his messianic identity (Matt. 11:2–6). In fact, in one instance, after Jesus healed a demonized man who could neither hear nor speak, the crowds responded with amazement and wondered aloud whether Jesus was the Messiah (Matt. 12:22–23). But the Pharisees could not accept their conclusion. Their minds were already made up; Jesus could not be the Messiah. Yet Jesus was performing such great miracles (like the one the crowd had just witnessed). What could they do? Exactly what cesssationists do. They narrowed their constraints for "authentic messianic signs" to align with their predetermined conclusion—constraints, of course, that excluded the signs Jesus performed.

48. Gaffin, "View," 42. Schreiner, *Spiritual Gifts*, 164, likewise, deems "miracles and healings" less relevant to cessationism "since there are no claims to new revelation."

The Pharisees' responses betrayed such fixed results. First, in the face of a clear miracle, they blamed Jesus for using satanic power (Matt. 12:24). Then, after Jesus denounced such foolish and rebellious thinking (Matt. 12:25–37), they simply requested another sign from Jesus (12:38)! In other words, Jesus's signs did not meet their criteria. So they demanded a sign that did—a sign "from heaven" (Matt. 16:1; Mark 8:11; Luke 11:16). Ironically, the reference to "heaven" may refer to signs like calling fire from heaven or parting the sea—the same signs some cessationists use to limit their own tests.[49]

### Other Problems with the "Rare Miracle" Hypothesis

This "rare miracle" argument fails on several other points as well.

First, cessationists claim that the purpose of miracles is to "confirm the credentials of a divinely appointed messenger to establish the credibility of one who speaks for God." But weren't Joel, Amos, Micah, and Obadiah divinely appointed messengers? Where are their "miracles"? What's more, John the Baptist—the last prophet under the old covenant, the greatest man born of women and the one who announced the arrival of the Lord himself—"performed no sign" (John 10:41).[50] Pennington replies that though "many true prophets never perform a miracle, . . . only true prophets . . . did perform miracles."[51]

So how closely tied are miracles really to canonical prophecy? Scripture does not call Joshua a prophet, yet the sun stood still when he commanded it, and "there was no day like that before it or after it, when the LORD listened to the voice of a man; for the LORD fought for Israel" (Josh. 10:14 NASB). But perhaps there is some other reason why this does not count, such as that, say, his lifetime overlaps with that of Moses. But neither is Samson's nonprophetic gift of strength allowed to count (Judg. 13–16).[52]

Conversely, if the point is attesting the canon of the prophets, why tie this uniquely to the messages of Elijah and Elisha, who didn't compose Scripture? Why not the prophets *who authored major portions of our Bibles*? Further, even in the case of the special miracle workers mentioned—like Moses, Elijah, and Elisha—what makes Pennington believe that their miracles were exclusively intended to confirm their credentials? And if only the most dramatic miracles in the Old Testament count, should we limit the gift of miracle

49. For seeking a celestial portent, see, e.g., Plummer, *Matthew*, 221; Davies and Allison, *Matthew*, 2:580; Schnabel, *Mark*, 182; Gibson, "Refusal," 45. Alternatively and somewhat less likely, it might be a circumlocution for a sign "from God" (e.g., Marcus, *Mark 1–8*, 499; Stein, *Mark*, 375).

50. Also Ruthven, *Cessation*, 184.

51. Pennington, *Cessationism*, 41.

52. We might mention healing through Abraham (Gen. 20:17) and partial exorcism through David (1 Sam. 16:23), but they were in some sense prophets (Gen. 20:7: Acts 2:30).

working in 1 Corinthians 12:28–29 to calling down fire from heaven or parting bodies of water? Even though Jesus includes, say, exorcism as a miracle (Mark 9:38–39), and makes available mountain-moving to anyone gifted with such faith (11:22–24)?[53]

Undoubtedly, miracles did confirm the "credentials" of true prophets who worked them. Yet many of their miracles had benefits that went beyond mere confirmation. When Elijah miraculously sustained the little flour and oil for the widow of Zarephath, or then raised her son from the dead, were these intended *only* to confirm his credentials as a prophet (and thereby simply the canonical status of prophets who authored much later books)? When Elisha made the axe head float or purified the deadly pottage, was it merely to confirm his credentials? What about the benefit to people's health and families? Are these lucky coincidences? And if God sometimes used his servants to help people in such ways then, why not today?

Finally, unless we accept its narrow definition, this "rare miracle" theory explicitly contradicts Scripture. Jeremiah 32:20 says, "You performed signs and wonders in Egypt and have continued them to this day, in Israel and among all mankind, and have gained the renown that is still yours" (NIV).[54] Scripture itself is clear that it does not report every miracle that happened (John 21:25). It covers only particular events and persons, and so presumably offers a mere sampling.[55] Based on the passages above, we can be sure that miracles and revelations took place far more widely than the three-periods hypothesis proposes.

It appears that the "rare miracle" hypothesis fails on every one of its own points:

1. God performed many miracles outside of the theory's specific time periods.
2. Miracles were not exclusive to prophets.
3. Miracles often had no connection to any special message.
4. Many who were special messengers speaking for God did not in fact "work miracles" (by the cessationist definition for the sake of this argument).
5. The "rare miracle" theory explicitly contradicts the plain text of Scripture (e.g., Jer. 32:20).

53. Note "whoever" in 11:23. On the hyperbolic character of mountain-moving (though not the "whoever"), see further Keener, "Casting Mountains."

54. MacArthur, *Chaos*, 113n19, dismisses this interpretation; Deere, *Still Surprised*, 291–92n2, responds as to why it should be taken literally.

55. One may also read Heb. 1:1 as saying that God spoke through the prophets at many *times* (if one renders the term with the NIV, ESV, KJV, NJB, WEB, though the Greek text could simply refer to many *passages*, as in the ASV, NASB, NET).

It is true that the ministries of Elijah and Elisha looked different from those of Jeremiah and Isaiah. But there is no need to read a doctrine into this distinctiveness that Scripture does not indicate. In reality, all of the prophets' ministries were supernatural. They all received revelatory knowledge and words. God worked directly through them all. That is the point. God is always working, speaking, and moving in supernatural ways among people. It has always been his nature and always will be.

But even if this "rare miracle" theory stood up to scrutiny, it still would not mean that miracles should be rare *today*. According to Joel, we are living in the last days in which the Spirit of God is being poured out on all who believe. These are the days when sons and daughters will prophesy, young men will see visions, and old men will dream dreams. Jesus declared the breaking in of God's kingdom accompanied by signs, wonders, and miracles—and he never withdrew that declaration! There is no biblical indication that there would be some days within the "last days" when the Spirit who had been poured out on all flesh would be withdrawn again. There is no biblical indication that the last days would ultimately descend into a time of no miraculous activity (or no special divine activity through God's children) at all.

A theory based on deductions, especially weak ones, should never trump explicit statements of fact and direct commands of Scripture (such as 1 Cor. 14:1, 39). The only thing that should eclipse those direct orders is another direct order. And in all of Scripture, there is none!

## Decline Even Within the New Testament?

MacArthur opines that "the last recorded miracles in the New Testament occurred around AD 58, with the healings on the island of Malta (Acts 28:7–10)." From then until Revelation, the New Testament records no more miracles. "Two later epistles, Ephesians and Romans, both discuss gifts of the Spirit at length—but no mention is made of the miraculous gifts."[56]

Aside from the fact that Paul authored Romans well *before* his time on Malta,[57] MacArthur's division is arbitrary here, since he also wants to limit prophecy and certainly apostles, one or both of which do appear in these letters (NASB):

> Romans 12:6: "However, since we have gifts that differ according to the grace given to us, *each of us is to use them properly*: if prophecy, in proportion to *one's* faith."

56. MacArthur, *Chaos*, 231.

57. Why would Paul send Romans via Phoebe, who lived in one of Corinth's port towns (Rom. 16:1–2), while he himself was on Malta or further along an itinerary to Rome? Perhaps MacArthur means that Romans was written later than 1 Corinthians, which mentions gifts of miracles, but clearly miracles were occurring later than Paul's letter to the Romans.

Ephesians 4:11: "And He gave some *as* apostles, some *as* prophets, some *as* evangelists, some *as* pastors and teachers."

MacArthur's argument is essentially a tautology that proves nothing here. It is like saying, since miracles occur only in narrative at the end of our latest book that might narrate them, they must have stopped occurring after that book concludes its narrative. Should we suppose that conversions stopped after Acts 28 because Acts stopped narrating them then? Again, this hermeneutic, applied consistently, would render all biblical narrative useless for teaching (in contradiction to 2 Tim. 3:16–17).

"Nothing is said about miraculous gifts in any of the later epistles of Paul," MacArthur admonishes. "Nor does he bring up the subject in any of his pastoral epistles."[58] Paul does not mention the Lord's Supper after 1 Corinthians; perhaps we should suppose that God discontinued it? Neither does Paul explicitly mention "justification" by faith in the Pastoral Epistles; perhaps God was now inaugurating a new and different approach to salvation? And if date matters so much, why exclude prophesying and visions in Revelation, probably the last New Testament book written?[59] (And if one objects that John could still prophesy only because he was an apostle, why should we assume that Paul as an apostle had lost his healing gift?)

Miracle reports are indeed less frequent in the final quarter of Acts, but this is because Paul spends most of that time in custody. When he has opportunity on the island of Malta, however, he suffers a snakebite unharmed (Acts 28:5), resumes his healing ministry (28:8), and then "the rest of the people on the island who had diseases were coming to him and being cured" (28:9 NASB). Occasionally someone cites Luke's use of the Greek verb *therapeuō* to suggest that these cures were accomplished medically through Luke the physician, though he does not mention his activity here. But this argument is specious: In the vast majority of other occurrences, Luke elsewhere uses this Greek term for "cured" (*therapeuō*) for special divine action through Jesus (Luke 4:40; 5:15; 6:18; 7:21; 8:2; 9:1, 6; 13:14; 14:3) or his agents (10:9; Acts 4:14; 5:16; 8:7).[60] Acts concludes twenty-one verses later.

Particularly tautological is Pennington's argument that "the New Testament records only one brief time period during which God granted men miracle-working power: the time of Jesus and His apostles."[61] And what other time period should the New Testament record than that of Jesus and his apostles—particularly if one believes that the canon closed with the last apostle's death?

58. MacArthur, "Foreword," iv.
59. With Alt, "Cease," 403.
60. Cf. Keener, *Acts*, 4:3692.
61. Pennington, *Cessationism*, 49.

Other cessationist arguments here are no stronger. Jon Ruthven aptly critiques the argument "that because 'Jews seek signs and Greeks seek wisdom' (1 Cor. 1:22), . . . Christian evangelism moved from an evangelism characterized by miracles to one characterized by reasoned discourse (and remained there for the rest of church history)." Signs were never limited to Jewish audiences. Scripture is clear that Paul's ministry among gentiles included massive signs (Acts 15:12; Rom. 15:19; 2 Cor. 12:12; cf. 1 Cor. 2:4–5; 1 Thess. 1:5).[62]

## A "Gift" of Miracles

The *charisma*, or grace-gift, of miracles appears in 1 Corinthians 12:10, 28, 29. In 12:10, it is called "workings" or "operations" of miracles; the plural might indicate that each one is a special grace, or that there are varied "specialist" gifts of miracles (cf. the plural "gifts of healings," "discernments of spirits"), or perhaps it merely reflects stylistic variation. In 12:28–29, it is abbreviated as simply "miracles."

The term translated "miracles" itself means simply "powers" or "expressions of power." The New Testament nowhere defines the term, but elsewhere in the New Testament it includes exorcism (Mark 9:39; cf. 6:13–14; Acts 8:7, 13; 19:11–12) without being limited to it (Matt. 7:22). It apparently includes healings as well (Mark 6:5; cf. 6:13–14; Acts 8:7, 13; 19:11–12). It seems roughly equivalent to "signs" and "wonders," with which it is often paired (Acts 2:22; 8:13; 2 Cor. 12:12; Heb. 2:4), so it might refer to something more visibly dramatic than gradual or invisible forms of healing (cf. Mark 6:5).

Although the debate is often framed as regarding "miracle workers," the primary debate involves those with a *gift* of miracles—that is, *God* sometimes performs miracles through them. Like all grace-gifts, working of miracles is God's activity through his agents. God is the one who works miracles or signs among us (Exod. 10:1–2; 34:10; Num. 14:11, 22; 2 Kings 20:9; Neh. 9:10; Ps. 78:12, 43; Isa. 38:7; Dan. 6:27; Gal. 3:5; Heb. 2:4), including through apostles (Acts 14:3; 19:11; cf. the divine passive in 2 Cor. 12:12). Jesus does miracles or signs (Matt. 13:58; John 6:2, 14; 12:18, 37; 20:30; cf. Mark 6:2; Luke 23:8) with God the Father working through him (Acts 2:22).

But the language is fluid enough to allow us to speak more generically of some people performing God's miracles or signs, with the understanding that it is really God who does so. Some might perform miracles in Jesus's name (Matt. 7:22; Mark 9:39). Agents of God's miracles include Moses and Aaron (Exod. 4:17, 21, 30; 11:10; Deut. 34:11; Ps. 105:26–27; Acts 7:36), Stephen (Acts 6:8), and Philip (Acts 8:6). We also read of evil miracle workers (Rev. 13:13;

62. Ruthven, *Cessation*, 184–85. For the argument for miracles in 1 Thess. 1:5, see, e.g., George, "Spirit in Thessalonians," 187.

19:20) and demons (16:14) that perform signs by God's permission (13:14). We should note (especially in view of Stephen and Philip) that the language is not limited to apostles.

If miracles still happen today, we have no reason to exclude them from sometimes happening when people pray for them or, moved by the Spirit, command them (Mark 11:23, not limited to apostles; see discussion in the next section). God often worked this way in Scripture to confirm that it was himself acting rather than a random freak of nature. Again, without explicit biblical evidence to the contrary, we should allow that God still works at times according to the patterns we see in Scripture—where he often performed miracles in conjunction with the action of his servants, more often associated with some people than with others. As these events dominated in settings of groundbreaking advances for the kingdom in Scripture, we might expect them to be more common in such settings today. It should therefore be no surprise that we *do* in fact see this in many such cases today.

## Promises for All Believers

Aside from narrative examples, we also have promises that, on the surface, should apply to all believers. Consistency requires this, except for those who consistently relegate all Jesus's instructions in the Gospels to a now-past era.

We mentioned John 14:12 in chapter 3. But Jesus also gives other wide-ranging promises regarding prayer in the Gospels (e.g., Matt. 7:7–11; Mark 11:24; John 14:13–14; 15:7, 16; 16:23–26; cf. also James 5:16b–18). Here we note especially Mark 11:22–24: "Keep trusting God. I assure you firmly: Whoever says to this mountain, 'Be snatched up and hurled into the sea,' and does not question inside but instead trusts that what they declare happens, it will happen for them. Therefore, I tell you: All the things you pray and ask for, trust that you've been granted them, and they'll be yours." Although Mark's Gospel elsewhere qualifies the promise here (note especially 10:38; 11:22), it nevertheless involves a range of answers to prayer (11:24) and some authorization to command (11:23). Such confidence may come with divine leading rather than personal desires. But we should not use some people's abuse of such sayings to ignore what Jesus explicitly says.

The occasion is the recognition that Jesus's mere words cursed a fig tree (11:12–14, 20); in response to Peter marveling (11:21), Jesus encourages his disciples that they, in dependence on God (11:22, 25), could also speak authoritatively, not to a mere fig tree but even to (speaking hyperbolically) a mountain (11:23). This promise is not limited to apostles; it is explicitly for "whoever" (11:23), no less than is the instruction for forgiveness that follows (11:25). Soon after this, Jerusalem's elite, angry about Jesus's action in the temple (11:15–18), question his authority (11:27–33)—a question that will appear absurd to those privy to Jesus's authority over spirits (1:27), forgiveness (2:10), wind (4:39–41), donkeys (11:7),[63] and, most recently, a fig tree (11:13–14). Jesus explicitly granted authority to cast out demons to the Twelve in 3:15; 6:7. Surely the authority to cast out mountains, addressed here to "whoever," is no less than this.[64]

## History of Cessationist Argument Regarding Miracles

Ruthven's PhD dissertation at Marquette University was a survey and critique of the historical cessationist argument against miracles, focused especially on Warfield's polemic. (We revisit Warfield's approach in more detail in chap. 21.) We follow here Ruthven's treatment of the subject.

In the second and third centuries, Christians used miracles and prophecy polemically to show the Jewish community that God had transferred the prophetic Spirit of God from Israel to the church.[65] This argument presupposes that Christians continued to exercise these gifts. The polemic developed (in an unfortunately more supersessionist direction) the approach of the New Testament, which drew from Christians' experience of the Spirit the logical corollary that God was with Jesus's movement (e.g., Acts 2:33), an approach maintained by continuationists today. Early apologists also used miracles to counter heretical sects; around AD 180, Irenaeus points out that mainstream Christians, in contrast to gnostics, continue to experience miracle working.[66]

Centuries later, the Roman church, with a long history of miracle claims, unfortunately turned this polemic against the emerging Protestant movement, which was mostly led by scholars rather than miracle workers (although the categories are not intrinsically mutually exclusive; Acts 19:9–12).[67] Catholic apologists argued that miracles accredited true—namely, Roman Catholic—doctrine. Further unfortunately, Protestants responded roughly in kind, yet without miracle claims to cite. Protestants had not been around very long, so they did not have a whole history of miracle claims to which they could appeal. Making a virtue of necessity, John Calvin insisted that miracles accredit

63. For the extraordinary character of being able to ride an unbroken (Mark 11:2) colt, see Keener, "Colt."

64. See the full argument (including in dialogue with other interpretations) in Keener, "Casting Mountains." On the passage, see in detail Dowd, *Prayer*. Regarding the passage's warning against doubt, the only way I (Craig) know how to avoid doubt entirely is to have a full inner conviction, driven by the Holy Spirit, that God will answer in a given case, though that is no reason to restrict prayer to such occasions. (Given the usual meaning of the Greek word, however, I am not certain that "doubt" is the correct translation; see again my article.)

65. Ruthven, *Cessation*, 11, cites, e.g., Justin, *Dial.* 82 (*ANF*, 1:240); 87 (*ANF*, 1:244); Origen, *Cels.* 2.8; 7.8 (*ANF*, 4:614); *Comm. Matt.* 14.19 (*ANF*, 9:508).

66. Irenaeus, *Haer.* 2.32.4–5.

67. Cf. Keener, "Teaching Ministry."

apostles in order to accredit their writings.[68] And since the Reformers had Scripture, they had the prophetic and apostolic message that true miracles accredit, and thus, he contended, most Catholic miracles did not count anyway. (Given all the spurious relics floating around medieval Europe, the Protestant rejoinder did help motivate the Catholic Counter-Reformation to test miracle claims more strenuously.)

Calvin was not as dogmatic as some of his subsequent followers.[69] He did not delve into extensive biblical argumentation against continuing miracles but developed existing theological tradition from Aquinas, which belonged to his adversaries' arsenal.[70] His interest was apologetic, countering Catholic attacks and also explaining the biblically curious paucity of miracles among the current chosen.[71]

Cessationism has often served such a valuable apologetic purpose since the Enlightenment as well; it has given Christian academics a handy answer to skeptics who charge, "If miracles are real, then where are your miracles today?" Unfortunately, it also has long inhibited the welcome and recognition of genuine miracles, contrary to its original apologetic function. Rightly concerned not to marginalize the sick, it has sometimes marginalized those who testify of miracles. Thus one friend in the Philippines was initially reticent to share her story at all because she had encountered others' extreme skepticism. After being healed from liver cancer and resuscitated after over an hour in the morgue, she was thrown out of her Baptist church for testifying about it![72] Apologetics are necessary but need to be updated as the culture's questions shift. Some apologetic teaching, being responsive, may also argue from experience, and a traditional argument from lack of miracles also would have exemplified such an argument (see part V, below).

Calvin's teaching, reinforced and further fortified during the Enlightenment, became a dominant line of Reformed tradition inherited by the Princeton scholar Warfield: Miracles accredit true doctrine and Scripture, and therefore they long ago served their entire function.[73] As Ruthven complains, Warfield embraces "an exclusively evidentialist purpose for miracles

68. Ruthven, *Cessation*, 22.

69. Ruthven, *Cessation*, 22n53, notes Calvin's concessions regarding miraculous or revelatory gifts: the category "either does not exist today or is less commonly seen" (citing *Inst.* 4.3.4, p. 1057). "Apostles, prophets or evangelists, he says, are not ordinary offices in the church today, but the Lord 'now and again revives as the need of the times demands'" (citing p. 1056; Hejzlar, "Calvin and Cessation").

70. Ruthven, *Cessation*, 24; on Aquinas, cf. 20.

71. For Calvin's apologetic context, see, e.g., Boys, *Evidence*, 107–10; for that of the Reformers generally, 111–14.

72. I (Craig) recount her story in Keener, *Miracles*, 1:569–70.

73. Warfield's Princeton teacher, Charles Hodge, associated the *necessity* of miracles only with the apostles but allowed that they could continue at times afterward (Ruthven, *Cessation*, 84n187, citing Hodge, *Systematic Theology*, 3:452).

(his designation of certain gifts of the Holy Spirit). Accordingly, the function of biblical miracles determine their duration: if their sole purpose is to accredit the initial presentation of New Testament doctrine, then they must perforce cease when the doctrine is established."[74] Because Warfield tied miracles so exclusively to apostles and the giving of the canon, he insisted that "had any miracles perchance occurred beyond the Apostolic age they would be without significance; mere occurrences with no universal meaning."[75]

Yet cessationism offers no real reason that miracles (full cessationism) or even miracle working (classical cessationism) would need to stop unless their function was *exclusively* to confirm apostles and thereby the canon.[76] When Deere was questioning his cessationism inherited from Warfield, he decided to search Scripture carefully and determine the biblical purpose(s) of miracles. His conclusion resonates with what we have already seen:

> If the primary purpose of miracles was to authenticate the apostles, why did God let so many other people do miracles? . . . Only three of the original twelve apostles wrote Scripture, and almost half of the New Testament was written by people who were not apostles and have no recorded miracles. If apostolic miracles confirmed Scripture, this would mean that almost one half of the New Testament is unconfirmed and therefore inferior to the part written by the apostles. Miracles do not authenticate the Bible. . . . The Scriptures list ten to twelve purposes of miracles, none of which have anything to do with authenticating Scripture.[77]

## Conclusion

That not all writers of Scripture or prophets had signs shows that God did not depend on signs to authenticate Scripture. More important, God often performed miracles through non-apostles and certainly nonwriters of Scripture. That false prophets existed with false signs shows that signs by themselves do not guarantee that anyone is an apostle or prophet. And Scripture is clear that prophecy (though not Scripture writing) continues as a key sign of the last days (Acts 2:17), which surely did not end at Pentecost.

So in the next chapter, let's look at what Scripture provides as the actual *biblical* purposes for miracles.

74. Ruthven, *Cessation*, 44–45.
75. Warfield, *Counterfeit Miracles*, 27–28.
76. Cf. Wilson, *Spirit and Sacrament*, 112–13.
77. Deere, *Still Surprised*, 99. He argues that Scripture is self-authenticating without miracles, citing Westminster Confession 1.4. Brown, "Miracles and Kingdom," 32, cites seven purposes.

# 10

# Purposes for Miracles

Those who follow B. B. Warfield's full cessationism associate miracles exclusively with canonical revelation. Most cessationists today recognize that God continues to perform miracles, so they associate them only *primarily* with the canon. But let's examine their purposes according to canonical revelation itself.

## Some Biblical Reasons for Miracles

Some of the following purposes for miracles overlap, but it is noteworthy that none of them is limited to the beginning of the church.[1] While their accreditation of the gospel message provides us good reason by analogy to respect the Scriptures written by many agents of that message, the Bible does not directly specify accrediting Scripture as a purpose for miracles. It appears again that cessationism is not only a postbiblical idea but an idea that depends on our acceptance of a number of other postbiblical ideas. In the name of honoring Scripture, full cessationism fails to observe what Scripture actually teaches.

1. Here following esp. Deere, *Still Surprised*, 106–15, 281–82; Brown, "Miracles and Kingdom," 32; Turner, *Gifts*, 291; cf. already Dale, "Healing," 108–9. Two of Deere's other reasons include pedagogic miracles (*Still Surprised*, 279–80, citing, e.g., Mark 11:12–25); miracles to bring repentance and salvation (280–81, citing Luke 5:8; Acts 8:6; 9:35, 42; this overlaps with our category of drawing attention to the gospel).

### *1. God Acts from Compassion*

The Lord has *compassion* on people's needs. Tom Pennington agrees that many miracles display God's compassion, but he denies that this was "the chief reason for Jesus's miracles."[2] Whether the "chief" reason or not, it was certainly a *real* reason, which is the question at hand. If compassion was a real reason then, and God's compassion continues rather than having ceased, it can remain a real reason now. The following examples illustrate this point (here using the NIV):

> Genesis 19:16: "When he hesitated, the men grasped his hand and the hands of his wife and of his two daughters and led them safely out of the city, for the LORD was merciful [cf. NASB, NET: "compassion"] to them."
>
> Exodus 3:7–8: "The LORD said, 'I have indeed seen the misery of my people in Egypt. I have heard them crying out because of their slave drivers, and I am concerned about their suffering. So I have come down to rescue them from the hand of the Egyptians and to bring them up out of that land into a good and spacious land, a land flowing with milk and honey.'"
>
> Matthew 14:14: "When Jesus landed and saw a large crowd, he had compassion on them and healed their sick."
>
> Matthew 15:32: "Jesus called his disciples to him and said, 'I have compassion for these people; they have already been with me three days and have nothing to eat. I do not want to send them away hungry, or they may collapse on the way.'"
>
> Matthew 20:34: "Jesus had compassion on them and touched their eyes. Immediately they received their sight and followed him."
>
> Mark 8:2, 7–8: "'I have compassion for these people; they have already been with me three days and have nothing to eat.' . . . He gave thanks for them also and told the disciples to distribute them. The people ate and were satisfied."
>
> Luke 7:13–15: "When the Lord saw her, his heart went out to her and he said, 'Don't cry.' Then he went up and touched the bier they were carrying him on, and the bearers stood still. He said, 'Young man, I say to you, get up!' The dead man sat up and began to talk, and Jesus gave him back to his mother."

Depending on the textual variant, one might also add Mark 1:41 (NASB):

> Mark 1:41: "Moved with compassion, *Jesus* reached out with His hand and touched him, and said to him, 'I am willing; be cleansed.'"

2. Pennington, *Cessationism*, 54.

When God does not heal, in the Bible or today, it does not mean that God lacks compassion. But the Bible is clear that when he does heal, this healing often reflects his compassion.

### 2. God Acts for His Honor[3]

God heals and does other acts for his glory, as the following examples may illustrate (here using ESV):

> Exodus 9:16: "But for this purpose I have raised you up, to show you my power, so that my name may be proclaimed in all the earth."

> Exodus 14:4, 17–18: "And I will harden Pharaoh's heart, and he will pursue them, and I will get glory over Pharaoh and all his host, and the Egyptians shall know that I am the Lord. . . . And I will harden the hearts of the Egyptians so that they shall go in after them, and I will get glory over Pharaoh and all his host, his chariots, and his horsemen. And the Egyptians shall know that I am the Lord, when I have gotten glory over Pharaoh, his chariots, and his horsemen."

> John 2:11: "This, the first of his signs, Jesus did at Cana in Galilee, and manifested his glory. And his disciples believed in him."

> John 9:3, 7: "Jesus answered, 'It was not that this man sinned, or his parents, but that the works of God might be displayed in him.' . . . And [Jesus] said to him, 'Go, wash in the pool of Siloam.' . . . So he went and washed and came back seeing."

> John 11:4, 40, 43–44: "But when Jesus heard it he said, 'This illness does not lead to death. It is for the glory of God, so that the Son of God may be glorified through it.' . . . Jesus said to her, 'Did I not tell you that if you believed you would see the glory of God?' . . . When he had said these things, he cried out with a loud voice, 'Lazarus, come out.' The man who had died came out."

Note also some of the many other passages where miracles lead to God's glory (continuing with ESV):

> Matthew 15:30–31: "And great crowds came to him, bringing with them the lame, the blind, the crippled, the mute, and many others, and they put them at his feet, and he healed them, so that the crowd wondered, when they saw the mute speaking, the crippled healthy, the lame walking, and the blind seeing. And they glorified the God of Israel."

3. God's glory is a central, essential biblical theme rightly emphasized by continuationist John Piper (e.g., Piper, *Reading Supernaturally*) as well as by cessationist Tom Schreiner (*Apostle of Glory*).

Mark 2:12: "And he rose and immediately picked up his bed and went out before them all, so that they were all amazed and glorified God, saying, 'We never saw anything like this!'"

Luke 7:16: "Fear seized them all, and they glorified God, saying, 'A great prophet has arisen among us!' and 'God has visited his people!'"

Luke 19:37: "As he was drawing near—already on the way down the Mount of Olives—the whole multitude of his disciples began to rejoice and praise God with a loud voice for all the mighty works that they had seen."

Acts 4:21: "And when they had further threatened them, they let them go, finding no way to punish them, because of the people, for all were praising God for what had happened."

### 3. God Attests His Gospel

God heals and does other signs to draw attention to the good news about Jesus (here using the NASB):[4]

Acts 2:11–12: "'Cretans and Arabs—we hear them speaking in our *own* tongues of the mighty deeds of God.' And they all continued in amazement and great perplexity, saying to one another, 'What does this mean?'"

Acts 3:16: "And on the basis of faith in His name, *it is* the name of Jesus which has strengthened this man whom you see and know; and the faith which *comes* through Him has given him this perfect health in the presence of you all."

Acts 4:10, 12: "Let it be known to all of you and to all the people of Israel, that by the name of Jesus Christ the Nazarene, whom you crucified, whom God raised from the dead—by this *name* this man stands here before you in good health. . . . And there is salvation in no one else; for there is no other name under heaven that has been given among mankind by which we must be saved."

Acts 4:29–30: "And now, Lord, look at their threats, and grant *it* to Your bond-servants to speak Your word with all confidence, while You extend Your hand to heal, and signs and wonders take place through the name of Your holy servant Jesus."

Acts 14:3: "Therefore they spent a long time *there* speaking boldly *with reliance* upon the Lord, who was testifying to the word of His grace, granting that signs and wonders be performed by their hands."

4. Pennington warns that evangelism was not "the chief reason" for Jesus's miracles (Pennington, *Cessationism*, 54). It is certainly a key reason in Acts.

> Hebrews 2:3–4: "How will we escape if we neglect so great a salvation? After it was at first spoken through the Lord, it was confirmed to us by those who heard, God also testifying with them, both by signs and wonders, and by various miracles and by gifts of the Holy Spirit according to His own will."

The signs testify not to the apostles or Scripture per se but to the good news about Christ, inviting attention to that message that people must either embrace (as in John 11:45; Acts 9:35, 42) or reject (John 11:46). It is the same good news that we preach to nonbelievers today, so we have every reason to believe that God still bears witness to its truth, often in the same ways we see in Scripture. Certainly he has not changed (Heb. 13:8).

Relatedly, one could add a fourth point, though we merely subsume it under the third point here: Miracles reveal God's reign (Matt. 11:4–6 // Luke 7:22–23; Matt. 12:28 // Luke 11:20). We mention this point only briefly here because we addressed it in detail in chapter 3. As to whether miracles are valuable for getting attention for the kingdom, Jesus says that they would have brought Sodom to repentance so that it would have remained even into his own day (Matt. 11:23).

#### *4. God Responds to Our Intimate Trust in Him*

God sometimes acts dramatically in response to people's trust in him. Here are some examples from one Gospel (here using AT):

> Mark 5:34: "He said to her, 'Daughter, your trust has delivered you. Go in peace, and be healed of your illness.'"

> Mark 5:36: "But when Jesus overheard what they said, Jesus told the synagogue leader, 'Don't be afraid. Just trust.'"

> Mark 9:23: "Jesus said to him, 'What do you mean: "If you're able!" All things are able to be for the one who trusts.'"

> Mark 10:52: "And Jesus said to him, 'Go. Your trust has delivered you!' And immediately he regained his sight and followed him on the way."

> Mark 11:24: "Therefore, I tell you, regarding anything you ask for in prayer, trust that God has granted them to you, and they will be yours."

And just a few more (still AT), lest one think the idea exclusive to Mark:

> Matthew 15:28: "Then Jesus told her, 'Ma'am, you have great trust. As you wish, so shall it be done for you.' And her daughter was healed from that very hour."

Luke 7:9–10 (cf. also Matt. 8:10, 13): "When Jesus heard these things, he was surprised at him. Turning to the crowd who were following him, he said, 'I tell you, not even in Israel have I found such trust.' And when those who had been sent returned to the house, they found the servant whole."

John 4:50: "Jesus told him, 'Go; your son will live.' The man trusted the promise that Jesus gave him and went."

John 11:40: "Jesus said to her, 'Didn't I tell you that if you believed you would see God's glory?'"

### *5. Opposing the Devil*

Jesus invaded Satan's kingdom with God's reign; he came to destroy the devil's works (Heb. 2:14; 1 John 3:8). He did so partly by delivering the demonized and healing the oppressed (using the NRSV):

Mark 1:24: "[The demonized man] cried out, 'What have you to do with us, Jesus of Nazareth? Have you come to destroy us?'"

Mark 3:22–24, 27: "And the scribes who came down from Jerusalem said, 'He has Beelzebul, and by the ruler of the demons he casts out demons.' And he called them to him, and spoke to them in parables, 'How can Satan cast out Satan? If a kingdom is divided against itself, that kingdom cannot stand. . . . No one can enter a strong man's house and plunder his property without first tying up the strong man; then indeed the house can be plundered.'"

Luke 10:17–19: "The seventy returned with joy, saying, 'Lord, in your name even the demons submit to us!' He said to them, 'I watched Satan fall from heaven like a flash of lightning. See, I have given you authority to tread on snakes and scorpions, and over all the power of the enemy; and nothing will hurt you.'"

Luke 13:11, 13, 16: "And just then there appeared a woman with a spirit that had crippled her for eighteen years. She was bent over and was quite unable to stand up straight. . . . When [Jesus] laid his hands on her, immediately she stood up straight and began praising God. . . . [Jesus replied,] 'Ought not this woman, a daughter of Abraham whom Satan bound for eighteen long years, be set free from this bondage on the sabbath day?'"

Acts 10:38: "[The message spread] how God anointed Jesus of Nazareth with the Holy Spirit and with power; how he went about doing good and healing all who were oppressed by the devil, for God was with him."

Jesus not only proclaimed and explained the kingdom; he demonstrated God's authority by healing the sick and expelling demons.[5] As George Ladd

5. Ladd, *Gospel of Kingdom*, 47.

emphasizes, "The exorcism of demons was no mere peripheral activity in Jesus's ministry but was a manifestation of the essential purpose of the coming of the Kingdom of God into the evil age."[6]

Has the devil gone quiet since Jesus's ministry? Or has he invaded the earth more forcefully, recognizing that his time is limited (cf. Rev. 12:12)? Evil certainly remains in the world (e.g., 1 John 4:3, 6; esp. 5:19). Hebrews 2:14–15 states that Jesus came to deprive the devil of his power over death, and so we no longer need fear it; yet death continues. Jesus defeated the devil decisively, but we continue to engage in spiritual warfare (e.g., Eph. 4:27; 6:13–17; James 4:7; 1 Pet. 5:8–9; Rev. 12:10–11).

While John MacArthur rightly acknowledges that Jesus used his power "to combat Satan's kingdom," he quickly warns, "Today we deal with evil spirits not by finding someone with the gift of powers to cast them out," but by following other spiritual warfare instructions in the epistles.[7] The instructions in the epistles, addressed to believers, are indeed necessary for our daily lives (again, Eph. 4:27; 6:13–17), for resisting false ideologies (2 Cor. 10:4–5; James 3:15; 4:4, 7), and for withstanding persecution (1 Pet. 5:8–9). But can anyone really suppose people can have demons like those in the Gospels *taught* out of them? When Jesus instructed the Twelve and apparently the Seventy(-Two) how to deal with resident demons, he taught them to cast them out (Matt. 10:8; Mark 6:7, 13; Luke 10:17). Deliverance was the procedure followed in Acts, by both apostles (Acts 5:16; 16:18; 19:12) and others (8:7). That the epistles, written to believers, lack direct instructions for exorcism hardly means that fuller demonization ceased with the death of the apostles.

As you might have noticed in some verses cited above, this pattern is sometimes relevant also for healing. Michael Brown notes hearing a radio preacher back when Brown was still a cessationist: "You know, in Bible days, it was the devil who made people sick and Jesus who made people well. Today, some preachers tell us it's Jesus who makes people sick and the devil who makes them well!" This is not to claim that sickness is the fault of those who are sick, but to suggest that health and healing are gifts from God and it is good for us to work for those goals when we can.[8] Jesus was combatting the devil's work by restoring people (Acts 10:38).

Certainly both demons and exorcising them continued to be issues in later centuries. "For every demon, when exorcised in the name of this very Son of God," Justin Martyr (ca. 100–ca. 165) insists, "is overcome and subdued." No other name, he continues, can accomplish this.[9] Jesus came for the devil's

6. Ladd, *Theology*, 53.

7. MacArthur, *Chaos*, 201.

8. Brown, "Miracles and Kingdom," 34–35; the preacher's quote is 34. This appears also in Brown, *Authentic Fire*, 186.

9. Justin, *Dial.* 85.1–2 (*ANF*, 1:241); brought to our attention in Williams, "Following Christ's Example," 70.

destruction, he says. "And now you can learn this from what is under your own observation. For numberless demoniacs throughout the whole world, and in your city, many of our Christian men exorcising them in the name of Jesus Christ . . . have healed and do heal, rendering helpless and driving the possessing devils out of the men, though they could not be cured by all the other exorcists, and those who used incantations and drugs."[10] Tertullian (ca. 155–ca. 220) even challenges the authorities to bring in a demon-possessed person to court; any Christian will make short work of the demon, forcing it to confess its deceit. If the demons do not immediately confess their identity, he insists, then execute that impudent Christian immediately![11] The leading cause of conversion to Christianity in the 300s (long after the death of anyone on whom the first apostles laid hands) was healing and exorcism in Jesus's name.[12]

### 6. Power Encounters

One particular expression of opposing the devil is what missiologists call "power encounters." Whereas MacArthur compares charismatic healing to occult or psychic healers to suggest that such healing can come from nondivine sources, one biblical function of miracles is to demonstrate that God's power is greater than that of occult forces. The biblical pattern is that God's agents wield greater power than those of the evil one. Should we suppose that occult forces continue to perform miracles but that God no longer grants greater signs to his own servants for his honor? Note the following (ESV):

> Exodus 7:12: "For each man cast down his staff, and they became serpents. But Aaron's staff swallowed up their staffs."
>
> Exodus 8:18–19: "The magicians tried by their secret arts to produce gnats, but they could not. So there were gnats on man and beast. Then the magicians said to Pharaoh, 'This is the finger of God.' But Pharaoh's heart was hardened, and he would not listen to them, as the LORD had said."
>
> Exodus 12:12: "For I will pass through the land of Egypt that night, and I will strike all the firstborn in the land of Egypt, both man and beast; and on all the gods of Egypt I will execute judgments: I am the LORD."
>
> Numbers 33:4: "[The people of Israel went out] while the Egyptians were burying all their firstborn, whom the LORD had struck down among them. On their gods also the LORD executed judgments."

10. Justin, *2 Apol.* 6 (*ANF*, 1:190); brought to our attention in Williams, "Following Christ's Example," 70–71.

11. Tertullian, *Apol.* 23.4–6; MacMullen, *Christianizing*, 27.

12. MacMullen, *Christianizing*, 61–62; Frend, *Rise*, 566–67 (also emphasizing the prevalent fear of demons in this period); Frend, "Place of Miracles" (on 11 noting Sozomen's explanation that his family was converted in his grandfather's day through a successful exorcism).

> 1 Kings 18:26, 37–39: "And they took the bull that was given them, and they prepared it and called upon the name of Baal from morning until noon, saying, 'O Baal, answer us!' But there was no voice, and no one answered. And they limped around the altar that they had made. . . . [Elijah cried] 'Answer me, O LORD, answer me, that this people may know that you, O LORD, are God, and that you have turned their hearts back.' Then the fire of the LORD fell and consumed the burnt offering and the wood and the stones and the dust, and licked up the water that was in the trench. And when all the people saw it, they fell on their faces and said, 'The LORD, he is God; the LORD, he is God.'"

> Acts 8:6, 9–11: "And the crowds with one accord paid attention to what was being said by Philip, when they heard him and saw the signs that he did. . . . But there was a man named Simon, who had previously practiced magic in the city and amazed the people of Samaria, saying that he himself was somebody great. . . . And they paid attention to him because for a long time he had amazed them with his magic. But when they believed Philip as he preached good news about the kingdom of God and the name of Jesus Christ, they were baptized. . . . Even Simon himself believed, and after being baptized he continued with Philip. And seeing signs and great miracles performed, he was amazed."

> Acts 13:8–12: "But Elymas the magician (for that is the meaning of his name) opposed them, seeking to turn the proconsul away from the faith. But Saul, who was also called Paul, filled with the Holy Spirit, looked intently at him and said, '. . . Behold, the hand of the Lord is upon you, and you will be blind and unable to see the sun for a time.' Immediately mist and darkness fell upon him, and he went about seeking people to lead him by the hand. Then the proconsul believed, when he saw what had occurred, for he was astonished at the teaching of the Lord."

Many early American Presbyterian missionaries to Korea had learned in seminary that spirits were not real, but most came to believe otherwise in the context of ministry alongside indigenous Korean believers.[13] Thus, for example, Charles Clark was astonished in the face of a violent demonstration of spirit possession; quickly changing his doctrine, he invoked Jesus's name and the man immediately became rational, completely unaware of his prior state.[14] Other missionaries also reported exorcisms (usually led by Korean believers), and noted that in the early, groundbreaking years exorcisms similar to those in the New Testament accompanied the start of many or most churches.[15]

---

13. Kim, "Healing," 270. This paragraph follows Keener, *Miracles*, 2:835.

14. Kim, "Healing," 270–71. In 1908 the same missionary reported an exorcism, after extended prayer, of a spirit so powerful that three nonbelievers outside were hurled to the ground when it came out (271, citing Clark's report).

15. Kim, "Healing," 272–73. The best known Korean exorcist was also the most popular Korean Protestant preacher of the day, Presbyterian Kim Ik-tu (Kim, "Healing," 273–74).

While we need to take into account cultural differences between the first century and today, none of the purposes we list above for miracles depend on cultural factors. As Jack Deere concludes, "They are rooted in the character and eternal purposes of God."[16]

## Purposes of Prophecy

Although we address prophecy further a few chapters hence (chaps. 12–14), we must address the issue in a preliminary way here because Warfield and others limit prophecy to a canonical function. As discussed regarding apostles in Ephesians 2:20, the purpose of New Testament prophecy was not *exclusively* laying a foundation for the universal church. That could be one purpose, but those who contend that it was the only purpose, making all subsequent prophecy superfluous, would have a difficult case justifying this position from Scripture.

Here are some other functions of prophecy, visions, and other revelations, in Acts alone (cf. Acts 2:17–18), though we add to them some additional supporting references:[17]

1. Getting people ready for famine (Gen. 41:25; 45:7; 50:20; Acts 11:28)
2. Warnings for the sake of safety (Matt. 2:12–13, 19–22) or preparedness (Acts 21:4, 11)
3. To call out sin and preserve holiness (2 Sam. 12:7; Acts 5:3–4, 8–9)
4. To guide in cross-cultural evangelism (Acts 8:29; 10:19; 16:9–10)
5. To send someone with a message (Acts 9:10)
6. To point someone to a source for the good news (Acts 10:3)
7. To encourage one to continue in boldness rather than fear (Acts 18:9–10)
8. To guide someone where their mission must go next (Acts 16:9–10; 19:21)
9. To encourage one in danger for himself and others (Acts 27:24–25)
10. To protect people from destruction at sea (Acts 27:31)

Paul points to the primary functions of prophesying in Christian gatherings in 1 Corinthians 14:3, none of which have to do with writing Scripture:

1. Building up the church
2. Exhorting or encouraging them (cf. also Acts 15:32)
3. Consoling or comforting them

16. Deere, *Still Surprised*, 115.
17. Here following many points in Ruthven, *Cessation*, 66.

Against those who assume that prophecy's exclusive function was to establish universal, foundational revelation (citing Eph. 2:20), Andrew Wilson notes several other explicit purposes for prophecy in 1 Corinthians 14 alone:

4. To "bring unbelievers under conviction (14:24)"
5. To "witness to the presence of the Holy Spirit in the assembly (14:25)"
6. To "enable the congregation to learn and be encouraged (14:31)"[18]

While 14:3 need not require revealing specific information, prophecy can sometimes involve that too, as in 14:24–25 (ESV):

> But if all prophesy, and an unbeliever or outsider enters, he is convicted by all, he is called to account by all, the secrets of his heart are disclosed, and so, falling on his face, he will worship God and declare that God is really among you.

Usually when I (Craig) have prophesied, it fits more the sort of functions listed in 14:3, but it has sometimes fit that in 14:24–25, whether in public meetings (bringing some to repentance) or individually (revealing an unbeliever's background and inviting conversion). Tongues also build up the individual (14:4) and can build up the church if interpreted (14:5–6, 26). God gives *each* of the *charismata* for the common good (12:7).

It is therefore surprising that MacArthur, referring in context to prophecy and tongues, declares, "Charismatics believe that the spectacular miraculous gifts were given for the edification of believers. Does God's Word support such a conclusion? No."[19] This claim merits no comment apart from Paul's own words about edification through spiritual gifts (here from the NASB):

> 1 Corinthians 14:3–5: "But the one who prophesies speaks to people *for* edification, exhortation, and consolation. The one who speaks in a tongue edifies himself; but the one who prophesies edifies the church. Now I wish that you all spoke in tongues, but rather that you would prophesy; and greater is the one who prophesies than the one who speaks in tongues, unless he interprets, so that the church may receive edification."

> 1 Corinthians 14:12: "So you too, since you are eager to possess spiritual *gifts*, strive to excel for the edification of the church."

18. Wilson, *Spirit and Sacrament*, 112n68.

19. MacArthur, *Chaos*, 117. Contrast, e.g., Martin Bucer: "God's spiritual gifts are given not only to impart faith but also to strengthen it" (*Metaphrasis et Enarratio* 42, in Adams, *Romans*, 37).

1 Corinthians 14:17: "For you are giving thanks well *enough* [if you pray only in a tongue], but the other person is not edified."

1 Corinthians 14:26: "What is *the outcome* then, brothers *and sisters*? When you assemble, each one has a psalm, has a teaching, has a revelation, has a tongue, has an interpretation. All things are to be done for edification."

## Further Considerations of Compassion

As mentioned earlier, Warfield determined that "had any miracles perchance occurred beyond the Apostolic age they would be without significance; mere occurrences with no universal meaning."[20] This clinical view of miracles misses a central aspect of God's heart. Jesus was "moved with compassion" for the people (Matt. 9:36). He wept at the tomb of Lazarus (John 11:35) and had compassion on the widow of Nain (Luke 7:13). Is it really "without significance" when a sick child is healed? Is it trivial when a person tormented by demons is delivered? Is it inconsequential when the Holy Spirit speaks words of life, direction, affirmation, rebuke, and love to God's people? Is it insignificant when God's children manifest God's kingdom in a fallen world? Is it insignificant when a person comes to faith in Christ because he or she witnessed God's power?

Perhaps Warfield and I (Daniel) have a different definition of what is "without significance." Warfield's point is that miracles were essential for Christianity's initial establishment in the world. Granted, but after that he sees them as no longer needed. So here lies the crux of the issue: *What is the purpose of miracles?* Were they temporary provisions meant to tide the church over till the canon closed and Rome became an ally? Or are they ongoing expressions of God's grace like internal transformation and gifts such as teaching?

Conyers Middleton declared, "This, I say, seems to be the most prevailing notion, . . . that miracles should then cease, when the end of them was obtained and the church no longer in want of them; being now delivered from all danger, and secure of success, under the protection of the greatest power on earth."[21] Yet I believe these convictions (once more common in the bosom of Christendom) breed a false sense of security. It is a dangerous delusion to imagine that we are "no longer in want" and "delivered from all danger." Without the presence and power of the Holy Spirit in our lives we are nothing and we have nothing. (Danger and desperate need remain a living reality for hundreds of millions of Christians around the world today.)[22]

20. Warfield, *Counterfeit Miracles*, 27–28.
21. Middleton, *A Free Inquiry*, xlvii.
22. See, e.g., Keener, *Suffering*, esp. chaps. 6–9.

I often preach to crowds that stretch to the horizon. I see the desperate needs all around me. I see sickness, poverty, and death—scenes I cannot adequately describe. People bring me demonized persons who are sometimes bound in physical chains. Desperate, weeping mothers bring me emaciated children who suffer at death's doorstep. Family members bring me the recently deceased bodies of their husbands, wives, or children. I see their tears and their desperate needs. I hear their sobs and their earnest prayers.

How should I respond? What are Jesus's biblical demands in such scenarios? This is not theoretical to me, nor is it a matter of this or that doctrine. It is life or death. Should I send them away with a sermon and a song? Should I say, "Be warmed and well fed"? Or, "I hope you feel better"? Is that the power of the gospel I proclaim?

Then I wonder what Jesus would do if he were here. Now that the Bible is complete and "Rome" is our friend (at least in some nations), would Jesus promise good news about the future and send them away demonized and sick? Would he turn to his disciples, smile, and say, "These people are 'no longer in want' of God's power"? Would he see miracles as theological matters only? Wouldn't he be overwhelmed with compassion?

Without Jesus's power I have nothing to offer a world dying in its sin, sickness, and bondage. Yes, the gospel itself is God's power for salvation (Rom. 1:16; 1 Cor. 2:4). But that is not just a slogan. It is a reference to tangible power that does more than enable people to preach; it also performs miracles, heals, and transforms (Rom. 15:19; Gal. 3:5). Everything of eternal significance is God-breathed. We serve God not by human might or power "'*but by my Spirit*,' says the LORD Almighty" (Zech. 4:6). If God's miracle-working power has indeed "ceased" and God has entrusted the church "to be maintained by ordinary ways,"[23] we are doomed! I need hardly mention the supernatural forces arrayed against both humanity and the gospel, forces that also lead to thousands of Christian martyrdoms each year.

Most theologians who advocate cessationism live in the Western world where current relative safety and security sometimes blunt our spiritual senses and blind us to the desperate straits of our world. Imagine trying to tell Christians who endure persecution under Islamists in parts of Africa or the Middle East, or under nationalist repression in parts of Asia, that their secure situation has "abated the necessity of miracles," that they have been "delivered from all danger" and therefore "those extraordinary assistances were discontinued."[24]

23. So Tillotson, *Works*, 48.

24. Nathaniel Marshall, as cited in Warfield, *Counterfeit Miracles*, 7. Warfield demurs from Marshall's cutoff in the age of Constantine, meanwhile himself tracing it instead earlier to the end of the apostolic era.

Meanwhile, I have observed that most believers around the world (especially in the Majority World) tend to be charismatic regardless of their denomination.[25] Missionaries from all kinds of denominations are often charismatic due to the real-world demands they face. For Christian workers who minister to people held captive by the powers of darkness, Warfield's cessationism offers little help. I have known Christian missionaries from the West who started out very noncharismatic—until they began to preach the gospel among villages filled with idolatry and witchcraft. The demonized people, persecution, and overarching spiritual resistance promptly persuaded them of their need for the Holy Spirit's raw power. Miracles display the power of God's kingdom and bring restoration to a broken creation. And that purpose applies to every generation.

25. Cf., e.g., retired Methodist bishop Hwa Yung, in *Quest* and "Pentecostalism"; also Chan, *Asian Theology*; for exorcisms, e.g., "Islam and Christianity," 30.

# 11

# Little Miracles Don't Count?

## *Uneven Criteria*

Does a claim that God merely healed your headache mean that miracles have ceased?

Sometimes critics of continuationism, instead of grappling with biblical arguments, focus on critiquing examples of modern miracle or prophecy claims that fall short of what they consider biblical examples. There are some problems with this approach. One is that this is an argument from experience, which the critics normally reject when used (as they massively can be) to support continuationism. If Scripture leads us to expect continuing miracles or prophecies, then we should welcome the occurrence of the genuine articles even if we have not yet seen full-fledged cases ourselves.

Another problem with the critique is that it is selective, focusing on weaker cases or claims today rather than stronger evidence. Stronger evidence exists[1] and should not be faulted for the fact that critics usually ignore it. Most problematic, the critique uses uneven criteria, glamorizing biblical examples while using a completely different standard for subsequent cases. The skepticism normally used against modern miracles would, as Enlightenment history demonstrated, be deployed even more easily against ancient, including biblical, miracles. Do Christians really want to honor a skeptical approach that, whenever applied consistently, has a long and continuing track record of undermining Scripture?

1. See, e.g., Romez, Zaritzky, and Brown, "Report"; Keener, *Miracles Today*.

## Extrabibical Standards for Miracles

Some modern critics employ extrabiblical criteria for miracles, sometimes unaware of how these criteria developed historically and apparently unaware that these criteria screen out a number of biblical miracles as well as modern ones.

### *Must Healing Always Be Instant?*

John MacArthur insists that, in contrast to modern healing claims, Jesus healed instantly.[2] Thus he rejects modern charismatic healings, "since no charismatic healer can come up with genuinely verifiable cases of instant healing involving organic disease."[3]

Likewise Tom Pennington asserts: "In the New Testament when someone with the New Testament gift of healing used his gifts, the results were complete, immediate, permanent, undeniable, every kind of sickness, every kind of illness. The purported healings of today's faith healers are the antithesis: incomplete, temporary, and unverifiable."[4]

Historically, it was Thomas Aquinas who introduced this element to the definition of miracles, using Aristotelian metaphysics: True miracles had to be "beyond any 'means' of nature," hence beyond dispute; this meant they should be, for example, "instantaneous" and visible.[5] Of course, not all ailments are visible, nor can one be certain of all permanent cures instantaneously. Certainly many of Jesus's miracles were also disputed, though more often by attribution to malevolent rather than natural agencies (e.g., Mark 3:22; cf. John 11:46–50).

Aside from the fact that some cures today *are* instant, not all miracles in Scripture are instant. Note, for example, the following:[6]

- Why did God create the world progressively rather than all at once in Genesis 1:1–2:4?
- Obviously, miraculous pregnancies required some time between conception and birth, or even becoming physically evident (Gen. 21:1–2; 25:21; Judg. 13:24; 1 Sam. 1:20; 2 Kings 4:16–17; Luke 1:57; 2:6).

2. MacArthur, *Chaos*, 211.
3. MacArthur, *Chaos*, 216.
4. Pennington, "Case." Cf. Pennington, *Cessationism*, 124: "With the real New Testament gift of healing, the results were complete, immediate, permanent, and undeniable"; he notes the "faith healers" antithesis on 125.
5. Ruthven, *Cessation*, 20–21. Such requirements eventuated in Lambertini's criteria, which can be applied so strictly that most of Jesus's miracles would not have passed muster. The need for such a level of strictness responds to Protestant polemic against excessive medieval gullibility. Cf. also Warfield, *Counterfeit Miracles*, 108–10.
6. Some would add Acts 16:18 but although the term *hōra* typically means "hour," it could have a more immediate sense in this case. Cf. also John 9:2–7, included by Turner, *Gifts*, 337.

- The widow of Zarephath's sustenance continued to be renewed daily rather than being supplied all at once (1 Kings 17:15–16).
- Oil continued to flow from the jar of a prophet's widow to pay a debt (2 Kings 4:1–7).
- Raising the Shunammite's son took some stages (2 Kings 4:33–35).
- Jesus healed one case of blindness in two stages (Mark 8:22–26).[7]
- Jesus delivered a youth from a demon and then healed him (Mark 9:25–27).
- Jesus cursed a fig tree and his disciples found it withered the next day (Mark 11:14, 20–21).
- Jesus declared healed ten men with skin diseases, and they were healed as they were going (Luke 17:14).

Granted, to be effective in getting attention (a key element of their purpose), "signs" were usually immediate. Signs predominate in the Gospels and Acts, which narrate the kingdom breaking new ground; this is also why Paul mentions them in the context of church planting (Rom. 15:19; 2 Cor. 12:12) rather than of church assemblies. No such parameters are necessary (stated or implied), however, for gifts of healings (1 Cor. 12:9) or healings in answer to collective prayer (James 5:14–16).[8] In those cases, recovery fulfills the need for healing, which differs from the need to attract attention for the gospel. Scripture nowhere implies that gifts of healings must be instant before they merit praise to God for his action.

In terms of verifiability, I (Craig) apply to miracle claims today the same standards I use in historiography, critically evaluating witnesses, preferring memories closest to the event, and so forth; I have catalogued hundreds of eyewitness claims. While I am qualified to make historiographic judgments, I depend on doctors' reports for medical judgments. Besides the various physicians cited in my books, one particularly helpful resource is Global Medical Research Institute, which publishes the strongest medically attested cases in journals.[9]

7. This was probably for symbolic effect, but it does illustrate that God does not require all healings to occur in a single moment.

8. Cf. also Turner, *Gifts*, 338.

9. See, e.g., Romez, "Case Report"; Romez, Zaritzky, and Brown, "Report." Online, see esp. the account of neuroscience professor Joshua Brown in the pilot episode of Angel's series Miracle at www.angel.com/shows/miracle; see also Brown, *Proving a Miracle*.

### *Always Complete and Organic Healing?*

MacArthur says that in contrast to modern healing claims, Jesus healed totally.[10] "The blind were given 20/20 vision, the lame could run and jump, the deaf could hear a pin drop."[11]

By what means biblically does MacArthur know this? Twenty-twenty is average perfect vision today, an arbitrary standard to impose on ancients; vision even keener than twenty-twenty is possible. One need not imagine Tolkien's elves to suppose being able to see at forty feet as well as most people today see at twenty; some people today have twenty-fifteen or even twenty-ten vision. Surely blind and deaf people received *adequate* sight and hearing, but Scripture itself nowhere quantifies the level needed to count as God's gift. When someone improves partially or gradually, some might not consider this a "sign" in the usual sense, but it may still constitute a *healing*.[12]

Moreover, MacArthur says that in contrast to modern healing claims, "Jesus healed organic disease."[13] For Pennington, "The purported healings of today's faith healers are . . . incomplete, temporary, and unverifiable."[14]

Aside from the fact that some modern cures *are* organic and a number *are* medically verified, how would we know that all cures effected by Jesus were organic? Since he healed every kind of sickness (Matt. 4:23; Mark 1:32–34), as Pennington also notes,[15] presumably some were not organic or externally verifiable (cf., e.g., severe pain in Matt. 4:24).[16] Even those that were organic and potentially verifiable are not all verified on the spot; although the bleeding woman is aware of her healing (Mark 5:29), for example, the narrative offers no external physical proof of that change, which would presumably require time.

Healings of blindness and other serious disabilities are normally organic, and we have evidence for a number of these today.[17] When skeptics turn to modern miracle claims, however, they usually protest that "faith" cures of blindness and the like are of merely psychosomatic or psychogenic

10. MacArthur, *Chaos*, 211.

11. MacArthur, *Strange Fire*, 167–68; for healings being "complete," see also Pennington, "Case."

12. Even Warfield acknowledges some "faith healings," provided they are not miraculous (Warfield, *Counterfeit Miracles*, 190–91). But cessationists generally hold gifts of healings to the standard of miracles.

13. MacArthur, *Chaos*, 212.

14. Pennington, "Case."

15. Pennington, "Case."

16. Some today estimate that only half the illnesses for which patients even in the West seek medical treatment are organic (Frye, "Faith Healing," 18; Markle, "Body," 16–17; Baroody, "Healing," 87–88; Benson, *Healing*, 49).

17. E.g., Romez, "Case Report"; Brown et al., "Study"; Brown, *Testing Prayer*, 207–9, 214–20, 223–30; Gardner, *Healing Miracles*, 202–5; further accounts in Keener, *Miracles*, 1:508–99; Keener, *Miracles Today*, esp. 93–105.

disorders. Here hard cessationists such as B. B. Warfield adopt skeptics' criteria for all postbiblical claims.[18] Since they place a virtually insurmountable burden of proof entirely on anyone claiming healing yet are ready to dismiss almost any healing claim as psychosomatic or fake, they claim victory in any argument before the argument can begin. Such skepticism is impervious to evidence. Must we discount all healings that occur during prayer if on some other occasions similar recoveries have happened without prayer? These are not allowed to count even if the former is instant and the latter gradual.[19]

This kind of standard would exclude most of Jesus's healings in the Gospels. The skin conditions translated in Scripture as leprosy sometimes go away (Lev. 14:2, 9). So Jesus healing a man's skin disease (Mark 1:40–44) does not count. On a few occasions, blindness may reflect psychogenic causes,[20] so we can rule out healing claims regarding blindness (though cures of psychogenic illnesses are rarely rapid). Rare cases of misdiagnosed death occur today, followed by a person's spontaneous resuscitation;[21] there go all of Jesus's raisings. Nor is the accumulation of evidence (such as multiple cases, with multiple independent witnesses) sufficient; one can protest that these were all faked or misinterpreted. But finally, even if something meets Warfield's other criteria, if it occurs among groups he mistrusts, or indeed at any time after the death of the apostles' associates, it simply cannot count: "Simple inexplicability . . . is not an adequate ground on which to infer miracle."[22]

Schreiner affirms that God heals today but tentatively doubts gifts of healings today because he doubts that there is a regular "pattern of healing" in particular ministries. Yet one friend of ours in Congo witnessed three raisings through her prayers, in two cases confirmed by other eyewitnesses we consulted (one of them my [Craig's] brother-in-law, a university science professor).[23] Another friend has seen large numbers of deaf and blind people

18. Cf. here even Saucy, "View," 129: "Extraordinary healings can have other explanations. Some illnesses, including blindness, deafness, and paralysis, may be symptoms of psychological trauma or hysteria, not genuine organic diseases. . . . These are not genuine miracles." Skeptics apply the same criteria to any biblical accounts they do not dismiss historically.

19. Warfield also defined miracles in a specific and arbitrarily complex way: a "force outside of nature, and specifically above nature, intruding into the complex of natural forces and producing, therefore, in that complex, effects which could not be produced by the natural forces themselves. These effects reveal themselves, therefore, as 'new'—but not as neo natural but rather as extra natural and specifically as super-natural" (Ruthven, *Cessation*, 46).

20. See, e.g., Capps, *Village Psychiatrist*, passim, esp. xii–xiv, 5, 64–65.

21. Hannig, Hauritz, and Grove, "Autoresuscitation."

22. Warfield, *Counterfeit Miracles*, 120. In context, Warfield is insisting that the context must be not simply Christian but theologically orthodox by his standards, a criterion by which he dismisses a well-attested miracle in a Catholic context.

23. See Keener, *Miracles*, 1:558–60; Keener, *Miracles Today*, 168.

healed as she has prayed, precipitating many conversions.[24] Would that not constitute a pattern?

"And the healings should be on the same level that we see in the New Testament: healing of the blind, of those who are unable to walk, of those who are deaf, and of those who are near death."[25] The New Testament naturally reports the more dramatic healings (why waste scroll space on temporary headaches when you can report healing of blindness?). But since Jesus healed all who came to him, we may assume that he healed a range of conditions. The legitimate question is not whether we can appreciate less dramatic healings. The legitimate question is whether we do see today "healing of the blind, of those who are unable to walk, of those who are deaf, and of those who are near death."[26] And the answer is clearly yes.[27]

## No Raisings Today?

MacArthur claims that "Jesus healed everyone."[28] Despite potentially hyperbolic claims of healing everyone in Syria (Matt. 4:24), probably understood as all the illnesses of those who came to him,[29] MacArthur probably does not mean *everyone*. That is, he probably does not mean that Jesus would have emptied out hospitals, as some cessationists challenge modern persons with gifts of healing to do. Jesus healed only one out of many people at the pool of Bethesda (John 5:3–9) and apparently left a disabled man in the temple precincts for Peter and John (Acts 3:2). But he did heal all who *came* to him. Whether this pattern always held true for Jesus's disciples, even outside evangelistic contexts, is more questionable (see discussion below).

What MacArthur surely demands is some dramatic cases, such as resuscitations from death. "Jesus," he points out, "raised the dead." "People who tout the gift of healing today do not spend much time in funeral parlors. . . . The reason is obvious."[30] The New Testament does not depict Jesus as spending much time around cemeteries either; but because people were buried almost immediately after death, the healer had to be brought to the corpse immediately after death (Mark 5:35–43; cf. Acts 9:37–38), happen upon a funeral procession (Luke 7:12–15), or raise someone entombed—a special case that is recorded in his ministry just once (John 11:17, 39).

24. See Keener, *Miracles*, 1:331–32; 2:716; Keener, *Miracles Today*, 97–98, 135–36, 211.
25. Schreiner, *Spiritual Gifts*, 164.
26. Schreiner, *Spiritual Gifts*, 164.
27. See, e.g., Keener, *Miracles*, 1:508–99; Keener, *Miracles Today*, 93–174; Moreland, *Guide*.
28. MacArthur, *Chaos*, 212.
29. Blomberg, *Matthew*, 92n5.
30. MacArthur, *Chaos*, 212.

MacArthur therefore dismisses a continuing gift of healing, or of evangelistic signs worked through God's human agents, "since no charismatic healer raises the dead."[31] MacArthur recognizes that continuationists claim raisings, but he insists that these cases are much weaker. "It is one thing to revive someone whose vital signs stopped on a surgeon's table. It is entirely another matter to come out of the grave four days after being buried or to climb out of one's casket at the funeral (see Luke 7)."[32] Keep in mind that Lazarus was the only such case in the Gospels after so many days; all others were almost immediately after death. The case in Luke 7 was not a "casket" but an open bier and, more relevantly, like other burials, would follow death almost immediately. As for the surgeon's table, one will have medical certification of death only if a medical context was available. If such a context was available, doctors normally will have (rightly) used medical means to seek to resuscitate the patient. So today one must choose: Do you demand formal medical certification, or that the raising happen outside a clinical setting? If you demand both, you rule out the possibility of much evidence even if such events happen. In Jesus's context, medical certification would have been impossible,[33] so without using uneven criteria you must rule out all *biblical* cases from the start.

### *Raisings Today?*

One could devote multiple chapters or even a book to accounts of raisings (see, e.g., chaps. 24–31 in my [Craig's] book *Miracles Today*).[34] I borrow just a few samples from that book here. Reports of divine resuscitations from death are not new.[35] For example, the early second-century bishop Quadratus reported that some people whom Jesus raised remained alive into Quadratus's own lifetime.[36] Similarly, an apparently second-century source reports that the first bishop of Arbil in Mesopotamia was converted through witnessing the Syrian evangelist Addai raising a man from the dead in the year 99.[37]

In the late second century, Irenaeus, a church father in France, argued that God was with true followers of Jesus rather than with cults that misrepresented Jesus. One of Irenaeus's arguments was that cultists could not raise the dead like some members of the true church could and periodically did.[38]

31. MacArthur, *Chaos*, 216.

32. MacArthur, *Chaos*, 212.

33. For weaknesses in much ancient medicine, see, e.g., McKeown, *Cabinet*; Keener, *Excursuses*, 285–303.

34. See *Miracles Today*, 137–74; further Keener, "Dead Raised"; Keener, *Miracles*, 1:551–79.

35. For a particularly extensive collection of testimonies through history (though more recent ones are generally more strongly attested), see Hebert, *Raised*.

36. Eusebius, *Hist. eccl.* 4.3.1–2.

37. Young, "Miracles in History," 110.

38. Irenaeus, *Haer.* 2.31.2.

Augustine and other leaders of the ancient church cite eyewitness reports of raisings through prayer.[39] John Wesley reports his direct experience with what he understands as a raising from the dead in his journal on December 25, 1742;[40] firsthand accounts also surround the ministry of nineteenth-century German Lutheran pastor Johann Christoph Blumhardt.[41]

Accounts today are far too numerous to include here.[42] To mention just a few, in Romania, Charlie and Florentina Mada were converted through the raising of their son Marius, after seven hours.[43] In Rwanda, Swidiq (now Cedric) Kanana was an imam converted through a raising—his own.[44] Sri Lankan pastor Noel Fernando returned to life roughly thirty hours after being declared dead.[45] In the Philippines, Elaine Panelo died of liver cancer, and the hospital sent her to the morgue. When her friend's Baptist pastor prayed over her an hour and forty-five minutes later, Elaine suddenly became conscious. The cancer was now gone, her physician was converted, and Elaine remains well close to four decades later.[46]

### *Doctors Who Attest Raisings*

Doctors also attest raisings. In what follows, keep in mind that after just six minutes without oxygen, irreparable brain damage sets in, and after twenty minutes the brain is dead. Thus Dr. Michael Fleischer recounts a patient's fatal experience with an amniotic fluid embolism, in which amniotic fluid leaks into the mother's bloodstream. Doctors did their best to resuscitate this young mother, but after she had no pulse for forty-five minutes, they allowed the family to enter the operating room to say their goodbyes. Fleischer

39. Augustine, *City* 22.8.

40. Cf. Kidd, "Healing," 159; Tomkins, *Wesley*, 106.

41. See Ising, *Blumhardt*, 207, 219.

42. See, e.g., De Wet, "Signs," 110–11; Bush and Pegues, *Move*, 57–58, 59, 60; Miller and Yamamori, *Pentecostalism*, 151–52; Beam, *Miracles*; Piper, *Minutes*, 13–20, 37, 42–45; Smith, *Impossible*; Merrill, *Miracle Invasion*, 13–18.

43. Cotton, *Raised*; interview with the Madas, Phoenix, Arizona, January 15, 2019; personal correspondence with the Madas, January 14, 27, 29, February 11, 16, and March 9, 2019; with Margaret Cotton, June 18, August 23, December 5, 6, 7, and 26, 2018; January 14 and February 16, 2019.

44. Kanana, *Dying in Islam*, esp. 93–100; Kanana, *Once Dead*; Cedric Kanana, personal correspondence, February 18, 2020; Benjamin Fischer, personal correspondence, February 16, 2020.

45. Shelley Hollis, phone interview, January 10, 2009; personal correspondence, November 6 and 8, 2009; April 23, 2010; fuller details from Noel's wife, Shanthi Fernando, October 7, 2019.

46. Elaine Panelo, interview, Baguio, Philippines, January 30, 2009; elsewhere in the Philippines, see Chester Allan Tesoro, interview, Baguio, Philippines, January 30, 2009. For others in Asia, see, e.g., Young, "Miracles in History," 117–18; Gardner, *Healing Miracles*, 138; Gardner, "Miracles," 1932; Pytches, *Come*, 242–44; Mullins, "Empire," 91; Lambert, *Millions*, 109, 118–19; Jenkins, *New Faces*, 114; Khai, "Pentecostalism," 270; Zhaoming, "Chinese Denominations," 451; Kim, "Pentecostalism," 32; Ma, "Mission," 31; Venter, *Healing*, 294–95.

describes as "heart-wrenching" their loud pleas with God not to take her, and he quietly joined them in prayer.

Afterward, recognizing the futility of further attempts at resuscitation, the medical team stopped chest compressions. But Fleischer continues: "Then the impossible happened. . . . Somehow, Ruby's heart started to pump on its own, now with a normal rhythm. And just as impossibly, her blood pressure was suddenly normal." Still, after forty-five minutes without a heartbeat, she would surely have brain damage and other organ failure. Yet she soon opened her eyes, sustained no damage, and after three days "went home with her healthy baby and entire family."[47]

Dr. Dave Walker recounts his experience with Andrew, a four-year-old boy lifeless for more than twenty minutes before CPR even began.[48] Andrew's dilated pupils did not respond to light, and his body began stiffening, his "head back in the posture of severe brain damage."[49] Once Walker knew how long the brain had been deprived of oxygen, he realized that it could not survive. The parents rallied their friends to pray; Walker also prayed, but, given his knowledge of normal medical expectations, he did not pray with much faith. Yet when he saw the child the next day, the boy was conversing with him. The following day the boy was sitting upright and playing with toys. Doctors treated his chest infection, but he suffered absolutely no brain damage. This experience shifted Walker's understanding of what God might do.

Cardiologist Chauncey Crandall provides another account. In fall 2006, physicians in a Florida emergency room labored for almost forty minutes to try to revive Jeff Markin, following all the American Heart Association protocols. Despite shocking Markin seven times, they were unable to revive him. Dr. Crandall confirmed that Markin was beyond resuscitation, and Markin was declared dead shortly after 8 a.m.

After writing his assessment, Crandall was returning to his rounds, when, he reports, he felt an unusual prompting from the Holy Spirit to return to the body—which the nurse was then preparing for the morgue. Markin's eyes were fixed and dilated, and his face and extremities had turned black with cyanosis; he was unquestionably dead. Without feeling much faith, Crandall obeyed the prompting.

Crandall prayed aloud for God to resuscitate Markin, giving him a second chance to know the Lord. When Markin was shocked one more time, the flat line on the monitor jumped to a normal heartbeat—which does not normally occur even when the heart stops for a short time. "In my more than twenty years as a cardiologist," Crandall notes, "I have never seen a heartbeat

47. Keener, *Miracles Today*, 159–60.
48. Walker, *God in ICU*, 99–104.
49. Walker, *God in ICU*, 100.

restored so completely and suddenly."[50] With no help, Markin started breathing immediately, and in just a few minutes his extremities were moving and he was speaking. Markin had no brain damage, and he did indeed come to know the Lord.

Dr. Sean George, head of the Department of General Medicine at Kalgoorlie Hospital, now Kalgoorlie Health Campus, Australia, has all the medical documentation posted for the account of another raising—his own. On October 24, 2008, he went into full cardiac arrest.[51] After half an hour workers normally give up trying to revive the patient, but for nearly fifty-five minutes, his friends struggled in vain to revive him. They administered some four thousand chest compressions during that period and shocked him thirteen times, leaving burns on his abdomen.

Notified of his condition, his thirty-eight-year-old wife Sherry Jacob, also a medical professional, and emergency room doctors from his Kalgoorlie hospital reached the clinic. George's body was now cold; by this time he had been dead for an hour and twenty-five minutes. Sherry then took Sean's hand and pleaded for God to restore him. Immediately, his heart began beating!

Though moved by Sherry's devotion, one of his colleagues recoiled. "This is the worst thing that could happen," he thought. "Sooner or later his wife will now have to decide when to disconnect life support." Three days later, however, he awoke with full brain function and began talking. He had not experienced loss of memory, and he began reading his own medical charts. Two weeks later he was discharged from the hospital, and within three months, he was back to working full-time. Three of the doctors who witnessed George's death were Christians, but two others were Hindu and one was Muslim. All recognize the miracle their colleague experienced. Of course, those who accept only instant healings as miracles must discount the value of this and some other accounts.

### Accounts from Our Circle

Two accounts of raisings related to my (Daniel) and my mentor's ministries appear in chapter 23 below.[52] Craig has researched scores of accounts, including eyewitness reports from among his friends and aquaintances globally, such

50. See Crandall, *Raising*, esp. 4; Chauncey Crandall, phone interview, May 30, 2010. Cf. further Fazzina, *Divine Intervention*, 203–6; Garlow and Wall, *Miracles for Real*, 164–67. Although the local and national secular media links are no longer posted at the same web addresses (cited in Keener, *Miracles*, 1:578–79), they were available in 2009, when I reviewed them. An explicitly Christian report remains posted at http://www.cbn.com/tv/1432634071001 (accessed May 26, 2014; July 24, 2020).

51. Sean George, personal correspondence, November 8, 2013; see George, "Miracle Story," which has the full account, with accompanying medical documentation. The account appears also in Garlow and Wall, *Real Miracles*, 22–28.

52. See also Kolenda, *Impact Africa*, 36, 150–51.

as Professor Ayodeji Adewuya;[53] Professor Debbie Watson and her father, Baptist Pastor James Watson;[54] Anglican missions leader Timothy Olonade;[55] Pastor André Mamadzi;[56] Lutheran Pastor Dimbiniaina Randrianasolo;[57] Pastor Margufta Bellevue;[58] medical doctor Ifeanyichukwu Chinedozi;[59] and nurse Sarah Speer.[60]

For example, when I (Craig) asked my Nigerian friend Leo Bawa, who now has a PhD from the Oxford Centre for Mission Studies, whether he had witnessed any miracles, he apologized at the beginning of his response that he did not have much to share. The seven pages of testimonies that he then provided included an account involving a dead child in a village where he was doing ministry in Adamawa State. His host's neighbors brought the child to him. After his initial dismay, he prayed for the child for a few hours. Afterward, he explains, the child revived and Leo handed him back to his parents alive.[61]

Jeanne Mabiala shared three accounts, just one of which I share here.[62] As a trained midwife in Congo-Brazzaville, she helped deliver a baby that had apparently died in the womb hours earlier. The infant's body was white, with the umbilical cord wrapped around her neck. Mabiala led two other women in prayer. Soon the baby opened her eyes and mouth, and after Mama Jeanne started patting her she cried. The baby's grandfather had gone out to build a coffin. When he returned, he was dumbfounded: The child was now fine and remains so.

For personal reasons, the one most compelling to me (Craig) was the following. One day when Thérèse Magnouha was two years old, she cried out about a snake.[63] Most snakes in the area were very poisonous, so her mother,

53. J. Ayodeji Adewuya, phone interview, December 14, 2009; personal correspondence, December 16–17, 2009.

54. James Watson, correspondence, November 27, 2009; sent by Deborah to me with correspondence, November 30, 2009; Deborah Watson, personal correspondence, December 9, 2009.

55. Also Timothy Olonade, personal correspondence, May 12, 13, 16, 22, 2014; Timothy Olonade, interview, February 20, 2015, Wilmore, Kentucky; Francis Kashimawo, personal conversation, Lagos, Nigeria, May 2013; Chinyereugo Adeliyi, personal correspondence, May 10, 11, 12, 2014.

56. André Mamadzi, interview, Yaoundé, Cameroon, January 17, 2013.

57. Dimbiniaina Randrianasolo, interview, Wilmore, Kentucky, April 18, 2019.

58. Margufta Bellevue, personal correspondence, January 30, 31, 2020.

59. Ifeanyichukwu Chinedozi, interview, Lynnfield, Massachusets, November 22, 2017; personal correspondence, February 24, 2018. See also the interview in Worthen, "Prove."

60. Sarah Speer, phone interview, January 7, 2009; personal correspondence, August 20, 2009.

61. Leo Bawa, personal correspondence, August 10, 2009; October 13, 2010.

62. Jeanne Mabiala, interview, Brazzaville, Congo, July 29, 2008. For two of the raisings we were able to consult another witness, one of them my brother-in-law, a scientist. I referred to these accounts earlier in the chapter.

63. Antoinette Malombé, interviews, Dolisie, Congo, July 12–13, 2008; Ngoma Moïse, phone interview, May 14, 2009.

Antoinette Malombé, panicked. Her daughter had stopped breathing, and there was no medical help available in this village. Malombé strapped the lifeless toddler to her back and ran to a nearby village, where family friend Coco Ngoma Moïse was doing ministry. Moïse prayed for Thérèse, who then started breathing again; the next day Thérèse was fine, playing as if nothing had ever happened.

When I asked Malombé how long Thérèse was not breathing, she calculated how long it took to get from the first village to the second, with the hills in between. "About three hours," she concluded, and I was aghast. You see, Malombé was my mother-in-law, and Thérèse is my wife's big sister. Thérèse has no brain damage and later earned a master's degree. Not to question one's mother-in-law, but we also did confirm the story with the other witness, Coco Moïse.

In science, when one encounters too many cases that violate the rule, one has to nuance the rule. Today, one would be hard-pressed to deny accounts of raisings. One might deny that they happen often in particular circles, but then one faces cases such as those of Mabiala, who witnessed three people raised through prayer during her ministry (two of them also attested by other witnesses we knew). All three of those were fairly immediate, although one did require some medical treatment afterward. But if one defines a gift of miracles as being able to raise anyone all the time, it is true that no one claims this today. Neither did first-century apostles, nor anyone we know of who might have had first-century gifts of healings.

## Everyone Healed at Will?

"According to Scripture," MacArthur proclaims, "those who possessed miraculous gifts could use their gifts at will. Contemporary healers do not heal at will. They cannot."[64] Indeed, he claims, "no charismatic healer heals everyone who comes for healing and hundreds go away from their services as sick or as crippled as when they came."[65] Here he apparently thinks of television evangelists. On the cutting edge of evangelism, however (breaking ground for the kingdom, the kind of setting described in the Gospels and Acts), a majority in some villages are healed, including of deafness or blindness.[66] Meanwhile, if it is just a majority healed, are we supposed to deny that God is doing these things because not all are healed or the person praying is charismatic? When

64. MacArthur, *Chaos*, 215. Cf. MacArthur, *Strange Fire*, 167: "The healing miracles of Jesus never failed. Neither did those done by the apostles in the book of Acts."

65. MacArthur, *Chaos*, 216.

66. See Brown et al., "Study"; Brown, "Testing Prayer"; Brown, *Testing Prayer*, 207–9, 214–20, 223–30.

even a minority are healed, must we deny that God is doing the healing and hearing the prayers?

In any case, is MacArthur correct that anyone gifted should be able to heal at will, "according to Scripture"? Jesus did heal everyone who came to him, and we are aware of no one with that track record today. But in some places Jesus was limited in his miracles, perhaps because he was unwilling to heal those without the faith to come to him (Mark 6:5). Some argue that even Jesus did not heal automatically, but remained subject to the Father: "Why would Luke say that the power of the Lord was present for Jesus to heal if Jesus could heal at any time, under any condition, and solely at his own discretion?"[67] (noting Luke 5:17; cf. 6:19; 8:46). Whether or not this is the case, Scripture does show that Jesus did not heal everyone near him (Mark 6:5; John 5:3).

MacArthur claims that it "is self-evident" that "no one anywhere today can credibly claim to have a healing gift comparable to Peter's (Acts 5:12–16) or Paul's (19:11–12)."[68] The passages to which MacArthur refers are portrayed by Luke as peak times of (explicitly) "extraordinary" miracles (Acts 19:11–12; cf. 5:15). Yet this was not always the case even in Paul's ministry. Paul could not always heal at will even his own companions (Phil. 2:25–27; 1 Tim. 5:23; 2 Tim. 4:20).[69]

Some cessationists imagine a New Testament utopia so extreme that they find problematic the biblical accounts that describe something other than the exceptional picture in Acts 5:15 or 19:11–12. Thus they suggest that the lack of immediate healing in Philippians and the Pastorals stemmed from God revoking Paul's healing gift later in his life: "Paul no longer had the gift of healing, and was no longer able to heal as he did only a few years earlier in Acts 28:9. The sign gifts were no longer operating."[70] But even by cessationist standards, this explanation makes no sense. The canon is still being written as Paul writes Philippians, which describes Epaphroditus's illness and recovery. Weren't the gifts supposed to continue till the canon's closure? Further, if the principle in Romans 11:29 applies ("God's gifts and his call are irrevocable"), it seems unlikely that Paul, Peter, or anyone had the gift of healing at one point but later "no longer" had it.

As Jack Deere notes, "This is an incredible explanation. Here we would have to admit that miracles had ceased even before the death of the apostles.

67. Deere, *Still Surprised*, 60.

68. MacArthur, "Foreword," iii.

69. Deere, *Still Surprised*, 65, notes that some claim that Paul could use healing only on unbelievers; but then how would he have raised Eutychus (Acts 20:9–12)? Certainly the gifts of healings are, like other *charismata*, designated for building up the church (1 Cor. 12:7). For nonhealing in Scripture and today, see, e.g., Keener, *Miracles Today*, 222–28, esp. 224–25; Keener, *Suffering*, 99–115, esp. 109–11; Gen. 32:31–32; 1 Kings 14:4; 2 Kings 13:21.

70. Kiszonas, "Tongues Cease."

There is no biblical argument to back up such an interpretation."[71] It also fails to account for Paul's own bodily sickness early in his ministry, a sickness apparently serious enough to account for why he preached in one area at that time (South Galatia) rather than another (Gal. 4:13).[72] Acts does not report his sickness; an apostle's sickness was not as relevant to Luke's point as were signs. Yet we do learn from Acts that for purposes of mission, God also worked through Paul in signs and wonders in that same period of his ministry (Acts 14:3, 10) and caused him to survive stoning (14:19–20). (Some also mention his "thorn in the flesh" in 2 Corinthians 12:7, but this case may have been something different from a physical affliction.)[73] Miracle working is not incompatible with simultaneous illness.

Using the same sort of hermeneutic used to exclude healing, perhaps we could say that the gift of *teaching* died out once we had the canon: In the *later* New Testament, John says, "You don't need anyone to teach you" (1 John 2:27; cf. 2:7), and only false "teachers" continue to be mentioned explicitly (2 John 1:9–10; Rev. 2:14–15, 20, 24). This conclusion would be absurd, but it conforms to the cessationist hermeneutic just mentioned.

Nor did Jesus suggest that everyone would be healed through his followers' ministry; we would need to care in other ways for those whose disabilities remained (Luke 14:13). If there is a conflict between biblical expectation and what we see today, it might be most with James 5:14–15, since it sounds like it *promises* that the prayer of faith will heal the sick. Whether it is cessationists or continuationists praying, that does not always happen.

How could Paul the apostle be sick (Gal. 4:13) or have close friends and colleagues who were sick (Phil. 2:26–27; 1 Tim. 5:23; 2 Tim. 4:20)? Maybe Paul was human just like us, and not every single person he prayed for was instantly healed. Maybe having apostolic signs for evangelism or gifts of healings for the church doesn't guarantee that every person you pray for is going to be healed immediately, completely, permanently, and undeniably.

## A Matter of Degree?

Thomas Schreiner argues that "charismatics must show that miracles are really happening to the same extent today as in the New Testament, and that there are people who have the gift of healings and miracles."[74] In terms

71. Deere, *Still Surprised*, 65. Moreover, revelatory gifts continue to be mentioned as part of church practice in the Pastorals (1 Tim. 1:18; 4:14; 2 Tim. 1:6).

72. Although, against the proposal that this was necessarily an eye problem (based esp. on Gal. 4:14), see Keener, "Note"; Keener, *Galatians*, 375. Galatians 4:13 also militates against an argument from a healer's illness (as perhaps implied in Warfield, *Counterfeit Miracles*, 184).

73. Cf. Num. 33:55; discussion in Keener, *Corinthians*, 240; cf. Keener, *Galatians*, 374.

74. Schreiner, *Spiritual Gifts*, 164–65.

of patterns, some do experience them more often than others, as we have already illustrated. In terms of extent, is there anything in the description in 1 Corinthians 12:9 that suggests that *everyone* will *always* be healed? If Paul envisioned that, would he not expect that all Christians could remain alive until Jesus returned, barring certain spiritual deficiencies in the church (1 Cor. 11:30)? Yet this is not the case (1 Cor. 15:22, 26; 1 Thess. 4:13). The same gifts may also differ in intensity from one person to another (cf. "proportion" in Rom. 12:6).[75]

Here a more moderate cessationist such as Schreiner comes closer to continuationists than do more traditional cessationists. "If a continuationist says that the gifts are operating today but to a far inferior degree than what we see in the New Testament, then they seem to be saying that the gifts aren't operating as they did in the New Testament. . . . The argument actually sounds like a form of cessationism to me."[76] A continuationist, meanwhile, may object that Schreiner's approach sounds like a form of continuationism, so long as he allows that *sometimes* they do meet the level we see in most New Testament narratives. He does allow that "perhaps God is pleased in cutting-edge missionary situations to grant the same signs and wonders we see in the New Testament era," while rightly warning that we should investigate claims before circulating them.[77]

## Healing like Jesus?

No one we know claims a perfect score like Jesus. No one represents God's kingdom as perfectly as Jesus. Moreover, no one will disagree with one cessationist's observation: "The high point in biblical revelation, of course, is the ministry, death, and resurrection of Jesus Christ."[78] Less fair is the claim that the apostles' "healing ministry is the standard by which all reported miraculous healings are to be compared. Anything short of that standard is not the biblical gift of healing."[79] Says who? On what authority?

75. Scholars debate the sense of Rom. 12:6. For what we take as the likeliest sense, see, e.g., Keener, *Romans*, 145–46; in agreement with Schreiner, *Romans*, 656. On the historic misappropriation of the phrase to support the (otherwise valuable) "analogy of faith" principle, see Menzies, *Romans*, 325–33.

76. Schreiner, *Spiritual Gifts*, 165.

77. Schreiner, *Spiritual Gifts*, 165. It is appropriate to evaluate miracle claims, like prophecy (1 Cor. 14:29), despite the problem in his particular analogy for this: Jesus's skeptical enemies in John 9:15–34 were hardly impartial investigators!

78. Schreiner, *Spiritual Gifts*, 166.

79. Pennington, *Cessationism*, 125. In the same paragraph he reads the apostles' recorded highlights as if they characterize all their healing, which would require us to assume that less dramatic conditions were unworthy of their attention.

### *Did Even the Apostles Heal Everybody?*

Certainly the apostles failed sometimes despite learning directly from Jesus (Mark 9:28–29). But some may suppose that they always succeeded in healing or deliverance after Pentecost, so our focus will be on those examples.

Not everyone around Paul or the Twelve was instantly healed (Gal. 4:13; Phil. 2:27; 2 Tim. 4:20), but even if they were, that hardly institutes a rigid standard for everyone who would ever exercise gifts of healings or miracles. We might actually expect the apostles, who were mentored by Jesus himself, to become above average in the effectiveness of their ministries. (It's no surprise, for example, that believers in Joppa sent for Peter, known for his ministry of signs, when Tabitha died; Acts 9:38.)[80] Nor need we expect gifts of healings in the church (1 Cor. 12:9) to be as dramatic as apostolic "signs."[81]

Cessationist teacher Sam Waldron defines "a miracle-worker" as someone "permanently gifted to do miracles."[82] Yet he concedes, "I am not implying that a miracle-worker can do miracles any time he or she wishes, any more than a prophet might prophesy any time he wishes."[83] Nearly all charismatics would agree with his concession.

Sound charismatics do not claim that everyone always is healed. Deere recounts that he was sick during an entire conference when he spoke on healing.[84] For five of the first six times I (Craig) spoke about miracles or healing at conferences after my first book on miracles came out, I was sick with one ailment or another, such as a cold at Oxford and a clogged left ear throughout a Vineyard Scholars conference.

Groundbreaking evangelism in new areas continues to lay new "foundations" (Rom. 15:20), and not surprisingly, genuinely dramatic miracles seem to flourish especially (though by no means exclusively) in such areas, as "signs" confirming the message of Christ's grace (cf. Acts 14:3).[85] Iris Mozambique offers examples of widespread healings of deafness and blindness, though admittedly not in every case.[86] Some friends in India and Mongolia have shared with me (Craig) that they witnessed many miracles as the first churches were planted in unevangelized areas, with these slowing down once the church was established.[87]

80. This is on the assumption that they were soliciting a miracle rather than comfort; see Keener, *Acts*, 2:1717–18.

81. So also Storms, "Response to Saucy," 159.

82. Waldron, *Continued*, 12.

83. Waldron, *Continued*, 17n7.

84. Deere, *Still Surprised*, 118.

85. Here I draw on Keener, *Gift & Giver*, 213.

86. Keener, *Miracles*, 1:515; Keener, *Miracles Today*, 30, 135–36; Stafford, *Miracles*, 151–59; Deichmann, "Lessons"; supplemental information from personal correspondence, May 27, 2016.

87. For this pattern in a particular region of India, I learned esp. from Ebenezer Perinbaraj, interviews, December 25, 2012; May 10, 2014; personal correspondence, May 11 and 14, 2014.

Mostly the same range of miracles we see in the Bible—except for the original creation, the exodus, the virgin birth, and Jesus's resurrection, which inaugurated a new creation—continue to be experienced today. (See again Craig's two-volume work, *Miracles: The Credibility of the New Testament Accounts*.)

Unlike "signs," which by definition are designed to get attention, healings need not be dramatic or instant to constitute answers to prayer (1 Cor. 12:9, 28–29; James 5:15–16). In churches, we usually see gifts of healings and prayer for the sick, which need not be dramatic. They can be gradual, through the way God created our bodies, through medicine (cf. 1 Tim. 5:23), rest, nutrition, and so on. MacArthur is right to point out that "genuine healings may come as a result of prayer and most often involve simple natural processes. Other times, God speeds up the recovery mechanisms and restores a sick person to health in a way that medicine cannot explain." "Certainly God heals . . . in answer to prayer and in order to reveal his glory."[88] Yet MacArthur denies that "the biblical gift of healing" can be expressed when God answers the petitioners' prayers through such ordinary means. His denial, however,[89] depends on his ideal that God always heals instantly when someone so gifted prays. Where does Paul so define this gift? MacArthur's denial fails to distinguish typical gifts of healings in churches from typical signs and wonders in evangelizing.

Because gifts of healings always appear only in the plural (1 Cor. 12:9, 28, 29), Carson is among those who argue, "This strongly suggests that there were different gifts of healings: not everyone was getting healed by one person, and perhaps certain persons with one of these gifts of healing could by the Lord's grace heal certain diseases or heal a variety of diseases but only at certain times."[90]

### *Either You're the Best or You're Fake*

Jesus was the best teacher. Does this mean that someone must lack the gift of teaching if they cannot teach like Jesus, even the first time they teach? If a teacher may grow in his or her gift, why not allow maturation in other gifts? (This is even aside from the matter of God's sovereignty in healing.) Where in the Bible does it say that gifts are genuine only if we deploy them fully or perfectly? What would such a requirement do for those who "know in part"

88. MacArthur, *Chaos*, 210.

89. MacArthur, *Chaos*, 216.

90. Carson, *Showing Spirit*, 39. See also Fee, *Presence*, 33: "Here he probably refers not to some 'gift' that enables people to heal others, but to the various concrete expressions of the Spirit's power bringing physical healing to members of the community; hence 'gifts of healings.'" Also Storms, "View," 212: "either many different gifts or powers of healing, each appropriate to and effective for its related illness, or each occurrence of healing constituting a distinct gift in its own right."

and "prophesy in part" (1 Cor. 13:9)? For Paul, even confessing Jesus as Lord is led by the prophetic Spirit (1 Cor. 12:3).

Deere points out,

> When I was a seminary professor, we argued that none of the contemporary "faith healers" healed like Jesus healed (if they were healing at all). . . .
>
> Our reasoning was faulty. Nowhere else in life would we take the stellar example in any category and use it as the qualification for membership in that category. No one has ever loved like Jesus or taught like Jesus. Should we conclude that God is no longer giving the gift of teaching or that our experience of love is an illusion?[91]

Andrew Wilson develops the analogy:

> Yes, the apostles were more successful at healing and prophecy than we are. There is, indeed, a discrepancy between our experience and what is described in the New Testament. But the apostles were also far more successful at evangelism. And church planting. And leadership. And cross-cultural mission. And church discipline. And teaching. And standing firm under persecution. And handling disappointment. Yet in none of these cases do we conclude that the gulf is so wide, their "success" so much greater than ours, that to tell people how to share the gospel or teach or lead more effectively, is to encourage people to be satisfied with sub-biblical Christianity. Rather, we acknowledge the disparity and seek to learn from it. . . . The same, surely, should apply to miraculous gifts.[92]

The same Spirit who provides us with "gifts" also produces "fruit" in us. The fruit of the Spirit is the virtues of Christlike character that God nurtures in us: love, joy, peace, patience, kindness, goodness, faithfulness, gentleness, and self-control (Gal. 5:22–23).[93] Both continuationists and cessationists would agree that all true Christians have the Spirit, and all are called to produce this fruit of the Spirit. But do we expect all believers to be flawless all the time? What if a born-again believer fails to live perfectly in the Spirit, losing his temper here or judging her fellow believer there? Do we say this is because the fruit of the Spirit has passed away? Of course not. Even though every true Christian has the Holy Spirit, we know that it takes time to develop life in the Spirit. That's the nature of our relationship with the Holy Spirit. Why would we allow ourselves room to grow in the fruit of the Spirit but deny others room to grow in particular gifts of the Spirit? Cessationists' claims that the gifts of the Spirit have passed away because charismatics operate in

91. Deere, *Still Surprised*, 59.

92. Wilson, *Spirit and Sacrament*, 110–11, cited approvingly in Allison and Köstenberger, *Holy Spirit*, 433–34n34.

93. For discussion of Paul's list in its ancient context, see, e.g., Keener, "Fruit"; Keener, *Galatians*, 515–24.

them imperfectly make no more sense than claims that the fruit of the Spirit has passed away because certain cessationists are so unloving, impatient, and unkind to some fellow believers.

### Exceptional *Miracles (Acts 19:11–12)*

Some[94] compare charismatic healing today with something unreasonably flawless. The high points celebrated in Acts 5:15 and 19:11–12 do not always happen today and were not always happening in the first century. I (Daniel) have heard testimonies in Africa of the sick being healed as we drove past on the road. Many times people carried to the meeting on their deathbeds were instantly healed upon their arrival to the field. Many others have been healed as they listened to the meeting on the radio or watched on television. Sometimes sick relatives in other cities were healed as we prayed for their loved ones who were present in the service. I have witnessed breathtaking miracles, signs, and wonders.

But I have yet to see the day when every single person—without exception—was healed! I long for it and pray for it. But I admit that I have not yet seen it. Yet I think some cessationists imagine that in the first century every day was exactly like the scenes described in Acts 5:15 and 19:11–12. They seem to think the apostles healed everyone at will.

But do these romanticized concepts of the gifts of the Spirit hold up to scriptural scrutiny? The very fact that Luke tells us about one season where particularly "extraordinary" displays of power came through Paul seems to suggest that, while the gifts remained constant, the levels of intensity for miracles seemed to spike at times. During Paul's ministry in Ephesus, for example, Luke tells us that God performed "extraordinary" miracles through his hands (Acts 19:11). The Greek phrase literally says, "God was performing no ordinary miracles."[95] Hence most versions translate the phrase "extraordinary." See also the NKJV's and NLT's "unusual miracles," KJV's "special miracles," and NCV's "very special miracles." These phrases describe uncommon acts of power, like the healings and deliverances that occurred through Paul's garments (Acts 19:12). Further evidence of the overall exceptional nature of Paul's ministry in Ephesus includes the entire province hearing the gospel (19:10); fear falling on "everyone" in the city (19:17); many occultists repenting, confessing, and burning their magical scrolls (19:18–19); and the idol industry getting so disturbed by conversions to Christ that a dangerous riot broke out (19:23–41). The local demonic stronghold was dethroned. These events for this season differ from the notable but less dramatic impact earlier

94. E.g., Pennington, "Case."

95. This is an example of the rhetorical device called "litotes," a negative understatement meant to accentuate its positive equivalent (see also Acts 28:2 for the same phrase used to describe the Maltese natives' "extraordinary kindness," or literally, "no ordinary kindness").

in Paul's ministry in the interior of Asia Minor (Acts 13–14), Macedonia (16:14–17:34), and Achaia (18:1–17).

As powerful as Paul's ministry ordinarily was, this was no ordinary season. For a period of two to three years (19:10; 20:31), Ephesus experienced a season of exceptional outpouring in the wider messianic era already characterized by the outpouring of the Spirit (2:17–18). Rainstorms vary in intensity even if they occur during the same rainy season.

But these stories are highlights in the lives of highly gifted servants of God during extraordinary times. Even the disciples had to grow in their supernatural ministries. Early on, they successfully healed some people (Luke 10:9, 17), and other times they failed (Matt. 17:19). Apart from one summary about Paul and Barnabas (Acts 14:3), Paul's recorded miracles begin one or two at a time (Acts 13:11; 14:9–10), well before the massive healings of Acts 19:11–12. While many signs followed his ministry among gentiles (15:12), Luke records none in the years between his conversion and his first mission from Antioch. Luke surely does not report every miracle through Paul's ministry (cf. 2 Cor. 12:12, in Corinth, where Luke reports no miracles), but if we see a pattern, it is that even Paul grew in his gift.

If I (Daniel) gave you a narrative of my life, with all the highlights compressed together, it would sound unbelievable. The same could probably be said of your life. But to assume I had no less dramatic days makes an excessive argument from silence on the other end of the spectrum from the claim that miracles were limited to three or four eras because more are mentioned there! Perspectives like those of Tom Pennington strike me as the opinions of people with strictly a priori knowledge about a ministry of healing rather than much firsthand experience. Why should we assume that the apostles' "highlight reel" ought to set the minimum threshold for what constitutes operating in an authentic gift of healing for all Christians of all times?

## Practical Experience and Healing

Whereas charismatic and noncharismatic professors have much in common, gifts such as healing and prophecy may look quite different than gifts that cessationist teachers are used to. Not all God's gifts look like our own.

### *Do Cessationist Critics Understand "Gifts of Healings" Better Than Charismatic Practitioners?*

Cessationist critics often claim they know about the gifts of the Spirit better than do charismatics because they know the Bible. But the Bible talks about the presence of the gifts, not the absence of the gifts. How can they base their cessationist comments on continuationist Scripture, missing the forest for the trees? Further, if these cessationists know the Bible, then they should also know that the Bible does not give us detailed instruction about all of the practical operations of spiritual gifts.

Most of what such cessationists claim to know is purely theoretical. For example, the gift of healing is never defined in Scripture. So when cessationists draw a distinction between "healing" (which in their view might happen in rare cases if God is so inclined), and the "gift" of healing (which some cessationists see as the ability to heal at will),[96] that distinction is mere speculation. Nobody in Scripture is explicitly described as possessing the "gift" of healing. So we cannot even infer from the biblical stories of healing what might constitute a "gift of healing" as opposed to a random, benevolent, sovereign miracle. There is even some question about whether we are talking about one gift or many, since Scripture talks about "gifts of healings" (1 Cor. 12:9, 30). Cessationist critics will often define and determine ad hoc what is and is not miraculous, what does and does not constitute the gift of healing, and so forth. All the while the more strident cessationists insist that those who claim a gift of healing must be deceived or are deceiving. Yet who will have more practical experience of healings than those regularly engaged in praying for the sick?

### *Empty Some Hospitals*

"If you have the gift of healing, why don't you go to the hospital and heal everyone?" This is a common objection to gifts of healings.

While we are talking about "gifts" as opposed to healing more generically, it may be helpful to address what may be a semantic issue, and perhaps a misunderstanding between charismatics and cessationists. This represents what is probably the number one question I (Daniel) get from skeptics when they hear testimonies of miracles that occur in our meetings.[97] It's usually posed as a rhetorical question rather than a sincere inquiry. It's meant to be a "gotcha" question—something that proves beyond a shadow of a doubt that I am a charlatan. Usually it's asked as if it were the knockout blow that silences every charismatic. But it simply betrays ignorance. It shows how little these skeptics understand what charismatics like myself believe, much less how the gifts of the Spirit actually operate.

When people ask me why I don't empty out hospitals, have they stopped to wonder whether that expectation is reasonable—even for someone with the gift of healing? We don't read that the apostles emptied out any ancient infirmaries either. Why did Jesus heal only one man at the pool of Bethesda? Within the five colonnades of that pool "lay a large number of

96. MacArthur, *Chaos*, 214.
97. For this objection, cf., e.g., Lanphere, *Cessationist*.

the disabled—blind, lame, and paralyzed" (John 5:3). They all awaited a miracle. But Jesus healed only one. Or how is it possible that in Nazareth, Jesus "could not" do any great miracles (Mark 6:5)? Why is it that even some of the apostles and members of the early church suffered with sickness from time to time? I am not trying to downplay the miracles of Jesus or the apostles, and by no means am I suggesting that I or my colleagues are on their level in any way. God forbid! I am only drawing attention to the facts conveniently overlooked by cessationists when they try to describe their imaginary utopia of the early church.

Just for the record, I do often go to the hospital and pray for people. Does everyone get healed? No. Do some get healed? Yes. Why doesn't everyone get healed? I don't know. I don't have all the answers. I don't parade around triumphantly waving a magic healing wand. In fact, my work in ministry is very painful at times. Few people, other than medical doctors and nurses, come face-to-face with as much sickness, suffering, and tragedy as those of us that are often called upon to pray for the sick. Contrary to the caricatures cessationists draw of us, based on their most hated villains from Christian television, ministering to the sick is not a flamboyant business. It requires a willingness to be vulnerable, to hurt with people, to be moved deeply with compassion, to weep tears, to grieve for other people's loved ones and feel their loss and their pain as though they were our own—all the while standing with them in faith.

There are many great victories along the way, and many glorious breakthroughs. We rejoice when that happens and give God all the glory. But there have been other times when the person I prayed for died. I don't want to say too much about this, but I think you need to understand what it's really like to be labeled as a "healing evangelist." We all have enough pain in our own lives. Who needs more? Who needs to feel other people's pain and loss? Yet Scripture calls us to "bear one another's burdens" (Gal. 6:2). We pray for the sick not because we think we are special but because it's what Jesus told us to do. We obey him and we trust him to do his part.

Even when people get healed and miracles take place, I don't claim them as my own. I don't claim to have ever performed a miracle. Although many have called me a "faith healer" and a "healing evangelist," I don't identify myself by these kinds of titles. Actually I don't like these titles. I don't even claim to have the gift of healing. Jesus is the healer. I am just a vessel, and an ordinary one at that. Although I have seen countless miracles, I don't take credit for a single one. All the glory belongs to Jesus. And this has always been the case in real healing (Acts 3:12; 14:15).

I am speaking for myself here, because that is all I can do. But these sentiments are not rare in the charismatic world. In my experience, these are the prevailing charismatic views on healing—even among the charismatic "faith healers" so vehemently condemned by cessationists.

### *Praying for the Sick*

Here's where cessationists and continuationists agree: We all believe in healing. That's a great start! But the cessationist will object to someone's claim to have a gift of healing—as though he or she can heal at will. Yet as I've already said, I (Daniel) do not believe that *I* have the ability to heal anyone at will. I do believe, however, that it is normally God's will to heal and that he still heals today. That means that when I pray, I pray with the expectation that God will heal. So here is the real difference. The typical cessationist prays for healing with much less expectation that God will heal. The typical continuationist prays *with* an expectation that, other factors being equal, God will heal. It looks like praying with the expectation that God desires to heal results in more healings.[98]

How can we account for this? It is what Scripture declares. James says that "the prayer offered in faith will restore the one who is sick, and the Lord will raise him up" (James 5:15). Notice that James is careful to describe the prayer that heals the sick person as a "prayer offered in faith." And James derives his "faith" theology from Jesus himself. Jesus made it clear that the reason some of the disciples' prayers did not work was because of their lack of faith (Matt. 17:19–20); he also often links faith with healing (see Matt. 8:10, 13; 15:28; Mark 5:34, 36; 9:23; 10:52; 11:22–25; Luke 17:19; John 4:50; 11:40; Acts 3:16; 14:9). This does not logically entail that lack of healing reflects lack of faith; Job offers one of the most conspicuous examples to the contrary (James 5:11). Jesus also sometimes performs miracles despite lack of faith (Mark 4:39–40), though on some occasions lack of faith hinders blessing (6:5–6; Luke 1:20). What the association of healing with faith does suggest clearly is that genuine confidence in God's power to heal is biblical.

When typical charismatics look at a verse like James 5:15, most see that God will raise up the sick person through the prayer of faith. They take it as a promise to grasp in faith. They stand on it and act on it. But some cessationists can look at the same verse and see something totally different. For example, Warfield says, "If any is sick among you, we read, let him call for the elders of the church and let them pray for him, rubbing him with his oil in the name of the Lord, and the prayer of faith shall save him that is sick. Where is there promise of miracle in that? What James requires of us is merely that we

98. See, e.g., Newman, "Discovering the Spirit," 49: Newman used to "pray and hope for the best," but when she began praying more confidently for healing, she "saw miraculous things happen, over and over." Although I (Craig) did not always list church affiliations in *Miracles*, I did encounter miracle accounts more often in circles that prayed for them more often (which were also the circles more apt to talk about them). The Gospels also highlight some occasions of desperate, committed prayers rather than anyone approaching Jesus nonchalantly (or skeptically, as in Mark 8:11–12).

shall be Christians in our sickness as in our health, and that our dependence then, too, shall be on the Lord."[99]

It seems to us that Warfield has completely missed the point of James 5:15. But then again, many cessationists agree with him. Most charismatics see here a promise of healing or divine intervention. Different interpretations of texts are common in theology, but the difference is very important when it comes to healing. If you hold Warfield's view, why bother to pray for those so sick or impaired that it would take special divine action to restore them? Why put yourself in the uncomfortable situation? Why subject yourself to the virtual certainty of continual disappointment? This is the reason Warfieldian cessationists don't pray for the sick the way typical charismatics do (or even the way some less strict cessationists do). If charismatics are praying for more people, more often, with more confidence that God will heal, is it any wonder that we tend to see more healings?

A couple of years ago, I (Daniel) heard about a brother in the Lord, about my age and also a minister, who had been diagnosed with a terminal disease and given only a few months to live. I knew he was from a cessationist background, and for all I knew he did not believe that healing was for today. But my heart became heavily burdened for him. So I contacted him and asked if I could visit and pray for him. To my surprise he agreed. I flew across the country and went to visit him in his home. When we began to talk, he said something I will never forget: "Whenever my evangelical friends come to visit me, they all pray with hesitation and reservation, almost like they're already saying their last goodbyes." He continued, "When I hear that, it makes me angry. I feel like telling them, 'If that is how you're going to pray, don't even bother. I don't need that kind of sympathy. I need someone who will fight for me.'" "Yes!" I said. "That's why I came. I'm not here to say goodbye. I'm here to fight for you. I'm here to pray in faith that God will heal you and raise you up."

If you were struggling with illness, how would you want someone to pray for you? You might be a cessationist. But I would wager that, if you were lying on your deathbed and felt that the Lord had more work for you to do, you would rather have a fervent charismatic praying for you than a resigned cessationist. If it were your child, spouse, or loved one in desperate need of a miracle, would you want someone praying for you who simply went through the motions without much expectation? Or would you want someone who believes it is normally God's will to heal and who will pray for you as though God were ready to heal?

99. Warfield, *Counterfeit Miracles*, 172. We have John Wesley's response to this interpretation in his letter to Conyers Middleton (Wesley, "Middleton"), in which he says, "Be pleased to try how many you can cure thus that are blind, deaf, dumb, or paralytic; and experience, if not philosophy, will teach you that oil has no such natural efficacy as this."

## Does God Delight in Healing?

Granted that not everyone gets healed, whatever the reasons, it is certainly biblical to seek healing for people. There is good reason to pray not resignedly, but with bold confidence in God's compassion and power. Even though we don't see healing every time, we may also pray eagerly, looking forward to seeing what our gracious God may do for his glory and for our precious brothers and sisters.

Charismatics do not all share identical views of healing, but all believe that we can pray for it and that some (with gifts of healings) may witness healing more often than others. Many affirm that Jesus's atoning death paid not only for our spiritual salvation but also for the restoration of our health (Matt. 8:17) and indeed for a new creation. We recognize that we will not inherit the full benefits of his sacrifice—such as our immortal resurrection bodies and a new earth—until his return.[100] But the "already" side of the already/not yet kingdom means that we pray with much greater confidence for people's physical welfare, a welfare that Jesus's ministry shows us that God actually does care about.

What we believe about God's concern for our physical welfare will greatly impact the way we approach prayer for healing. How can we pray in faith for something if we're not even sure whether God does it today? Cessationists will often cover their bases by prefacing their prayer with the phrase, "If it be thy will . . ." Theologically, such a preface might be superfluous, in that if something is not God's will, he will not do it, with or without our permission. He knows what we need better than we do (Mark 10:38). Based on Scripture, however, we have good reason to trust that God *does* care about our physical well-being. For that principle, note the following verses (NIV):

> Exodus 15:26: "[The Lord] said, 'If you listen carefully to the Lord your God and do what is right in his eyes, if you pay attention to his commands and keep all his decrees, I will not bring on you any of the diseases I brought on the Egyptians, for I am the Lord, who heals you.'"

> Exodus 23:25–26: "Worship the Lord your God, and his blessing will be on your food and water. I will take away sickness from among you, and none will miscarry or be barren in your land. I will give you a full life span."

> Deuteronomy 7:12–15: "If you pay attention to these laws and are careful to follow them, then the Lord your God will keep his covenant of love with you,

100. See discussion in Carson, *Showing Spirit*, 156–57; Keener, *Matthew*, 273; cf. Keener, *Peter*, 199–200. For historical debates about how atonement applies to healing, see Keener, *Miracles*, 1:391–400; Keener, *1–2 Peter, Jude*, 26.

as he swore to your ancestors. He will love you and bless you. . . . The LORD will keep you free from every disease."

Psalm 103:1–3: "Praise the LORD, my soul; all my inmost being, praise his holy name. Praise the LORD, my soul, and forget not all his benefits—who forgives all your sins and heals all your diseases."

Isaiah 53:4–5: "Surely he took up our pain and bore our suffering, yet we considered him punished by God, stricken by him, and afflicted. But he was pierced for our transgressions, he was crushed for our iniquities; the punishment that brought us peace was on him, and by his wounds we are healed."

Matthew 4:23–24: "Jesus went throughout Galilee, teaching in their synagogues, preaching the good news of the kingdom, and healing every disease and sickness among the people. News about him spread all over Syria, and people brought to him all who were ill with various diseases, those suffering severe pain, the demon-possessed, those having seizures, and the paralyzed, and he healed them."

Matthew 8:16–17: "When evening came, many who were demon-possessed were brought to [Jesus], and he drove out the spirits with a word and healed all the sick. This was to fulfill what was spoken through the prophet Isaiah: 'He took up our infirmities and bore our diseases.'"

Luke 9:1–2: "When Jesus had called the Twelve together, he gave them power and authority to drive out all demons and to cure diseases, and he sent them out to proclaim the kingdom of God and to heal the sick."

Acts 5:14–16: "More and more men and women believed in the Lord and were added to their number. As a result, people brought the sick into the streets and laid them on beds and mats so that at least Peter's shadow might fall on some of them as he passed by. Crowds gathered also from the towns around Jerusalem, bringing their sick and those tormented by evil spirits, and all of them were healed."

1 Corinthians 12:7–9: "Now to each one the manifestation of the Spirit is given for the common good. To one there is given through the Spirit the message of wisdom, to another the message of knowledge by means of the same Spirit, to another faith by the same Spirit, to another gifts of healing by that one Spirit."

James 5:14–15: "Is anyone among you sick? Let them call the elders of the church to pray over them and anoint them with oil in the name of the Lord. And the prayer offered in faith will make the sick person well; the Lord will raise them up."

Most charismatics look at verses like these throughout Scripture and ask, "Has not God already revealed his concern for our physical restoration and healing?" Shouldn't we believe his written Word (*sola scriptura*!) and pray from a position of faith on that basis? When we pray for people's restoration, we are not twisting God's arm to do something he'd really rather not do. Someone might then respond, "If this is the case, why isn't everyone healed?" Nearly all charismatics realize that not everyone is healed. Indeed, it is obvious that no one in this present body is immortal. So it makes sense for readers to look for biblical explanations as to why healing doesn't always happen. But our *default* (normal) expectation should be that God is ready to hear our prayer for healing. This expresses confidence in God's character and power more than in the power of illness. What he does in response to our prayer is up to him. God may also lead us to pray in certain ways at certain times.

Scripture invites us to pray for healing with expectancy (James 5:14–16). Granted, there are cases like Job, where, for reasons unknown from our earthly perspective, God allows illness to continue at great length. But if we are using the model of Job to explain the nonhealing of 95 percent of the people we pray for, either there may be a serious problem among our group sample or culture (as in 1 Cor. 11:29–30) or we are approaching God with an anti-expectancy, expecting God *not* to heal.

That God does not always heal people for whom we pray doesn't change the pattern that Scripture declares. If we are going to "err" on one side or another, wouldn't it be better to err on the side of faith in God's promises, of taking God at his Word and at least asking? Of course, I do not believe it is literally possible to "err" on the side of trusting God's Word. My point is that we should not turn our experiences into doctrines. I've prayed many times for people who weren't healed. But my experience does not change the Word of God. I'm going to keep praying for the sick as though everyone I've ever laid hands on was instantly healed. God's Word is our standard and invites us to care about what he cares about—people's spiritual and physical well-being.

Whether one believes that Scripture affords us such confidence in prayer or not, the model it does provide is one of trust in God's faithfulness. Certainly Scripture welcomes us to expect that God heals. My primary point here is that one cannot make a *sola scriptura* argument that healing is not for today. The best one can do is to turn to subjective experience to support such a claim. But that is what cesssationists insist we should not do—base truth on experience or feeling rather than God's Word! If we are going to follow Scripture, we must believe that God graciously does heal and that his healing is not limited to the merely naturalistic processes that Warfield (a full cessationist) allowed.

## Semantics and Style

I think ordinary cessationists will probably find that many of their objections to our charismatic beliefs were based on mischaracterizations and misunderstandings. There are differences between what I believe and what the typical cessationist believes. And those differences are very important. But those differences are often smaller than what many cessationists realize or have even considered.

Often when cessationists talk about the "gift of healing," they envision something no one believes in—namely, the power to heal anyone, anytime at will. The apostles did not have that ability, and even Jesus was limited by people's unbelief on at least one occasion (Mark 6:5). I (Daniel) have heard cessationists reject "faith healers" because they claim the ability to heal everyone at will. I can tell you as a personal friend to many of the most well known "faith healers" in the world—even some of the most controversial ones—not one of them believes this. I have my share of disagreements with many of these individuals. But I can assure you, I have never known any charismatic "faith healers" who believe they can heal at will.

This will come as a surprise to many cessationists. But it is just one area among many in the cessationism-continuationism debate where we simply misunderstand one another. I have a feeling that many of the disagreements about healing boil down to semantics. In some cases, cessationists and continuationists are actually saying the same things but using different terminology and perhaps with a different emphasis. In reality, many times our differences are quite small. I should probably add that style is also a factor. I think it's important to separate our semantics and style from actual doctrinal objections. Only then can we see what is worth arguing about.

Our disagreements are not always doctrinal or even logical. Often there is more of a visceral reaction against styles of ministry that some find unappealing. For example, many of the more conservative cessationists often take issue with our practice of bringing those healed in our meetings up to the platform to testify publicly. But this concern is a matter of style. If God has genuinely healed someone, why should we be silent about it? In the Gospels and Acts, a very common response to healing was glorifying God for it (e.g., Mark 2:12; Luke 7:16; 13:13; 17:15; 18:43; Acts 3:8–9). Where and how they testify is simply a matter of preference. I hope we can all agree that what really matters is the authenticity of the miracle claim.

But miracle claims are no small issue either. The skeptic tends to doubt that most miracle claims are genuine. They will often ask, "Where is the evidence?" They want to see a doctor's report. They want documentation to verify the healing. They will often say that we (charismatics) do not have a single verified healing testimony. They usually get this line from other skeptics—like particularly skeptical investigative journalists looking to do a hatchet job. Presupposing that miracles cannot happen, they are positive that we are somehow faking it and are determined to prove it. I once had a woman ask me during a question-and-answer session if I pay actors to pretend that they've been healed!

Let me just address this objection head-on. To say there are no documented healings is preposterous. The assertion is simply untrue. We actually encourage people who have been healed in our meetings to go to the doctor and get checked. Night after night in our gospel campaigns people bring me the reports from the hospitals—often one from before prayer and the other from after prayer—that show they have been inexplicably healed from things like HIV/AIDS, cancer, and other serious ailments. Every day after our meetings in Africa, I send a team to follow up on those who testified to being healed the night before. They interview not only the person who was healed but also their family, friends, and neighbors. The footage of those interviews can be seen online.

Further, anyone can check YouTube right now and watch miracles happen in our meetings right before his or her eyes on a platform in front of hundreds of thousands of witnesses. Such miracles include formerly deaf ears hearing, blind eyes opening, and disabled persons walking. You do not need to rely on merely paper "documentation." Through this technology, you, too, can be an eyewitness!

Beyond that, secular news channels and noncharismatic Christian journalists have followed up on some of our testimonies, both in the Majority World and in the West. Our ministry has an entire book that consists of nearly three hundred pages of documented miracles in our ministry.[101] I could take you to visit many people, who have now become dear friends, who were healed in our meetings from incurable infirmities, handicaps, and diseases. In many cases, we can show that these miracles have stood the test of time, lasting for decades.[102] But our ministry is by no means the only one with verified healings. I know many other ministries that have experienced authentic miracles so often that to document them all would be impossible.

Still, I (Daniel) am not obsessed with the subject of documentation for one simple reason. Miracle testimonies do not warrant skepticism. I know miracles happen, and I expect miracles to happen. As I mentioned earlier, we have tried to be good stewards of the miracles we experience by providing what documentation is available. But I am not trying to prove anything to the skeptics. Those who already decided to disbelieve will not be convinced anyway. Those skeptical about Jesus weren't convinced even when he rose from the dead. My main interest is to bring the power of God's kingdom into people's lives. Those who experience the kingdom know the truth—and God knows the truth.

My hard cessationist critics could see the same miracles I see if they would stop being so bitter and cynical. As remarkable as they are, miracles *are supposed to happen*. Likewise, the church should operate in the Spirit's gifts

101. Kolenda, *Impact Africa*.
102. See, e.g., Warner, *Evangelist*, 180–81.

regularly. They may be awe-inspiring and mind-blowing, but they should still be the norm.

## What About Those Who Don't Get Healed?

While we celebrate the "already" side of the kingdom, we also await its "not yet." There are wonderful, godly men and women who love Jesus and serve him faithfully, who are also sick or disabled. What about them? What about those who haven't been healed or who have died from their sicknesses without an answer to prayer for healing in this life?

These questions bother me as well. I won't pretend to have the answers. As unsatisfying as that may sound, it is the truth and the best I can do. To offer an explanation in those situations seems trite and cliché. I do not believe that, as a general principle, a person is sick because of sin or his or her lack of faith. My own sister, a precious and godly woman, has suffered from a physical disability her whole life. We have prayed for her many times without a healing. On the other hand, she could have died several times as a child. We thank God for sparing her life, and one day we will understand. (Craig does offer some further discussion in his book, *Miracles Today*.)[103]

There is coming a day when all of God's children will be restored in every way. One day even the most severe disabilities and infirmities will vanish as we receive new, glorified, resurrected bodies. But until then, despite the mysteries of unanswered prayer and despite many disappointments and questions, we continue to stand on God's Word. And we continue to see miracles day after day.

103. Keener, *Miracles Today*, 217–28.

# IV

# Prophecy and Tongues

A key cessationist objection to continuing gifts is that the gift of prophecy would now compete with the canon of Scripture, even though it never competed with Scripture in biblical times. Although Paul explicitly describes tongues especially as prayer, cessationists often associate it with prophecy so as to dispense with both gifts together.

Chapter 12 argues for postbiblical prophecy. Chapter 13 shows that it does not compete with the canon. Chapter 14 addresses the objection that modern prophecy is imperfect. Chapter 15 addresses some experiences somewhat analogous to prophecy, such as hearing God's voice and being led by the Spirit. Chapter 16 examines the purpose of New Testament tongues and its continuance in history. Finally, chapter 17 examines whether modern tongues may correspond to those in the New Testament.

# 12

# Postbiblical Prophesying

Imagne this scenario: Around the year 95, a prophet's message is suddenly interrupted. "I can't say any more," the prophet acknowledges. "I think God must have just closed the canon." Most cessationists presumably allow for a more gradual disappearance of prophecy than this scenario depicts, but in any case, it would happen without prior biblical warning, since the Bible nowhere predicts or announces it.

Isn't it *more* biblical—more consistent with what we learn *throughout* Scripture—to expect that God continues to speak as he did in the Bible? There he did so in various times and places as he deemed best, particularly when his people welcomed his work. As I (Craig) wrote elsewhere, "Ruling out continuing prophetic messages suggests a radical break with the practice of the entire biblical tradition, without biblical forewarnings of such. Such a break would simplify addressing the frailty of persons who claim such messages and absolve us of the need for discernment, but that is not the biblical approach to such problems."[1] Why would God work one way throughout Scripture in various times and places but then suddenly stop, without prior warning, at or soon after the end of the first century? That is not how we ordinarily treat other New Testament models. God delights to work through his people in a range of ways.

The gift of prophecy is a central target of cessationism. Many objections are the same as those given to "apostolic" miracles (our discussion in chaps. 8–9), but sometimes they are more pointed.

Thus Richard Gaffin notes, "My main concern is the cessation of all revelatory or word gifts. By word gifts I have in mind . . . prophecy and its

1. Keener, *Spirit Hermeneutics*, 321n84.

assessment, tongues and their interpretation, the word of wisdom, and the word of knowledge."[2]

Likewise, Thomas Schreiner deems "miracles and healings" less relevant to cessationism than prophecy is because the former involve "no claims to new revelation."[3]

## Postbiblical Prophecies

The New Testament seems to envision continuing prophecy, even beyond the obvious and oft-cited discussions in Acts 2:17–18; 1 Corinthians 12–14; and 1 Thessalonians 5:19–22. See Matthew 23:34 ("I'm sending you prophets . . . , some of whom you'll beat in your synagogues") and the parallel in Luke 11:49 ("I'll send them prophets and apostles"). The book of Revelation also seems to envision continuing prophets (11:10, 18; 16:6; 18:20, 24; 19:10; 22:9).

Such pictures were striking in a first-century context. Many academics in Jesus's day were effectively cessationists. While some streams of Jewish thought allowed for the continuance of prophecy, especially on the popular level (Mark 6:15; 8:28; 11:32; Luke 7:16; 24:19),[4] many leaders doubted the continuance of prophets in any sense like the sense in the Old Testament;[5] later rabbis were often explicit about prophecy's suppression in the present era,[6] or they considered no one in their generation worthy of it.[7]

The Mishnah collects the opinions of early rabbis, especially regarding legal matters. If you look at a Scripture index to the Mishnah, you'll see that it's primarily dominated by the Torah. While the Old Testament trajectory chronologically climaxes in the prophets, who flow naturally into Jesus's ministry, later rabbis believed that the era of prophecy was over for now, so the real leaders—namely, themselves—were just the experts who could explain the Torah. Many members of the educated elites were the cessationists of Jesus's day, whereas members of Jesus's movement were the hypercharismatics, the ones who prophesied a lot. Among early Jewish movements, Jesus's movement was distinctive in applying the title of "prophet" without hesitation "to contemporary figures"[8] (see, e.g., Matt. 11:9 // Luke 7:26; Acts 11:28; 21:9–11; 1 Cor. 12:28–29; 14:29, 32).

2. Gaffin, "View," 42.

3. Schreiner, *Spiritual Gifts*, 164.

4. Josephus, *War* 1.78–80; 2.159; 6.300–309; in the diaspora, see esp. Wis. 7:27; Philo, *Heir* 259.

5. 1 Macc. 9:27 (cf. 4:45–46; 14:41); Josephus, *Ag. Ap.* 1.41; 2 Esd. 12:42; *2 Bar.* 85:3; cf. Isaacs, *Spirit*, 49–51. For Josephus, see further Leiman, "Josephus and Canon"; Bamberger, "Prophet," 305; Best, "Pneuma," 222–25; Isaacs, *Spirit*, 49; Aune, "Προφήτης."

6. *T. Soṭah* 12:5; 13:3; *b. Sanh.* 11a, bar.; *b. Soṭah* 48b, bar.; *b. Yoma* 9b; *Song Rab.* 8:9, §3; *Pesiq. Rab Kah.* 13:14.

7. *T. Soṭah* 14:3; *b. Sukkah* 28a; *y. ʿAbod. Zar.* 3:1, §2; *y. Hor.* 3:5, §3; *y. Soṭah* 9:16, §2; *Song Rab.* 8:9, §3.

8. Aune, *Prophecy*, 195.

Nor did prophetic communication stop with the following generation. Vision and dream reports feature in subsequent Christian history,[9] including, for example, accounts about early Christian martyrs,[10] Augustine's reports of his mother's experiences,[11] or experiences in early Methodism.[12] They were common in early evangelicalism;[13] early radical Puritans claimed direct revelations, including in dreams and visions.[14] (See further comment on visions and dreams in chap. 15.) Many Christians in the Radical Reformation also emphasized the Spirit's "inner voice,"[15] as did early Quakers and others.[16] Prophecy also appeared among seventeenth-century Jansenists,[17] an Augustinian sect in France that emphasized grace and predestination.

### *Prophecy in Early Church History*

Prophecy clearly appears in the Apostolic Fathers. The *Didache*, from the late first or very early second century, speaks extensively about the continuing gift of prophecy and how to distinguish true prophets from false ones (advice useful for modern discernment as well).[18] It was spiritually dangerous to judge a true prophet, but one who did not live right was a false prophet (*Did.* 11.7–11). In the early second century, Ignatius claims that the Spirit inspired his exhortation, exposing a sin in a particular church that he could not have known naturally (Ignatius, *Phld.* 7.1–2). Polycarp reportedly experienced divine revelation and spoke prophetically (*Mart. Pol.* 12.3). Many early Christians affirmed the Shepherd of Hermas, a book that claims many revelations, although most Christians did not accept it as Scripture.[19]

9. See, e.g., Bovon, *Studies*, 155–61; Keener, *Miracles*, appendix E.

10. Robeck, "Prophecy," 736, noting, e.g., the martyrdom of Perpetua. He cites Cyprian, *Ep.* 10.4; 58.1; 78.1–2, 6.1–3. He also notes "visions/prophecies that were given to provide comfort to the Confessors."

11. Herum, "Theology," 35–36, cites Monica's dream of Augustine in *Conf.* 3.11.19; her vision of safety despite the storm in 6.1.1.

12. See Webster, "Salvation"; Asbury's prophetic dream in Wigger, *Saint*, 188; John Wesley's reports of visionary experiences of some people he knew in Huyssen and Huyssen, *Saw*, 106–7. Noll, *Shape*, 46, notes early Methodists' use of "dreams, portents and special revelations."

13. Noll, *Rise*, 267.

14. Kidd, "Healing," 160. Turner, *Gifts*, 290, notes how Warfield differs "from (e.g.) a Puritan or Pietistic spirituality which gave considerable scope for such experiences."

15. Burgess, "Evidence," 29.

16. Burgess, "Evidence," 29.

17. Burgess, "Evidence," 30.

18. See *Did.* 10.7; 11.3–11; 13.1–6; 15.1–2.

19. Robeck, "Prophecy," 735, cites Irenaeus, *Her.* 4.20.2; Clement of Alexandria, *Strom.* 1.1.1; 1.85.4; 2.3.4; 4.74.4. See also Shogren, "Prophecy," 414–18, also noting *Barn.* 16.9. Hermas advocated discernment of prophets, though I (Craig) recommend discernment of some of Hermas's own prophecies.

Prophecy is well documented in the early church fathers in the second century and later.[20] Andrew Wilson summarizes some of the claims:[21]

- Justin Martyr (ca. 100–ca. 165)
  - "For the prophetical gifts remain with us, even to the present time. And hence you ought to understand that [the gifts] formerly among your nation [Israel] have been transferred to us."[22]
  - Moreover, he lists among the continuing gifts "the Spirit of understanding, and of counsel, and of power, and of healing, and of foreknowledge, and of teaching, and of the fear of the Lord."[23]
- Irenaeus of Lyons (ca. 120/140–ca. 200/203, writing ca. 180)
  - "Therefore, also, those who are in truth His disciples, receiving grace from Him, . . . have foreknowledge of things to come: they see visions, and utter prophetic expressions. . . . And what shall I more say? It is not possible to name the number of the gifts which the Church, [scattered] throughout the whole world, has received from God, in the name of Jesus Christ."[24]
  - He also notes "many brethren in the Church, who possess prophetic gifts, and who through the Spirit speak all kinds of languages, and bring to light for the general benefit the hidden things of men, and declare the mysteries of God."[25]
  - One element of Marcion's heresy was that he and those like him "set aside the gift of prophecy from the Church."[26]
- Tertullian (ca. 155–ca. 220)
  - "Let Marcion then exhibit, as gifts of his god, some prophets . . . ; let him produce a psalm, a vision, a prayer—only let it be by the Spirit, in an ecstasy, that is, in a rapture, whenever an interpretation of tongues has occurred to him. . . . Now all these signs (of spiritual gifts) are forthcoming from my side without any difficulty."[27]

20. For academic treatments, see, e.g., Shogren, "Prophecy and Canon"; Robeck, *Prophecy*.

21. Wilson, *Spirit and Sacrament*, 103–7. We supplement his list also with three sources noted in Hyatt, *Years*, 17, 20–21.

22. Justin, *Dial.* 82, noted in Shogren, "Prophecy," 418; Wilson, *Spirit and Sacrament*, 103. See further Justin, *Dial.* 35; 85. One need not adopt Justin's supersessionist expression here to contrast nonmessianic Jewish and Christian self-claims in that period.

23. Justin, *Dial.* 39, adapting the list in Isa. 11:2 for gifts. Shogren, "Prophecy," 418, adds *Dial.* 51–52, 87–88.

24. Irenaeus, *Haer.* 2.32.4 (*ANF*, 1:409).

25. Irenaeus, *Haer.* 5.6.1 (*ANF*, 1:531).

26. Irenaeus, *Haer.* 3.11.9 (*ANF*, 1:429). Robeck, "Prophecy," 736, adds that "Irenaeus . . . spoke against those who rejected the gift" (*Demonstration of the Apostolic Preaching* 99).

27. Tertullian, *Marc.* 5.8 (*ANF*, 3:446–47).

    - Tertullian also mentions a sister who receives many "gifts of revelation," experiencing visions and auditions of angels and sometimes the Lord, and revealing the hearts of some.[28]
    - Provided the postbiblical prophecy was consistent with Scripture and the rule of faith, Tertullian justified even some postbiblical theological claims based on John 16:12–13: The disciples were not ready for all understanding yet, so more would be revealed later.[29]
- Origen (ca. 185–ca. 254)
    - Origen speaks of "signs and wonders which we must believe to have been performed," noting that "traces of them are still preserved among those who regulate their lives by the precepts of the Gospel."[30]
    - He later notes that in his day, Christians still "foresee certain events."[31]
- Cyprian (195–258) reported that visions remained common.[32] He also spoke of the practice of some church appointments confirmed by prophecy,[33] and his own experiences of personal guidance.[34]
- Novatian (210–80): The Holy Spirit "places prophets in the Church, instructs teachers . . ."[35]
- Hilary of Poitiers (310–67): "*God has set some in the church, first apostles*, in whom is the word of wisdom; *secondly prophets*, in whom is the gift of knowledge; *thirdly teachers*, in whom is the doctrine of faith; *next mighty works*, among which are the *healing of diseases*, . . . and gifts of either speaking or interpreting *various kinds of tongues*."[36]
- Basil of Caesarea (330–79): "As is the power of seeing in the healthy eye, so is the operation of the Spirit in the purified soul. . . . The Spirit is ever present with those that are worthy, but works, as need requires,

28. Tertullian, *An.* 9 (*ANF*, 3:188).

29. Robeck, "Prophecy," 736, citing Tertullian *On Monogamy* 2.2–3; 4.1. But even most Montanist prophecies were not doctrinal; they usually involved guidance (Robeck, "Prophecy," 736, citing Tertullian, *On Flight in Persecution* 9.4) or supplements for what Montanists believed Scripture already taught (comparing Tertullian, *On Modesty* 21.7; *On Chastity* 10.5; *On the Resurrection of the Flesh* 11.2).

30. Origen, *Cels.* 1.2 (*ANF*, 4:397–98).

31. Origen, *Cels.* 1.46 (*ANF*, 4:415); on prophecy, see also Origen, *Comm. Rom.* 9.3.2, 6, 9 (on Rom. 12:6–8). Hippolytus also supported prophecy (Shogren, "Prophecy," 426).

32. Cyprian, *Ep.* 9.4 (even among children); 57.5.

33. Robeck, "Prophecy," 736, noting Cyprian, *Ep.* 39.1, 4; 40; 48.4; 63.1; 66.5, 10; 70.

34. Robeck, "Prophecy," 737, citing Cyprian, *Ep.* 16.4; cf. *Life and Passion of Cyprian* 7.

35. Novatian, *Trinity* 29 (*ANF*, 5:641). Novatian's rigor led to his excommunication by Rome, but (at least for Protestants) this should not undermine his testimony concerning current practice.

36. Hilary of Poitiers, *On the Trinity* 8.33 (*NPNF*$^2$, 9:147), quoted in Laurito, *Speaking in Tongues*, 95.

in prophecies, or in healings, or in some other actual carrying into effect of His potential action."[37]

- Cyril of Jerusalem (313–86): God works differently among different believers, "for He employs the tongue of one man for wisdom; the soul of another He enlightens by Prophecy."[38]

### *Reduction in Prophecy Reports After the Fourth Century*

Reports of prophecy persist well after Constantine; nevertheless, they seem less common after the fourth century and may have already been declining in the third. Various factors help account for this decline. The transition to more hierarchical structures, restricting more of the exercise of spiritual gifts to clergy, as well as the hagiographic focus on particularly endowed "saints," created less of a role for laity.[39] Influential Anglican author William Law (1686–1761) complained that when people stopped believing in baptism in the Spirit, then worldly education, power, and striving after honor replaced the gifts.[40] Wesley likewise attributed the diminution especially to the church's increasing spiritual weakness and the self-centeredness of "dry, formal, orthodox men" who "began even then to ridicule whatever gifts they had not themselves."[41] Even in the Bible, prophecy's temporary diminution at times could stem from judgment (Ps. 74:9; Amos 8:11) or neglect (1 Sam. 3:1).

The church's reaction to late second-century Montanist claims of unique prophetic authority (as opposed to simply prophesying without such claims) may be another factor.[42] Most contemporary scholars regard Montanists as orthodox in their key theology,[43] despite their idiosyncrasies (especially regarding asceticism) and the excesses of some members.[44] The original objection of Montanus's contemporaries to his prophesying was apparently its form: "frenzy and ecstasy, . . . prophesying in a manner contrary to the constant custom of the Church."[45] Whatever the Montanists' theology,[46] their critics condemned specifi-

37. Basil, *On the Spirit* 26.61 (*NPNF*², 8:38).

38. Cyril of Jerusalem, *Catechetical Lectures* 16.12 (*NPNF*², 7:118), writing ca. 350. Likewise, 17.37 (in Shogren, "Prophecy," 432): "May you be worthy of the gift of prophecy!"

39. Cf. Robeck, "Prophecy," 737; Burgess, *Holy Spirit*, 14; MacNutt, *Crime*; Laurito, *Speaking in Tongues*, 96.

40. Hunter, *Spirit Baptism*, 166, citing Law, *Power*, 128–29.

41. Wesley, *Journal*, August 15, 1750, cited in Burgess, *Peoples*, 180; Billman, *Thread*, 58.

42. Carson, *Showing Spirit*, 166; Hyatt, *Years*, 30; Laurito, *Speaking in Tongues*, 96; cf. Kelsey, *Tongue Speaking*, 159.

43. Robeck, "Prophecy," 736, notes also Hippolytus, *Ref.* 8.12; Epiphanius, *Pan.* 48.1; Jerome, *Epist.* 41.3.

44. Robeck, "Prophecy," 736, notes alleged date-setting for Christ's return (citing Epiphanius, *Pan.* 48.2) or a local city as the site of the new Jerusalem (Eusebius, *Hist. eccl.* 5.18.1).

45. Eusebius, *Hist. eccl.* 5.16.7 (*NPNF*², 1:231). See further Shogren, "Prophecy,"423–24. Orthodox churches already experienced prophecy (Eusebius, *Hist. eccl.* 5.3; Shogren, "Prophecy," 419–20).

46. The ancient charges might be slander, but their modern defenders must argue that case mostly from silence. Still, Tertullian insists that the bishop of Rome embraced this Phrygian

cally Montanist prophesying, not prophesying generally; thus a mainstream Christian critic of Montanism asked why their prophetic activity died out with that of their last chief prophetess, whereas Paul insisted "that the prophetic gift should continue in all the Church until the final coming."[47]

### Continuing Prophecy After the Fourth Century

Nevertheless, visionary claims continue unabated through the Middle Ages, although the rise of late antique hagiography requires us to take into account genre and date when evaluating them. Certainly mystical experiences and hearing from God remained welcome, although then, as today, discernment often fell short of the ideal. Lidwina of Schiedam (1380–1433) had astonishingly accurate prophecies and could even see people's hidden sins.[48] One man who visited her suddenly became overcome by an awareness of his own sinfulness and began to repent spontaneously.[49] Early Protestant writer John Foxe attributed prophecy to Hildegard of Bingen (1098–1179).[50]

The Franciscan theologian Bonaventure (1221–74) attributes prophecy as well as healings to Francis of Assisi (ca. 1181–1226).[51] Colette of Corbie (1381–1447) was a French nun who reportedly had a prophetic gift that not only predicted the future but also accurately revealed specific information about people and exercised discernment of spirits. Colette was understood as prophesying many future events, including the Protestant Reformation that began a couple generations later.[52] Philipp Melanchthon also cites the prophecies of an earlier faithful Franciscan that Melanchthon believed also included the Reformation;[53] Foxe attributes another such prophecy to Jerome of Prague (1379–1416).[54]

---

movement until he was wrongly influenced by Praxeas, who was in fact himself heterodox (Tertullian, *Prax.* 1, highlighted by Hyatt, *Years*, 27–28). Wesley also defended them (in his journal for August 15, 1750; cited in Burgess, *Peoples*, 180; Billman, *Thread*, 16).

47. Eusebius, *Hist. eccl.* 5.17.4 (*NPNF*$^2$, 1:234).

48. Bynum, *Feast*, 129. On one occasion, for example, she received a revelation about a priest in adultery.

49. Cruz, *Mysteries*, 260–61. See also Bynum, *Feast*, 126, who links the confession to a sweet aroma coming from Lidwina's left hand.

50. Boys, *Evidence*, 89, 237. For her visions, see Worthen, *Spellbound*, 5.

51. Bonaventure, *Life of St. Francis of Assisi*, chap. 11; Doles, *Miracles*, 116; Oliver, *Movements*, 200–201.

52. Cruz, *Mysteries*, 191.

53. Boys, *Evidence*, 88; so also Luther in Holland, *Dominion*, 320. Although Johann Hilten predicted an antipapal reformer for 1514 or 1516, he also predicted Turkish conquest of Italy and Germany and the world's end in the 1650s (Holland, *Dominion*, 301, noting on 304 that Columbus echoed the dating). Date-setting has never been wise (cf. Mark 13:32), and hearers have generally seized on predictions that favored them; the point here is simply that some early Protestants could acknowledge even foretelling when it proved useful.

54. Boys, *Evidence*, 237.

Sources also associate visions, prophecies, and healing prayer with the Waldensians.[55] Meanwhile, John Calvin's biographer Theodore Beza indicates that Calvin himself, who is often cited against the continuation of gifts, sometimes accurately predicted events beyond natural knowledge.[56] Martin Luther sometimes claimed to speak by the Spirit,[57] and some allies respected his accurate predictions to the extent of comparing him with Elijah.[58] In 1707, George Joeschke reportedly prophesied the safe emigration of the Moravians, fulfilled in 1722.[59]

One reason early Anabaptists cited for gathering among themselves and not attending state churches was that the biblical model for church practice in 1 Corinthians 14 allows members to practice their respective spiritual gifts,[60] including prophecy.[61]

Scripture provides safety rails for discernment, and its neglect (sometimes inadvertent, due to lack of access) risks the proliferation of falsehood. Mainstream Anabaptists recognized miracles but protested false prophets.[62] Trying to rethink Christian doctrine from scratch and neglecting some clear safety rails in Scripture, some early Anabaptists moved beyond orthodox Christology in teaching the "celestial flesh" of Christ before his resurrection. Some Anabaptist prophecies also proved self-serving. Anabaptist false prophets, such as at Münster, brought discredit on and further persecution to the Anabaptist movement as a whole, but the Münster leaders were far from the mainstream.[63] The French prophets, too, displayed excesses and error, especially as the movement developed (see discussion below). John Wesley and George Whitefield, however, had initially hoped for better from them;[64] they saw no intrinsic reason that God would not speak prophetically in their day.

In Wesley's ministry, he reports "angelic visitations, prophecies, divine dreams, visions," and the like.[65] So intimately related were such dreams, visions, and trances to the spreading of the gospel that he did not believe the

55. Hyatt, *Years*, 68, citing Douglas, *Dictionary of Church*, 1026.

56. Boys, *Evidence*, 124–27.

57. Boys, *Evidence*, 184, 189–92. He also credited another's accurate prediction (188).

58. Billman, *Thread*, 32, following Horsch, "Faith," 16.

59. Boys, *Evidence*, 296–97.

60. Hyatt, *Years*, 80, citing the early Anabaptist document (ca. 1532–34) *Answer of Some Who Are Called (Ana)Baptists Why They Do Not Attend the Churches*; Peachey and Peachey, "Answer," 10.

61. Burgess, "Evidence," 28; see Burgess, *Peoples*, 142.

62. Hyatt, *Years*, 84, noting Klassen and Klaassen, *Writings of Marpeck*, 50, 60–61, 96.

63. Bainton, *Reformation*, 106; Chadwick, *Reformation*, 191; Worthen, *Apostles*, 44; Hyatt, *Years*, 81–84.

64. Carson, *Showing Spirit*, 167, 179.

65. Xhemajli, *Supernatural*, 51, citing Wesley, *Works* (AM), 3:22, 115, 134, 199, 370, 376, 418, 437, 639; Wesley, *Miscellaneous*, 566; Jennings, *Supernatural Occurrences*, 110–11. See also Xhemajli, *Supernatural*, 56, citing Wesley, *Works* (AM), 3:134; 5:200. See further discussion in Taves, *Fits*.

work would be going forward without it.[66] Early Methodists reported many dreams, visions, and trances, often providing guidance[67] and sometimes providing safety from a coming attack.[68] They also felt God's call internally, often as an inner voice.[69] Sometimes they reported witnessing the Spirit as fire,[70] wind,[71] or other visible manifestations.[72] (Tongues of fire reportedly appeared above the heads of some girls at the outpouring of the Spirit at Pandita Ramabai's orphanage in 1905;[73] the sound of a powerful wind also is said to have accompanied the outpouring among Reformed believers in West Timor, Indonesia, in 1965.)[74]

In 1855, an eleven-year-old Russian boy living in Armenia experienced a series of visions warning that Turks would eventually turn on Armenians. In 1900, he felt that these visions were about to be fulfilled, and many who believed him, including a significant number of Armenian Presbyterians, began emigrating until all of the group had left by 1912.[75] The Armenian genocide began in 1915, killing an estimated six hundred thousand to 1.2 million Armenians.

### French Reformed Continuationists

Because many cessationists today claim the Reformed mantle for their cessationism, we pause here to note some early Reformed prophets, whatever one makes of some of their prophecies. This is important because polemical Reformed cessationists have loudly claimed that those loyal to Reformed tradition must be cessationist, so that some non-Reformed charismatics have felt that Reformed Christians are uniformly hostile to them. In fact, many Reformed Christians today are not cessationists, and even many, or most, who *are* cessationist are not hostile to all charismatics. Although neither of this book's authors come from Reformed backgrounds, we affirm that tradition's many valuable contributions to the wider church, including its emphasis on God's glory and sovereignty and careful attention to Scripture. This book

66. Xhemajli, *Supernatural*, 56, citing Wesley, *Works* (AM), 5:200; 7:375; cf. Xhemajli, *Supernatural*, 169.
67. Xhemajli, *Supernatural*, 166–69.
68. Xhemajli, *Supernatural*, 168.
69. Xhemajli, *Supernatural*, 101–12.
70. Xhemajli, *Supernatural*, 145–47.
71. Xhemajli, *Supernatural*, 118, 147–48.
72. Xhemajli, *Supernatural*, 148–51.
73. June 20, 1905, in Synan, *Voices*, 137–38; Ma, "Mission," 24; Jones, "Fire," 214.
74. September 26, 1965, in Tari, *Wind*, 24–25; Tari, *Breeze*, 6. Cf. also "an audible wind" in the 1930s Shandong revival (with Southern Baptist participation; Bays, "Revival," 173); another on August 27, 1970, in the Solomon Islands revival (Koch, *Zulus*, 50).
75. Kelsey, *Tongue Speaking*, 65–67; cf. 59.

challenges not the Reformed tradition in general but only the cessationism that some inflexibly associate with it.

During waves of often deadly persecution against Reformed Christians in France, Calvin's original homeland, many fled abroad. French Reformed Christians were divided. Many refugee ministers mistrusted the prophecies reportedly being given among Reformed Christians in their homeland;[76] most London ministers proved skeptical, given the dominant cessationism among contemporary Anglicans.[77] Eventually the more hostile established Reformed ministers in London seem to have applied ecclesiastical pressure to seek to discredit the earlier testimonies.[78]

Cultural factors played into this. As Boston University historian Michèle Sigg observes, the earlier "refugees could not relate to the French Prophets who came from the rural south because they were mostly peasants or artisans, less educated than the exiles who represented an urban, upscale population that had avoided protracted suffering by fleeing the country." But they also mistrusted their millenarianism, limited theological sophistication, charismatic gifts, and sometimes-erroneous prophecies.[79] Conversely, others felt drawn to them, across denominational boundaries,[80] and they provided one of the streams that influenced the nineteenth-century French evangelical renewal.[81]

Many refugees with firsthand experience of the prophets were more hopeful. François-Maximilien Misson, son of a refugee minister, collected sworn depositions from refugees in London, published in 1707 as *Le Théâtre sacré des Cévennes*.[82] They regarded their prophecies as fulfillments of Joel 2:28.[83] Estimates of those experiencing such inspiration in the regions in question were above eight thousand, and "hundreds of children as well as adults were thrown into prison or the dungeons because of their inspirations."[84] Though imprisoned, most continued to prophesy; one witness detained in 1703 noted an eight-year-old boy prophesying eloquently.[85] Some of their captors reportedly tortured the child prophets unsuccessfully in attempts to make them

76. Cosmos, *Huguenot Prophecy*, 60, 154. The main primary source (in English) is Misson, *Cry*.

77. Cosmos, *Huguenot Prophecy*, 164, noting Schwartz, *French Prophets*, 70. Like dissenters in England (such as Baptists), Camisards were derided as "Knaves, Fools, and Madmen" (146) and ridiculed (like early Methodists generations later) for "enthusiasm" (165). Hume, of course, later liberally applied the language of "knaves" and "fools" to those testifying of miracles (Hume, *Miracles*, 43, 52; cf. 27, 29, 32, 34, 36–39, 43, 52–55).

78. Cosmos, *Huguenot Prophecy*, 166–71, esp. 168. For libels against them, see 127–57.

79. Sigg, *Revival*, 39.

80. Sigg, *Revival*, 39–40. For their mission work, see 40–41.

81. Sigg, *Revival*, 42–43.

82. Cosmos, *Huguenot Prophecy*, 23.

83. Cosmos, *Huguenot Prophecy*, 32.

84. Cosmos, *Huguenot Prophecy*, 53.

85. Cosmos, *Huguenot Prophecy*, 54.

confess that adults had taught them how to pretend they were prophesying ecstatically.[86]

Particularly remarkable were the many young children speaking articulately under putative inspiration.[87] In one particularly extraordinary case a child in a cradle, no more than fourteen months old, was said to speak distinctive French.[88] The witness testified that some twenty people were present to listen to the child on the occasion that he came; the toddler had neither walked nor spoken otherwise, yet was exhorting repentance in French not unlike the other child prophets.[89] Another testified of witnessing a toddler of fifteen months speaking under inspiration in good French,[90] although he later recanted this testimony under pressure.[91] One even reported, albeit secondhand, a six-month-old infant imprisoned with its mother for prophesying, and the infant exhorting repentance.[92] Whatever one makes of the rare reports of infants prophesying, eyewitness accounts of other children prophesying during this time are pervasive. One witness, for example, recounted seeing "sixty other children between three and twelve years of age" calling for repentance and predicting future events.[93] (Nor are reports of young children prophesying accurately limited to this movement.)[94]

Prophecies often encouraged those who got lost looking for the secret nocturnal worship gatherings in the forest.[95] One youth in a clandestine assembly

86. Cosmos, *Huguenot Prophecy*, 60–61 (citing Abel Boyer), 96; cf. 64–66. The persecutors often favored the idea of adult instruction rather than inspiration (Cosmos, *Huguenot Prophecy*, 145).

87. Citing the eyewitness testimonies, see, e.g., Cosmos, *Huguenot Prophecy*, 33, 80–81; also briefly Cutten, *Speaking with Tongues*, 58; Kelsey, *Tongue Speaking*, 53; Hyatt, *Years*, 87 (citing Lacy, *Cry*, 15); Davis, *War of Camisards*, 42. Some exhortations to repentance may have involved public participation in the Mass as secret Protestants, which Reformed Christians at the time would have believed required repentance (82–83). Physicians lacked medical explanations for the children's ecstatic states (Cosmos, *Huguenot Prophecy*, 70).

88. Cosmos, *Huguenot Prophecy*, 51. Perhaps the child was a prodigy (children can often say a couple actual words by this age), but the linguistic feat presupposed in the report seems astonishing.

89. Cosmos, *Huguenot Prophecy*, 68.

90. Cosmos, *Huguenot Prophecy*, 68.

91. Cosmos, *Huguenot Prophecy*, 172. He claimed that the testimony attributed to him included statements he had not made—yet he had earlier signed the deposition in his own hand confirming its truth (173).

92. Cosmos, *Huguenot Prophecy*, 69, citing Mary Rouvirere's deposition that reported her brother's account of events in the late 1680s.

93. Burgess, *Peoples*, 163. Rather than recognize that God's Spirit empowered these illiterate children, Heath, "Little Prophets," 123–24, supposes that they were uttering memories of sermons heard by their ancestors, something medical science affirmed possible at the time. Cf. 130: "the degree to which this sacred lore had been burnt into the soul of a long-suffering people."

94. See, e.g., Wesley, *Works* (1872 ed.), 2:499, 506–7; 10:22–23 (as cited in Billman, *Thread*, 17, 56, 97); others in Billman, *Thread*, 133, 187–88.

95. Cosmos, *Huguenot Prophecy*, 46.

prophesied about some who were lost outside, before the latter were safely brought in.[96] Also important were prophetic warnings of danger. During one clandestine assembly of fifteen believers in a basement, a young woman warned that they should disperse; shortly after they did so, local authorities raided the house.[97] On another occasion, too, an eyewitness recounted a girl's prophecy: "There are people now, intending to seize you: retire hence forthwith." A raid swiftly followed, but the believers had scattered safely.[98] Prophecy also apparently exposed spying traitors in their midst.[99]

While many of these early prophecies seem more veridical, discernment apparently declined as some topics became conventional. Prophecies that France would restore freedom to Reformed Christians[100] may have proved wishful thinking. Calls to arms may have proved even more so.[101] The earliest prophecies, in 1686, called for repentance and prepared for martyrdom, but later ones further included a call to war.[102] Some children assured the Camisards that God would destroy Babylon and then deliver his church.[103] Only in July 1702 did the prophetic command go forth, from multiple inspired persons at the same time, to take up arms.[104] One leader prophesied a strike to avenge the torture and apparent killing of colleagues,[105] and while it fit the values of the era,[106] it did not fit Jesus's teaching. Early Camisard victories drew international attention, but without foreign support the resistance eventually collapsed after its young prophet leaders were killed.[107] Some believe that their military resistance preserved their community in the long run.[108] Be that as it

96. Cosmos, *Huguenot Prophecy*, 53.

97. Cosmos, *Huguenot Prophecy*, 51, citing the deposition of Jacques Du Bois.

98. Cosmos, *Huguenot Prophecy*, 51, citing the deposition of Jean Vernet.

99. Cosmos, *Huguenot Prophecy*, 113; cf. Sigg, *Revival*, 27. Witnesses also claimed a trial by fire soon afterward in which the prophet stood in the midst of a fire for fifteen minutes and emerged unharmed as a sign (115–16), though others were doubtful (172).

100. E.g., Cosmos, *Huguenot Prophecy*, 59.

101. On the call to arms, see Cosmos, *Huguenot Prophecy*, 85–105 (esp. 89–90, 96–97, 101), noting esp. the deposition and memoirs of Abraham Mazel.

102. Cosmos, *Huguenot Prophecy*, 34; Davis, *War of Camisards*, 33–34, 41. Prophesying surfaced particularly notably in the Dauphiné in 1688 and soon spread to other vicinities (Cosmos, *Huguenot Prophecy*, 43, 57, 181–82), but esp. in the Cévennes from 1701 forward. Not all later prophecies were militant; contrast an eight-year-old's in 1703 in Cosmos, *Huguenot Prophecy*, 54.

103. Cosmos, *Huguenot Prophecy*, 35, 48, 69–70. The book of Revelation declares Babylon's doom, but it did not occur on the Camisards' anticipated timeline.

104. Cosmos, *Huguenot Prophecy*, 96–97.

105. Cosmos, *Huguenot Prophecy*, 101; cf. 144.

106. Cosmos, *Huguenot Prophecy*, 101, 103–4.

107. Sigg, *Revival*, 29.

108. Cf. discussion in Davis, *War of Camisards*, 87, and esp. Bosc and Allier, "Guerre," 353–54, cited there. Given Calvin's response to armed resistance in France in his own day (Parker, *Calvin*, 181–83), Calvin likely would have disapproved. Whatever one's views on defensive warfare, we should invalidate the French Prophets because of the emergence of a militant

may, the earlier prophecies are less controversial. What is clear in any case is that not all Calvinists have been cessationists.

Although most of the Camisards were poor and lacked much education (unlike many Huguenots in other regions), their Calvinist trust in God's sovereignty shone through. One witness noted that some believers, though warned that martyrdom awaited, gathered for worship in the face of imminent danger. Likewise, another witness pointed out that Camisard soldiers, warned of impending "death in battle by prophets among their troop, resigned themselves to their fate with great humility."[109]

### *Scottish Reformed Prophets*

While B. B. Warfield followed a more hardened development of Calvin's approach (see chap. 21 below), some other elements of the post-Calvin Reformed tradition have followed Calvin's own more open approach. In addition to Camisards, some other early streams of the Reformed tradition also allowed postbiblical prophesying. Some writers have traced prophetic claims, for example, among Scottish Reformers.[110] These include, for example,

- George Wishart (1513–46)
- John Knox (1514–72)
- John Welch (1570–1622)
- Robert Bruce (1554–1631)
- Alexander Peden (1626–85)

Among the Scottish Reformers, John Knox used Old Testament prophets as a model for his ministry.[111] While we may disagree with some of his prophecies, there is no denying that he believed prophecy continued in his day.[112] *The Scots Worthies* recounts various prophecies by Knox and others. For example, in a context recounting many instances of Knox's accurate predictions, the work declares that when he was in the castle at St. Andrews, Knox "foretold both the manner of their surrender, and their deliverance from the French

faction among them no more than we invalidate Protestantism because of the wars some of its adherents fought. We cannot simply negate their rich spiritual legacy.

109. Cosmos, *Huguenot Prophecy*, 35.

110. Deere, *Voice*, 69–78; noted also in Storms, *Language*, 225. For prophecy among the Scottish Covenanters, see also Lloyd-Jones, *Spirit*, 45, 88. Already in 1858, Bushnell, *Nature*, cites *The Scots Worthies* against cessationism (Burgess, *Peoples*, 208).

111. For comparing himself to Elijah at times, see Yonge, *Cameos*, 226, found online at https://archive.org/details/cameosfromengli07yonggoog/page/n225.

112. Oss, "Response to Saucy," 168, citing Johnson, "John Knox," chap. 6; Ridley, *John Knox*, esp. 517ff. See also Sweeney, "John Knox."

gallies," predicting various deaths, and the like.[113] Facing execution in 1581, the earl of Morton recalled John Knox's warning and confessed that in this Knox "had been a true prophet."[114] Likewise, Knox's son-in-law John Welch warned how a rich man had profaned the Sabbath and that the man would lose his estate without passing it to his children; it happened, and the man confessed "that he had found Mr. Welch a true prophet."[115] Robert Bruce, moderator of the General Assembly of the Church of Scotland, "was also a man who had somewhat of the spirit of discerning future events, and did prophetically speak of several things that afterward came to pass."[116]

The Westminster Confession of Faith certainly sounds cessationist: "The whole counsel of God concerning all things necessary for his own glory, man's salvation, faith and life, is either expressly set down in Scripture, or by good and necessary consequence may be deduced from Scripture: unto which nothing at any time is to be added, whether by new revelations of the Spirit, or traditions of men."[117]

Yet not even all its framers meant the Confession to rule out prophecies, so long as no one tried to add them to Scripture. That is, for at least some, the statement was meant to address the canon rather than prophecy per se (or for that matter learning fresh truth from natural revelation, e.g., in physics).[118] One of the Confession's framers, Scottish Presbyterian Samuel Rutherford, declared that Jan Hus, John Wycliffe, Martin Luther, and others were among those "who have foretold things to come even since the ceasing of the Canon of the word."[119] He likewise attributes predictive prophecies more locally to various figures: "In our nation of Scotland, Mr. George Wisehart foretold that Cardinal Beaton should not come out alive at the Castle of St. Andrews, but that he should die a shameful death; . . . Mr. [John] Knox prophesied of the hanging of the Lord of

113. Howie, *Scots Worthies*, 64 (all page references to this work are from the Kindle edition). For Knox's prophecies, see also Boys, *Evidence*, 215–25. Knox's experience of the Spirit apparently narrowed the constraints of his "cessationism" (cf. Boys, *Evidence*, 235).

114. Quoting from Howie, *Scots Worthies*, 68.

115. Howie, *Scots Worthies*, 108.

116. Howie, *Scots Worthies*, 127.

117. Westminster Confession 1.6 (cited in Oss, "Response to Saucy," 169). Ruthven, *Cessation*, 30, sees the Confession as "a definitive denial of continuing revelation." It reacted to Quaker visions and manifestations (Ruthven, "Response," 11–12, noting esp. Milne, *Confession*).

118. See Oss, "Response to Saucy," 168–70. On this approach, "private spirits" (Confession 1.10) simply subjects prophecies to the authority of Scripture, like "all decrees of councils, opinions of ancient writers, doctrines of men" (Oss, "Response to Saucy," 170). The "former ways of God's revealing His will unto His people now being ceased" then refer to revelations "wholly unto writing" (Confession 1.1), i.e., the canon, rather than prophecies like those at Corinth that were never added to the canon.

119. Luther often associated the gift of prophecy with predicting the future (Luther, gloss on Rom. 12:6, in Luther, *Romans*, 106), as did Johannes Brenz, in 1564 (in Adams, *Romans*, 430, citing Brenz, *Epistolam*, 194); cf. also Fiddes, *Romans*, 312 (adding Melanchthon, *Romans*, 214) and 311 (noting William of Saint-Thierry and Aquinas)

Grange; Mr. John Davidson uttered prophecies, known to many of the kingdom, diverse Holy and mortified preachers in England have done the like."[120]

Rutherford accepted prophecy and simply required fair guidelines for discernment:

1. They did not require anyone to accept "their prophecies as scriptures. Yea they never denounced Iudgement against those that beleeve not their predictions."
2. Their revelations do not contradict God's Word.
3. Those prophesying "were men sound in the faith."[121]

How many other framers shared Rutherford's approach is open to question (probably most did not), but Rutherford's thinking leaves open the possibility that from the beginning, the Confession was capable of at least being *construed* as cessationist regarding merely the canon, without applying to all revelation.[122] In practice, the Spirit blows where he wills; in August 1742, at the height of the evangelical awakening in Scotland, many experienced visions and various manifestations that came to characterize the revivals in North America.[123]

Many Reformed thinkers doubt that Reformed theology obligates all its adherents to support cessationism. Many modern Reformed churches have recognized the exegetical weaknesses of cessationism. In 1970, a Presbyterian position paper supervised by Bruce Metzger declared the doctrine's lack of exegetical support and concluded, "We cannot . . . follow the view of some theologians that the purely supernatural gifts ceased with the death of the apostles."[124] The then-Southern Presbyterian Church subsequently issued a similar assessment.[125] The Evangelical Presbyterian Church "affirms the gifts of God's Spirit as biblically valid for today."[126]

120. Rutherford, *Survey*, 42, as quoted in Oss, "Response to Saucy," 169. For Wycliffe, see also Boys, *Evidence*, 62; for Wisehart (spelled in various ways), 230–34.

121. Rutherford, *Survey*, 43–45, as quoted in Oss, "Response to Saucy," 169.

122. Early Reformed confessions understood that while Scripture was God's *written* Word, the Word existed also as unwritten oracles, preaching, and of course Christ (Adhinarta, *Doctrine*, 31), but they deny subsequent revelation (while allowing the Spirit's continuing illumination of and testimony to Scripture; 37, 39).

123. Schmidt, *Fairs*, 42, 145–46, cited in Billman, *Thread*, 40; Dallimore, *Whitefield*, 2:125, cited in Billman, *Thread*, 67.

124. Ruthven, *Cessation*, 84n187; Cottle, "Tongues," 492, both citing "Report of Assembly," 150.

125. Ruthven, *Cessation*, 84n187, citing Williams, "Person"; see also McDonnell, *Presence*, 3:287–317.

126. "Position Paper." The Presbyterian Church in America is more conservative but allows for some differences regarding tongues and miracles, provided the former offers no new revelation and the latter acknowledges the completed role of miracle clusters that attested Scripture ("Report of Interim Committee").

Widely known Reformed continuationists today include John Piper, Sam Storms, Wayne Grudem, R. T. Kendall, and D. A. Carson. Unfortunately, some of the harsh cessationists noted earlier in this book, while accepting these continuationists as genuine brothers in Christ, denounce their continuationist position as minimizing Scripture and occasionally even find their view on this point comparable to that of Benny Hinn![127] Polemic is not the ideal breeding ground for nuance.

#### *Was George Whitefield Really a Cessationist?*

Some argue that Whitefield was a cessationist, quoting statements like this: "The *karismata*, the miraculous gifts conferred on the primitive church, . . . have long since ceased."[128] This is, however, a highly misleading and disingenuous way to characterize his position. Reading Whitefield's thoughts about the "*karismata*" in context, including the quote above, reveals that he was actually arguing *against* a form of cessationism. In the quote above, Whitefield was responding to a pamphlet called *Observations upon the Conduct and Behavior of a Certain Sect Usually Distinguished by the Name of Methodist*. It was an attack on Methodists in general, and on Whitefield personally. The author of the pamphlet was "anonymous," but Whitefield had good reason to believe it was either composed or commissioned by the bishop of London himself.[129]

The pamphlet quotes Whitefield's journals extensively and accuses him of falsely claiming that "God's presence was with and among them" and that he had received personal "communications with God" as well as having divine "revelations and directions."[130] In response, Whitefield defends himself with biblical examples of supernatural guidance and miracles. He then asks, "Are not all these things, and whatever else is recorded in the book of God, written for our learning? Is not God the same yesterday, today, forever? And may he not now, as well as formerly, reveal his arm and display his power in bringing sinners home to himself as suddenly and instantaneously as in the first planting of the gospel church?"[131]

Whitefield then challenges the author to bring evidence for his accusation that what was written in Whitefield's journals is false. "Can he bring any proof against the matters of fact recorded in these journals? Or will he venture to affirm, that I did not feel the divine presence in an extraordinary manner, that is, more at one time than another? Or that I have not been directed in a more immediate manner, at certain times, when waiting upon God? Were not such-like queries put by the heathens to the primitive Christians?"

127. As at one point in Lanphere, *Cessationist*.
128. Cloud, "Charity."
129. Green, *Publications*, 43.
130. Gibson, *Observations*, 18.
131. This and the following quotes are from Whitefield, *Works*, 166–68.

And here is where we arrive at his famous, and often-cited, quote about the "*karismata*." Whitefield asks, Does the author agree with some of his other critics that "the indwelling, and inward witnessing of, as also praying and preaching by the Spirit, among the *karismata*, the miraculous gifts conferred on the primitive church, and which have long since ceased? If so, no wonder the expressions referred to [in Whitefield's journals] are strong and extraordinary to him."

He goes on to defend his claims of the supernatural, saying that he and his fellow evangelists

> believe that Jesus is the same yesterday, today, and forever: and that he is faithful, who hath said to his Apostles, and in them to all succeeding truly Christian ministers, "Lo, I am with you always, even to the end of the world." Consequently, they believe the Comforter will abide with them forever, witnessing with their spirits that they are children of God; leading them by a diligent search of the holy scriptures into all truth; guiding them together with the world, the voice of friends and Providence, in all circumstances by his counsel; giving them utterance when called to speak to the people from God, and helping their infirmities, and assisting them in prayer when called to speak to God for the people. Inwardly moved by this Spirit . . . and his blessed influences they have from time to time happily experienced, as thousands whose eyes have been opened to discern spiritual things, can testify.

In other words, Whitefield's mention of the charismatic gifts was not meant as an attack on the continuation of the work of the Spirit but as a defense of it. He was not claiming the gifts have ceased; *he was quoting his critics who said they ceased*. While he apparently felt, as would be expected in his milieu, that some gifts belonged exclusively to the apostolic age, he passionately refuted the extreme cessationism of his day and believed in the ongoing work of the Holy Spirit in outward, tangible, and extraordinary ways. His views were radical in those days and caused him a great deal of difficulty. Yet he stood firm in his affirmation that Jesus is the same yesterday, today, and forever.

Whitefield preferred the wild frontier of America to the cobbled streets of London.[132] Perhaps the persecution from the rigid leadership of the Church of England at the time is one reason why. It was in America that Whitefield met another Calvinist whose ministry was marked by these unusual manifestations of the Holy Spirit: Jonathan Edwards, whose insights we address in chapter 20.

### *Cessationists Who Prophesied: Spurgeon*

God's gifts are gifts, dependent not on our precise theology or moral perfection. Not all charismatics who prophesy are skilled exegetes; certainly that was

132. Philip, *Life*, 363.

true of the young church in Corinth. Likewise, one need not believe that certain gifts are for today, according to one's understanding of those gifts, to exercise them as the Spirit leads. For example, frontier evangelist Peter Cartwright rejected the possibility of modern prophets—but then prophesied himself.[133]

In a day when most preachers were cessationists, Charles Spurgeon was apparently one too.[134] Yet he testifies of God working through him in ways that nearly all charismatics today would consider prophetic.[135] On one occasion while preaching, "he suddenly broke off from his subject, and, pointing in a certain direction, said, 'Young man, those gloves you are wearing have not been paid for; you have stolen them from your employer.' At the close of the service, a young man, looking very pale and greatly agitated, came to the room which was used as a vestry, and . . . placed a pair of gloves upon the table, and tearfully said, 'It's the first time I have robbed my master, and I will never do it again.'"[136]

Spurgeon also recounts learning of a conversion that occurred through his prophetic preaching:

> A city missionary . . . asked this question: "Do you know Mr. Spurgeon?" . . . "Yes," he said. . . . "The man [Spurgeon] looked at me as if he knew me, and in his sermon he pointed to me, and told the congregation that I was a shoemaker, and that I kept my shop open on Sundays; and I did, sir. I should not have minded that; but he also said that I took ninepence the Sunday before, and that there was fourpence profit out of it. I did take ninepence that day, and fourpence was just the profit; but how he should know that, I could not tell. Then it struck me that it was God who had spoken to my soul through him." . . . I could tell as many as a *dozen* similar cases in which I pointed at somebody in the hall without having the slightest knowledge of the person, or any idea that what I said was right, except that I believed I was moved by the Spirit to say it; and so striking has been my description, that the persons have gone away, and said to their friends, "Come, see a man that told me all things that ever I did [cf. John 4:29]; beyond a doubt, he must have been sent of God to my soul, or else he could not have described me so exactly." And not only so, but I have known many instances in which the thoughts of men have been revealed [1 Cor.

133. Cartwright rejected prophetic gifts, probably partly in response to activities of groups such as Shakers, Mormons, and con artists (Watters, *Peter Cartwright*, 53–55, 343–45)—ironic in view of his embrace of extrabiblical manifestations such as the "jerks" (see our chap. 20). Yet on occasion he himself confronted such sectarians with genuine prophetic insight into their actions and future (Cartwright, *Autobiography*, 341–46). On Mormon tongues, see Worthen, *Spellbound*, 117–20.

134. Spurgeon, "Receiving."

135. For him, preaching was prophetic and Spirit-led, so the leap may not have been far. The following quotations from Spurgeon are from Spurgeon, *Autobiography*, 2:226–27; also in Spurgeon, *Sermons*, 173–74. They are often cited by continuationist authors (Deere, *Voice*, 88–90; Storms, "View," 201–3; Storms, *Guide*, 89–90; Wilson, *Spirit and Sacrament*, 113–14; Storms, *Language*, 226–27). Deere also cites Fullerton, *Spurgeon*, 206. For Spurgeon's ministry in praying for healing, Clark ("Strange Fire," 63) cites Conwell, *Life*, chap. 7, "Wonderful Healing."

136. Spurgeon, *Autobiography*, 3:88–89.

> 14:25] from the pulpit. I have sometimes seen persons nudge their neighbours with their elbow, because they had got a smart hit, and they have been heard to say, when they were going out, "The preacher told us just what we said to one another when we went in at the door [cf. perhaps 2 Kings 6:12]."[137]

Spurgeon's testimony includes two clear biblical allusions: One evokes Jesus's revelation of the Samaritan woman's condition; the other is a passage specifically concerning New Testament prophecy! He may have viewed his experience as analogous to but lesser than biblical prophecy. In today's environment, however, he might well have acknowledged this as the prophetic gift of the Spirit. What matters more than labels is that he welcomed God's Spirit to work through him. Incidentally, in 1857 Spurgeon declared that "in a few more years . . . the Holy Spirit will be poured out in a far different style," when God's children would prophesy and have visions and dreams, as in Acts 2:17–18.[138] This does not sound like a very hard cessationist.[139]

## Prophecies Can Still Be Quite Accurate

How do we evaluate prophecy? Paul's lengthiest discussion of spiritual gifts provides a Christocentric basis for evaluation toward the beginning: "Therefore I make known to you that no one speaking by God's Spirit says, 'Cursed be Jesus!' Likewise, no one is able to say, 'Jesus is Lord!' without the Holy Spirit" (1 Cor. 12:3; cf. 2 Pet. 2:1; 1 John 4:1–6). Moral tests are also relevant (Jer. 23:14; Lam. 4:13; Matt. 7:15–23; 2 Pet. 2:2–3).

I (Craig) personally appreciate more general prophetic words that echo the message of Scripture, as biblical prophecies often did, since that makes discernment easier (at least for me as a biblical scholar!). These have been the sorts of prophecies I have often given: entirely biblical in substance yet often confirmed as precisely what the person was struggling with or what the church pastor was preparing to preach about (sometimes down to the very passage). Often they talk about God, his heart, or his calling to trust or turn to him.

### *Personal Examples*

Nevertheless, there are in fact plenty of examples of accurate, more concrete prophecy today. Many reports claim accurate prophecies (with a higher

137. See Spurgeon's sermon "God, the All Seeing One," February 14, 1858 (Spurgeon, *Sermons*, 173–74). See also Storms, "Cessationist Prophesies."

138. Spurgeon, *Sermons*, 129–30, quoted in Oliver, *Reformations*, 245.

139. Some of his contemporaries also associated him with healing. Baptist Temple pastor Russell Conwell (1843–1925), founder of Philadelphia's Temple University, also commented that thousands were healed through Spurgeon's ministry (King, "Gifts," 95–96).

degree of accuracy in some circles than in others).[140] Some cases may be a matter of chance (given other inaccurate prophecies), but some are specific and important. For example, in some cases prophecies have been said to expose government agents secretly infiltrating services.[141] One message spoke of someone planning to commit suicide, even giving some details of their plans. Afterward a visitor confessed that she had decided to visit a church one more time before killing herself; God intervened.[142]

As in Scripture (Matt. 2:12–13, 22), dreams have sometimes also provided safety, telling fugitive Christians exactly when to flee their oppressors.[143] Dreams or other leadings have also motivated mission calls; this is said, for example, for Patrick as motivating his evangelism of Ireland. One could fill entire books with examples, as I (Craig) have done with miracle reports, but a handful of samples should suffice to demonstrate that God does continue to work this way at times.

I (Craig) focus here on some firsthand cases known to (and mostly experienced by) my wife Médine or myself.[144] For example, when my wife was in her home country, Republic of Congo, she experienced many prophecies among the mainstream Evangelical Church of Congo. In one case, before it was obvious that war would come to Médine's hometown in Dolisie, a friend visited Médine's family on January 9, 1997. "I wanted to move here to Dolisie, but the prophet was adamant. 'Don't stay more than two weeks. If you stay till past midnight, Sunday, January 24, you won't be able to get out.'"

Médine's family could not easily relocate, however, since her father was disabled. Médine herself had recently barely escaped fighting in the capital, and she and her sister Thérèse were both recovering from medical procedures. Monday, January 25, began as usual. Thérèse was preparing to leave for the elementary school where she taught. Around six in the morning, however, they heard a deafening sound. Dolisie was being bombarded; war had come to their town.[145]

140. For popular modern claims of charismatic Christian prophecy, sometimes accurate to the detail, see, e.g., Anderson, *Pentecostalism*, 71–72; McKenna, *Miracles*, 6–7, 9–13, 23; Libersat, "Epilogue," 140; Gutierrez, *Mujer de Milagros*, 76–77; Jones, *Wonders*, 67; Koch, *Zulus*, 219–20, 232, 234–35, 240–41; Marszalek, *Miracles*, 43–44, 166, 244–45; Deere, *Surprised*, 36–37, 133, 210–12; Pytches, *Come*, 97–100; Baker and Baker, *Enough*, 27; Moreland and Issler, *Faith*, 198–99; Numbere, *Vision*, 453; Anderson, *Miracles*, 232–34; Tsivoery, "History," 40, 52–53; Vigen, "Interpretation," 112; Fish, *Road*, 83, 91, 102, 174–75.

141. In postwar Nigeria, during a military government, in Numbere, *Vision*, 81.

142. Dubose, "Foreword," x, describing the public interpretation the Spirit gave him of an utterance in tongues. Dubose is assistant general superintendent of the Assemblies of God (USA). I (Craig) was present on a different occasion in Ohio ca. 1977 when Pastor Chuck Schumacher prophesied about someone who had come planning to commit suicide unless God met her that night, and she came forward to receive Christ.

143. Doyle, *Dreams*, 156; Doyle, *Killing Christians*, 121.

144. Here I use Keener, "Ongoing Evidence," 355–56.

145. I borrow the wording from Keener and Keener, *Impossible Love*, 123–24.

On three other occasions, despite very few white people in the country (and none in her region during war), individuals independently prophesied to Médine, without knowledge of each other, that she would marry a white man with a big ministry. Médine and I were not dating, and I didn't have a visibly big ministry at that point. One of those prophecies was given when she was a refugee in the forest. Another was given by a woman who was annoyed by what she felt led to say because *she* did not personally *approve* of marrying white people![146]

Later, Médine and I became engaged, but I initially kept the matter secret at my Baptist seminary. At that time, a charismatic staff worker took me aside. "You have found your future wife," she explained. "Don't worry that you are from different cultures or continents." Others also gave similar unsolicited prophecies. When Médine was trying to get a valid passport so she could leave her country and we could be together, her country's passport office had no record that the passport had even been filed for. That in turn meant that her supporting documents needed to acquire a passport were also lost. We panicked, but Rosamund, a Ghanaian Baptist, told me, "I feel that God is saying that the passport is done." I protested, but she remained insistent. The next day an official informed Médine that he had her passport. "It's been ready for a long time," he explained. Rosamund was right and I was wrong.

One brother from Ethiopia, Mesfin Nigusse, who had not been informed that I was a writer, prophesied to me about two big books I was writing, the second of which would be larger than the first. At the time, I thought him only partly correct, because I could not imagine writing a larger book than the (ultimately 4,500-page) Acts commentary on which I was then working. I myself did not yet know that my large (ultimately 1,100-page) book on miracles, which was taken from a growing chapter in my Acts commentary, would come out first and the second book—the four-volume Acts commentary—would indeed be the larger one.

Riely Mikrut led worship for about a decade but became concerned that perhaps she was doing it in her own strength. So she gave up doing it, and on February 10, 2023, she told her worship leader friends, "The Lord would have to force a microphone in my hand right now for me to get up and lead again." The next day, she visited the spontaneous outpouring of the Spirit that Asbury University was experiencing, and she felt the Lord assure her that her gift for leading worship was from him. The day after, she was among those praying at the altar there when suddenly one of the key worship leaders at the outpouring approached her and said, "You're a worship leader, aren't you? You're anointed and humble, so come up and join us in leading worship."

146. In much of Africa, between one-fifth and one-third of Christians claim to have prophesied ("Islam and Christianity," 212), and even more to have received direct revelation from God (213).

She then shoved a microphone into Riely's hand. Although Riely had led hundreds of hours of worship before, she had never felt the fear of the Lord and the presence of the Lord the way she did during those next two hours.[147]

While working on this book, I was at a dinner for the speakers at a conference. I was sitting across from my new friend Melissa Chalhoub, a fellow speaker, when she began feeling that God had a word for the waiter. He was initially poker-faced when she began to prophesy to him, but soon his face betrayed his amazement. As he soon shared, everything she said was spot-on. He explained that he had been seeking a closer walk with God and had asked God just that morning for a sign. He had also been wanting to find a church, so she connected him with a local pastor who was also at our table. "I'll see you this Sunday," the waiter announced to him.[148]

On a later occasion I talked with someone to whom I had once seen Melissa prophesy. He didn't remember her name, but her prophecy dramatically changed the course of his life in providential ways he could not have guessed when she prophesied. So the next time I was teaching in a venue where she was also ministering, I took notice. After publicly warning against sin, in a crowd of fewer than two hundred people Melissa publicly called out very specific points: God wanted to touch someone with a mark on their left inner leg just above the ankle, someone who had broken his right hand multiple times, a Chlorissa and Tom together, someone who fixes old clocks, someone who builds bunk beds, and someone with a ministry to clothe the homeless. In every instance, someone was present to whom the message she gave directly applied. In the last case, the pastor addressed had begun ministry to the homeless the preceding week.[149]

While Melissa and I were talking about this afterward, one woman who had suffered for several years with complex regional pain syndrome came up to her and announced that God had completely healed her when Melissa prayed for her the preceding day. Long unable to run or jump before the healing, she tested out her new experience by running a mile afterward and doing cartwheels.[150]

I was at the conference as a Bible teacher, but other friends also prophesied there. Jerame Nelson, whose international evangelism meetings have seen millions come to Christ, prophesied to one Methodist woman, with whom I spoke afterward. He told her that she paces back and forth in her home praying and occasionally hits her feet on things there. He said she had been reading Ephesians 1 over and over, putting her name into it in her

147. Riely Mikrut, interview, March 12, 2023; also used in Keener, "People Met Jesus." I also confirmed this with the worship leader who prophesied to Riely, but who, in keeping with the spirit of the outpouring, requested to remain unnamed.

148. October 4, 2024.

149. August 29, 2025.

150. Danielle Wright, August 29, 2025.

prayers and underlining it in her Bible. "How do you know this?" she asked, dumbfounded. He told her that God wanted her to know that he had heard and was answering her prayer.[151]

I also think of a number of people over the years who have accurately and independently prophesied to me details of my calling that I have not shared (and continue not to share) with anyone.[152] I could mention some other dear, trustworthy, humble friends whom I have watched prophesy with amazing and detailed accuracy to people they did not know. Admittedly, not all prophecy is like that; it must always be evaluated, and I could also give examples of unfulfilled prophecies. But there is enough of the real thing that I would be a fool to doubt it after what I have witnessed.

### *Conversions*

Sometimes prophecies lead to conversions. I've even experienced the gift myself. When I worked at a small street mission, one prophecy led to two nonbelievers rushing forward to repent. On another occasion, while I was doing Bible study with a young believer, one of his friends from high school dropped by. I knew nothing about her, but I felt led to begin sharing with her about the pain in her background, and for about half an hour I felt the Spirit strongly pouring through me information about her and especially God's love for her and comfort about her past. Finally, she began to weep and surrendered her life to Christ, knowing that God had revealed the secrets of her heart.[153]

Romeo Pelle from Romania acknowledges many excesses among charismatics, but he rejects cessationist polemic against charismatics. "I was saved 34 years ago when God sent a Hungarian prophet to my home to speak to me. . . . In Oradea, Romania, a city 5 miles from the Hungarian border, . . . I was an atheist and addicted to alcohol, tobacco and women. . . . God pierced my heart when [through] that 73 year old prophet—exactly as 1 Corinthians 14:24–25 states . . . —God disclosed the deepest secrets of my heart, and 3 days later I gave my life to Christ (Jan. 12, 1986)."[154]

Yusuf Herman, a friend from Indonesia, shared that when he and a friend named Samuel came to do ministry in a new village, they met a boy who was disabled and his mother. Samuel immediately felt that the disability was caused by an attempted abortion. When Samuel inquired, the mother admitted that she had tried to abort him before his birth. Yusuf and Samuel then ministered to the family.[155]

151. August 29, 2025. For another collection of examples, see Greig, "Purpose," 317–18.

152. For prophecy and others' callings or confirmations, see, e.g., Acts 13:2, 4; Sanusi, *Gloria*, 62–63.

153. Noted in Keener, *Gift & Giver*, 51.

154. Romeo Pelle, personal correspondence, April 12, 2020.

155. Yusuf Herman, personal correspondence, September 3, 2014, including a photo and names of the mother and son.

## Conclusion

Sometimes in Scripture disobedient people told true prophets to stop prophesying, or at least to stop prophesying what they did not want to hear (Isa. 30:10; Amos 7:12). This is a significant potential danger for cessationists. Meanwhile, some other prophets gained followings by telling people what they *did* want to hear. This is a significant potential danger for charismatics.[156]

156. See discussion in Keener, *Suffering*, chap. 3.

# 13

# Prophecy Versus the Canon?

Some cessationists charge that charismatics devalue the canon by adding new revelations, which, despite charismatics' intentions, must surely compete with Scripture itself.[1] Regarding prophecy, John MacArthur complains that charismatics "add—however unwittingly—to God's final revelation." Thus "they undermine the uniqueness and authority of the Bible."[2] MacArthur must know an interesting fringe of charismatics, because in our decades of experience in charismatic circles, we have never met the sort that he describes: "New revelation, dreams, and visions are considered as binding on the believer's conscience as the book of Romans or the gospel of John."[3]

## The Logic (or Not) of the Prophecy-Versus-Canon Argument

To grant the incompatibility of prophecy and a completed canon, one must accept a number of premises not clear in Scripture itself:[4]

1. All prophecy must be of inerrant quality worthy of inclusion in the canon.
2. Despite being of inerrant and potentially canonical quality, most prophecies during the canonical period were never included in the canon.

1. For prophecy undermining the canon, see, e.g., MacArthur, "Revelation." Against it, see, e.g., Storms, "Revelatory Words."
2. MacArthur, *Chaos*, 64.
3. MacArthur, *Chaos*, 64.
4. Cf. somewhat similarly Wilson, *Spirit and Sacrament*, 111–12.

3. Even though prophecy never competed with Scripture during the entire period of Scripture's formation (since most prophecy was never included or meant to be included in Scripture), prophecy somehow threatens Scripture's uniqueness today.
4. Prophecy, unlike teaching, is so closely tied to canon (though narrative rather than prophecy is the canon's dominant genre) that a completed canon requires prophecy to cease.

Remove any of these premises, none of which appear in the Bible itself, and the argument collapses.

#### *Add to the Bible Everything God Speaks?*

The argument that the finality of Scripture precludes further prophecy seems to run like this:

1. All Scripture = inspired.
2. All true prophecy = inspired.
3. Therefore, all true prophecy = Scripture.

Besides treating all "inspiration" as equivalent to Scripture, some cessationists further treat Scripture as the sole locus of "revelation," though this is not how the Greek term translated "revelation" is actually used in Scripture itself. Thus they postulate that since the canon of Scripture has been closed, there can be no new revelation of any kind. Therefore there can be no prophecy.

1. New revelation = new Scripture,
   but . . .
2. The closed canon = no new Scripture,
   so . . .
3. No new Scripture = no new revelation,
   therefore . . .
4. No new revelation = no more prophecy.

You may have noticed a logical problem in these syllogisms. Apples are fruit and oranges are fruit, but that does not mean that apples are oranges. Likewise, Scripture is inspired and true prophecy is inspired. But that does not mean that prophecy is equivalent to Scripture.[5] The English word "inspired"

5. Although we have never met charismatics who treat prophecy as equivalent to Scripture, some "prophets" condemned by classical Pentecostals as heretical did hold that position (noted in Menzies, *Romans*, 211)—an equation of the two expressions of inspiration ironically held by these cessationists, who then use it to criticize mainstream Pentecostals and charismatics.

can be used different ways. In several translations, it appears in 2 Timothy 3:16.[6] Most conservative believers understand this to mean that God enabled the authors of Scripture to produce those writings that constitute his final, revelatory, and authoritative written Word. But when charismatics or Pentecostals refer to modern prophecy as inspired, they do not mean it is expressed perfectly or that it equates with Scripture. Rather, they simply mean—to use Paul's language—that the prophecy came from the Spirit (1 Cor. 12:8–11). In Corinth Paul expected the church's prophetic words to bring "edification and exhortation and comfort" (1 Cor. 14:3 NKJV). He did not expect them to bring new Scripture or divine law. He even expected the Corinthian believers to evaluate prophecies (1 Cor. 14:29), whereas Scripture was already pre-tested.

Likewise, when charismatics use the language of "revelation" in prophetic contexts, they generally mean it in the sense in which it sometimes appears in English Bibles rather than the narrower sense reserved for Scripture in some systematic theologies. In this sense, it is something that God has revealed to someone, apparently in a form such as in prophecies or visions (1 Cor. 14:6, 26; 2 Cor. 12:1, 7). The same is true for the cognate verb "reveal" (1 Cor. 14:30; cf. 2:10), which can apply even to the way God reveals Christ to us when bringing us to himself (Matt. 11:25, 27 // Luke 10:21–22; cf. Matt. 16:17; Gal. 1:16)—which clearly has not ceased.

### *Denying Scripture's Sufficiency?*

MacArthur complains that "Third Wave teaching, for example, flatly denies the sufficiency of Scripture. To say that God is giving the church fresh revelation today is in effect to deny that the Bible is complete and sufficient."[7] Cessationist scholar Richard Gaffin also sees charismatic use of "revelation" in the same way: "In view is additional, immediate revelation that functions, especially where guidance is concerned, beyond Scripture and so unavoidably implies a certain insufficiency in Scripture that needs to be compensated for."[8]

Other cessationists largely agree,[9] generally conflating canon with prophecy even though Scripture itself shows this conflation to be impossible. As Gaffin maintains,

6. A newer study raises lexical questions regarding the meaning of the terms in the verse itself, but more generally, ancients did understand key ancient sources as inspired, and Jews and Christians certainly so regarded Scripture; for some ancient conceptions of inspiration, see Keener, "Inspiration."

7. MacArthur, *Chaos*, 140. Scripture's sufficiency, meanwhile, appears first in the list of doctrines of the Assemblies of God, the world's largest Pentecostal denomination!

8. Gaffin, "View," 52.

9. E.g., Snoeberger, "Tongues."

- "The continuation of the prophetic gifts today . . . relativizes the sufficiency and authority of Scripture."[10]
- "But if prophecy today, as claimed above, is of divine inspiration and authority, then, whatever the intention, in effect Scripture has been added to."[11]
- The charismatic approach may affirm "the authority of Scripture," but "it denies its sufficiency."[12]

Some early Protestants applied this argument very firmly against other early Protestants. Detractors of early Anabaptist Felix Mantz, for example, accused him of claiming special revelation (in addition to rebaptizing persons). He denied claiming special revelation, affirming simply that occasionally God showed him something in a special way in Scripture. He was condemned and summarily executed by drowning.[13] Happily, most misunderstandings regarding extrabiblical "revelations" are treated less harshly today.

### *Scripture Is Sufficient—but for What?*

God led Paul's mission team to Macedonia through a dream and an interpretation; Scripture did not specify that he should go to Macedonia, but it did offer models of learning from God through dreams.[14] Now that the canon is complete, would we know God is sending us to Macedonia (or Moscow, or Mauritania) simply by reading the Bible? Or might some additional guidance help, especially through biblically sanctioned means such as dreams? David inquired of the Lord before major decisions (1 Sam. 23:2–4; 30:8; 2 Sam. 2:1; 5:19, 23); do we now, in the age of the Spirit, have *less* access to God's special leading? Should we not seek guidance in a key way the New Testament models (e.g., Acts 8:29; 10:19)?

Although Scripture speaks of the Spirit leading his people in a variety of ways (Ps. 143:10; Matt. 4:1 // Luke 4:1; Rom. 8:14; Gal. 5:18), MacArthur appears to confine this leading to learning Scripture.[15] Gaffin concedes, "Obviously, the Bible does not give specific answers about all sorts of individual life concerns and daily decisions that have to be made (whom to marry, what ministry opportunity to take, whether our church should expand its building, what the real problem in a particular counseling situation is, and the like)."

10. Gaffin, "View," 44.
11. Gaffin, "View," 47.
12. Gaffin, "Statement," 337.
13. Williams, *Radical Reformation*, 145; cited along with other material in Hyatt, *Years*, 80.
14. Cf. Alt, "Cease," 410: "Where in Scripture would Paul have learned that he should go to Macedonia or to Jerusalem?" On a personal note, many times the Spirit led me (Craig) in personal evangelism in ways that brought people to Christ whom I would not have even met otherwise.
15. MacArthur, *Chaos*, 65.

Yet he denies that we need God to show us answers for such matters beyond creation and Scripture.[16]

Robert Saucy, who often shares the cessationist suspicion of continuing revelation, nevertheless demurs from Gaffin: "While Scripture is the canon of truth, does not the Spirit reveal his will in specific situations, both personally and corporately as a church, beyond what anyone can legitimately exegete from any Scripture passage?"[17]

Clarifying how different voices are using terms such as "revelation" and "sufficiency" may advance the discussion. (Charismatic scholar Sam Storms helpfully clarified such matters in his presidential address to the Evangelical Theological Society several years ago.)[18] If you want to define "sufficiency" as sufficient for all details where we might need God's guidance, then yes—though we may be quoted out of context by those eager to score a cheap point—Scripture *is* often insufficient for some matters. It is insufficient by itself to tell me whether to move to Cleveland or to Columbus (indeed, it doesn't even tell me whether there *is* a Cleveland or Columbus), whether to marry Leah or Shakesha, or the kinds of daily decisions for which we depend on the Spirit to somehow lead our steps.

Scripture is also insufficient to tell me whether I have diabetes, am driving on the correct road, or have the right name for a postbiblical historical figure. Does getting a medical checkup, using a map, or consulting a reference work mean that I deny the sufficiency of Scripture *for the purpose for which God gave it*?[19]

### Confusion of Categories

Gaffin argues that "if inspired speech continues today, then, as our canon, Scripture is not complete; no matter how highly we may otherwise view it, the Bible is but a part of that canon."[20] This claim confuses categories. Scripture itself reveals that many prophecies were offered that were never recorded in Scripture;[21] it is thus nonsensical to confuse canon with inspiration or prophecy.[22]

16. Gaffin, "Statement," 337.

17. Saucy, "Response to Gaffin," 70; cf. also Grudem, "Expect," 244–45; Robeck, "All-Sufficiency"; Hodges, "Authority"; Greig, "Sufficiency."

18. Now published as Storms, "Gifts," 79–97.

19. Even the Westminster Confession of Faith, usually understood as cessationist regarding prophecy, restricts to the revelation of Scripture explicitly only "all things necessary for [God's] own glory, man's salvation, faith and life" (1.6). It does not thereby explicitly exclude complementary epistemic approaches for the knowledge of nature and the like.

20. Gaffin, "Response to Storms and Oss," 292.

21. Also noted against the biblical case for cessationism in Saucy, "Response to Gaffin," 68. See, e.g., 1 Kings 18:4; 1 Cor. 14:29; see further references and discussion below.

22. Oss, "Statement," 312, suggests a problem with some of Gaffin's other categories as well, observing "a hardening of the categories (history of salvation and order of salvation). . . . To

Many argue that, while Scripture is silent about prophecy ceasing, it is also silent about the closing of the canon, so we cannot deny that some things have changed since the death of the apostles.[23] They could not predict the close of a canon, these cessationists argue, without denying the imminence of Christ's return.[24]

But the link this argument presupposes between prophetic revelation and canon compares apples and oranges. The observation that the canon is closed is virtually tautological, since the "canon" is by definition what the church has historically accepted as the agreed-on, closed measuring stick for other claims. By choosing for our New Testament the books that early Christians believed originated from Jesus's immediate or outlying circle, all from within living memory of Jesus's ministry, they made what we recognize as sound, Christocentric choices. Their acceptance of works within living memory of the events also fits what we recognize today as sound historiography. But canon is by no means coextensive with divine revelation, as even a simple survey of Scripture itself shows (see discussion below).

Yet some cessationists' conflation of prophecy and canon goes so far that, to counter the contrary biblical evidence, they conflate *potential* canonicity with canonicity. Thus some claim that all Old Testament and New Testament prophecy "was in principle canonical," even if not included in the canon. The same was true for all apostolic writings, included in the canon or not.[25] But while we cannot evaluate the level of inspiration in Paul's letter to Laodicea (Col. 4:16) or his earlier letter to Corinth (1 Cor. 5:9), Scripture is clear that apostles did not always get it right (cf. Peter's need for correction in Gal. 2:11–14). Similarly, the prophet Nathan had to walk back something he spoke with confidence to David as the Lord's will (2 Sam. 7:3–5). Rather than treating everything an apostle or prophet spoke as if it were necessarily of "canonical" quality, is it not better to affirm that God's providence arranged for us to have the right and not the wrong works?

Prophecy serves a different purpose than canon. Judah had God's promises to the house of David, celebrated in many psalms. They had promises of the covenant in the Torah. But the Torah also included curses for those who disobeyed. True prophets could discern whether covenant blessings or curses applied in their generation; false prophets tended to cite only the blessings people wanted to hear. These biblical principles apply today as well. We need Scripture (cf. 2 Kings 22:10), we need correct interpretation (22:11), and we

argue that because something belongs to the history of salvation it can never have continuing results in the life of the church (e.g., experiences of the Spirit's empowering work) is to draw the lines too rigidly." This is true of both Jesus's resurrection and Pentecost, for example.

23. Gaffin, "Response to Saucy," 152; Saucy, "Response to Storms," 228.

24. Saucy, "Response to Storms," 228.

25. Waldron, *Continued*, 77.

often need confirmation and elaboration of the correct application for our day also by the prophetic Spirit (22:13–20).

A pair of leading Southern Baptist scholars writing on pneumatology rightly show that prophecy competes with Scripture only "if it possesses Scripture-level authority." They recognize that "responsible continuationists deny that it does."[26]

## Prophecy ≠ Scripture—in Scripture

Scripture itself does not equate all prophecy with Scripture.

### *Extracanonical Revelation Recognized by Scripture*

Here are some examples of prophets whose prophecies are not recorded for us in Scripture (NIV):

> Numbers 11:25–26: "Then the Lord . . . took some of the power of the Spirit that was on [Moses] and put it on the seventy elders. When the Spirit rested on them, they prophesied—but did not do so again. However, two men, whose names were Eldad and Medad, had remained in the camp. . . . Yet the Spirit also rested on them, and they prophesied in the camp."

> 1 Samuel 19:20: "So [Saul] sent men to capture [David]. But when they saw a group of prophets prophesying, with Samuel standing there as their leader, the Spirit of God came on Saul's men, and they also prophesied."

> 1 Kings 18:4: "While Jezebel was killing off the Lord's prophets, Obadiah had taken a hundred prophets and hidden them in two caves, fifty in each, and had supplied them with food and water."

> 1 Kings 19:10: "[Elijah] replied, 'I have been very zealous for the Lord God Almighty. The Israelites have rejected your covenant, torn down your altars, and put your prophets to death with the sword.'"

> 2 Kings 4:38: "Elisha returned to Gilgal and there was a famine in that region. While the company of the prophets was meeting with him, he said to his servant, 'Put on the large pot and cook some stew for these prophets.'"

> 2 Kings 6:1: "The company of the prophets said to Elisha, 'Look, the place where we meet with you is too small for us.'"

> Luke 2:36: "There was also a prophet, Anna."

26. Allison and Köstenberger, *Holy Spirit*, 433n34; see also Grudem, "Expect," 243–46.

Acts 11:27: "During this time some prophets came down from Jerusalem to Antioch."

Acts 13:1: "Now in the church at Antioch there were prophets and teachers."

Acts 21:9: "He had four unmarried daughters who prophesied."

One might also compare the unrecorded revelation in Revelation 10:4: "And when the seven thunders had spoken, I was about to write, and I heard a voice from heaven saying, 'Seal up the things that the seven thunders have spoken, and do not write them.'"[27]

We could also mention many prophets just one or two of whose prophecies are recorded, though they presumably prophesied more often (hence their title as prophets). For example:

- Gad (1 Sam. 22:5; 2 Sam. 24:11–19)
- Ahijah (1 Kings 11:29–30; 14:4–16)
- An anonymous man of God in 1 Kings 13:1–6
- An anonymous prophet in 1 Kings 20:13, 22
- Another anonymous prophet in 1 Kings 20:38–42
- Micaiah (1 Kings 22:8–28; 2 Chron. 18:8–27)
- An anonymous prophet in 2 Kings 9:1–10
- Huldah (2 Kings 22:14; 2 Chron. 34:22)
- Iddo (2 Chron. 9:29; 12:15; 13:22)
- Shemaiah (2 Chron. 12:5, 15)
- Azariah (2 Chron. 15:8)
- Uriah (Jer. 26:20)
- Agabus (Acts 11:28; 21:10–11)

Some prophets composed books that may have served as sources for the canon but were not preserved or canonized themselves (1 Chron. 29:29; 2 Chron. 9:29; 12:15; 13:22). But we cannot insist that all prophecies were only universal prophecies regarding salvation history. Although Scripture appropriately focuses on prophecies regarding salvation history, Israelites resorted to prophets even to locate lost donkeys (1 Sam. 9:3, 6, 9). And granted that Rebekah's pregnancy served a key salvation-historical purpose (Gen. 25:23), she might not have thought to inquire of the Lord (25:22) if the Lord was known to address only salvation-historical questions. Most prophets must have barely ever prophesied if they addressed only the sort of

27. Cf. possibly also the two prophets in Rev. 11:3, 10, depending on how we interpret them.

salvation-historical matters on which Scripture is primarily focused. Certainly most prophets never prophesied if Scripture contains—much less is coextensive with—all prophecies.

### *Hundreds of Thousands of First-Century Prophecies*

Most important, Paul expects prophecies in local congregations (NASB):

> 1 Corinthians 11:4–5: "Every man who has *something* on his head while praying or prophesying disgraces his head. But every woman who has her head uncovered while praying or prophesying disgraces her head."
>
> 1 Corinthians 14:29: "Have two or three prophets speak, and have the others pass judgment."
>
> 1 Corinthians 14:31: "For you can all prophesy one by one, so that all may learn and all may be exhorted."
>
> 1 Thessalonians 5:20: "Do not utterly reject prophecies."
>
> 1 Timothy 1:18: "This command I entrust to you, Timothy, *my* son, in accordance with the prophecies previously made concerning you, that by them you fight the good fight."
>
> 1 Timothy 4:14: "Do not neglect the spiritual gift within you, which was granted to you through *words of* prophecy with the laying on of hands by the council of elders."

If we envision just two to three prophecies (1 Cor. 14:29, 31) per week per average house congregation in the Roman Empire, by the end of the first century there were probably more than nine hundred thousand prophecies. No one saw the need to add them to the Bible then. Why then should any subsequent prophecies be added to or compete with Scripture? If prophecy could occur while Scripture was being written, without prophecy needing to be on the same level as Scripture and hence included in it, why should anyone suppose prophecies would need to challenge Scripture now?

Some respond to our objection by arguing that the prophecies not canonized need not have contained errors.[28] That is a different matter for discussion (already treated in terms of potential canonicity above, under "Confusion of Categories"), but it is beside the present point. The point here is that prophecies did not compete with Scripture in biblical times so there is no reason to suppose that they would compete with it now.

28. Schreiner, *Spiritual Gifts*, 111.

Meanwhile, just as the Bible doesn't contain all prophecies, it contains genres besides prophecy, such as history and proverbs. Narrative is the largest genre in the Bible, and we recognize biblical narrative as no less inspired than the prophetic books. Again, canon and prophecy are in no way coextensive.

Storms thus responds rightly to Gaffin: "If noncanonical revelation was not a threat to the ultimate authority of Scripture in its emerging form, neither should it pose a threat to Scripture in its final form. If first-century Christians were obligated to believe and obey Scripture in the open-canonical period, simultaneous with and in the presence of noncanonical prophetic revelation, there is no reason to think noncanonical revelation in the closed-canonical period of church history would present any more of a problem."[29]

### *The New Testament Does Not Act as If New Testament Prophecy Were Scripture*

Paul fails to give instructions that would have been essential if New Testament prophecy were the same as Scripture. For example, given his many instructions regarding prophecy, if prophecy in the churches were equal to Scripture, wouldn't Paul have urged believers to have someone write those prophecies down? With all the believers prophesying in Corinth—so many that they had to be told not to interrupt one another—if not a single one is recorded as Scripture, it should be clear that this was not the purpose or intent for prophecy in Paul's churches. Again, Paul encourages them to "keep silent" rather than prophesy when someone else is doing so (1 Cor. 14:31). This would be very unwise if the fate of the nation or the church rested on a prophet's utterances (as with some Old Testament prophets)—or if they were equal to Scripture.

More to the point, there is no passage in the New Testament that suggests prophecies in the church ought to be treated as Scripture or given any binding authority. One could take personal encouragement for one's calling from accepted prophecies, but their content was not universal for all the church (1 Tim. 1:18; 4:14). Whereas Paul urges the testing of prophecies (1 Cor. 14:29; 1 Thess. 5:20–22), he would never do so regarding Scripture, which was inspired like true prophecies but already tested and thus accepted as a standard.[30]

## The Danger of New Doctrines?

Some fear that postbiblical prophesying allows for new doctrines. Most biblical prophecies, however, did not introduce new doctrine. They could summon God's people back to Scripture (as often in the books of the prophets). They could warn

29. Storms, "Response to Gaffin," 82.
30. Oss, "View," 279.

the king where danger awaited (2 Kings 6:8–12) or tell people their lost donkeys were found (1 Sam. 9:20). Such prophecies do not introduce new doctrine.

We all should agree that Christ's first coming is the fullest revelation we'll get until his next one (Heb. 1:1–2). The Spirit continues to teach us also (John 14:26; 16:12–14; 1 John 2:27), but prophecy is not meant to introduce new doctrines today. Paul mentions prophecy (for edification, exhortation, and comfort, 1 Cor. 14:3), but he does not give examples. Note therefore the two explicit examples of New Testament prophecy in the book of Acts:

- "A severe famine will come on the world" (Acts 11:28).
- "The Jews in Jerusalem will bind this man" (Acts 21:11).

Do *either* of these involve new doctrine? Certainly praying in tongues (which its detractors often lump with prophecy) has nothing to do with new doctrine. In contrast to prophecy or prayer in tongues, *teaching* is far more apt to introduce new doctrine (since *doctrine* by definition is *teaching*). Should we therefore exclude the gift of teaching as for today? Likewise, should we reject the teaching gift for today because some have abused it? Second Peter 2:1 roughly equates false teachers with false prophets.

Of course, if one treats prophecy as merely preaching, then it might run as much risk of introducing new doctrine as teaching would. Some cessationists believe that preaching is prophecy, while insisting that any other kind of prophecy has ceased.[31] Throughout Scripture, prophecy was speaking what one heard from God or was moved by him to say. While even prepared preaching certainly can be prophetic and Spirit-led, biblical prophecy was at least sometimes spontaneous (e.g., 1 Cor. 14:30). Paul regularly distinguishes prophecy from teaching (Rom. 12:6–7; 1 Cor. 12:28–29; Eph. 4:11). With believers in Corinth being so new in the faith, and most gentiles lacking Old Testament knowledge, Paul even recommended prophecy rather than teaching as something all the believers there could do to edify one another (14:1, 3–5, 31, 39).

## Prophecy Is Not the Same Thing as Teaching

We agree with cessationists that no one should introduce postbiblical doctrines. This is, however, precisely why we strongly oppose cessationism. *Cessationism*

31. Cf. Calvin, *Romans*, on 12:6 (see also the citation in Oss, "Response to Saucy," 167); MacArthur, *Chaos*, 69; cf. Origen, *Romans* 2.208–9; Diodore of Tarsus, *Romans* 106, both cited in Fiddes, *Romans*, 310). Schreiner, *Spiritual Gifts*, 93, 95, correctly demurs, at least regarding the usual specific sense in the NT. Against identifying prophecy with preaching, see Ahn, *Interpretation*, 175–84. Note also that those who complain about some charismatics making NT prophecy different from OT prophecy would be grossly inconsistent to make prophecy only preaching. Meanwhile, early church fathers expected continuing prophecy but did not expect prophecy to include new doctrine (Shogren, "Prophecy," 413, 422–23, 425).

*is, as even most cessationists today agree, itself a postbiblical doctrine*. As a *postbiblical doctrine*, cessation is epistemologically self-defeating. (That is, it is what it complains about.) Obeying biblical injunctions, such as "Zealously desire spiritual gifts" (1 Cor. 14:1) and "Zealously desire to prophesy, and do not forbid speaking in tongues" (14:39), is far more biblical than to forbid the practice of such gifts on the basis of postbiblical inferences now hallowed merely as part of many churches' tradition.

Sadly and sinfully, some popular-level, biblically ungrounded charismatic teachers (in teachings far more than in prophecies) do feel the need to come up with novel teachings so as to market their ministries as special. This fault is not limited to charismatics, however; popular-level traditional dispensational prophecy teachers, for example, have been indulging this practice for well over a century.[32] For that matter, we seem to require novelty of doctoral students and monograph writers (sometimes with good results but often with bad ones!).[33] Craving novelty is actually not a novel problem (Acts 17:21).

One study of modern prophecies found that they rarely even addressed doctrinal issues; like biblical prophecies, most addressed assurance, exhortation, guidance, and the like.[34] I (Craig) used to prophesy much more often than I do now, though I continue to follow the Spirit's leading as I seek to share God's message in various other ways. When I have prophesied, whether in church or to individuals, usually the messages God laid on my heart were biblical messages, in biblical vocabulary, addressed to current local situations. In church, sometimes the prophecy echoed the very passage or theme that the pastor, unknown to me, was going to preach later during that service, reinforcing the point. In another case, to my own dismay I had to prophesy to an apparently vibrant church that its lampstand was about to be removed if they did not catch a vision for outreach. This church seemed to me strong in other areas except on this single point. Yet within a year the church ceased to exist. None of these prophecies contradicted Scripture or added to it. In one case, several of us were traveling to a ministry destination when I felt a peculiar urge from the Spirit. I asked the others in the car, "What would you say if I said, 'Thus says the Lord, "You're going the wrong way?"'" They laughed and said they'd say I was crazy. Eventually we stopped at a gas station and the attendant said, "You're on the right road, but you're going the wrong direction." Would the Bible by itself have warned us of that? (Though the gas station attendant's verdict sufficed for our driver, we would have saved some gas had we reversed direction earlier.)

Meanwhile, I've never prophesied a new doctrine.

32. See surveys in, e.g., Wilson, *Armageddon Now*; Kyle, *Last Days*. For that matter, Luther expected human history to conclude in 1558 (see Cohen, "Contemporaries," 197).

33. Most of this paragraph reflects Keener, *Gift & Giver*, 212–13.

34. Turner, *Gifts*, 319–20.

## Cessationism Versus the Canon

Taking the matter of canon further, some cite Deuteronomy 4:2 and Revelation 22:18–19 to warn against adding words to Scripture.[35] In context, these passages (like Deut. 12:32; cf. Prov. 30:6) simply refer to adding to the books in question; others indeed attempted the same claims for other, less genuinely inspired books.[36] Revelation, which warns against adding words to it, expects prophets until the Lord's return (11:10, 18; 16:6; 18:20, 24; 19:10; 22:9), as in Matthew 23:34 and Luke 11:49 and, of course, 1 Corinthians 14, where Paul uses the title "prophets" for anyone who prophesies (1 Cor. 14:29, 32) without always attributing to them unusual authority.

Nevertheless, the principle that some find here makes sense: Don't add your own views to what God has inspired. Certainly that would exclude adding them to the canon.

The deeper problem is the misapplication of Scripture's sufficiency for doctrine to prohibit God's continuing speaking for our lives or normal, local-church charismatic prophecy. Schreiner warns, "The sole and final authority of Scripture is threatened if so-called prophets today give revelations which have the same authority as Scripture."[37] "Such claims," he worries, "would compromise the unique authority of Scripture."[38] We would agree wholeheartedly. But in decades of experience with Pentecostal and charismatic churches, neither of us has ever directly witnessed a prophecy on a local-church level that would be accorded the authority of Scripture. Scripture comes to us pre-tested and written down to guide the universal church. Local church prophecies often echo Scripture, applying its message to personal or local situations. On our view, those who claim prophecies on the level of Scripture are cults and false prophets—not ordinary charismatics.

Responding to the cessationist charge that continuationists violate the principle of *sola scriptura*, Robert Graves and Gary Greig suggest that continuationists, who at least try to apply New Testament teachings about spiritual gifts today, may hold to that principle "more consistently than do Cessationists."[39] On extrabiblical grounds, cessationists exclude from required obedience biblical teachings surveyed in earlier chapters of this book from the Gospels, Acts, and even commands in Paul. How much of the canon does their doctrine leave operative?

35. Pennington, *Cessationism*, 139–40.

36. *Let. Aris.* 310–11; *1 En.* 104:11–13; 108:6; Keener, "Ongoing Evidence," 353. For wider application of the principle, cf. Jos. *Ag. Ap.* 1.42; *b. Sanh.* 107ab; *y. Sanh.* 2:6, §2; *Pesiq. Rab Kah. Sup.* 1:8; *Gen. Rab.* 47:1; cf. Matt. 5:18.

37. Schreiner, *Spiritual Gifts*, 160.

38. Schreiner, *Spiritual Gifts*, 161.

39. Graves and Greig, "Cessationism," 81.

The Bible itself never offers the hard cessationist rule that God should not speak outside of Scripture. Instead, it provides scores of examples that violate the alleged rule. "It is indeed ironic," Steve Alt laments, "that the bibliocentric doctrine that God only speaks to man objectively through Scripture [is] itself an unbiblical doctrine."[40]

Or as Sam Storms rightly asks, "Which view more greatly honors the authority of Scripture: the one that aims to reproduce the pattern of church life and experience expressed in the New Testament, or the one that relegates substantial portions of the New Testament record to contemporary irrelevance?"[41]

40. Alt, "Cease," 411.
41. Storms, "Statement," 325.

# 14

# Stoning Fallible Prophets

When Paul does not follow through with his word to visit as soon as he had planned, Corinthian Christians complain that his word is unreliable. Granted, perhaps he faced unforeseen circumstances (inability to foresee the future was a common excuse in antiquity,[1] and not a bad one at that); but they might suppose that he as a prophet (1 Cor. 14:37) *should* have foreseen them. If Paul cannot keep his word to visit, how can the Corinthians trust his gospel (see 2 Cor. 1:17–23)? Yet prophets, like teachers, know only in part (1 Cor. 13:9), and plans change (Rom. 1:13). Is it realistic to hold fallible humans to the standard of infallibility?

Whatever "a true prophet . . . prophesies must *always* come true," insists Sam Waldron.[2] Since New Testament prophecy is like Old Testament prophecy, he says (on which claim, see discussion below), "all professed prophecy must be held to the standard of Deuteronomy 18:15–22. Such prophecy must be prepared to pass the test of absolute infallibility."[3] Tom Pennington agrees: "A true prophet's predictions always come true."[4] New Testament scholar Thomas Schreiner declares that "the test of whether one was truly a prophet of God was whether his words came to pass (Deut. 18:21–22). If they did not, he was to be regarded as a false prophet."[5]

1. E.g., Pliny, *Ep.* 5.9.7; Quintilian, *Decl.* 301.16; Hermogenes, *Issues* 68.10–69.21 (esp. 69.15–17); Libanius, *Declam.* 36.42; 44.50–52, 61.

2. Waldron, *Continued*, 52.

3. Waldron, *Continued*, 69. For use of Deut. 13:1–5; 18:15–22, see also Waldron, *Continued*, 50–52.

4. Pennington, *Cessationism*, 38 (see more fully 38–41).

5. Schreiner, *Spiritual Gifts*, 101. "*The*" test is surely too narrow, since moral and theological tests dominate the context in Deuteronomy.

## When to Kill Your Prophet (Deut. 18:20–22): Rebellion or Mistakes?[6]

Deuteronomy 18:20–22 (ESV) says: "'But the prophet who presumes to speak a word in my name that I have not commanded him to speak, or who speaks in the name of other gods, that same prophet shall die.' And if you say in your heart, 'How may we know the word that the LORD has not spoken?'—when a prophet speaks in the name of the LORD, if the word does not come to pass or come true, that is a word that the LORD has not spoken; the prophet has spoken it presumptuously. You need not be afraid of him."

The passage about executing a prophet who speaks something that does not come to pass (18:20–22) contrasts this false prophet with the true prophet like Moses earlier in the same context (18:15–19). More specifically, the kind of prophet to which it refers in context is a prophet who speaks in the name of other gods or speaks presumptuously what God has not said (18:20, 22). This reiterates the warning about a false prophet who leads God's people away from him in Deuteronomy 13:1–5 (NASB): "If a prophet or a dreamer of dreams . . . spoke to you, saying, 'Let's follow other gods (whom you have not known) and let's serve them,' . . . that prophet or that dreamer of dreams shall be put to death, because he has spoken falsely against the LORD your God."

This part is clear enough, but what does it mean to speak "presumptuously"? Does it refer to stoning a prophet who *thought* Israel's God was speaking and misunderstood him or made a mistake on some point? This seems to be how many cessationist critics take this passage. Yet the Hebrew word translated "presumptuously" usually means "rebelliously against" (as in Jer. 50:29; Neh. 9:16, 29), certainly in Deuteronomy (Deut. 1:43; 17:13). As specified clearly in the context of the statement noted above, it refers to someone seeking to lead God's people away from God. If it actually referred to anyone who makes a mistake in speaking for the Lord, then it would sentence to death Nathan, who had to correct himself (2 Sam. 7:2–5). If it refers to anyone whose word does not come to pass, it would sentence to death Jonah, who prophesied judgment before the judgment was averted by the people's repentance (Jon. 3:4). (No wonder Jonah was so upset!) Jeremiah teaches that in fact most prophecies are conditional (Jer. 18:5–10).

Of course, we all recognize that we're not called to literally stone even genuinely *false* prophets today. The New Testament commutes the Old Testament death penalty to throwing the person out of church (1 Cor. 5:11–13, using Old Testament capital-punishment language for excommunication).[7] If a person has prophesied falsely, even publicly, but is not leading us toward other gods or counseling rebellion against the Lord, some discipline may be in order, allowing for a time of seeking where they got it wrong. But if a

6. I adapt some of this material from Keener, "Strike."
7. See Deut. 13:5; 17:7, 12; 19:13; 21:21; 22:21, 22, 24; 24:7.

person has prophesied rebelliously against God's true message, then, whether their words come to pass or not, the full discipline of putting them outside the church is in order. We always need to be pretty sure we get it right before exercising that full discipline, which is quite serious (Matt. 18:15–17; 1 Cor. 5:5; 1 Tim. 1:20).

While we don't execute church members today, we do need to take prophecy very seriously. On the local level, we grow and mature as best as we can. Before we say definitively, "The Lord says," we'd better be pretty sure we're right. (That's why many charismatics today insist that it's safer to say, "This is what I feel like the Lord is saying.") And before going public on a massive scale (as sometimes happens on social media), prophets should have a pretty good track record of hearing God rightly.

### *Old Testament Standards?*

Discussion of whether potentially fallible prophecy today, prophecy that needs to be evaluated, is biblical turns largely on whether the same was true for prophecy in the first generation of the church. This question in turn often depends on another: Was New Testament prophecy expected to be infallible like Old Testament prophecy? And that's if in fact infallibility was the standard even for prophecy from the Old Testament period.

### *Conditional Prophecy*

While we rightly expect true prophecies to be accurate—otherwise why pay them any attention at all?—not all true prophecies come to pass. Indeed, we may sometimes act to *prevent* them from coming to pass—though without repentance, attempts to evade their judgment will prove futile (1 Kings 22:28–37).

John MacArthur complains about a charismatic who claims that all prophecies are ultimately conditional.[8] Yet while some biblical prophecies are surely unconditional (e.g., 2 Sam. 7:15; Ps. 89:33–37; Heb. 6:17), it is clear that at least some and surely many prophecies are in fact conditional.[9] God articulates the principle most explicitly in Jeremiah:

8. MacArthur, *Chaos* (1992), 70.

9. Theological explanations vary. Because God deals with humans within time, specific directions may, as with a GPS, change if one fails to implement the first instructions; yet on our view God knows the final outcome. I (Craig) mentioned my view in Keener, "Political Prophecies": "My own opinion is that God foreknows human choices or final outcomes, but he also accommodates time-bound people within time"; again in Keener, "Trump Prophecies." In those articles I suggested, however, that the political prophecies in question were not conditional but mistaken—at the least in their timing. When Balak wants Balaam to change his prophecy, Balaam declares that God does not change his mind (Num. 23:19); but when Balaam strategizes

Jeremiah 18:7–10 (NIV): "If at any time I announce that a nation or kingdom is to be uprooted, torn down and destroyed, and if that nation I warned repents of its evil, then I will relent and not inflict on it the disaster I had planned. And if at another time I announce that a nation or kingdom is to be built up and planted, and if it does evil in my sight and does not obey me, then I will reconsider the good I had intended to do for it."

But it can be exemplified in numerous passages:

Genesis 18:26–32: God promised Abraham not to destroy Sodom *if* he found a certain number of righteous people there.[10]

1 Samuel 2:30 (NASB): "Therefore the Lord God of Israel declares, 'I did indeed say that your house and the house of your father was to walk before Me forever'; but now the Lord declares, 'Far be it from Me—for those who honor Me I will honor, and those who despise Me will be insignificant.'"

1 Samuel 9:16 (NIV): "About this time tomorrow I will send you a man from the land of Benjamin. Anoint him ruler over my people Israel; he will deliver them from the hand of the Philistines." But because of his disobedience, Saul fails (e.g., 1 Sam. 31); God uses David instead (2 Sam. 3:18; 19:9).

1 Samuel 13:13–14 (ESV): "For then the Lord would have established your kingdom over Israel forever. But now your kingdom shall not continue."

1 Kings 2:4 (NJB): "If your sons are careful how they behave, and walk loyally before me with all their heart and soul, you will never want for a man on the throne of Israel."

1 Kings 19:15–16, 19–21; 2 Kings 8:13; 9:1–3: Two of the three assignments God gave Elijah on Mount Horeb were delegated to his successor or the successor's agent.

1 Kings 21:29 (ESV): "Have you seen how Ahab has humbled himself before me? Because he has humbled himself before me, I will not bring the disaster in his days; but in his son's days I will bring the disaster upon his house."

2 Kings 20:1, 5–6 (AT): "About then Hezekiah fell ill and was at the point of death. The prophet Isaiah son of Amoz came and said to him, 'Yahweh says this, "Put your affairs in order, for you are going to die, you will not live."' . . . 'Go back and say to Hezekiah . . . "Yahweh . . . says this: I have heard your prayer and seen your tears. . . . I shall add fifteen years to your life."'"

---

to get Israel to sin and so face judgment, he succeeds in the short term (31:16), albeit at the cost of his life (31:8).

10. God's angel also was given freedom to spare Zoar at Lot's request (Gen. 19:20–23; Deut. 34:3), although Lot ended up leaving it anyway (Gen. 19:30).

Isaiah 1:19–20 (NASB): "If you are willing and obedient, / You will eat the best of the land; / But if you refuse and rebel, / You will be devoured by the sword."

Jeremiah 22:24–30: The Lord declares that Jehoiachin (Coniah) would die childless (or as if childless) and none of his descendants would sit on his throne (22:30); yet God later restores the royal line of Jeconiah (1 Chron. 3:17; Matt. 1:11–12; cf. 2 Kings 25:27–29; Jer. 52:31–33).

Jeremiah 26:18–19: Micah prophesied Jerusalem's destruction, but after Hezekiah prayed, God relented of that judgment (at least in that generation).

Jeremiah 38:20–23 (NIV): "'They will not hand you over,' Jeremiah replied. 'Obey the Lord by doing what I tell you. Then it will go well with you, and your life will be spared. But if you refuse to surrender, this is what the Lord has revealed to me: . . . All your wives and children will be brought out to the Babylonians. You yourself will not escape from their hands.'"

Ezekiel 18:30–32 (NRSV): "Therefore I will judge you, O house of Israel, all of you according to your ways, says the Lord God. Repent and turn from all your transgressions; otherwise iniquity will be your ruin. Cast away from you all the transgressions that you have committed against me, and get yourselves a new heart and a new spirit! Why will you die, O house of Israel? For I have no pleasure in the death of anyone, says the Lord God. Turn, then, and live."

Jonah 3:4, 10 (NASB): "Then Jonah began to go through the city one day's walk; and he cried out and said, 'Forty more days, and Nineveh will be overthrown.' . . . When God saw their deeds, that they turned from their evil way, then God relented of the disaster which He had declared He would bring on them. So He did not do *it*."

Acts 27:10–34: Paul foresaw that not only cargo (27:10, 21) but also the passengers (27:10) would be lost if the ship set out; but (probably in light of his prayers; cf. 27:24) he soon corrected this to all 276 passengers surviving (27:22, 34)—though not if the sailors were allowed to abandon the ship (27:31).

Revelation 2:5 (AT): "So remember where you've fallen from and turn back and do again the first works. And if you don't, I'll come and move your lampstand from its place, if you don't turn back."

Prophecy today can also be conditional. I (Craig) illustrate here with what I understand to be my own experience. Once I felt the Lord warning me of a coming trial more difficult than the hardest one I had yet faced, one that had nearly killed me. In the following weeks I humbled myself with prayer and fasting in preparation for the coming testing. One day, however, I was surprised, as I felt him encourage me that because I had humbled my heart before him, that test now wouldn't be necessary.[11] (I still don't know what the test would have been, but I'm happy I didn't have to find out the hard way.)

Sometimes, as my wife Médine comments about the understanding in Africa, prophecies are conditional warnings about situations that often should be averted through prayer or obeying the warning.[12] When my wife was a girl in Congo, Coco Moïse, a prayerful family friend, had a vision of her leaving the country, hardly possible for people of her family's means at the time. He then saw her returning while the airport was being bombed, even though at the time of the vision the nation had long been at peace. The family thus prayed concertedly that God would avert this crisis. Some twenty years later, when she finished her PhD and was returning to Congo, her flight plans were diverted. She was disappointed, only to learn afterward that the airport where she would have landed was bombed at this time.[13] (She did later have to escape the capital's airport in a hail of gunfire, but in this case as in the former one God protected her.)

Besides prophecies often being conditional, they can be fulfilled differently than we might expect. Many biblical prophecies unfolded in phases; the most obvious case in point involves grand prophecies of Israel's restoration, which unfolded partly in the return from Babylon, partly in Jesus's ministry (e.g., Isa. 35:5–6 and 61:1–2 in Matt. 11:5 // Luke 7:22; Luke 4:18–19), and finally in the future (with either one or two future phases depending on one's millennial views). God promises Zerubbabel and Joshua (Hag. 2:2, 4) that he will very soon shake all creation, shake the nations, and fill the new temple with glory (2:6–9, 21–22) and that he will make Zerubbabel like a signet ring on that day (2:23). When did this happen? Zerubbabel, from the house of David, lived in the sixth century BC. Some prophetic language is obviously figurative, but the prophecy might also foreshadow a fuller son of David (cf. Zech. 3:8; 4:14). In any case, the prudent will not infer too much from prophecies prematurely; God used and exalted Zerubbabel, but a fuller shaking of the nations and creation is yet to come (Heb. 12:26). And while we're on the topic, some visions, which normally require interpretation, can look very strange (e.g., Dan. 8:3–14; Zech. 1:18–21; 5:1–11). Prophecies can be parabolic as well (e.g., Ezek. 17:2–10).[14] And who would really expect to die from a lion

11. For humbling at least delaying judgments, cf. 1 Kings 21:29; 2 Kings 22:19.

12. See also, e.g., Burgess, *Revolution*, 161.

13. Coco Moïse still remembered her especially by this prophecy when they talked around November 30, 2008. Among other long-range prophecies, one might compare the prophecy given to Moses Tay's mother when she was pregnant with him about his significant future ministry; he became a doctor but eventually became the Anglican archbishop of the province of South East Asia (Green, *Asian Tigers*, 101–2).

14. In the late first or early second century, the *Didache* uses the strange *behavior* of some OT prophets (cf., e.g., Isa. 20:2–3; Jer. 13:1–5; Ezek. 4:1–8; Hosea 1:2) to exclude judging negatively *contemporary* prophets on the basis of strange symbolic actions (*Did.* 11.11).

attack for not punching an apparently (but not really) masochistic prophet (1 Kings 20:35–36)? Apart from *spiritual* wisdom, many prophecies make little sense (1 Cor. 2:13–14).

We recognize that in the New Testament even in small house churches, like those in Corinth, prophecies had to be evaluated each week (1 Cor. 14:29). That suggests that those prophecies remained fallible and not all of them passed muster in all their details (see more discussion on this below).

But how does that square with Old Testament teaching about stoning a prophet if their word doesn't come to pass? As we discuss further below, some argue that all Old Testament prophecies were of "Scripture quality." But we should remember that not all prophecies in Old Testament times, just like not all prophecies in New Testament times, automatically qualified for inclusion in the Bible, even if true prophets uttered them. We don't hear the prophecies of the true prophets whom Jezebel killed, or of the hundred whom Obadiah hid in a cave (1 Kings 18:4; cf. 2 Kings 9:7).

In the Old Testament, senior prophets often mentored junior prophets, probably supervising their prophesying (1 Sam. 19:20; 2 Kings 2:3–7; 4:38). That is, there was also a process of review as younger prophets were maturing. (It was considered noteworthy when a prophet arose like Samuel, none of whose words failed—1 Sam. 3:19; or Moses, who talked with God face-to-face—Num. 12:6–8.) New Testament prophets often arose in the first generation following Acts 2's Pentecost, so they lacked senior prophets to mentor them. Prophecy in Corinth, where the believers were just two or three years old in the Lord, had to get vetted through a process of peer review (1 Cor. 14:29).

Words coming to pass was one measure, but it was not *the* decisive criterion for prophecy. Prophets were false even if their words came to pass, if they sought to lead God's people to worship other gods (Deut. 13:1–5); they spoke "rebellion" against the Lord (13:5). The test of "coming to pass" is also not always relevant, even conditional prophecies aside. Although some New Testament prophecies are predictive (Acts 11:28; 21:11; Rev. 2:21–22), for example, many are not (1 Cor. 14:3; Rev. 2:2–4, 13–15), though they often directly address matters of people's hearts (1 Cor. 14:24–25; cf. Rev. 2:19, 23).

Israel's history does not give us much indication of true prophets who prophesied *publicly* and spoke what was not truly the word of the Lord. After being mentored by senior prophets, by the time that newer prophets were speaking, they seem to have been fairly mature in their prophetic callings. Prophecies in local congregations must be evaluated, but in the Old Testament we never see a true prophet who prophesies wrongly on a massive national scale (apart from false prophets, as those in 2 Kings 22:6–12 seem to be). So while an error might not always make a person the kind of false prophet who prophesies *rebellion* against God, it is still very serious business. True prophecy is about honoring God and revealing his heart.

Some kings may have *thought* prophecies false when they produced trouble. After the Judahite king dismissed hired soldiers from the Northern Kingdom in obedience to a prophecy, he did win the battle, but the dismissed soldiers plundered his towns. He was less ready to heed prophets after that (2 Chron. 25:6–16). True prophecies may yield trouble in the short run (1 Sam. 22:5–6). Prophetic instructions do not guarantee prosperity and ease.

### *Is New Testament Prophecy the Same as Old Testament Prophecy?*

Many cessationists reject the idea that prophets might be fallible. They contend that we should hold New Testament prophets, and thus modern charismatic prophets (if they exist), to the same standard as Old Testament prophets. These cessationists say the standard for Old Testament prophets, and therefore for New Testament prophets and any subsequent prophets, is infallibility. Since prophets today are not infallible, they say, this proves that prophets do not exist today.[15] (And if infallibility is the standard, most of us would be afraid to venture even to say, "I feel like God might be saying something like . . .")

After all, the background for New Testament prophecy is clearly Old Testament prophecy, a point they emphasize (I believe rightly) by noting the use of Joel 2:28–29 in Acts 2:17–18.[16] Ironically, the same passage assumes that prophecy should characterize this age until the day of the Lord. So *if* prophecy should be infallible and charismatics aren't doing it right, perhaps instead of arguing for prophecy's cessation, which this passage contradicts, we should all be praying for (cf. 1 Cor. 14:39) the gift of infallible prophecy. That is, instead of being cessationists, critics should show how prophecy should be done properly.

Cessationists point out that "the Bible never explicitly or overtly distinguishes New Testament prophecy from Old Testament prophecy."[17] If we grant the point, it seems quite ironic methodologically that it comes from cessationists. Cessationists reject the belief in a change in prophecy as unbiblical since there is no "overt" Scripture that says the Old Testament prophetic gift has ceased. Yet with much less biblical warrant, they not only believe the Old Testament prophetic gift is obsolete. They also believe the New Testament prophetic gift is obsolete! Cessationists condemn charismatics for rejecting one expression of prophecy, while cessationists reject both. Where is the "overt testimony" and "explicit precedent" for cessationism that they demand of charismatics? In other words, if cessationists criticize charismatics for lack of overt testimony that Old Testament prophecy has ceased, shouldn't they

15. MacArthur, *Strange Fire*, 119; Waldron, *Continued*, 15, 65–69; Pennington, *Cessationism*, 116–23; Schreiner, *Spiritual Gifts*, 105.

16. MacArthur, *Strange Fire*, 120; Schreiner, *Spiritual Gifts*, 105.

17. Waldron, *Continued*, 65–66 (quotation from 65); see also Schreiner, *Spiritual Gifts*, 105.

doubly criticize themselves for claiming *both* Old and New Testament prophecy have ceased?

### Is New Testament Prophecy Different from Old Testament Prophecy?

Certainly Old Testament prophecy is the background for New Testament prophecy, as the cessationists noted above argue. Whether Old Testament prophecy itself was always perfect is a point to be discussed further below. But we must observe some dimensions of New Testament prophecy that go beyond Old Testament prophecy, not least because the gift is now for all believers (Acts 2:17–18). This positive advance may also introduce some complications, since not all believers are fully mature today—nor were they in the New Testament (at least, not in Corinth).

Notice that the Old Testament never encourages the children of Israel to prophesy one by one (as in 1 Cor. 14:31) or tells prophets to be quiet at times to allow someone else to prophesy (as in 1 Cor. 14:30). Moses *wished* that all of God's Old Testament people would prophesy precisely because he knew that was not the case (Num. 11:29)! Old Testament prophets were specially chosen from among God's people. But in the New Testament, "you can *all* prophesy one by one" (1 Cor. 14:31, our emphasis).

Today the prophetic gift is meant to be pervasive. Joel predicted the Spirit of God would be poured out on all flesh to the extent that youth would prophesy and ordinary people would receive divine communication (Joel 2:28–29; Acts 2:17–18). This is clearly a different dimension of prophetic revelation than what had been the standard for public prophets in the Old Testament and what would be written as Scripture in the New. But it seems impossible to imagine a situation in which every believer is able to prophesy yet there are never any mistakes, or that we would never mistake ordinary dreams for prophetic ones.

The very widespread availability of the prophetic gift suggests more potential for mistakes and demands a different role than what we see in senior prophets such as Elijah or Isaiah. We don't depend on prophets to hear God's voice for us in the same way as in the Old Testament (cf. Exod. 20:19; Deut. 5:27). Every true believer has the Holy Spirit living within; we are all able to hear God's voice for ourselves. That is why the New Testament calls for the evaluation of prophecy in the church, rather than its automatic acceptance or rejection. And it is why prophecy is guided by some new rules never found in the Old Testament.

This is not to say that Old Testament–style senior, national prophets are necessarily *obsolete*. Scripture does not explicitly teach this. God can do whatever he wants to do. He can raise up major prophetic voices like Jeremiah and Isaiah if he desires. Such prophets would certainly not write new Scripture; they would only affirm the truth already in Scripture. But they could prophesy this biblical truth on a major, national level. They might pronounce judgments and predict the future at times with great accuracy. This has indeed been said to happen in the church age—such as with Girolamo Savonarola or John Knox. Our main point, and what seems clear from Scripture, is that this is not the normative pattern for prophetic expression in the church. It has different characteristics than what was commonly expressed by the most public prophets under the old covenant.

D. A. Carson suggests that prophets in New Testament congregations rarely commanded the authority granted New Testament apostles or "the writing prophets" in the Old Testament.[18] Paul's limits on prophecy in 1 Corinthians 14:29, 30, and 36 present a "gift of prophecy . . . considerably tamed"[19]—tamed, at least, if we compare it with public Old Testament prophecies rather than the training sessions where junior prophets were being mentored (1 Sam. 19:20).

## Were Old Testament Prophets Infallible?

Cessationists often claim that true prophets must be infallible, like (they say) biblical prophets.[20] One cessationist, for example, readily grants that most prophecies offered in the Old and New Testament periods do not appear in the canon (he cites 2 Kings 2:3, 5, 7, 15; 4:1, 38; 5:22; 6:1; 9:1). He nevertheless contends that such prophecies were without error: "*Everything* they prophesied was true!"[21] But how would we know that? Indeed, the prophets in 2 Kings 2 wrongly supposed that Elijah had been cast on a mountain (2:16); their level of prophetic acuity was clearly less than that of Elisha.

### *Israelite Prophets Limited*

Samuel was extraordinary in that God never let any of his words fail (1 Sam. 3:19). Yet even Samuel made a wrong *mental* assumption that God had to correct (16:6–7). After God corrected Nathan, Nathan had to correct the assurance he had given to David (2 Sam. 7:3–5). Even godly court prophets like Nathan could make wrong assumptions in times of royal favor.[22]

This problem is not, however, limited to court prophets or even the Old Testament. When John the Baptist heard that Jesus was healing people, he questioned Jesus's identity (Matt. 11:2–3, Luke 7:18–20). Probably John did

18. Carson, *Showing Spirit*, 96.
19. Carson, *Showing Spirit*, 98. See further Kay, "Perspectives," 447–48.
20. E.g., Gaffin, "View," 48–51; MacArthur, *Strange Fire*, 119; Waldron, *Continued*, 15, 55; Schreiner, *Spiritual Gifts*, 101–10.
21. Schreiner, *Spiritual Gifts*, 111.
22. Some of these paragraphs develop Keener, "Political Prophecies."

so because he earlier heard from God that the coming one would baptize in the Spirit and in fire (Matt. 3:11; Luke 3:16). John, however, drew a faulty inference about the timing. John also recognized Jesus as the coming one (Matt. 3:14; John 1:6–7, 15, 29–36; 3:26; cf. Acts 19:4). Yet so far as John could tell from the reports he was hearing, Jesus was not baptizing anybody in fire, leading to some confusion. What John heard from God was right, but John's inference was wrong because he, like all prophets, had only a piece of the larger picture (1 Cor. 13:9).

Scripture is clear that Old Testament prophets did not ordinarily hear God as directly as Moses did, face-to-face. Instead, they experienced visions, dreams, and riddles (Num. 12:6–8). Besides his more dramatic revelations, Elijah also was ready to discern God's quiet voice (1 Kings 19:12). Nor were visions all necessarily external; Saul saw one when he was physically blind (Acts 9:12). Like riddles, dreams and visions may require interpretation; prophets did not always understand them immediately. Besides John the Baptist, note, for example, the following:

- Prophets often needed a direct interpretation alongside their vision (e.g., Jer. 1:11–15; Amos 7:8–9; 8:1–3).
- Jeremiah did not always understand the lesson behind a command until after he carried it out (Jer. 13:1–7; 35:2, 14).
- Alarmed by visions, Daniel had to request an interpretation (Dan. 7:16).
- Daniel did not initially understand a vision, which left him exhausted and ill (Dan. 8:27).
- An angel told Daniel that some things shown to him were not yet meant to be understood (Dan. 12:8–9).
- Zechariah had to ask the revealing angel the meaning of his visions (Zech. 1:9, 19; 4:4; 5:10; 6:4–5), and he had to admit his ignorance when the angel asked him if he knew the meaning of symbols he was seeing (4:5, 13).
- Also Acts 10:17: "Peter was greatly perplexed in mind as to what the vision which he had seen might mean."

Besides all this, a prophet (Gen. 20:7) might not understand even a more direct word from God. God directly promised Abram a son from his own body (Gen. 15:4). After some years Abram did have a son from his own body, through Hagar. When that son, Ishmael, was thirteen, God spoke to Abram again and promised him a son through Sarai (17:16). Abram had been assuming the promised heir was Ishmael (17:17–18) but now discovered it would be Isaac (17:19). In Genesis 15, God hadn't told Abram that the promise had to be through Sarai. He knew only in part, because God had shown him only in part.

Limited understanding might imply fallibility (or at least potential fallibility), but it need not imply promulgation of error. At the same time, some cessationists read the assumption of infallibility from that doctrine of Scripture back onto biblical prophets even when they were not writing Scripture. This assumption may reflect the logical fallacy of affirming the consequent. Affirming that God providentially preserved Scripture without error does not require one to affirm that all prophets were always inerrant.

### *Different Levels of Israelite Prophecy*

Certainly ancient Israelite prophets had limitations; these may have even included fallibility. Some prophecy in the Old Testament period was never intended to be canonical, foundational, or even public. Leading prophets such as Samuel, Elijah, and Elisha mentored prophets-in-training or junior prophets (1 Sam. 19:20–25), sometimes called "sons of the prophets" (1 Kings 20:35; 2 Kings 2:3, 5, 7, 15; 4:1, 38; 6:1; 9:1). Even Isaiah may have had some disciples (Isa. 8:16). Their level may be similar to that of the junior prophets in Corinth or Thessalonica, except that in the young churches, lack of senior prophetic mentors entailed the need for peer review (1 Cor. 14:29).

Consider cases such as the following (ESV):

> Numbers 11:25–26: "Then the Lord came down in the cloud and spoke to him, and took some of the Spirit that was on him and put it on the seventy elders. And as soon as the Spirit rested on them, they prophesied. But they did not continue doing it. Now two men remained in the camp, one named Eldad, and the other named Medad, and the Spirit rested on them. They were among those registered, but they had not gone out to the tent, and so they prophesied in the camp."
>
> 1 Samuel 10:5: "As soon as you come to the city, you will meet a group of prophets coming down from the high place with harp, tambourine, flute, and lyre before them, prophesying."
>
> 1 Samuel 19:20: "Then Saul sent messengers to take David, and when they saw the company of the prophets prophesying, and Samuel standing as head over them, the Spirit of God came upon the messengers of Saul, and they also prophesied."
>
> 1 Samuel 19:24: "And [Saul] too stripped off his clothes, and he too prophesied before Samuel and lay naked all that day and all that night. Thus it is said, 'Is Saul also among the prophets?'"
>
> Acts 19:6: "And when Paul had laid his hands on them, the Holy Spirit came on them, and they began speaking in tongues and prophesying."

Besides fallibility, we also have an Old Testament prophet with an integrity problem: He's so eager to spend time with another prophet that he lies to him—before prophesying accurately (1 Kings 13:18–22). Yet he's not called a false prophet (1 Kings 13:11, 20, 25–26, 29; 2 Kings 23:18). Not all prophecy in the Old Testament was equally authoritative or, as in the instances cited above, even heard by all the junior prophets' colleagues (since all were prophesying together; cf. a similar situation with tongues in Acts 2:4, 11; 10:46; 19:6). Those addressing the question of Old Testament prophecy's function often cite the observations of Old Testament scholar Iain Duguid.[23] He draws attention to many of these same passages as well as to others. Abraham is a prophet (Gen. 20:7), presumably because he listens to God, but his prophethood is mentioned in this single passage only in connection with prayer. (Cf. the patriarchs more generally in 1 Chron. 16:22; Ps. 105:15.) We learn of prophetically inspired worship in 1 Chronicles 25:1–3 (cf. also 1 Sam. 10:5; 2 Kings 3:15; Hab. 3:19). As Gregg Allison and Andreas Köstenberger conclude, "None of the second [less authoritative] type of prophecy undermines the authority and sufficiency of Scripture."[24]

Our cessationist Reformed friends may be interested to know that Martin Luther himself held that Old Testament prophets "often erred" and were not always under the influence of the Holy Spirit.[25] Ideas about prophetic infallibility have sometimes become romanticized over time.

Paul not only describes our prophesying, like our knowledge, as partial, but he also describes our partial knowledge in terms of seeing through "a mirror dimly" (ESV, NASB, NRSV) as opposed to "face to face." Ancient mirrors did not reflect as accurately as do modern ones.[26] In translation, however, we may especially miss the biblical allusion in the term "dimly" (KJV, "darkly"). It is the Greek term *ainigma*, "riddle, obscure communication." In the Greek version of Numbers 12:8 known to Paul's audience in Corinth, the term contrasts this *ordinary* experience of prophets with Moses's extraordinary, fuller experience of God "face to face." As already noted, the Lord revealed himself to ordinary prophets in intermediary ways such as dreams and visions (Num. 12:6) rather than directly.

23. Duguid, "Kind of Prophecy." Duguid is cited in Wilson, *Spirit and Sacrament*, 112n67; Allison and Köstenberger, *Holy Spirit*, 433n34. Schreiner, *Spiritual Gifts*, 95–96n5, however, acknowledges the case but remains unconvinced "that the small p. prophet erred in their prophecies." The evidence shows neither that they did or did not, but without the prior premise that they could not (because they must be like Scripture), it would seem to allow for normal human responses.

24. Allison and Köstenberger, *Holy Spirit*, 433n34.

25. Thompson, *Sure Ground*, 130.

26. See Forbes, *Studies in Technology*, 184–85. For background on the passage, see further Hollander, "Seeing God." For the image positively, see Wis. 7:26.

Were prophets like Elisha and Agabus more reliable than most of those who prophesy today? That is likely the case, since both were senior prophets. Moreover, Elisha had Elijah as his mentor, and Agabus came from Jerusalem (Acts 11:27–28), probably in a time when Jesus's own disciples were leading the church (2:42; 5:42; 8:1). We might expect most of today's prophets, without mentoring by such leaders, to be more like those in Corinth, needing to practice peer review. While some are more mature, we learn who they are by testing their prophecies and observing their lives.

According to the likeliest sense of Romans 12:6, those who prophesy do so "according to the proportion of faith" allotted them, suggesting that some may prophesy at higher levels than others. Robert Saucy notes C. E. B. Cranfield's suggestion that mostly genuine prophecies could be "adulterated" by sources other than the Spirit.[27]

## Prophecy as Perfect as the Canon?

Many cessationists don't just hold modern prophets to the standard of Old Testament prophets. They hold prophecy in the church to the standard of Scripture itself: infallible and inerrant! Such cessationists would have you believe that if modern prophecy is not on the level of Scripture, it is false prophecy. The Bible never says that prophets (even in the Old Testament) were required to be "infallible and inerrant." It only says their predictions were required to come true (Deut. 18:22), and with the various sorts of qualifications we have noted earlier.

Many continuationists counter that prophecy in the early church *was* potentially fallible, thus requiring testing. To grant the inerrancy of all prophecy and thus the danger of postbiblical prophecy, Andrew Wilson notes, requires the acceptance of some significant prior premises:

1. All Old Testament prophecy "was infallible divine revelation."
2. All New Testament prophecy was likewise "infallible divine revelation."
3. The sole purpose of New Testament prophecy was to lay the foundation for the universal church.
4. We may be sufficiently confident of these premises to contradict "Paul's instruction to pursue the *charismata*."

Wilson doubts each premise and finds the acceptance of all together as incredible.[28]

27. Saucy, "View," 147, citing Cranfield, *Romans*, 2:620.
28. Wilson, *Spirit and Sacrament*, 111–12.

As Wilson points out, "It remains difficult to read 1 Corinthians if we assume that Paul is speaking of infallible, foundational revelation throughout (with numerous Corinthian prophets chipping in, . . . often talking over each other, with their prophecies weighed by those sitting down, and none of it ever recorded or transmitted to another church), and there is a broad scholarly consensus that he is not."[29]

This is the case because all prophecy is "in part," just as teachers "know in part" (1 Cor. 13:9). As noted in chapter 5, until Jesus returns, our knowing is limited and partial (13:9–12). Saying that all the prophecies that made it into the Bible are perfect doesn't mean that none of God's servants ever uttered imperfect prophecies. It just means that after the fact and with the benefit of hindsight and additional prophetic perspectives, they were never made part of the canon. That's why Paul insists that each prophecy must be evaluated (1 Cor. 14:29). He warns us not to quench the Spirit or despise prophecies; instead, we are to test them, keeping what is good and rejecting what is evil (1 Thess. 5:19–22).[30]

### *Did Agabus Miss It?*

Many continuationists argue that Agabus offers a case in point of fallible prophecy.

Agabus prophesied in Acts 21:11 to Paul, "The Holy Spirit says, 'In this way the Jewish leaders in Jerusalem will bind the owner of this belt and will hand him over to the Gentiles'" (NIV). The main point of Agabus's prophecy was accurate, but his word was not "infallible and inerrant" by the strictest standard to which some cessationists hold charismatics. If cessationists held Agabus to the same standard by which they judge charismatics, he might well be deemed a false prophet. In reality, it was Roman soldiers—not Judean antagonists—that bound Paul (Acts 21:33; 22:29). After Jewish assailants tried to kill Paul, Roman soldiers from the Fortress Antonia inadvertently rescued him from the mob. Then they bound him with chains (Acts 21:31–32).

After Agabus's prophecy (Acts 21:11), Luke says that "we all"—Luke, Agabus, Philip and his prophetic daughters, and Paul's other companions—begged Paul not to go to Jerusalem (21:12). Paul insisted, however, based on what the Spirit had already shown him (19:21), so his friends acquiesced: "The Lord's will be done" (21:14). Instead of following Agabus's and others' interpretation of the prophecy, Paul evaluated it and remained convinced that it was not God's ultimate will for him to avoid Jerusalem. Paul did not treat Agabus's prophecy, and certainly not its general interpretation, as Scripture.

29. Wilson, *Spirit and Sacrament*, 112n68, citing Thiselton, *Corinthians*, 956–65, 1087–94, esp. 965; Garland, *1 Corinthians*, 583; Ciampa and Rosner, *Corinthians*, 581.

30. I adapt this paragraph from Keener, "Political Prophecies."

At the same time, no doubt Agabus's prophecy still helped Paul. It warned him of what awaited him in Jerusalem and therefore helped prepare his heart. We might then ask, Would that prophecy still have helped Paul if the canon were complete? And the answer would be, Of course. Agabus's prophecy to Paul has nothing to do with foundational truth and everything to do with one man's specific situation. Scripture is sufficient to establish doctrine. But we still need the Spirit's voice for guidance and encouragement for our personal lives in every era until we know as we are known.

Yet was Agabus's prophecy itself *wrong*? Cessationist scholar Richard Gaffin rightly observes that such a verdict "suffers from the demand for pedantic precision imposed on Agabus."[31] He cites an Old Testament scholar accordingly: "If one's judgment is rigid enough, similar 'errors' in OT predictions can also be cited."[32] Fellow New Testament scholar Tom Schreiner likewise warns against "interpreting the fulfillment of prophecy in a rigid way."[33] "Modern Western conceptions of accuracy must not be applied to the Scriptures when we speak of accuracy."[34] "Those who think that Agabus erred define error too narrowly and rigidly."[35]

Paul himself summarizes his experience in the same way after the fact in Acts 28:17 that Agabus did beforehand, and nobody thinks Paul forgot his experience.[36] Ordinary speech condenses experiences like this all the time.[37]

In this case we agree with Gaffin and Schreiner about the need to allow this flexibility, just as we evangelical New Testament scholars allow, for example, for different Gospel writers narrating the same event or New Testament quotations of the Old Testament. Our continuationist response, however, is to ask why most cessationists will not allow *similar* flexibility for prophecy in charismatic churches today. Why not allow such latitude to prophecy today when it gets the substance right but the wording is less than precise by wooden Western standards?

There are genuine false prophecies; an obvious case in point might be (whatever your political predilections) the chorus of prominent voices insisting that Donald Trump would be inaugurated on January 20, 2021. Telling people what they want to hear builds one's social media platform (cf. 2 Tim. 4:3–4),

31. Gaffin, "View," 49.

32. Gaffin, "View," 49n65, citing Hilber, "Diversity," 256. Cf., e.g., Judg. 9:57 on the fulfillment of the curse in 9:20, though in 9:53–54 it is not by fire.

33. Schreiner, *Spiritual Gifts*, 113.

34. Schreiner, *Spiritual Gifts*, 114, citing the Chicago Statement on Biblical Inerrancy and also Craig Blomberg's work. See helpfully Blomberg, *Reliability*; Blomberg, *Believe Bible*.

35. Schreiner, *Spiritual Gifts*, 115.

36. Schreiner, *Spiritual Gifts*, 113; so also Keener, *Acts*, 3:3105–6, 3334n1789; 4:3739.

37. See Keener, *Christobiography*, 123. Even human memory condenses to fit schemas; see Kirk, "Tradition," 196. For conflating details to condense accounts in antiquity, see, e.g., Derrenbacker, *Practices*, 94, 100–113; Licona, *Differences*, 20, 48, 52, 56, 67, 91, 95, 109.

so it's no surprise that these voices scored massive hits.[38] (Given the outcome of the 2024 election and the rareness of presidents with nonconsecutive terms, however, at least some of those expecting Trump to become president again may well have heard *something* right, even if they wrongly supposed the terms to be consecutive.) Doctrinally unsound churches that suggest that God will give people whatever they want also lend themselves to false prophecies.[39] But insofar as our observations are representative, most prophecies in theologically sound charismatic churches are within the same range we allow for Agabus.

### God Versus Prophets as Infallible

Cessationists rightly denounce the idea that God speaks fallibly. That God speaks infallibly, however, does not guarantee that we always *hear* infallibly. Hearers were not infallible in the Old Testament, the New Testament, or today. Analogously, we may affirm that Scripture is infallible without pretending that all our understanding and teaching of Scripture are infallible. Just as teachers grow in the gift of teaching, prophets need to mature in the gift of prophecy.

Despite insisting that true prophecy should be free of error, biblically informed cessationists recognize that God worked through prophets' personalities. As Sam Waldron points out, "God's control of the prophet is intimately organic, not externally mechanical. God accommodated the prophet to the prophecy. . . . It is no contradiction of the full divinity and authority of the prophetic word that it is permeated with marks of Isaiah's or Amos' personality."[40] Likewise, Schreiner allows that prophets, like other people, could make mistakes, except when they were prophesying.[41]

This raises a semantic question. Most continuationists and cessationists alike agree that prophets as individuals were fallible but might disagree over whether they may have ever been mistaken when they *believed* that what they were saying was God's message. Granted that God protected the words that were canonized, and the words of mature prophets to Israel. But were there never lapses in the junior prophets mentored by Samuel, Elijah, and Elisha? Bringing them to maturity may have been one of the reasons for the mentoring (cf. 2 Kings 2:15–18; 4:38–44; 6:1–7) and supervision (1 Sam. 19:20). This process was impossible in Corinth, where those prophesying, like the rest of the church, had been Christians

38. One of the experts on the *Cessationist* video proclaims (perhaps hyperbolically) that "all" charismatic prophets proclaimed that President Trump would be reelected in 2020 (Lanphere, *Cessationist*). That is certainly not true; YouTube's analytics together with many charismatic Republicans gave those prophets a large platform, but some people known for prophecy said nothing of the sort (e.g., Julian Adams, Stacey Campbell, Cindy Jacobs) and some of us (such as Ron Cantor and, for what little it may be worth, myself [Craig]) felt that the election was going to go the opposite direction.

39. See Keener, *Suffering*, ch. 3.

40. Waldron, *Continued*, 55.

41. Schreiner, *Spiritual Gifts*, 111n5.

for only a few years when Paul first wrote. So there may be a semantic issue: A person may believe that he or she speaks the word of the Lord, but in retrospect Scripture may reserve the label (true) "prophecy" for when they were right.

As Carson writes, careful treatments of biblical inspiration distinguish "between the *mode* of inspiration and the *result* of inspiration in order to avoid all mechanical theories of dictation. The *result* of inspiration is a text truly from God, right down to the words, while also being in the words of the human author; but that does not mean the *mode* of inspiration required God to dictate the text."[42] "This raises the possibility, at least, that revelation, whatever the mode, might well *not* be *communicated* accurately unless the *results* are guaranteed. In that case the prophecy that has actually come by revelation might well have to be evaluated, *without reflection on the quality of the revelation itself*."[43] Canon is the end product of consensus regarding a minimum of revelation that all mainstream Christians recognize as fully inspired; it is no guarantee that every prophetic attempt in prior history was inspired at the same level. Nor need we suppose that it is today.

### Testing Prophecy

Most telling are the instructions Paul gives for guarding against errant prophecies in the New Testament. He doesn't say to *execute false prophets as a deterrent for other, would-be, false prophets*. (Modern continuationists and cessationists share a consensus against executing people in church today. But Paul doesn't even suggest throwing someone out of the church if they make a mistake; contrast 1 Cor. 5:13.) Instead, he says, "Let two or three prophets speak, and let the others judge" (1 Cor. 14:29). Prophecy should be evaluated by other believers, who are able to do this because they have the Spirit of God dwelling inside of them, just as the prophet does. Prophets do not stand above the church, speaking down with absolute authority. Instead, they stand on the same level with their fellow believers, who must evaluate their message. This is very different from what we see with the leading, senior prophets to Israel in the Old Testament.

Paul encourages the Corinthians to prophesy (1 Cor. 14:5). He commands hearers not to "treat prophecies with contempt" (1 Thess. 5:20). He tells them to test every prophetic word (1 Thess. 5:21). As mentioned earlier, he exhorts us to judge one another's prophecies (1 Cor. 14:29). But he also encourages the Corinthians, "You can all prophesy one by one, that all may learn and all may be encouraged" (1 Cor. 14:31). Can Paul be describing the same level of prophecy as Isaiah when he pronounced judgment on the nations, or Jeremiah when he delivered the word of the Lord to the king of Judah, giving divine direction to all of God's people?

42. Carson, *Showing Spirit*, 161.
43. Carson, *Showing Spirit*, 161.

If inaccurate prophetic words deserved capital punishment (even though Roman law no longer permitted it to be carried out in the first century), would it make sense for Paul to encourage the people to prophesy and to desire earnestly the gift of prophecy (1 Cor. 14:1) and not to despise prophecy (1 Thess. 5:20)?

Astonishingly, Gaffin denies that Paul's requirement to test prophecy recognizes its fallibility.[44] Why else would it need to be tested? If the average house church gathered some fifteen to fifty people, we should not expect them to find new false prophets among themselves on a regular basis.[45] I do not rule out the possibility of such happening on occasion. Decades ago shudders went down my (Craig's) spine as I heard a completely false prophecy, demonically inspired, in a public assembly, but this utterance did not come from a regular attender or constitute a regular occurrence that would have to be discerned every week. In this rare case the false spirit was so blatant that everyone except the speaker recognized it as false. I also had this experience when hearing a visiting minister in another church. Afterward I confirmed my suspicion that he belonged to the same cult as the aforementioned visiting "prophet." In this case it was not false prophecy but false teaching, yet my spiritual sense of the demonic spirit was the same.

The need to examine prophecies was not simply to screen out false prophets each week; it was especially to discern and perhaps adjust the accuracy of prophecies from generally trusted members of the congregation. Against some, then, in 1 Corinthians 14 Paul likely envisions evaluating prophecies rather than evaluating prophets (for the latter, see Matt. 7:15–23; 1 John 4:1–6). Again, whereas senior prophets such as Samuel and Elisha often mentored junior prophets in the Old Testament, the Corinthian Christians were just a few years old in the Lord, and Paul was no longer with them to supervise. Peer review was the best they could do. As Jack Deere notes, false prophets are not beginning-level prophets who make a mistake; as in the Bible, they "are those who *contradict* the teaching and predictions of true prophets and attempt to lead people away from God and his Word."[46]

## Conclusion

Even beyond variation in detail (as with Agabus's prophecy), prophets, like teachers, are capable of making mistakes. Their messages thus must be tested.

44. Gaffin, "View," 50. He compares use of the term for the action of the Bereans in Acts 17:11. But the Bereans' examination is not to determine whether the Scriptures they examine are correct, but to determine whether Paul's interpretation of them is correct!

45. As Carson, *Showing Spirit*, 95–96, points out, Paul describes such prophetic evaluation as "normal operating procedure."

46. Deere, *Voice*, 68.

Scripture, by contrast, has already withstood the tests, and therefore constitutes the theological standard by which we can evaluate other claims to hear God. Some situations go beyond mere mistakes. Thus, the prophets who prophesy "presumptuously" in Deuteronomy are explicitly those who seek to lead people away from God and therefore must be removed from harming God's people.

We should also distinguish between the sort of prophecy in 1 Corinthians 14, practiced by relatively new believers in small groups and house churches, and the sort of prophets prophesying on a national level such as some Israelite prophets in the Old Testament. Anyone who assumes the latter sort of role today without being first proved in local church settings, exalted courtesy of social media or other means, risks bringing reproach on the church. Not accredited to speak for the church, they act out of order and must assume responsibility for any consequences of their actions. In biblical terms, their judgment is on their own heads.

Don't stone fallible prophets. But do keep your (exclusively figurative) stones ready for the false ones.

# 15

# Analogous Experiences?

Some more generous cessationists view as legitimate some experiences claimed by charismatics without regarding them as genuinely prophetic. Sometimes they view them as somewhat analogous to the biblical experiences but on a lesser level. For example, many who reject the gift of prophecy for today nevertheless often allow for intuitive experiences they consider somewhat analogous to prophecy, or similar to what charismatics consider prophecy.

Likewise, continuationists also consider analogies for biblical gifts, though sometimes from different angles than the above-mentioned cessationists. Given our limited biblical information about some gifts, we may be able to learn more about them by making analogies with other gifts, such as teaching, as we will suggest at times in this chapter.

## Teaching

Already in this book we have hinted at analogies between prophecy and teaching in matters such as growing in gifts and evaluating them.

### *Growing in Gifts*

Thus, for example we may grow in prophetic sensitivity to the Spirit in a manner similar to how we grow in teaching. Paul, after all, speaks of how we lack perfect knowledge as well as perfect prophesying until we see Jesus face-to-face (1 Cor. 13:9, 12). We find the analogy already also in Paul's lists in 1 Corinthians 13:2, 8; 14:6, because we understand teaching to be Paul's usual sense in that letter for communicating "knowledge" (see especially 1:5:

"enriched in all speech and all knowledge"; and see the discussion in chap. 5 above).

> 1 Corinthians 13:2: "And if I have prophecy and I know all mysteries and all knowledge . . ."
>
> 1 Corinthians 13:8: "But if there are prophecies, they will end; . . . if there is knowledge, it will end."
>
> 1 Corinthians 14:6: "revelation or knowledge or prophecy or teaching"

Those who assume that one's exercise of a gift must be perfect to be genuine would (hopefully) never assume that standard for the gift of teaching. Can someone with the gift of teaching teach *any* passage and answer *any* linguistic or background question on command? While I (Craig) love to answer many kinds of Bible questions on the spot, I'm grateful that neither my charismatic nor my cessationist friends expect me to be able to answer all of them.

### *Equal Strictness*

God has a strict standard for both gifts, commensurate with the degree to which we are influencing people. Compare James 3:1 (NRSV): "Not many of you should become teachers, my brothers and sisters, for you know that we who teach will be judged with greater strictness." That is another reason why those of us with the gift of teaching must mobilize the body of Christ to use their scriptural gifts and not, as we have often done, merely try to train fellow teachers.

When we claim "The Bible says . . ." among those for whom those words mean "The Lord says . . . ," we owe our hearers appropriate cautions. If the biblical gift of prophecy requires infallibility, shouldn't we say the same for the biblical gift of teaching? Again, if prophecy says, "This is what God is saying," so does teaching if it says, "This is what the Bible is saying, and the Bible is what God is saying." (Cf. Jer. 29:24–32, esp. 31.)

Perhaps a very unusual cessationist might protest (though I have never heard this) that the modern act of teaching differs from having the biblical gift of teaching, so that the modern practice, unlike the ancient one, is allowed to be fallible. But then why should such a cessationist not allow the same for prophecy? As Jack Deere puts it, "I trust teachers, pastors, evangelists, and friends who all make serious errors. None of the people I trust are right all the time. None of them claim that. Neither do any of the mature prophetic people I know."[1]

1. Deere, *Voice*, 68.

Teaching, like prophecy, incurs strict judgment, since other people often depend on what we say as being from the Lord. (This is a good reason to avoid dogmatism on matters about which we are unsure.) One might reply that our hearers have Bibles and so are responsible to test our teaching for themselves. That is true. That is also what we argue for prophecy. Our hearers have the Spirit and so are responsible to test our prophetic words for themselves.

Not everyone appreciates this analogy. Thomas Schreiner protests, "Sometimes continuationists say that prophecy is like teaching since teachers aren't infallible, but there is a key difference between prophecy and teaching. Teachers, as noted earlier, expound and explain the biblical text. Prophets, however, bring an immediate word from God."[2] That does make teachers easier for us fellow teachers to evaluate, insofar as we understand Scripture rightly; but then, discerning prophets may be equally equipped to discern what errs in other prophets' prophesying (1 Cor. 14:29). Moreover, sound charismatics would never consider a prophecy outside Scripture, which must be tested, to be a "word from God" on the level of Scripture. We take it less seriously than a direct word from Scripture and often have to wait and see what comes of it. The only groups that explicitly place prophecy on the level of Scripture are cults. In practice, some less careful Christians may implicitly but wrongly accept prophecy at that level—just as they do with their pastors' teaching, with Scofield reference notes, or with some apparent academic tour de force in linguistics or theology.

As I (Craig) wrote elsewhere, "There are errors in much of the charismatic movement, but humbly serving with one's gift of teaching will bring change much better than denunciations will. . . . Teaching error in the name of Scripture seems as vulnerable to critique as mistaken affirmations in the name of the Spirit, so long as we claim to be speaking for God. Vocal dismissal of brothers and sisters and their God-given gifts seems to me to fall into that category" of error.[3]

## Impressions

As noted in this chapter's opening words, some cessationists do allow for analogous sorts of experiences today. John MacArthur, for example, believes that Bible expositors like himself fill today's prophetic mantle, so long as they understand that the "revelatory aspect of prophecy" has ended.[4] For MacArthur, then, his preaching effectively plays a role analogous to some elements

2. Schreiner, *Spiritual Gifts*, 106.

3. Keener, *Gift & Giver*, 211–12. By such vocal dismissal I refer not to conciliatory cessationists such as Schreiner but to the sort noted in the introduction.

4. MacArthur, *Chaos*, 69. Cf. similarly Calvin in Oss, "Response to Saucy," 167.

of biblical prophecy. (Schreiner, however, rightly objects that prophecy in the narrowest sense differs from "charismatic exegesis or preaching.")[5] While Richard Gaffin denies that the New Testament teaches ongoing "revelatory word gifts," he does "not deny that experiences may occur today" somehow *resembling* those in the New Testament.[6] We charismatics can surely welcome such common ground as overtures to dialogue.

Some cessationists, however, believe that God speaks *only* through Scripture; he does not even prompt "believers through inward impressions and feelings."[7] But is one "led by the Spirit" or does one "walk by the Spirit" only by reading the Bible?[8] In the name of Scripture, this approach seems to nullify the reality of the outpoured Spirit (Acts 2:17–18, 33) to which Scripture abundantly testifies. From a charismatic perspective (and that of many other Christians), this extreme approach sounds almost akin in practice to deism. Other cessationists, while denying that such promptings reflect the biblical gift of prophecy, properly recognize that God can lead people through impressions so long as we do not depend on them as if they were always accurate.[9] One can hardly read the stories of nineteenth-century figures of great faith such as George Müller or Hudson Taylor and fail to recognize the importance of inner promptings that they understood in terms of God's voice.[10]

Schreiner suggests that "what happens in charismatic churches today is . . . the sharing of *impressions* rather than prophecy."[11] Actually, we have witnessed charismatic sharing in some congregations that does seem to be on no higher level than impressions; such congregations have seemed startled when what we would consider a more typical prophecy happens. We believe that impressions are at least a legitimate place to start (and should be accordingly *expressed* as impressions), though "impression" is sometimes too tame a way to express the Spirit's moving. Sometimes we have experienced an overwhelming inner compulsion and certainty to the extent that we felt we could not have withheld the message without sensing God's disappointment or discipline.

5. Schreiner, *Spiritual Gifts*, 93, 95. In the more *general* sense of God "prophetically" leading our speech, my (Craig's) expositions of Acts have argued for this taking place whenever we preach the gospel (see Keener, "Spirit and Mission"; cf. 1 Thess. 2:13).

6. Gaffin, "Response to Saucy," 153.

7. Pennington, *Cessationism*, 19. Pennington further warns that believers should "reject all forms of supposed continuing revelation, including subjective impressions of God's will" (172).

8. This leading can be especially moral (Rom. 8:14; Gal. 5:18) but also applies to specific direction (Matt. 4:1 // Luke 4:1; cf. Ps. 143:10; Isa. 63:14; 2 Cor. 3:6, 18; Gal. 5:16, 25); see Keener, *Galatians*, 504–6. Cf. Luther's gloss on Rom. 8:14 (LW 25:71), where he equates being led with being "moved or directed."

9. Schreiner, *Spiritual Gifts*, 90–92. Cf. also Saucy, "View," 143; the summary in Grudem, "Conclusion," 343–44.

10. See, e.g., Müller, *Autobiography*; Taylor and Taylor, *Secret*. Note also the early Moravians in Boys, *Evidence*, 286–99.

11. Schreiner, *Spiritual Gifts*, 118.

Schreiner helpfully adds that "impressions may be a mixture of truth and error. Sometimes, in a most remarkable way they might be completely right! God may lay something on someone's heart, and it may be exactly right and exactly what a person needs to hear. Sometimes the impression may be quite astonishing and clearly miraculous, though this is quite rare. On the other hand, sometimes impressions are totally wrong. . . . And some impressions may be a mixture of truth and error. Those whose impressions are wrong aren't false prophets. After all, in my view, impressions aren't prophecies anyway!"[12]

In particular, he warns that naturally overconfident persons may "confuse their own certainty with the leading of the Spirit." God may use them, but they are fallible.[13] All his points about impressions here are well taken. This is not to say that all impressions are on the same level. I have found that even prophecies driven by overwhelming compulsion can begin as unexpected impressions, which, after some internal testing, one begins to recognize as much more than that. Such impressions might initially seem like mere ideas popping into one's head, but in time one becomes more apt to recognize when it is the Lord himself speaking. John Calvin, for example, believed that the Spirit can guide us in prayer "and regulate our affections."[14]

Sometimes "impressions" can be a matter of life and death. During war in Congo, my brother-in-law Aimé felt a sudden urge to run back up the hill instead of continuing on to the market. Moments later, the market erupted in gunfire. Is his survival merely a coincidence, or might God have designed such an urge for his benefit? Aimé is an associate pastor and seminary professor. Others also report timely impressions that provided safety—for example, preventing the burning down of a house.[15]

A woman told R. T. Kendall that she felt something was wrong with his (physical) heart. Because of this, he requested a test, which showed his need for "immediate open-heart surgery. . . . That was a word from God for me that saved my life."[16] A sadder case happened in his youth, when a holiness preacher refused to close the service, warning that this was someone's final chance to be saved. Patsy, one of R. T.'s friends, just mocked. The next day she died in a traffic accident.[17]

Korean Christian Esther Ahn Kim felt certain that God was telling her to go to Pyongyang,[18] where a preacher independently felt God leading him to

12. Schreiner, *Spiritual Gifts*, 118–19.
13. Schreiner, *Spiritual Gifts*, 121, following Edwards, "Distinguishing Marks of Work," 282.
14. Calvin, *Inst*. 3.20.5 (Adams, *Romans*, 467).
15. Sheikh, *Call Him Father*, 150–51.
16. Kendall, *Prophetic Integrity*, 93.
17. Kendall, *Prophetic Integrity*, 94–95.
18. Kim, *If I Perish*, 45.

go to find her.[19] Kim also felt led to warn the Japanese government that if its leaders continued to oppress other nations and their Christians, fire from heaven like "sulpher fire" would devastate them.[20] Later, after she learned that Americans had relentlessly bombed Japanese cities, with atomic bombs on two of them, she felt that God had vindicated that message for which she had first been arrested.[21]

Shukri, a new believer in Iraq, shared Christ boldly with Muslims, as the Lord would lead him. One day he told his wife, "I felt like the Lord said to me that I am going to see Him today."[22] Later that day soldiers from ISIS captured, tortured, and executed him.[23] Yet when his body was recovered, "he was smiling."[24]

Kamal, an Egyptian believer, "felt a compelling urge" to go to the Friday market.[25] There a Muslim woman draped in black ran up to him; in a dream, Jesus had shown her Kamal, in the very clothes he was wearing, and said that this man could explain Jesus to her.[26] (Needless to say, he did so.)

Chidimma Nwaedi was not sure where or in what subject to do her PhD. When she prayed and fasted, she heard just three words: "strategic—leadership—Evangel." Never having heard of Evangel University or a doctorate in "strategic leadership," she eventually googled the three terms and learned of Evangel and that it offered a PhD in this subject. That was how she ended up at one of my (Craig's) alma maters.[27]

At the same time, Schreiner is right that impressions can mislead. If people's hearts are not right, their biases can even lead them to seriously false prophecy. As I (Craig) warned elsewhere, some "risk drawing on the vaguest of impressions or inclinations, thus filling in with 'visions from their own minds, not from the mouth of the Lord' (Jer. 23:16). Judah's false prophets prophesied what they wished to be true. 'I did not send the prophets, yet they ran; I did not speak to them, yet they prophesied. But if they had stood in my council, then they would have proclaimed my words to my people, and they would have turned them from their evil way, and from the evil of their doings' (Jer. 23:21–22, NRSV)."[28]

19. Kim, *If I Perish*, 56.
20. Kim, *If I Perish*, 63, 73, 78, 92.
21. Kim, *If I Perish*, 263, 277. The second atomic bombing may have been literal overkill; sadly, it struck the center of Christianity in Japan (Kantowicz, *Rage*, 1:433–34; Keener, *Suffering*, 141).
22. Doyle, *Killing Christians*, 97.
23. Doyle, *Killing Christians*, 99.
24. Doyle, *Killing Christians*, 101.
25. Doyle, *Dreams*, 4.
26. Doyle, *Dreams*, 7. Others also recount being approached by seekers who dreamed about them (e.g., Doyle, *Dreams*, 223–24).
27. Evangel University, "Confirmed."
28. Keener, "Trump Prophecies."

Even outside of the "gift of prophecy," there is nothing in Scripture that suggests God no longer speaks, leads, guides, and gives revelation to his people today. The book of Acts is filled with examples of revelation, divine guidance, and direction that might not technically be "prophecy" but are legitimate and authentic direction by the Spirit just the same. Acts, focused on the mission to the nations, naturally highlights especially the Spirit's guidance for cross-cultural mission. For example:

- In Acts 8:29, the Holy Spirit told Philip to approach the Ethiopian eunuch.
- In Acts 10:19, the Holy Spirit showed Peter that three men were looking for him.
- In Acts 15:28, the apostles and elders sent a message of instruction to gentile believers, saying, "It seemed good to the Holy Spirit and to us not to burden you with anything beyond the following requirements . . ."
- In Acts 16:7, the Holy Spirit would not allow Paul and his companions to enter Bithynia.

So even if prophecy in its strictest sense were not for today (a point inconceivable in view of Acts 2:17–18), there would still be nothing in the New Testament to preclude the Holy Spirit from leading people through impressions, visions, dreams, supernatural awareness, hidden knowledge, and the like. This is an important point. God's leading and voice are not restricted to "prophets" and prophecy, whether in the Old Testament or the New. David sought the Lord's direction before major decisions (1 Sam. 23:2, 4; 30:8; 2 Sam. 2:1; 5:19, 23); we who have the new-covenant experience of the Spirit surely should not be less guided. Yet many cessationists not only claim that the closed canon eliminates the need for prophets. More disturbingly, the strictest cessationists also claim that God doesn't speak anymore at all—outside of what is written in Scripture. From this perspective, God would be like a husband who refuses to talk directly to his wife because he's said everything he feels in a love letter long ago. This fits neither biblical teaching nor most Christians' experience of God's character.

## Semantics

Some differences may be semantic. "Open but cautious" theologian Robert Saucy does not deny that in some ways God continues to lead and that believers continue to hear. He does deny that personal leading relates to biblical gifts such as prophecy, but he recognizes, "It is difficult to see how the thought in my mind that I believe to be God's direction and the answer to my prayer, if it is truly guidance from God, is not revelatory. Moreover, if it concerns an issue that is not revealed in Scripture—and there are many, both personal (e.g., marriage, career) and corporate (for the church)—then it is new or fresh."[29] "This voice of God is in our hearts and minds, which are still a mixture of the new work of God and our old sinful egos."[30] God the revealer and leader is infallible in speaking and leading; we humans are fallible in hearing and understanding.

If we define prophecy as only what God speaks, then of course it is without error, since God does not make mistakes. Our hearing is the problem. The Bible does seem to reserve the language of "prophecy" for prophecies considered authentic (despite being spoken by fallible prophets) or wholly inauthentic, rather than merely partly correct. When people speak to Paul by God's Spirit in Acts 21:4, Luke may avoid calling it "prophecy" per se because the speakers were not completely correct.[31] Luke does, however, tell us that these "disciples" were speaking "through the Spirit." Paul's friends rightly heard that he would suffer in Jerusalem (20:23; 21:11) but wrongly inferred from this information that he should not go there (cf. 21:12–14; 2 Kings 2:3–5, 16–18). God had already told Paul himself to *go* to Jerusalem (the probable meaning of Acts 19:21).[32] Subjectivity is messy; but so long as we need wisdom from the Lord, we have to live with some subjectivity. As fellow members of Christ's body who each know in part, it seems best to get all the wisdom and guidance on the table and then discern how it fits together.

Schreiner allows that "the definition of prophecy is crucial to the argument made here. If the prophecies of New Testament prophets could be mixed with error, then I would have no quarrel with New Testament prophets existing today."[33] His concern then would be that "we would then have the task of discerning where they speak truth and where they err."[34] Well, imagine that! This is precisely what Paul calls for in 1 Corinthians 14:29.

Schreiner suggests, "The difference between cessationists and continuationists is in some ways insignificant at the practical level when it comes to prophecy, for what continuationists call prophecy, cessationists call impressions. As a cessationist, I affirm that God may speak to his people through impressions."[35] We would suggest that being sensitive to impressions, growing in the ability to distinguish between what is from God and what isn't, is one

29. Saucy, "View," 143.

30. Saucy, "View," 143.

31. Schreiner, *Spiritual Gifts*, 117, regards the prophecy as correct (if we choose to call it a prophecy) but its interpretation as incorrect; I would agree, and further advocate allowing such a distinction *today* as well.

32. See discussion in Keener, *Acts*, 3:2861; with, e.g., Bruce, *Acts: Greek*, 361; Arrington, *Acts*, 200; Kee, *Every Nation*, 233; Dunn, *Acts*, 262.

33. Schreiner, *Spiritual Gifts*, 159. He also acknowledges that charismatics do not claim that God's own voice is fallible; the fallibility arises in our hearing of God's voice (102n1).

34. Schreiner, *Spiritual Gifts*, 159.

35. Schreiner, *Spiritual Gifts*, 119.

of the ways that prophecy comes, like visions, dreams, or riddles that need to be interpreted. Scripture seems explicit that this was the norm among biblical prophets except Moses (Num. 12:6–8). Schreiner and we would not differ on modern impressions being fallible; we would only differ on whether biblical prophets were also fallible, but that is more a question of exegesis than of modern praxis. Our approaches overlap significantly: Fallible, real Christians seek to be led by God, and God does desire to lead us.

A cessationist might insist that only word-for-word, direct quotes from God constitute prophecy (though Scripture itself often more flexibly paraphrases earlier prophets). But that would actually change very little in a practical sense. In my (Daniel's) experience, most prophetic activity in the charismatic community occurs when people express what they sense from God. Whether anyone technically calls it a prophecy or something different is immaterial on a practical level. The bottom line is that God communicates to his people what they need to hear for exhortation, encouragement, or consolation (1 Cor. 14:3).

## God Still Speaks

Intimacy with God shapes the Christian life, from providing assurance of the Spirit in our hearts to calling us to various ministries to growing us in God's love (e.g., Rom. 5:5–10; 8:16; Gal. 4:6; 1 John 1:3, 7; 3:19; 4:7–8).

### *Who Called You?*

Mark Rutland, former president of Southeastern University and subsequently Oral Roberts University, shares an entertaining experience he had. He was flying home from an intense ministry trip and found himself in a discussion with a cessationist minister on an airplane. I (Daniel) recount his experience in another book:

> [Rutland] was tired and feeling rather unspiritual at that particular moment, but the man sitting next to him wanted to make conversation. "What do you do for a living?" this gentleman asked, to which Dr. Rutland replied, "I'm a Bible college president and a minister." The gentleman, who was also a minister, automatically assumed they were part of the same denomination. He continued to probe inquisitively until he discovered that Dr. Rutland was, in fact, affiliated with a Pentecostal denomination.
>
> It was then that the gentleman realized they held very different doctrinal positions, and his demeanor immediately changed. His tone became argumentative, and he decided to take advantage of the opportunity to debate a real-live Pentecostal. "I have something I want to ask you," he said. Dr. Rutland was not in the mood for a debate. "Friend, can't we just relax and drink our Diet Coke?" he asked. But the man was insistent. "No," he said, "there is something

I need to know. Please just answer this question: Since the canon of Scripture is closed, do you believe God still speaks? Because we don't."

Dr. Rutland reluctantly responded, still not wanting to engage in a debate. "Okay," he said, "I'll answer your question if you'll answer mine: Are you or are you not called to preach?"

"Yes, of course, I'm called to preach," the man shot back.

"Then let me ask you," Dr. Rutland said. "Who called you?"

The gentleman had no reply. He turned his face to the window and never spoke to Dr. Rutland again for the rest of the trip.[36]

### *Jesus's Sheep Hear Him*

Jesus said that those who belong to him hear his voice. When Jesus first talks about his sheep knowing his voice (John 10:3), the case most directly in view is the formerly blind man who has now come to follow him (9:35–38). (In 9:40–10:12, the leaders who threw the man out of the religious community function as the thieves, robbers, and wolves, at whose hands Jesus lays down his life for the sheep.) Strictly speaking, then, we begin heeding God's voice when we respond to his invitation to salvation. And that experience initiates us into a whole life of hearing and knowing the voice of our Good Shepherd.

Jesus also says, "My sheep hear My voice, and I know them, and they follow Me" (John 10:27 NASB). This voice of the Good Shepherd is, in fact, the voice of God speaking to individual believers under the new covenant. This is a relationship in which God wants us to grow. It's not a relationship from which he wants us to shrink because we've been taught to fear intimacy with him.

Cautions are appropriate, but fear can inhibit trust. Whereas we must evaluate individual prophecies (1 Cor. 14:29), we should not be "cautious but merely open" about their possibility. As Michael Brown has ventured, how many evangelicals would want to be described as "cautious but open" about evangelism, or Bible reading, or prayer, despite our potential fallibility in all these areas. Paul does not urge us to hold prophecy in general at a cautious arm's length; rather, he encourages us to pursue it diligently (1 Cor. 14:1, 31, 39).

Jesus declares, "My own know me *just as* the Father knows me and I know the Father" (John 10:14–15). Naturally the knowledge is not perfect from our end, but it is perfect from his. In the incarnation, Jesus has made God known. In the cross, Jesus has made God available. And in the resurrection, and by the Spirit, Jesus has made God dynamically present in our lives. God's presence is not something we have to work up. We don't have to wait for a special feeling to acknowledge he is there. John 14–16 emphasizes that because Jesus has gone to the Father and provided the Spirit, the Spirit (and the Father and Jesus, 14:23) live within us. And just as Jesus called his first

36. Kolenda, *Live*, 99–100.

disciples friends because he made known to them whatever he heard from the Father (15:15), so now the Spirit reveals Jesus to us, making known to us whatever he hears (16:13–14). Of course, the heart of our hearing is not simply daily guidance, as if we are the focus of our relationship with him. The heart of our relationship with him is the revelation of his heart for us (16:14–15). It's about knowing *him*.[37]

### *Traditional Evangelical Devotion*

None of this discussion of hearing God or intimacy with him involves a specifically novel or Pentecostal teaching. Consider, for example, the following lines of a familiar hymn from 1875, the lyrics composed by Fanny Crosby (1820–1915):

> I am Thine, O Lord,
> I have heard Thy voice,
> And it told Thy love to me;
> But I long to rise in the arms of faith,
> And be closer drawn to Thee.

In another stanza it continues: "When I kneel in prayer, and with Thee, my God, I commune as friend with friend." The song, sometimes called "Draw Me Nearer," appears, for example, in the original *Trinity Hymnal* (number 713) of the Orthodox Presbyterian Church as well as in hymnals of the United Methodist Church (number 419) and others. It comes from an era when many songs celebrated personal intimacy with the Lord, an approach also celebrated at times in medieval and Pietist devotion. Compare, for example, Crosby's lyrics "Blessed assurance, Jesus is mine" (1873).

Consider also the refrain from C. Austin Miles's 1912 hymn, "In the Garden."

> And He walks with me, and He talks with me,
> And He tells me I am His own,
> And the joy we share as we tarry there,
> None other has ever known.

Whatever one thinks of the song "In the Garden,"[38] one can hardly dismiss its intimate perspective as limited to charismatics. It appeared, for example, in *The Broadman Hymnal* (1940), the 1975 *Baptist Hymnal*, and the 1991 *Baptist Hymnal* (where it is number 187).

May we celebrate, rather than shy away from, the precious gift of intimacy with God that Jesus has provided for us by the Holy Spirit.

37. See further Keener, *Gift & Giver*, chaps. 1–2; Keener, "Function of Pneumatology."
38. See historical discussion in Fenner, "Garden."

## Visions and Dreams

The prophetic era of Joel and Acts 2 includes not only prophesying in the narrower sense but also revelatory visions and dreams. (Again, we use "revelatory" not in the sense of new doctrine but in the sense of God showing us things related to our lives.) We treat this in somewhat more detail than some other expressions of prophecy simply because I (Craig) have accounts of them already on hand from research I undertook for an earlier study.[39]

Vision and dream reports feature often in Christian history.[40] For example:

- Constantine apparently claimed a vision or dream.[41]
- Cyprian recounts boys having not only dreams but visions.[42]
- Saint Patrick was guided by dreams and visions,[43] and he describes his experience as a missionary in light of various biblical passages, including Acts 2:17–18.[44]
- Augustine's reports of his mother's experiences[45] (his own experience with *tolle lege* is itself notable as a supernatural sign).[46]
- Many monks claimed visions or dreams.[47]
- Many medieval mystics did as well.[48]

39. I take the following material from appendix E in Keener, *Miracles*.

40. E.g., in 1097 in Hamilton, "Signs," 98; see Wiebe, *Visions*, 15–24. Vision accounts appear even among women who knew that men were skeptical of women's reports (see Van Dijk, "Miracles," 248). Sixteenth-century physician Girolamo Cardano found portents in dreams (Duffin, *Miracles*, 22–23). In some cases, the vision experience is explicitly subjective or appears ambiguous yet real to the person experiencing it: Charles Finney (Huyssen and Huyssen, *Saw*, 91, an extended experience; Prather, *Miracles*, 126–28); F. B. Meyer (Huyssen and Huyssen, *Saw*, 111–12, less subjective); in some cases the language might be partly figurative, but may point to visionary experiences: John Bunyan (109, at conversion); Catherine Marshall (125–26); Reinhard Bonnke (140). Cf. also Alcoholics Anonymous founder Bill Wilson's transforming experience of heaven (Kent and Waite, *Beyond*, chap. 28, citing Robert Thomsen's biography of Wilson).

41. For discussion, see, e.g., Price, "*Signo*."

42. Cyprian, *Ep.* 9.4.

43. Patrick, *Confession* 21, 23, 24, 29; cf. 43.

44. Patrick, *Confession* 40.

45. Herum, "Theology," 35–36, cites Monica's dream of Augustine in *Conf.* 3.11.19; her vision of safety despite the storm in 6.1.1. Augustine's own ecstasies (Herum cites *Conf.* 7.10.16; 7.17.23; 9.10.24–25) resemble Neoplatonist contemplation of the divine.

46. See Augustine, *Conf.* 8.12. Some pagans used children's words at play to divine the will of deities (e.g., Dio Chrysostom, *Or.* 32.13; Plutarch, *Is. Os.* 14, *Mor.* 356E; Xenophon of Ephesus, *Eph. Tale* 5.4; cf. Matt. 21:16), though this was apparently a sort of divination. Children were also often thought more susceptible to inspiration (Stamps, "Children," 197).

47. Oliver, *Movements*, 124.

48. Worthen, *Spellbound*, 5. Beyond the medieval period, also note Teresa of Avila (e.g., Oliver, *Reformations*, 45; Eire, *Flew*, 73).

- Thomas Aquinas (ca. 1225–1274) apparently experienced an ecstatic vision of God toward the end of his life.[49]
- Waldensians accepted visions and prophecies.[50]
- Jan Hus (1369–1415) claimed visions and dreams.[51]
- Early Anabaptist leader Hans Hut depended much on visions and dreams.[52]
- There were various precise prophetic dreams among Dutch Reformed Christians from the 1600s and 1700s.[53]
- Early radical Puritans also claimed direct revelations, including in dreams and visions.[54]
- They were common in early evangelicalism.[55]
- Such experiences were documented in early Methodism, especially among circuit riders.[56]
- Francis Asbury reported a prophetic dream.[57]
- There were revelatory dreams among some mid-eighteenth century Baptists.[58]
- Salvation Army founder William Booth also reports such a revelation.[59]
- They are also reported during the Welsh Revival of 1904.[60]
- Visions also figured in the Shandong Revival (1927–37).[61]

49. Some attribute his final three months of silence instead to a nervous breakdown, but quite early sources suggest instead (or at the same time) a spiritual vision of God that he claimed made all his prior academic work seem trivial in comparison; see Burgess, *Peoples*, 120–21, citing Bernard Gui (1261–1331), Aquinas's biographer.

50. Toon, "Waldenses," 1026.

51. Boys, *Evidence*, 77–78; Oliver, *Reformations*, 5–6, following Doles, *Miracles*, 132–33.

52. Murray, "Anabaptism."

53. Boys, *Evidence*, 304–15.

54. Kidd, "Healing," 160.

55. Noll, *Rise*, 267.

56. See Webster, "Salvation"; Xhemajli, *Supernatural*, 166–69; Ruth, *Methodist Life*, 177; Billman, *Thread*, 90–95; John Wesley's reports of visionary experiences of some people he knew (Huyssen and Huyssen, *Saw*, 106–7); early Methodist women preachers such as Zilpha Elaw and Jarena Lee (Riggs, *Witness*, 6; Pope-Levison, *Pulpit*, 27; Andrews, *Sisters*, 35; Wigger, *Heaven*, 120–23; Billman, *Thread*, 75; Bowens, *Readings*, 78, 84–85, 167; cf. 294); among children in Billman, *Thread*, 97–98 (citing Wesley, *Journal*, February 21, 1742; August 29, 1746; July 14, 1759; August 6, 1759; June 10, 1788). Noll, *Shape*, 46, cites early Methodists' use of "dreams, portents and special revelations"; these were central to and pervasive in early Methodism (Wigger, *Heaven*, 110, 123; Ruth, *Methodist Life*, 161; Taves, *Fits*, 85, 92–93, 109; as cited in Billman, *Thread*, 65, 76, 91–92).

57. Wigger, *Saint*, 188.

58. Kidd, *Awakening*, 246.

59. Huyssen and Huyssen, *Saw*, 80–82.

60. Pytches, *Come*, 133; esp. Harvey, "Agony"; for Evan Roberts, e.g., White, "Revival," 1.

61. Crawford, *Revival*, chaps. 4–6.

### *Visions and Dreams Globally Today*

Historian Mark Noll points out that African Christians "are not surprised when Jesus speaks to them in dreams and visions," a pattern consistent with narratives in Acts.[62] Researcher Kurt Koch reports cases where God provided visionary revelation to illiterate new believers who lacked full access to Scripture.[63] Koch himself preached for years against visions, dreams, and the like until he encountered genuine revelatory ones in places of revival.[64] Asian examples appear in a range of countries that include Myanmar,[65] China,[66] India,[67] Indonesia,[68] Singapore,[69] and the Philippines.[70] Globally, many ministers experience calls to ministry through dreams.[71] Elisée Ouoba, professor at an evangelical university in the United States, was called to ministry through a repeated, audible voice in his younger days in Burkina Faso.[72]

Some dreams provide warnings. The day a converted Korean prisoner had dreamed that her husband said goodbye, she learned that he had just

62. Noll, *Shape*, 23–24. See now esp. Droll, *Dreams*. These experiences flourish despite many early missionaries' condemnation of attending to dreams (Lagerwerf, *Witchcraft*, 17–18).

63. Koch, *Zulus*, 138–39, 200–201.

64. Koch, *Zulus*, 232.

65. See Khai, "Pentecostalism," 269, 270.

66. Yamamori and Chan, *Witnesses*, 9, 39, 59; Aikman, *Jesus in Beijing*, 101. For popular-level claims about dreams in China, see Yun, *Heavenly Man*, 32, 35, 135, 137, 178, 180, 181, 189, 197, 305–6, 315, 341; Danyun, *Lilies*, 84; Jones, *Wonders*, 75, 103 (recognizing the foreigner, a missionary, seen in a dream). About visions, see Yun, *Heavenly Man*, 58, 60, 68–69, 73, 103, 108–9, 122–23, 124, 254; Baker, *Visions*; Danyun, *Lilies*, 43, 49–50, 195, 210, 351–52. For visions in the Manchurian revival of 1908, see Shaw, *Awakening*, 185.

67. E.g., nineteenth-century and early twentieth-century examples in McGee, *Miracles*, 34, 36, 82.

68. In Timor, see, e.g., Wiyono, "Timor Revival," 284 (following, e.g., Brougham, "Work," 167).

69. Green, *Asian Tigers*, 56, 96.

70. Ma, "Manifestations"; Ma, "Vanderbout," 135.

71. In Africa, e.g., Burgess, *Revolution*, 160; Walls, *Movement*, 88; Kalu, *African Pentecostalism*, 151; Emmanuel Itapson, interview, April 8, 2011; in Latin America, e.g., Alamino, *Footsteps*, 23; Marostica, "Learning," 210; in India, e.g., Huyssen and Huyssen, *Saw*, 93–94; in Korea, e.g., Kim, "Healing," 275; in Iran, e.g., Voice of Martyrs, *Hearts of Fire* 2, 254; in the West, e.g., the visions reported in Poloma, *Assemblies*, 73–74; Ten Boom, *Hiding Place*, 234–36; Shaw, *Awakening*, 138; Huyssen and Huyssen, *Saw*, 54–55, 80–82 (William Booth), 176; Tallman, *Shakarian*, 147; McGee, *Miracles*, 70; Zagrans, *Miracles*, 4; the dream in Alexander, *Fire*, 114. Note also a visionary call behind the Indonesian Timor revival in Wiyono, "Timor Revival," 278; the call of Indonesian evangelist Petrus Octavianus by a vision (Crawford, *Miracles*, 73); another in Indonesia in Tari, *Wind*, 159.

72. Elisée Ouoba, interview, March 16, 2009. He is from the Evangelical Church of SIM in Burkina Faso (Eglise Evangélique SIM au Burkina Faso), which was heavily influenced by earlier cessationist Western teachers. For other callings through an audible voice in Africa, see, e.g., Burgess, *Revolution*, 79; Hanciles, *Beyond Christendom*, 329; in Asia, e.g., Tari, *Wind*, 142–43; in the United States, e.g., John Stewart, who ministered among the Wyandot people in 1816 (McGee, *Miracles*, 10); Amanda Berry Smith (Pope-Levison, *Pulpit*, 89); Anna Gulick, on her experience (interview, March 10, 2011).

died.[73] The day another recent convert in the cell dreamed about meeting Jesus, she was taken out and executed.[74] Another dream warned the cell's leading Christian the life-threatening test of faith that awaited her that day.[75]

Visions and dreams seem to proliferate particularly in times of spiritual intensity. For example, they figured heavily in the Nias Revival in Indonesia in 1916.[76] They also appear in orphanages and among other groups of children in Asia.[77] They flourished in China some time ago, particularly conspicuously during an intense period of persecution that lasted about three years.[78]

Such claims also do appear in the West and Western sources[79]—for example, the revivals among thoroughly Reformed Christians in the Hebrides in 1939.[80]

### *Healing Through Visions and Dreams*

Reports also include healings in conjunction with visions[81] and dreams.[82] Gregory of Nazianzen's mother was healed through a dream.[83] For example,

73. Kim, *If I Perish*, 189.
74. Kim, *If I Perish*, 216.
75. Kim, *If I Perish*, 218.
76. Dermawan, "Study," 260.
77. See Baker, *Visions*; cf. also comment in McGee, *Miracles*, 147; among children in the Philippines, Ma, "Vanderbout," 135; among young women at Ramabai's mission for "orphan brides," see, e.g., Anderson, "Signs," 201; in Myanmar, see Khai, "Pentecostalism," 270; in Indonesia, see Koch, *Zulus*, 207 (prophecies); Tari, *Wind*, 51–54 (various experiences, including visions); in Africa, see Koch, *Zulus*, 208–16 (a girl's accurate visions), 217–18 (prophecy through a child).
78. Aikman, *Jesus in Beijing*, 83.
79. See, e.g., Ten Boom, *Tramp*, 189 (Ten Boom's vision of angels); visions in Wiebe, *Visions*, 42–86; Huyssen and Huyssen, *Saw*, 24, 79, 118–19, 122, 127, 132–33, 150, 183, 186, 195–201; dreams in Huyssen and Huyssen, *Saw*, 102–3, 119–20, 137; cf. Llewellyn, "Events," 251–52, 258–59; White, *Spirit*, 98; Alexander, *Signs*, 115–30 (esp. 115–17, 124–25); Deere, *Voice*; Williams, *Signs*, 141–42; Storms, *Convergence*, 60–61, 64, 78–80; Stibbe, *Prophetic Evangelism*, 95; Baker and Baker, *Enough*, 49–50, 55, 181; Baker and Baker, *Miracles*, 31, 199; Moreland and Issler, *Faith*, 198–99; Anderson, *Miracles*, 94–95; Pullinger, *Dragon*, 28–29, 106, 123, 135, 200, 232. Even I (Craig) periodically have dreams of Jesus.
80. Peckham, *Sounds*, 107, 234.
81. E.g., Duffin, *Miracles*, 172–74; Wiebe, *Visions*, 84; Zhaoming, "Chinese Denominations," 450–51; Yamamori and Chan, *Witnesses*, 59–60; Young, "Miracles in History," 117; McGee, *Miracles*, 219; Bush and Pegues, *Move*, 51, 61; Polkinghorne, *Science and Providence*, 55; Chesnut, *Born Again in Brazil*, 87–88; Tari, *Breeze*, 58–59 (raising); Anderson, *Pelendo*, 111–12; Eusbarina Acosta Estévez, interview, August 7, 2010; Wilson, "Miracle Events," 271; Karnofsky, "Vision," 15–16 (a medieval example); Anderson, *Miracles*, 179–81; Huyssen and Huyssen, *Saw*, 27–28, 144–48, 157–62; Moolenburgh, *Meetings*, 72–84 (though none here are naturally inexplicable).
82. For dreams and healings (or prescriptions or instructions where to seek healing), see, e.g., Bush and Pegues, *Move*, 51, 61; Tomkins, *Wesley*, 60 (Charles Wesley's healing); Burgess, *Revolution*, 224; Alexander, *Fire*, 114; Woodard, *Faith*, 94; Koch, *Zulus*, 76, 121 (marital reconciliation). Cf. Jacques Moussounga, personal correspondence, September 8, 2005; Joshua Obeng, interview, January 28, 2009; Antoinette Malombe, interview, July 13, 2008; Jeanne Mabiala, interview, July 29, 2008; Lakshmi Devi, personal correspondence, October 29, 2010; Anonymous, "History in Indonesia," 137.
83. Burgess, *Holy Spirit*, 159, citing Gregory, *On the Death of His Father* 28–29.

Bari Malto was a village shaman, but after he contracted leprosy, his village cast him out. A couple women doing evangelism came and prayed for him, and that night two angels touched his hands in a dream. When Bari awoke the next day, he was completely healed. He ran into the village and showed them what had happened. As a result, the entire village became followers of Jesus.[84]

When Anna Gulick was an evangelical Lutheran missionary in Japan in the mid-1950s, she was receiving penicillin in various forms for her allergies. One night after spraying it in her nose, however, her "heart went into fibrillation due to anaphylactic shock from penicillin." She knew she had only five minutes to live in this state, and it was too late for her friends to get help, but suddenly she could see only Jesus at the foot of her bed. Without speaking, she communicated from her heart that "if He still had work for me to do, I was willing to stay." Then the room returned to normal, and her heart was beating fine. The next day the doctor warned her not to take penicillin again in any form. From that time forward she lost her fear of death, knowing that Jesus would be with her again.[85] My (Craig's) neighbor, Anna passed away only at the age of ninety-six several years ago.

Similarly, Australian Markan scholar Rikk E. Watts recounts an incident that followed an extended time of prayer when he was about eighteen years old. A man visiting their church noted that he was not a Christian but that he had seen the church's name in a dream, in which he also heard that he would be healed there. Although the man had not identified his specific health problem and Watts had not observed his entrance, he felt led to pray for the man's lower legs. Suddenly the man began shouting that he was healed and afterward inquired how Watts knew that the problem was with his feet.[86]

### Personal Experiences

Although I (Craig) have never yet had a vision, I do have dreams. I periodically have the joy of being with Jesus in my dreams, which also sometimes contain prophecies and often ecstatic worship as I experience God's presence. Some serve other purposes. For example, they often provide encouragements for what God has called me to do. Thus, sometimes when I arrive at some venue nervous about speaking but recognize that I saw the venue in a dream the night before, it gives me fresh courage that the Lord is with me.

84. See Keener, *Miracles Today*, 126–27; Craig's source is Ebi Perinbaraj, one of his MDiv students who worked closely with Malto and thereafter did his PhD at TEDS.

85. Anna Gulick, personal correspondence, August 10, 2009; further details, August 13, 2009; interview, March 10, 2011. Dr. Nicole Matthews notes that the arrythmia can often be reversed medically through electric shock or high-dose steroids, but it would not normally reverse itself spontaneously, as here (personal correspondence, August 16–17, 2009).

86. Rikk E. Watts, interview, November 17, 2010.

Sometimes dreams come as warnings. On November 10, 2008, for instance, I dreamed of a vehicle from the oncoming lane forcing my wife Médine off the road; I warned her and then prayed. An hour or so afterward, as she was driving to teach her French class at Eastern University, a car from the oncoming lane pulled out from behind a truck and nearly hit her.

On January 23, 2011, I dreamed that I visited my first pastor and found him very happy and with his wife, who had previously died. I cannot recall dreaming of them in the roughly thirty-five years since I had met them; I had not been in contact for a long time. That evening his granddaughter wrote to inform me that he had passed away two days before. When Pastor Daniel Ndoundou passed away in Congo, my wife, then a student in France, was among many who dreamed of his passing before receiving word about it.[87]

### *Conversion Through Dreams*

Sometimes, as in Acts 10:5–6; 11:13–14, a vision or dream can lead to people receiving the gospel. Some cessationists, however, claim that God no longer speaks through visions or dreams. God speaks through studying the Bible, they contend, but he does not reveal things "through visions and dreams."[88] This raises the question about what to do regarding people being converted through such experiences today.

Many report that in some underevangelized regions, large numbers or even most of those converted to Christianity today testify that they were converted at least partly through dreams or visions;[89] individual examples could be multiplied around the world[90] (with cases from many years, for example,

87. On Pastor Ndoundou, see Keener, "Ndoundou."

88. Pennington, *Cessationism*, 19.

89. E.g., Trousdale, *Movements*; Moreland, *Triangle*, 169; Moreland and Issler, *Faith*, 151–53; Doyle, *Dreams*, 127, 130, 202; Kraft, *Worldview*, 493; cf. Becken, "Healing Communities," 233; Guthrie, "Breakthrough," 26; Morgan, "Impasse," 61; Kure, "Light," 184 (revelations); Hausfeld, "Understanding," 75. In Indonesia, see, e.g., Anonymous, "History in Indonesia," 147; Crawford, *Miracles*, 92, 94; Knapstad, "Power," 82–83, 87–88.

90. E.g., Voice of Martyrs, *Hearts of Fire 2*, 247, 249–50, 255; Sheikh, *Call Him Father*, 30–32, 39–41, 52, 178, 185 (cf. also warning dreams in 149, 152); Doyle, *Dreams*, 3–4, 8, 44–45, 49–51, 58, 65–66, 166, 239; Doyle, *Killing Christians*, 37, 63, 69–70, 104–5, 109, 111, 131, 135–36, 160; Bush and Pegues, *Move*, 54, 62; Kwan, "Argument," 499 (conversion through a vision in nineteenth-century China); Goforth, *Goforth*, 216 (a conversion through a dream, after a request for one, in early twentieth-century China); Anderson, *Pelendo*, 33–36 (a voice, in central Africa, with an attendant sign); Burgess, *Revolution*, 250; Chesnut, "Exorcising," 181–82 (Brazil); Kim, "Healing," 273 (Korea); Olson, *Bruchko*, 151 (a vision, leading to most of a Yuko village's conversion in South America); Bush and Pegues, *Move*, 53, 62; Yun, *Heavenly Man*, 50; Stearns and Stearns, *Vision*, 17, 151, 185 (many among unevangelized peoples); Filson, "Study," 150 (a postmortem vision; after the woman returned to life she was converted and [151] engaged in evangelism), 154 (a dream preparing one for a particular witness); Tari, *Wind*, 143–45; Tari, *Breeze*, 19; Koch, *Zulus*, 34, 143, 150, 202, 224 (through dreams; converted

in India).[91] In Fiji, for example, Rita Jeet prayed to Hindu deities and was a popular radio personality.[92] At a point of deep brokenness in her life, she prayed for Jesus to show himself to her if he was real, whereupon she saw a bright man coming from the sky. She became a follower of Jesus, and various miracles started after that.[93] After Jesus appeared to the sixteen-year-old Jewish adolescent Hugh Montefiore, Montefiore became a follower of Jesus and eventually both a Cambridge New Testament instructor and Anglican bishop.[94]

The Gospel Coalition website mentions a *Mission Frontiers* study in which a quarter of Muslim converts interviewed came to faith in Christ at least partly through a dream.[95] On some occasions, multiple persons have the same dream about Jesus the same night.[96] Some are converted through an extensive series of dreams;[97] one tough customer, for example, started with thirty in a row before converting.[98] Another, in Syria, had periodic dreams for about a year and then one every night for forty-five nights before he visited a Christian friend and joined his faith.[99] No place is immune to God's presence (Ps. 139:7–12); some even witnessed Jesus when in Mecca during the hajj.[100]

On one occasion, it is reported that many persons who venerated the sun were converted through an Indonesian preaching team when a vision of Jesus appeared just above the sun, seen by everyone present.[101] On another, a Hausa man recounted that an angel appeared to him three times and read to him from a book, then sent him on a long journey to Christians for an explanation, where he heard the same passage as they discipled him.[102] In gospel-deprived Somalia, Azzam Azziz Mubarak became a follower of Jesus

---

through visions in 141–42, 159, 225; cf. dreams for repentance in 227–31); Pope-Levison, *Pulpit*, 51 (Sojourner Truth); Marszalek, *Miracles*, 57–58, 133; dreams in the Jesus Film newsletter, January 15, 2010; visions associated with (before, during, or immediately after) conversions in Huyssen and Huyssen, *Saw*, 35–36, 42, 48–49, 54–55, 89, 104–5, 170–72, 175; Levitt, *Beef*, 1–3, 48. Cf. an example in early Methodism (Wigger, *Saint*, 93); Ekechi, "Medical Factor," 294, notes the influence of a vision on corporate conversion in 1873 Onitsha.

91. E.g., McBane, "Bhils," 139 (two people both having visions the same night urging them to accept Christ, leading to twenty-two baptisms in November 1901); Lynch-Watson, *Robe*, 18 (also in Davey, *Robe*, 23–24); Boehr, *Medicine*, 55–56; Huyssen and Huyssen, *Saw*, 56–58; see esp. now Iyadurai, *Experience*, 13–56.

92. Phone interview, April 15, 2019; personal correspondence, April 21, 25, 2019; April 30, 2020.

93. Keener, *Miracles Today*, 34.

94. Wiebe, *Visions*, 82.

95. Carlson, "Dream"; see also Doyle, *Dreams*, 127, allowing for as high as one-third.

96. E.g., Doyle, *Killing Christians*, 63, 83. Cf. Doyle, *Dreams*, 66–67.

97. E.g., Doyle, *Dreams*, 88, 90, 105, 120–21, 201, 216–17, 224, 233.

98. Doyle, *Dreams*, 141.

99. Doyle, *Dreams*, 154.

100. Doyle, *Dreams*, 44–45, 65.

101. Koch, *Revival*, 143.

102. Talbot, "Vision," 276–77.

after eight visions;[103] he now risks his life regularly to share the gospel.[104] In Egypt, ten imams had dreams about Jesus, became rudimentary followers of Jesus, and commandeered an unsuspecting Christian to disciple them.[105] In Syria, Muhammad, from the secret police, was assigned to follow a Muslim-background believer named Adel, but Muhammad kept having dreams about Jesus. Adel explained to Muhammad what these dreams meant, and his pursuer became his brother in Christ.[106]

Dina, an officer in Iran's Female Secret Police, often called in to a Christian call-in show to mock Christians. Yet her mother was dying of cancer and the two of them planned suicide. Hormoz Shariat, the call-in host, challenged her to give Christ a chance for one week.[107] Several days into that week, Dina's mother dreamed of Jesus and found herself healed.[108] They became Jesus followers.

Conversion through dreams naturally leads also to valuing the Bible.[109] Those so converted also share their faith.[110] And the most fundamental test of their conversion is that they are willing to die for Jesus.[111]

What percentage of these conversions and conversion accounts do full cessationists need to discount, often in agreement with the converts' persecutors? On a hard cessationist view, is Satan converting these people? Why would Satan work against Satan (Mark 3:23–26)? It seems much simpler to accept an explicit biblical explanation: Acts 2:17 specifies dreams and visions from God's Spirit as among the characteristics of last-days experience.

103. Doyle, *Killing Christians*, 4–5.
104. Doyle, *Killing Christians*, 1–17.
105. Doyle, *Dreams*, 21–22.
106. Doyle, *Dreams*, 147.
107. Doyle, *Dreams*, 75–77.
108. Doyle, *Dreams*, 80–82.
109. Doyle, *Dreams*, 92, 120–21, 172–73; Doyle, *Killing Christians*, 94, 105, 136–37, 160–61. Even with dreams, Scripture is central in conversion; see fuller discussion in Doyle, *Dreams*, 133–35.
110. E.g., Doyle, *Dreams*, 157, 175; Doyle, *Killing Christians*, 94.
111. Doyle, *Dreams*, 11.

# 16

# Tongues in the New Testament and History

We address tongues in this book's wider section on prophecy for two reasons. First, both involve a sort of "inspired" (by which we mean, Spirit-led) speaking. Second, we do so because many cessationists reject tongues precisely because they believe that it is a form of prophecy. The New Testament form of tongues, however, is normally a form of prophetic (i.e., Spirit-led) *prayer*.[1]

## Not Languages Native to the Speaker

Contrary to suggestions that Paul applies "speaking in a tongue" to speaking in a language the speaker knows and interpretation refers to natural translation or paraphrase, most recognize that the languages are unknown to the speakers. This is already clear from the expression "*other* tongues" (Acts 2:4) and the impossibility that the disciples knew all the dialects presupposed in Acts 2:5–11.

Likewise, Paul treats the languages as unknown to the speaker. If no interpreter is present, the person praying in tongues should pray that they may interpret (1 Cor. 14:13). That they need to *pray* to have the interpretation makes clear that the tongue is not a language that the speaker understands

1. For more extensive discussion of tongues in the New Testament, esp. Acts, see Keener, *Acts*, 1:805–31; briefly, cf. Keener and Vaughan, "Tongues." On a more accessible and practical level, see Storms, *Language*. Mills, *Glossolalia: Bibliography*, includes more than 1,150 entries already in 1985.

and can explain on command; the interpretation requires supernatural help, just as the tongue does. If the speaker in a tongue knew the language, how could we envision a situation in which the speaker should keep quiet in the assembly because no "interpreter" is present (14:28)?

Interpretation here is not, as some later premodern commentators supposed, merely explaining a liturgical language.[2] Many Judean synagogues included Scripture readings in Hebrew followed by paraphrase in the Aramaic vernacular,[3] but Paul's descriptions of Spirit-moved tongues and interpretation differ significantly from that known custom:

> 1 Corinthians 14:2 (NIV): "For anyone who speaks in a tongue does not speak to people but to God. Indeed, no one understands them; they utter mysteries by the Spirit."
>
> 1 Corinthians 14:14 (NJB): "For if I pray in a tongue, my spirit may be praying but my mind derives no fruit from it."

The worshiper requires a special spiritual charism at the time whether to pray in a tongue or to offer the interpretation, a situation not necessary for a liturgical language.

## Tongues as Prophecy—or Prayer?

Citing 1 Corinthians 14:5, cessationists often see tongues as a form of prophecy and therefore deny that tongues continue today because they deny that prophecy continues today.[4] For them, prophecy competes with the canon and so must have passed away (an argument we have already demonstrated as fallacious in chap. 13). Thomas Schreiner concedes that if tongues are not for the purpose of prophetic revelation, then tongues are not a problem. But he wonders "what function interpreted tongues actually play in the congregation if the word shared doesn't reveal God's truth."[5] How about them serving the function of prayer—which is exactly what Paul says in 1 Corinthians 14? Worship and prayer belong to Christian gatherings no less than teaching does (14:26; cf. Eph. 5:18–19; Col. 3:16).

2. An interpretation that fit more the setting of those commentators. Cf. Blosser and Sullivan, *Speaking in Tongues*, 129 (cf. 124): "Greek was the language of liturgical readings and instruction in indigenous Syrian church assemblies, while another priest stood nearby who would immediately translate the Greek into Syriac" (citing Egeria). Cf. Epiphanius in Vellacott, *View*, 8–11; but even Diaspora synagogues normally used Scripture in Greek, and why would anyone in churches be using older Greek dialects? See esp. Gresham, "Tongues."

3. Neh. 8:8; in a later period, *Targum Onqelos* and still later targumim.

4. Gaffin, "View," 42 (cf. Grudem, "Conclusion," 344); Waldron, *Continued*, 15–16, 88–89; Schreiner, *Spiritual Gifts*, 163 (cf. 128); cf. MacArthur, *Chaos*, 231.

5. Schreiner, *Spiritual Gifts*, 163–64.

### *Tongues as Prophecy?*

Against common claims, 1 Corinthians 14:5 does not identify tongues with prophecy in terms of specific function (i.e., prophecy but in another language); it merely says that interpreted tongues *edify* the church, just like prophecy edifies the church:

> 1 Corinthians 14:5 (NASB): "Now I wish that you all spoke in tongues, but rather that you would prophesy; and greater is the one who prophesies than the one who speaks in tongues, unless he interprets, so that the church may receive edification."

But then, during corporate gatherings *all* spiritual gifts are meant to edify the church (14:26).

This is not to deny that speaking in tongues is a form of prophetic speech in the broader sense. Peter regards it as a legitimate fulfillment of Joel's promise about prophesying, as are visions and dreams (Acts 2:4, 17–18). But the particular form this Spirit-moved speech *usually* takes in the New Testament is prayer and praise. Just as the psalms are inspired worship (cf. 1 Chron. 25:1–3; 2 Chron. 29:30) in which God occasionally has direct speaking parts (e.g., Pss. 2:7–9; 12:5; 32:8; 46:10; 75:2–5; 81:6–16; 89:19–37; 91:14–16; 110:1–4; 132:14–18), so apparently are tongues.

If we had only Acts 2:11, we could potentially understand the description of tongues at Pentecost—"declaring God's magnificent acts"—as either proclamation or praise (cf. Ps. 71:19), yet the context clearly indicates that it is Peter's message, rather than the tongues, that functions as evangelistic proclamation (Acts 2:37–41). Still more clearly, the most unambiguous occasions of tongues in the New Testament all involve praise rather than proclamation.[6] In Acts 10:46, the members of Cornelius's household speak in tongues and extol God. The Greek term for extolling God here is cognate to the "magnificent acts" declared in 2:11; it is frequent in biblical psalms and with the Lord as its object appears in praise in Luke 1:46. The Greek construction in Acts 10:46[7] allows for overlap between the two activities (speaking in tongues and extolling God), and the gentiles are certainly not addressing their speech in tongues to Peter and his colleagues. Nor are the tongues in 19:6 preaching to Paul or recognized by hearers.

6. So also Storms, *Language*, 73–75. Most scholars reject the tongues at Pentecost as evangelistic in character; see, e.g., discussion in Turner, *Gifts*, 226, 313. For one balanced approach to tongues as prophetically inspired prayer as a foretaste of the global church (Rev. 5:9; 7:9), see Johnston, "Speaking in Tongues."

7. The Greek term *kai* can function not only as "and" but also epexegetically as "even." The noticeably different *te . . . kai* construction in Acts 19:6 is more likely to differentiate tongues and prophecy as distinct activities.

### *Tongues as Prayer in 1 Corinthians*

The primary biblical function of tongues is prayer. Particularly clear are the explicit instances in 1 Corinthians (NASB):

> 1 Corinthians 14:2: "For the one who speaks in a tongue does not speak to people, but to God."
>
> 1 Corinthians 14:14–16: "For if I pray in a tongue, my spirit prays, but my mind is unfruitful. What is *the outcome* then? I will pray with the spirit, but I will pray with the mind also; I will sing with the spirit, but I will sing with the mind also. For otherwise, if you bless *God* in the spirit *only,* how will the one who occupies the place of the outsider *know to* say the "Amen" at your giving of thanks, since he does not understand what you are saying?"

Where Paul is most specific, then, speaking in tongues involves

- speaking to God (14:2),
- praying (14:14–15),
- singing (14:15),
- blessing God (14:16), and
- giving thanks (14:16–17).[8]

Moreover, Paul speaks in tongues more than do all the Corinthians (14:18)—yet apparently not in church (14:19). If Paul rarely if ever uses tongues in church, where is he using it? Unless he is prophesying in tongues to people outside church or just into the air, this suggests that Paul's personal speech in tongues was mostly directed toward God rather than other people.[9]

Certainly we should not be surprised that the Spirit is active in worship as well as in prophecy. Worship by the Spirit characterizes the new covenant in contrast with other forms of worship (John 4:24; Phil. 3:3), and the Spirit also generates "spiritual songs" in Ephesians 5:19 and Colossians 3:16[10] (cf. also 1 Corinthians 14:26). This is one of the expressions of being filled with the Spirit (Eph. 5:18–19), certainly consonant with prophesying in worship in the Old Testament (1 Chron. 25:1–3). We surely should not expect *less* Spirit-filled worship under the Spirit-empowered new covenant (Ezek. 36:26–27; Joel 2:28–29; 2 Cor. 3:3, 6)! Because the Spirit inspires both tongues and interpretation (1 Cor. 12:7–11), and the former is prayer with one's spirit and the latter

8. For tongues as prayer rather than prophetic message, see also Fee, *Presence*, 218; Laurito, *Speaking in Tongues*, 41.

9. Cf. also Ruthven, *Cessation*, 67; esp. Wilson, *Spirit and Sacrament*, 112–13n69.

10. If, as is likely, *pneumatikos* refers to God's *pneuma*, that is, the Holy Spirit; see Fee, *Presence*, 28–32.

with one's mind (14:13–15), singing with one's spirit (in tongues) and with one's mind (the interpretation; 14:15) are both forms of worship by the Spirit. Both the tongue and the interpretation come from God's Spirit (12:8–11).

This is not to deny the possibility of tongues *ever* functioning more specifically as a message from God. Because Paul usually uses the Greek term *laleō*, "speak," with tongues rather than a phrase *specifying* prayer, it may well have wider functions, though these are less explicit. That a tongue may also be used to communicate *from* God is a possible meaning in 1 Corinthians 14:6: "Now, brothers and sisters, if I come to you and speak in tongues, what good will I be to you, unless I bring you some revelation or knowledge or prophecy or word of instruction?" It might also be implied in "speaking to oneself" in 14:28, if that means something like prophesying to oneself (as in 2 Sam. 23:2–3; Jer. 27:2; Hosea 1:2), though it might mean simply "quietly, so no one else can hear."[11]

Fairly widespread charismatic experience supports the belief that God can also speak to us through tongues, and we accept that likelihood. Nevertheless, prayer to God is much more explicit and, insofar as we can tell from 1 Corinthians 14, more central as its function.

## Personal Use of Tongues

Paul supports the personal use of tongues in multiple ways.

First, that Paul distinguishes between tongues utterances in an assembly and those in private devotion makes clear that he knows both uses. If tongues were intended only for congregational use, they would always need an interpreter. Then the way most charismatics use tongues today—as a devotional prayer language—would be unbiblical. But Paul shows us that this devotional use is not only legitimate but also the primary way he exercised the gift himself. Paul declares that he speaks in tongues more than any of the Corinthians (1 Cor. 14:18). In the gathered assembly of believers, he would rather speak "five intelligible words to instruct others than ten thousand words in a tongue" (14:19). Yet Paul speaks in tongues so frequently that he can boast that he prays this way more than the Corinthians (of all people!). Paul clearly does not speak in tongues very much as a public gift (without interpretation). It is therefore obvious that his prayers in tongues (more than all of them, 14:18) are largely private.

Second, Paul says that, if there is no interpreter, the person speaking in tongues should "speak to oneself and to God" (1 Cor. 14:28). If tongues are only for congregational use, why should the person speak to oneself and God?

11. For addressing oneself, see, e.g., Pss. 103:1; 104:1; 116:7; Luke 12:19; *Pythagorean Sentences* 22.

Third, he speaks in mysteries and *no* one understands him (1 Cor. 14:2) without a supernaturally gifted interpretation (14:13). Paul thus acknowledges that when his spirit prays in a tongue, his mind is unfruitful (14:14). Some cessationists take Paul's claim of the mind being unfruitful during tongues prayer (14:14) as indicating that it has no value, but this inference makes little sense of Paul's claim to pray in tongues more than all the Corinthians (14:18)![12] Rather, Paul points out here that his mind does not understand what he is saying so he will also pray with his mind. But far from demeaning prayer in tongues as worthless, he insists that he will also pray with his spirit, in a tongue. He thus indicates that this sort of prayer complements more cognitive prayer, adding a dimension missing in exclusively cognitive prayer.

See 1 Corinthians 14:14–15 (here NASB): "For if I pray in a tongue, my spirit prays, but my mind is unproductive. What is *the outcome* then? I will pray with the spirit, but I will pray with the mind also; I will sing with the spirit, but I will sing with the mind also." As Gordon Fee points out, "Contrary to the opinion of many, spiritual edification can take place in ways other than through the cortex of the brain. Paul believed in an immediate communing with God by means of the S/spirit that sometimes bypassed the mind; and in vv. 14–15 he argues that for his own edification he will have both. But *in church* he will have only what can also communicate to other believers through their minds (vv. 16–19)."[13]

Finally, if that were not enough, Paul explicitly says, "Anyone who speaks in a tongue edifies himself" (1 Cor. 14:4). Paul prayed in tongues personally and recommends such prayer as the most common use for tongues.

## Was Paul *Against* Tongues?

John MacArthur insists that "in 1 Corinthians 14:2 Paul was *criticizing* the Corinthians for using their 'gift of tongues' to speak to God and not to men."[14] It "is condemnation, not commendation. The context demands that."[15] Sadly, this assertion reflects simply abominable, dogmatically driven exegesis. Here is the verse:

> 1 Corinthians 14:2 (NIV): "For anyone who speaks in a tongue does not speak to people but to God. Indeed, no one understands them; they utter mysteries by the Spirit."

12. Laurito, *Speaking in Tongues*, 39.

13. Fee, *Presence*, 219. For neurological study of glossolalic release, see, e.g., Brahinsky, *Tongues*, 117–19.

14. MacArthur, *Chaos*, 228.

15. MacArthur, *Chaos*, 228n17.

Here are samples of the verse's context (AT), a context that MacArthur believes *condemns* tongues:

> 1 Corinthians 14:5: "I want all of you to speak in tongues, but even more want you to prophesy."
>
> 1 Corinthians 14:18: "I thank God: I speak in tongues more than all of you."

Does this not suggest the *opposite* of what MacArthur claims? That Paul condemns *abuse* of tongues is obvious, but it is hardly possible that he condemns prayer in tongues itself, since he regards it as a divine *charisma*—a grace-gift from God's own Spirit (1 Cor. 12:7–11). Paul lists tongues among God's "gifts" (12:10). Surely all God's gifts are good, even if some are greater than others (12:31). Admittedly, some of us have received ill-conceived holiday gifts, but who would dare say, "*God* gave me a bad gift"?

MacArthur further insists that "Paul would never extol prayers that bypass the mind. . . . That was—and still is today—a pagan practice. In the Greco-Roman mystery religions, ecstatic utterances were commonly employed as a way to circumvent the mind in order to commune with demonic entities. So it is likely that Paul's words in these verses include a sarcastic tone."[16] For MacArthur, use of tongues seeks "deeper spiritual intimacy with God through *mystical*, *muddled*, and even *mindless* experiences. This is a dangerous practice for believers, who are called to *renew* their minds, not *bypass* their intellectual faculties or subjugate reason to raw emotion."[17]

Treating Paul's words as sarcastic is an ingenious way to make the text mean the exact opposite of what it says![18] Paul most certainly does emphasize the Spirit's renewal of our minds[19]—but not to the exclusion of his work in the affective aspect of our person (cf., e.g., the emotive imagery of biblical psalms). Paul does not present prayer in tongues with one's spirit as *hostile* to prayer with one's mind. Compare 1 Corinthians 14:15: "I'll pray with the spirit, and I'll also pray with the mind." If God can lead our hearts to pray in our own language or by groaning, why not in another language, especially if, as Paul says, this is a way of praying with one's spirit? Some cessationists seem to believe, contra Paul (again 1 Cor. 14:15), that only prayer with the mind, not with one's spirit, is appropriate.

Nor for that matter do Paul's other comments demean the human spirit:

16. MacArthur, *Strange Fire*, 150. He compares mystery cults also in MacArthur, *Chaos*, 228.
17. MacArthur, *Strange Fire*, 244.
18. Here see Fee, *Presence*, 219n527: "MacArthur, 372, whose biases intrude on his interpretation, considers it sarcastic here." See the critique of this position in Carson, *Showing Spirit*, 102n89. Cf. similarly Oss, "View," 280n79, regarding MacArthur's "convoluted exegesis."
19. I (Craig) dedicate an entire book to this subject: Keener, *Mind*.

Romans 1:9–10: "God, whom I serve/worship in my spirit in the good news of his Son, is my witness how I unceasingly mention you, always in my prayers."

Romans 8:16: "The Spirit himself testifies along with our spirit that we are God's children."

For MacArthur, tongues today are like "counterfeit tongues at Corinth."[20] Yet Paul could easily have insisted on stopping tongues speech at Corinth had he regarded it as counterfeit; rather, he critiques merely the gift's *abuse*, just like he critiques *abuse* of the Lord's Supper a couple chapters earlier. There Paul protests that they have turned the Lord's Supper into their own supper (1 Cor. 11:20–21), but he still differentiates the table of the Lord from the table of demons (10:21).

More critically, MacArthur's view misses the point of Paul's argument. Paul himself prayed in tongues privately more than all the Corinthians, though he did not make a big deal about it (1 Cor. 14:18). Although the abuses in the Corinthian church require him to emphasize that tongues be kept in their place and be offered in proper order (14:40), he qualifies his words lest anyone overreact on the other side (as MacArthur has done): He explicitly forbids the church to prohibit tongues in their public worship services (14:39)![21]

Paul would hardly add this warning against forbidding tongues if forbidding tongues were actually what he wished to do! As Sam Storms puts it, "If tongues was not a spiritual gift for the church, why did Paul allow it to be exercised and used in the church at all? Yet he did; if interpreted, speaking in tongues was entirely permissible."[22] If Paul guards against too negative a view of tongues even when he is correcting an abuse of the gift, how much less negative would he have been where no abuse existed? Paul is instead addressing public order: The public use of *uninterpreted* tongues is not helpful to the gathered church. Not only with regard to tongues but with regard to other gifts and practices as well, many churches today would do well to heed Paul's admonition that "the spirit of the prophet is subject to the prophet" (1 Cor. 14:32–33).

Although God may allow us more of a particular gift than we need, we must be prepared to limit even how we exercise the gift of prophecy (14:29–33), which Paul treats as particularly edifying. In a similar way, I might be *able* to teach from Scripture for ten hours straight (and have sometimes done so), but this does not mean that God always wants me to do so. The need of the church, rather than simply the availability of divine inspiration and enablement, should determine the public use of any spiritual gift. (Inspiration itself

20. MacArthur, *Chaos*, 231.
21. This and the following paragraphs are from Keener, *Gift & Giver*, 107–9.
22. Storms, "View," 219.

can be expressed even when others are not listening; see, e.g., Num. 11:25; 1 Sam. 10:5, 10; 19:20.)[23]

MacArthur insists, "The fact modern glossolalia parallels pagan religious rites should serve as a dire warning of the spiritual dangers."[24] Against MacArthur's association with pagan cults, scholars have shown that no evidence supports the idea that tongues appeared in pre-Christian mystery cults.[25] Depending on one's definition of "ecstasy" more generally, some find ecstasy even in some Israelite prophecy (including Num. 11:25–26;[26] 1 Sam. 19:20–25; 2 Kings 9:11),[27] or even spiritually something like tongues there.[28] (Nor by any means are all tongues experiences ecstatic.)[29] Others have looked for some early Jewish analogies for tongues,[30] though these at best would simply serve to show that the first disciples could recognize what God was enabling them to do. Peter himself grounds the phenomenon in Joel's prophecy about God empowering his people to hear and speak for him (Acts 2:17–18). Aside from tongues *not* being documented in pre-Christian paganism,[31] the same guilt-by-association principle could be used to discredit teaching, biblical instances of prophecy, giving thanks for our food, or virtually any other practice.

23. See, e.g., comments in Gane, *Leviticus, Numbers*, 585–86.

24. MacArthur, *Strange Fire*, 154.

25. Forbes, *Prophecy*, 124–48; Ruble, "Tongues," 15.

26. The proximity of Num. 12:6 may suggest something like visionary experience, but in any case expressed in speech.

27. E.g., Albright, *Stone Age*, 42, 44; Bright, *History*, 187; Levine, *Numbers 1–20*, 325; Ashley, *Numbers*, 214; Budd, *Numbers*, 129; Hertzberg, *Samuel*, 85, 168; Ackroyd, *Samuel*, 83–84; Arnold, *Samuel*, 291. In the wider environment, Mesopotamians and Hittites preferred divination, but some ecstatic prophetism appears (Gurney, *Hittites*, 158–59; Haran, "Continuity and Change," 181; Huffmon, "Prophecy," 111–12; Paul, "Prophets," 1159–60; Parke, *Sibyls*, 216–20; elsewhere, *ANET*, 26; Albright, *Yahweh*, 212), and it was somewhat common among Greeks (Plutarch, *Dial. L.* 16, *Mor.* 759B; Aelius Aristides, *Def. Or.* 34–35, §11D; Parke, *Sibyls*, 219; Parke, *Oracles*, 85, 256–57); in Diaspora Judaism, see *Sib. Or.* 2.1–5; 3.1–7, 295–99, 489–91; 11.315–18; 12.295–96.

28. For something like tongues there, see, e.g., Wenham, *Numbers*, 109; Neil, *Thessalonians*, 129; cf. comparison in Cole, *Numbers*, 193–94. Note esp. the use of the probably reflexive *hitpael* (Cotton, "Spirit in Numbers 11," 12–13), though this form of the verb does not always entail ecstasy (Cole, *Numbers*, 193n55).

29. See Turner, *Gifts*, 305–6, and sources cited there.

30. See the survey in Keener, *Acts*, 1:808–9, 811.

31. Regarding the Pythia, Forbes, *Prophecy*, 103–19 (esp. 104–6 for terminology and 107–19 for the phenomena); Aune, *Prophecy*, 31; Aune, "Magic," 1551; Fontenrose, *Delphic Oracle*; Sourvinou-Inwood, "Delphic Oracle," 445. Magical papyri offer a somewhat closer analogy (Williams, "Glossolalia as Phenomenon") but remain later and quite different (Forbes, *Prophecy*, 153–54; Aune, "Magic," 1550–51; cf. the truly analogous lists of vowels in gnostic texts in Burgess, *Holy Spirit*, 41). See the survey in Keener, *Acts*, 1:809–11.

## How Often Must One Mention It Before It Counts?

Some cessationists use a sieve for evidence about tongues so constricted that they force a case from ordinary silence (that is, an argument from silence where the silence is not in any way unexpected). Tom Pennington, for example, points out that Paul does not mention tongues in any letter written after 1 Corinthians, including the Pastorals, which "contain the permanent instructions for ministry in the church age (1 Tim. 3:14–15)." From this silence he infers that tongues died out before the end of the 50s of the first century.[32]

It's easy to see how the logic is fallacious. Instead of taking New Testament mentions as samples, he assumes that it occurred only in the passages that mention it. Paul addresses tongues in 1 Corinthians because of its abuse, just as he addresses the Lord's Supper there because of its abuse. Were it not for problems in Corinth, we would not know from the New Testament that Christians actually continued to practice the Lord's Supper that Jesus modeled in the Gospels (1 Cor. 11:23–26).[33] Paul does not address the Lord's Supper in later letters. Did the practice of the Lord's Supper die out by the late 50s? (We do not know the date of Jude 12, but the *Didache*, Ignatius, and other sources very clearly indicate that it did not die out.)[34]

Or how would Pastor Pennington's logic work for other practices such as weekly meetings (1 Cor. 16:2)? If a problem did not, and was not expected to, arise in this or that church, Paul did not ordinarily bring it up. For example, Paul addresses Christians with unbelieving spouses in the Corinthian church (1 Cor. 7:12–16). This seems like an important matter that would have general relevance, since people were often converted after marriage. It probably came up often (see Matt. 10:35–36; 1 Pet. 3:1–2). But Paul addresses it only once because no other church wrestled with that issue so much that it required Paul to address it.

Tongues was not a central issue, but even issues as close to Paul's heart as justification by faith do not appear in precisely those terms in the Pastorals (though it is implied in Titus 3:5, 7). Did God change the means of salvation with a new dispensation in the time of the Pastorals? Paul's letters normally address specific situations, and we read them to learn both about how Paul dealt with these situations and about the faith and experience of the earliest Christians. The latter information is often assumed rather than articulated by Paul and his audiences, because he does not need to tell them what they already know.

This is why 1 Corinthians is our main source of information for examining tongues as a gift. Indeed, had the Corinthians not made mistakes in their use of tongues, we might not know anything about tongues' intended operation in

32. Pennington, *Cessationism*, 161–62; cf. MacArthur, *Chaos*, 233.

33. So also Richardson, *Theology*, 364.

34. See, e.g., *Did*. 9.1–5; Ignatius *Phld*. 4.1; *Smyrn*. 6.2; 8.1.

the church. Perhaps our cessationist brothers and sisters could take some cues from Paul. Instead of assuming the gifts have ceased or complaining about them—neither of which Paul did—maybe they could look beyond whatever oddities and abuses come with the territory and reiterate scriptural wisdom on how to employ such precious gifts for God's glory.

To downplay tongues, some cessationists find other ways to limit it outside Acts especially to troublesome Corinth. Pennington argues that Luke knew about the character of tongues only from Corinth.[35] Yet Luke's "we" in Acts does not extend to Corinth, where Paul spent eighteen months the first time (Acts 18:11). Luke doesn't even report Paul's miracles in Corinth, though we know they happened there (2 Cor. 12:12). Acts and the longer ending of Mark indicate that tongues was not limited to Corinth. The continuation of tongues does not *depend* on this inference that prayer in tongues occurred in other churches, but its wider occurrence seems highly probable nonetheless, even though Paul lacked reason to correct its abuse in his other surviving letters. Here are some concrete reasons for this inference:

- Paul himself prayed in tongues regularly (1 Cor. 14:18). He seems to have regarded prayer in tongues as a special form of prayer, "praying with one's spirit" (14:14–15). Does that not sound like a positive practice he would have encouraged elsewhere?[36] From whom else would the Corinthians have learned about the experience, not least what to call it?
- Acts suggests that tongues evidenced divine inspiration in many early Christian communities, and that Luke's target audience[37] would recognize this point.
- Paul's occasional letters confirm that some other gifts listed in 1 Corinthians 12 were standard practice in Paul's other churches. Paul expected prophecy to occur (1 Thess. 5:20), even in churches he had never visited (Rom. 12:6). This expectation should not surprise us, since his Jewish contemporaries believed that prophecy would accompany the outpouring of the Spirit (see Joel 2:28–29).[38]

## Demon Tongues?

Before moving forward, we should address one side issue. In earlier generations some critics considered all Pentecostal speaking in tongues to be demonic.

35. Pennington, *Cessationism*, 108; Pennington, "Case."
36. With, e.g., Barrett, *Acts*, 116; cf. Neil, *Acts*, 73; Downing, *Cynics*, 220–21.
37. Possibly in Macedonia, and certainly not limited to Corinth; see discussion in Keener, *Acts*, 1:430–32.
38. I follow here Keener, *Gift & Giver*, 107–9.

Although critics today more often explain it as a psychological phenomenon (we can be grateful for the upgrade),[39] some do mention demonic associations in passing, even if only to assure readers that this is not their view.

MacArthur concedes that tongues could be just "a learned behavior," but only after he manages to elaborate on tongues in cases of demon possession and the occult.[40] Sam Waldron, too, regards most modern tongues as simply natural "free vocalization," though "some of it may indeed be demonic."[41] Although we currently lack evidence for tongues in pre-Christian paganism, it does indeed appear in many cults and in some cases of spirit possession today, where it obviously comes from spirits other than God's.[42]

Of course, analogies need not suggest causality or invite guilt by association. For example, many cults also have teachers, which does not suggest that all teaching is cultic. After the Christian experience of tongues, it was inevitable that it would also turn up elsewhere. Polytheism is syncretistic, incorporating elements of other religions, and the Bible says that Satan takes on some elements of truth to make his deception more appealing (2 Cor. 11:13–15). Church fathers understood even the ancient mystery cults as a demonic imitation of Christianity.[43] Tertullian claims that Christianity has the true mysteries, of which others are poorer and later copies.[44] As the mysteries began to lose devotees to Christians in a later period, they adopted some features from Christianity, many of them attested in the mysteries only from that later period.[45]

Schreiner, who does not believe that modern tongues correspond to the biblical gift, nevertheless recognizes that they need not be demonic; he welcomes J. I. Packer's suggestion that they may be a way of relaxing the mind.[46] (They do indeed relax the mind, as one might infer from 1 Corinthians 14:14. Prayer in tongues has also been reported as reducing the pain of drug withdrawal and can greatly increase the probability of long-term recovery.)[47]

39. For a survey of psychological studies and explanations, generally moving from hostile a century ago to much more favorable today, see Keener, *Acts*, 1:818–20; esp. Kay, "Glossolalia."

40. MacArthur, *Chaos*, 239–40.

41. Waldron, *Continued*, 91.

42. See the brief survey and sources cited in Keener, *Acts*, 1:817.

43. Benoit, "Mystères," 79–81.

44. Tertullian, *Apol.* 47.14.

45. Metzger, "Considerations," 10–11; Eliade, *Rites*, 115.

46. Schreiner, *Spiritual Gifts*, 130–31, noting Packer, *Keep in Step*, 168–70. Turner, *Gifts*, 290, summarizes Packer as even commending "Pentecostal glossolalia as an aid to spirituality," so long as it does not compete with the power of its NT counterpart.

47. Wilkerson, *Cross*, 154–68 (regarding Teen Challenge, the success rate of which has been supported by other studies); and, regarding Jackie Pullinger's work in Hong Kong, Storms, *Guide*, 145–46; Pullinger, *Dragon*, 83, 149, 158–60, 166, 169, 173, and especially 174; external corroboration in sociologists Miller and Yamamori, *Pentecostalism*, 99–105 (esp. 104, 109; against any supposition of their starting with favorable bias, see 99, 147). I myself (Craig) have experienced glossolalia's utility in dealing with short-term severe pain in a bloody injury.

## Tongues, Order, and Edification

So, what *does* Paul say about speaking in tongues in 1 Corinthians? We find most of his teaching on this subject in chapter 14. Here is a list of key verses on the subject (from the LEB).

> 14:1–2: "Pursue love, and strive for spiritual *gifts*, but especially that you may prophesy. For the one who speaks in a tongue does not speak to people but to God, because no one understands, but by the Spirit he speaks mysteries."
>
> 14:5: "Now I want you all to speak with tongues, but even more that you may prophesy. The one who prophesies *is* greater than the one who speaks with tongues, unless he interprets, in order that the church may receive edification."
>
> 14:6: "But now, brothers, if I come to you speaking with tongues, how do I benefit you, unless I speak to you either with a revelation or with knowledge or with a prophecy or with a teaching?"
>
> 14:13: "Therefore the one who speaks in a tongue must pray that he may interpret."
>
> 14:14–15: "For if I pray in a tongue, my spirit prays but my mind is unproductive. *Therefore what should I do?* I will pray with my spirit, but I will also pray with my mind. I will sing praise with my spirit, but I will also sing praise with my mind."
>
> 14:18–19: "I give thanks to God *that* I speak with tongues more than all of you, but in the church I prefer to speak five words with my mind, in order that I may instruct other *people*, than ten thousand words in a tongue."
>
> 14:26: "*Therefore what should you do*, brothers? Whenever you come together, each one of you has a psalm, has a teaching, has a revelation, has a tongue, has an interpretation. All *things* must be done for edification."
>
> 14:27–28: "If anyone speaks in a tongue, *it must be* on one occasion two or at most three, and *one after the other*, and one must interpret. But if there is no interpreter, he must be silent in the church, but let him speak to himself and to God."
>
> 14:39–40: "So then, my brothers, desire to prophesy, and do not prevent speaking with tongues. But let all *things* be *done* decently and according to proper procedure."

A key text that underlines the overarching theme of this chapter is verse 12 (still LEB): "In this way also you, since you are zealous of spiritual *gifts*, seek for the edification of the church." Paul's main point was not to suppress or downplay the importance of any of the gifts of the Spirit—including tongues. On the contrary, his interest lies in the *proper use* of those gifts. He understands that, when properly employed, the Spirit's gifts edify the church. His interest in 1 Corinthians 14 fits that of Paul's larger argument in 1 Corinthians 12–14, in which Paul encourages the diversity of spiritual gifts for the common good (12:1–31), led by love (13:1–13). Paul emphasizes that the diverse gifts, like the many different instruments in a symphony, must be harmonized by love. Without love, the gifts create a cacophony of discord (13:1–14:40). Again, Paul's primary concern is the edification of the church.

Thus, in the corporate gathering, two or at most three should speak in tongues, only one at a time, and someone must interpret. Everything must be done in a way that builds up the church. During a worship gathering, a few intelligible words will edify more than will a thousand unintelligible words. So if there is no interpreter, the person speaking in tongues should do so privately. Everything must be done in a fitting and orderly way. Ensuring that (almost) no one will misunderstand his point, Paul prefaces his concluding summary about order (14:40) by warning them to seek the gift of prophecy and not to forbid speaking in tongues (14:39).

### *Is Edifying Oneself Bad?*

Astonishingly, MacArthur denies Paul's explicit claim that God gives all gifts to build up the church. He says, "Charismatics believe that the spectacular miraculous gifts were given for the edification of believers. Does God's Word support such a conclusion? No. In fact, the truth is quite the contrary. . . . Tongues never were intended to edify believers."[48] By contrast, consider again what Paul actually explicitly declares in 1 Corinthians 14 (AT):

> 14:4: "Those who speak in a tongue edify themselves; but the one who prophesies edifies the church."
>
> 14:5: "One who prophesies is greater than one who speaks in tongues unless he interprets, so the church may receive edification."
>
> 14:12: "Even so, you also, because you're zealous for spiritual matters, be zealous to abound for the edification of the church."
>
> 14:26: "When you gather, each has . . . a teaching, . . . a tongue, an interpretation. Let all things be for edification."[49]

48. MacArthur, *Chaos*, 141.

49. That each one "has" a gift to contribute is not a rebuke, but recalls the same terminology in 12:7, 11, 18, indicating that they *should* contribute these gifts for the common good (12:7).

MacArthur claims that tongues "cannot edify the church in a proper way."[50] Paul, by contrast, says that "the one who prophesies is greater than the one who speaks in tongues, *unless one interprets, so that the church may be edified*" (1 Cor. 14:5 AT).[51] When conjoined with interpretation, tongues edifies the church, like prophecy and other rightly used gifts (1 Cor. 14:12, 26; Eph. 4:12, 16). But of course MacArthur also rejects the gift of prophecy, which Paul specifies as *particularly* edifying to Christ's body (1 Cor. 14:3, 5).

Meanwhile, Paul notes that individual prayer in tongues edifies individual believers; in 14:4 Paul says (NASB): "The one who speaks in a tongue edifies himself; but the one who prophesies edifies the church." That is why Paul argues that prophecy is better: In *church*, edifying other believers is the priority. Yet Paul also says that he wishes they all spoke in tongues (14:5)!

Edifying oneself is inferior to edifying the church, but it is far from *negative*. If personal edification is wrong, then pastors should study the Bible only for sermon preparation, not for personal devotions! Indeed, in the face of error and spiritual danger, Jude 20 exhorts believers to build themselves up in their faith, praying by the Spirit.[52]

### *Don't Forbid Speaking in Tongues*

There isn't space to elaborate on every cessationist argument against speaking in tongues, but we have addressed the most common and substantial ones. The conclusion can only be that it is biblical to speak in tongues. Glossolalia is a precious and powerful gift that Paul wishes that all believers would practice (14:5) and that he commands them not to forbid (14:39).

Are there abuses of tongues? Of course. There are also abuses of teaching—many of which we have witnessed in this chapter from some cessationist theologians. Yet we do not say that teaching ought to be discouraged because some do it poorly. The same applies to all the spiritual gifts. Human abuse does not negate the reality of the divine gift. The Corinthians abused the gift of speaking in tongues—as they abused the gift of knowledge (1 Cor. 8:1, 11). But Paul does not invalidate the gift; he confirms it. Then he teaches its proper and powerful operation. Our response should be the same. In other words, our response should be biblical rather than cessationist.

Perhaps a good way to conclude our primary discussion concerning tongues in the New Testament is with a quote from Billy Graham. Though expressing caution because of potential for abuse and error, he concludes that there is no scriptural reason to suppose the gift of tongues is not for today: "Although there is honest disagreement among Christians about the validity of tongues

50. MacArthur, *Chaos*, 232; also, Waldron, *Continued*, 87.

51. See also Oss, "View," 280n79 (despite the apparent typo pointing to 14:15).

52. See discussion in Keener, *1–2 Peter, Jude*, 146. Cf. also Menzies, *Speaking in Tongues*, 135; Amoafo, *Stand Up*, 164.

today, I personally cannot find any biblical justification for saying the gift of tongues was meant exclusively for New Testament times. . . . Indeed, tongues is a gift of the Spirit. . . . Today there are Presbyterians, Baptists, Anglicans, Lutherans and Methodists, as well as Pentecostals, who speak or have spoken in tongues."[53]

## Tongues as a Sign

Because 1 Corinthians 14:22 is among the most debated and debatable passages in 1 Corinthians 14 (next to 14:34–35), few scholars would base a case solely on this passage, but because it enters into the discussion here, we address it as well.

### *Tongues for Preaching to Jews?*

First Corinthians 14:22 declares, "Tongues are for a sign, not to those who believe, but to unbelievers." MacArthur therefore contends that "tongues never were intended to edify believers" (a point we have repeatedly refuted already), "but to convince Jewish unbelievers of the truthfulness of the gospel."[54]

In fact, the opposite of MacArthur's claim is likelier. On a more likely reading, Paul's assertion that tongues comprise a sign for unbelievers is *not* "to convince Jewish unbelievers of the truthfulness of the gospel." Paul declares that "tongues" would actually deter Jewish (or any) unbelievers from the gospel. Therefore, he discourages the Corinthians from treating tongues as an evangelistic tool. A careful reading of 1 Corinthians 14:20–25 reveals this. Here is the passage (NASB):

> Brothers *and sisters,* do not be children in your thinking; yet in evil be infants, but in your thinking be mature. In the Law it is written: "By men of strange tongues and by the lips of strangers I will speak to this people, and even so they will not listen to me," says the Lord. So then, tongues are for a sign, not to those who believe but to unbelievers; but prophecy is not for unbelievers, but for those who believe. Therefore if the whole church gathers together and all *the people* speak in tongues, and outsiders or unbelievers enter, will they not say that you are insane? But if all prophesy, and an unbeliever or an outsider enters, he is convicted by all, he is called to account by all; the secrets of his

53. Graham, *Holy Spirit*, 110. For one example of a spontaneous charismatic prayer meeting consisting of an Anglican, Baptist, Catholic, Presbyterian, and Pentecostal, see Keener, *Gift & Giver*, 171–72.

54. MacArthur, *Chaos*, 117–18. Catching more of the sense of the Isaiah quote, Waldron, *Continued*, 86, suggests that "Paul's whole point in 1 Corinthians 14:21 is that the gift of tongues was a sign of judgment on the Jews."

> heart are disclosed; and so he will fall on his face and worship God, declaring that God is certainly among you.

As Sam Storms points out, the context's contrast "is between believer and unbeliever, not Jew and Gentile"; with most commentators, we believe that the unbelieving visitor is likelier a gentile than a Jew.[55]

### *A Sign of Judgment*

Paul's biblical citation is also relevant to his purpose, at least for those hearers who were most biblically knowledgeable. Paul cites Isaiah 28:11–12. In that context, the rebellious people of Judah—particularly its leaders—had rejected the word of the Lord coming through prophecy. They give excuses, such as being unable to read or not being allowed to read (29:11–12). Isaiah the prophet had invited the people of Judah to repent and find rest (Isa. 28:12; see also 30:15). But the people refused this invitation. So God determined to give them a more direct message, now as simple as baby talk (Isa. 28:9–10, 13). This message, however, would not come to them in a language they would understand. It would come in "other tongues." The Assyrians, speaking "a foreign tongue," would enter the land as God's instrument of judgment (Isa. 28:11); while Judah might not understand the language any more than baby talk (28:9), the judgment would be clear. The strange language of the Assyrians embodies God's judgment against his prophecy-resisting people, "that they may go, and fall backward, and be broken, and snared, and taken" (28:13 ESV).

Paul would hardly quote this passage to support tongues as a sign to convince unbelieving Jews. The point of both Isaiah and Paul is that "other tongues" would *not* convince Jewish unbelievers of the truthfulness of the gospel, at least not before judgment strikes. On one very plausible view, that is precisely what Paul is trying to tell the Corinthians in verses 20 and 21. He's essentially saying: "If tongues were signs of judgment that would not convince the Judeans in Isaiah's day, they will not convert unbelievers in your day." Why, then, does Paul call tongues a sign to unbelievers but not believers (1 Cor. 14:22)? Scholars have long debated the verse's meaning.[56] But most recognize that it must relate somehow to Paul's illustrations in verses 23–25.

Notice that Paul's illustrations show the impact of *both* prophecy and tongues *only on unbelievers*. That is Paul's sole concern in this passage. He is imagining two scenarios, both of which have to do with the impact of *two*

55. Storms, "View," 219, who also suggests that Paul's allowance of the gift in church "seems difficult to explain if its only or even primary purpose" was directed toward "unbelieving Jews."

56. For varying views, see, e.g., Keener and Vaughan, "Tongues," 1061; Sweet, "Sign"; Roberts, "Sign." Some see the passage as quoting, then refuting, a Corinthian claim; see Johanson, "Tongues."

separate gifts on *one* group: outsiders visiting a Christian assembly in Corinth. His first illustration answers the question, "How do tongues affect unbelieving visitors?" (1 Cor. 14:23). The answer suggests that it will repel the visitors.

His second illustration answers the question, "How does *prophecy* affect unbelieving visitors?" (1 Cor. 14:24–25). The answer here is wholly positive. Put another way, Paul is addressing the "evangelistic" power of both tongues and prophecy when visitors attend a Christian meeting. Prophecy will convert them; tongues will drive them away.

Up to this point in chapter 14, Paul was concerned about the way tongues and prophecy affected only believers (1 Cor. 14:1–19). As we have seen, tongues without interpretation would fail to edify gathered believers while prophecy would succeed. Now in this passage, Paul addresses the impact of those same two gifts—tongues and prophecy—on a different group: unbelievers rather than believers (14:21–25).[57] Just as uninterpreted tongues would not edify believers, neither will they convict unbelievers. Visiting outsiders will simply think an assembly with various unintelligible utterances is mad (14:23). Prophecy, however, *will* convict unbelievers, just as it would edify believers. When outsiders visit and hear prophecy, they become convinced that God is really among those Christians (14:24).

### *Tongues Normally Not for Nonbelievers*

Thus most understand the assertions in verse 22 in light of the illustrations in verses 23–25. Tongues are not the kind of sign that benefits unbelievers. Some contend that the point, in fact, is that they are rather the kind of sign that *results* in unbelievers. Prophecy, on the other hand, is not a sign that results in unbelievers, but one that results in believers. When visitors hear prophecy, they turn toward God and his people.[58] On a slightly different interpretation, tongues are a sign that, like in Isaiah 28, signifies judgment (for "signs" of judgment, see 1 Sam. 2:34; 1 Kings 13:3–5; Isa. 20:3; Jer. 44:29; Ezek. 4:3; 12:6, 11; 14:8; 24:24, 27).[59] Granted, the matter may be different when someone recognizes the tongue in Hebrew, as has happened on occasion even today (see chap. 17 below), but this situation is exceptional rather than typical, and is never mentioned in the New Testament, including in Acts 2.[60]

57. The believers should not be like the unbelievers, like infants (14:20) who need a message so direct that even infants might understand (Isa. 28:9).

58. For this interpretation of verse 22, see Gladstone, "Sign Language." See also Fee, *Corinthians*, 677–78; Heil, *Role*, 200–202.

59. See, e.g., Dunn, *Jesus and Spirit*, 230; Fee, *Presence*, 241–42; Witherington, *Conflict*, 285; Garland, *1 Corinthians*, 650–51; Horton, *Corinthians*, 137–38; Hays, *First Corinthians*, 240; Keener, *Corinthians*, 114–15; cf. earlier Chrysostom, *Hom. Cor.* 36.2 (Bray, *Corinthians*, 142).

60. As a fisherman, Peter would not likely be sufficiently fluent in Hebrew to preach in it, and the only possible reference to hearers recognizing Hebrew, the mention of residents of Judea in Acts 2:9, may refer to their use of Aramaic.

Therefore, a careful reading of this passage proves the exact opposite of MacArthur's conclusion that "tongues never were intended to edify believers, but to convince Jewish unbelievers of the truthfulness of the gospel."[61] Paul's point is *not* that tongues convince unbelieving Jews—or any unbeliever—of the gospel's veracity. Tongues as a public display rather solidify or at least signify unbelief, as the Isaiah quotation and Paul's illustrations both demonstrate. Because tongues were a sign of unbelief and judgment in Isaiah's day, the Corinthians should *avoid* using tongues as a public evangelistic tool and focus their use of tongues on its value for private self-edification.

## Tongues Continued in History

For MacArthur, "history records that tongues did cease."[62] Even if this were correct (as we shall see, it is not), it could simply mean that subsequent generations failed to embrace the biblical gift and teaching about it.[63] Moreover, while the individual gift appears in subsequent literature less frequently than mention of charismatic gifts in general, one would hardly have reason to suppose that God would withdraw tongues while continuing the gift of prophecy (even on the cessationist view that God would withdraw tongues as a *form* of prophecy), yet prophecy, healing, and so forth are also reported to continue.[64]

By contrast, historian Harold Hunter observes, "An exhaustive research for records of tongues-speech suggests there may not be a major period of church history without this phenomenon occurring among Christians."[65]

### *Tongues in the Patristic Era*

So is MacArthur correct about tongues ceasing in the first century? The focus of surviving writings from the next century was apologetics or debated theological questions rather than particular spiritual manifestations, but we do have references. Mark 16:17, probably from the early second century,[66] suggests that tongues did not die out, and certainly not (against a common cessationist position) when the last of the original twelve apostles died. This passage refers to

61. MacArthur, *Chaos*, 117–18. Contrast Paul's words: "One who speaks in a tongue edifies himself" (1 Cor. 14:4).

62. MacArthur, *Chaos*, 242.

63. Here with Laurito, *Speaking in Tongues*, 89.

64. Laurito, *Speaking in Tongues*, 96.

65. Hunter, *Spirit Baptism*, 24.

66. See Bird, *Gospel of the Lord*, 313. Against it being an original part of Mark, see, e.g., Edwards, *Mark*, 497 ("virtually certain"); Bock, *Mark*, 384; Voelz, *Mark 8:27–16:20*, 1222–37; Gladd, *Handbook*, 202.

"new" tongues alongside exorcism and healing (16:17–18), so it emphatically does not refer to mere translation of known languages in a bilingual church setting. It surfaces too early, with acceptance too widespread, to attribute its origin to Montanists or some other fairly local sect. (Nor need one attribute it to Phrygia or any other supposedly "enthusiastic" region when 1 Cor. 14 attests such enthusiasm over tongues already in a major urban center on the Greek mainland.)

Indeed, Mark 16:9–20 was accepted as canonical by the time of Irenaeus and thus provides solid second-century evidence for the phenomenon.[67] As Christopher Forbes points out more generally, tongues was widespread enough to continue for some time over a wide geographic area.[68]

Moreover, writing around the year 180, Irenaeus claimed that the gift continued in his day. He speaks of those who are spiritual as those who have God's Spirit and currently "possess prophetic gifts, and who through the Spirit speak all kinds of languages, and bring to light for the general benefit the hidden things of men, and declare the mysteries of God."[69] When skeptic Conyers Middleton complained that Irenaeus's testimony does not count because Irenaeus does not claim to have experienced the gift himself, John Wesley exposed this as an argument from silence; Acts never reports Paul speaking in tongues (even in Acts 9:17–18) and yet he spoke in tongues more than all the Corinthians (1 Cor. 14:18). Peter and John do not mention such gifts in their letters, yet we know from Acts that they experienced them![70]

Some try to undermine the significance of Irenaeus's mention of tongues from its slightly earlier omission in Justin Martyr; this tactic elevates an argument from silence over explicit evidence[71]—an argument especially precarious when we consider how much else Justin omits, including use of some key sources now regarded as canonical. For example, should we assume that John's Gospel was not yet in circulation because Justin never mentions and barely alludes to it?[72] One cannot expect tongues in Justin's list of gifts, since his list reflects not 1 Corinthians 12 but Isaiah 11.[73] Meanwhile, specifically describing

67. See Forbes, *Prophecy*, 76–77.

68. Forbes, *Prophecy*, 75–84.

69. Irenaeus, *Haer.* 5.6.1; also noted in Forbes, *Prophecy*, 78–79, who further notes Eusebius, *Hist. eccl.* 5.7.6. Cf. also Palma, "Glossolalia," 42; Ruble, "Tongues," 18; Shogren, "Prophecy,"427–28 (citing also *Demonstration of the Apostolic Preaching* 99). Contrast the speculative and error-riddled case of Rogers, "Tongues," (academic but polemical) soundly refuted in Shogrun, "Gift of Tongues," 403–5 (showing Irenaeus's testimony to be firsthand and that it lacks Montanist influence).

70. See Wesley, "Middleton"; Oliver, *Reformations*, 121 (following Tuttle, "Wesley and Gifts"); Billman, *Thread*, 15 (citing Wesley, *Works*, 10:21).

71. Forbes, *Prophecy*, 77–78. For continuing prophecy in Justin, see *Dial.* 82; exorcism in *Dial.* 85; miracles in *Dial.* 35.8 (on which see Williams, *Justin Martyr*, 71n3).

72. Excepting perhaps Justin, *1 Apol.* 61; contrast other sources that are not much later (Keener, *John*, 93; cf. Braun, *Jean*, 136–44; Osborn, *Justin*, 137; Barnard, *Justin Martyr*, 60–62).

73. Hunter, "Tongues-Speech," 127, on Justin, *Dial.* 39: "a 'Christianized' version of Isa 11:2–3"; cf. Justin, *Dial.* 87.

Christian worship,[74] Celsus complains that besides various prophecies in the first person, some utter "strange, fanatical and quite unintelligible words, of which no rational person can find the meaning."[75] Clement of Alexandria (ca. 150–ca. 215) includes tongues among the gifts that distinguish those who are perfected in knowledge.[76]

Tertullian (160–240), before he became a Montanist,[77] also argued that tongues, interpretation, and prophecy continued among the orthodox. His description suggests that they often appear in an intense spiritual state associated with prayer; he contrasts their persistence among the orthodox with the lack of such gifts among Marcion's followers.[78] Sources claim that the Egyptian monastic leader Pachomius (d. ca. 346) spoke the language of angels.[79] Hilary of Poitiers (310–67) continues to list speaking in and interpreting tongues among spiritual gifts, alongside miracles, prophecy, and teaching.[80] Eusebius (d. 339) includes tongues among the gifts with which God adorns his church.[81] Other reports also exist.[82]

### *Later Decline in Reported Tongues*

In some areas reports of this gift, like reports of some other gifts, apparently declined over time. Augustine rightly understood and repeatedly emphasized a key feature of the Pentecost narrative: When the first Christians

74. The prophecies are explicitly trinitarian, making the Christian character of the gatherings difficult to dispute.

75. Origen, *Cels.* 7.9. Whether in a genuine human language or not, the utterances sound to the outsider like gibberish (1 Cor. 14:23).

76. Clement of Alexandria, *Strom.* 4.21 (*ANF*, 2:433–34); and comment in Burgess, *Holy Spirit*, 72.

77. Meanwhile, pace some (note Rogers, "Tongues"), no ancient source associates tongues with Montanism (Forbes, *Prophecy*, 79–80, 160–62; Burgess, "Ancient Churches," 11; Shogren, "Gift of Tongues," 401–3; also Cutten, *Speaking with Tongues*, 35). The primary analogy with Montanism involves its prophetic character (see, e.g., Kim, "Montanism," who argues that its detractors misrepresented it).

78. Tertullian, *Marc.* 5.8, in Forbes, *Prophecy*, 79–80; Kelsey, *Tongue Speaking*, 38; Shogren, "Gift of Tongues," 407. For exorcism, cf. Tertullian, *Spect.* 26. Cf. also Origen in Robeck, "Charismata," 120.

79. Kelsey, *Tongue Speaking*, 38, citing Sozomen in the fifth century. Others claimed he received supernatural knowledge of Latin and Greek (Cutten, *Speaking with Tongues*, 38, 41).

80. Hilary of Poitiers, *On the Trinity*, 147, as quoted in Burgess, *Holy Spirit*, 171; Thiselton, *Spirit*, 194; Laurito, *Speaking in Tongues*, 95.

81. Burgess, *Holy Spirit*, 104, noting Eusebius, *Comm. Isa.* 6.2; Eusebius, *Comm. Ps.* 65.4; 77.18; cf. Floris, "Charismata," 370–71.

82. E.g., Basil, *Shorter Rules* 278, in Floris, "Charismata," 373. Although the wording might be interpreted differently, it is possible that Patrick experienced something like tongues and interpretation in his sleep (Patrick, *Confession* 24): "Whether it was within me or beside me—I heard authoritative words which I could hear but not understand, until at the end of the speech it became clear"; translation at https://www.confessio.ie/etexts/confessio_english#. Patrick apparently connects this experience with the Spirit's groanings within him (*Confession* 25), but in 24 the wording is articulate.

received the Holy Spirit, they spoke "with the tongues of all nations,"[83] fitting Acts' emphasis on the mission to the ends of the earth. This was, he thought, "the chief and most necessary sign" of the Spirit's coming on believers.[84] Even though Acts 8:17–18 does not explicitly specify that the Samaritan believers spoke in tongues when they received the Spirit, Augustine is confident that they did: "For the Holy Ghost was at that time given in such sort, that He even visibly showed Himself to have been given. For they who received Him spake with the tongues of all nations"; this is, he affirms, what Simon witnessed.[85]

If this makes Augustine sound like a classical Pentecostal, his other comments would disabuse us of such a notion. Whereas the earliest Christians demonstrated that they had received the Spirit by speaking in the tongues of all nations, now Christians demonstrated receiving the Spirit by being part of the true, universal church, which by virtue of its universality speaks the tongues of all nations.[86] Because Augustine believed that speaking in tongues involved preaching in languages that the preachers had not learned, he believed that this no longer happened simply by the laying on of hands.[87] Since the gospel had spread among the nations, he thought, preaching in unlearned languages was no longer needed.[88] Augustine's context was at least partly polemical,

83. See Augustine, *Sermons on the New Testament* 21.33 (on Matt. 7:32); 27.4 (on Matt. 15:21); 30.5, 9 (on Matt. 17:19); 39.1 (on Matt. 21:19); Augustine, *Ep.* 137.16 (to Volusianus); Augustine, *City of God* 22.5; Augustine, *Tractates on John* 32.6 (on John 7:37–39); 92.2 (on John 15:26–27); 93.4 (on John 16:1–4); Augustine, *Homilies on First John* 2.3 (on 1 John 2:12–17); Augustine, *On the Psalms* 55.10; 59.14; 67.9; 95.5; Augustine, *Trin.* 15.19.34.

84. Augustine, *City of God* 18.49; all my references to Augustine here follow the *ANF* translation. For tongues as the necessary (but now ceased) "sign" of receiving the Spirit, cf. also Augustine, *Tractates on John* 32.7 (on John 7:37–39); Severus of Antioch, *Catena on Acts* 10.44 (Martin, *Acts*, 140). Irenaeus already suggests that the Spirit descended on the disciples at Pentecost "that they all might prophesy and speak with tongues" (Irenaeus, *Haer.* 3.12.1). More recently, cf. Barrett, *Acts*, lxxxiv: "Speech is in Acts the characteristic mark of the Spirit's presence, sometimes in glossolalia (2.4; 10.46; 19.6), sometimes in prophecy (2.17, 18; 11.27; 13.1–3; 21.(4), (9), 10, 11), sometimes in proclamation (e.g. 4.31)." For Pentecostal discussions of initial evidence, including early Pentecostal detractors from the doctrine, see McGee, *Initial Evidence*; brief survey in Keener, *Acts*, 1:825–28.

85. Augustine, *Sermon* 49.10 (on Luke 7:37); cf. Chrysostom, *Hom. Acts* 18. In more recent times, see, e.g., Dunn, *Jesus and Spirit*, 188–89; Carson, *Showing Spirit*, 145; Rackham, *Acts*, 116; Haenchen, *Acts*, 304; Arrington, *Acts*, 89; Palma, *Spirit*, 152–53 (and sources he cites); Stronstad, "Baptized," 174–75; Magruder, "Reading" (esp. 299); Starner, "Co-Laborers," 232 (plausibly noting that readers will fill the silences from the previous and subsequent occasions in Acts; cf. Stonehouse, *Areopagus*, 80 ("prophecy and tongues"); Faw, *Acts*, 104–5 (tongues, prophecy, or ecstatic praise); Packer, *Acts*, 65; discussion in Keener, *Acts*, 2:1529.

86. Augustine, *Sermon* 21.28 (on Matt. 7:32); Augustine, *Tractates on John* 32.7 (on John 7:37–39).

87. Laurito, *Speaking in Tongues*, 97–98 (quoting from Augustine, *Retractions* 55).

88. Laurito, *Speaking in Tongues*, 98, citing Augustine, *Expositions of the Psalms*, 489; see also Augustine, *Homilies of 1 John* 6.10; Kelsey, *Tongue Speaking*, 40; Burgess, *Holy Spirit*, 189. Luther followed Augustine's understanding (Burgess, "Evidence," 27; Burgess, *Peoples*, 136). Zwingli's tradition seems friendlier to tongues (cf. Ellingsen, *Roots*, 80).

insofar as he was seeking to counter the Donatists. Donatists apparently claimed that their individual tongues speech confirmed God's blessing among them; Augustine countered by claiming that the church as a whole now spoke the languages of the nations.[89]

That is, Augustine's understanding of tongues was tied very closely to a particular understanding of Acts 2. He rightly understood Luke's emphasis on mission to the nations, but he was likely wrong in thinking that the apostles evangelized in tongues at Pentecost. He was clearly mistaken exegetically if he limited tongues to such a function; *certainly none* of the other New Testament mentions of tongues involve preaching in tongues to people who would understand their words.

Meanwhile, Novatian[90] and Ambrose[91] spoke of tongues in the present tense, in the very period when Chrysostom and Augustine apparently thought that the gift had finally died out.[92] These later traditions also challenge the assumption of some more skeptical modern scholars[93] that already the evangelist Luke's church must have no longer known what genuine tongues experiences were.[94]

### Continuing Tongues

Those who thought that the gift had died out largely also understood tongues not as languages given for worship but as languages given for evangelism (based on their understanding of Acts 2).[95] Although there is reason to suppose that even the latter has happened on some subsequent occasions in history (see some examples in chap. 17 below), this phenomenon (like natural ability to translate in a bilingual setting) is plainly not what 1 Corinthians describes, nor what Acts describes in 10:46 or 19:6. Neither Cornelius's household, nor the Ephesian disciples, nor the assembled worshipers in

89. Blosser and Sullivan, *Speaking in Tongues*, 103–5; Kelsey, *Tongue Speaking*, 40; cf. Boys, *Evidence*, 24–25. Burgess, "Ancient Churches," 8–9, notes that Augustine specifically and repeatedly denies the current connection of tongues with Spirit reception, and suggests that he seems to be reacting against something, but Burgess does not attribute that to a known sect.

90. Novatian, *Trinity* 29. Although we should not weigh too much grammatically on the tense, the context of his argument about gifts perfecting Christ's body in fact suggests that he believes they continue (Burgess, *Holy Spirit*, 79).

91. Ambrose, *Holy Spirit* 2.150–51. Cf. also Thiselton, *Spirit*, 199.

92. Forbes, *Prophecy*, 80–84. For Chrysostom's perplexity, see Cutten, *Speaking with Tongues*, 36–37; Burgess, *Holy Spirit*, 126; Thiselton, *Spirit*, 116. Chrysostom did attribute a recent experience of "tongues" to a persecuted witness who, after his tongue was plucked out, testified even more vocally (Floris, "Chrysostom," 381, on Chrysostom's *Encomium to Martyr Romanus*). For the long duration of Christian tongues-speaking in late antiquity, see, e.g., Ruble, "Tongues," 17–25; Carson, *Showing Spirit*, 165–68; cf. Wimber, *Power Evangelism*, 157–74.

93. E.g., Goulder, *Type and History*, 77.

94. Forbes, *Prophecy*, 50n14; see also Menzies, "Luke-Acts," 97. As Bovon, *Theologian*, 237, notes, the Spirit's early activity was remembered but continued to function in Luke's own day.

95. With Kelsey, *Tongue Speaking*, 40; Laurito, *Speaking in Tongues*, 98; Blosser and Sullivan, *Speaking in Tongues*, 103–5.

1 Corinthians are preaching in tongues to anyone. To argue otherwise, based on the text's silence and in the face of what the passages actually say, is exegetically untenable by any standard of grammatical-historical exegesis used today. In 1 Corinthians the language is naturally unknown to the speaker, even while speaking it, and is explicitly used in prayer (e.g., 1 Cor. 14:2, 14–17).

But to the extent that many came to understand tongues only as a gift of preaching in other languages, we cannot expect to find them attesting the usual New Testament use of tongues attested by that label. This does not mean that the biblical gift ceased, but that when people experienced it, they would usually not use the label "tongues." Thus Augustine himself, especially in his exposition of the Psalms, spoke often of jubilation, an esctatic, joyful worship that he described as too deep to articulate linguistically.[96] Such experiences continue to be reported in subsequent centuries.[97] Indeed, after tracing cases of *jubilatio* through patristic and medieval sources,[98] Catholic theologian Eddie Ensley observes, "In certain passages in Franciscan literature we find the sounds of certain jubilations actually written out. These descriptions are amazingly like descriptions of present-day glossolalia within the Charismatic Renewal."[99]

Others have shown instances of tongues sporadically through history.[100] For example, the twelfth century abbess and visionary Hildegard of Bingen (1098–1179) created (or was given) her own private language, with a recorded, unique alphabet, probably especially for worship and speaking with God.[101] Some also report that Colette of Corbie (1381–1447) spoke in tongues.[102] Teresa of Avila (1515–82) speaks of a "strange and mysterious kind of prayer."[103] Some have also associated Ignatius of Loyola's gift of heavenly *loquela* ("speech") with singing in tongues.[104]

96. Augustine, *Conf.* 12.16.23; Augustine, *Ennar. Ps.* 47.6; 66.2; 81.3; 100.4. Cf. Aquinas (in Ensley, *Sounds*, 234; Oliver, *Movements*, 53); comment on Elizabeth's ecstatic speech in Gregory Thaumaturgos, *Second Homily on the Annunciation to the Holy Virgin Mary*.

97. Many link the practice of *iubilatio* with tongues (Parmentier, "Zungenreden"); see Underhill, *Jacopone*, 77–78, in Ensley, *Sounds*, 50; Oliver, *Movements*, 232. Both are at least precognitive expressions of worship. On tongues as typically precognitive and paralinguistic, see Thiselton, "Interpretation," 23–24, cited in Ahn, *Interpretation*, 162.

98. Ensley, *Sounds*, 6–7.

99. Ensley, *Sounds*, 50; see also xiii (cited in Oliver, *Movements*, 229).

100. See the five-part series of Riss, "Tongues." Cf. also Bouyer, "Movements," 113–31; Williams and Waldvogel, "History," 61–113 (cited in Carson, *Showing Spirit*). Tongues never died out in Eastern Orthodoxy (Ward, "Argument," 90, citing Kelsey, *Tongue Speaking*, 7).

101. See, e.g., Burgess, "Evidence," 21; Burgess, *Peoples*, 99; "Letter? I 'Ardly Know 'Er"; "Vox Inauditae." Burgess records a basic glossary of some one thousand words, imposed onto a Latin grammatical structure. Some have reasonably compared her worship in this language to tongues (e.g., Kelsey, *Tongue Speaking*, 47–48; Hyatt, *Years*, 59), though more skeptical interpreters view it as a jumble of known languages (Cutten, *Speaking with Tongues*, 41).

102. Oliver, *Revivals*, Kindle location 3266.

103. Teresa of Avila, *Castle or Mansions*, 197. She speaks of words without order during jubilation (Oliver, *Reformations*, 46, citing multiple early sources).

104. See Oliver, *Reformations*, 40–41.

Some report that tongues-speaking occurred among thirteenth-century Waldensians.[105] Some early Anabaptists reportedly spoke in tongues,[106] possibly including Menno Simons, one of their most influential leaders.[107] (Luther apparently deemed tongues allowable so long as an interpreter was present.)[108] George Fox (1624–91) and early Friends (Quakers) experienced healing, prophetic knowledge, and speaking "with new tongues, as the Lord gave us utterance."[109] Moravians experienced an outpouring of the Spirit that led to them becoming the first significant Protestant missions movement. One of their early critics complained about them speaking "some disconnected Jargon" that they attributed to the Spirit.[110] Sources also suggest tongues-speaking of various sorts among seventeenth-century Jansenists.[111] One learned coworker whom Wesley greatly respected was Thomas Walsh, who reports, "This morning the Lord gave me language that I knew not of, raising my soul to Him in a wonderful manner."[112] More reports from the 1740s Great Awakening, however, involve groanings, which some commentators consider "protoglossolalia."[113]

### *Tongues Between Cane Ridge and Azusa Street*

Because sources for recent centuries are fuller than for earlier ones, we naturally have more reports from the nineteenth century than earlier. Tongues are reported on occasion early in the Second Great Awakening,[114] even at Cane Ridge.[115] They appear, for example, among Presbyterians in North Carolina in 1801.[116] Likewise, University of Georgia students in 1800–1801, overwhelmed by the Spirit in nearby camp meetings, "shouted and talked in unknown

105. Synan, *Tradition*, 110.

106. Williams, *Radical Reformation*, 133 (reported by detractors who associated it with various excesses); Worthen, *Spellbound*, 58 (citing Byrd, *Aspects*, 101, 204); Burgess, "Evidence," 28; Hyatt, *Years*, 79, citing Littell, *Origins*, 19.

107. Hunter, *Spirit Baptism*, 162, and sources cited there, also noting that some modern Anabaptist thinkers, including John Howard Yoder, classify many of the early Anabaptists favorably as charismatic (cf. also Oliver, *Reformations*, 23, citing Davis, "Anabaptism," 221).

108. Worthen, *Spellbound*, 58.

109. Hall, *Worship*, 88; Hyatt, *Years*, 92, citing Fox, *Works*, 3:13; see further Kelsey, *Tongue Speaking*, 55; Oliver, *Reformations*, 71. But Fox himself "eventually discouraged such ecstatic utterances" (Burgess, "Evidence," 29), perhaps due to abuses.

110. Hyatt, *Years*, 96, citing Burgess, "Evidence," 32.

111. Burgess, "Evidence," 31. This was already noted by Bushnell, *Nature* (Burgess, *Peoples*, 208).

112. Riss, "Tongues"; Hyatt, *Years*, 104; Oliver, *Reformations*, 121. A Pentecost hymn by Charles Wesley seems to describe tongues as a "new strange language" (Billman, *Thread*, 59).

113. King, "Gifts," 95.

114. Synan, *Movement*, 24, noted by Hyatt, *Years*, 115.

115. Synan, *Tradition*, 110. More common was "protoglossolalia," as also in what became the Cumberland Presbyterian Church (King, "Gifts," 95).

116. Oliver, *Reformations*, 160.

tongues."[117] One 1858 work mentions tongues-speaking occurring among people of lower class.[118] Likewise, during Charles Finney's initial experience of the Spirit, he "bellowed out the unutterable gushings of my heart."[119] This might be closer to the groanings of Romans 8:23 than to articulate tongues.[120] He also describes the experience in terms of unquenchable joy. Sources show that speaking in tongues continued to surface periodically in camp meetings and revivals through the nineteenth century.[121]

On the other side of the Atlantic, it appears among believers in Prussia in 1817.[122] It also broke out among groups of believers in Britain in 1830–31.[123] Edward Irving concluded that this was a sign of a subsequent empowerment of the Spirit[124] and useful for personal edification.[125] Irving became a controversial figure,[126] but the first reported occurrences of tongues occurred well before Irving began to theologize about them.[127] Far less controversial was the influential US Baptist leader A. J. Gordon, founder of Gordon College, who rejected cessationist arguments regarding tongues, prophecy, and healing.[128] Influential on both sides of the Atlantic, Dwight L. Moody emphasized empowerment by the Spirit, and a witness reports that after Moody's preaching some were "speaking in tongues" and "prophesying."[129] Gordon came to expect the restoration of all the gifts "after observing instantaneous healings

117. Coulter, *College Life*, 195, quoted in Synan, *Tradition*, 13; see also King, "Gifts," 95; Billman, *Thread*, 113.

118. Burgess, *Peoples*, 204, citing Horace Bushnell (1802–76). Many of us would object to elements of Bushnell's theology, but here we are citing his observation of people's experiences.

119. Finney, *Memoirs*, 20; for another person, 305. Finney treated this as his baptism in the Spirit, which he viewed as necessary for ministry (see Hunter, *Spirit Baptism*, 173–74).

120. So also King, "Gifts," 96 (noting that Finney also prophesied). Hunter, *Spirit Baptism*, 174n104, doubts that Finney's "gushings" refer to tongues.

121. Synan, *Tradition*, 13n29. Synan also cites Johnson, "Camp Meeting," "for a description of speaking in tongues in early North Carolina camp meetings."

122. Oliver, *Reformations*, 179.

123. Hyatt, *Years*, 118–20, noting firsthand sources cited in Strachan, *Theology of Irving*, 13, 66, 58; see also Kelsey, *Tongue Speaking*, 56–57.

124. Dorries, "Irving and Spirit Baptism"; Strachan, *Theology of Irving*; cf. Synan, *Voices*, 85–87. Some argue that he viewed prophecy as well as tongues as such an evidence (Hunter, *Spirit Baptism*, 24, 181), though tongues does seem preeminent (see the quotation of Irving in Hunter, *Spirit Baptism*, 181–82).

125. Hyatt, *Years*, 120–21.

126. Defending his orthodoxy, see Dorries, "Controversy" (cited in Dorries, "Irving and Spirit Baptism," 55n1; Hyatt, *Years*, 207n8). Irving had a positive impact on others for spiritual renewal (e.g., Sigg, *Revival*, 158–59).

127. Cutten, *Speaking with Tongues*, 89–91.

128. Hyatt, *Years*, 127, citing Gordon, *Ministry of Spirit*, 72; Gordon, *Ministry of Healing*, 53. Gordon defended Irving theologically (Hyatt, *Years*, 128, citing Gordon, *Ministry of Healing*, 101–3).

129. Synan, *Tradition*, 88, citing Hollenweger, "Handbuch," 2:360; Pollock, *Moody*, 90–91; cf. also Oliver, *Reformations*, 220.

at Dwight Moody's meetings."[130] Tongues appeared alongside other gifts in the early Salvation Army,[131] and the movement's founder, General William Booth, valued such gifts.[132]

The indigenous 1860 Christian awakening in Tirunelveli, India, included praise "by unknown tongues, with their interpretations."[133] Many Russian Christians experienced tongues in the 1800s;[134] Armenians particularly experienced an outpouring of prayer in tongues in 1880.[135] Independently, it also continued in the United States in this period. William James, a US philosopher often called the father of American psychology, reports an encounter in Boston in the early 1870s with one whose circle believed she was speaking in tongues.[136] Tongues occurred elsewhere in the late nineteenth-century United States, including a northern midwestern Methodist church, a Swedish Mission church, and in some interdenominational revivals.[137] It was even more common in the Holiness movement as early as 1875, though at that time it belonged to a range of emotional expressions of revivalism not yet emphasized in terms of its specific New Testament context.[138] It appeared in the 1890s in the early Fire-Baptized Holiness Church.[139] Reportedly more than a hundred people spoke in tongues during the 1896 Camp Creek Revival in North Carolina.[140] Holiness preacher Maria Woodworth-Etter insisted that tongues occurred in her meetings well before Azusa Street, and observers also recount it in African American churches before Azusa Street.[141]

Some observers reported tongues during the 1904–5 Welsh Revival,[142] though especially in the form of non-Welsh speakers preaching in fluent Welsh.[143] During

130. King, "Gifts," 95.

131. Billman, *Thread*, 161, citing Ryan, "Signs and Wonders," by a Salvationist officer in one of the movement's publications. The article highlights General Booth's affirmation of divine healing, which also characterized many Holiness circles at the time.

132. Billman, *Thread*, 158 (citing *The War Cry* [November 21, 1914]): "Specifically concerning tongues, healings and miracles, Booth wrote: 'There is not a word in the Bible which proves that we may not have them in the present time. . . . I long for them myself. I believe in their necessity, and I believe they are already among us. The poor infidel world would be made to see all of God that is possible, in order that it may believe.'"

133. Quoting John Christian Aroolappen (1810–67) in Aroolappen, *History*, reproduced in Burgess, *Peoples*, 212 (see 210–13).

134. Burgess, *Peoples*, 213–14, 218.

135. Kelsey, *Tongue Speaking*, 66.

136. Kelsey, *Tongue Speaking*, 60–61, citing William James in James, "Introduction," 277.

137. Kelsey, *Tongue Speaking*, 61.

138. Kelsey, *Tongue Speaking*, 69; Synan, *Tradition*, 52, 109 (noting 1881), 110–11 (noting documented examples from 1890, 1896, and 1899); Worthen, *Spellbound*, 179.

139. Oliver, *Reformations*, 211.

140. Synan, *Tradition*, 111. It is also known as the Shearer Schoolhouse Revival.

141. Worthen, *Spellbound*, 176.

142. Kelsey, *Tongue Speaking*, 65.

143. Cutten, *Speaking with Tongues*, 114, noting their prior inability to understand it, their English accent when preaching in Welsh, and suggesting (114–15) that they probably absorbed

the revival, one Dutch visitor allegedly even preached in English without having learned the language.[144] Tongues occurred among Methodists in India in 1905,[145] and are well documented at Pandita Ramabai's orphanage in India in 1906–7. An observer at India's Mukti Mission heard some girls who did not know English praying in English, plus other articulate, language-like prayers unintelligible to the observer.[146] They were also appearing elsewhere in India in 1906;[147] one missionary declared, "Young men and women are receiving the gifts of the Spirit, speaking with tongues, interpreting tongues previously unknown to them; the sick are being healed, and unclean spirits cast out in answer to prayer."[148]

Most of the above accounts are available only because they happened collectively or appear in someone's memoirs, so the latter should be taken as merely samples of a wider range of private experiences that no one recorded. In a Hebrew course I (Craig) took with Assemblies of God scholar Stanley Horton (1916–2014), he recounted that his maternal grandmother spoke in tongues in the 1800s. I would not want to depend very much on my memory of someone else's account I heard forty-five years ago, but happily I learned that Lois Olena also reported the story in her biography of Professor Horton. In the mid-1880s Clara Daisy Sanford Fisher (1866–1945) experienced an overwhelming sense of the Spirit "and suddenly began to speak in a language she had never learned." The other women present inquired about the language, but she did not know what it was. "She continued to pray in tongues when she was alone," but it was not until tongues became more widely known that she understood and talked openly about her experience.[149]

Unknown to me (Craig) in my youth, my Methodist aunt and grandmother had been praying for my family's conversion (in my case, from atheism). I did know that they would be thrilled to learn that I had met Christ and that I now appreciated rather than despised churches. Nevertheless, I worried that my grandmother, Beatrice Young Keener (1905–95), might be upset to discover that I prayed in tongues. Instead, when we could talk privately, she shared with me that she was instead delighted. She had never experienced

---

some unconsciously (cf. Synan, *Tradition*, 88n12). Less skeptically, see Synan, *Tradition*, 88, citing Vivier, "Glossolalia," 117, which drew on *The Yorkshire Post*, December 27, 1904; *West Africa* 9, no. 219 (February 25, 1905): 163.

144. Synan, *Tradition*, 88, citing Penn-Lewis, "Revival," 6–7. Joseph Smale's Baptist church in Los Angeles was also reporting visions and groanings before Azusa Street (King, "Gifts," 97).

145. Billman, *Thread*, 135, citing Oconer, "Methodism in Asia," 163.

146. Hyatt, *Years*, 154 (citing Frodsham, *Signs*, 107–8); Burgess, *Peoples*, 244; Billman, *Thread*, 133. A Western witness attributed claims of identifiable languages to Pandita Ramabai's own direct testimony (Ellis, "Tongues," cited in Cutten, *Speaking with Tongues*, 116). Ramabai herself was certainly sufficiently linguistically proficient to evaluate some of the languages in question.

147. Burgess, *Peoples*, 248, noting cases in Manmad in June and Bombay (Mumbai) in July.

148. Abrams, *Baptism*, 3–4, reproduced in Burgess, *Peoples*, 249.

149. Olena, *Horton*, 25.

the gift herself, but she said (presumably hyperbolically) that all the Baptists and Methodists prayed in tongues where she was growing up in Georgia. I later read the brief autobiography of her father, Jim Young (1880–1967), a Methodist deacon and Sunday school superintendent, where he recounted the date in 1912 on which he initially and unexpectedly experienced that gift.[150] These various examples all occurred outside the modern Pentecostal and charismatic movements.

One could of course multiply modern instances in tongues by the millions, but in the next chapter we will explore specifically only the less common cases in which someone present recognized the language spoken.

## Conclusion

Biblically and even historically, a case against tongues clearly fails. That tongues are an available biblical gift, however, does not automatically mean that all instances of tongues today are the biblical gift. While technically the genuineness of some people's belief that they exercise tongues differs from the biblical question of whether the gift should continue, its centrality in the argument of many cessationists merits it at least some discussion. To this subject we now turn.

150. "Autobiography of James Louis Young," unpublished paper in author's possession (written 1956), 4: "It was the last of October 1912," with a mule-drawn wagon in Lincoln County, Georgia, "when I was driving along the road, that God baptized me with the Holy Ghost according to Acts 2 and other places in the Bible." I later checked the itinerary of G. B. Cashwell in that area and discovered that he had preached the message of Azusa Street just upriver from where my great-grandfather lived.

# 17

# Tongues Recognized as Languages?

The interest of this book is more about whether the Bible leads us to expect spiritual gifts for today than about how often modern practices are genuine biblical gifts. If the Bible says we should welcome the full range of God's gifts to build one another up, then we should pursue such gifts even if others are not doing them properly. But as cessationism becomes increasingly less significant, the discernment question of what is real will become more and more prominent. For example, while various academic venues in the West invite me (Craig) to lecture about the possible reality of miracles, academic venues in Asia have invited me instead to lecture about how to distinguish divine from demonic activity. Important as the question is, that would require a separate book. That discussion will be vital for continuationists in the rising generation of the global church.

Nevertheless, at some points the cessationist critique depends so heavily on an alleged contrast between a biblical gift and the modern one that some discussion of the latter is necessary. That is the case in a key cessationist critique of tongues, which we must explore briefly here. Some of that argument turns on linguistics, but as neither the critics nor the two of us respondents are trained linguists, we will not explore that question in full, linguistic detail. We can, however, offer some observations.

## Biblical Tongues as Existing Languages?

Despite their different emphases, Luke and Paul surely describe the same phenomenon of speaking "languages."[1] The Greek term *glōssa* normally

1. So also most patristic commentators (Kovacs, *1 Corinthians*, 229n1). For charts listing the parallels and distinguishing the emphases, see Keener, *Acts*, 1:814–15.

*means* "language," and it makes little sense that Luke and Paul would coin the expression for completely unrelated experiences.[2]

Cessationists often insist that modern charismatic expressions of the Spirit's gifts do not line up with Scripture. Tom Pennington says, "If the Spirit were still gifting believers today with the miraculous gifts, they would be the same gifts that we find in the New Testament. However, the Charismatic gifts claimed today bear almost no resemblance to their New Testament counterparts." As an example, he points to the modern practice of tongues.[3] Likewise, John MacArthur contends that "biblical tongues are not gibberish," as he considers modern tongues to be, "but languages."[4]

To what extent, and how often, should Spirit-led tongues be real human languages? And, given the vast multitude of human languages (cf. 1 Cor. 14:10), how often, when they are real human languages, should we expect someone present to happen to recognize the language?

### Tongues in Acts 2 as Real Languages

Nearly everyone today recognizes that Luke views the tongues spoken in Acts 2 as real languages.[5] But scholars debate whether this was the case for all New Testament instances of speaking in tongues. Cessationists often regard Acts 2 as the template for all other cases of tongues. It is "the first and pivotal reference,"[6] and thus tongues are always "the miraculous ability to speak a foreign language not learned by normal human methods."[7]

Cessationists make Pentecost's tongues paradigmatic for other New Testament tongues even though elsewhere cessationists emphasize the uniqueness of Pentecost as a "once for all" event. They say it is not intended as a repeatable paradigm.[8] There is some truth in both approaches, but neither is decisive for the question at hand. While Pentecost's unique historical role at the beginning does not preclude it from being a template in other respects, neither does it guarantee which aspects are normative. The wind? The fire? At Pentecost, it made sense for God to give languages people would understand, since there were people present whose understanding and consequent amazement would facilitate Peter's message of salvation. That is not the case in *any* of the other biblical instances of tongues.

2. With Dunn, *Jesus and Spirit*, 151, 243; Forbes, *Prophecy*, 50, 56–72; Gundry, "Ecstatic Utterance?"; Cartledge, "Glossolalia."
3. Pennington, "Case."
4. MacArthur, *Chaos*, 227.
5. But against the rare view that he didn't, see appendix 2.
6. Waldron, *Continued*, 84.
7. Pennington, "Case"; Pennington, *Cessationism*, 96.
8. Gaffin, *Perspectives*, 22.

The human languages spoken on the day of Pentecost did serve a special redemptive historical purpose. Among other purposes, they were, we believe, prophetic signs of the evangelistic and missional significance of that outpouring. Those international languages were signs that pointed to the nations. The miraculous but intelligible languages announced a new era in which not only Israel but "whoever shall call upon the name of the Lord shall be saved" (Acts 2:21; Rom. 10:12–13). Jewish people, miraculously worshiping in languages from outside their land, began to fulfill their mandate to be a "light to the nations" (Isa. 42:6; cf. Acts 13:47). This experience thus foreshadowed the fulfillment of the commencement of the Great Commission (Acts 1:8). The day of Pentecost was in some respects unique, and the outpouring of the Holy Spirit never happened exactly that way again in the New Testament.

A template does not mean that every aspect was identical; certainly in Acts 10 and 19, in contrast to Acts 2, we have no mention of hearers present who recognize the languages. The template allows for significant variations in how a sovereign God expresses his power, but it nevertheless remains a template in various ways for subsequent collective outpourings of the Spirit. For example, disciples are filled with the Spirit after prayer in Acts 4:31, with some of the same effects as at Pentecost two chapters earlier: external signs (here an earthquake instead of wind and fire), Spirit-led speech (here bold proclamation rather than tongues), sharing possessions (2:44–45; 4:32, 34–35), and apostolic witness with power (2:43; 4:33). In a broader sense, it serves as a template for the Spirit in the lives of subsequent Christians as well (Acts 9:17; Rom. 8:23, noting "first fruits," which relates to the festival of Pentecost; Spirit-filled praise in Eph. 5:18–19).

### Biblical Tongues as Human Languages

Thomas Schreiner makes a good case for the position that tongues are real human languages,[9] which independently corresponds to some arguments in my (Craig's) commentary on Acts 2.[10] Schreiner argues that in neither Acts nor 1 Corinthians are tongues ecstatic speech "with no discernible code or linguistic pattern."[11] The point is rarely disputed in Acts 2, and he points out that Acts 10:46–47 is clear that tongues is the same gift: "They heard them speaking in tongues. . . . They received the Holy Spirit in the same way we did." "The Spirit fell on them just as he did on us at the beginning" (11:15).

Peter and Luke use the tongues link to confirm that Cornelius's household received the Spirit rather than to confirm the precise nature of the tongues (i.e., it need not be all the languages represented in 2:9–11). Nevertheless, I

9. Schreiner, *Spiritual Gifts*, 123–32.
10. Keener, *Acts*, 1:819–23; Keener, *Acts* (Cambridge), 125–29.
11. Schreiner, *Spiritual Gifts*, 123.

agree that we should normally take it to be a linguistic or at least communicative phenomenon barring evidence to the contrary. Yet tongues ultimately represent simply languages unknown to the speaker (1 Cor. 14:2, 14–15), not languages that must be recognized by others present. The less multilinguistic settings after Pentecost lack hearers who recognize the languages. There are subsequent occasions in history of recognizing the languages involved.[12] That tongues confirms reception of the Spirit in this case is explicit (Acts 10:45–47), but God did not duplicate every aspect of the original event (such as fire or wind, 2:2–3). When I (Daniel) preach in Africa, the Holy Spirit falls in Nigeria "the same way" he does in Ghana. That doesn't mean they are identical occurrences in every detail.

More importantly, Schreiner emphasizes that the very term "tongue (*glōssa*) points to a language, to some kind of code."[13] The Greek language has other ways to speak of inarticulate speech, such as the term *barbaroō*. Greeks in fact originally called foreigners "barbarians" because their speech sounded inarticulate to Greeks, although these foreign languages were real languages.[14] In 1 Corinthians, those who do not understand the tongues experience them as barbarian speech (Greek *barbaros*, 1 Cor. 14:11).

Schreiner notes that the angelic tongues of 1 Corinthians 13:1 may be just hyperbolic.[15] While scholars divide sharply on this issue,[16] I (Craig) am on record as supporting the hyperbole interpretation.[17] Still, the hyperbole makes sense only because Paul does not limit tongues to human languages; they are languages in the sense of being communication to God. God can even create new linguistic structures or communication through affectively loaded syllables or through sign language if he wishes.[18] Paul allows for different "*kinds* of tongues" (1 Cor. 12:10, 28),[19] though this expression probably refers especially to the diversity of languages (14:10).[20]

12. See esp. May, *Witnesses to Pentecost*; discussion below.

13. Schreiner, *Spiritual Gifts*, 126. See also Keener, *Acts* (Cambridge), 125–29.

14. See, e.g., Plato, *Crat.* 409DE; Sextus Empiricus, *Pyr.* 3.267; Philo, *Conf.* 6, 190; Quintilian, *Inst.* 1.5.5–33; Plutarch, *Educ.* 6; *Mor.* 4A; Maximus of Tyre, *Or.* 8.8.

15. Schreiner, *Spiritual Gifts*, 127.

16. Some interpret "tongues of angels" literally, whether from Paul's or the Corinthians' perspective (e.g., Fee, *Corinthians*, 598; Witherington, *Acts*, 135).

17. Keener, *Corinthians*, 108; so also Horsley, *Corinthians*, 176.

18. Lest one suppose that God is limited to vocal languages, in an account from the 1940s Aimee Ada Coryell preached for two hours in sign language, which she had never learned (Grenholm, *Dokumenterade Språkmirakler*, 70–71).

19. Thiselton, *Spirit*, 114. Note various "kinds" of spirits (Mark 9:29), and, without using *genos*, various kinds (heavenly and earthly) of bodies (1 Cor. 15:39–41). Heavenly (ambrosial) food (manna) was special in kind (Wis. 19:21).

20. Fitting the world's many peoples (cf. the use of the same term *genos* in 2 Cor. 11:26; Gal. 1:14; Phil. 3:5).

### *Not Languages in 1 Corinthians?*

In my (Craig's) view, church fathers who saw tongues as real languages for evangelism, as did the earliest year or two of Pentecostals, rightly understood Luke's theological emphasis: Tongues point to cross-cultural mission.[21] But they misunderstood the *practice* of tongues elsewhere in both Acts and 1 Corinthians. Nowhere in Acts 10:46; 19:6; or 1 Corinthians 12–14 are tongues used to preach the gospel, and probably also not in Acts 2, where Peter must preach the gospel in Greek.

The earliest Irvingites believed tongues to be foreign languages but soon shifted toward understanding them as a distinct spiritual phenomenon;[22] this was also the pattern of early Pentecostalism. The first Pentecostals belonged to a wider movement of people praying for "missionary tongues" to help them evangelize the world.[23] Following this expectation, many of Pentecostalism's early exponents understood tongues as a form of missionary xenoglossia.[24] Apart from Charles Parham,[25] most early Pentecostals fairly quickly abandoned the "missionary tongues" view after it failed the empirical test.[26] Many (perhaps most) Pentecostals today do understand them as real languages,[27] but not, like the earliest Pentecostals, as a means of preaching cross-culturally without prior linguistic training.

Nevertheless, those who mock the first Pentecostals for having to learn about their gift should not question their Spirit-empowered zeal for missions: Indeed, there are now far more charismatic and Pentecostal missionaries in

21. For this understanding of Acts 2:4, see Keener, "Tongues"; Keener, *Acts*, 1:828–31; Miller, *Tongues*. William Seymour viewed tongues speech "as an ecumenical and international sign of freedom and unity," "as a *crossing of boundaries*" (Thiselton, *Spirit*, 331).

22. Cutten, *Speaking with Tongues*, 103–5; Hunter, *Spirit Baptism*, 176.

23. E.g., Anderson, *Pentecostalism*, 33–34; McGee, *Miracles*, 61–76; and some sources in our following note on early Pentecostal views of xenoglossia. This was also the view of early Moravians (Burgess, "Evidence," 32).

24. See McGee, "Hermeneutics," 102; McGee, "Strategy," 52–53; Goff, "Theology," 64–65; Jacobsen, *Thinking in Spirit*, 25, 49–50, 74, 76, 97; Robeck, *Mission*, 41–42, 236–37, 243, 252; see especially McGee, "Shortcut"; McGee, "Logic"; Anderson, "Signs," 195–99. Before Pentecostalism, some evangelical missions advocates like A. B. Simpson, the early Christian & Missionary Alliance, and three members of the famous "Cambridge Seven" sought missionary tongues, apparently usually unsuccessfully (McGee, "Radical Strategy," 77–78, 80–83).

25. Anderson, *Pentecostalism*, 190.

26. E.g., Wacker, *Heaven*, 47–51; McGee, *People of Spirit*, 77–78; Hudson, "Strange Words," 61–63; Anderson, "Points," 167; Goff, "Theology," 69; Ma, "Eschatology," 100 (noting Goff, *Fields*, 16). Note especially the shift in the Indian mission context, after which Garr emphasized that the point was not tongues themselves but how they symbolized baptism in the Spirit (McGee, "Calcutta Revival," 138–39). The xenolalia interpretation "was already waning by 1906," shortly after the movement's beginning (McGee, "Strategies," 204).

27. Hollenweger, *Pentecostals*, 342.

the world, and with far more disciples to show for their efforts, than all cessationist denominations combined.[28]

#### ARGUING FOR METALINGUISTIC TONGUES

"Open but cautious" scholar Robert Saucy is more skeptical that tongues in 1 Corinthians are human languages. He cites several factors against this:

1. "They require the equally supernatural gift of interpretation for their understanding."
2. "In cosmopolitan cities such as Corinth there were undoubtedly many languages present, but" Paul does not entertain "the possibility of someone present who could understand the language naturally."
3. "Paul uses foreign 'languages' (a different word than used for 'tongues') as an analogy for tongues (1 Cor. 14:10–13). Something is not usually identical to that with which it is said to be analogous (cf. the other analogies used in vv. 7–9)."
4. "Mark's use of the word 'new' (*kainos*) in Mark 16:17 to describe tongues, a term that is commonly used to refer to the 'wholly different and miraculous' things that belong to the new age, also suggests that tongues are not simply other human languages."

Saucy even argues for something "more than human languages" in Acts 2, citing various scholars.[29]

Robert Graves suggests that tongues must transcend earthly languages. "If my native language (English) is not capable of conveying my heart's praise or petition, then how could it achieve that by a non-English speaker in a xenolalic utterance? In other words, if Spanish is insufficient for the Hispanic, how could it suffice for the German as an utterance in tongues? If the S/spirit is limited by one's learned language, how would speaking in someone else's learned language accomplish more?"[30] British scholar Mark Cartledge suggests that tongues "transcends" natural language, functioning as "a language of the spirit rather than of the mind."[31] While some consider it pseudolinguistic, others respond that it is genuinely linguistic in that it functions communicatively.[32] Some Pentecostal theologians also define tongues

28. Kolenda, "Embarrassing Story."

29. Saucy, "View," 131–32n57. He notes, e.g., Behm, "καινός," 449; Montague, *Holy Spirit*; Kling, "Corinthians"; Moody, *Spirit of God*; Kuyper, *Work of Spirit*.

30. Graves, *Praying in the Spirit*, 58. See further Graves, "Nature," 108–16.

31. Cartledge, *Charismatic Glossolalia*, 135, as quoted in Laurito, *Speaking in Tongues*, 76.

32. Laurito, *Speaking in Tongues*, 79, in light of James K. A. Smith's appropriation of speech-act theory (in Smith, "Resistance Discourse," 83).

as "pneumatic speech" with intelligible (perhaps affective) content but not human languages.[33]

Ben Witherington argues against a human language partly on the basis of 1 Corinthians 14:2: "For one who speaks in a tongue isn't speaking to people but rather is speaking to God. For nobody understands what the speaker is saying, since the person speaks mysteries by the Spirit." He views this as "a clear indication that glossolalia was seen as a prayer language or as a way to talk to God, not as a human language. Paul calls it the Spirit speaking mysteries. Here *mystēria* surely means 'unknown or secret things,' probably, that is, what is unintelligible."[34] Even the speaker does not understand (14:14), so Paul commends praying both with our spirit (in tongues) and with our understanding.

### COMMUNICATION, WHETHER LINGUISTIC OR METALINGUISTIC

Schreiner concedes the strength of an argument from 1 Corinthians 14:2.[35] But he notes that this does not mean they are not real languages. There were people present on the day of Pentecost who recognized the languages spoken, but even if no one is present to recognize a language, that does not make it any less a language.[36] Here I (Craig) would agree—and I would just want to add that this may be also the main reason why a tongue is usually unintelligible today without an interpretation. The denial that any tongues speech today is linguistic depends entirely on linguistic studies of various groups of tongues speakers generalized to all tongues speech.

A couple responses are possible, depending on whether we view tongues as a transcendental form of communication or actual languages. When we read Paul on his own terms, in context, we come to the conclusion that "tongues" refers to unknown languages that "*no one*" understands (14:2). Here are some questions I (Daniel) ask of Paul's instructions that illustrate my point:

- Does it make any sense to say that "anyone who speaks in a [foreign language] does not speak to people but to God"?
- Does it make any sense to say that, when people speak in a human foreign language, "no one understands them"? Paul's statement in fact contrasts with the understanding in Acts 2:8.

33. Williams, *Renewal Theology*, 2:215–16, 221–22. Cf. Anglican thinker C. S. Lewis, who is cited as affirming that the phenomenon could be babbling but useful when energized by the Spirit (*Transposition*, 9–19).

34. Witherington, *Conflict*, 281. Witherington himself prays in tongues (see Witherington, *2 Corinthians*, 123–24).

35. Schreiner, *Spiritual Gifts*, 127.

36. Schreiner, *Spiritual Gifts*, 128.

Two additional arguments are weaker, since the abundance of earthly languages makes routine recognition less likely, but they are sometimes mentioned:

- Why would Paul say that, if unbelievers or outsiders hear the Corinthians speaking in tongues, they would say the Corinthians are out of their minds? What if someone from cosmopolitan Corinth ventured in who might recognize the language? They might have seen them instead as "highly educated."[37]
- Further, would a gift of supernatural interpretation be necessary if tongues are just foreign languages? If both tongues and interpretation of tongues are spiritual gifts, it makes sense that tongues could be a spiritual language.

Some Pentecostal theologians also define "tongues" as "pneumatic speech" with intelligible (perhaps affective) content but not human languages.[38] Various linguistic studies of glossolalic speech suggest that it functions as "free vocalisation" that, on the one hand, comes short "of the complex suprasegmental sound-patterning associated with natural language," yet, on the other, proves more phonologically structured than what occurs "in comparable phenomena like baby talk and schizophrenese."[39] Clusters of sounds resemble the sorts of words and groups of words known in other languages, but they are not coherent enough at a semantic level for full language.[40] This may suggest a nonpropositional communication by the speaker heavily dependent on formulaic implicatures.[41]

37. Storms, *Guide*, 182.

38. Williams, *Renewal Theology*, 2:215–16, 221–22.

39. Hilborn, "Glossolalia," 111.

40. Hilborn, "Glossolalia," 112; Wacker, *Heaven*, 52. Hilborn, "Glossolalia," 112–13n6, notes one study where a speaker's structures belonged not to a language the speaker knew but to some other known languages.

41. Hilborn, "Glossolalia," 114, 128–29; for "decoding," cf. 131. In pragmatic linguistics, "implicatures" involve what a speaker implies beyond the literal sense of words, due to context or other factors. If the speech is to God, as in 1 Cor. 14:2 (Hilborn, "Glossolalia," 113), partial implicatures could symbolize a larger communication. Hilborn, "Glossolalia," 132–45, goes beyond the code model of language to relevance theory's contention that evidence of speaker intention is paramount (cf. also the summary in Cartledge, "Tongues-Speech," 217–18). Hilborn seems to lay more emphasis on the act than the phonological content, and I am not convinced that this is quite right; the sounds might communicate through inference the way musical rhythm, keys, and so forth can communicate in some (neurophysiological) ways cross-culturally but in most ways within the framework of particular cultural expectations (not necessarily the speaker's own). Malina and Pilch, *Acts*, 28, follow Goodman and emphasize tongues "not as language but as communication" (see also Malina and Pilch, *Letters*, 119–20).

On my (Craig's) view, biblical tongues are languages, at least in the sense of being linguistically communicative. Yet granted that God gave languages on the day of Pentecost that people present could recognize, he clearly does *not* give tongues that anyone recognizes in any of the other cases in the New Testament. Given the number of languages in the world (cf. 1 Cor. 14:10: "many kinds of languages in the world"), that is not surprising; nor need it be a language that *anyone* speaks for it to be a sort of language that is a genuine communication intelligible to God.[42] They are noncognitive, affective expressions that communicate our heart to God.

### Not All Tongues Are Necessarily Tongues[43]

That some cases of tongues are not the genuine biblical experience, of course, would not indict all other cases, especially when many of the challenged cases predominate in heterodox or syncretistic groups.

In contrast to some other charismatics, we believe that biblical "tongues" are normally languages (of at least some sort) unknown to the speaker. Nevertheless, we recognize various possible caveats:

- We do find plausible D. A. Carson's case that they may usually be further encoded (more on this below).
- We also recognize that God can provide some form of languages that allow communication with him even if no one has ever spoken them naturally.
- New Testament "language" could include communication lacking fuller linguistic features.
- Further, we do not deny that God could work through something on a lesser level than the biblical gift.
- Nor would we suggest that charismatics should supervise one another to make sure the words *sound* like a genuine language; we have heard real foreign languages that sounded like gibberish from our own linguistic limitations. (Indeed, others mocked one student's "tongue" until a visiting missionary recognized its "clicks" as a southern African language.)[44]
- We also have to allow those who are young in a gift to mature in their use of it, as with prophecy or teaching or any other gift.

The speaker's focus should be on sincerely praying with his or her spirit to God, depending solely on the Holy Spirit to make sure the words come out right for this purpose.

42. See Kolenda, "Tongues."
43. The following is mostly from Keener, *Gift & Giver*, 124–25.
44. May, *Witnesses to Pentecost*, 123–24.

Nevertheless, one early Pentecostal leader did warn that when the focus shifted more toward tongues utterance itself than to worshiping God, tongues "did not sound right."[45] Some tongues speakers do seem to perform their "gift" out of habit or rote rather than by cultivating sensitivity to the Spirit. When one hears a particular phrase repeated ten times (especially if followed by a much more lucid "interpretation") one is often tempted to be skeptical at least concerning the fluency of the "tongue." Accepting the reality of the genuine gift does not require us to accept as genuine all purported manifestations of the gift. Jonathan Edwards warned of spiritual counterfeits during genuine times of revival, and William Seymour argued that one who focused on signs more than on God and his holiness would get a counterfeit. We intend this observation to motivate us to a deeper sensitivity to the Spirit rather than leading sincere but insecure seekers to doubt the reality of their spiritual experience. (Meanwhile, prayers in English are not always particularly articulate either. "Help!" can be a real prayer!) As prophecies of even accepted church prophets had to be tested, as teachers may mature in their gift, as we "know in part and prophesy in part," tongues-prayers presumably may grow more fluent and Spirit-led as well. I (Craig) recognize that I articulate my own prayers in tongues more fluently and sensitively to the Spirit at some times than others.

Thirty-five years ago, when I (Craig) was experiencing the deepest crisis I had ever faced since my conversion, a family took me to a charismatic church. During prayer someone came up to my seat unsolicited and started praying for me. He was making a buzzing sound like a bee, which I supposed he thought was tongues. I did not want him to pray for me; I wanted him to go away and allow me to pray by myself undisturbed! Perhaps noting my perplexity, he explained, "I felt that the Lord showed me you were going through something and I should come and pray for you." I allowed him to pray but was so annoyed by his buzzing that I did not tell him I was in fact facing a crisis. Afterward I complained to one of the people who brought me that the buzzing was certainly not tongues. "He has a bee anointing," she explained. Then I was even more annoyed! I did not and do not believe he was praying in biblical tongues. Yet the man had enough sensitivity to the Spirit and concern for a brother to pray for me. While I am sure he didn't have a "bee anointing," I also think it likely that he was my brother in Christ, probably doing the best he knew to follow the Spirit's leading.

### *Groaning and Jubilating*

Many scholars believe that Paul refers to tongues in Romans 8:26.[46] I believe that "groaning" refers to an even deeper prayer, one too deep for us to articulate in words, in *any* language. When the struggle of still living in the present age is

45. John G. Lake, cited in Hyatt, *Years*, 185.
46. I borrow this paragraph from Keener, *Suffering*, 200–201.

too painful for us to even know how to pray about it, the Spirit intercedes for us with "inarticulate groanings" (Rom. 8:26). We groan (8:23) along with creation (8:22) and the Spirit (8:26) in birth pangs for the coming world.[47] Possibly some of the less articulate tongues today might be more like the experience in Romans 8:26 (what some have called "protoglossolalia")[48] than full-fledged tongues.

Augustine speaks of worshiping the ineffable God with songs and "groaning with groaning unutterable."[49] He spoke of a wordless celebration that some interpreters compare with tongues; perhaps it is more like a positive counterpart to groaning (Rom. 8:26). "What is jubilation, but admiration of joy which cannot be expressed in words?"[50] "Into the voice of rejoicings break forth if ye cannot into that of words. For 'jubilation' is not of words, but the sound alone of men rejoicing is uttered, as of a heart labouring and bringing forth into voice the pleasure of a thing imagined which cannot be expressed."[51] "Whatsoever ye cannot explain in words, ye do not therefore forbear exulting: what ye shall be able to explain, cry out: what ye cannot, jubilate."[52] "One who jubilates, uttereth not words, but it is a certain sound of joy without words: for it is the expression of a mind poured forth in joy, expressing, as far as it is able, the affection, but not compassing the feeling. A man rejoicing in his own exultation, after certain words which cannot be uttered or understood, bursteth forth into sounds of exultation without words, so that it seemeth that he indeed doth rejoice with his voice itself, but as if filled with excessive joy cannot express in words the subject of that joy." He compares the exuberance of harvesters, who "among the songs which they utter in words, they put in certain cries without words in the exultation of a rejoicing mind; and this is what is meant by jubilating."[53]

Augustine believed that tongues referred to evangelizing in others' languages, and he was unfamiliar with that phenomenon in his day. But he was quite familiar with the overflow of a heart too full of God's Spirit for his human words to contain.

## Modern Tongues Are Not Languages?

MacArthur complains that "what passes for tongues in the Pentecostal and charismatic movements . . . are not true languages."[54] Many others

47. Tongues similarly may express longing for the future (see Fee, *Listening*, 117). Cf. tongues' connection in the late 1800s with eschatological anticipation (Faupel, "Speaking in Tongues").
48. King, "Gifts," 95–97.
49. Augustine, *Conf.* 12.16.23.
50. Augustine, *Ennar. Ps.* 47.6 (*NPNF*¹, 8:162).
51. Augustine, *Ennar. Ps.* 66.2 (*NPNF*¹, 8:274).
52. Augustine, *Ennar. Ps.* 81.3 (*NPNF*¹, 8:391).
53. Augustine, *Ennar. Ps.* 100.4 (*NPNF*¹, 8:488).
54. MacArthur, *Chaos*, 227; cf. likewise MacArthur, *Strange Fire*, 134–35.

agree.[55] Many writers who argue that modern tongues are not real languages appeal to the wide-ranging study of William Samarin.[56] MacArthur quotes Samarin at length, noting that all studied glossolalia consists of "*strings of syllables, made up of sounds taken from among all those that the speaker knows, put together more or less haphazardly but which nevertheless emerge as word-like and sentence-like units because of realistic, language-like rhythm and melody*. . . . Yet in spite of superficial similarities, glossolalia is fundamentally *not* language."[57]

### *More Realistic Expectations?*

We have heard plenty of tongues that do not sound like language, but we have heard conversations in genuine languages that sound no different to us. Admittedly, we are not linguists, so we must attend to Samarin's conclusions with academic respect.

Even in vernacular prayer, however, one notably encounters predominantly vocative forms and titles, often repetitive and formulaic expressions, and often very limited vocabulary. It can be repetitive in a way that conversations or debates are not. Many offer prayers such as, "Thank you, Jesus! Thank you, Lord! I just praise you, Jesus!"[58] How much more when no one expects one's prayers to be articulate? Would this sound like what others consider linguistic communication? Indeed, Paul's citation of Isaiah 28:11's unintelligible speech in 1 Corinthians 14:21 may evoke its context (including the short repetitive syllables of Isa. 28:13), which may suggest very simple speech. Moreover, in terms of many tongues speakers pronouncing sounds only native to their language, one might expect more precise articulation only in a higher level of fluency in tongues. (I here assume our argument from chap. 15 that we may grow in praying in tongues just as we may grow in gifts of teaching or administration.) Nonfluent speakers of languages not their own will differ significantly in accents and other pronunciation from native language speakers; that is why my (Craig's) Francophone wife laughs when I speak French.

The brain's frontal lobes, the brain's control center, and its linguistic center show decreased activity during tongues-speaking, suggesting that this is not the part of the brain generating tongues. Andrew Newburg, MD, concludes,

55. E.g., Schreiner, *Spiritual Gifts*, 126, 130.

56. Samarin, *Tongues*, xii, 227; expanded in 103–28. Samarin's study included snake handlers but also those who would be considered more orthodox.

57. MacArthur, *Strange Fire*, 134, citing Samarin, *Tongues*, 127–28.

58. Note the basic structure of the glossolalic prayer that emerged in English among non-English speakers at Mukti Mission in India: "O Lord, open the mouth; O Lord, open the mouth; O Lord, open the heart; O Lord, open the heart" (Hyatt, *Years*, 154, quoting Frodsham, *Signs*, 107–8). For tongues as more like repetitive, liturgical forms than conversational speech patterns, see Johnston, "Speaking in Tongues," 777.

"Our brain imaging research shows us that these subjects are not in control of the usual language centers during this activity, which is consistent with their description of a lack of intentional control while speaking in tongues."[59]

### *Encoded Communication*

Carson, building on the work of Vern Poythress, suggests a category for modern tongues that differs from both noncommunicative sounds and recognized languages.[60] This is coded language. He offers an example of his point:

> Suppose the message is: "Praise the Lord, for his mercy endures forever." Remove the vowels to achieve: PRS TH LRD FR HS MRC NDRS FRVR. This may seem a bit strange; but when we remember that modern Hebrew is written without most vowels, we can imagine that with practice this could be read quite smoothly. Now remove the spaces and, beginning with the first letter, rewrite the sequence using every third letter, repeatedly going through the sequence until all the letters are used up. The result is: PTRRMNSVRHDHRDFRSLF-SCRR. Now add an "a" sound after each consonant, and break up the unit into arbitrary bits: PATARA RAMA NA SAVARAHA DAHARA DAFARASALA FASA CARARA. I think that is indistinguishable from transcriptions of certain modern tongues. Certainly it is very similar to some I have heard. But the important point is that it conveys information provided you know the code. Anyone who knows the steps I have taken could reverse them in order to retrieve the original message.[61]

On this approach, "tongues may bear cognitive information even though they are not known human languages—just as a computer program is a 'language' that conveys a great deal of information, even though it is not a 'language' that anyone actually speaks."[62] Indeed, since God knows the mind of the Spirit that produces the prayer, the code could exist on an entirely different level than we might expect, also incorporating nonlinguistic affective cues.

Thus, pace many cessationists, "the alternative is not as simple as 'human languages' or 'gibberish.' . . . The fact that Paul can speak of different kinds of tongues (12:10, 28) may suggest that on some occasions human languages were spoken (as in Acts 2), and in other cases not—even though in the latter eventuality the tongues were viewed as bearing cognitive content."[63]

59. "Language Center."

60. Carson, *Showing Spirit*, 84–87, drawing on Poythress, "Nature of Glossolalia," 131; Poythress, "Analyses," 369, 375. He also notes "the cautious essay" of Sullivan, "Speaking in Tongues."

61. Carson, *Showing Spirit*, 85–86. Many observers note that the "word" units in most utterances in tongues each end in vowels. I do not find this to be the norm with my own prayers in tongues or those of some others I know.

62. Carson, *Showing Spirit*, 86.

63. Carson, *Showing Spirit*, 86–87.

MacArthur critiques Carson's suggestion by complaining that, "while such a suggestion is innovative, it has no exegetical basis."[64] This is a remarkable complaint coming from an advocate of cessationism, which itself, as we have repeatedly observed, lacks any "exegetical basis." Carson's suggestion at least attempts to wrestle with how the gift of tongues *might* function, and it accounts both linguistically and theologically for both ancient and modern evidence. Nowhere does the New Testament describe the mechanics of tongues or what qualifies as genuine tongues, so here, as in cases like the Spirit bearing witness with our spirit that we are God's children, exegetical information is limited and may be helpfully informed by spiritual experience.

Continuationists tend to side with Carson here. For Sam Storms, tongues is normally not a language like German, yet it is "linguistic," communicating real information. What is important is that "God understands, that the 'coded' speech of the believer contains meaningful, substantive truths that are known to God."[65] He cites also prolific New Testament scholar David Garland: "Paul understands [tongues] to be a language inspired by the Spirit and not a noncognitive, nonlanguage utterance. . . . Tongues consist of words . . . , which, though indecipherable, are not meaningless syllables strung together."[66]

Likewise, New Testament scholar Max Turner notes that "even the more hostile analyses admit that 'tongues speech' conveys meaning in its prosodic contour (metre, stress, intonation, etc.) and one can distinguish pleading, grieving, thanking, praising 'tongues speech.'"[67] Suggesting the Spirit's work with the human subconscious (Paul's "my spirit"), he follows C. S. Lewis's application to tongues of a fuller system communicated through more limited symbols (like a perceiver recognizing a three-dimensional reality in a two-dimensional depiction).[68]

## Real Languages

Cessationists often insist that biblical tongues were human languages because they see it as a fatal flaw in the case for continuationism. Their rationale goes something like this:

1. All biblical tongues were human languages.
2. No tongues today are human languages.
3. Therefore, no tongues today are biblical.

64. MacArthur, *Strange Fire*, 235–36, quotation from 236.
65. Storms, *Language*, 72.
66. Garland, *1 Corinthians*, 584.
67. Turner, *Gifts*, 309–10.
68. Turner, *Gifts*, 310, noting Lewis, *Transposition*, 9–20. Considering Paul's treatment of "secrets of the heart" (1 Cor. 14:25; cf. 2:11; 4:5) in terms of the subconscious, Thiselton, *Spirit*, 120, 388, cites Theissen, *Aspects*.

This rationale is, however, open to challenge in both its premises. First, out of more than twenty references to tongues in Scripture, only one instance connects them explicitly with unlearned human languages. Most others are silent on the issue or in some cases could even support the thesis that a tongue is potentially an unknown or heavenly language. Certainly they are unknown to the speaker and (in the vast majority of instances) to the hearers.

Second, although many do not believe that the modern gift of tongues comes in human languages, this phenomenon does indeed surface from time to time, although some cessationists boldly claim otherwise. Various Christians have testified to this miracle throughout history and in the modern era.

### Genuine "Missionary Tongues"

Cessationists deny that when modern charismatics speak in tongues, they speak in actual, unlearned foreign languages. But that is not necessarily true in every case. Credible testimonies abound of Christians who have spoken in unlearned languages known to some who were present. Given the vast number of possible languages, recognizing one would be rare, just as it was rare in the first-century church (unattested in the New Testament outside Acts 2). But in contrast to what our cessationist friends suggest, there are cases.

Augustine believed that God gave the earliest church xenolalia to reach the nations, but now that the church spoke all languages, the individual gift was superfluous; it was now manifested collectively in the church's worship.[69] But did the church already speak *all* languages?

Meanwhile, Pachomius, a renowned fourth-century Egyptian monk, "was widely reputed to have spoken miraculously in Greek and Latin though he had never learned these languages."[70] God reportedly miraculously enabled Ephrem the Syrian, who spoke only Syriac, to communicate with Basil the Great in Greek and with the Egyptian bishop Abba Bishoy.[71] In more recent times, an African American preacher in the 1700s cried out in Cherokee, a language unknown to him, bringing his release from Cherokee captors.[72]

Missionary accounts from the late Middle Ages also recount occasions of preaching to local peoples in their languages unlearned by the speakers.[73] Reports exist of some missionaries who preached in or understood languages they had not learned, or who were heard in local languages they

69. Blosser and Sullivan, *Speaking in Tongues*, 105–8, 117. Note also Cyril of Alexandria, Thomas Aquinas, and Thomas Cajetan (Blosser and Sullivan, *Speaking in Tongues*, 117). For tongues and global evangelism, see also Theodoret of Cyrrhus, *Comm. Rom.*, on Rom. 1:15.

70. Cutten, *Speaking with Tongues*, 38, 41; Oliver, *Movements*, 124; Blosser and Sullivan, *Speaking in Tongues*, 117.

71. Blosser and Sullivan, *Speaking in Tongues*, 167.

72. Marrant, *Narrative*, cited in Oliver, *Reformations*, 141.

73. Hyatt, *Years*, 61.

were not speaking: for example, Saint Vincent Ferrier (ca. 1350) and early sixteenth-century missionaries Saint Louis Bertrand and Saint Francis Xavier.[74] Francis Xavier reportedly acquired some languages miraculously (though having to study others) for the purpose of mission.[75] Some Jansenists reportedly spoke "Arabic and other languages they had never learnt."[76] Some reports of missionary tongues also circulated in late nineteenth-century evangelical missions.[77]

Some sources today likewise report this phenomenon on occasion. Nenilava, who led a major twentieth-century revival in the Lutheran Church of Madagascar, believed that Jesus himself taught her French and the other languages she would need to communicate beyond her own mother tongue.[78]

Asbury Old Testament PhD student Shiby Thomas, from Kerala, a Malayalam-speaking state in South India, explained his own experience to Craig. Even though he had studied some Hindi in school from ages twelve to eighteen, it was not at a level that allowed him to speak or understand it. He had not used it for eight years when God sent him to a state that used a special form of Hindi. From his second week there, however, he received a special ability to preach in Hindi.[79]

More dramatically, my friend Micael Grenholm, of Sweden, followed up another case. After praying extensively for Albania when it was a closed country, Rickard Lundgren wanted to reach Albanians. He had never studied their language, but when visiting he awoke and suddenly had a name for everything he looked at. He was now speaking such flawless northern Albanian that everyone assumed that he was from there. He retained that gift permanently, and many witnesses continue to attest his perfect Albanian, which he has used for the gospel.[80]

In a different twist on language miracles (a hearing miracle), Jonas Andersson was preaching in Benin in 2005 with interpreters in French and Bariba. People responded to various verbal cues, showing their attentiveness, and about half streamed forward to accept Christ. After he finished leading them to Christ, however, no one could understand him, and the ministry team soon discovered that most of those present knew neither French nor Bariba, but only

74. Cutten, *Speaking with Tongues*, 39, 42–46 (and others on 38–41, 46–47); Kelsey, *Tongue Speaking*, 50–51; Burgess, *Peoples*, 127, 152–53 (citing much earlier sources; also noting the Protestant response on 155); cf. Cruz, *Mysteries*, 241, 529–30. Kelsey, *Tongue Speaking*, gives other examples, albeit noting the greater difficulty of substantiating them, on 51; cf. also John of the Cross (1542–91) and Anthony of Padua (1195–1231) in Cutten, *Speaking with Tongues*, 39, 45.

75. Blosser and Sullivan, *Speaking in Tongues*, 10–40, esp. 27, 34–35; Oliver, *Reformations*, 51.

76. Knox, *Enthusiasm*, 372, as quoted in Burgess, *Peoples*, 170.

77. E.g., Goff, "Theology," 64.

78. Tsivoery, "History," 18–19.

79. Shiby Thomas, personal correspondence, March 5, 7, 2025.

80. Grenholm, *Dokumenterade Språkmirakler*, 132–35.

other languages, such as Yom, Berba, and Fulani. On the following nights, they divided people into seven language groups with seven interpreters, but that first night, everyone heard him in their own language despite the lack of translation into those languages.[81]

Surprise Sithole has experienced xenolalia many times, including when preaching. Chichewa (a language dominant especially in Malawi) first came to him miraculously when he was preaching to people who could not otherwise understand him, and since that time he has been fluent in the language.[82] He acquired Nhungue and English the same way.[83] My friend Will Hart was present before to witness this spontaneous gift.[84]

### *The French Prophets?*

When the rationalist cleric Conyers Middleton (1683–1750) complained that tongues speaking had never occurred since apostolic times, John Wesley pointed to the French Prophets among the Camisards, Reformed Protestants in southern France.[85] Many believe that they valued speaking in tongues as a divine sign.[86] Witnesses among Huguenot refugees testified "how infants and young children moved their hearers to repentance with their inspired pronouncements—usually spoken in French, a language which they had not previously been known to speak."[87] Various witnesses testified of "inspired children under three years of age" exhorting in French. Most were considered illiterate and unable to speak French apart from inspiration.[88] As noted earlier, in one particularly extraordinary case a child in a cradle, no more than fourteen months old, was said to speak distinctive French.[89]

81. Grenholm, *Dokumenterade Språkmirakler*, 128, citing both Jonas Andersson and Clause Sossa, the latter being missions director for Fondation Missionnaire Évangélique.

82. Sithole, *Voice*, 53.

83. Sithole, *Voice*, 90, 103; for other languages, 183. His wife Tryphina also acquired English facility supernaturally (137).

84. Will Hart mentions this during an interview with Surprise on September 26, 2024, "Surprise Sithole: Supernaturally Learning Languages, Witchcraft, and Fasting," at https://www.youtube.com/watch?v=x2ikchgd3nk (accessed Oct. 24, 2024).

85. Kelsey, *Tongue Speaking*, 54; Hyatt, *Years*, 88; cf. Hunter, *Spirit Baptism*, 163. Middleton is also quoted in Cutten, *Speaking with Tongues*, 32, with Wesley's response on 56–57. For a skeptical approach to the child prophets, see Cutten, *Speaking with Tongues*, 48–66. Bushnell, *Nature*, also cited tongues among the Camisard Huguenots (Burgess, *Peoples*, 208).

86. So Blosser and Sullivan, *Speaking in Tongues*, 15. Astonishingly, Blosser and Sullivan, *Speaking in Tongues*, 8, then exclude them from discussion as being a "separatist" sect.

87. Cosmos, *Huguenot Prophecy*, 32; emphasizing the articulate French, also 48, 51, 68; see, e.g., Misson, *Cry*, 14, 103. The French word *enfant* can mean "infant" or "child." On such speech in French versus the local patois, see also Sigg, *Revival*, 27. In the 1700s, Occitan was more like Spanish than French.

88. Cosmos, *Huguenot Prophecy*, 67.

89. Cosmos, *Huguenot Prophecy*, 51, 68.

One witness reports his astonishment at hearing his mother prophesy in French, a language in which he had never heard her try to utter a single word before or after.[90]

Whether we should treat the French Prophets' experience as actual xenolalia is debatable. Most spoke only the local patois of their villages,[91] but most adults probably did *understand* French, in which Reformed congregations heard Scripture and liturgy.[92] As many early US Pentecostals prophesied in King James English ("Thus saith the Lord"), Huguenot utterances probably evoked "the archaic French of the Geneva Bible."[93] So even if we grant that the Spirit enabled young children to prophesy in a language they could not ordinarily speak, it is not quite the same as full-fledged xenolalia. Nevertheless, a well-educated English nobleman reported hearing some of these uneducated refugees in London also speaking in Hebrew and Latin, which they could not do when not in spiritual ecstasy.[94] Some sources report the occurrence of unknown tongues.[95]

## Xenolalia Today

There are oral and written reports of such xenolalia (also called xenoglossia or xenoglossy) occurring in a minority of modern cases.[96] For example:

- One US author, a French major, recognized one tongues speaker praying in perfect French.[97]
- One Pentecostal tongues utterance in a Western church proved to be a dramatic message in Sinhalese to visiting missionaries.[98]

90. Cosmos, *Huguenot Prophecy*, 74–75, citing Jean Vernet.
91. Cosmos, *Huguenot Prophecy*, 75–76; cf. Cutten, *Speaking with Tongues*, 61.
92. Cosmos, *Huguenot Prophecy*, 76.
93. Cosmos, *Huguenot Prophecy*, 78 (but the comparison with the KJV is our own).
94. Cutten, *Speaking with Tongues*, 56–57; Kelsey, *Tongue Speaking*, 54.
95. Burgess, "Evidence," 30.
96. E.g., Stibbe, *Prophetic Evangelism*, 75; Olson, *Bruchko*, 152; Synan, *Voices*, 147; see also some possibly relevant examples in McGee, "Shortcut" (some after minimal acquaintance with a language); McGee, "Radical Strategy," 78–79, 84–85 (including pre-Pentecostal missionary claims in the 1880s and 1890s). In many instances in early Pentecostalism and subsequently, it was believed that genuine xenoglossia was recognized in prayer (see, e.g., Yeomans, *Healing*, 119, understood "a little" by the author; more significantly, Woodworth-Etter, *Miracles*, 110; McGee, *People of Spirit*, 24, 46–47, 57, 61, 64, 75; Robeck, *Mission*, 268–69; Blumhofer, "Portrait," 96, 99; Sherrill, *Tongues*, 19, 20, 42–43, 45, 90–91, 93, 94, 95, 96–97, 99–100; Synan, *Voices*, 60, 76–77, 84, 101–2; Gardner, *Healing Miracles*, 38). For a reported case of independent yet identical "interpretations" of tongues in two different languages, see Pullinger, *Dragon*, 69–70 (the second interpreter did not know the first's language).
97. Mansfield, *Pentecost*, 50.
98. Gardner, *Healing Miracles*, 142–43.

- One author I (Craig) knew, whose course I once took, recounted some twenty-five cases he had collected.[99]

Despite scholars suggesting alternative explanations for many purported cases,[100] as well as attribution to coincidence when only a few words appear,[101] cases continue to be reported, many of them not easily dismissed. For example, Professor Del Tarr, a scholar of linguistics, notes about ten cases, some with considerable supporting evidence, especially cases where he was one of the eyewitnesses. On such occasions people recognized the language being spoken by someone speaking in tongues, and not just mere snippets.[102]

Hwa Yung, a missiologist and retired Methodist bishop of Malaysia, shared with me (Craig) the experience of a friend of his, Randy Singkee, that he had verified personally.[103] Singkee

> runs . . . the largest Malay language Christian publisher catering primarily to the indigenous churches in Malaysia. In 1990 . . . he was offered a place to do a Master's degree in computerized mapping at the University of Edinburgh. . . . But as the date of departure drew near, the confirmation letter for the scholarship still had not arrived. Without the scholarship he simply had no money to go to Edinburgh. In a state of desperation, he went to a prayer meeting where a visiting group from the Lun Bawang church had come to speak on the revivals in their midst.
>
> A Lun Bawang woman prayed for him, knowing nothing of the dilemma he was in. To his great surprise, she started praying in tongues—in Mandarin Chinese, to be exact. Now this was a woman with little formal education from the Borneo jungles and [who] only spoke her own mother tongue, Lun Bawang, and the national language, Malay. Clearly, she did not know what she was saying as she prayed in tongues. But Singkee, also an indigenous person, had gone to a Chinese primary school and understood exactly what God was saying to him through her prophetically.

He flew to Edinburgh the next day and God miraculously supplied his need. "Years later, and after careful checking, Singkee found that the woman who

99. Harris, *Acts Today*, 108–30; on 7 he refers to his earlier book with seventy-five cases.

100. Hilborn, "Glossolalia," 115–16, on some tested incidents; Wacker, *Heaven*, 47–48. Hudson, "Strange Words," 61, suggests that most accounts are based on snippets here and there recognized by hearers (which could be random) or the sorts of sounds speakers could have heard before and unconsciously verbalized (one so inclined could offer the same proposal regarding the diaspora hearers' perception at Pentecost). Goff, "Theology," 66, attributes some language-like patterns and words to cryptomnesia.

101. Turner, *Gifts*, 308n27.

102. Tarr, *Foolishness*, 401–3. I note this also in Keener, "Ongoing Evidence," 357; an example also in May, *Witnesses to Pentecost*, 37.

103. Hwa Yung, interview, Boston, Massachusets, November 17, 2025; personal correspondence, November 18, 2025. I have condensed to essential elements for the sake of space.

had prayed for him was one Ibu Maria, who was a deeply prayerful person with a wonderful prophetic gift."

### *Various Incidents*

The most extensive collection of examples, to our knowledge (eighty-nine cases)—and again some of them well-supported with multiple attestation—appears in a work by my (Craig's) friend Jordan Daniel May.[104] Although the reader will find fuller details in May's book, a number of cases he recounts seem providentially directed for specific encouragements to the hearers present on those occasions. That is, the phenomenon may be more common but simply revealed in cases where it proves most relevant for edification. A majority of the accounts reflect recognition of fairly familiar languages simply because those that are best known are most apt to be recognized by someone present. These then would be the tip of the iceberg of occasions in which a genuine human language could be involved in tongues.[105]

For example:

- In 1994, after Moses Cao, from Vietnam, spoke in a church about the needs of Christians in Vietnam, he was amazed to hear local US Christian Sandra Kirschner utter in tongues a message of great encouragement in the South Vietnamese dialect, and then shift to the North Vietnamese dialect in interceding for and promising the preaching of the gospel in North Vietnam. This message ultimately encouraged Vietnamese Christians to continue evangelizing during a period of persecution.[106]
- Invited by fellow college students, an Iranian Muslim visitor to a church was astonished to hear a member praying in tongues; the visitor recounted that "the member was praising God in perfect Farsi."[107]
- When a recent convert who knew only English began unexpectedly worshiping God in tongues, a hearer opposed to tongues was astonished to hear the new believer "speaking about God's love in perfect German"; the former opponent of tongues requested prayer and received the gift himself that day.[108]

104. May, *Witnesses to Pentecost*. May notes that he sought multiple attestations and omitted testimonies that he could not confirm with witnesses (xiii).

105. Cf. Collins, *Charismatic Christianity*, 135. In one report, the tongues were unknown, but different persons were saying the same words at the same time (Billman, *Thread*, 136–37, citing Waugh, *Fires*, 96).

106. May, *Witnesses to Pentecost*, 121–22, citing multiple witnesses, including Cao and Kirschner.

107. May, *Witnesses to Pentecost*, 45. For a Dutch Reformed Christian's dream containing two Persian words that proved prophetic, see Boys, *Evidence*, 306.

108. May, *Witnesses to Pentecost*, 52, attested by five witnesses.

- On the English Isle of Wight, Dr. Ian Hall recognized a church member's utterance in tongues as 1 Corinthians 13, word for word, in Koine Greek; someone who did not know this then felt led to read that very chapter in English, functioning as the interpretation.[109]
- Not knowing what to pray for specifically, a minister prayed in tongues for a young man, who was excited that the minister had prayed for him in perfect Haitian Creole, the young man's language.[110]
- A missionary familiar with Chadian Arabic confirmed that an American worshiper, unfamiliar with Arabic, gave an utterance in a tongue in this language that another American worshiper unfamiliar with the language then accurately interpreted.[111]
- A different missionary confirmed that a tongues utterance in a different church was, unknown to the speaker, in the Upper Egyptian dialect of Arabic, with a completely accurate interpretation.[112]
- A Palestinian Christian international student, disheartened to be away from home, was excited to hear a non-Arabic-speaking young woman beside her praying the Lord's Prayer "in perfect Arabic."[113]
- In a number of cases, Jewish visitors recognized Hebrew being spoken or sung when someone was worshiping in tongues.[114]
- In 1980 a visitor named David Legere heard Marigold Cheshier worshiping in tongues and explained to her that she had declared authoritatively and repeatedly in Hebrew, "I'm saved by the blood of the Lamb!" He did not know that she had struggled with assurance of her salvation before that point.[115]

109. May, *Witnesses to Pentecost*, 54, noting that this was the prelude to a revival there. Praying in tongues, another believer on a different occasion shared the message of Christ in Greek to a Greek speaker (May, *Witnesses to Pentecost*, 57).

110. May, *Witnesses to Pentecost*, 23.

111. May, *Witnesses to Pentecost*, 10, confirmed with three witnesses.

112. May, *Witnesses to Pentecost*, 11, confirmed with three witnesses.

113. May, *Witnesses to Pentecost*, 12.

114. See May, *Witnesses to Pentecost*, 58–69; one of these confirmed to me (Craig) by Byron Klaus, personal correspondence, March 10, 2025, regarding the experience of his father. I learned of a very probable case from David Boskey and Aron Williams (personal correspondence, March 30, 2025). William Caldwell reported a similar situation that convinced a young rabbinic student who encountered a pastor speaking fluent Hebrew without realizing it (Kelsey, *Tongue Speaking*, 157). Kelsey also reports a seminary Hebrew professor telling "a close friend" of Kelsey's that her utterance in tongues was "a reasonably good talk in Hebrew, of which she had no knowledge" (Kelsey, *Tongue Speaking*, 163).

115. May, *Witnesses to Pentecost*, 65, confirming with both persons. In August 2006, I met Marigold Cheshier in Kenya, where she and her husband were doing effective evangelism; she is also the sister-in-law of my undergraduate institution's former president.

- An Estonian immigrant who did not believe in tongues heard a message in tongues in Estonian from a US believer unfamiliar with Estonian; he became a regular attender after that.[116]
- A homesick international student celebrated the encouragement when in chapel he recognized an utterance in tongues as Mandarin Chinese; he testified that "the interpretation was a perfect translation."[117] (The biblical term for interpretation of tongues is looser than translation,[118] so "a perfect translation" is not the norm.)
- Unable to communicate in a language his hearer knew, a missionary began speaking in tongues; suddenly the man became alert and they conversed for fifteen minutes, so that the man was deeply moved, even though the missionary had no idea what he had said.[119]
- A Japanese woman heard a simple, five-sentence utterance in tongues that she recognized as Japanese, followed by the same sentences in English during the interpretation. Neither the tongues speaker nor the interpreter knew any Japanese.[120]
- In another church, a Japanese visitor to a church heard a tongues utterance in Japanese from a non-Japanese speaker, followed by a correct interpretation, which led to the Japanese visitor becoming a follower of Jesus.[121]
- When Bill Shrader first received the gift of praying in tongues, his friends recognized the language as French. The next year, he was praying in tongues for a woman needing direction, and she, startled, noted that he had just given her God's answer in French. Another French speaker understood his prayers as he prayed, and two North African missionaries recognized it too; his accent was not Parisian but North African.[122]
- A former missionary to Brazil understood a Bible college student's praise in tongues, recognizing it as Portuguese; the interpretation uttered by another student captured "the essence of the message."[123]
- In 1982, Gary Royer, then a missionary to Brazil, heard a teenager in Argentina prophesy in tongues that, unknown to her, was fluent Portuguese; she prophesied about a coming revival in Argentina that would

116. May, *Witnesses to Pentecost*, 43–44.

117. May, *Witnesses to Pentecost*, 96, recalled by Dr. George O. Wood, on whom it made "a 'remarkable impression,'" and a witness close to the family of Arthur Cao, the student.

118. With, e.g., Menzies, *Romans*, 194, 206.

119. May, *Witnesses to Pentecost*, 83.

120. May, *Witnesses to Pentecost*, 80–81.

121. May, *Witnesses to Pentecost*, 82.

122. May, *Witnesses to Pentecost*, 46, 49, 50.

123. May, *Witnesses to Pentecost*, 101.

soon bring millions to Christ, a revival that indeed began four years later.[124]

- When a white teenager in Arizona began praying in tongues for the first time, some Apache Christians around him recognized him repeatedly shout, "God is good!" in the Apache language.[125]
- A visitor who had been a Latin major heard a tongues utterance in Latin and confirmed that the interpretation was an excellent translation of it.[126]
- In Singapore in the summer of 1993, four Buddhist monks were so amazed by an utterance in tongues, which they recognized as a rare dialect preserved in their monasteries, and the matching interpretation by a visiting American, that the monks committed themselves to Christ.[127]
- Other languages recognized include Bahasa Indonesia,[128] Gujarati,[129] Hindustani,[130] Italian,[131] Korean,[132] Kusaal,[133] Malay,[134] Quechua,[135] Russian,[136] Urdu,[137] and Zulu.[138]

### *Tongues in English*

Likewise, English speakers (who provide many accounts particularly accessible to us fellow English speakers) have often heard non-English speakers speaking in tongues in English.[139]

- In Côte d'Ivoire, Dr. Willard Teague, a native Texan and my (Craig's) classmate in seminary, was shocked to hear his Francophone colleague praying in English, and with a Texas drawl no less, only to discover that

124. May, *Witnesses to Pentecost*, 104; also confirmed for me with further details by Gary Royer, personal correspondence, March 11, 2025.
125. May, *Witnesses to Pentecost*, 7–8, confirmed with three witnesses; the dialect was the White Mountain dialect of Western Apache.
126. May, *Witnesses to Pentecost*, 93.
127. May, *Witnesses to Pentecost*, 130.
128. May, *Witnesses to Pentecost*, 70–71.
129. Turner, *Gifts*, 308n27.
130. May, *Witnesses to Pentecost*, 128–29, noting multiple witnesses.
131. May, *Witnesses to Pentecost*, 72–79.
132. May, *Witnesses to Pentecost*, 85–88, also noting Keener, *Miracles*, 1:328n126.
133. The language of the Kusasi people in northern Ghana; May, *Witnesses to Pentecost*, 89–92.
134. May, *Witnesses to Pentecost*, 98–99.
135. May, *Witnesses to Pentecost*, 105.
136. May, *Witnesses to Pentecost*, 106–7.
137. May, *Witnesses to Pentecost*, 120.
138. May, *Witnesses to Pentecost*, 123–24, citing three witnesses.
139. May, *Witnesses to Pentecost*, gives examples on 16–44.

his colleague had simply been praying in tongues and had no idea the prayers were in English.[140]

- In 1994 in Togo, where the official language is French, many people in one service began speaking in tongues for the first time, and missionary Charity Harris testifies that he "heard many praising God in perfect English."[141]
- Over a span of years a missionary often heard a particular Spanish pastor in Barcelona, who knew no English, praying in tongues in English, and with a Caribbean rather than Spanish accent.[142]
- A Vietnamese man who knew no English praised God in perfect English while speaking in tongues.[143]
- A young teenager in Argentina in 1996 wanted to thank an Anglophone mission team and, trusting God to help her, shared with them excitedly how God had blessed her; only after her testimony did they learn that she knew no English but had spoken spontaneously.[144]
- Other examples could be multiplied, from Argentina,[145] Burkina Faso,[146] Chile,[147] Colombia,[148] Senegal,[149] Tunisia,[150] and Venezuela.[151]

### *Tongues in Spanish*

Because Spanish is widely spoken, it is no surprise that it is among languages more often recognized. Missionary Rick Ryan, fluent in Spanish, confirmed that Kathy Buckles's prayer in tongues came out in perfect Spanish, which she didn't know; the Spanish-speaking woman for whom Buckles prayed gave her life to Christ.[152]

Around 1980, Mark Rutland, now a former president of two universities, tried to greet a Mexican congregation with several Spanish phrases he had learned, but more Spanish started coming to him, and he found himself preaching the entire sermon in Spanish, though he never took courses in

140. May, *Witnesses to Pentecost*, 22.
141. May, *Witnesses to Pentecost*, 23.
142. May, *Witnesses to Pentecost*, 29.
143. May, *Witnesses to Pentecost*, 31, confirmed with three witnesses.
144. May, *Witnesses to Pentecost*, 25, confirmed with three witnesses.
145. May, *Witnesses to Pentecost*, 39 (noting the "perfect California accent"). He notes as one of his sources Jones, *Filled*, 54; Jones and I were classmates in seminary.
146. May, *Witnesses to Pentecost*, 37.
147. May, *Witnesses to Pentecost*, 41.
148. May, *Witnesses to Pentecost*, 34.
149. May, *Witnesses to Pentecost*, 42.
150. May, *Witnesses to Pentecost*, 36.
151. May, *Witnesses to Pentecost*, 32.
152. May, *Witnesses to Pentecost*, 110, citing three witnesses, including Ryan and Buckles. For other accounts of tongues being Spanish, see May, *Witnesses to Pentecost*, 111–17.

Spanish. He understood what he was saying and this ability in Spanish remains with him.[153]

In summer 2008, when working with teen apologetics with Focus on the Family, professor and apologist Alex McFarland took four hundred teenagers to Peru. They saw fifty thousand conversions in one month. When they were ministering in a slum area of Miraflores, a brother named Apolinario joined them. Apolinario could speak neither Spanish nor English, but only Quechua. Everybody else spoke Spanish, so Juan Carlos was Alex's translator, but because Juan Carlos's grandmother spoke Quechua, he was able to translate a little bit for Apolinario, who hung around Alex at meals. One day after Alex had given an altar call and others were busy following this up, Alex saw four soccer players drinking a lot of vodka. He went and tried to talk with them, but naturally they couldn't understand him. So Apolinario came up behind him and offered—in perfect English—to translate into Spanish for him! Apolinario translated for him for an hour, and all four soccer players accepted Christ. When Alex told them that if they were serious, they should pour out all the rest of the vodka, they did so. Now, Alex had been with Apolinario for nine or ten days, and Apolinario couldn't speak any English or Spanish. But now he was speaking perfect English and translating to and from Spanish! When Juan Carlos was able to come up, he exclaimed, "This is Pentecost!" God had given Apolinario this ability. Everyone celebrated, but by the time they all got back to Lima, Apolinario could no longer speak English or Spanish. It was a temporary gift.[154]

### *Swedish Tongues Reports*

In addition to Jordan May, Swedish author Micael Grenholm has explored a variety of linguistic tongues experiences, interviewing multiple witnesses in most instances.[155] I include here just a few of his accounts.

- Several witnesses confirmed that in 2012, retired psychiatrist Henny Palmér heard and translated into Swedish an extensive utterance in perfect academic Latin by Åke Bäckström. Bäckström, an uneducated and humble man who had never heard Latin, much less studied it, was astonished to learn that this was the language he had been speaking.[156]
- Attested by multiple witnesses, Peter Allerberg prophesied about the gospel to two Turkish women in perfect Turkish, although he had never learned Turkish or even interacted with Turks.[157]

153. May, *Witnesses to Pentecost*, 108–9.

154. Alex McFarland, interview, March 20, 2025; confirmation, August 5, 2025.

155. Grenholm, *Dokumenterade Språkmirakler*.

156. Grenholm, *Dokumenterade Språkmirakler*, 97–98, citing as firsthand witnesses Grenholm's parents-in-law and Anita Eriksson, all of whom knew Bäckström well.

157. Grenholm, *Dokumenterade Språkmirakler*, 57–58, citing as witnesses Örjan Armgren, Simon Ådahl, Grete Lauritzen, and Peter Allerberg.

- In Sri Lanka, a Methodist Christian who did not know whether he had the gift of tongues suddenly felt led to speak words he did not know, introducing his Swedish guests as agents of the gospel—in perfect Swedish, a language he did not know.[158]
- On October 30, 2019, when Jonas Andersson was praying in tongues, Maria Gergis experienced him praying and prophesying to her extensively in fluent North African Arabic.[159]
- In 2012, when Jonas Andersson was preaching in Vietnam, Mary Tran began translating for him fluently, even after long monologues, and testified that she was *hearing* him speak in Vietnamese, and so was just repeating what he was saying.[160]
- In fall 2010, Tuula Petersson was among those present when "Frans," a Swede who knew no Finnish, began prophesying in Finnish at Rosenius Church, and she could understand all that he was saying about the Lord. Ola Hössjer, mathematics professor at Stockholm University, calculated the odds of these precise sentences emerging by mere coincidence at something like one in 368 trillion.[161]

### *Tongues Among Acquaintances*

Here are some examples of testimonies of recognized linguistic tongues among my (Craig's) own friends and acquaintances:

- In Togo in 1949, a missionary couple had experienced multiple failed pregnancies when the wife overheard a Togolese boy who knew no English praying in tongues: "You're going to have another baby, and it will be a boy. When he is born you will know that nothing is impossible with God!"[162] The boy, Murray Brown, was my undergraduate classmate and confirmed the account for me![163]
- Derek Morphew told me that around 1975, an elder in the church they pastored approached wide-eyed after Derek's wife, Karin, gave an

158. Grenholm, *Dokumenterade Språkmirakler*, 43–44, citing as witnesses Micael Lahtinen and Benny Lindqvist.

159. Grenholm, *Dokumenterade Språkmirakler*, 99–100, citing as witnesses Jonas Andersson and Maria Gergis.

160. Grenholm, *Dokumenterade Språkmirakler*, 127, citing as witnesses Jonas Andersson and Mary Tran.

161. Grenholm, *Dokumenterade Språkmirakler*, 5–6. Frans had earlier witnessed someone else who often spoke in tongues when someone present understood and translated by knowledge of the language.

162. May, *Witnesses to Pentecost*, 28.

163. Murray Brown, personal correspondence, March 10, 2025. I have full confidence in Murray and thus that this is the story he knew from his parents.

utterance in tongues in the church. The elder, who had grown up in Italy and whom they knew well and long-term, recognized the Portuguese dialect and told her what she had said (very similar to the interpretation).[164]

- My seminary student Joseph Hardy provided me access to his aunt's account of his grandmother in Guyana. As a midwife she prayed in tongues during a mother's difficult, potentially fatal delivery; after the successful delivery, the mother marveled at the midwife's Arabic—which the midwife had never learned.[165]
- Pastor David Workman told me that his mother, without much formal education or any exposure to French, was understood to be praising God in an old dialect of French.[166]
- Workman also noted that about fifteen years before our discussion a friend of his had prayed for someone in Mexico who apparently knew no English, and the person began praising God in glossolalia—in this case, fluent English.
- My wife tells of a well-known Congolese minister, a close friend of her parents, Daniel Ndoundou, who was said to have preached in Swedish in Sweden without knowing the language.[167]

The following cases among my acquaintances suggest more direct knowledge:

- After Byron Klaus, a seminary president, prayed in tongues for a young woman in Portugal, a missionary there told him that the woman noted that Klaus prayed in Portuguese "very specifically for an unmentioned need . . . she had not shared with anyone."[168] I know Byron quite well and he confirmed this account for me.[169]
- When my friend Joseph Castleberry, now a former seminary dean and university president, heard a believer in Bolivia worshiping God joyfully in English, he approached her, only to discover that she knew no English.[170] I confirmed this account with him.[171]
- When Doyle Jones (one of my former seminary classmates) was praying in tongues in the presence of Jawahar Samuel and Sheba Kulothungan,

164. Derek Morphew, personal conversation, Corona, California, November 12, 2007.

165. Personal correspondence from Joseph Hardy and his aunt, Yvonne Cummings, October 29, 2024. Cummings knew the story both from her mother, the midwife (Joseph's grandmother), and from the Indian Muslim woman.

166. David Workman, personal conversation, Wynnewood, Pennsylvania, April 30, 2008.

167. On whom see Keener, "Ndoundou," but she did not include this claim in the article, since it was not in her written sources.

168. May, *Witnesses to Pentecost*, 103. This was before he knew any of the language.

169. Byron Klaus, personal correspondence, March 10, 2025.

170. May, *Witnesses to Pentecost*, 16.

171. Joseph Castleberry, personal correspondence, March 11, 2025.

they both excitedly explained to him that he was praising God in their language of Tamil.[172]

- When Leah Macinskas-Le, who recently finished her PhD in the study of early Judaism and the New Testament, was my seminary student, she told me how her Jewish agnostic mother became a follower of Jesus.[173] Raised in a traditional Jewish household and having attended Hebrew school, the mother visited a Full Gospel church with her husband's cousin, a member of a Brethren church. She was shocked to hear the pastor, who did not know any Hebrew, singing the Shema in Hebrew, and realized that something supernatural was taking place.[174]
- My friend Leo Bawa, from Nigeria, tells me of his own temporary ability to understand and speak some local tribal languages.[175]
- Chris Baumgartner, whom I met through Orbis Ministries, shared that his first experiences praying in tongues astonished him so much that he recorded them, sending a couple clips to a translator and inputting others into translation software; they came out in classical Hebrew, as words of encouragement or the same sorts of prayers he had been praying in English. On one of the occasions, what came to him in tongues turned out to be the very words in Hebrew that those around him in church were then singing in English.[176]

Of course, I realize that this is not how tongues always works, and that usually there is no one present who knows the language. But then, only one of the several biblical passages about tongues reports it coming in languages recognized by anyone present.

## Craig's Not-Learned Experience

MacArthur allows for tongues as "a learned behavior."[177] Yet the experience sometimes comes spontaneously to those unacquainted with it. In my (Craig's)

172. Jones, *Filled*, 54–55 (a copy of which Doyle gave me); May, *Witnesses to Pentecost*, 118–19, who collected four witnesses, including Dr. Kulothungan. Doyle and I also corresponded further; Jordan May had been one of his students (personal correspondence, March 11, 2025).

173. Leah Macinskas-Le, interview, April 25, 2010. Noting my mention in *Miracles*, 1:328n126, May, *Witnesses to Pentecost*, 60–61, also provides the account with fuller details.

174. Leah Macinskas-Le, personal correspondence, after Leah consulted with her mother, September 30, 2024; October 1, 2024.

175. Leo Bawa, interview, August 10, 2009.

176. Chris Baumgartner, discussion, Nashville, Tennessee, October 3, 2024; personal correspondence October 9, 2024; phone interview, March 7, 2025. Chris provides the account more publicly (conversing with other witnesses) in Baumgartner, "Gifts."

177. MacArthur, *Chaos*, 240.

case, there was no one from whom I could have learned it.[178] I was converted from atheism and an unchurched background. I had very little knowledge of Christianity apart from the basic gospel message through which I had been converted two days earlier; I had never heard of speaking in tongues.

Yet I was so overwhelmed with a sense of God's majesty that I had to praise him, and God was so great that I felt that only he could inspire me with the words to praise him. Since it was obvious that God knows all languages, I welcomed the worship coming from my heart and mouth in another language. This is a gift that has remained dear to me in my private prayer life, one that has at times helped protect my faith in the God of the Bible when I faced many academic challenges to that faith. Many others also have experienced tongues without prior knowledge of the experience. Indeed, some studies have shown that those who come to the experience from backgrounds ignorant of or antagonistic to it tend to emphasize it more than those who grew up with it.[179] (Maybe that's why this book has two chapters about it?)

By contrast, I have barely ever given a *public* utterance in tongues (i.e., in church). Once it happened after a three-day fast, and twice it happened a week after I emphasized that I *never* give public utterances in tongues. (That should teach me not to dictate what God will not lead me to do.) The most recent time I recall was at one of the African American Baptist churches where I served as an associate minister in the 1990s. The pastor asked me to open the service in prayer, but from our pre-service time of prayer I felt overwhelmed by the Spirit. Barely[180] able to restrain myself, I warned him that it was likely to come out in tongues. "Go ahead," he urged supportively, so I warned everyone what was coming, opened the service with a prayer in tongues, and then interpreted. Everyone was excited, though I don't think that had ever happened there before. Happily it was not the sort of Baptist church that might have thrown me out!

So I do have an experiential bias for tongues; no one can convince me that my initial experience of the gift (and the spirtual renewal I experience when I pray in tongues) is not real. Some who have never experienced it might have an experiential bias against something that seems to them so unusual. But

178. Although Marziyeh Amirizadeh read about tongues in Acts, her experience in Voice of Martyrs, *Hearts of Fire 2*, 249, also seems spontaneous, accompanied by a vision that confirmed her new faith and that soon led to spreading the gospel. Some new Roma believers in Thessaloniki belonged to a church that did not teach about tongues, but some of the women, who were illiterate, experienced it anyway (Debbie Dimitriadi shared this with Craig in Thessaloniki, August 15, 2025).

179. Laurito, *Speaking in Tongues*, 75, citing also Hine, "Glossolalia," 212.

180. We are able to control ourselves (1 Cor. 14:32). But that is easier at some times than others (as we might note from some of the unplanned, collective experiences with tongues during special outpourings in Acts, as in 2:4; 10:46; 19:6).

what can we say about "arguments from experience"? That is the subject of chapter 18.

## Conclusion

While all tongues are meant to be communication, they need not all function in the same way or on the same level. Some may be human languages (though given the massive number of such languages, they would be recognized only occasionally); others may be encoded; others may be simply affective communication. Most important is that they are prayers from the heart to God. But cumulatively enough cases exist to show that, at least occasionally, tongues are languages that can be recognized by hearers present.

# V

# Arguments from Experience and History

Empiricism, used in exploring general revelation, depends on arguments from experience. Because doctrine depends especially on special revelation, however, Scripture takes pride of place. We do not base doctrine on postbiblical experience. Some therefore wish to discount altogether arguments from postbiblical experience. Curiously, however, while cessationists generally criticize charismatic arguments from experience, they commonly appeal to other experiences to make their case for cessationism. One of their most common and persuasive arguments is a postbiblical argument from eccentric charismatics; another common argument is based on revulsion toward emotional manifestations that appear at times. Arguments from postbiblical history are also arguments from postbiblical experience.

Chapter 18 is the book's shortest and introduces the argument from experience. Chapters 19 and 20 turn to cessationist arguments based on erratic charismatics and emotional manifestations. Chapter 21 turns to a history of cessationism, climaxing in the early twentieth-century hard cessationism of B. B. Warfield. Chapter 22 then counters with a history of postbiblical miracles, which on occasion cluster around individuals who become known for praying for such. Those whose position is rooted in particular periods in church history can usually find support for their position somewhere there. Again, however, those who embrace Scripture as God's Word should subordinate their traditions to Scripture, which, as already shown, offers no quarter to cessationism.

# 18

# Arguments from Experience

"Experience," Luther believed, "is necessary for the understanding of the Word," which must "be believed and felt."[1] Sometimes Peter (e.g., Acts 11:5–15, 17; 15:8–10) and Paul (e.g., Acts 22:17–21; 26:12–19) argue by appealing to charismatic experience—and to more general experience as well (e.g., Acts 2:32; 1 Cor. 15:8). Most cessationists, however, do not accept such experiences today, much less arguments from them (except perhaps for experiences of the Spirit that can be correlated with conversion, such as in 1 Cor. 2:4–5; Gal. 3:1–5; 1 Thess. 1:5).

Interestingly, anticharismatic arguments from some charismatics' behaviors (chaps. 19–20) and even anti- or procharismatic arguments from history (chaps. 21–22) are all arguments from experience. Despite cessationists' regular critiques of charismatic arguments from charismatic experience, the dominant and rhetorically most powerful weapons in these critics' arsenal are themselves arguments from experience.

John MacArthur warns that experience is not a "valid test of truth."[2] While I may "know that I know" something with certainty because of my experience with the Spirit (e.g., Rom. 8:16), someone outside me cannot measure

1. Luther, WA 5:108, as quoted in Bartholomew, *Hermeneutics*, 198; Luther insisted that he had learned to abandon his own wisdom and depend on the Spirit to hear Scripture (WA 4:519.3–4, as quoted in Bartholomew, *Hermeneutics*, 199). Luther notes Paul's appeal to his audience's experience in Gal. 3:5 (*First Lectures on Galatians*, on 3:5, in Bray, *Galatians, Ephesians*, 93).

2. MacArthur, *Chaos*, 23–46. We do gain empirical knowledge from experience, but it is publishable only when it remains constant over a significant sample size, not simply personal experience. He also correctly notes that "no matter what kind of experience" a charismatic thinks they have, they "still face the same challenge given to every Christian: the need to walk by the Spirit in obedience to the Word" (253).

that. When discussing doctrine, then, we Christians depend on Scripture, a shared source the authority of which we Jesus followers all affirm, rather than simply our own experience. In his own appeal to Scripture, MacArthur articulates a solid biblical hermeneutic that would benefit general charismatic (and other popular-level) Bible readers.[3] (We believe that, unfortunately, he does not follow it himself when it comes to passages about spiritual gifts!)

MacArthur and many fellow cessationists decry charismatics' appeal to experience. Cessationists, however, also often depend on experience. The cessationist argument from the inferiority of expressions of gifts today (chap. 11) is an argument from experience. If we follow Scripture alone, the range of gifts, not least prophecy, is needed to build up the church. Thus if the church is weak in some gifts, such weakness should motivate us to pursue those gifts more (with charismatics) rather than less (with cessationists). Nor do gifts such as prophecy take a single form or express themselves with identical intensity everywhere in Scripture.

Arguments against gifts based on selective accounts of charismatic abuses and abusers (sometimes the most publicized practitioners of certain gifts) are also arguments from limited experience. Those who were not present to experience the Spirit's outpouring on Cornelius's household (Acts 10:44–48; 11:15–16; cf. 10:9–19, 22, 30–33; 11:5–13) were initially quick to judge Peter's actions (11:2–3), in contrast to those who experienced the incident with Peter firsthand (10:45–46; 11:12).

Those who have left behind or discount circles that practice some gifts based on bad experiences there, yet lack genuine biblical support that gifts have ceased, may act hypocritically to criticize charismatic appeals to experience. We should take warning and learn lessons from bad experiences, but trying to generalize from them to all cases functions in logic as an inductive, hasty generalization fallacy or fallacy of composition. Such an argument also demonstrates the fallacy of exclusion (reflecting selection bias) and is often deployed in a form of the misleading vividness fallacy. That is to say, the typical cessationist argument from (bad) experience is shot through with fallacious logic.

## Cessationists Should Stay Closer to Scripture Regarding Gifts

Historically, those who were not seeing miracles and gifts felt the need to justify this situation that seemed so different from what they read in the New Testament.[4] Even when they made theological arguments, then, they were

3. MacArthur, *Chaos*, 85–96.

4. As is often noted; see, e.g., Deere, *Still Surprised*, 47, 50; Keener, *Gift & Giver*, 107. Oss, "View," 272, adds also the role of theological presuppositions, though some of these may have originated in experience.

responding to their own experience. Certainly, as one former cessationist points out, one does not "become a cessationist [simply] by reading the New Testament."[5]

Although B. B. Warfield claimed to stand on both Scripture and history, his polemic against postbiblical miracles treated Scripture only cursorily. He addressed his supposed biblical basis in "hardly more than a half-dozen pages [out] of over three hundred," very little of it exegetical.[6] In 1974, the editor of the *Presbyterian Journal* rightly insisted, "It can be rather categorically stated that the New Testament simply does not affirm that the Church should expect God to stop working miracles among his people. To take that position is to come perilously close to the approach which is anathema to Reformed hermeneutics, namely, conclusions based on what is said to be the experience of the Church rather than the clear teaching of Scripture."[7]

One might respond that addressing Scripture was not Warfield's intention in the book; perhaps he intended to simply supplement an established groundwork.[8] To which we might respond in turn: *What* established groundwork? *No one* has succeeded in making a viable *biblical* case for cessationism; the raw material for it in Scripture is simply not there. As we have seen, the argument has to rest on multiple levels of inference at multiple removes from the biblical text. MacArthur's Strange Fire conference is noteworthy for following the same pattern: Critiquing various charismatic figures was far more central than any biblical case for cessationism.

## Our Experience Is Too Limited to Pass Judgment on Scripture

Daniel has experienced many miracles in his ministry on the cutting edge of evangelism. By contrast, there have been times in my (Craig's) life as a Christian when my experience would have tempted me to affirm cessationism in some form—times of disappointment at apparently unanswered prayers and even disgust at abuses in the name of the Spirit.[9] People have, however, also abused the Bible, family relationships, and other spiritual treasures that God has given us; we do not for this reason ordinarily reject these treasures. I have never yet had a vision. I have interviewed a number of people who have witnessed the raising of the dead,[10] but I have never witnessed it directly myself. The main reason that I could never embrace cessationism, however,

5. Deere, *Still Surprised*, 47.

6. Ruthven, *Cessation*, 77; cf. 174.

7. Aiken, "Miracles," 9, as quoted in Ruthven, *Cessation*, 84n187.

8. So Gaffin, "View," 28.

9. In this paragraph I reuse Keener, "Ongoing Evidence," 325–26.

10. See Keener, *Miracles Today*, 137–74; further Keener, "Dead Raised"; Keener, *Miracles*, 1:551–79.

is that I am convinced that the biblical evidence is uniformly against it. That is, my limited experience has sometimes tempted me toward cessationism, but clear biblical authority has always prevented me from accepting it. Still, if I move beyond my personal experiences from some times in my life to a larger consideration of God's work in the world (and even in my life), even experience rules against cessationism.

As I wrote more than two decades ago, "The argument that gifts ceased and therefore should cease is an argument based on one kind of experience. Yet those who make this argument simply dismiss the experience of hundreds of millions of [other] Christians today." Granted, "some people's claims of spiritual experiences are inauthentic," but dare one simply dismiss all of them?[11]

At that time I also wrote:

> Although I have heard of miracles such as those in Acts happening regularly in some places, I frankly confess that I have not witnessed many miracles on that scale. I could seek theological rationalizations for this lack, contending that God simply does not want to do such miracles today, but seeking an argument to validate my experience would violate my commitment to read my experience in light of Scripture. . . . As a biblical scholar who by conviction determines the meaning of the text first and then asks its implications for today, I must conform my experience to the Bible rather than the Bible to my experience. In other words, I remain committed to spiritual gifts because I am committed to Scripture, rather than the reverse. . . . The Bible's message does not simply confirm my own experience of miracles; it summons me to be more open to appropriate signs and wonders than I already am.[12]

Since that time I have indeed witnessed some more fairly conspicuous miracles. I have also had considerably more opportunity to consult scores of eyewitnesses and follow up on more than enough reports.[13] I have no doubt that God continues to do miracles as he did in biblical times, especially in locations of groundbreaking evangelism. Unlike Warfield, most cessationists today also recognize that God does continue to work miracles. Yet I have often encountered evidence of such groundbreaking miracles in evangelism particularly among those who expect them, as well as a wider range of spiritual gifts, in accordance with what the expectant read in Scripture. This does not mean that all of us have or need to have the same gifts. Nor are the flashiest gifts necessarily the most important (1 Cor. 12:22–25). It does mean that we shouldn't begrudge others their gifts (12:21, 26).

11. Keener, *Gift & Giver*, 92.
12. Keener, *Gift & Giver*, 111.
13. E.g., Keener, *Miracles*; Keener, *Miracles Today*.

## Arguments from Experience Versus Arguments from Lack of Experience

Mark Rutland tells the story of his visit to a village deep in the Peruvian rainforest when a jet coursed through the sky.

> The chief asked if that is how I came to Peru, which launched a long, comic community discussion of air travel. The kibitzers around us joined in with ludicrous comments on how airplanes looked and worked, all of which were utterly absurd. Finally, I paced off what I thought were the dimensions of a 707, which may have been as far off as their ideas were. When they realized what I was showing them could have held every person in their village, the arguments and denials went up in intensity. Finally, the chief raised his hand and spoke what to this day seems like great wisdom:
>
> "I have never seen an airplane except up there in the sky. I cannot imagine what something like that looks like on the ground. They look very small to me in the sky, but birds look smaller to me in the sky."
>
> His own wife objected, "Why should we believe this man?"
>
> He answered her with a question: "Why should we doubt him? He got here somehow. I hope someday to see an airplane on the ground. Until then I will just wait."
>
> Remarkable and memorable wisdom from a man who lived in a hut.[14]

If anyone should speak from the authority of experience, should it not be those who have that experience rather than those who lack it? (Those who lack it, of course, can attest from their experience that not everyone shares the first group's experience.) Would we not be wise to apply that principle to those who experience abuse, racism, or proficiency in a given language?

Vocal cessationists may have opinions about "miraculous" gifts of the Spirit, but they lack actual experience with them. They would be hard-pressed to claim otherwise, since they don't believe they exist today. And one cannot have practical experience with something that doesn't exist. Perhaps an ex-charismatic would say, "Well, I prophesied and spoke in tongues and I can tell you it is fake." Actually, all you can confirm is that what *you* did was fake. No one can convince me that the miracles I (Daniel) have seen are fake. If you are convinced that what you experienced was fake, maybe you are right. But that doesn't speak to the occurrence of miracles outside your sphere of experience (see chaps. 22–23).

So we are right back at my earlier statement: Cessationists have no practical experience with certain of the Spirit's gifts. Beyond the limited statements in Scripture, they should not be pontificating about the nonexistence of certain gifts any more than the villagers of Rutland's story could teach pilots or

14. Rutland, "MacArthur"; also Rutland, "Cessation Theology," 3–4.

flight attendants about airplanes. Until they accept the Bible's testimony and experience their own miracles, the plane will continue to fly without them. Meanwhile, some vocal cessationists will gaze up from the ground and explain how flying is just not possible—as the real airplane soars by.

But what if these cessationists had the wisdom of the hut-dwelling Peruvian chief? They would then say, "I haven't seen valid prophecy or clusters of healing and miracles, but that doesn't mean they don't exist. Since I haven't seen them, perhaps my opinions, and those of my other hut-dwelling brothers, are not correct. Perhaps by listening to someone who has seen clusters of healings and miracles, I could learn something that I didn't know before."

Instead of imbibing Jesus's teaching, many academic critics in his day simply assumed that he must be wrong. After all, they had studied Torah for many years and learned it from others who had studied it for many years. Jesus was a young man without accreditation in their circles of sages. Surely, if God were going to act, he would do it among *them*. But God often prefers the humble and the lowly, and today he is using many of the lowly while some more precise theological experts scoff. Granted, many of the lowly are also being exploited by the proud, by those we rightly recognize as false apostles and teachers. That's why we need more of the critics to humble themselves, embrace what God is doing, and bring to bear their expertise on serving and protecting the humble instead of dismissing their genuine experiences with God.

# 19

# The Argument from Wacky Charismatics

Spiritual gifts could be perfectly biblical in principle and abused or neglected in exercise. Yet vocal cessationist critics often insist that the mishandling of the gifts by some charismatics indicates the cessation of those gifts. There are conspicuous errors among many charismatics today. These do not, however, justify misappropriating Scripture so as to deny that we should expect biblical gifts to continue today. Yet John MacArthur readily confuses these two issues in his books.

As mentioned in chapter 18, wacky charismatics have sometimes tempted me (Craig) to be a cessationist. (For purposes of this book, we are pretending that "wacky" is a theological term.) Cessationism would be so much neater and simpler. The *biblical* solution to wackiness, however, is discernment (1 Cor. 14:29; 1 Thess. 5:20–22), not throwing out the baby with the bathwater. I have witnessed my share of charismatic craziness over the decades, but I have also witnessed in most noncharismatic churches various divergences from what is taught in Scripture (even apart from their teaching and practice regarding spiritual gifts). So as a Bible teacher I want to call all the church back to biblical norms—yet patiently and graciously (2 Tim. 2:24–25), especially when the craziness is due to inadequate teaching rather than deliberate defiance of Scripture.

Other charismatic teachers also recognize the need to challenge errors in charismatic circles. This is true, for example, of Ken Fish and many other proteges of John Wimber, as well as many denominational Pentecostals and others. In his works, charismatic teacher Michael Brown has often challenged shallow or worldly charismatic practice.[1] R. T. Kendall affirms the continuance of prophetic and healing gifts but criticizes the state of the current charismatic movement as "Ishmael," waiting for God to send an "Isaac" that brings together Word and Spirit.[2]

Although many parts of the church separate those, we desperately need both. Rice Broocks, author of *God's Not Dead*, likewise affirms all the gifts but rightly laments the distortions often practiced in the name of "charismatic" teaching. He emphasizes that Scripture provides our script, but much of the charismatic world in the United States today is like professional wrestling: The bad guy knocks out the referee so no rules remain.[3] One does not have to be a cessationist to challenge charismatic extremes, though our varied experiences with the Spirit and examinations of Scripture influence what we consider "extreme."

## Most MacArthurian Charismatics Are Wacky

Both MacArthur's *Charismatic Chaos* and his Strange Fire conference focused not on exegetical support for cessationism—which is, as we have seen, beyond scarce—but on wacky examples of charismatics (plus some charismatics misrepresented out of context as wacky). In this approach he and his compatriots follow the model set by B. B. Warfield, whose focus in *Counterfeit Miracles* was not exegesis but attempting to debunk all miracle claims throughout history.[4]

MacArthur rightly critiques the excesses of prosperity teachers and positive confession,[5] and, insofar as his information is accurate, many other errors among charismatics on a popular level. (Although these appear among many biblically untrained Christians on a popular level, they are issues that need to be confronted pastorally.) At the same time, many of his comparisons risk caricature, cumulatively supporting an *ad hominem* argument.[6]

1. E.g., Brown, *Holy Fire*; Brown, *End*. For excellent balance, see Collins, *Charismatic Christianity*.

2. See esp. Kendall, *Receiving Promise*; on some prophetic circles, see Kendall, *Prophetic Integrity*.

3. Craig Keener, conversation with Rice Broocks, Nashville, Tennessee, October 6, 2024.

4. While acknowledging the relative soundness of A. J. Gordon and A. B. Simpson (Warfield, *Counterfeit Miracles*, 159, 195), Warfield shows more interest in John Alexander Dowie (196), who by all standards, including those of mainstream Pentecostals and charismatics, went off the deep end.

5. MacArthur, *Chaos*, 264–90. Clark, "Strange Fire," 65–66, acknowledges MacArthur's correct challenge to extreme Word of Faith and prosperity teaching but responds (61–62, 66) that most charismatics do not embrace it. Some who do value prosperity mean it in the same sense that Puritans did (67, citing their work ethic).

6. As rightly emphasized in Clark, "Strange Fire," 59–61.

### *Pentecostal History*

Seeking to discredit Pentecostalism, MacArthur focuses on Charles Parham (including some unproved allegations about him) and E. W. Kenyon, because, he says, "these two men are responsible for the theological foundations upon which the entire charismatic system is built. They represent its historic roots."[7] Parham, to be sure, was influential on William Seymour's view of tongues as Spirit baptism's "Bible evidence," but Pentecostalism never depended on his leadership and in most of the country moved on without him. (Certainly Seymour did.)[8]

And while many have argued that Kenyon may stand behind some elements in Word of Faith teaching (a connection initially pointed out by a specifically charismatic critic of the teaching),[9] Kenyon was hardly a central influence on Pentecostalism as a whole. Early Pentecostals mostly followed the well-worn paths of the late nineteenth-century radical evangelical healing movement.[10] Kenyon became a Baptist minister originally brought back to faith through the preaching of leading Baptist pastor A. J. Gordon. If one assigns guilt by association, does Kenyon taint all Baptists?

MacArthur's "foundations" and "roots" argument seems to deliberately isolate potentially vulnerable figures to the neglect of others. For healing, what about key nineteenth-century supporters such as Dorothea Trudel, Johann Christoph Blumhardt, A. J. Gordon, or A. B. Simpson? Gordon, a Baptist, was theologically balanced and portended the ultimate mainstream of the movement. (Gordon was convinced about healing through witnessing the instant healing of a jaw during D. L. Moody's 1877 campaign.)[11] For baptism in the Spirit, whatever one's views on the subject, what about John Wesley (in his later years),[12] Charles Finney, Holiness preachers, Moody, R. A. Torrey, and among Pentecostals themselves, Seymour and William Durham?[13] These views originated with neither Parham nor Kenyon. While not treating tongues

7. MacArthur, *Strange Fire*, 31. Parham was a racist, but so was Luther, and Seymour was not; the unproved sexual accusation against Parham should be admitted only if MacArthur also admits the unproved accusation that John Knox "had an affair with his mother-in-law" (De Arteaga, "Parody," 30).

8. See Robeck, "Seymour," esp. 79–89.

9. McConnell, *Gospel*. Cf. also other early charismatic critiques of Word of Faith teaching, e.g., Farah, *Pinnacle*; Fee, *Disease*. Some others question the alleged influence of New Thought on Kenyon's single year at Boston's Emerson School of Oratory (see McIntyre, *Kenyon*), noting that A. J. Gordon and A. B. Simpson were stronger influences (Bowman, *Controversy*, cited in Oliver, *Revivals*, 238).

10. On which see, e.g., Chappell, "Healing Movement"; Hardesty, *Faith Cure*; Baer, "Bodies"; Alexander, *Healing*; Curtis, *Faith*; Curtis, "Character"; for one collection of some primary sources from the period, see Graf, *Healing*.

11. Hartley, *Evangelicals*, 58.

12. See Wood, *Pentecost* (e.g., 145).

13. Spirit reception distinct from and subsequent to initiation also characterized most later patristic sources, although normally in routinized, sacramental form (see, e.g., Hunter, *Spirit*

as evidence of baptism in the Spirit, Simpson "urged the value of tongues" before the rise of Pentecostalism.[14] And for radical faith, George Müller and Hudson Taylor provide some of the seminal nineteenth-century models.[15]

Most of the many academic historians regarding the history of healing movements, evangelicalism, the Holiness movement, and Pentecostalism would take issue with MacArthur's radically disproportionate representation of Pentecostalism's roots.[16]

### Guilt by Association

MacArthur says that most of the charismatic world accepts Oneness Pentecostals;[17] in fact many Trinitarian Pentecostals consider Oneness Pentecostalism heretical. While many ordinary Christians on a popular level switch back and forth between addressing the Father and Son in prayer, some denominations articulate the distinction particularly clearly. The longest part of the doctrinal statement of the Assemblies of God, the world's largest Pentecostal denomination,[18] is an affirmation of the Trinity originally formulated to guard against the Oneness teaching; its statement on the Trinity appears second in sequence, only after its statement on the inspiration of Scripture.[19] Trinitarian Pentecostals also rightly reject any connection of tongues to salvation.[20]

MacArthur includes in his critique of charismatics some evangelists whom all acknowledge as fakes, such as Peter Popoff.[21] MacArthur compares with charismatics false New Age prophecies[22] and false prophecies by the Watch Tower Society.[23] He also discusses figures that mainstream Pentecostals and charismatics would consider cultic, such as Hobart Freeman, William Branham,[24] and certainly Joseph Smith[25] and the United House of Prayer for

---

*Baptism*, 137–38); so also many later sources, including Aquinas (154); cf. even C. I. Scofield (Ward, "Argument," 82).

14. Thiselton, *Spirit*, 312, also noting that "he strongly opposed all 'Cessationist' beliefs, appealing to Joel 2 and 1 Cor. 12:8–10 and 12:28–30."

15. See King, *Moving Mountains*.

16. See, e.g., Synan, *Movement*; Dayton, *Roots*; Synan, *Tradition*; Anderson, *Pentecostalism*; Opp, *Lord for Body*; Robeck, *Mission*; Porterfield, *Healing*; Anderson, *Ends of the Earth*. For Seymour's major role beyond Parham, see also Hunter, *Spirit Baptism*, 28–29.

17. MacArthur, *Strange Fire*, 52–53.

18. Assemblies of God World Missions, "Vital Stats," suggests 88.9 million members and adherents, only 3.5 percent of whom live in the US.

19. See Assemblies of God, "Truths."

20. Cf. Keener, *Gift & Giver*, 93: "Adding any condition to salvation—whether tongues-speaking or anything else—distorts the sufficiency of Christ."

21. MacArthur, *Chaos*, 208.

22. MacArthur, *Strange Fire*, 127.

23. MacArthur, *Strange Fire*, 128.

24. MacArthur, *Chaos*, 194–95.

25. MacArthur, *Strange Fire*, 51, noting "tongues, prophecy, and . . . visions."

All People.[26] "Most churches do not go to that extreme," he concedes, but "such examples represent the logical end of the charismatic insistence that God is giving new revelation to the church today."[27] Yet the vast majority of charismatics with even the slightest biblical training reject such groups.

Meanwhile, guilt by association is a fallacious means of reasoning. Some cults use holy books or have rules against sexual immorality. The Watch Tower Society (Jehovah's Witnesses), by the way, strongly opposes the ideas of miracles or healing today—and certainly tongues. Should continuationists use them to deploy guilt by association against cessationism?

MacArthur also compares charismatics to occultic and psychic healers.[28] Scripture does talk about displays of occult power, but usually in a context where God goes on to demonstrate how his power is greater (Exod. 7:11, 22; 8:7, 19; Dan. 2:27; 4:9; Acts 8:11–12; 13:8–12; cf. 1 Kings 18:22–40). Should we expect that God would tell us today to stop healing (or caring about health) because occult healers do it? Or should we expect, as often in Scripture, a greater display of God's power that trumps occult power? Likewise, when applied to ordinary charismatic Christians praying for healing, anecdotes of fake "faith healers" or fraudulent healings merely amount to logically fallacious, ad hominem attacks. Do we respond to false *teaching* by rejecting all teaching? Most cults have prayer, preaching, leaders, and afterlife promises. Should we reject all these actions or beliefs today because cults have them? Shall we reject all money because counterfeits exist? My first periodontist lost his license for malpractice; happily, my current periodontist repaired the damage inflicted by the first one. It would be foolhardy to reject all doctors or medicine because of the mistakes of some (these mistakes were more common before modern regulations).

### Exploiters

"The tragic irony," MacArthur complains, "is that the movement labeling itself as 'Spirit-filled' is notorious for sexual immorality, financial impropriety, and ostentatious worldliness in the lives of its most visible leaders."[29] But other evangelicals also have their share of horrendous scandals, from Jerry Falwell Jr. to Ravi Zacharias, and even to leaders in MacArthur's own circle. Is it fair to paint all evangelicals with the same brush? Or to paint the Christian movement or religion as a whole with the brush of child-molesting priests and adulterous pastors? Various individuals and groups, including in religious spheres, exploit the advantage of potential independence and especially lack of accountability.

26. MacArthur, *Strange Fire*, 69.
27. MacArthur, *Strange Fire*, 69.
28. MacArthur, *Chaos*, 203–4.
29. MacArthur, *Strange Fire*, 205.

The scandal involving Zacharias does not rightly discredit all apologetics ministries; the scandal surrounding Falwell does not rightly discredit all Christian colleges; scandals around fallen pastors cannot discredit all pastoral ministry. Such scandals do provide a significant warning against celebrity Christianity and putting preachers on pedestals. Our leaders wouldn't fall off pedestals so often if we'd quit putting them up there. Even when people are touched through a ministry (such as Zacharias's apologetics), God may be responding to the recipients' need or faith rather than the vessel he uses. Hannah went away happy after Eli prayed for her (1 Sam. 1:17–18), not realizing that Eli himself stood under judgment (2:29); but God granted her request for a son (1:20, 27; cf. 2:21), and perhaps Eli's because of his office (cf. 2:20).

Tragically, some false prophets and exploiters have gotten away with heinous crimes before being exposed. With prophecy as well as with other ministries, this more often happens with those on pedestals than with garden-variety "lay" prophecy or other gifts in local churches. One prophet in one of the Evangelical Church of Congo congregations was known for being very accurate, but over time he became very inaccurate, and finally it came to light that he had begun sexually harassing young women who worked with him.[30] In the United States, Craig's friend Elijah Stephens experienced devastating consequences when he followed what turned out to be a fabricated prophecy from Shawn Bolz, now widely accused of extensive unethical conduct.[31]

Likewise, at International House of Prayer of Kansas City (IHOPKC), "prophet" Bob Hartley had his children doing research on people who would be at a conference so he could "prophesy" to them deceptively.[32] That it is better to hear God in part (1 Cor. 13:9) than to not hear at all is no excuse to *pretend* to hear what God is not saying. Also at IHOPKC, but far more famous, was Paul Cain.[33] Jack Deere notes that Cain could be so precise that once when Cain was rambling and Deere's mind wandered to his old bird dog, Cain turned to him and exclaimed, "Jack, what are you doing thinking about your bird dog when I am preaching?"[34] Yet Deere also testifies about what he subsequently learned: Cain not only sometimes prophesied

30. Shared with us by Médine Moussounga Keener, September 28, 2024.

31. See, e.g., Winger, "Insider"; "Important Letter."

32. One of his children, Jed, who at the time was too young to understand the ethical dimension of the research, has since publicly exposed his father; see Hartley, "Deception"; now esp. helpfully Winger, "Going Public." Some of those who come out of the wreckage left by such false prophets may paint with too broad a brush, but the trauma they endured makes this understandable.

33. Citing Cain's assistant Reed Grafke, Scott, *Blundered*, 74–75, notes that while Cain had an extraordinary, naturally inexplicable gift, when feeling pressure, he also sometimes "cheated."

34. Jack Deere, conversation in Nashville, Tennessee, October 19, 2023; used with his permission, granted September 29, 2024. Deere provided other examples no less difficult to explain naturalistically.

deceptively but also sexually abused his apprentices.[35] Some other prophetic voices at IHOPKC, however, apparently had a different character; two private sources thus informed me that John Paul Jackson tried to warn others about those there he discerned as false prophets, though his warnings largely went unheeded.

On February 7, 2025, Sam Storms released "My Heartfelt Apology to the Body of Christ." He confesses that, despite his close relationship with IHOPKC founder Mike Bickle, he never suspected Bickle's involvement in sexual sin.[36] Apart from the women Bickle exploited, however, few people—even Bickle's harshest theological critics—were aware of that. Some of IHOPKC's most characteristic elements were not primarily dependent on Bickle; 24/7 prayer, for example, also characterized the Moravian revival, starting in 1727.[37] The unexpected revelation of Bickle's sin certainly surprised and grieved me (Craig). Far more, it devastated many deeply godly people who were involved with IHOPKC, whose trust Bickle had also exploited. After learning of his behavior, some of them, such as Allen Hood, were central in exposing him.[38] But I was also surprised by the revelations about Zacharias and Philip Yancey. Surely John MacArthur and Phil Johnson were also surprised by the revelation about their associate Steve Lawson. Happily, they acted appropriately in supporting church discipline.[39] We must lament and never celebrate such abuses.

We do our best to discern, but some things we just don't see coming; we don't know others' hearts.[40] Paul warns us neither to embrace accusations prematurely (1 Tim. 5:19) nor to endorse someone's ministry prematurely (5:22). We recognize some sins in this life, whereas others will become obvious only at the judgment (5:24). Once matters are clear, however, church discipline is essential, and some charismatic circles need to develop more appropriate accountability structures.

The most persuasive argument against charismatic experience is indeed wacky charismatics. But the reasoning is flawed. By analogy, the most persuasive

35. See Deere, "Power." Deere notes Mike Bickle's resistance to exposing more about Cain, both here and in Deere, "Opinion." Bickle also very gently defended Cain in my interview with him on November 9, 2019.

36. See now esp. Storms, *Rise and Fall*.

37. Burkholder, "Remembering Revival," 11.

38. Insider Scott, *Blundered*, 158–59, though writing from a limited perspective as we all do, believes that "while some aspects of [IHOPKC's] prophetic history are true," Bickle reshaped them thoroughly to his own advantage.

39. Master's Seminary dean Steven Lawson, at age 73, was exposed in September 2024 for a "five-year relationship with a woman in her late twenties" (see Roys, "Lawson"). Phil Johnson appears to have responded with integrity.

40. On God as searcher of hearts, see, e.g., 1 Chron. 28:9; Ps. 139:23; Jer. 17:10; Rom. 8:27; Rev. 2:23. Among examples, Joseph could not have foreseen how centralizing all power under Pharaoh (Gen. 47:19–20) would later be used against his own people; David and even his prophet Nathan could not foresee the apostasy of Solomon so as to prevent his accession.

argument detractors raise against Jesus today is the behavior of some who claim to be Jesus's followers, often including the savage attacks of some Christians against others. We periodically meet those who reject the Christian faith because they feel they must accept all or nothing of their parents' conservative Christian beliefs. Does that always make all those beliefs wrong?[41]

Those who criticize charismatics by highlighting only the worst examples are dishonestly selective and are resorting to the ad hominem fallacy, a sort of argument that merits being dismissed at the outset as illogical. Using a similar strategy, Israel's enemies invited the Persian king to check the records for Jerusalem's past revolts (Ezra 4:15), and sure enough, the search revealed such revolts (4:19). Jerusalem did not necessarily revolt more than most other cities, and they had never revolted against *Persia*, but the narrow search criteria created the impression that Israel's enemies wanted.

Again, by analogy, in 2018, a journalistic investigation found 412 abuse claims against 168 independent Baptist church leaders.[42] In 2019, revelations of ministerial abuse rocked the Southern Baptist Convention, with more than seven hundred victims and hundreds of offenders, reportedly including former SBC president Johnny Hunt.[43] These revelations are terrible, but they do not properly discredit all Baptists or all Baptist pastors. Anyone in a position of power or influence over others, particularly without accountability, can become vulnerable, especially if oblivious to the dangers of transference and countertransference.[44] Scandals in individual denominations usually pale numerically compared to their larger secular counterparts; for example, more than eighty thousand claimed that they experienced sexual abuse in the Boy Scouts of America.[45]

As long as people sin, abuses will happen, but some continuationist ministries that have been around for a long time have developed much clearer accountability structures for addressing them than those typical of completely independent ministries. For example, the US Assemblies of God, a denomination that globally belongs to the largest Pentecostal fellowship, made the news when a number of cases of sexual abuse surfaced among local or regional affiliates of its college and youth ministries. At the same time, the national

41. Against dismissing Christianity or evangelicalism because of the scandals of some of their agents, see, e.g., Werntz, "Scandals."

42. Shellnut, "Hundreds," citing findings from the *Fort Worth Star-Telegram*; also "Abuse of Faith."

43. See, e.g., Downen, Tedesco, and Hennes, "Need to Know."

44. On potential risks in pastoral countertransference, see, e.g., Cooper-White, *Wisdom*; Hinksman, "Transference."

45. Confidential internal records over roughly a century include nearly 8,000 abusers and more than 12,000 victims; although the organization barred predators from further participation, they often failed to inform police. Now rebranded Scouting America, the organization now has some of the strictest protections in place, protections few imagined necessary a century ago. For order of magnitude, the organization had some 5 million youth members in 1979 and 2.3 million in 2017, with nearly 900,000 adult volunteers in the latter year (Wikipedia, "Boy Scouts").

level follows strict protocols not only for such circumstances but even for many forms of moral deviation that lack legal prohibitions.[46] It removes ministerial credentials for sexual misconduct for two years, during which time rehabilitation is obligatory if credentials are to ever be restored. Districts are required to retain and transfer offenders' records.[47] Despite Jimmy Swaggert's donations of millions of dollars to the denomination's missions program, the denomination's leaders upheld their standard of discipline and Swaggert's refusal to comply cost him his credentials in 1988.

Different interpreters will differ as to the severity of and appropriate discipline for different offenses.[48] Certainly I (Craig) want to stay in my lane as an expositor of Scripture rather than trying to defend contemporary figures. The scandals of recent years (charismatic and noncharismatic, religious and secular) show how little we know of the private lives of even the most publicly respectable leaders; God alone fully knows people's hearts. Yet even apart from that, I want to stake my theology on Scripture rather than on any contemporary's current reputation. And when there are questions, I would rather grant someone the benefit of the doubt (as in the US legal system) until investigation proves otherwise, even when (as often in, for example, marriage counseling situations) that entails holding in tension conflicting stories.

### Prophets Aren't Omniscient

Some complain more specifically that with all the "prophetic" people around Bickle, surely some should have prophetically discerned his infidelities.[49] But prophets are not omniscient; they know only what God chooses to reveal, in his time (2 Kings 4:13–14, 27, 39–40; Matt. 13:17 // Luke 10:24; Acts 18:21; 1 Cor. 4:19; 2 Cor. 1:15–17). For example:

- Although God showed Joseph that his brothers would eventually bow to him (Gen. 37:5–10), God apparently did not warn him what his brothers would do to him when he visited (37:13–17).

46. Neglecting such protocols violates the denomination's explicit standards. Despite various advantages of local church autonomy, one disadvantage is that, as with Baptists and other churches with congregational polity, it has sometimes complicated church discipline at a higher level.

47. Assemblies of God Bylaws, Article X, esp. X.3a (p. 214).

48. E.g., we do not equate the nonphysical offense of Michael Brown, apparently limited to no more than a single year more than two decades ago (based on our reading of the fullest report), with the long-term affair of Steve Lawson or the multiple affairs of Mike Bickle over the course of many years.

49. One of those prophetic people did share with me that it was becoming clear that something was going on, but the Lord did not show him what, and Bickle's infidelities just seemed too hard to believe (personal correspondence, July 11, 2024). I (Craig) can understand that; in early 1987 I felt that I heard the Lord explicitly tell me that one of my dearest associates was committing adultery, but because of my respect for the person I did not take it *literally* until circumstances forced me to do so.

- Although Samuel knew (maybe without needing prophetic revelation) that Saul was dangerous (1 Sam. 16:2), and the prophet Gad gave David specific warning afterward (22:5), no prophet warned David to expect that Saul would seek his life.
- Although Nathan announced coming judgment in David's family and through one of David's acquaintances (2 Sam. 12:10–11), none of David's prophets informed him in advance that specifically Absalom or Ahithophel would revolt.
- David apparently also lacked specific warning of the revolt of Sheba son of Bichri (20:1–2).
- Nathan warned David of Adonijah's conspiracy only after it had become public (1 Kings 1:8–11, 24).
- Although Elisha knew Gehazi's sin when he committed it, he apparently did not foresee it, since he did not replace him beforehand (2 Kings 5:25–27; cf. 4:31).
- Paul probably did not foresee the failure of Demas (2 Tim. 4:10; cf. Philem. 24).
- While Paul knew that some of the Ephesian elders would eventually become false teachers (Acts 20:30), had he known which ones he might have removed them from leadership beforehand.

Perhaps God is so courteous as to give some people many chances (as in the case of Samson) before exposing their sin and shaming them before others. The book of Judges suggests that God often made use of very fallible people (e.g., Judg. 8:27; 11:30, 39; 16:1; also 1 Sam. 2:29).[50] In the end, though, sin catches up with sinners (Num. 32:23; Judg. 16:20–21; 1 Sam. 2:31–36; 2 Sam. 12:10–14; 1 Tim. 5:24). Even the most gifted of prophets (1 Kings 13:2–6) could die for personally (albeit unwittingly) disobeying God (13:21–24), without harming the otherwise godly prophet who lied to this fellow prophet (13:18, 28–32).

Similarly overgeneralizing is a remark attributed to MacArthur on Twitter: "I'll start believing the truth prevails in the Charismatic Movement when its leaders start looking more like Jesus Christ."[51] Such a statement reflects at best a very limited acquaintance with ordinary, genuine charismatic believers. As two examples, Brown mentions charismatic Dutch Reformed Christian Corrie ten Boom and one of his own former students martyred for his loving witness for Christ.[52] We could mention countless others.

50. See also Martin, "Judging"; Martin, *Judging*.

51. See John MacArthur (@johnmacarthur), Twitter (now X), October 16, 2013, https://x.com/johnmacarthur/status/390563678350606336.

52. Brown, *Authentic Fire*, 74, although the link he cites to MacArthur's post is now dead. Beth Fish shared an example of someone brought to Christ through their Vineyard small group

Nor is such shallowness limited to charismatics. As Deere warns, in contrast to persecuted churches desperately needing real miracles, "the Western church often has more in common with the Laodicean church. . . . Nobody really persecutes the church in America because it doesn't threaten anyone. And it won't until it becomes a praying church."[53] Biblical illiteracy and consequent infidelity are growing; whether it is zeal without knowledge or knowledge without zeal, we together must confront this growing challenge.

### Caricaturing a Movement

While MacArthur exempts from his criticism of heresy his "reformed continuationist" friends,[54] he complains that they represent only a small minority and that they simply provide cover to the wider movement.[55] He insists that his critiques, by contrast, involve not "the wacky fringe" but "the *mainstream* Charismatic Movement."[56] Scholars and sound Bible interpreters are a minority in *most* parts of the church. Yet one might suppose that those of us who have spent decades inside the movement—Daniel, Craig, Brown, and others—have a broader knowledge of what is mainstream than does MacArthur.

MacArthur worries that "the continuationist position severely limits the ability of its advocates to confront others who fall into charismatic confusion."[57] In fact charismatics with wrong teaching are far more likely to welcome correction from fellow continuationists than from cessationists, especially harsh cessationists such as MacArthur. They may not always know whom to trust, but they definitely know not to trust those whom they view as adversaries of the Spirit's work in their lives.

Moreover, while MacArthur is right to critique errors where they are present, this does not justify jettisoning the baby with the bathwater. While populist online platforms have proliferated unfounded teachings, Pentecostal denominations are among the firmest in upholding the authority of Scripture, supporting mission, and being active in evangelism. The Barna Group's research revealed that the Assemblies of God, the world's largest Pentecostal denomination, is the denomination with the highest commitment to the essential Christian doctrines. Barna also found that there were only three types of churches in America that "had a majority of adherents who had shared their faith in Christ with a non-Christian in the past year [2001]." They were Pentecostal, Assemblies of God, and

---

who eventually smuggled Bibles to North Korea and finally was martyred there (shared October 5, 2024); examples could be multiplied.

53. Deere, *Voice*, 87–88 (quote from 88).

54. MacArthur, *Strange Fire*, 231–34.

55. MacArthur, *Strange Fire*, 234.

56. MacArthur, *Strange Fire*, 234–35.

57. MacArthur, *Strange Fire*, 238.

nondenominational churches.[58] (And since the Assemblies of God is Pentecostal, there really are only two groups.) Likewise, charismatic renewal has tended to make Christians in traditional denominations more committed to Scripture rather than less.[59] MacArthur's use of wacky charismatics to criticize the whole movement is indeed a case of severe misrepresentation.

### *Supportive Reformed Voices*

"I thought it was a bad idea," notes Reformed pastor John Carpenter: "a conference hosted by one group of Christians to explain how bad another group of Christians is. But the rationale was that since the troubled group wasn't correcting their own troubles, someone had to do the dirty work. Hence was hatched John MacArthur's 'Strange Fire' conference."[60]

Lest one suppose that MacArthur believes that he speaks for the entire Reformed community, he himself acknowledges his Reformed continuationist friends, as already noted. Particularly noteworthy in the North American context is well-known pastor-scholar John Piper,[61] along with other noteworthy Reformed continuationists such as Wayne Grudem and former cessationist Storms. MacArthur viewed their continuationist position as inconsistent with Reformed theology, despite his own decidedly non-Reformed eschatology.

Charismatic scholar Brown, though not Calvinist himself, notes Reformed pushback against MacArthur's fire. Reformed Baptist and supremely gracious church historian and evangelical leader Timothy George quotes Reformed Anglican J. I. Packer's appreciation of the charismatic movement, though Packer was not charismatic himself:

> When we apply these tests to the charismatic movement, it becomes plain at once that God is in it. For whatever threats and perhaps instances of occult and counterfeit spirituality we may think we detect around its periphery (and what movement of revival has ever lacked these things around its periphery?), its main effect everywhere is to promote robust Trinitarian faith, personal fellowship with the divine Savior and Lord whom we meet in the New Testament, repentance, obedience, and love to fellow Christians, expressed in ministry of all sorts towards them—plus a zeal for evangelistic outreach that puts the staider sort of churchmen to shame.[62]

58. Barna Group, "Findings."
59. De Arteaga, "Parody," 25.
60. Carpenter, "Recovering."
61. See, e.g., Piper, "Prophecy and Tongues" (accessed Aug. 29, 2024); see further "Spiritual Gifts."
62. Brown, *Authentic Fire*, 154–55, citing George, "Strange," which in turn cites Packer, *Keep in Step*, 150. Graves, "Nature," 108, also notes 224–25 of the 1984 edition of Packer, *Keep in Step*.

Continuationists citing Packer's book to challenge the Strange Fire conference drew an unfortunate reaction. Namely, cessationist pastor Dan Phillips responded that Packer embodied the very problem that Strange Fire sought to address, abusing his respectability to support a corrupt movement.[63]

### *Chauncy Versus the First Great Awakening*

Each outpouring of the Spirit is different, and the charismatic movement has its problems. Without equating the twentieth-century Pentecostal and charismatic movements with the First Great Awakening, however, we can at least note that in their first century these movements have been one of history's greatest forces for evangelizing the world. Church historians often consider global Pentecostalism possibly "the fastest-growing movement that the church has ever seen."[64] At the very least, the strong majority of Christian observers consider its contribution to global mission beneficial.

For Brown, the contrasting responses such as those mentioned above echo those during the First Great Awakening. "It appears that just like Charles Chauncy, the chief critic of the Great Awakening, the Strange Fire camp has focused on the chaff whereas J. I. Packer, like Jonathan Edwards before him, has focused on the wheat."[65] Brown then quotes from his own *Revival Answer Book*:

> Professor Conrad Cherry observed that "Chauncy meticulously assayed and reported the abundant improprieties of the revival . . . , screamings and writhings by the congregations. . . . Chauncy's list was endless." . . . Yet this is precisely where Chauncy made his fatal mistake, since, as Cherry notes, "These things in his judgment constituted the very nature of the revival itself; the Awakening was not a work of God's Spirit but a despicable instance of wanton emotionalism." Sadly, this very same error is being repeated by some leaders today who seek to protect the Church from errors and extremes but are actually turning the hungry and thirsty away from the Spirit's life-giving streams.[66]

For Chauncy, Brown continues, "there was no revival taking place at all; it was a sham, a counterfeit, a fraud. Critics of the Great Awakening were unanimous in their verdict: It was not a true awakening, nor was it great."[67]

63. Phillips, "Packer on Charismatics" (cited in Brown, *Authentic Fire*, 155).

64. Sweeney, *Story*, 153. Cf. Tomkins, *History*, 220: "the fastest-growing form of Christianity ever." Similarly, evangelism aided by signs and wonders eventually contributed to the young Anglican Province of South East Asia being "one of the fastest growing parts of the Anglican Communion" (Green, *Asian Tigers*, 1).

65. Brown, *Authentic Fire*, 155.

66. Brown, *Authentic Fire*, 155–56.

67. Brown, *Authentic Fire*, 156. He cites Brown, *Revival Answer Book*, 17; and suggests further De Arteaga, "Strange Fire."

Chauncy constituted Edwards's main challenger[68] and led the attacks on George Whitefield as the source of the disorder.[69] Critics suggested that the revival waned too quickly to be genuine, and insisted that the radicals were not merely in error but were agents of Satan.[70] As Mark Noll points out, Chauncy (1705–87) "was as quick to spy the brambles of enthusiasm as some of the revival's supporters were to spot the fruits of the Spirit."[71] Complaining that participants in the revival were following internal impressions about Scripture and the like, Chauncy and other rationalistic "Old Lights" collected all the negative stories they could to demonstrate the revival's supposed "antinomian and enthusiastic excesses."[72] He used guilt by association with fringe movements,[73] and denounced "Screamings . . . Tremblings" and other bodily manifestations.[74] Whereas moderates suggested that excesses were relatively rare, Chauncy considered them pervasive.[75]

One comment that Chauncy found particularly offensive was one radical revivalist's query as to whether Chauncy was born again.[76] Edwards warned against questioning professing Christians' salvation in this manner—while also himself warning that the revivals' critics risked committing the unpardonable sin against the Holy Spirit.[77]

Impressed by British Enlightenment thinkers, Chauncy also led his followers away from traditional Puritan theology.[78] His criticisms (of both genuine and perceived excesses) divided some supporters of the awakening, as some sought to appease him or forestall his criticisms.[79] Some cautious moderates thus withdrew support from Whitefield.[80] When one long-bedridden woman was healed after prayer, even moderates were concerned that the incident would challenge the then-widespread belief that miracles stopped after the apostles, while critics mocked that it was a fake miracle like those

68. E.g., Kidd, *Awakening*, 161–62.
69. Kidd, *Awakening*, 169.
70. Kidd, *Awakening*, 166.
71. Noll, *Rise*, 129.
72. Noll, *Rise*, 129; Kidd, *Awakening*, 130. Because James Davenport (1716–57) was excessive for a time, he became a prime feature in Chauncy's criticisms (Noll, *Rise*, 130; Kidd, *Awakening*, 62, 140, 162).
73. Noll, *Rise*, 129.
74. Kidd, *Awakening*, 162.
75. Kidd, *Awakening*, 162. For other reactions against excesses in revivalism, such as common emotional subjectivism (rooted in Puritan introspection) and perceived anthropocentric methods, see Evans, "Pursuit," 26–28. Some may also involve repeated attempts to reconvert the converted.
76. Chauncy believed "that Davenport would judge him unconverted" (Kidd, *Awakening*, 145).
77. Kidd, *Awakening*, 120.
78. Noll, *Rise*, 180.
79. Cf. Kidd, *Awakening*, 67, 156–57.
80. Kidd, *Awakening*, 169–70.

of Catholics![81] Chauncy also denounced, with some moderates supporting him, the practice of some revival supporters allowing women and African Americans moved by the Spirit to exhort.[82] (Later, by the 1820s, secular science had provided critics a supposedly empirical explanation for the religious enthusiasm displayed at Methodist and Baptist meetings: Now it could be blamed on "animal magnetism.")[83]

Chauncy thus missed out on what God was doing. More sinfully, he also led many others to miss out on it too.

## Charismatics Break Rules for Exercising Gifts?

Tom Pennington says, "Tragically most charismatic practice today completely disregards those clear biblical commands [Paul's directives in 1 Cor. 14]. So not only are today's charismatic gifts not the New Testament gifts, but the clear directives the apostle laid down for the practice of the New Testament gifts are largely ignored. In most of the contemporary charismatic practice, the Holy Spirit is not honored. Instead, He is routinely grieved and disobeyed. The result is not the work of the Spirit, but it is a work of the flesh, clear rebellion even if it were the New Testament gifts."[84]

From our charismatic perspective, it seems ironic that a cessationist would accuse charismatics of ignoring aspects of Paul's instruction regarding spiritual gifts. Cessationists, after all, discard Paul's instruction about them altogether. In this case, however, the ad hominem claim cannot even be substantiated. Pennington denounces "most" charismatic practice as dishonoring and "routinely" grievous and disobedient to the Holy Spirit. One might hope for evidence to support such a claim. Given estimates of hundreds of millions of Pentecostals and charismatics globally,[85] it seems speculative for him to characterize "most" of their practices with a passing, undocumented statement. Gathering firm data to support Pennington's criticism would require him to observe or cite a respectable survey of hundreds of thousands of Pentecostal and charismatic churches, or at least take a fairly diverse random sample. Only a tiny percentage of Spirit-filled churches broadcast their services on television for Pennington to observe. Yet Spirit-filled churches pepper the entire globe, including very remote, underground, and persecuted areas, as well as large cities and population centers.

81. Kidd, *Awakening*, 162–63; Kidd, "Healing." Chauncy maintained the traditional Protestant view that the pope was the antichrist (Kidd, *Awakening*, 172).

82. Kidd, *Awakening*, 127, 213. For concerns about African American women's visions during the Awakening, see Worthen, *Spellbound*, 41.

83. Worthen, *Spellbound*, 135.

84. Pennington, "Case."

85. Johnson, Barrett, and Crossing, "Christianity 2010," 36; Johnson and Ross, *Atlas*, 102.

At best, then, all this statement could legitimately argue is that *some* charismatics today do not use the gifts correctly. It cannot demonstrate widespread charismatic abuse of the gifts. Moreover, even were such abuse pervasive in a contemporary movement, it could not speak to the continuation or cessation of the gifts at all. Even so, since Pennington's point is one of the most common objections I (Daniel) hear from cessationists, it is still worth addressing—so long as, again, we ignore the irony of one who rejects gifts for today while insisting on their proper practice.

### *Pennington's First Rule: Just Two or Three Prophecies*

Pennington highlights the areas where he believes charismatics violate Paul's instructions about prophecy in 1 Corinthians 14.[86] He says,

- "Rule number one, two or at the most three were to prophesy at a church service. Notice verse 29, 'Let two or three prophets speak.'"
- "Secondly, other prophets and the congregation were to evaluate those prophecies against previous revelation. Verse 29 says, 'Let the others pass judgment.'"
- Thirdly, "they were to speak one at a time, verse 30."
- "Fourthly, women are not allowed to prophesy in the corporate worship, verse 34 again."[87]

#### CHURCH "SERVICES"?

There are a couple problems with Pennington's first "rule." On our understanding, Paul actually does not limit the number of prophets who can speak "at a church service." We say this for two reasons. First, Paul's churches did not have "services" the way we think of them. They rather had house meetings gathered around a sacred meal and centered on the Lord Jesus's presence by the Spirit.[88] For Pennington to assume something like a modern church ser-

86. Just prior to the following rules on prophecy, Pennington recounts Paul's similar regulations of tongues. I will focus on Pennington's discussion of Paul's regulations on prophecy because the same basic rebuttal applies to both. See Pennington, "Case."

87. Pennington, "Case."

88. Calling the Corinthian gathering a "service" at all is anachronistic. Paul addresses the Corinthians' church gatherings in 1 Cor. 11:17–14:40, a passage that reflects a mode of gathering that is far more simple, familial, cooperative, and charismatic than the typical modern church "service" in the Western world—whether cessationist *or* charismatic—to which Pennington seems to refer. The early Christians' gatherings would include the Lord's Supper as a full meal (see also Acts 2:42 and Jude 12), as well as the whole body's participation in sharing the Spirit's gifts with one another (see further Keener, *Background Commentary*, 722). Paul's concept of a church gathering appears in 1 Cor. 14:26: "Therefore what should you do, brothers? *Whenever you come together, each one of you* has a psalm, has a teaching, has a revelation, has a tongue,

vice as the context for Paul's instruction changes the frame of reference from apostolic, biblical practice to traditional, evangelical practice.

Paul is not concerned about disrupting the tidy flow of a church "service" led by platform leaders and structured after the pattern of congregational singing, offering, and sermon. He is rather concerned that a covenantal family is able to gather and benefit from everyone's participation in the Spirit. That is why he wants the prophets to speak in turn and then have their prophecies judged.

#### TWO OR THREE AT A TIME

Which leads to our second and more important reason that Pennington's first rule is less than accurate biblically.

Paul actually does not say that only two or three prophets may speak per "service." Pennington stops short, in the middle of Paul's statement, and therefore misses his point. What does Paul actually say? "Let two or three prophets speak, *and let the others pass judgment*" (1 Cor. 14:29 NASB, my emphasis). Paul's limit is not on the number of prophets who can speak in a given meeting. It is on the number of prophets who should speak *before the others evaluate their prophecies*.[89]

One of Pennington's mistakes is to separate verse 29 into two separate "rules." Paul does not give two rules. He gives one. After two or three prophets have spoken, others should then evaluate what was said. If we stop reading after the first half of verse 29, then it sounds like Paul may be limiting the number of prophets allowed to speak during a church meeting. But when we allow Paul to finish his thought, we see the verse is actually one compound thought, not two separate rules. We should also allow that verse to speak within its larger context. Then we would know what "two or three" means. It is a guideline to allow evaluation before too many prophets speak. It is not a restriction on the number of prophets to speak in a gathering.

Otherwise the next verses make no sense: "But if a revelation is made to another who is seated, the first one must keep silent. For you can *all* prophesy one by one, so that all may learn and all may be exhorted; and the spirits of prophets are subject to prophets; for God is not a God of confusion but of peace, as in all the churches of the saints" (1 Cor. 14:30–33 NASB, my emphasis). Paul tells the gathered community that they can "all" prophesy—not just two or three. His only restrictions are that they take turns and that they pause

---

has an interpretation. All things must be done for edification" (LEB, my emphasis; original italics omitted).

89. Paul gave the same basic guidance to those speaking in tongues earlier in v. 27: Two or three should speak, and then someone should interpret. Interpretation should follow tongues just as evaluation should follow prophecy. So Paul, again, might not be limiting the number of those who speak in tongues for a meeting (of a given size and length).

for evaluation. But again: *All* can participate so that all may learn. Similarly, Paul had already told the Corinthians that *all* members of the church may contribute to the meeting. "Each one" of them—not just two or three—has a significant gift to offer the other members (see 1 Cor. 14:26). So Paul has no interest in limiting the number of prophets to speak. He wants everyone to contribute. But in order for that to happen, Paul prohibits interruptions and requires order.

### VIOLATIONS OF PENNINGTON'S RULE?

Now that we see what Paul actually means by the first two "rules," do Pennington's implied criticisms of the charismatic world apply? In my (Daniel's) view, to speak honestly, I would say both no and yes. I first say no, based on the argument I just made. According to Paul's instructions for a charismatic worship gathering, everyone is allowed to participate. Paul gives no limit to the number of people who may prophesy in a gathering. Admittedly it is difficult, if not impossible, to allow total participation in large gatherings. But Paul does not have in mind the kind of large gathering that we often see in a modern church building or conference event.[90] His concern in this passage is for the kind of local, charismatic gathering that he taught his converts to have. Paul's expression of "church" would meet in someone's house around a meal and mutually share in the activity of the Spirit through prayer and the gifts.[91] First Corinthians 11:17–14:40 offers the clearest and most direct scriptural teaching we have on the subject of church gatherings. In this context, the "all" who may prophesy extends to all believers present in a church meeting (see Paul's use of the same Greek term in 14:5, 18, 23–24, 26).[92] Therefore,

90. The New Testament seems to leave room for various kinds and sizes of Christian assemblies. For example, Luke tells us about meetings among the early Jewish believers both in the temple precincts and in individual homes (Acts 2:46; 5:42). This appears to indicate larger, citywide gatherings for teaching (Acts 2:42), as well as more intimate meetings around meals. Keep in mind, however, that the temple area was a public place, not a privately owned church building. Luke also tells us that Paul used a "school" for instructing disciples in Ephesus after he was driven from the synagogue (Acts 19:9). Paul probably rented this lecture hall, which was associated with "Tyrannus"—either the owner or regular lecturer. In any case, it seems Paul conducted meetings there that gave more formal instruction to new believers, or held informative discussions, rather than the sort of meeting he taught established churches to hold (1 Cor. 11:17–14:40). Though our larger, modern services may not be wrong, neither are they precisely what Paul envisioned for a typical first-century church gathering. And it is the latter sort of gathering that Paul addresses in 1 Cor. 11–14.

91. Both 11:20 and 14:23 indicate gathering together, using a phrase that can also mean "*in the same place*" (as in NET; trans. from Dr. Robert Gladstone, private correspondence, July 16, 2018; cf. Acts 2:1).

92. Some would argue that Paul's encouragement for "all" to prophesy cannot possibly refer to one meeting but rather refers to the general principle that all church members are now qualified to prophesy at various times. But that argument does not take into account

against Pennington, when charismatics have more than three prophets speak, they do not violate Paul's instructions.

Nevertheless, even if we accept Pennington's rule, it is actually rarely violated. In the course of my life, I (Daniel) have attended many hundreds of charismatic meetings. My family has been in charismatic church ministry for five generations. Now that I lead an international evangelistic ministry and help lead large conferences around the world, I also help lead perhaps a hundred charismatic meetings per year. I rarely witness a meeting where more than three prophetic words are given. (I, Craig, second Daniel's observation.)[93] I have never witnessed people interrupt one another or jockey for position while they prophesy.[94] Based on this experience, Pennington's insinuation that charismatics violate his stipulated protocol makes little sense. I'm sure such violations do occur on occasion, but in the overall scheme of charismatic gatherings as a whole, these are relatively quite rare. So between Paul's clear instructions in Scripture and typical experience, no, Pennington's implied criticism does not apply to modern charismatic gatherings. Where did he derive his "expertise" regarding charismatic practice?

### Pennington's Second Rule: Evaluating Prophecies

But I give a qualified yes to Pennington's implied criticism that charismatics do not judge their own prophecies. I say "qualified," because charismatics do sometimes judge prophecies given in their meetings. I myself have had to help judge prophetic words in a gathering and help prophetic people remain accountable. Further, I know leaders who plant charismatic churches that practice corporate prophecy regularly. It is their constant practice to weigh every prophecy carefully. They do this not only to discern whether the messages line up with Scripture but also to perceive the practical applications of what God is saying to their churches through the collective force of the prophecies. I also personally know key leaders in the charismatic movement who are balanced in their approach to prophecy. They highly value and welcome

---

the fact that, in context, Paul *is* talking about what happens during a single meeting. As Fee notes, "This language [that 'all' may prophesy] makes almost no sense at all if he is referring to what should take place over several different meetings; the concern throughout, beginning with the verb 'you assemble' in v. 26, is with what takes place in a given gathering" (Fee, *Corinthians*, 695).

93. I (Craig) cannot recall seeing more than three in a church meeting. Where I did experience (and participate in) more was in an occasional gathering of three to four persons meeting together for an extended time of prayer. This is different than a public gathering and was designed for the specific purpose of praying to and hearing from God; cf. the group Samuel was mentoring in 1 Sam. 19:20; the prophets in 1 Sam. 10:5; and occasions in Acts such as 19:6.

94. That does not mean that it has never happened; see Graves, "Nature," 105, who rightly condemns an example he witnessed.

prophetic ministry in their midst, but they also hold prophetic people and their prophecies accountable.

Sadly, however, I admit that such accountability is often not the case. We charismatics can do a much better job at judging our own prophecies and helping to keep prophetic people accountable. Of course, I do not mean that we should start with default suspicion. Scripture teaches us not to despise prophetic ministry but to value it (1 Cor. 14:1; 1 Thess. 5:19–20). Yet it also teaches us to exercise discernment, not assuming that every prophetic word is accurate (1 Cor. 14:29; 1 Thess. 5:21–22; 1 John 4:1). And all of this should be done in love (1 Cor. 13). To add to the problem, the digital age has made putatively prophetic messages even more prolific with even fewer safeguards. So we should exercise special caution beyond those we know well, without succumbing to cynicism.

On the one (cessationist) side, there is automatic skepticism toward prophetic words. On the other (continuationist) side, there is often automatic acceptance of prophetic words. We need the balance of more accountability. My (Daniel's) early academic mentor Michael Brown has written an entire book to address these kinds of issues within the charismatic movement.[95] Brown says about judging prophecy: "All too often prophets deliver words with little or no accountability, even if [those words] are inaccurate or never come to pass."[96] He also says, "Without question the New Testament calls for prophetic words to be tested, which indicates that in this era, when everyone can potentially prophesy, we cannot take everything at face value. Prophecies must be judged."[97]

So Pennington has a point. Charismatics must do better at judging prophecy. I am happy to receive this criticism and to encourage my fellow charismatics to be more responsible. But again, what does this prove about cessationism? It only shows that we charismatics should be more conscientious about Paul's instructions—not that we should become *less* so by discounting the very gifts about which he so carefully instructs us. Paul does not hold the Corinthians' excesses against them—or against the Spirit's gifts!—the way Pennington does to charismatics today. Instead, Paul lovingly corrects the Corinthians *based on his conviction that the gifts should operate during Christian worship*. Ironically, some of Pennington's corrections can ultimately help the charismatic community improve their exercise of the gifts for the body's sake.

95. Brown, *Holy Fire*.

96. Brown, *Holy Fire*, 81. Brown goes on to note that, in fact, there may be extenuating circumstances that hinder a prophecy's fulfillment. So these things must be considered. But when the prophecies still collapse under scrutiny, they must be addressed and the prophets held accountable.

97. Brown, *Holy Fire*, 83.

### *Pennington's Third Rule: Interpreting Tongues*

Another area where cessationists may have a legitimate complaint, specifically on matters of protocol, is Pennington's third point—interpretation of tongues. Paul says that if someone is going to speak in tongues during the worship gathering, there must be an interpreter. But "if there is no interpreter, the speaker should keep quiet in the church and speak to himself and to God" (1 Cor. 14:28). This rule is clear enough. Wherever charismatics have violated this rule, Pennington's repetition of Paul's instruction is warranted. However, in all my years of participating in charismatic worship meetings, I have never seen this rule violated. (Insofar as I, Craig, may chime in here: I also have never seen it violated. I did witness two people starting to interpret simultaneously with the same words—despite there ordinarily being multiple ways to phrase an idea—but in line with Paul's instruction against two speaking at once, one stopped.)

In fact, in meetings I (Daniel) have attended that included spontaneous messages, those messages were usually prophecies, not tongues. But when tongues did occur, the normal pattern followed Paul's instructions. It was simple and orderly. Someone would normally speak out in tongues during a silent moment in the meeting. Then that same person or someone else would interpret. Nothing like the Corinthian abuses implied by Pennington ever occurred. In mainstream charismatic practice, they are not common. Wherever these abuses do occur, Pennington's criticism would be well taken. But as with the last rules, by itself this criticism would not indicate that these gifts have passed away.

Pennington might be thinking of times in corporate gatherings when (at least in many circles) charismatics will pray or worship simultaneously. During such moments, everyone glorifies God at the same time, singing or praying in the Spirit. This can include people's singing or praying in tongues at the same time. But these are not with one or two persons speaking out to be heard above others. In this kind of meeting, when people are singing and praying at the same time, it is understood that everyone is speaking to God in the context of worship or prayer. This is similar to when, in many vibrant Korean churches, Christians pray passionately and spontaneously at the same time, typically in Korean; no one is listening for someone else's words or language. When Christians pray together without any voice rising above all the others, for all any visitor need know everyone may be praying in their own language. The language is not what makes the difference.

This sort of collective prayer to God is not out of order the way it would be if someone were leading out in uninterpreted tongues. Indeed, when Paul urges a member without an interpreter to speak in a tongue "to oneself and to God" (1 Cor. 14:28), he envisions a form of tongues-praying in a meeting that is not drawing others' attention. This kind of worship is not chaotic or disorderly. It is a heartfelt overflow of love to the Lord in a congregational setting, and it is edifying for the whole group. Insofar as experience might count for anything, both of us, Daniel and Craig, have found these moments as some of the most edifying and orderly (in the sense of divinely orchestrated, not chaotic) corporate experiences we have had. I (Daniel) have been in many services over the years when such worship seemed to enrapture thousands of people for extended periods of time. I've also seen how sinners have been overwhelmed in these environments to the point that, without an altar call or even a word preached, they run to the altars and prostrate themselves in repentance saying, "God is in your midst."

Neither of us view this worship as violating Paul's prohibition in letter or spirit. Paul was specifically addressing the intelligibility of spontaneous utterances, which is not an issue with simultaneous prayer. However, if during one of these meetings, someone seeks to give a public message or lead out in prayer heard by all others, we would have the right to demand intelligible speech. Paul's overarching point was that everything should be done in love, to edify one another. This would include preferring one another, edifying the body, being respectful for other speakers, and avoiding unnecessary confusion for unbelievers.

Some cessationists would strongly disagree with this point of view. They will insist that every word of 1 Corinthians 14 must be followed to the letter in every kind of gathering, large or small, public or private, and regardless of the principle of order. Anything less would be, as Pennington says, "clear rebellion." If this is your perspective, as you have already seen, we read 1 Corinthians 14 somewhat differently than you do. However, we will still respect your practice when we visit your churches, celebrating wherever God's Word is preached (cf. Phil. 1:18). Just keep something in mind. The Lord requires you to submit yourself to the same standard by which you judge others (Matt. 7:1–2 // Luke 6:37–38). You cannot say that the protocol for the gifts ought to be followed to the letter, and at the same time reject altogether biblical teaching supporting the use of the gifts in church. Such a judgment strains at a gnat and swallows a camel.

Remember that the same apostle who insists that tongues be interpreted (1 Cor. 14:13, 27–28) also insists that tongues not be forbidden (14:39). So if you feel we charismatics are getting it wrong, I will make you a deal—in all sincerity. Acts 2:17–18 declares this the era of the prophetic Spirit. If charismatics' attempts to follow this reality are inadequate, you are more than welcome to model a better way for us. Alternatively, join us in the Spirit-filled community. Allow us to pray for you to experience worship in tongues, prophesy, and believe for healings and miracles. In return, you can use your gift in teaching to help us apply scriptural principles to our meetings with greater care, and to demonstrate by example how to exercise the gifts with greater excellence. Let's work together as Christ's body, contributing our varied gifts for the edification of his church.

### Pennington's Fourth Rule: Women Don't Prophesy in Church

For his final point, Pennington refers to 1 Corinthians 14:34 by saying, "Women weren't allowed to prophesy during corporate worship."[98] But is that what Paul actually says? To quote the apostle directly: "The women are to keep silent in the churches; for they are not permitted to speak, but are to subject themselves, just as the Law also says" (1 Cor. 14:34 NASB).[99]

The context is tongues, prophecy, and order, but the issue here must be order rather than praying in tongues or prophesying. Why? Because we know explicitly from the same letter that Paul *does* permit women to prophesy in church. Just a few chapters earlier Paul permits women to pray and prophesy in church, so long as their heads are covered. Women don't cover their heads in most churches today, most of which understand head coverings as a cultural practice.[100] Praying and prophesying, however, are not merely cultural practices; they pervade biblical history, and Scripture associates godly prophecy and some prayer with the guidance of the Holy Spirit.

In 1 Corinthians 11:5, Paul takes for granted that women will publicly pray and prophesy in a worship gathering. This is especially clear in light of the previous verse where Paul cites the proper prophetic etiquette for men (1 Cor. 11:4). He says it is disgraceful for a man to pray or prophesy with his head covered. Then, in a balanced comparison, he says that it is disgraceful for a woman to pray or prophesy with her head *un*covered. The difference there is not between men speaking and women refraining. Both men and women may prophesy. The difference is between the physical attire of men and women. Paul assumes that women can prophesy during a meeting. "You can all prophesy" (1 Cor. 14:31) thus includes both genders, fitting our expectation from Pentecost (Acts 2:17–18).

So the silence Paul insists for women in church must be qualified rather than absolute. Otherwise Paul contradicts himself between these two passages. (Any church that allows women to participate even in congregational singing recognizes that the requirement of silence is not absolute, to whatever extent beyond this they mandate silence.) He allows women to prophesy in the first

98. Pennington, *Cessationism*, 134.

99. This section is largely from Daniel. I (Craig) have devoted significant earlier work to 1 Cor. 14:34–35 (Keener, *Paul*, 70–100; Keener, "Learning"). But since nearly all cessationists are also complementarians or gender traditionalists, and they tend to dislike egalitarians at least as much as charismatics, and I (Craig) am publicly known as egalitarian, I thought it better to mostly sit this section out and hear Daniel's approach. Gender debates require appeal to ancient background, whereas the cessationism debate can be settled simply by reading passages in their literary context. There are notable complementarian charismatics such as Wayne Grudem and Sam Storms, so for the sake of argument I mostly (apart from some light documentation) recuse myself here.

100. See, e.g., Keener, "Head Coverings"; Keener, *Paul*, 19–69; for further background, see Llewellyn-Jones, *Tortoise*.

passage, so in what respect does he forbid them to speak? Paul contextualizes his restriction on women's speaking, applying it to a particular situation. Notice the next verse: "If they desire to learn anything, let them ask their own husbands at home; for it is improper for a woman to speak in church" (1 Cor. 14:35 NASB). Paul puts his restriction on some women's speech in light of their desire to "learn," not on their desire to prophesy.

Prophecy is acceptable, but "speaking" in order to "learn" during a meeting is not. Scholars offer various suggestions about why or how this is happening. They often point out that women received less education in Paul's day. For example, Jewish boys were raised to recite the Torah, whereas girls were not. As a result, some women may not have understood something said or done in a meeting. They had not been fully versed in the new Christian way. Meanwhile, the husbands in that culture would have been more knowledgeable. We may not appreciate this state of unequal affairs from our modern vantage point, but it was a situation unavoidable in Paul's day. So based on his response in these verses, it appears that when the women would seek answers, they would also disrupt the meeting. Perhaps they were asking their husbands in church, or perhaps they were even interrupting the Bible lesson. It was customary in antiquity to interrupt lectures with questions,[101] but unlearned questions were unwelcome.[102]

Whatever the specifics, this fits the context precisely because this is a problem of order. Precisely out of concern for order, Pentecostals today normally do not allow prophecies or utterances in tongues to interrupt sermons.[103] This was surely also Paul's concern even with the much less formal Bible lessons in ancient house churches. Remember that Paul's overarching concern for his church gatherings is love in practice. He wants all to participate, but only in a way that respects and edifies everyone. Paul's advice here is similar to other instructions he gives (1 Cor. 11:22, 34). Though his gatherings were cooperative and intimate, they were still sacred. Behavior that may be appropriate at home may not be appropriate during "church," even if it happened to be meeting in one's home. So Paul's simple adjustment for these women allows them to support the meeting's overall purpose while still learning what they need to learn. Read in this light, Paul's instructions actually made provision for the women to receive instruction they may not have ordinarily received. What sounds restrictive from our modern Western framework actually may have empowered women in its original framework.

101. Seneca, *Lucil.* 108.3; Musonius Rufus, 3, p. 38.25–26; Aulus Gellius, 1.26.2; 8.10; 12.5.4; 16.6.1–4; 20.10.1–6; Lucian, *Dem.* 14, 39; Macrobius, *Sat.* 7.2.3, 5; in Jewish pedagogy, *t. Sanh.* 7:10; *Abot R. Nat.* 6A; Safrai, "Education," 2:966; Goodman, *State*, 79.

102. Plutarch, *Lect.* 4, *Mor.* 39CD; 11, *Mor.* 43BC; 18, *Mor.* 48AB; Lucian, *Dem.* 14, 39; Jeffers, *World*, 252.

103. Although God has been known to interrupt messages on occasion with unanticipated signs; Acts 10:44–46!

But whatever the exact nature of the original situation, Paul's injunction for women to be silent is qualified by a particular phrase ("if they want to learn"). It is not an unqualified, absolute command to be quiet during church. Further, Paul's use of the word translated "to be silent" in fact lends support to this conclusion.

This is consistent with how Paul uses the word earlier in the same chapter: "If anyone speaks in a tongue, two—or at the most three—should speak, one at a time, and someone must interpret. If there is no interpreter, the speaker should *keep quiet in the church* and speak to himself and to God" (1 Cor. 14:27–28 NIV). In this context, Paul tells the person speaking in tongues to "be silent" in the exact same way he tells the women to be silent—same word, same tense, same mood. But Paul is not telling a tongues-speaker never to speak; the tongues-speaker is free to speak if there is an interpreter. The silence relates to the conditions, in this case, asking questions.

The next example is even clearer: "Two or three prophets should speak, and the others should evaluate. But if something has been revealed to another person sitting there, the first prophet *should be silent*" (1 Cor. 14:29–30 CSB). Again, same word, tense, and mood as regarding the women. Paul is not telling anyone to refrain from every kind of speech. He is telling the Corinthians to be polite and defer to one another. If someone is giving a prophetic message, he or she should not dominate the meeting. Rather, if another person indicates he or she has a message to share while someone else is speaking, the first person should wrap it up and allow the other person to speak. "Silence" does not mean, "You are never allowed to speak in church." It means, "Stop speaking and give someone else a turn." This is exactly the limited way Paul uses the word for the inquiring women. They should cease from certain kinds of talk but are free to speak out within the boundaries of love and edification defined by the apostle, which include praying and prophesying (11:5).[104]

On our approach, then, Pennington's fourth implicit criticism fails to hold any water. Women in Paul's day, as well as our day, are more than welcome to prophesy. That is what the Bible teaches. In all fairness to Pennington and other cessationists with similar arguments, Peter says Paul's writings have "some things hard to understand" (2 Pet. 3:16). At first glance, it may seem that Paul does indeed restrict both the number of prophets in a meeting and the speech of all women. But upon careful reading of Paul's instructions, in context, both conclusions fail. In turn, half of Pennington's implied criticisms

104. 1 Cor. 11:1–16 might offer some clues to Paul's reference to law-based submission. Some of the women in that previous situation—who were free to prophesy—were also risking blurring the lines of distinction between the two genders and disrespecting their husbands. Perhaps the sort of situation in chapter 11 also lay behind chapter 14. In any case, Paul teaches with balance throughout: Honor God and honor one another by maintaining God-given distinctions, order, and the right for everyone to contribute to the meeting in love.

are wrong. The other half of his criticisms are somewhat valid and helpful. But none of them support a cessationist perspective.

While we are discussing 1 Corinthians 14, I would like to point out that, while charismatics certainly are imperfect in their stewardship of the gifts of the Spirit, at least we are trying. We wrestle with these instructions in the real world (not simply as a matter of theory). One of the important lessons we learn from Paul is that, while the operation of the gifts might be messy at times, it is worth the effort invested. This is a lesson cessationists should ponder. Despite the problems Paul had in Corinth, not only did he encourage the Corinthians to continue their operation of the Spirit's gifts, but he actually encouraged them to seek—indeed "covet"—the gifts even more! He valued these gifts as indispensable aspects of life in the Spirit. So he was happy to deal with the problems, not to eliminate certain gifts but to enhance and encourage authentic expressions for the sake of the Lord's body. Cessationists who see a blanket prohibition of women prophesying cannot simultaneously claim to honor 1 Corinthians 11.[105]

## What About the Fakes and Flakes?

How should we respond to all the abuses that can be pointed out in the charismatic world? Examples of moral turpitude and financial scandals, shady fundraising techniques, questionable doctrines, and false prophecies abound in our community, along with a healthy dose of weird people. Shouldn't those examples of bad fruit discredit the movement? (Craig adds that if being ADHD, extremely introverted, or a nerd counts as weird, he is weird himself.)

Without making any excuses for legitimate grievances, I would like to remind the critic that the charismatic movement is not an organized association. We are literally hundreds of millions of people from all over the world and every denomination. Theologically there are Reformed charismatics, Roman Catholic charismatics, and everything in between. Anyone can claim to be charismatic. By virtue of the designation's generic character (meaning those who try to follow Paul's teaching about gifts), there is no vetting process or application procedure. The only thing that unites us as charismatics, strictly speaking, is our belief that the gifts and power of the Holy Spirit are still available, as we see plainly taught in Scripture. It is unfair to paint any large movement with a broad brush, but much more so one that is as diverse as

105. Universalizing Paul's regulations here also makes little sense if, as cessationists claim, these gifts were about to become obsolete in just a few short years. Though Paul was still expecting that the Lord might return soon (in his lifetime, 1 Cor. 15:51), he could not guarantee this (Matt. 24:36, 50; 25:13; Mark 13:32; Luke 12:46; 1 Thess. 5:2). Paul had taught in Corinth for eighteen months (Acts 18:11); any new regulations Paul adds in 1 Corinthians, therefore, were likely new to this situation.

ours. One could do the same thing with still wider groups such as evangelicals, or with Protestants, or with Christians generally, or with people from any culture or nation. The scandals of some do not properly incriminate all without ultimately incriminating everybody.

Even so, one could raise the question of whether a common theme of bad fruit among charismatics indicates the influence of an ungodly spirit. If indeed bad fruit characterizes the entire movement, I would be inclined to agree. But many cessationists have been terribly misinformed on this topic. During the Strange Fire conference, a disturbing pattern emerged. Presenters routinely cherry-picked snippets of video and audio clips that were either taken out of context or came from the worst, most fringe elements of the charismatic community. Most charismatics themselves reject the latter groups. The same techniques of slander could be used to discredit any denomination, group, or local church in the world.[106] We see this practice regularly when politicians demonize their opponents. In reality, the charismatic movement, despite its flaws, is full of amazing and godly people who love Jesus, honor the Scriptures, and serve God with their whole hearts.

Charismatic ministries with large congregations, television programs, multimillion-dollar budgets, and celebrity pastors receive more than their share of media coverage. This means that if things go wrong, they do so in a spectacular and very public way. But cessationist denominations are not without their share of scandals either. It is no secret that Martin Luther's writings, for example, instigated antisemitism and bloodshed (see discussion in chap. 20 below). Some churches that deny spiritual gifts are liberal, denying not only spiritual gifts but also biblical sexual ethics for today. Some others, conversely, are so rigid on various matters that they alienate young people, women, divorced people, scientists not persuaded by young-earth views, those who vote differently, and so forth. We all have our issues to deal with. Let's not allow hypocrisy to be one of them.

Moreover, of course there are frauds and charlatans, fake healers and imposters. No one suffers because of these pretenders more than those of us incriminated with them in the court of public opinion. And we often have to follow their scorched earth in ministry. Then there are those who may be sincere, but their theology, approach, and style leave much to be desired. There are also those who bring reproach upon the name of Christ through foolishness and sin. We grieve over these situations as much as anyone. They will answer to God for how they conducted their ministries and carried his name (Matt. 7:21–23). But *all* of us will answer for how we've handled his Word (James 3:1). We don't respond to receiving counterfeit bills by discarding money, or

106. Sometimes conservative Christians have slandered even their own peers; for example, Josh Buice was discovered slandering some of his fellow Reformed Baptists; see, e.g., Shellnut, "Founder."

to getting food poisoning by rejecting food. Even if every minister of healing you've ever seen was false, that does not mean no one else has experienced the authentic article. Nor does it justify your rejection of God's true gifts that Scripture supports. Our standard is God's Word, not human flesh.

Even if charismatics were completely wrong, that would still not solve the cessationist's problem. Even if every charismatic prophet was a charlatan and we could dismiss the whole movement as aberrant, that would not erase the claim of Scripture that in the last days the Spirit will be poured out on all flesh, sons and daughters will prophesy, young men will see visions, and old men will dream dreams. Even if every charismatic prophecy was false, that would do nothing to prove cessationism, because, as cessationists themselves acknowledge, no amount of experience can trump Scripture.

In fact, it would only make the cessationists' dilemma worse. If these charismatic practices should not match the biblical gifts, cessationists would still need to explain something crucial: Where is the true prophecy that, according to Joel, is supposed to be profuse and happening everywhere? If charismatics are doing this wrong, then the proper response should be to set the right example by showing us how it *ought* to be done. But ruling out Joel's prophecy, Acts 2:17–18, or 1 Corinthians 14:31 altogether does not seem an option for those who take the biblical text's claims seriously.

# 20

# "Manifestations," History, and Scandals

Both continuationists and cessationists alike should agree that, regardless of how many gifts remain today, the Spirit's *fruit* in our character matters more than those gifts. Likewise, all of us know of some gifted preachers, teachers, apologists, and the like whose fruit falls short of their gifts. Gifts and fruit are not the same thing, sort of like comparing apples and oranges (or in this case maybe leaves and oranges). Fruit reveals our relationship with God, our character in him; God gives us gifts, *especially* (though not exclusively) for Christ's body. Such gifts, therefore, don't belong to or define us; we can't boast in them (cf. 1 Cor. 4:7). Believers should use gifts in the service of love (12:31–13:8; 13:13–14:1); but, as in Corinth, sometimes they abuse gifts. It is therefore no surprise that some advocates of gifts today—like some detractors—fail on the issue of fruit. Neither supporters nor detractors of particular gifts should confuse these categories.

Scripture is clear in support of the continuance of prophecy, tongues, and (not normally disputed) teaching. Those of us who recognize this continuance are therefore by definition continuationists. But critics of charismatics sometimes focus on other public demonstrations that, if they appear in Scripture with reference to divine activity at all, do so only incidentally. They are also often incidental to ordinary charismatic church life—that is, they are not central to charismatic identity for mainstream charismatic Christians. One can be charismatic and never experience these demonstrations. But they are flashy, attract attention, and hence often feature heavily in antagonistic cessationist critiques.

These experiences have a long, pre-Pentecostal history in what we call revivals, and they have come to be called "manifestations." They include responses such as laughing, weeping, and (often more controversially) falling. These manifestations have nothing to do with spiritual gifts themselves and as such are not directly relevant to this book's question of cessationism and continuationism. Because they are a common issue in cessationist critiques of charismatics, however, they bear at least brief discussion.

One speaker in the movie *Cessationist*, for example, claims that laughing in Hindu kundalini yoga looks exactly like the charismatic practice.[1] (I, Craig, question the speaker's spiritual discernment in this case; the movie's clips of Hindu practice neither look nor feel like what I have experienced as a charismatic.) But my students also laugh at my jokes (admittedly perhaps only as a reprieve from my content-heavy lectures); should a guilt-by-association suggestion then condemn seminary education? Or should we prohibit expressions of joy during a religious gathering (against, e.g., Neh. 8:10; Pss. 9:2; 42:4; 149:3)? Humans have a limited range of potential responses to spiritual and other experiences; assuming that all responses of a particular kind can reflect only a single form of stimulus is questionable logic. Moreover, the devil regularly imitates God's activity (think of pagan prophets in the OT; or Rev. 13:11; 17:10). Why would some give more credence to the imitation than to the reality it counterfeits?

## Testing "Manifestations"

Biblically, some kinds of experiences are always good (such as being born again), some are always bad (such as sex outside of marriage), but many others can be good or bad depending on their context. Some may also be unnecessary or weird without being sinful or demonic.

Four questions can help sort through many of these experiences:

1. Is the experience explicitly endorsed in Scripture? If the answer is yes, the manifestation is acceptable in principle (assuming that it passes tests of discernment, as Paul requires for local church prophecy).
2. Is it forbidden in Scripture? Any manifestation or practice that conflicts with the written Word of God should be prohibited. All believers should agree on this point.
3. Does it fit the larger pattern of Scripture? In other words, even if it is not explicitly mentioned in Scripture, is it consistent with similar things that God has done in the past?

1. Lanphere, *Cessationist*.

4. Does it conform to biblical principles? For example: Does it produce the fruit of the Spirit? Does it reflect God's character?

For many believers, cessationists and charismatics alike, this approach feels too uncertain. Their mentality might call for more rigid rules and more clearly defined categories that make all spiritual matters simple, safe, and predictable. But this is just not the way life in the Spirit works, any more than the way that life in general works. Jesus explained the spontaneous nature of the life of the Spirit to Nicodemus when he said, "The wind blows wherever it pleases. You hear its sound, but you cannot tell where it comes from or where it is going. So it is with everyone born of the Spirit" (John 3:8).[2] Scripture reveals the truth about God, salvation, the human condition, spiritual life, the end times, and many other issues. But it does not pigeonhole the way people should or should not physically react when the Spirit manifests himself with intensity. He is full of surprises. We know this because Scripture sets the precedent for it (e.g., 1 Sam. 19:23–24; Jer. 23:9; Ezek. 1:28; Dan. 10:11).

To be a person of the Spirit involves a certain amount of risk, because God's work is in many ways beyond our understanding and ability to control. Following the Spirit requires a willingness to deal with mistakes and human error, just as Paul had to address them in Corinth. It can be messy and difficult at times, and there are those who would just prefer a "tidy, comfortable little package."[3] And yet, despite the challenges, risks, and unknowns, we affirm with confidence that encouraging and praying for the Holy Spirit to work mightily among his people is more than worthwhile. He can do more in one moment than we can do in one hundred years. His gifts are just that: gifts—not curses, not burdens, not embarrassments. They are wonderful, glorious, and desirable gifts. If God has something to give, let us desire it with all our hearts.

## Laughing or Weeping

Responses to the Spirit are not always calm. In the Old Testaments, observers sometimes supposed prophets were insane (2 Kings 9:11; Jer. 29:26; Hosea 9:7), a charge also leveled against Jesus (Mark 3:21; John 10:20). Festus suggested that Paul was insane (Acts 26:24), though perhaps for his content as well as his delivery style.[4] Paul requires order in public assemblies, such as the courtesy of not interrupting others' speech. But he also contrasts being filled

2. As cessationist Richard Gaffin also put it, "The Spirit is like the blowing wind, sovereign and ultimately incalculable" (Gaffin, "View," 25).

3. Gaffin, "View," 25.

4. See discussion in Keener, "Madness."

with the Spirit with being drunk (Eph. 5:18) in what may be an independent witness to the observers' misunderstanding on the day of Pentecost that the disciples were drunk (Acts 2:13).[5]

### *Laughing*

The Bible never lists laughing as a result of the Spirit—but it does list joy right after love as a fruit of the Spirit (Gal. 5:22). One of the outpourings of the Spirit in Acts is accompanied by noteworthy joy (Acts 13:52), and the Holy Spirit generates joy in Romans 14:17 and 1 Thessalonians 1:6. At least some people do laugh when they experience joy! The following references are from the NASB:

> Acts 13:52: "And the disciples were continually filled with joy and with the Holy Spirit."
>
> Romans 14:17: "For the kingdom of God is not eating and drinking, but righteousness and peace and joy in the Holy Spirit."
>
> Galatians 5:22: "But the fruit of the Spirit is love, joy, peace, patience, kindness, goodness, faithfulness."
>
> 1 Thessalonians 1:6: "You also became imitators of us and of the Lord, having received the word during great affliction with the joy of the Holy Spirit."

In addition to weeping and leaping, laughter characterized some medieval mystics' ecstasies.[6] One commentator notes that it has occurred in many revivals, reflecting there "an overwhelming joy in the experience of God's love and acceptance";[7] in the Great Awakening, it occurred "among those claiming to have visions of Heaven."[8] Some early Methodist converts experienced hours of laughter, one woman for a day and night.[9] John Wesley mentions one woman who "was so overwhelmed with the love of God that

5. For the latter observation, cf., e.g., Oss, "View," 281; Deere, *Still Surprised*, 199n1.

6. Farges, *Phenomena*, 155, quoted in Webber, "Mystics"; for Catherine of Siena, see Ensley, *Sounds*, 102; Oliver, *Movements*, 233; further discussion in Francis, "Encounter." See also dancing with Teresa of Avila and fellow nuns (Oliver, *Reformations*, 45) and jumping among some Russian Orthodox mystics in the 1800s (Oliver, *Reformations*, 191, 193) and Welsh (Calvinist) Methodists in the 1760s (Oliver, *Reformations*, 121).

7. Wagner, "Laughing," 241.

8. Wagner, "Laughing," 242.

9. Xhemajli, *Supernatural*, 164–65; cf. Oliver, *Reformations*, 119. This may be the best explanation also for the Wesley brothers' own experience of lengthy, uncontrollable laughter during private worship on one occasion (Hyatt, *Years*, 102; Oliver, *Reformations*, 119; Billman, *Thread*, 57; Wesley, *Works*, 1:271–72).

she sunk down, and appeared as one in a pleasant sleep . . . ; she frequently laughed while she saw His glory."[10] An ecstatic "holy laugh" was among the common experiences reported at the 1801 Cane Ridge Revival.[11] It also occurred in early Salvation Army meetings,[12] and in China's Shantung Revival, associated with Baptists.[13]

Well before people talked about "holy laughter" or associated it with a particular kind of teaching, I (Craig) experienced laughter at a holy moment in my life. Two days after my conversion from atheism, knowing nothing about tongues or other spiritual gifts, I was, as I noted in an earlier book, "so overwhelmed with the awesome majesty and presence of God that I understood that only he could provide me adequate words with which to praise him. And because I intuitively understood that God knows all languages, it somehow did not surprise me when the Spirit gave me another language in which to praise him." Yet tongues was not the only part of this experience. As an atheist without authentic hope for the future, I had been despondent. Although I had some earlier moments of happiness (e.g., over some birthday presents), they were nothing like what I first experienced on this occasion. "For an hour or two I worshiped God in tongues—often punctuated with deep, cathartic laughter (which has recurred on occasion since)—experiencing a joy I had never known before. When I finished, I was convinced that the purpose in life I had long sought must be to promote the glory of Jesus Christ alone."[14]

I note this not to suggest that this is or should be other people's experience. I note this only to illustrate that the experience of joy in the Spirit can be expressed at times in laughter.

### Weeping

Both joy and weeping are possible responses to God's work. When God's people heard his law being read, they started weeping (Neh. 8:9), perhaps in sorrow for their sins. Ezra the priest and scribe insisted that they needed to shift to joyous celebration because it was a festival sacred to the Lord. "Don't mourn," he urged them. "For the Lord's joy is your stronghold!" (8:10 AT).

10. Wesley's journal for July 9, 1759, in Wesley, *Journal* (Culley), 334. Wesley discouraged levity, and he often notes crowds that laughed in derision or inattention, but laughter from spiritual joy belongs to a different category (see Wesley, *Works* [1872 ed.], 9:27, cited in Billman, *Thread*, 57).

11. Synan, *Tradition*, 12; Wagner, "Laughing," 242; Boles, *Revival*, 67; Oliver, *Reformations*, 159; Billman, *Thread*, 109 (citing Synan, *Movement*, 24).

12. Oliver, *Reformations*, 208.

13. Billman, *Thread*, 51, citing Crawford, *Revival*. In our Kindle edition it appears in chaps. 3 and 4 (in one chapter, it is called "holy laughter").

14. Keener, *Gift & Giver*, 175–76.

Yet weeping was also often appropriate, especially when it expressed genuine repentance, as at times in Scripture and the First Great Awakening. See for example the following (NRSV):

> Ezra 10:1: "While Ezra prayed and made confession, weeping and throwing himself down before the house of God, a very great assembly of men, women, and children gathered to him out of Israel; the people also wept bitterly."
>
> Joel 2:12: "Yet even now, says the LORD, return to me with all your heart, with fasting, with weeping, and with mourning."
>
> Zechariah 12:10: "And I will pour out a spirit of compassion and supplication on the house of David and the inhabitants of Jerusalem, so that, when they look on the one whom they have pierced, they shall mourn for him, as one mourns for an only child, and weep bitterly over him, as one weeps over a firstborn."
>
> James 4:8–10: "Draw near to God, and he will draw near to you. Cleanse your hands, you sinners, and purify your hearts, you double-minded. Lament and mourn and weep. Let your laughter be turned into mourning and your joy into dejection. Humble yourselves before the Lord, and he will exalt you."

Strong emotions affect different people differently. Sometimes people weep for joy (e.g., Gen. 29:11; 33:4). Ephrem the Syrian (d. 373) valued the gift of tears,[15] and Symeon the New Theologian (949–1022) saw the gift of tears as an evidence of receiving the Spirit.[16] Some other individuals, such as Margery Kempe (ca. 1373–after 1439), also recount receiving the gift of tears.[17] Late medieval audiences could respond emotionally to passionate sermons with weeping and swaying.[18] The seventeenth- to eighteenth-century Huguenot young prophets often wept during inspiration.[19] So did many Moravians during the Moravian Pentecost of August 13, 1727.[20] Jonathan Edwards (1703–58) and many of his congregation wept through George Whitefield's (1714–70) first message at their church.[21]

When I was praying with a good friend from the Friends (Quaker) movement, I was worshiping in tongues while he was quietly weeping. Frequent weeping also characterizes some Christian movements in China and elsewhere.

15. Burgess, *Peoples*, 51.
16. Burgess, "Ancient Churches," 14; Burgess, *Peoples*, 87.
17. Burgess, "Evidence," 23.
18. Holland, *Dominion*, 290.
19. Cosmos, *Huguenot Prophecy*, 67–68. See, e.g., Misson, *Cry*, 60.
20. "One Spirit"; Greenfield, *Power*, 35; Oliver, *Reformations*, 105.
21. Oliver, *Reformations*, 130.

### *Spiritual Emotion*

Anna Gulick, a French professor at the time of the 1970 Asbury College outpouring, told me (Craig) that she could feel God's presence even blocks away from the campus. I experienced this spontaneous sense at least a block away during the 2023 outpouring at the same university. On a more massive scale, during the 1850s prayer revival in the United States, voyagers recounted feeling God's presence "when coming within 100 miles" of the coast, sometimes all of a ship's passengers being converted by the time of arrival.[22]

Complaining about religious emotion generally, some critics protest repeating lines of a song over and over. Regarding repetition that reinforces the point and expresses honor to God, I would reply with Revelation 4:8: "And the four living creatures . . . do not rest day or night from saying, 'Holy! Holy! Holy! is the Lord God Almighty, who was and is and is to come!'"[23]

Some people are more reserved by nature and may express significant emotion only in times of deep catharsis. This is not wrong, but neither should such reticence be imposed on others; indeed, we often weep with those who weep (John 11:33–35; Rom. 12:15). Eli was wrong to misjudge Hannah's passionate prayer (1 Sam. 1:13). Most preexilic biblical collections of prophecy are in poetry, and examples of emotion abound there. Emotion is particularly clear in the Psalms, which mention joy, gladness, and the like more than ninety times and celebrate praise with dancing (Pss. 149:3; 150:4) and lifting hands (28:2; 63:4; 119:48; 134:2; 141:2; cf. 1 Tim. 2:8). "If anyone is cheerful, let them sing!" James instructs (James 5:13). Some Levitical invitations to praise in the Psalms appear rousing (e.g., Ps. 150).

Likewise, perhaps a third of the psalms are laments, pouring out grief and fear to God. Certainly psalms invite us to let our hair down (at least for those who, unlike Craig, still have some). Some of us show our emotions more than others, but Scripture recognizes us as whole persons and engages every aspect of our beings.

As to religious emotion, ancient Stoics disapproved of the use of *pathos* (appeal to emotion) in persuasion, in contrast to most ancient communicators. While Paul agreed with Stoics on some points, he was not shy about stirring emotions for the Lord. He appeals freely to his hearers' feelings (e.g., 2 Cor. 6:11–13; Gal. 4:12–20; Philem. 9). At times his celebration could rise to a rousing crescendo, for example:

> 1 Corinthians 15:51–57 (NRSV): "Listen, I will tell you a mystery! We will not all die, but we will all be changed, in a moment, in the twinkling of an eye, at the last trumpet. For the trumpet will sound, and the dead will be raised

22. Oliver, *Reformations*, 198–99, citing Orr, *Prayer*, 18.
23. Parallelism also pervades the psalms (e.g., Ps. 85:2–3), lingering on a worthy point to express it thoroughly.

imperishable, and we will be changed. For this perishable body must put on imperishability, and this mortal body must put on immortality. . . . Then the saying that is written will be fulfilled: 'Death has been swallowed up in victory.' 'Where, O death, is your victory? Where, O death, is your sting?' . . . Thanks be to God, who gives us the victory through our Lord Jesus Christ."

In more recent times, evangelical Holiness preachers at the turn of the twentieth century were often known for antics that held crowds spellbound, including "holy jumping."[24] In the early twentieth century, baseball-player-turned-preacher Billy Sunday engaged his athletic skills in preaching, while radio preacher and pastor Aimee Semple McPherson dramatized her preaching as well. Whatever some readers think of such approaches to holding attention, emotionally rousing, dramatic preaching was hardly new in the twentieth century. In the eighteenth century, mild-mannered Edwards was close friends with Whitefield, who was so known for his emotionally rousing, theatrical preaching that his most authoritative modern biography calls him "the divine dramatist."[25] It is said that one time Whitefield even had a trumpeter blast his trumpet as Whitefield preached about Jesus's return, evoking panic among those who had not yet repented![26]

But certainly the harsh cessationists cannot oppose all emotion in any case, since they stoke fear of and laughter about charismatics when they compare them to non-Christian movements.[27]

## "Slain in the Spirit"

The charismatic experience that arouses the most comment from cessationists is what has come to be called being "slain in the Spirit." In the most spiritually edifying cases, a person is so overcome by the Spirit's presence that he or she collapses to the ground or temporarily loses awareness of the world around them. A broader definition that can encompass all cases is falling down in a spiritually and emotionally intense setting.

John MacArthur declares that the New Testament nowhere shows that God's Spirit might cause "Christians to fall into a trance, faint, or lapse into frenzied behavior."[28] Incredulous, Jack Deere responds, "Are we reading

24. Book, "Heel Kicking," 25. The article also mentions occasions of "holy laughter" in such circles, particularly in the context of conversions.

25. Stout, *Dramatist*. Wesley tolerated more manifestations in his meetings than Whitefield did, but he preached more calmly (Billman, *Thread*, 56).

26. Kendall, *Prophetic Integrity*, 23.

27. E.g., a clip of MacArthur at the Strange Fire conference, provoking laughter by comparing "nice" charismatics with "nice" Mormons, or, as noted above, comparisons with kundalini practice and the like.

28. MacArthur, *Chaos*, 168.

the same Bible?" and cites the trance visions of Peter (Acts 10:10) and Paul (22:17).[29] "Trance" is the term used to translate the Greek term *ekstasis* in these cases in, for example, the KJV, ESV, NASB, NET, NIV, WEB, NJB, and NRSV. Perhaps MacArthur was using a different translation that day.

So let's take being "slain in the Spirit" as a test case and apply our four questions. Scripture contains no passages that show masses of people being "slain in the Spirit" or collapsing when hands are laid on them. So, on the one hand, the Bible does not explicitly teach being "slain in the Spirit." But on the other hand, neither does the Bible prohibit such a manifestation. So our next question should be, Is there any biblical precedent for this experience in the wider scope of Scripture? Put another way, does the Bible teach or illustrate any experience that corresponds in principle to this phenomenon?

### *Some Biblical Incidents*

Although these experiences are not related to spiritual gifts per se, in circles that welcome them people sometimes collapse to the ground or become too overwhelmed by God's presence to notice what occurs around them. One need not assume that all such experiences reflect the impact of the Spirit today to recognize that the Bible talks about divinely connected experiences like this. For example:

- Daniel fell on his face overwhelmed when he saw angels (Dan. 8:17–18).
- Ezekiel fell on his face when he witnessed the Lord's glory (Ezek. 1:28; 3:23; 43:3; 44:4).
- Ezekiel fell on his face when overwhelmed with God's message (9:8; 11:13).
- Jesus's top disciples fell in terror when God spoke from heaven (Matt. 17:6).
- When a brilliant angel showed up at Jesus's tomb, the guards "shook from fear of him and became like dead men" (Matt. 28:4 NASB).
- The soldiers who came to arrest Jesus fell backward onto the ground (John 18:6).
- Before the Lord's glory, Saul of Tarsus fell to the ground (Acts 9:4; 22:7).
- When John witnessed the risen Lord in glory, "I fell before his feet like someone dead!" (Rev. 1:17 AT).

Other instances may perhaps seem more relevant to some cases today:

29. Deere, *Still Surprised*, 199n1.

- Abram fell unconscious during a vision (Gen. 15:12).[30]
- Balaam fell down in a trance (Num. 24:4, 16).
- Those overwhelmed by the Spirit of prophecy could also fall down, oblivious to their surroundings (1 Sam. 19:20–24, especially 24).
- When the Lord's glory filled the Lord's house, the priests could not get up and stand because of the glory (1 Kings 8:11; 2 Chron. 5:14).[31] Someday, with glorified bodies, we will be better suited to stand before his glory, but our frame of flesh, including our finite nervous system, is not now equipped to endure this spiritual intensity unaffected.
- Peter fell into a trance (Acts 10:10; 11:5).
- Paul fell into a trance (Acts 22:17).

As for being weak after a profound spiritual experience, one might compare these occurrences:

- Daniel 8:27: "Then I . . . was exhausted and sick for days" (NASB).
- Daniel 10:8: "I had no strength left, my face turned deathly pale and I was helpless" (NIV).

So this phenomenon of someone's falling on the ground or becoming unconscious when encountering God's presence is consistent with experiences that sometimes occurred in Scripture. Therefore, (1) although it is not specifically endorsed per se, (2) neither is it forbidden, and (3) there is indeed precedent for it. It does fit within the broader pattern of Scripture.

But there is one more question: (4) Does it conform to biblical principles? This is the point where theory meets reality. The true, final test of physical manifestations is not what they look like outwardly, but what happens in the hearts of the people having the experience. It's not so much about whether they fall down or not but about what happens when they get back up. Have their lives changed? Are they falling more in love with Jesus? Is there any evidence of the sanctifying work of the Holy Spirit? We may examine that only on a person-by-person basis.

30. He later fell on his face and laughed at God's promise (though this was not "holy" laughter! Gen. 17:17). Sometimes falling before the Lord was for intercession or honor, as with any superior (Deut. 9:18, 25; cf. 2 Chron. 20:18). Someone overwhelmed by others' prophetic insight might also fall on their face to worship God (1 Cor. 14:25).

31. The Hebrew term *amad* here normally means "stand" (with, e.g., ESV, NRSV). Indeed, Israelites bowed low and priests could not enter the Lord's house because of the glory (2 Chron. 7:1–3; even Moses could not enter the tabernacle under similar circumstances [Exod. 40:35]). The Hebrew term for glory is also the term for heaviness (2 Cor. 4:17 may suggest a possible play on words in Paul's mind).

### *Making Analogies*

Instead of considering the biblical examples, MacArthur compares being "slain in the Spirit" to occult practices and alternative-religion founder Joseph Smith's experience.[32] Such comparisons are not new. Critics of the Great Awakening complained that falling down, trembling, and other bodily manifestations resembled the behavior of groups despised in that era. Jonathan Edwards replied to such criticisms: "It is a weak objection, that the impressions of enthusiasts have a great effect on their bodies. That the Quakers used to tremble, is no argument that Saul, afterwards Paul, and the jailer, did not tremble from real convictions of conscience. . . . The root and course of things is to be looked at, and the nature of the operations and affections are to be inquired into, and examined by the rule of God's word, and not the motions of the blood and animal spirits."[33]

To be sure, people fall down in settings other than among charismatic Christians, but does this mean that falling down reflects the same spirits as in those settings? Some of those same settings share some of our affirmations (e.g., sometimes monotheism) or denials (e.g., often materialism), without that shared feature contaminating our beliefs. Ancient Israelites lifted their hands to the true God (Ezra 9:5; Pss. 28:2; 63:4; 119:48; 134:2; 141:2; Isa. 1:15; Lam. 1:17; 2:19; 3:41),[34] even though other peoples throughout antiquity lifted their hands to other gods.[35] Israelites also danced in worship (2 Sam. 6:14; Pss. 149:3; 150:4), bowed, and sang psalms, as did their pagan

32. MacArthur, *Strange Fire*, 201. Outside Christian orthodoxy, Shakers and Mormons also reportedly experienced tongues and prophecy (see Kelsey, *Tongue Speaking*, 57–58). Critics (cited in Ward, "Argument," 79) reviled early Pentecostals by comparing their experiences with pagan ones.

33. Edwards, "Distinguishing Marks."

34. Cf. other Jewish depictions in 1 Esd. 9:47; 2 Macc. 3:20; 14:34; 15:12, 21; 3 Macc. 5:25; 4 Macc. 4:11; *1 En.* 84:1; *Sib. Or.* 3.559–60, 591–93; 4.162–70; Josephus, *Ant.* 3.26, 53; 4.40; *Ag. Ap.* 1.209; *Ps. 155* 2; *T. Mos.* 4:1; *t. Moʿed Qat.* 2:17; *Mek. Pisha* 1.38 [Lauterbach, p. 4] on Exod. 9:29. Among Christians, see, e.g., 1 Tim. 2:8; *1 Clem.* 2.3; 29.1; *Acts of John* 43.

35. Cf. *Hymn to Aton* (*ANET*², 370); ancient Near Eastern practice in Ross, "Prophecy," 3; Homer, *Il.* 1.450; 3.275, 318; 5.174; 6.257; 7.130; 8.347; 15.368–72; 19.254; *Od.* 9.294, 527; 17.239; 20.97; Euripides, *Elec.* 592–93; Polybius 3.62.8; Apollonius Rhodius 1.248; 4.593, 1702; Justinus, *Epit.* 19.3.2; Diodorus Siculus 14.29.4; Dionysius of Halicarnassus, *Rom. Ant.* 3.175; 15.9.2; Ovid, *Metam.* 2.477, 580; 6.261–62; 9.702–3; 11.131; 13.410–11; Livy 7.6.4; Virgil, *Aen.* 1.93; 4.205; 9.16; 12.195; Valerius Flaccus 2.255; 4.473; Seneca E., *Controv.* 1.1.11; Quintus Curtius 4.10.34 (Persians); 6.7.28; Silius Italicus 4.669; 6.466; Statius, *Silv.* 4.1.15–16; Epictetus, *Diatr.* 4.10.14; Chariton, *Chaer.* 3.1.8; Plutarch, *Cam.* 5.5; *Demosth.* 26.4; 28.5; *Alex.* 19.4; 30.6 (Persians); *Cleverness of Animals* 17, *Mor.* 972B; Tacitus, *Ann.* 14.30 (Druids); Suetonius, *Nero* 6.41; Arrian, *Alex.* 4.20.3; Appian, *Hist. rom.* 2.5.5; *Bell. civ.* 2.12.85; Heliodorus, *Aeth.* 10.11; Mitchell, "Archaeology," 156 (prehistoric); Gordon, *Civilizations*, 259; Finegan, *Archeology of Religions*, 91 (Zoroastrian); Deissmann, *Light*, 415; Wright, "Inscription," 58 (line 10 of a Greek inscription); Graf, "Prayer," 792; Shiell, *Reading Acts*, 67.

neighbors[36]—but to different deities. Closer to the subject here, such circles may recount visionary trances. But while that was also true in ancient Near Eastern and Greek paganism,[37] this shared feature did not stop Israelite or early Christian prophets from also recounting visions or prophecies.

Cautious but open scholar Robert Saucy offers a more balanced approach than MacArthur here: Scripture does not speak of "any supernatural physical manifestation, such as shaking or falling down," accompanying spiritual gifts. "Because we are psychosomatic beings," however, "spiritual experiences directed toward the heart will always, if they truly reach the heart, impact the physical dimension. The effect at times could be very obvious, e.g., weeping or various bodily expressions of joy. But these manifestations are not the direct work of the Spirit on the body, any more than the leaping of the man healed by Peter (Acts 3:8)." They may be human responses to divine activity.[38]

### *Learned Responses or Real Encounters?*

I (Craig) have barely even a minuscule percentage of Daniel's experience with these matters, so I offer merely my own two cents here (though with inflation, perhaps the idiom could now be adjusted to twenty-five cents). I have had many dramatic experiences with the Spirit, including being so overwhelmed with God's honor and glory that I have fallen on my face before him (whether during corporate worship or private prayer). I don't recall ever being knocked unconscious when someone laid hands on me ("slain in the Spirit"), though, and I have occasionally experienced being gently (though in my case never roughly) pushed.

When I have prayed for people, on rare occasions *they* have fallen, taking me by such surprise I grabbed their hands to try to slow their descent! I do not

36. See, e.g., *Instruction of Ani* (*ANET*², 420); Schoville, "Dance," 376–78; Kaiser, "Pantheon," 127.

37. For Mari, see Haran, "Continuity and Change," 181; Huffmon, "Prophecy," 111–12; in Wen-Amon, Albright, *Yahweh*, 212; cf. the possible evidence of Ebla in Pettinato, *Archives*, 253; see further Keener, *Acts*, 1:900–902. This is relevant even if the ecstasy was controlled and not a full ecstasy, as some have suggested due to the forms of the prophecies (Moran, "Prophecy," 27–28). Among Greeks and Romans, see, e.g., Dionysius of Halicarnassus, *Rom. Ant.* 1.31.1; Virgil, *Aen.* 6.77–102; Lucan, *Civ. W.* 5.97–193 (albeit exaggerated poetically); Plutarch, *Dial. L.* 16, *Mor.* 759B. For Greek prophetic "madness," see Chevallier, *Ancien Testament*, 40; Lucian, *Alex.* 12; see the perception of Cassandra in Euripides, *Alex.* frg. 62g; in Israel, cf. 2 Kings 9:11; Jer. 29:26; Hosea 9:7. For Israelite ecstasy, cf. Schmid, "Geistwirkungen"; Aune, *Prophecy*, 86–87; for alleged connections between Israelite and Mari models, see Holladay, "Statecraft," 11–12; Bright, *History*, 88–89. Wilson, "Ecstasy," 323–25, finds further cases of ecstasy based on more subtle phraseology in the prophets; Parker, "Possession Trance," views the experience as only marginal in Israelite prophetism. More recent studies challenge some earlier ones (see Michaelsen, "Ecstasy").

38. Saucy, "View," 142.

know whether theirs were learned reactions or they were literally overwhelmed by the Spirit, but they certainly responded as if the latter was the case.

Yet I know others who have often witnessed this phenomenon, sometimes even despite trying to prevent it.[39] One Church of Christ congregation was experiencing spiritual renewal, but the pastor was worried because when he laid hands on people to pray, they would fall to the ground. This was getting him in trouble with some other Church of Christ pastors in the area. He asked my advice; I suggested he urge people to try not to fall. He explained that he had already done that and they were falling anyway. The only suggestion I could think of besides that was to have them sit while he prayed, in hopes that they would either remain upright or have less distance to fall. But refusing to pray for them because they might fall seems a severe and unbiblical overreaction. And as Daniel pointed out above, Scripture does offer examples of the Spirit overwhelming people in ways like this, and there were also examples during the Great Awakenings. While we should not cultivate falling as if dropping by itself had intrinsic value beyond demonstrating gravity, neither should we prohibit God sometimes touching people in this way.

### *Examples in Pre-Pentecostal History*

In the late Middle Ages, congregations wept loudly and some people fell to the ground as a Dominican preacher proclaimed repentance, while others were healed.[40] Teresa of Avila (1515–82) often entered ecstatic "raptures" for hours at a time.[41] Seventeenth- and eighteenth-century Jansenists also experienced trance states.[42] Early Quakers would often shake or fall to the ground, overwhelmed by God's Spirit.[43] Overwhelmed by God's presence, Moravian worshipers fell to the floor in 1727 at the beginning of a spiritual outpouring that led to the first full-scale Protestant missions movement.[44]

The Reformed Camisards often regarded "violent agitations of the body" as signs of inspiration.[45] Often these agitations included falling, even sometimes from a height without injury,[46] though weeping during inspiration was more common.[47] Falling and trances also accompanied the Scottish evangelical

39. I also have other friends who have witnessed people not just falling but also being thrown backward for many feet uninjured because of God's overwhelming power. But I place this testimony only in a note rather than risk my credibility on a point of at best peripheral import here!

40. Hyatt, *Years*, 61, regarding Vincent of Ferrier (more often, Vincent Ferrer; 1350–1419).

41. Teresa of Avila, *Castle*, 10.

42. Burgess, *Peoples*, 170; Billman, *Thread*, 43 (noting also, e.g., Talbot, *Universe*, 129–31).

43. Ingle, *Friends*, 59 (cited in Oliver, *Reformations*, 73).

44. Hyatt, *Years*, 95.

45. Cosmos, *Huguenot Prophecy*, 33; cf. 47, 49–50, 53, 67–74, 113.

46. Cosmos, *Huguenot Prophecy*, 50, 71; Sigg, *Revival*, 27; Hyatt, *Years*, 87.

47. Cosmos, *Huguenot Prophecy*, 67–68.

awakening in 1742.[48] Sinners under conviction fell to the floor in various Baptist[49] and Methodist[50] meetings in the colonies in the 1700s. Mass numbers fell to the floor during a revival that broke out among Presbyterians in 1796, expressions even more common at the Cane Ridge Revival of 1801, again led partly by Presbyterians; thousands fell there.[51] Falling also accompanied the evangelical Irish Revival of 1859–60.[52] During the indigenous Christian awakening in India in 1860, many of those under the Spirit's conviction "fell down and rolled on the ground" but then experienced joy as they came to Christ.[53] Many fell also in early Salvation Army meetings, alongside celebratory shouting and dancing,[54] as well as in some Holiness meetings.[55] Nor are twentieth-century examples limited to the Pentecostal trajectory; the experience also appeared in one of history's most famous Baptist revivals, in China's Shandong Province in 1927–37.[56]

### EDWARDS AND THE FIRST GREAT AWAKENING

One figure whom MacArthur clearly respects is the rightly renowned theologian Jonathan Edwards. As one scholar of US history notes,

> Edwards became the ablest apologist for revivals in Britain and America. When Boston's Charles Chauncy (very much a man of the Enlightenment) attacked the revivals as frauds because of their emotional excesses, Edwards replied that, although no emotional response, however intense, could prove by itself the presence of God in a person's soul, he insisted that intense feelings must always accompany the reception of divine grace. For Edwards an unemotional piety could never be the work of God. In effect, Edwards countered Chauncy's emotional defense of reason with his own rational defense of emotion.[57]

48. Schmidt, *Fairs*, 145–46, as cited in Billman, *Thread*, 40.
49. Kidd, *Awakening*, 251.
50. Taves, *Fits*, 86; sources cited in Oliver, *Reformations*, 138.
51. Hyatt, *Years*, 113–15, citing Johnson, *Camp Meeting*, 35, 64–65; see also Boles, *Revival*, 67; shortly before Cane Ridge, see Boles, *Revival*, 54. For the dominant Presbyterian influence at Cane Ridge, see Billman, *Thread*, 51.
52. Worthen, *Spellbound*, 165–66. Critics attributed the falling to hysteria, but tens of thousands were converted.
53. John Christian Aroolappen (1810–67) in Aroolappen, *History*, reproduced in Burgess, *Peoples*, 213 (see 210–13). Falling, overwhelmed by the Spirit, is also reported during the outpouring at the Mukti Mission on June 29, 1905 (Burgess, *Peoples*, 244).
54. Oliver, *Reformations*, 208. Cf. ecstatic dancing among early Methodists (Ruth, *Methodist Life*, 161; Schmidt, *Fairs*, xxv; Billman, *Thread*, 76, 110).
55. Oliver, *Reformations*, 226. Cf. esp. the Holiness meetings of Maria Woodworth-Etter, as well as critics' non-Christian analogies at the time (Worthen, *Spellbound*, 167–69).
56. Crawford, *Revival* (provided one consults the unabridged edition), noted in, e.g., Billman, *Thread*, 51.
57. Murrin, *Liberty*, 128, as cited in Brown, *Authentic Fire*, 294. Murrin's quotation appears on 157 in a 2006 edition.

Such responses to revival are typical throughout history (see already Acts 2:13). As John White notes,

> The irony of revivals is that while they are so longed for in times of barrenness, they are commonly opposed and feared when they arrive. . . . This increase in the Spirit's activity provides other reasons for our often less than enthusiastic endorsement of revival—it disturbs the community. Church dignitaries are particularly offended by two things. They deplore "hysterical behavior" in religious meetings. They also resent new leadership. Since revival is often characterized by both, vested interests within the church react with fear and hostility.[58]

Consistent with most expectations in his era, Edwards rejected the idea of a coming revival of spiritual gifts and "the 'enthusiastic delusion' of believing that laymen were capable of ministering to others,"[59] but he evaluated fairly what he witnessed. While Edwards, unlike "Separate Baptists, Radical Congregationalists, and, later, Methodists," did not promote bodily manifestations, he offered biblical precedents to show that they were permissible.[60] Edwards's wife, Sarah, experienced trances that Edwards recognized as a genuine work of the Spirit.[61] He observed many such experiences, including people fainting unconscious for hours, laughing, and being delighted with visions.[62]

Already in the late 1730s, people in the fields were overwhelmed when they heard Wesley's message of the new birth. People trembled at the Spirit's presence when Wesley preached from Acts 2.[63] On other occasions, many sobbed as they repented; others were so overcome they shook or fell down;[64]

58. White, *Spirit*, 39, cited in Billman, *Thread*, 220. White cites Martyn Lloyd-Jones for the nature of revival. On orthodox church leaders opposing nearly every fresh revival in history, see further De Arteaga, *Quenching*; briefly, "Parody," 17.

59. Billman, *Thread*, 31.

60. Wagner, "Manifestations," 55.

61. Brown, *Authentic Fire*, 294, noting Taves, *Fits*; for the descriptions of the religious ecstasies of Sarah Edwards and David Brainerd, see Taves, *Fits*, 66–67.

62. See Oliver, *Reformations*, 127 (citing Jonathan Edwards, "A Narrative of Surprising Conversions," in Edwards, *Revival*, 13; Jonathan Edwards, "Revival of Religion in Northhampton in 1740–1741," in Edwards, *Revival*, 154); Edwards, "Letter to Prince."

63. Wesley's journal, May 25, 1740.

64. Deere, *Still Surprised*, 184–85, providing an example from Wesley's journal for June 15, 1739; Burgess, *Peoples*, 179, quoting from Wesley's journal for January 1, 1739; Dunn, *Jesus and Spirit*, 192; White, *Spirit*, 181; Tomkins, *Wesley*, 72–74; Oliver, *Reformations*, 119. See also Xhemajli, *Supernatural*, 48–49 (citing Wesley, *Miscellaneous*, 608; *Works* [AM], 3:129, 134); Xhemajli, *Supernatural*, 57 (citing Wesley, *Works* [AM], 4:36), 59 (citing, e.g., Wesley, *Works*, 4:25). See further, e.g., Wesley's journal for April 26, 1739; May 1, 4, 1739; with trances, July 9, 1759; also Wesley, *Journal* (Culley), 334, 509. See a fuller listing in Fox, "Word and Power," 102–3; Billman, *Thread*, 53–57, 62, 96, 101–2, 110–11, 116; most fully and extensively Taves, *Fits*. Wesley warned against interfering with such divine works (Wood, *Pentecost*, 191).

many shrieked, roared, barked, and jerked.[65] Critics who were present often fell, overtaken themselves until set free.[66] Of the more than sixty gathered at Fetter Lane on January 1, 1739, at 3 a.m., including Wesley and Whitefield, "many fell to the ground"; the outpouring of the Spirit at that time marked a key spiritual transition for the Methodist movement.[67] (MacArthur can cite Wesley respectfully,[68] despite not being fond of his Arminianism.)[69] John White notes that Wesley expected such emotional expressions as works of the Spirit, and some occurred, in a more restrained fashion, in Whitefield's meetings.[70]

Wesley's *Arminian Magazine* unashamedly included a monthly section testifying of various incidents considered to be divine activity.[71] His successors in the movement in the United States, for example Francis Asbury's colleague Henry Boehm in 1801, witnessed the same sort of manifestations.[72] Sometimes people "fell under the power" in one location when others were praying for them in a different location.[73]

Hearing misrepresentations about what was happening (not uncommon with critics of revival!—cf., again, e.g., Acts 2:13), Wesley's colleague Whitefield protested, but the next day Whitefield experienced the same phenomenon: "For no sooner had he begun (in the application of his sermon) to invite all sinners to believe in Christ, than four persons sunk down close to him, almost in the same moment. One of them lay without either sense or motion; a second trembled exceedingly; the third had strong convulsions all over his body, but made no noise, unless by groans. The fourth, equally convulsed, called upon God, with strong cries and tears."[74]

65. Xhemajli, *Supernatural*, 59, citing, e.g., Wesley, *Works*, 4:25. For occasional "animal roaring and barking" in early Methodism, see Xhemajli, *Supernatural*, 164; Oliver, *Reformations*, 119 (among some Jansenists, 92; at Cane Ridge, 159; Billman, *Thread*, 109); Billman, *Thread*, 110 (citing Ferguson, *Organizing*, 131–32). For jerking, also Xhemajli, *Supernatural*, 162–63; Billman, *Thread*, 109.

66. See Wesley's letter to his brother Samuel (May 10, 1739), quoted in Burgess, *Peoples*, 184; see also Fox, "Word and Power," 102; Billman, *Thread*, 56.

67. Fox, "Word and Power," 96–100; Billman, *Thread*, 52–54, citing also Stevens, *History*, 3:501; Schmitt, *Floods*, 128.

68. See MacArthur, "Adoption." For his earlier respect for Wesley's evangelistic passion, however, see MacArthur, "Passion."

69. See MacArthur, "Battle."

70. White, *Spirit*, 181. Secular explanations vary; whereas Sargent regarded these convulsions as hysterical, Raymond Prince thinks the convulsions during Wesley's preaching on June 15, 1739, represent merely suggestion (see Prince, "EEG," 130, 132).

71. Wood, *Meaning*, 195 (as cited in Billman, *Thread*, 58). The original version of the magazine ran from 1778 to 1797. Wesley regularly collected testimonies that underlined divine activity in Christian experience (Taves, *Fits*, 74, in Billman, *Thread*, 65).

72. Ruth, *Methodist Life*, 194–95 (as cited in Billman, *Thread*, 71). Note also others, e.g., in Rowe, "Albright," 38–39; Wigger, *Heaven*, 108–9, 117 (Billman, *Thread*, 71–74).

73. Ruth, *Methodist Life*, 171 (Billman, *Thread*, 74–75).

74. Wesley's journal, July 7, 1739, in Deere, *Still Surprised*, 185; Oliver, *Reformations*, 117; Billman, *Thread*, 62 (giving the reference also as Wesley, *Works* [1872 ed.], 1:210); Fox, "Word

Whitefield's journal recalls many falling during his preaching in the American colonies because of the Spirit's conviction.[75] Whitefield did worry that some well-meaning believers' actions during revival played into critics' hands, but he also believed it inevitable that some "wild-fire will necessarily blend itself with the pure fire."[76] Meanwhile, Whitefield also marveled at the even more massive weeping and falling he witnessed during an outpouring in Glasgow, Scotland, in 1742.[77]

As the awakening spread to the American colonies, Jonathan Edwards recorded some of his observations.[78] "It was a very frequent thing to see a house full of outcries, faintings, convulsions, and such like, both with distress, and also with admiration and joy. . . . It was pretty often so, that there were some that were so affected, and their bodies so overcome, that they could not go home, but were obliged to stay all night where they were." Falling continued in evangelistic meetings of circuit riders.[79] Sometimes those who came to mock the meetings were struck down as if dead, leading to their conversions.[80]

### FINNEY AND THE SECOND GREAT AWAKENING

Falling continued to pervade mass conversion meetings during the nation's Second Great Awakening, as did shouting, jerking, and other ecstatic expressions.[81] At the University of Georgia in 1800–1801, for example, students began jerking or "fell prostrate as if shot down by a sniper."[82] Falling[83] and jerking[84] were also common, for example, in meetings of Peter Cartwright, a frontier circuit rider (whose example appears here not least because he is one of Daniel's ancestors on his mother's side). Michael McClymond, one of the leading scholars on historic US awakenings, notes common characteristics historically, which include physical effects, such as "weeping, shouting, fainting, dancing," and sometimes falling; these features have characterized

---

and Power," 102. Groans from conviction also accompanied the Awakening in the colonies (see the source in Lovejoy, *Enthusiasm*, 77; Hyatt, *Years*, 111). Prestigious Yale College withheld two degrees in 1741 to promoters of such "enthusiasm" (Billman, *Thread*, 66, following De Arteaga, *Quenching*, 28).

75. E.g., May 14–15, 1740, in Whitefield, *Journals*, 276; White, *Spirit*, 71 (in Billman, *Thread*, 66). See also the testimony in Marrant, *Narrative*, cited in Oliver, *Reformations*, 141.

76. Kidd, *Awakening*, 170.

77. Billman, *Thread*, 67, quoting Dallimore, *Whitefield*, 2:125.

78. Edwards, "Account of Revival," 150, in Deere, *Still Surprised*, 186.

79. E.g., Xhemajli, *Supernatural*, 149, 151–58.

80. Xhemajli, *Supernatural*, 155–58.

81. For hundreds (both believers and nonbelievers) at Cane Ridge even on a single occasion in 1801, see Synan, *Tradition*, 12. Some barked as if they were "dogs as they 'treed the devil'" (Hyatt, *Years*, 114, quoting Synan, *Movement*, 24). Cf. Wagner, "Manifestations," 56.

82. Synan, *Tradition*, 13, in turn quoting from Coulter, *College Life*, 194–95.

83. Watters, *Peter Cartwright*, 29–30, 33–34; Cartwright, *Autobiography*, 30–31, 121, 221–22.

84. Cartwright, *Autobiography*, 48–49.

a range of participants in revivals, "including Calvinists, Quakers, Baptists, Methodists, and adherents of the Holiness movement."[85]

The nineteenth-century mass evangelist Charles Finney (1792–1875) was a leading figure in the Second Great Awakening. Early in his Christian life, Finney was overwhelmed by God's Spirit, pouring out the depths of his heart in a deep experience with God.[86] Later, his ministry powerfully impacted many cities across the United States and England. Of the prominent revival he led in Rochester, New York, Finney wrote that "it seemed as if the whole city would be converted."[87] Indeed, Lyman Beecher, once a fierce opponent to Finney, estimated about one hundred thousand conversions directly or indirectly attributed to the revival in Rochester.[88] Finney made a significant contribution to the abolition of slavery, the temperance movement, and other social issues that would impact the nation for generations to come.[89] Dwight L. Moody praised Finney's ministry,[90] and Finney profoundly impacted other well-known leaders such as William Booth (founder of the Salvation Army),[91] Jonathan Goforth (prominent missionary to China),[92] George Williams (founder of the YMCA),[93] Charles Spurgeon,[94] and many others.

"Manifestations" were common in Finney's meetings. Finney himself, as well as those in his meetings, admitted that these could not be simple emotional reactions to persuasive preaching. Finney said, "It would probably not be possible, for one who had never witnessed such a scene, to realize what the force of the truth sometimes is under the power of the Holy Ghost."[95] He said, "The Spirit's work was so spontaneous, so powerful, and so overwhelming, as to render it necessary to exercise the greatest caution and wisdom in conducting the meetings."[96] He claimed to have been personally led by the voice of God, and even to have had several visions. He prophesied on a number of

85. McClymond, "Characteristics," 6. McClymond is also an Edwards historian; see McClymond and McDermott, *Theology*.

86. Finney, *Memoirs*, 20. Finney described his experience as "like a wave of electricity" and "waves and waves of liquid love" (Rogers, "Did You Know?," i).

87. Finney, *Memoirs*, chap. 32.

88. Miller, *Finney*, 75; Duewel, *Revival Fire*, 110.

89. Brand, *Addresses*, 17–18.

90. Rogers, "Did You Know?" Of Moody, R. A. Torrey insisted, "The seventh thing that was the secret of why God used D. L. Moody was that he had a very definite enduement with power from on High, a very clear and definite baptism with the Holy Ghost" (Torrey, *God Used Moody*, 51).

91. Woodall, *Price*, 56–57.

92. Goforth, *Goforth*, 179–80.

93. Pierson, *Review*, 339. See "Finney: Know": "George Williams, an English worker, was converted by reading Finney's writings. In London in 1844, inspired by Finney's social reform stand, Williams founded the YMCA."

94. Spurgeon, *Lectures*, 173–74.

95. Finney, *Memoirs*, 161.

96. Finney, *Memoirs*, 170.

occasions. He saw miracles of healing, miracles of provision, and miracles of nature. He even believed that on a number of occasions, certain people had been struck dead in divine judgment for opposing the revival![97]

Nevertheless, MacArthur's theologically meticulous circle rejects Finney as heretical.[98] Many in MacArthur's circle also reject the altar calls that Finney popularized, though they remain common in many Baptist and other churches today. (While many of us disagree with Finney on some theological points, sometimes even key ones, God surely used him as a major figure in the Second Great Awakening, which evangelized much of the United States in its generation.)[99] Given rejection of Finney's examples in MacArthur's circle, we now return again to Edwards and the First Great Awakening, which most of the harsh cessationists respect.

## Jonathan Edwards's Criteria Defending the First Great Awakening

As noted, the First Great Awakening drew criticisms from guardians of rationalism such as Charles Chauncy; such "manifestations" were naturally offensive to more sedate conventional ecclesiastical culture. Edwards produced a work designed to refute the criticisms while also refocusing the subject to the clearer evidences of the Spirit.

### *Manifestations That Neither Prove nor Disprove God's Working*

In laying out criteria, Edwards begins with the "negative signs" that do not allow one to either prove or disprove that a genuine work of God is occurring:[100]

1. "Nothing can be certainly concluded from this, That a work is carried on in a way very unusual and extraordinary; provided the variety or difference be such, as may still be comprehended within the limits of Scripture rules." That is, if it does not *contradict* Scripture, it does not impugn the work of the Spirit occurring.
2. "A work is not to be judged of by any effects on the bodies of men; such as tears, tremblings, groans, loud outcries, agonies of body, or the

97. See the many accounts throughout Finney, *Memoirs* (pagination varies by edition).

98. MacArthur, "Living"; Johnson, "Wolf." Nevertheless, Johnson may be calling "wolf" prematurely. Many in MacArthur's circle misunderstand or misrepresent much of Finney's theology (Flowers, "MacArthur"). See also Gueizo, "Making."

99. MacArthur, "Look at Awakening." The First Great Awakening impacted especially church people; the Second reached especially the unchurched and dechurched.

100. See Edwards, "Distinguishing Marks," cited in, e.g., Deere, *Still Surprised*, 193–94; Brown, *Authentic Fire*, 123–29. Anyone can read Edwards's essay directly at http://www.biblebb.com/files/edwards/je-marksofhs.htm (accessed Aug. 30, 2024).

failing of bodily strength. The influence persons are under, is not to be judged of one way or other, by such effects on the body; and the reason is, because the Scripture nowhere gives us any such rule." That is, bodily manifestations neither dispute nor prove the work of the Spirit.

3. "It is no argument that an operation on the minds of people is not the work of the Spirit of God that it occasions a great deal of noise about religion."
4. "It is no argument that an operation on the minds of a people is not the work of the Spirit of God that many who are the subjects of it have great impressions made on their imaginations." There was no biblical reason to reject without evaluation the trances and visions of his wife or others.
5. "It is no sign that a work is not from the Spirit of God that example is a great means of it." This might mean, Brown notes, that even though some people might be just imitating others, "learning by example is both reasonable and Scriptural, if, in fact, the work is from God," so "you can't prove anything either way from this."[101]
6. "It is no sign that a work is not from the Spirit of God that many who seem to be the subjects of it are guilty of great imprudences and irregularities in their conduct."
7. "Nor are many errors in judgment, and some delusions of Satan intermixed with the work, any argument that the work in general is not of the Spirit of God."
8. "If some, who were thought to be wrought upon, fall away into gross errors, or scandalous practices, it is no argument that the work in general is not the work of the Spirit of God."
9. "It is no argument that a work is not from the Spirit of God that it seems to be promoted by ministers insisting very much on the terrors of God's holy law, and that with a great deal of pathos and earnestness."

Contrary to how some cessationist critics have applied Edwards's list, Edwards did not provide these tests to disprove that anything was a work of God. Instead, Edwards is specifying that, against the awakening's critics, such manifestations do *not* disqualify something (such as the First Great Awakening) as a work of God, although neither do they prove it.[102]

101. Brown, *Authentic Fire*, 126.

102. See fuller discussion in Brown, *Authentic Fire*, 123–24, citing Edwards scholars and responding to MacArthur, *Strange Fire*, 34. De Arteaga, "Parody," 19–25, highlights how MacArthur misappropriates Edwards's criteria, which favor rather than refute most of the modern charismatic movement.

Edwards notes that an experience need not be specified in Scripture to be genuine, if it does not *contradict* Scripture:

> Some object against such extraordinary appearances, that we have no instances of them recorded in the New Testament, under the extraordinary effusions of the Spirit. Were this allowed, I can see no force in the objection, if neither reason, nor any rule of Scripture, exclude such things. . . . I do not know that we have any express mention in the New Testament of any person's weeping, or groaning, or sighing through fear of hell, or a sense of God's anger; but is there any body so foolish as from hence to argue, that in whomsoever these things appear, their convictions are not from the Spirit of God? And the reason why we do not argue thus, is, because these are easily accounted for, from what we know of the nature of man. . . . Nobody supposes that there is any need of express scripture for every external, accidental manifestation of the inward motion of the mind. . . . And there is also reason to think, that such great outpouring of the Spirit was not wholly without those more extraordinary effects on persons' bodies. The jailer in particular, seems to have been an instance of that nature, when he, in the utmost distress and amazement, came trembling, and fell down before Paul and Silas. His falling down at that time does not seem to be a designed putting himself into a posture of supplication, or humble address to Paul and Silas; for he seems not to have [yet] said anything to them then; but he first brought them out, and then he says to them, Sirs, what must I do to be saved? Acts xvi. 29, and 30. But his falling down seems to be from the same cause as his trembling. The psalmist gives an account of his crying out aloud, and a great weakening of his body under convictions of conscience, and a sense of the guilt of sin, Psal. xxxii. 3, 4.[103]

### Edwards's Positive Signs of the Spirit's Work

For Edwards, the ultimate test of experiences that Scripture does not specifically address is how one lives afterward—consonant with Matthew 7:16–20.[104] As an older generation of Pentecostals sometimes pointed out, what proves the Spirit's genuine work in you is not how high you jump or whether you fall down but how you live when you get up.

Following, then, are Edwards's positive signs that do confirm a divine work:[105]

1. "When the operation is such as to raise their esteem of that Jesus who was born of the Virgin, and was crucified without the gates of Jerusalem; and seems more to confirm and establish their minds in the truth of what the gospel declares to us of his being the Son of God, and the Saviour

103. Edwards, "Distinguishing Marks."

104. With Deere, *Still Surprised*, 194, citing Edwards, "Distinguishing Marks," 18.

105. Edwards, "Distinguishing Marks." Brown, *Authentic Fire*, 130–31, rightly draws attention to this.

of men; is a sure sign that it is from the Spirit of God." Edwards cites here 1 John 4:2–3.

2. "When the spirit that is at work operates against the interests of Satan's kingdom, which lies in encouraging and establishing sin, and cherishing men's worldly lusts; this is a sure sign that it is a true, and not a false spirit." Edwards cites here 1 John 4:4–5 and Matthew 12:25–26 (where Satan does not cast out Satan).
3. "The spirit that operates in such a manner, as to cause in men a greater regard to the Holy Scriptures, and establishes them more in their truth and divinity, is certainly the Spirit of God." Edwards rightly cites here 1 John 4:6.
4. "Another rule to judge of spirits may be drawn from those compellations given to the opposite spirits, in the last words of the 6th verse, 'The spirit of truth and the spirit of error.'" Edwards again points to 1 John 4:6.
5. "If the spirit that is at work among a people operates as a spirit of love to God and man, it is a sure sign that it is the Spirit of God." For the last point, note 1 John 4:8.

Edwards thus concludes that the awakening in his day is a work of God, and insists, "Let us all be hence warned, *by no means to oppose, or do any thing in the least to clog or hinder, the work; but, on the contrary, do our utmost to promote it*. Now Christ is come down from heaven in a remarkable and wonderful work of his Spirit, it becomes all his professed disciples to acknowledge him, and give him honour."

With Edwards, we recognize that human frailties impact all outpourings of God's Spirit on human beings.[106] Yet also with Edwards, we further recognize God's Spirit at work where people grow in loving God, God's Word, and one another, and where the work honors Christ and his kingdom versus that of Satan. Edwards chose to stand for such a work in his day. May we do the same in ours.

## Reformers' Scandals: Do Abuses Invalidate a Work of the Spirit?

Distancing himself from charismatic extremists, Sam Storms once used them to justify his cessationism. "I was faithful to the eleventh commandment of Bible-church evangelicalism: 'Thou shalt not do at all what others do poorly.'"[107] Inductive study of Scripture, however, eventually made cessationism impossible

106. So also Wesley; see Billman, *Thread*, 60–61, 198 (citing, e.g., Wesley, *Works* [1872 ed.], 2:519).

107. Storms, "View," 205.

for him. From then on he had to evaluate charismatic experiences rather than dismiss them wholesale.

Human errors and sins inevitably arise on the fringes of movements initiated by God, and sometimes they even manage to hijack them.[108] But these human failures should not discredit the work that God himself initiated. Gideon failed to destroy the ephod by which he celebrated his victory, even after his people went astray for it (Judg. 8:27; contrast 2 Kings 18:4). This failure does not mean that God (Judg. 6:11–26) had not genuinely provided Gideon's earlier victories (7:1–23; 8:4–21). The Spirit of the Lord continued to come on Samson (13:25; 14:6, 19; 15:14) until he had violated the last element of his Nazirite vow (16:17), despite such blatant sins as sleeping with a prostitute (16:1). We rightly denounce Samson's sins in Judges 16, but we dare not denounce God's prior work along with it. We also don't discard the book of Psalms because one of its chief authors committed adultery and murder.

Likewise, God's Spirit endowed the Corinthians with gifts (cf. 1 Cor. 1:7) despite their spiritual immaturity (3:1), blatant immorality (5:1–2), and heresy (15:12) (though their sin did limit some of his benefits; 11:30). Despite the Galatians' folly and susceptibility to heresy (Gal. 1:6; 3:1; 4:19; 5:4), God worked miracles among them (3:5).[109] Even Peter and Paul had their temporary conflict with each other (Gal. 2:11–14; cf. also Acts 15:39), not unlike Whitefield and the Wesleys. God's Spirit works through us frail humans, and very often also in spite of us.

What if cessationist critics held the Reformers to the same standard to which harsh cessationists hold charismatics? In this section, we follow a line of examination especially laid out by William De Arteaga, Michael Brown, and others.[110]

Harsh cessationist critics of charismatics often express confidence in their position in part because they view it as an inheritance from the Reformation. (As we shall see in chap. 21, this is only partly their inheritance.)

For MacArthur, "the Protestant Reformation is rightly regarded as the greatest revival in the last thousand years of church history. . . . Names like Martin Luther, John Calvin, and John Knox are still well-known today."[111] Tom Schreiner points out, "I think it is significant that the great teachers whom God used to bring about the Protestant Reformation were cessationists."[112]

108. As perhaps with later Jansenists several centuries ago or the self-centered "prosperity" (versus provision) emphasis among a significant sector of modern charismatics.

109. With Deere, *Still Surprised*, 197. On abuses generally, see *Still Surprised*, 197–203.

110. See further Kolenda, "False Prophecies."

111. MacArthur, *Strange Fire*, 213. As shown in chap. 12, Knox prophesied, whatever his theology. De Arteaga, "Parody," 30, notes the "probably true (but unproven)" accusation "that John Knox, the founder of Scottish Presbyterianism, had an affair with his mother-in-law."

112. Schreiner, *Spiritual Gifts*, 167.

Ironically, MacArthur uses the Reformers to denounce charismatics, comparing charismatics to the medieval church against which the Reformers reacted: "The modern charismatic counterfeit is following down that same perilous path—basing its belief system on something other than the sole authority of Scripture and poisoning the church with a twisted notion of faith. Like the medieval Catholic Church, it muddles the clear teaching of Scripture and obscures the true gospel," destroying lives.[113]

On many issues cessationists value the Reformers' emphasis on *sola scriptura*, Scripture alone, against earlier church traditions. And indeed the Reformers, while valuing ancient traditions, were distinctive for their commendable and needed emphasis on appealing to Scripture, God's own Word, above all else. Ironically, however, as we have shown, Scripture does not support cessationism, so those who appeal to a cessationist *tradition* from leading Reformers are not acting *hermeneutically* in accord with the best instincts of the Reformers. Whereas Catholic and Orthodox Christians (normally not cessationist anyway) are within their rights to appeal to tradition, Protestants who claim *sola scriptura* act hypocritically if they use "theology" (insofar as this represents merely a code word for their theological tradition) to deny explicit biblical teaching.

The magisterial Reformers not only reacted against Catholics but (surely to the annoyance of many modern Baptists and Mennonites) persecuted the often charismatic-style Anabaptists of the Radical Reformation. Calvin, Luther, and many of their colleagues had the gift of *teaching*, an essential gift for getting the church back on track. But then as today, teachers need the other gifts as well for us to be a whole body. From (for example) many Baptist, Church of Christ, or independent charismatic perspectives, the magisterial Reformers still retained too much of the clerical structure of the medieval church. Anabaptist house churches where members shared spiritual gifts did not fit the civil-ecclesiastical arrangements to which Europe was accustomed. Luther's approach to church and state not only cost the lives of many peasants but also, when isolated from his other teachings, facilitated the Nazi war effort in later Germany.

Cessationist critics who mock initial Pentecostal views about missionary tongues (as in the *Cessationist* movie),[114] despite Pentecostals and charismatics supplying the largest global missionary force today, should consider their own Reformation heroes and the first centuries of Protestantism.[115] The magisterial Reformers initially neglected or opposed missions, partly because they associated them with Catholics. Catholics noted that Catholic missionaries were converting thousands of pagans, while Protestants (at that time) were

113. MacArthur, *Strange Fire*, 217–18.
114. Lanphere, *Cessationist*.
115. Kolenda, "Embarrassing Story."

converting hardly any. Instead of responding that they would soon embark on such, Protestants "tended to say 'Missions are neither obligatory nor desirable,'" so don't use our deficiency in this area against us.[116] One of the first and most devoted missionary movements arose among the persecuted Moravians after their experience of the outpouring of the Spirit.[117] It was not only Catholic miracle claims against which Reformers overreacted but also Catholic missionary endeavors.

### *Luther on the Devil and Sin*

Grounds for scandal have shifted over the centuries. Luther's marriage, violating his monastic vow of celibacy, scandalized many Catholics in his day but is rarely cause for criticism today (especially among those of us who are married ministers). Luther's secret consent to Philip of Hesse's bigamous marriage (1540, because Scripture did not explicitly prohibit polygamy), alongside Melanchthon and Bucer,[118] produced scandal but has obviously long since blown over.

While we are right to acknowledge the good that Luther accomplished (and I, Craig, am happy to emphasize that *scholars* played such a pivotal role in sixteenth-century reforms), harsh cessationist critics judge charismatics by a standard that their own Reformation heroes would not survive. Virtually everyone recognizes that Luther sometimes spoke intemperately. Luther even lost his temper toward Calvin, souring the relationship from Luther's side.[119] Calvin continued to respect him but complained to Heinrich Bullinger about Luther's "restless uneasy temper which is so ready to boil over everywhere."[120] Scholars speak of "Luther's cultivated gift for invective" that "often went far beyond the rhetorical norms of his day."[121] Brown offers numerous examples of Luther's frailties. Some of these examples were highlighted by Roman Catholic detractors whose attitude toward Luther is similar to MacArthur's attitude toward charismatics.

116. Neill, *History of Missions*, 221–22. The Second Great Awakening helped propel free churches in the US into missions (Kling, "Model," 14).

117. See Neill, *History of Missions*, 237–38, 310. Even earlier, the Spirit-moved Pietist movement among German Lutherans also supported missions; see Neill, *History of Missions*, 227–28.

118. Chadwick, *Reformation*, 71–72; Bainton, *Reformation*, 259; Latourette, *History of Christianity*, 2:728. In principle, Cardinal Cajetan also preferred bigamy to divorce (Bainton, *Reformation*, 259).

119. Parker, *Calvin*, 169. In 1552–53 Joachim Westphal even denounced Calvin and treated as excommunicable anyone who did not strictly follow Luther's views (Parker, *Calvin*, 170).

120. Quoted in Parker, *Calvin*, 170. We might cut Luther at least some slack in view of his past traumas (though he himself would not regard this as an excuse; see Luther, *Romans*, 288); he was not paranoid in supposing that many people wanted him dead.

121. Midelfort, *History*, 83.

Luther (like many others of his day) was surely as demon-obsessed as a stereotypical modern hypercharismatic.[122] He credulously recounted that he heard that the devil "drained all the milk from the breasts of five women" in Saxony, though demons resided far more in Prussia.[123] The devil could drown those who swam in streams alone, and appeared in various animal forms, often that of an ape. Fearing that a dog he discovered in his room at the Wartburg was a demon, he hurled it out his window. Much of his demonology came from postbiblical monastic or German folklore.[124]

Luther is also known for his crudities (typically scatological, as opposed to eschatological), which sometimes further influenced his articulation of demonology. For example, when demons tempt him, he explained, "I show them my butt, for that's where they belong." He elsewhere taunts the devil with orders such as, "Lick my butt!" or "Eat my feces!"[125] "Almost every night when I wake up the devil is there and wants to dispute with me. I have come to this conclusion: When the argument that the Christian is without the law and above the law doesn't help, I instantly chase him away with a fart."[126] He frequently denounced his enemies as insane or demoniacs and their ideas as inspired by demons.[127]

His hyperbolic expressions of freedom sound almost like the most antinomian expressions of hypergrace. We would belong to Jesus "even if we were to kill or commit adultery thousands of times each day."[128] Such quips are not representative of his broader theology,[129] but they are representative of some of his rhetoric.

### *Luther and the Peasants*

Luther's theology of church and state ultimately overcame any of his early liberationist tendencies.[130] In an era in which partisan polemic proved

122. See, e.g., "Prince of Darkness"; Hendrix, *Martin Luther*, chap. 8 ("Angels and Demons"); Midelfort, *History*, 92–97.

123. Eire, *Flew*, 292.

124. See Eire, *Flew*, 292; cf. 301.

125. We have slightly reworded the quotations, all from Eire, *Flew*, 293, to avoid unduly offending the fainthearted.

126. Brown, *Authentic Fire*, 101, citing Beaumont, "From Farts to Faith," for this and other quotes, with references. Cf. similarly Eire, *Flew*, 293–94.

127. Midelfort, *History*, 83.

128. Brown, *Authentic Fire*, 101, noting the incompatibility with MacArthur's treatment of lordship salvation. Brown's source ("Myth of Luther") cites "Let Your Sins Be Strong," from "The Wittenberg Project"; "The Wartburg Segment," translated by Erika Flores, from *Dr. Martin Luther's Saemmtliche Schriften*, Letter No. 99, August 1, 1521.

129. Luther and other early Reformers did in fact expect transformation to follow justification; see, e.g., Chester, *Reading Paul*, 163, 193, 215, 300–301; Das, *Galatians*, 589n130; Luther, *Romans*, gloss on chap. 12, marginal note 2.

130. See Arnal, "Luther and Peasants," 459–61. Luther presupposed the continuance of feudalism in which serfs owed allegiance to lords (Arnal, "Luther and Peasants," 452).

a matter of life and death, Luther's growing entanglement in political matters led to some costly pronouncements.[131] While Luther initially supported some just demands from the peasants, he reacted to the violence of their extremists and soon "showed himself at his worst," says historical theologian John Dillenberger, who complains, "Some of his most vindictive writings came out of this period."[132] The revolts undermined the civic authority on which the political success of Luther's more epistemological revolution depended, and Luther could not risk being identified with the extremists' approach.[133]

Better to suffer from a single tyrant, he contended, "than from numerous tyrants, that is, from the mob."[134] Yet most of the peasants protesting in 1525 cannot be characterized as mobs.[135] Luther's knowledge of peasant protests unfortunately rested on very limited and not very representative sources.[136] In his *Against the Robbing and Murdering Hordes of Peasants* (1525), Luther wrote:

> Rebellion brings with it a land filled with murder and bloodshed. . . . Therefore let everyone who can, smite, slay, and stab, . . . remembering that nothing can be more poisonous, hurtful, or devilish than a rebel. It is just as when one must kill a mad dog.[137]
>
> It is also plain that these peasants have deserved death many times over. . . . One who perishes on the peasants' side is an eternal brand of hell, for he . . . is a member of the devil. . . . Stab, smite, slay, whoever you can.[138]

After the princes took Luther literally and massacred as many as a hundred thousand peasants, others challenged Luther. He replied that rebels had to be put down before they caused more harm. If anyone thought him too harsh in his instructions, he insisted:

> A rebel is not worth rational arguments, for he does not accept them. You have to answer people like that with a fist.[139]

131. On "his polemical streak," see Chadwick, *Reformation*, 61.

132. Dillenberger, *Martin Luther*, xxv.

133. See Holland, *Dominion*, 323.

134. As quoted in Arnal, "Luther and Peasants," 453.

135. As shown in Arnal, "Luther and Peasants," 455–58, noting their Twelve Articles; see also Sessions, "War," 27.

136. Porter, "Millenarianism," 396.

137. Lindberg, *Sourcebook*, 98 (from LW 46:49–50, 52); see further Arnal, "Luther and Peasants," 464; Porter, "Millenarianism," 398; Sessions, "War," 30.

138. From Rupp and Drewery, *Martin Luther*, 121–26.

139. *An Open Letter on the Harsh Book Against the Peasants* (1525), in Lindberg, *Sourcebook*, 98 (from LW 46:65). See also Arnal, "Luther and Peasants," 464–65.

> I, Martin Luther, have during the rebellion slain all the peasants, for it was I who ordered them to be struck dead. All their blood is upon my head. But I put it all on our Lord God: for he commanded me to speak thus.[140]

The peasants felt betrayed, while Catholic princes charged Luther as at fault for the revolt to begin with.[141] Anti-Luther sources (the veracity of which we have not directly confirmed in this case) even cite Luther as saying:

> To kill a peasant is not murder; it is helping to extinguish the conflagration. Let there be no half measures! Crush them! Cut their throats! Transfix them. Leave no stone unturned! To kill a peasant is to destroy a mad dog! If they say that I am very hard and merciless, mercy be damned. Let whoever can stab, strangle, and kill them like mad dogs.[142]

> A peasant is a hog, for when a hog is slaughtered it is dead, and in the same way the peasant does not think about the next life, for otherwise he would behave very differently.[143]

### *Magisterial Reformers Versus Anabaptists*

While Luther mistrusted Anabaptist "prophets," he affirmed the importance of the Spirit in interpreting the Bible correctly—which on matters he considered essential meant interpreting it the way he did.[144] Yet supporters of believers' baptism may cringe at Luther's denunciation of Anabaptists. His rhetoric had real effects. Lutherans today recognize that "approximately one thousand Anabaptists were killed in lands governed by Lutheran princes in the sixteenth century."[145] Nor was Luther alone on this point.

Baptists and other low-church Protestants often prefer Ulrich Zwingli to Luther regarding the Lord's Supper, but Zwingli stood with Luther and Calvin on infant baptism—if not necessarily in exegesis, then at least in supporting the state's right to enforce it. Zwingli combatted Anabaptists, who insisted on baptizing confessing believers rather than infants. Zwingli considered baptism only "an external ceremony," but he believed that the sectarian Anabaptists

140. In *Table Talk*, cited in Verres, *Luther*, 240; Murray, "Hermeneutics." See further Arnal, "Luther and Peasants," 465.

141. Bainton, *Here I Stand,* 281; for Luther's critics, see Edwards, *Printing*, 149, as cited in Holland, *Dominion*, 323.

142. Murray, "Hermeneutics." Most of these sources appear in Brown, *Authentic Fire*, 101–2, whom we follow here.

143. Luther in 1532, in O'Hare, *Facts*, 246.

144. See, e.g., Holland, *Dominion*, 328. For Luther's (commendable) emphasis on the Spirit in biblical interpretation, see Ramm, *Interpretation*, 98; Wyckoff, *Pneuma*, 22–24.

145. "Right Remembering," 3. For large numbers of Anabaptist martyrs, see also Horsch, *Mennonites*, 300.

were schismatic and could lead to anarchy.[146] Thus Zurich's city council, after banishing and imprisoning Anabaptists to silence them, finally gave the order on March 7, 1526: "If any one hereafter shall baptize another, he will be seized by our Lords and, according to the decree now set forth, will be drowned without mercy."[147] Zwingli himself wrote, "Whoever will be baptized hereafter will be submerged permanently."[148] An invitation to gallows humor?

Like some other rebel leaders at Münster, John of Leiden, the tyrannical and polygamous "king" of Münster, was a false prophet who ultimately suppressed religious freedom. His actions merited suppression in the interest of civil society (though the suppression took the form of literal overkill). But it's not fair to paint all Anabaptists with Münster's brush; most Anabaptists were, and nearly all today are, pacifists, and as a persecuted minority movement they became leading European voices for religious freedom and separating church and state.

#### *Luther on "the Jews"*

Although Europe had a long tradition of anti-Judaism, Luther's voice on this point proved particularly loud and hostile, exceeding that of his fellow Reformers.[149] As a Jewish believer in Jesus, Brown grieves particularly deeply over Luther's denunciations of the Jewish people in Luther's later years.[150] One theologian today laments that Luther's "qualified antipathy to ethnic Judaism becomes pathological in his late disgraceful tract *On the Jews and Their Lies*."[151] Brown highlights this 1543 work, noting that "Hitler and the Nazis implemented with zeal" its prescriptions.[152]

> I brief, dear princes and lords, those of you who have Jews under your rule— . . . so that you and we all can be rid of the unbearable, devilish burden of the Jews,

146. In Lindberg, *Sourcebook*, 131–32. For Bullinger's view that Anabaptists subverted proper civic authority, see Baker, "Dissent," 138. Initially, Bucer was more tolerant (145). Fear of anarchy helped motivate Luther's support of the princes in the face of the peasant revolt (Porter, "Millenarianism," 400).

147. Lindberg, *Sourcebook*, 131.

148. Harder, "Reaction," 52.

149. Martin Bucer was strongly intolerant of Jewish activity within Christendom; see Rowan, "Luther, Bucer," 82–85. More moderate are Calvin (Robinson, "Calvin and Jews") and esp. Andreas Osiander (Rowan, "Luther, Bucer," 90). Some, such as Bullinger, averred that Luther went too far (Rudnick, "Hate Speech," 423). MacArthur, who rightly takes issue with Parham's racism, ignores Luther's antisemitism (De Arteaga, "Parody," 29–30).

150. Luther earlier supported the Jewish people; for this and Lutheranism's repudiation of this work, see Brown, *Objections*, 127–35; also Brown, *Stained*, 239n34.

151. Fiddes, *Romans*, 299.

152. Brown, *Authentic Fire*, 103–4; similarly, Brown, *Stained*, 31–32. These quotations are widely cited (e.g., Holland, *Dominion*, 372) and freely available today online at, e.g., "Anti-Semitism." As Chester, *Reading Paul*, 359n103, notes, here "Luther utters intentional, vicious, and completely indefensible slanders against Judaism."

lest we become guilty sharers before God in the lies, blasphemy, the defamation, and the curses which the mad Jews indulge in so freely and wantonly against the person of our Lord Jesus Christ. . . . First, their synagogues . . . should be set on fire, and whatever does not burn up should be covered or spread over with dirt so that no one may ever be able to see a cinder or stone of it. And this ought to be done for the honor of God and of Christianity. . . . Secondly, their homes should likewise be broken down and destroyed. . . . For this reason they ought to be put under one roof or in a stable, like gypsies.[153] Thirdly, they should be deprived of their prayerbooks and Talmuds in which such idolatry, lies, cursing and blasphemy are taught. Fourthly, their rabbis must be forbidden under threat of death to teach any more. . . . Fifthly, passport and traveling privileges should be absolutely forbidden to the Jews. . . . Sixthly, . . . all their cash and valuables of silver and gold ought to be taken from them and put aside for safekeeping. Seventhly, let the young Jews and Jewesses . . . earn their bread by the sweat of their noses.

Other widely available quotations from this work include the following:

Did I not tell you earlier that a Jew is such a noble, precious jewel that God and all the angels dance when he farts?

We let them get rich on our sweat and blood, while we remain poor and they suck the marrow from our bones.[154]

They are just devils and nothing more, with no feeling of humanity for us heathen.[155]

At other times he uncritically repeated the historic blood libel against them and insisted that anyone should be allowed to beat them without penalty.[156]

Luther spewed venomous rhetoric, but not entirely creatively; as one author complains, his polemic against many groups regularly included "sows, devils and such like."[157] In the early 1520s Luther hoped that tolerance would bring about Jewish conversion, but once he viewed this approach as futile, he turned to polemic against them as toward Anabaptists and others, hoping to insulate Christians from what he regarded as their theological hostility.[158] As one writer notes, given all of Luther's writings and targets of abuse, his

153. Nazis also tried to exterminate the Roma people, whom others often called Gypsies.

154. The translation in these quotations appears in "Anti-Semitism."

155. Grisar, *Luther*, 286. For close connection between Jews and Satan in the later Luther, see Amaru, "Mirrors," 99.

156. Cohen, "Contemporaries," 198, citing, e.g., *Table Talk* (December 18, 1536). On the medieval blood libel, see, e.g., Johnson, *Blood Libel*; Teter, *Blood Libel*; Soyer, *Blood Libel*.

157. Grisar, *Luther*, 287 (e.g., "The peasants are the merest hogs"; Papist clergy are "like pigs"). Apparently devils were as pervasive in Luther's Germany as pigs were.

158. See Roynesdal, "Luther and Jews"; cf. Cohen, "Contemporaries," 196–98. For Amaru, "Mirrors," 97–99, Luther employs Jews, whether positively or later negatively, as theological

fixation on Judaism in his later life might have appeared relatively peripheral: "Luther's anti-Judaism might have been forgotten and even understood as a product of his times. After all, Luther preached in a Wittenberg church where anti-Jewish art—the notorious *Judensau* depicting Jews nursing on the teats of swine—had been installed hundreds of years before he was born."[159]

But his polemic continued to echo in later generations,[160] and antisemites mined Luther's writings for their purposes. Already in 1546 the Brunswig City Council expelled Jews from their community, citing Luther's essay.[161] Subsequent centuries of Lutherans forgot, but the tracts remained available for later exploitation. Carl Cohen understandably complains, "Not since the exgressions of St. John Chrysostom had any Christian engaged in such vituperation against Jews and Judaism as had Marin [sic] Luther."[162] Luther's anti-Jewish tracts may not have been widely available in twentieth-century Germany before the Nazis drew attention to them, and even then, very selectively.[163] But the Nazis may have coordinated Kristallnacht (Nov. 9–10, 1938), their first violent, public attack on Jewish institutions, with Luther's birthday (Nov. 10). Following Luther's rhetoric literally, Nazis set alight 191 German synagogues.[164] Two weeks later German Lutheran bishop Martin Sasse published a tract connecting the event with Luther's birthday and recounting Luther's anti-Jewish rhetoric. The first printing was of one hundred thousand copies.[165] (An aside here for nonauthors: That is normally considered an enviable sales volume.) At the Nuremberg trials, a noted antisemite defended himself by appealing to Luther.[166]

Because cessationists often condemn charismatics for allegedly undermining the canon, it may be relevant to note that Luther, unlike modern

symbols. On Luther's anti-Judaism, see also, e.g., Eckardt, "Reformation," 24–33; Rowan, "Luther, Bucer," 88–89.

159. Marans, "Luther"; see also Rudnick, "Hate Speech," 421–22. Luther did not systematize his theology (see Gupta, *Language of Faith*, 184), and his works do not always represent a single view.

160. A generation after Luther, Marcus Lombardus praises Luther for his intelligent and angry denunciation of Jews (Cohen, "Contemporaries," 198). Cf. already Caspar Güttel's 1527 reappropriation of Luther's anti-Judaism (Evener, "Reception").

161. Rudnick, "Hate Speech," 426.

162. Ages, "Luther and Rabbis," 195.

163. Many of the Nazis were anti-Christian as well as anti-Jewish, and Nazis' anti-Judaic concerns were more ethnic and Darwinist than religious (see Edwards, "Luther and Jews," 14–15; Holland, *Dominion*, 472–76, 481, 483–84; Poewe, *Religions*). Nor was Luther in a position in his day to expect compliance to his invective (Rowan, "Luther, Bucer," 89).

164. Brown, *Authentic Fire*, 104–5.

165. Marans, "Luther"; Edwards, "Luther and Jews," 15; Brown, *Authentic Fire*, 105. Contradictions within Luther may also find an analogy in Pastor Heinrich Fausel, who cited Luther's anti-Judaism yet later, in 1943, helped hide Jews from the Nazis (see Probst, *Demonizing*).

166. Marans, "Luther"; Brown, *Authentic Fire*, 105. Brown adapted some of the material from his earlier book, Brown, *Kosher Jesus*, 1–4.

charismatics, rejected apostolic authorship of James and treated it, Hebrews, Jude, and Revelation as disputed books.[167] He insisted that one should interpret these books in light of the undisputed ones.

### *Complaints About Calvin*

The standard that MacArthur uses to dismiss charismatics generally is used by some others to dismiss his own theological tradition. Calvin displayed a much calmer disposition than Luther and loved the life of an academic. (As an academic, I, Craig, find in Calvin a comforting model of a valuably influential scholar.) Calvin's modest lifestyle can hardly be faulted; indeed, Geneva's council owned the house and furniture he used.[168] Some of his family members were involved in sexual scandals, but while Calvin felt ashamed, none of them involved him personally.[169]

Those eager to find fault with him, however, manage to do so, particularly by examining the Geneva produced partly by his theological influence.[170] Calvin's circle of ministers, for example, sought to regulate what parents named their children, so that Calvin provided a list of forbidden names.[171] Calvin turned over Servetus to the authorities who executed him, but on theological grounds that at the time all of Europe regarded as deathworthy.[172] Calvin responded to a 1545 plague in Geneva by calling for the destruction of witches; that year Geneva executed twenty-nine accused of the crime.[173] While hostility to witches was virtually universal, the concern with them seems ironic from theologians who rejected continuing *divine* miracles. Brown cites the following examples from a Catholic website about Calvin:[174]

> Children were whipped or hanged for calling their mother a devil.
>
> Magicians and sorcerers were hunted down. . . . According to the city register, in 60 years, some 150 were burnt at the stake.

167. Brown, *Authentic Fire*, 106. For more mainstream charismatic views, see e.g., Keener, "Get the Bible."

168. Parker, *Calvin*, 129. For Calvin's emphasis on charity, especially toward Christian refugees, see Holland, *Dominion*, 331–32.

169. Parker, *Calvin*, 130.

170. Even missing a Sunday service warranted investigation (Holland, *Dominion*, 331).

171. Parker, *Calvin*, 128.

172. See Parker, *Calvin*, 148–53. Calvin wrote to Farel that if Servetus came to Geneva, "I will never let him depart alive, if I have any authority" (148). Geneva also tortured many people before executing them (e.g., 157).

173. Such activities continued; in 1571, Geneva executed thirty-six persons accused of witchcraft (Eire, *Flew*, 309).

174. Brown, *Authentic Fire*, 106–9.

> The number of dishes that could be served at table was regulated, as well as the shape of shoes, and the ladies' hair styles.[175]
>
> Sermons were given on Thursdays and Sundays. Attendance was obligatory under pain of fine or flogging. Not even children were excused. The spies would verify that the streets and houses were empty. Every year, the controllers of orthodoxy went house-to-house to have everyone sign the profession of faith voted that year.

Admittedly, the polemical website[176] might be executing partial revenge for similar Protestant denunciations of authoritarian Catholic regimes from the same period. Calvin wasn't the only voice at Geneva. But social control at Geneva may help explain why postmillennial dominionism originated not with charismatics (as some today suppose) but with Reformed reconstructionists![177]

## Conclusion

Matters peripheral to the question of the continuation of prophetic and miraculous gifts become central in many vocal cessationists' polemic. Many of these matters are also irrelevant to the question of whether the Spirit is active in charismatic experiences. Sometimes (though not always), many of the experiences could also be genuine human responses to the power of God's Spirit. Edwards's prudent observations on these matters remain valuable.

Meanwhile, the same standards that MacArthur's circle have employed against charismatics would discredit some of their own theological heroes, whose teachings in one prominent case even were pressed into service for mass murder. MacArthur's standards and his practice of guilt by association would discredit his own theological heritage—as well as virtually any tradition to which it was applied in the same tendentious way. Charismatics have their share both of frauds and of genuine ministers of Christ who failed in scandalous ways. Human failures, however, discredit neither the works of God nor the other human vessels whose records have proved far more faithful than those who failed.

175. As one proofreader pointed out, however, sumptuary laws were common in this era.

176. Marcille, "Think of Calvin."

177. See, e.g., Worthen, *Spellbound*, 343. Olasky, "Communism," 48, recounts his earlier encounter with hyper-Calvinist Theonomists celebrating the new proliferation of their ideals among Pentecostals.

# 21

# History of Cessationism

Although we are convinced that one cannot support cessationism from Scripture, one could make an argument from some lines of Protestant church tradition. Cessationism stems partly from church tradition—ironically, in a particular line of church tradition that rejected dependence on prior tradition—and partly, in its fullest (Warfieldian) form, from the legacy of deism.

Church history is not normative in the way that Scripture, God's Word, is normative. But church history, like biblical history, provides models. Some of these models are positive; others are negative. While the issue in this chapter is primarily the continuation of miracles, this information suggests implications for other divine activity as well. If God continued to perform miracles, often through individuals, why would we assume that he stopped granting other, often less "sensational," gifts?

B. B. Warfield, often cited by cessationists as having "discredited" modern miracles, inadvertently reveals why he does not try to build his case on Scripture. Miracles' "function thus confined them to distinctively the Apostolic Church, and they necessarily passed away with it. Of this we may make sure on the ground both of principle and of fact; that is to say both under the guidance of the New Testament teaching as to their origin and nature, and on the credit of the testimony of later ages as to their cessation."[1]

Warfield's case rests not on Scripture but first on his theory that he wrongly claims may be deduced from Scripture (but which he inadvertently concedes lacks direct biblical claims). Second, however, and the focus of his work, his case rests on postbiblical experience (in the above quotation, "the testimony

1. Warfield, *Counterfeit Miracles*, 6.

of later ages")—the very weakness (argument from experience) with which many cessationists today charge charismatics.

Before surveying Warfield more fully, however, we should consider some precursors. Some theological experts interviewed in the *Cessationist* movie claimed that the church historically has always been cessationist.[2] Simply reading Warfield's attempt to dismantle all miracle claims in history, however, would quickly disabuse anyone of believing that hard cessationism was ever dominant: Miracle claims pervade history, which is why Warfield was at such pains to respond to them! While thinkers who held various degrees of cessationism appear periodically through history, so do continuationists. Perhaps what the interviewees in the movie meant by the church historically was the *Protestant* church, and then mainly that of the Reformed persuasion. And since there have long been exceptions even in Reformed circles, then only the Reformed circles they consider orthodox. They could have saved us the trouble of writing this paragraph by stating their thesis more simply: All those in church history who agree with cessationists have been cessationist.

Nevertheless, some suggest that the earliest articulation of a cessationist position in church history may come from a claim attributed to the Montanist prophetess Maximilla: "After me there will be no more prophecy, but the end."[3] Church fathers challenged her alleged claim by citing 1 Corinthians 13:10, noting that gifts will continue until Jesus's return.[4]

## Some Decline in Gifts

Early church fathers noted continuing gifts (see chap. 22 below), although sometimes comparing their weakened present to the greater past. Some public gifts declined as authority became centralized in institutional leadership.[5]

### *Variations Among the Fathers*

Augustine initially sounded like he thought that tongues[6] and miracles had ceased, but he later explained that he merely meant that miracles had

2. Lanphere, *Cessationist*.

3. Epiphanius, *Pan.* 48.5.4 (PG 41:855). Here I follow Ruthven, *Cessation*, 15, 122. Even this quotation, however, seems to suggest that prophecy ends only at Jesus's return.

4. Eusebius, *Hist. eccl.* 5.17.4 (citing Miltiades); Ruthven, *Cessation*, 122, also notes Irenaeus, *Haer.* 2.28.7 and other sources for the unanimous patristic application of 1 Cor. 13:10 to the eschaton. On the passage, cf. also e.g., Origen, *Comm. Rom.* 1.2.4; 3.3.14; Augustine, *Spirit and Letter* 41, 49, 64.

5. Cf. Keener, *Gift & Giver*, 106.

6. Augustine, *Homilies of 1 John* 6.10. Augustine apparently countered Donatist appeals to individual tongues speech confirming God's blessing by claiming that the church as a whole now spoke the languages of the nations (Blosser and Sullivan, *Speaking in Tongues*, 103–5).

diminished.[7] True, he said, not everyone today speaks in tongues when hands are laid on at baptism, nor are the sick *always* healed; but even when he had written his apparent denial, he knew of a blind man healed by approaching martyrs' bodies, and countless other miracles.[8] Augustine in fact ended up completely affirming that many miracles were continuing to occur in his own day. His diocese collected dossiers of testimonies for those occurring locally, on average one miracle every ten days.[9]

Another leader often cited as noting "the loss of the miraculous gifts" was John Chrysostom, but he speaks of their decline, not of their ceasing.[10] Moreover, he is lamenting their decline rather than justifying it as theologically normative.[11] Alongside decline in gifts, Chrysostom laments the decline of Christian unity, but he is hardly prescribing either as the ideal state; he instead prefers emulation of earlier times.[12] Apparently like Origen before him, then, Chrysostom associates the diminution of charismata with diminished spiritual purity.[13]

Some cite later church fathers as claiming that certain gifts had declined or ceased. These early theologians, however, were usually making observations

7. His original intention was to express their diminution, not their cessation; see Blosser and Sullivan, *Speaking in Tongues*, 112.

8. Houston, *Miracles*, 9; Kelsey, *Healing*, 185 (citing Augustine, *Retractions* 1.13.7, in PL 32:604–5; *On the Advantage of Believing* 16.34; *Conf.* 9.7.16); cf. Billman, *Thread*, 24. On healing through relics (perhaps as points of contact for faith), see, e.g., Gardner, *Healing Miracles*, 78–81 (others find these more theologically problematic; e.g., Saucy, "View," 116; but cf. Deere, *Surprised*, 74); cf. Bentley, *Relics*, 65–66; already in Scripture unusual intermediary means of healing appear (cf. 2 Kings 13:21; Acts 5:15; 19:11–12), and agents of miracles including prophets' staffs (e.g., Exod. 7:19–20; 14:16; cf. Judg. 6:21; 2 Kings 4:29) or dipping in the Jordan (2 Kings 5:10, 14). On the ancient expectation of gifts, including prophecy and tongues, during confirmation and other initiation rites, see McDonnell and Montague, *Initiation*, 314.

9. Augustine, *City of God* 22.8.

10. Floris, "Chrysostom," 378–81.

11. John Chrysostom, *Hom. 1 Cor.* 29.1; 36.7; see Wilson, *Spirit and Sacrament*, 107; Boys, *Evidence*, 26. Chrysostom believed that miracles continued, but corporately, through the church and its rituals, such as oil, exorcism, and relics (Blosser and Sullivan, *Speaking in Tongues*, 119). Cf. Kelsey, *Tongue Speaking*, 39–40. Chrysostom included among the now ceased wonders even the Spirit's groaning; see *Hom. Rom.* 14, on Rom. 8:26 (trans. Morris and Simcox, pp. 324–25); but contrast Calvin, *Inst.* 3.20.5 (Adams, *Romans*, 467). Among patristic sources, Calvin depended esp. on Chrysostom for his cessationism (Gilbert, "Charismata," chap. 3); more helpfully, he also draws on Chrysostom as an exegete (Walchenbach, "Calvin").

12. See Chrysostom, *Hom. 1 Cor.* 36 (PG 61:312–15), in Kovacs, *1 Corinthians*.

13. For the association of the diminution of signs with the church's lack of holiness in Chrysostom, see Floris, "Chrysostom," 381–83; Wesley, "Letter to Middleton." See Origen, *Cels.* 7.8, though affirming their continuance among the pure and citing Wis. 1:5. Some decline is note cessation (Shogren, "Gift of Tongues," 408). Though recognizing the continuance of miracles and even claiming to have witnessed some (Cels. 1.46, 67, in Kelsey, Healing, 136; further on Origen, see Woolley, *Exorcism*, 20–23 [citing Origen, *Cels.* 1.22; 4.33; 7.4, 67; *Hom. Jos.* 24; *Comm. Matt.* 110]), Origen might have been, however, less familiar with contemporary prophecy or tongues (Kelsey, *Tongue Speaking*, 39; though cf. *Cels.* 7.8 [Shogren, "Gift of Tongues," 408]; Origen, *Comm. Rom.* 1.1.4 on Rom. 1:1).

about their surroundings, not theological statements about what *should* be the case. Some, like Augustine noted above, also made clear continuationist statements in other places in their writings. They also often prayed for miraculous graces as though these experiences were normal.[14] Although the prevailing understanding of tongues as preaching in unlearned languages left some with the supposition that this gift had stopped, for example, they could speak of Christians "jubilating," singing aloud with joy that burst the constraints of syllables.[15] Others freely reported continuing miracles, and it is no surprise that Catholic and Orthodox Christians, historically more committed to ancient Christian memory than to the demands of the radical Enlightenment, never adopted cessationism.

### *Reasons for Decline?*

Most recorded history comes from literate elites rather than the cutting edge of mission; what happened on a popular level is harder to document. Even so, the decline of particular gifts in various periods is not best explained by a divine decree to permanently end them, since such gifts resurface in other periods. Scripture shows that God's people have often lost his blessings at times. For one period in Israel's history, the book of the law was lost (2 Kings 22:8), yet God never intended this state of affairs to be permanent. Protestants often argue that the doctrine of justification by faith was lost until the Reformation.[16]

As already noted, many who remarked on the gifts' decline in their era specifically *attributed* such decline to the weak state of the church; this includes not only church fathers but some early evangelicals.[17] Those who appeal to some authors not *observing* particular gifts in particular periods of history (an argument from experience) generally reject even *massive* observations of these gifts in other, more recent periods of history, apparently regarding as normative the silence of some periods against the loud voice of others, such as today or in the New Testament. So, curiously, cessationists may regard the late fourth century and the Reformation period as normative, but not the New Testament, the early postapostolic period, or the recent era that includes the greatest shift in history toward the evangelization of all peoples.

14. Ruthven, *Cessation*, 18–22.

15. Storms, *Language*, 223, citing Oliver and noting that some understand this phenomenon as tongues. See further chap. 16, above. Some have also suggested that Calvin, while understanding tongues differently, may have found himself speaking what charismatics would understand as tongues (Warford, "Calvin Speaks"); but others note the absence of this claim in the English translation of Beza's *Life of Calvin*, the alleged original source.

16. See more fully Deere, *Still Surprised*, 50–53.

17. William Law, *Power*, 128–29 (in Hunter, *Spirit Baptism*, 166); Wesley, *Journal*, August 15, 1750 (Wesley, *Works* [1872 ed.], 2:204), cited in Burgess, *Peoples*, 180; Billman, *Thread*, 58 (also noting Wesley, *Works* [1872 ed.], vol. 7, Sermon 89).

There were also periods in the history of the church where it seems that fewer people were born again. Should we infer from these periods of decline that God no longer wants people to be born again and that people today claiming to be born again are merely deceived? Should we infer from periods deemphasizing justification by faith that the Reformers erred in recovering this emphasis? Moreover, the church continued to report miracles throughout even the periods when they seemed less common, especially in missionary settings. Even if we were to disbelieve all the reports of miracles, they clearly demonstrate that Christians continued to *believe* in miracles—that is, we cannot say that the church had yet adopted cessationism.

Aquinas constricted earlier definitions of miracles to refer to events beyond any potential natural "means," which were instantaneous, visible, and beyond dispute.[18] Later developed in Prospero Lambertini's criteria, these restrictions would necessarily exclude most miracles in the Bible. God parted the sea overnight rather than instantly, and by an east wind rather than without natural means (Exod. 14:21). Shaped by different theological presuppositions, the Egyptian army that charged into the sea after Israel seemed unpersuaded that Israel's God would deliver the Israelites fully. This aptly timed temporary parting to allow only Israel to cross alive (14:28–29) nevertheless appears more than a little fortuitous! Yet it was not a miracle if miracles must be instant, without natural means, and interpretively indisputable. Nor—for those who insist that Jesus's miracles were undeniable—did his critics mind contesting or doubting at least the *source* of Jesus's miracles (Mark 3:22; John 11:46–47; Acts 4:16–17), despite a much broader definition of miracles then that included even exorcism (Mark 9:38–39).

## Calvin's Apologetic Cessationism

As Reformation and New Testament scholar Stephen Chester notes, the sixteenth-century Reformers offer invaluable insights. Yet "this does not mean that they are right on every issue,"[19] an approach that would be unworkable in any event given some of their differences from each other. Something like cessationism as we know it, though not yet in its fully hardened dogmatic form, originated with John Calvin. The new Protestant movement was not (yet) demonstrating miracles, a point exploited by the movement's Catholic critics,[20] who appealed to a long history of Catholic miracle claims. Martin

18. Ruthven, *Cessation*, 20–21; Turner, *Gifts*, 286.

19. Chester, *Reading Paul*, 1.

20. An argument, one notes, from experience. Note Bishop Francis de Sales's criticism of lack of Protestant miracles in de Sales, Works, 3:19, found online at http://archive.org/stream/catholiccontrove00sain#page/19/; also e.g., Eire, *Flew*, 150–53, 294.

Luther and especially Martin Bucer blamed Catholic miracles on the devil,[21] and later Protestants carried this reproach even further.[22] The Reformers' constraints on supernaturalism,[23] never adopted by Roman Catholic or Eastern Orthodox Christians, served their immediate polemical situation against Roman Catholic apologetic use of miracle claims.[24] Early Protestants sought to discredit medieval miracles, for the most part wholesale; while critical inquiry might have proved more helpful, the reaction against miracles associated with the traditional Roman church was predominantly polemical.[25]

### *Calvin's Apologetic*

Reformers had already been repudiating the abuses and superstitions of the late medieval church.[26] But instead of denouncing medieval miracles as the devil's delusions, Calvin might have pointed to many of those miracles as demonstrating God's compassion or authenticating Christian faith generally, rather than proving specific doctrines.[27] That is, he could have countered the Catholic polemic of the era without discarding the baby with the bathwater. Moreover, the leading Reformers were scholars rather than frontline missionaries, so they could have pointed out that they simply had a spiritual gift different than miracle working (see 1 Cor. 12:28–29).

Though normally a careful scholar, Calvin chose a different response.[28] He developed the earlier argument that God gave miracles especially to validate the apostles and their writings, and he now tended to restrict miracles virtually to this purpose. By doing so, he could dismiss appeals to postbiblical (especially Catholic) miracles and insist that the sole basis of argument should be apostolic Scripture—hence returning the debate's playing field to

21. Ruthven, *Cessation*, 22; for Luther, see Eire, *Flew*, 61, 294, 393n31 (citing WA 6:447, already in 1520; also Morton, "Naturalism"); for Zwingli, see Eire, *Flew*, 321 ("many" cases); for Calvin, see Brown, *Miracles*, 15.

22. Soergel, "Legends," 22–29. The sixteenth- and seventeenth-century emphasis on demonic causes (Daston, "Facts," 98) served well the purposes of sectarian polemic (101) but also undoubtedly fed into the witch hysteria that led to thousands of killings. Witchcraft and demonic concerns led to first demonic and then more naturalistic explanations (106–7).

23. More among some than others; annoying Calvin, some Lutherans accused him of rationalism (Menzies, *Romans*, 330, following Starling, "Analogy of Faith," 12).

24. E.g., Harrison, "Miracles," 500–501; Daston, "Facts," 114; for the same purpose for sixteenth- and seventeenth-century Anglican cessationism, see Walsham, "Miracles," 279, 283. For the continuance of charismata in the Eastern Orthodox Church, see the sources in Floris, "Charismata," 374–75; Burgess, "Proclamation," 357–58.

25. See, e.g., Parish, "Histories"; Mullin, "Bushnell," 460–61; Lovelace, *Dynamics*, 269.

26. MacNutt, *Crime*, 140.

27. See Deere, *Still Surprised*, 73–74.

28. Ruthven, *Cessation*, 22; see also Ruthven, "Place." Yet "mostly, Calvin assumes the traditions enshrined in Aquinas, rather than attempts systematically to prove his contention" (Ruthven, *Cessation*, 24).

biblical scholars. His case was partly shaped by the polemic of his day between Protestants and Catholics.[29] Catholic miracles, or at the most extreme, all postbiblical miracles, were now from the devil.[30]

To make his case, as Derek Morphew notes, in his *Harmony of the Gospels* Calvin pares down Mark 16:17–18's "those who believe" "to 'certain people' who are so gifted. Then perhaps, even these gifts for certain people were but for a time." Still, Calvin seems somewhat ambivalent as to whether ending the gifts was God's ideal: "Perhaps this was not the purpose of God, but because of ingratitude."[31] Certainly ingratitude and other such sins can lead to withdrawal of blessings for a time[32]—though explaining away miracles when God does them would also express ingratitude. But Calvin goes on to contend that God probably intended these gifts only as temporary and so they finally passed away.[33] He states their cessation more directly in his *Institutes*.[34]

His approach forced him to challenge even the practice of anointing in prayer in James 5:14–16.[35] Because Catholics claimed that their anointing remained effective, Calvin replied, "We experience otherwise. . . . Therefore they make themselves ridiculous when they boast that they are endowed with the gift of healing. The Lord is indeed present with his people in every age; and he heals their weaknesses as often as necessary, no less than of old; still he does not put forth these manifest powers, nor dispense miracles through the apostles' hands. For that was a temporary gift, and also quickly perished partly on account of men's ungratefulness."[36]

Note Calvin's appeal here to experience ("We experience otherwise").[37] It is hard to blame Calvin, who wrote at a time when his movement was new and fellow Protestants had few firsthand healing claims to report. Whether Calvin would have taken the same line of defense today—when we have abundant evidence for miracles among Calvin's fellow Protestants—seems more open to question.

29. Turner, *Gifts*, 286–87, following esp. Ruthven, *Cessation*; on his polemic against Catholic and Anabaptist approaches, see further Gilbert, "Charismata," chaps. 3–4; Eire, *Flew*, 61, 294–95; cf. also William Tyndale (Eire, *Flew*, 61).

30. Eire, *Flew*, 17, 61, 294, 393n31, citing Calvin's prefatory letter to King Francis in *Inst.* 1.17–18. Bullinger associated Catholic miracles with witchcraft (Eire, *Flew*, 61); he also insisted on harsh punishments for witchcraft (Eire, *Flew*, 333).

31. Morphew, "Calvin and Kingdom," 128–29.

32. Cf. 1 Cor. 11:30; more tangentially, Rom. 1:21. Ps. 78 invites Israel to remember God's works (78:7, 11, 42; cf. 106:13, 21) rather than refusing to believe unless one can see more (78:18–20). One should also testify of God's past works to the next generation (78:4, 6, 8).

33. Morphew, "Calvin and Kingdom," 128, citing Calvin, *Harmony*, 3:254.

34. Morphew, "Calvin and Kingdom," 128–29.

35. In contrast to Luther's eventual position (Föller, "Luther on Miracles," 346; cf. Kelsey, *Healing*, 233), despite Luther's view of James!

36. Deere, *Still Surprised*, 75, quoting Calvin, *Inst.* 4.19.19.

37. See here Menzies, *Romans*, 329: "While Calvinists often accuse Pentecostals of deriving their theology from experience rather than scripture, here Calvin is guilty of that error."

### *Not a Dogmatic Cessationist like Warfield*

In any case, Calvin did not develop this apologetic extensively, despite his vast corpus of extant writings. His interest was defending the Reformation and its basis in Scripture, so he lacked the inflexible dogmatism of successors such as Warfield.[38] In another place he allowed, for example, that the class of miraculous or revelatory gifts "either does not exist today or is [simply] less commonly seen."[39] Calvin argued that prophets, with their special revelation, either no longer "exist, or they are less manifest."[40] When he comments on Romans 12:6, Calvin divides prophecy between predictive and interpretive functions, allowing that the latter continues.[41] (Although this approach is less cessationist than dismissing the gift entirely, it has its own problems. Beyond extrabiblically subdividing gifts into past and continuing ones, it now extrabiblically divides the single gift of prophecy into past and continuing elements. And some cessationists today support this completely postbiblical division even while insisting that charismatics should hold prophecy to what cessationist critics consider Old Testament standards!)

Further evidence suggests that Calvin, while using a form of cessationism for apologetic purposes, would not oppose sound charismatic activity if it were to occur in what he would consider a theologically orthodox setting. D. A. Carson cites Calvin's commentary on 1 Corinthians 12:28–31, where prophets may be those adept at revealing God's will, whether through prophecies or teaching; yet, he concludes, it is hard to be sure, since "such gifts or offices have been kept from the church for so long a time, except for traces or shades of them still to be found."[42] Calvin was a good exegete as well as systematician. Thus, while in some contexts he restricts miracles to confirming the apostles' teaching, elsewhere he affirms the explicit biblical position that spiritual gifts—which would include miracles—"were given for the edification of the church, and unless they contribute to this [purpose] they lose their grace."[43]

More surprisingly, he allowed that apostles and prophecy might recur as the gospel was breaking new ground in unevangelized regions, again confirming

38. Calvin insisted that people could understand God's Word only through the Spirit's enlightenment (see Wyckoff, *Pneuma*, 27; Osborne, *Spiral*, 340; George, "Introduction," xxix; esp. now Adhinarta, *Doctrine*, 38). Both Puritans and Pietists agreed (Oliverio, *Hermeneutics*, 85), as did many at Princeton Seminary until the rise of a conservative scholasticism there in the nineteenth century (Wyckoff, *Pneuma*, 43–45), which provided an academic context for Warfield's polemic.

39. Ruthven, *Cessation*, 22n53, citing Calvin, *Inst.* 4.3.4.

40. Carson, *Showing Spirit*, 168, quoting Calvin, *Inst.* 4.3.4. Cf. Boys, *Evidence*, 118.

41. Oss, "Response to Saucy," 167. For Calvin's transformation of prophecy into interpretation, see Menzies, *Romans*, 328–29.

42. Carson, *Showing Spirit*, 168, again citing Calvin, *Inst.* 4.3.4. See Calvin, *1 Corinthians*, 211 (Oss, "Response to Saucy," 168).

43. Deere, *Still Surprised*, 74, citing Calvin, *Inst.* 3.2.9. See also Calvin, *Epistles*, 1:395, cited in Adhinarta, *Doctrine*, 160.

the gospel as God had done for the Roman world.[44] While apostles, prophets, and evangelists in Ephesians 4:11 are no longer ordinary church offices, God "now and again revives [them] as the need of the times demands."[45] He also concedes, "I do not deny that the Lord has sometimes at a later period raised up apostles, or at least evangelists in their place, as has happened in our own day."[46] Calvin honors Luther with the title of a "distinguished apostle of Christ."[47] Calvin was not claiming that Luther was literally apostolic in the sense of one of the Twelve; but then, contrary to some critics, neither is that how orthodox continuationists define postbiblical apostolic ministry today.

Unfortunately, some who have claimed Calvin's mantle, like Warfield, developed his apologetic argument into a permanent dogma, one that, in our view, even contradicts Scripture while claiming to defend it. Some people today selectively canonize particular earlier Protestant teachings almost the way we expect Catholics to follow any *ex cathedra* pronouncements of the Pope. Such Protestants effectively make their Protestant forebears (or at least their favorite traditions from them) as inerrant as they claim Scripture to be. Doesn't that practice sound like something the Reformers accused Catholics of? If it didn't contradict our eschatology, we might expect Calvin and Luther to be turning in their graves.

## Luther

Reformers such as Luther, Ulrich Zwingli and Calvin held a softer and less dogmatic stance than that of modern classical cessationism. Though the magisterial Reformers did not expect to see many miracles in their day, Luther advocated discernment; until evaluation is possible, he urged, we should wait and see whether a claimed spiritual experience is from God (Acts 5:38–39).[48]

### *Potential Miracles, When Needed*

In 1522, Luther expounded Mark 16:17–18, declaring, "Where there is a Christian, there is still the power to work these signs if it is necessary." God uses such signs only where needed to support his Word. This was less necessary now in Europe because the gospel was known. But while he hoped it would

44. Ruthven, *Cessation*, 22.

45. Ruthven, *Cessation*, 22n53, citing Calvin, *Inst.* 4.3.4; and Hejzlar, "Calvin and Cessation."

46. Deere, *Still Surprised*, 76, citing Calvin, *Inst.* 4.3.4–9.

47. Deere, *Still Surprised*, 76, citing Calvin, *Inst.* 4.3.4.

48. Oss, "Response to Saucy," 167, citing Bainton, *Here I Stand*, 209. Luther apparently told a mystic that he had received revelations (Hyatt, *Years*, 74; Oliver, *Reformations*, 12, citing Hoffman, *Luther*, 190), and he certainly prayed for healings (Oliver, *Reformations*, 13–14).

never be necessary, if "need should arise, and men were to denounce and antagonize the Gospel, then we verily should have to employ wonder-working rather than permit the Gospel to be derided and suppressed."[49]

When he preached on Mark 16 again the next year, he appealed also to John 14:12, insisting, "We must allow these words to remain and not gloss them away, as some have done who said that these signs were manifestations of the Spirit in the beginning of the Christian era and that now they have ceased. That is not right; for the same power is in the church still. And though it is not exercised, that does not matter; we still have the power to do such signs."[50] Luther did believe in prayer for the sick and witnessed some of his confident prayers answered.[51] A year before he died, Luther taught on prayer for the sick, both privately and in churches, following James 5:14–15. In a letter he noted "prayer for healing by the laying on of hands" occurring in Wittenberg.[52]

Although not focused on charismatic signs, post-Luther Lutherans also produced wonder books based on natural anomalies, some revisiting ancient use of such features as apocalyptic portents.[53]

### Miracles Among Subsequent Lutherans

Many Lutherans around the world also have become more open to special divine action, not least in Ethiopia's very Spirit-filled Mekane Yesus church (the world's largest Lutheran church body). One of the best-known ministers of healing in the 1800s was the German Lutheran pastor Johann Christoph Blumhardt (1805–80). Blumhardt viewed healings as foreshadowings of the kingdom,[54] and though he labored in prayer on behalf of the sick, he recognized God's sovereignty.[55] Blumhardt's legacy remained well-known into the twentieth century, and his son Christoph continued his ministry in prophecy and healing.[56]

49. Oss, "Response to Saucy," 167, citing Luther, *Writings*, 12:207 (preached on Ascension Day 1522). For Luther on miracles and prayer for healing, see also Föller, "Luther on Miracles," 342, 344, 346.

50. Oss, "Response to Saucy," 167, citing Luther, *Writings*, 12:190 (preached on Ascension Day 1523); Burgess, *Peoples*, 141, citing the same sermon (but at 3:189–90 in Luther, *Writings*); Föller, "Luther on Miracles," 342, 344. Wesley also appropriated Mark 16 for healing (Wesley, *Works* [1872 ed.], 8:457–59; Billman, *Thread*, 80).

51. Boys, *Evidence*, 192–203, 243–45; Föller, "Luther on Miracles," 346; Kidd, "Healing," 149; Kirby, "Recovery," 113; Dod, "Healer," 174; Billman, *Thread*, 32–33.

52. Föller, "Luther on Miracles," 346; cf. Kelsey, *Healing*, 233.

53. See Soergel, *Miracles*.

54. Ising, *Blumhardt*, 234, 410; cf. Macchia, *Spirituality*, 76.

55. Ising, *Blumhardt*, 333–35. Although for a time against medicine, he changed (213–14, 267, 337–38). In contrast to some later teachers on healing, Blumhardt was moderate, recognizing that God does not heal everyone supernaturally (Reyes, "Framework," 88); even Warfield, *Counterfeit Miracles*, 195, respected him.

56. Moltmann, "Blessing," 149 (citing here Ragaz, *Kampf*).

Liberal theologian David Friedrich Strauss (1808–74), who dismissed biblical miracle claims as legends and myths, had to work hard to explain away his own friend's healing: Struggling to walk before visiting Blumhardt, the friend went hiking in the mountains afterward.[57] Likewise, Rudolf Bultmann (1884–1976), consistent with his skepticism about miracles, naturally considered the "legends" about Blumhardt "preposterous."[58] Yet today earlier letters, diaries, and the like provide firsthand evidence that healings actually did surround Blumhardt's ministry, often immediately after his prayers.[59]

For example, in 1845, a dying woman, vomiting large quantities of clotted blood, began recovering within a few minutes of prayer, still tired but regaining strength.[60] In 1846 a physician certified the healing of a previously incurable skin rash.[61] Other eyewitness reports of cures include blindness,[62] paralysis,[63] epilepsy,[64] and the like. When a woman whose "hand closed by seizures" found no help from her Tübingen physicians, she was cured after her first service at Blumhardt's church; her physicians initially refused to believe that she was the same woman.[65] In 1872, after a young man clubbed a boy in the head, the doctor warned that the boy's skull had been split open. Though expected to die within two hours, the boy recovered and from the next day forward treated Blumhardt like a grandfather.[66] Blumhardt's wife Doris revived from near death ("without breathing or pulse," he shared in a letter at the time) when he prayed,[67] as did another woman.[68] A witness confessed irritation when Blumhardt momentarily interrupted the liturgy to pray for

57. Ising, *Blumhardt*, 222–23 (regarding Eduard Mörike).

58. Kydd, *Healing*, 42n40 (citing Bultmann, *Kerygma and Myth*, 120). Other theologians, such as Karl Barth and Jürgen Moltmann, looked to Blumhardt as an influence (Kelsey, *Healing*, 236–37; Kydd, *Healing*, 34; Barth, *Letters*, 251; Barth, *Dogmatics*, 165ff. [noted in Kauffman, "Introduction," 7–8]; Moltmann, "Blessing," 149; for Bonhoeffer, see Macchia, *Spirituality*, 1, 4).

59. See the copious documentation in Ising, *Blumhardt*.

60. Ising, *Blumhardt*, 176.

61. Ising, *Blumhardt*, 210. Pressed for time, he prayed concisely for a man with a severe skin problem; the man was offended by the prayer's brevity (hence perhaps not likely cured psychosomatically), yet as he traveled home he discovered his skin beginning to clear (329).

62. Ising, *Blumhardt*, 209; partial blindness and deafness on 210; possibly partial healing of complete blindness on 329.

63. Ising, *Blumhardt*, 212–13.

64. Ising, *Blumhardt*, 329–30, noting two instantaneous cases (though also other cases where he was unable to help).

65. Ising, *Blumhardt*, 267. People were sometimes healed during the church's corporate prayer (279).

66. Ising, *Blumhardt*, 328–29.

67. Ising, *Blumhardt*, 207.

68. Ising, *Blumhardt*, 219.

God to withhold an impending hailstorm; yet "in an instant it grew light and in a few minutes we had blue skies and bright sunshine."[69]

Examples today could be multiplied. My late friend Anna Gulick experienced some miracles when she was a Lutheran missionary in Asia.[70] Lutherans in Madagascar have witnessed miracles, including raisings from the dead, especially through their ministry of exorcism.[71] One Lutheran writer in Tanzania notes, "The phenomenon of demon possession is a hard reality with which a good number of East African Christians struggle daily." Whereas Westerners tend to denigrate such views as "primitive," he notes, East Africans take them for granted, and "the biblical accounts are read not as myths, but as objective accounts of actual experiences."[72]

## Anabaptist Continuationists

Magisterial Reformers reacted not only against the medieval church but also against some Anabaptists who believed they could prophesy.[73] Although magisterial Reformers found Anabaptist prophecy threatening, Scripture provides a more helpful solution—namely, discernment. As charismatics of every generation relearn if they fail to learn from Scripture and history, discernment is vital; some Anabaptist prophecies (most conspicuously at Münster) and some medieval miracle claims (and the relics business they often advertised) clearly proved false.[74]

Most Anabaptists, taking *sola scriptura* further than some magisterial Reformers, were continuationists.[75] (That also proved true of some other minority movements such as Moravians.)[76] Expecting the continuation of all gifts, Anabaptists often experienced healing and other gifts, as well as spiritual

69. Ising, *Blumhardt*, 215. Hail would have devastated the harvest, but Blumhardt focused on the immediate distraction to the congregation.

70. E.g., Anna Gulick, personal correspondence, August 10 and 13, 2009; interview, March 10, 2011.

71. Dimbiniaina Randrianasolo, interview, Wilmore, Kentucky, April 18, 2019; Bennett, *Not Afraid*.

72. Mchami, "Possession," 17 (while conceding that East African interpretation could use more exegesis).

73. Cf. Calvin, "Fanatics, Abandoning Scripture and Flying Over to Revelation, Cast Down All the Principles of Godliness" in *Inst.* 1.9 (Oss, "Response to Saucy," 167).

74. On relics, see esp. Bentley, *Relics*.

75. Hyatt, *Years*, 80, citing other sources, including Peachey and Peachey, "Answer." See Michael Sattler (1490–1527) in "Schleitheim Confession"; Thomas Müntzer (1489–1525) in Baylor, *Reformation*, 24; Hans Denck (1459–1523) in Baylor, *Reformation*, 151. See also Murray, "Anabaptism." Some, like Müntzer, clearly went too far (see Arthur, *Tailor-King*; Holland, *Dominion*, 365; Worthen, *Spellbound*, 9–10).

76. See, e.g., Burgess, "Proclamation," 356. Note also Zinzendorf, in Boys, *Evidence*, 263; on miraculous Moravian escapes similar to those in Acts, see 266–71.

joy sometimes expressed in dancing or fainting.[77] A Swiss Anabaptist document from the 1530s explains why they would not attend the state churches; the main reason was that they desired to follow instead the biblical order of exercising spiritual gifts (1 Cor. 14:26).[78]

Nor did all other early Protestants follow the lead of some magisterial Reformers. Hugo Grotius, Heinrich Bullinger, John Foxe, and Johann Bengel all affirmed that miracles could continue in their day.[79] The Book of Common Prayer and other early Anglican sources appear to speak of miracles, healing, prophecy, and tongues as current gifts.[80]

## Enlightenment Challenges

In the 1590s Puritans sought to cast out demons, but Anglican leaders fiercely opposed their activities.[81] Yet because the Enlightenment shifted Protestants' epistemological foundation from Scripture to human reason, the Enlightenment "era is generally regarded as the watershed in thought about miracles."[82]

When people are conditioned to believe that God no longer intervenes supernaturally in our world, they often begin the slide toward viewing biblical miracles as fairy tales. This happened within Protestantism in Europe. Throughout the seventeenth century, rationalist theologians denied modern-day miracles while affirming biblical miracles. But by the end of the eighteenth century, they were also denying biblical miracles.[83]

### *Deist Denials*

Protestants rejected Catholic claims, but radical deists and David Hume carried the process further, rejecting *everybody*'s miracle claims, usually including those in the Bible.[84] Deists were the first conspicuous movement in the history of Christendom to (often) deny biblical miracles.[85] Even a number

77. Hyatt, *Years*, 79, citing Littell, *Origins*, 19.
78. Hyatt, *Years*, 80, citing Peachey and Peachey, "Answer."
79. Boys, *Evidence*, 96, 151–52, 236, 255–57.
80. Boys, *Evidence*, 316–30; Oliver, *Reformations*, 36–37.
81. Ruthven, *Cessation*, 24n60, cites here Walker, "Cessation," 111. Also, Walker, *Unclean Spirits*, 66–70, 72–73, and Thomas, *Religion*, 80, 124, 256, 479, and 485.
82. Ruthven, *Cessation*, 24. See Brown, *Miracles*. Ordinary Protestants in England were still reporting miracles even while the Enlightenment engaged elites; see Shaw, *Miracles*.
83. Spalding, "Protestantism."
84. For deist influence on Hume, see Burns, "Hume"; Burns, *Debate*.
85. Richardson, *Apologetics*, 158; on their rational religion tending to distance God apart from creation and providence, note also Smart, *Experience*, 471.

of early deists, however, argued not against miracles but against their use in a Christian apologetic defending special revelation, which assaulted deist premises.[86] Although Hume was apparently not a deist himself,[87] many of Hume's specific arguments were developed first in deism's polemic against Christian miracles.[88] Whatever his personal opinions at some points in his life, some of his arguments in *Of Miracles* reflect the worldview promulgated by deism.[89]

Hume fostered an environment that put Christians on the defensive, making even biblical miracles a liability rather than an apologetic tool.[90] As a result, many Protestants shied further away from miracles. Historian Thomas Kidd suggests that the current divide between global Pentecostalism and many noncharismatic evangelicals echoes the divide that existed between radical and moderate evangelicals already in the 1700s.[91] One might also compare the earlier mentioned polemical interaction between evangelist George Whitefield and the traditionalist bishop of London, Edmund Gibson.[92]

Some estimate that from Francis Asbury's arrival in the United States until his death, the number of Methodists grew one thousand times over.[93] By 1890, more than 8 percent of the United States was Methodist, but dramatic decline soon followed; 45,000 Methodist churches closed over the next century. One Methodist observer credits two complementary factors: Conservative cessationists and liberal antisupernaturalists made common cause to undercut the supernaturalism that had fueled Methodist growth at the beginning.[94]

86. Burns, *Debate*, 70. Eighteenth-century deists, including Toland and Tindal, differed, however, from later philosophic deism (Tennant, *Miracle*, 7, 96–97; cf. Nichols, *History*, 100), and some (again including Tindal and Toland) affirmed miracles (Burns, *Debate*, 14); thus, for example, John Toland (1670–1722) found NT miracles more plausible than OT ones (Loos, *Miracles*, 13).

87. Hume disclaimed the title of deist (from a testimonial anecdote about Hume cited in Fosl, "Hume," 171, 188n23), and some of his arguments undermined not only monotheistic orthodoxies but also deism (Fosl, "Hume," 174; González, *Story*, 2:190; Heimann, "Enlightenment," 476; Manschreck, *History*, 221–22).

88. See Brown, *Miracles*, 52–53, noting that Hume was simply more reserved than deists about targeting the gospel miracles specifically.

89. Some associate Hume with "attenuated deism" or a modern Epicureanism (see Brown, *Thought*, 256).

90. For Hume targeting the apologetic use of miracles, including in John Locke, see Houston, *Miracles*, 50; Earman, *Failure*, 14–15.

91. Kidd, *Awakening*, 323.

92. See again Whitefield, *Works*, 166–68.

93. See Noll, *Rise*, 190.

94. Billmann, *Thread*, 117–22, following esp. De Arteaga, *Quenching*, 130–34; Wood, *Pentecost*, 332.

### *Not-So-Middle-of-the-Road Middleton*

The polemic against miracles climaxed in the work of Conyers Middleton.[95] Middleton parodied an apologist for patristic miracle claims with precisely opposing arguments.[96] While Middleton explicitly aimed his polemic against Catholics,[97] most of his contemporaries suspected him of seeking "to overthrow the whole Christian system."[98]

John Wesley correctly warned that Middleton's critique, refusing all evidence, could be turned against the biblical record no less easily.[99] It did, in fact, facilitate the transition of some contemporary thinkers, such as the historian Edward Gibbon, out of Christianity. Wesley, who publicly challenged Middleton's claims,[100] lamented that Middleton "aims every blow, though he seems to look the other way, at the fanatics who wrote the New Testament."[101] Against skeptics, Wesley appealed to phenomena in his own meetings, "neither in private, but in the open air, and before more than two thousand witnesses."[102]

The only rational difference between a full cessationist and a deist methodologically is that the full cessationist lacks a consistent worldview. (As for partial cessationists, we argued in chap. 6 that they are inconsistent; but since they are being less consistent by embracing less of the fallacy, we won't complain.) As someone who has worked to provide evidence for miracles, I (Craig) have sometimes found antisupernaturalists and full cessationists (those of Warfield's persuasion) making common cause against a considerable body of evidence. (This is normally not true for moderate cessationists who allow for continuing miracles.)[103] The approach of Middleton and Warfield makes difficult any apologetic for New Testament miracles, because it has already surrendered any epistemological grounds that could defend them to nonbelievers.

Jack Deere summarizes Middleton's approach to church fathers and early Christian martyrs: They were all liars.[104] Deere also surveys Middleton's three main methods to dismiss their testimony to supernatural events:

95. Middleton, *A Free Inquiry*, iii–iv, opens with an appeal to John Locke; yet Locke affirmed biblical miracles (Burns, *Debate*, 57–69; McKenzie, "Miracles," 79; Brown, *Miracles*, 42–46), though, in keeping with opinions of his day, not postbiblical ones (Mullin, "Bushnell," 462).

96. Ruthven, *Cessation*, 27.

97. Middleton, *A Free Inquiry*, iii.

98. Ruthven, *Cessation*, 28, quoting from Wesley's *Journal*, January 28, 1749.

99. Brown, *Miracles*, 72.

100. See Wesley, "Letter to Middleton," 705–61.

101. Ruthven, *Cessation*, 28, quoting from Wesley's *Journal*, August 12, 1771.

102. Xhemajli, *Supernatural*, 49, quoting Wesley, *Works* (AM), 3:134.

103. E.g., my friend Darrell Bock, a very moderate cessationist, offered a public, fair, and favorable response to my presentation "Miracle Reports" (subsequently published as "Miracle Reports and Argument").

104. Deere, *Still Surprised*, 78–85.

1. The hostile authorities, who were wiser than the mere eyewitnesses, did not recognize the events as supernatural.
2. One should prefer any possible natural explanation to any supernatural one.
3. If a story is so supernatural as to be inexplicable naturally, it is too unbelievable to even merit the attention to refute it. (And given argument number 2, any event that is naturally explicable is not supernatural. Thus, heads I win, tails you lose: miracles never happen.)[105]

Because Justin Martyr was so foolish to accept such an "absurd and monstrous," "impious and heretical," doctrine as premillennialism,[106] for example, Middleton averred that one could disregard any claims he made as "pure flights of an enthusiastic fancy and heated brain."[107] Middleton ridicules patristic and martyrs' reports of miracles if they did not bother to specifically name their witnesses.[108]

Plenty of intellectuals pushed back against Middleton; Oxford University even honored William Dodwell with a doctor of divinity degree for his refutation of Middleton.[109] Dodwell complained that Middleton's criteria were so strict as to require a witness's infallibility, making any exploration of past miracles impossible.[110] One might add that such an approach makes nearly all historiography impossible. Less prone to disguise his consistent skepticism, Hume openly questioned all miracles.[111]

The modern theological argument that excludes all postbiblical miracles (while accepting biblical ones) rests on theological a prioris and an astonishing degree of philosophical inconsistency.[112] The modern historiographic principle of historical uniformity shattered cessationism's historically arbitrary barrier between biblical and postbiblical miracles, each evaluated by different rules

105. Cf. the complaint of Boys, *Evidence*, 31, regarding skepticism about an otherwise-well-attested miracle of tortured Christians whom God enabled to speak despite the extraction of their tongues: "This miracle has recently been impugned; for no other reason, which I can discover, except that it makes so decidedly against the unhappy cause of those who impugn it." Boys, *Evidence*, 32–33, names the witnesses; on 256–57 he also follows Bengel's son and editor in recounting Joseph Jenisch being born without a tongue (November 26, 1606), later healed through prayer, and a minister for forty years till his death in 1675.

106. Deere, *Still Surprised*, 83, citing Middleton, *A Free Inquiry*, 31.

107. Deere, *Still Surprised*, 83, citing Middleton, *A Free Inquiry*, 30.

108. Deere, *Still Surprised*, 85, citing Middleton, *A Free Inquiry*, 22–24.

109. Deere, *Still Surprised*, 80n4, citing William Dodwell's work, Dodwell, *Answer*.

110. Deere, *Still Surprised*, 83, citing Dodwell, *Answer*, 70. Warfield, *Counterfeit Miracles*, 31, sides with Middleton against Dodwell.

111. Craig addresses Hume and his aftermath in Keener, *Miracles*, 1:107–200; at a more detailed philosophical level, see, e.g., Houston, *Miracles*; Johnson, *Hume*; Earman, "Bayes"; Earman, *Failure*; Earman, "Hume."

112. See Ruthven, *Cessation*, 83–92; cf. 35–40, 64–71; cf. Jaki, *Miracles and Physics*, 38.

(and facilitating Hume's polemic against modern miracles); soon people usually either denied both or accepted both.[113]

## B. B. Warfield's War on Miracles

R. C. Sproul describes Warfield as "legendary," a "titan" of theology, "a mighty champion of the Reformed faith," and "second only to Jonathan Edwards as America's greatest theologian."[114] Warfield was a man of towering intellect, and he took an admirable stand against theological liberalism. But for all the theological good he did in that debate, his cessationist polemic aligned his philosophy and method with the very opponents he combated regarding biblical authority.[115] In 1918, Warfield wrote a famous cessationist book called *Counterfeit Miracles*. Although the book is not primarily exegetical, many cessationists who claim to be Bible-based nevertheless cite it in support of their position.[116]

Because Warfield's *Counterfeit Miracles* is so ensconced in subsequent cessationist thinking, we should point out briefly some of Warfield's many contradictions that still characterize the historical argument of full cessationism today. Again, some of these resemble Middleton's approach already noted. Warfield, opposing liberals regarding the miracles of the Bible, declared, "The atheist, the materialist, the pantheist are within their rights in denying the possibility of miracles. But none other is. As soon as we adopt the postulate of a personal God and a creation, so soon miracles cease to be 'impossible' in any exact sense of the word."[117] So what changed after the first century?

### *Warfield's Secular Philosophical Foundations*

Warfield's sentiments are humanly understandable. His wife was disabled, never healed, and passed away when he was working on the project.[118] Many of us who have experienced such tragic disappointments have struggled with

113. Mullin, *Miracles*, 30; Lawton, *Miracles*, 58. Cf. also Turner, *Gifts*, 298, noting here Brown, *Miracles*, 64–68, 198–204; Ruthven, *Cessation*, 82–92.

114. Sproul, "Warfield."

115. Ruthven, *Cessation*, 173. Warfield rightly valued science. Indeed, with contemporary evangelicals such as Asa Gray and Charles Hodge, Warfield viewed evolution as the clearest evidence of design, objecting only to attributing the patterns to pure chance (e.g., Livingstone, *Defenders*, 49, 63–64, 95, 104–5, 116, 135–38).

116. Cf. Wiggs, "Cessationism," and Wiggs, *Engines*, 170: "'Counterfeit Miracles' became the definitive statement of cessationism to the conservative fundamental segment of Christianity."

117. Warfield, "Question," 175–76, cited in Ruthven, *Cessation*, 52–53.

118. Mullin, *Miracles*, 214 (cf. also Brown, *Miracles*, 199). For the illness of A. C. Cooke's daughter and Cooke's hostility to Charles Price's healing campaigns after she was not healed, see Opp, *Lord for Body*, 162. Pelley, "Response," also notes Justin Peters's understandable disillusionment.

theodicy and other questions. We cannot know whether Warfield's approach to the subject might have been different otherwise, but we can at least express sympathy for him. Unfortunately, whatever the factors in his approach, his treatment of miracles was radical.

Shockingly, Middleton, who mocked miracle accounts and accused biblical writers of errors and inconsistency,[119] directly influenced Warfield's approach to miracles. Warfield in turn wrote the standard defense of full cessationism. Warfield appeals to Middleton's *Free Inquiry* at length in the opening chapter of *Counterfeit Miracles*.[120]

Jon Ruthven, whose dissertation evaluated Warfield's argument against miracles, notes that "Warfield's philosophical and historiographical approach to miracles was derived from the Enlightenment era and from Conyers Middleton respectively."[121] Theologically, various studies complain that Warfield contaminated his Calvinism with secular rationalism.[122] The worldview of classical cessationism, such as is found in Warfield, is closer to rationalism and deism than to anything in Scripture or the early church.[123] Ironically, his approach to postbiblical miracles follows Hume's epistemic skepticism rather than Scripture.[124] His recourse to skeptics' epistemology for all postbiblical cases has rendered comfort to skeptics and complicated any defense of biblical miracles. All evangelicals who lay claim to the sufficiency of Scripture for doctrine therefore ought to question Warfield's cessationism as a philosophically laden extrabiblical tradition.[125]

As Ruthven complains,

> Warfield . . . used many of the same critical techniques on historical miracles that his liberal opponents had used on Scripture. . . . He cites approvingly Adolf von Harnack's rationalization of exorcisms in the early Church; and dismisses every claim to miracles as human misperception, be it superstition, mental imbalance or mendacity. The very essence of Warfield's argument against post-biblical miracles seems formed from a template of Harnack's rationalistic liberalism, but also from Hume's *Enquiry:* all have their *a priori*, *i.e.*, that miracles cannot happen; . . . a highly critical evaluation of witnesses to miracles;

119. Middleton, *Works*, 31–47.

120. Warfield, *Counterfeit Miracles*, 28–31; cf. Ruthven, *Cessation*, 27.

121. Ruthven, *Cessation*, 28.

122. Ruthven, *Cessation*, 32, cites the following: Livingstone, "Princeton Apologetic," 342–43; Krause, "Principle of Authority," 113–34, 222–39 (for review) and 272–76 (for critique); and esp. Wolterstorff, "Reason"; Plantinga, "Reformed Epistemology"; Makarian, "Concept of Revelation," 107–8 and 226–33. For evaluation of Warfield's dependence on Scottish commonsense realism, Ruthven depends esp. on Vander Stelt, *Philosophy and Scripture*, 166–84, 304–13.

123. Ruthven, *Cessation*, 173.

124. Cf. Ruthven, *Cessation*, 25n61.

125. Even as early as the second and third centuries, Tertullian warned against the danger of corruption from worldly (Greek) philosophy into Christian doctrine: "Free Jerusalem from Athens and the church of Christ from the Academy of Plato" (Caram, *Fall*, 68).

and, a pre-ordained analysis of the (im-)probability of miracle occurrences on a case by case basis.[126]

Although Warfield's own professor at Princeton, Charles Hodge, doubted that miracles were *necessary* after they confirmed the apostles' testimony, he accepted the possibility of postbiblical miracles "on suitable occasions."[127] Warfield, however, demurred. For him, all New Testament miracle claims are authentic, because they are attested by apostles (who are circularly attested by their miracles). All later miracle claims, by contrast, must have some non-miraculous explanation, because subsequent testimony is untrustworthy and too often comes from Catholics and other groups whose theology he rejected.[128]

For Warfield, miracle claims subsequent to the apostles simply reflected "the curious power which preconceived theory has to blind men to facts," seemingly oblivious to the force his own presuppositions exercised on his evaluations of an abundant history of miracle claims, many of them more documented by testimony temporally close to the events than many in Scripture itself.[129]

Cessationists differ among themselves as to when "supernatural" gifts supposedly ceased. Warfield's historical argument thus suffers even at the hands of other cessationists—including some he cites in his book—who recognize that miracles continued beyond the first century, and some as late as the fifth century. Warfield notes but rejects what he considers the "Anglican" theory—namely that miracles persisted for several centuries after the New Testament to get the church on a good footing in the Roman Empire.[130] "If the usefulness of miracles in planting the church were sufficient reason for their occurrence in the Roman Empire in the third century," he reasons correctly, "it is hard to deny that it may be sufficient reason for the repetition of them in, say, the Chinese Empire in the twentieth century."[131] Allowing postapostolic miracles then naturally leads one to accept Catholicism instead of Anglicanism, he

126. Ruthven, *Cessation*, 76. See further *Cessation*, 57; Ruthven, "Cessation."

127. Hodge, *Systematic Theology*, 3:452, as quoted in Ruthven, *Cessation*, 84n187.

128. E.g., he rejects the testimony of twenty-eight physicians that Pierre de Rudder's healing was miraculous (Warfield, *Counterfeit Miracles*, 118–19; see discussion later in this chapter, under "Dismissing Historical Cases"). Warfield, *Counterfeit Miracles*, 71–124, challenges "Roman Catholic miracles," particularly (on 103–24) Lourdes (though on 107 apparently conceding a higher number cured than is actually likely); also Irvingite and related claims (Warfield, *Counterfeit Miracles*, 125–53). Warfield, *Counterfeit Miracles*, 110, concedes that genuine cures at Lourdes are undeniable yet (111) attributes them mostly to "hysterosis," while leaving other cures (117–18; such as the instant healing of a broken bone) as mere anomalies or falsehoods. One wonders why a theist must automatically prefer such psychological explanations, which themselves lack experimental confirmation, to theological explanations.

129. Deere, *Still Surprised*, 87, quoting from Warfield, *Counterfeit Miracles*, 20.

130. A theory he summarizes in Warfield, *Counterfeit Miracles*, 6–9.

131. Warfield, *Counterfeit Miracles*, 35.

insisted.[132] Warfield recognizes that he cannot concede some miracles beyond associates of the first-century apostles without compromising his entire case.

### The Rise of Skeptical Theology

When historians found specious an application of completely different rules of evidence for biblical and postbiblical miracles, the collapse of such a division invited one of two responses: a denial of biblical miracles or the possibility of postbiblical ones.[133]

Syncretism is where elements of one religion combine with another. In the West, we often think of ancestor veneration in Asia or elements of traditional African religion in Africa. Yet Christians from other cultures can also discern our Western blind spots, particularly our syncretism with deism. Compare one summary of the state of US Christendom: "moralistic therapeutic deism."[134]

What is most astonishing is the common cause that full cessationists made with modernists in rejecting postbiblical miracles. As one author put it, "In the early years of the 20th century, . . . new critical approaches to Christian theology began to suggest that biblical stories were more metaphorical than literal, and that Christianity's truths were mainly . . . symbolic."[135] That is why in 1910 the General Assembly of the Presbyterian Church in the United States, in an effort to distinguish liberal theology from biblical Christianity, came up with five required doctrines that all true believers must hold: (1) the inerrancy of Scripture, (2) the virgin birth of Jesus, (3) the doctrine of atonement, (4) the bodily resurrection of Jesus, and (5) the authenticity of biblical miracles.[136] The Assembly referred to these doctrines as "fundamentals."[137] These doctrines were highlighted, not only because of their centrality to the faith, but because they were the very doctrines under assault from liberal theologians of the day.

Do you think it's a coincidence that at least three of these five points are directly related to belief in the miraculous? Opposition to miracles had been the driving force behind much of Western culture's opposition to Scripture since the Enlightenment. The satanic deception of theological unbelief is pointed directly at the heart of "supernaturalism." I (Daniel) would argue that the dismissal of many central doctrines today reflects an underlying

132. Warfield, *Counterfeit Miracles*, 35–37.

133. Mullin, *Miracles*, 30; Lawton, *Miracles*, 58. By the early twentieth century, various writers allowed that miracles declined in character after the subapostolic age while affirming that there was no a priori reason to deny them happening in any age (Maclean, "Miracles," 42; Bernard, "Miracle," 395–96; cf. Wright, "Miracles," 191, arguing that some claims after the subapostolic era "are far too well attested to be scornfully and summarily dismissed").

134. See seminally Smith, *Soul Searching*.

135. McAdams, *Redemptive Self*, 142–43.

136. *Minutes of Assembly*, 1870, 272–23.

137. *Minutes of Assembly*, 1870, 271.

pathology. The real disease is a kind of unbelief working to attack *any* kind of miraculous work of God on earth.

### *Apologetic for a Currently Nonmiraculous Faith*

Even the most hostile full cessationists may well have a sincere, apologetic motivation. Ironically, however, in this they act much like the liberal theologians they typically detest. They want to save biblical Christianity from itself.[138] Consider healing, for example. Cessationists know that Jesus taught that "whoever believes in me will also do the works that I do" (John 14:12). They know James promises that "the prayer offered in faith will make the sick person well" (James 5:15). But if they have not witnessed divine healing, or have no real confidence it actually happens, hard cessationists need to save the Bible from itself by explaining why the healings do not occur in spite of Scripture's promises.

As we have noted, two hundred years after the Reformers, Enlightenment philosophers like Hume took skepticism about contemporary miracles to its logical conclusion. If miracles aren't happening today, why should we believe they ever happened? Maybe they were like stories from the Greek mythical past.[139] Highly influential thinkers argued against miracles and painted all supernaturalism as superstition. Sophisticated secular intellectuals rejected the miraculous, so Christian intellectuals went on the defensive.

Modernist theologians, in an attempt to rescue Christianity from what must have looked like an impending religious apocalypse, proposed an alternative approach to biblical interpretation. They reduced the miracle stories to fables. They proposed a new way of seeing biblical healings and exorcisms. Such stories represented spiritual principles rather than literal, physical realities. For example, leprosy in Scripture represented sin as defilement or religious impurity. So when a leper was healed in the Bible, it represented only a kind of *spiritual* healing—a cleansing of internal impurity.[140]

Like their liberal counterparts, by rejecting modern miracles hard cessationists tried to create a kind of defensive buffer for Christianity. After all, biblical miracles occurred almost two thousand years ago. They are beyond the reach of the scientific method to disprove. If you claim the time of miracles was unique and then distance yourself from modern miracle claims, your position cannot be disproved—it becomes unfalsifiable. This thinking appeals in a culture already saturated with deism. The full deist says, "God made the world miraculously and then left it alone to function according to the

138. For this characterization of liberal theology as apologetic, see Mohler, "Hell."

139. Unlike Greek myths, New Testament testimonies stemmed from within living memory of events, as we demand from historical sources (see Keener, *Christobiography*; see esp. Acts 20:9–12; 28:8–10; Rom. 15:19; 2 Cor. 12:12).

140. MacNutt, *Crime*, 146.

laws of nature. God no longer intervenes miraculously." The full cessationist says, "God gave us the gospel miraculously and then left the church alone to function according to Scripture. God no longer intervenes miraculously." The hardest cessationism—no postbiblical miracles—resembles deism, except with an updated cutoff point for embarrassing kinds of God's activity.

The door might remain open theoretically to random but unverifiable miracles, or internal supernatural phenomena, like salvation or character development. But these kinds of miracles carry no burden of proof for cessationists. They are off the hook. In healing the paralytic, Jesus himself taught that it is easier just to make a truth claim than to demonstrate it with a miracle (Matt. 9:1–8).[141] Warfieldian cessationists have taken that easier route—especially when they join the intellectually respectable liberals to attack the wingnut "fanatics" who hold on to the crazy notion of modern miracles. Some otherwise theologically conservative cessationists even used the critical methods of the skeptics or liberal rationalists like Hume (who were themselves denying biblical miracles) to refute modern miracle claims.

By attacking contemporary miracles, they probably hoped to establish their own credibility and protect themselves from guilt-by-association with Catholics, Christian Scientists, claims for healing among late nineteenth-century radical evangelicals, or anyone else claiming miracles. Their scheme resembles a kid who thinks, "I'll help the bullies beat up my brother so they won't pick on me." The problem is that theologically conservative cessationism is more self-contradictory than liberalism, on the one hand, and continuationism, on the other. Skeptics can reject modern miracles for the same reason they reject biblical miracles. They do not believe miracles ever occurred; they do not accept the Bible's testimony. But from a philosophical standpoint they at least apply their rejection of eyewitness testimony for miracles consistently across the board.

### *Warfield's Inconsistency*

We revisit here in greater detail a point introduced more than once earlier. Jon Ruthven's dissertation on Warfield takes him to task for his inconsistency. Warfield uses Hume's skeptical approach to postbiblical miracles, though more directly confessing the influence of Middleton.[142] He follows Aquinas's narrow definition of miracle, which excludes even God's use of nature to accomplish miracles.[143] (Again, this would exclude the miracle of the east wind blowing back the sea in Exod. 14:21.) Even if God healed a person in a way that seemed obviously supernatural, Warfield insists, this would not be

141. "Which is easier: to say, 'Your sins are forgiven, or to say, 'Get up and walk'?" (9:5).
142. Ruthven, *Cessation*, 25n61, 27.
143. Ruthven, *Cessation*, 46.

a miracle.[144] Sharpening the contrast between postbiblical miracles and Jesus, Warfield idealizes Jesus's ministry beyond the Gospels: "For a time disease and death must have been almost banished from the land."[145]

As Ruthven points out, "Warfield excoriates those who claim to examine carefully nature and history, declaring, on a posteriori grounds, that biblical miracles do not happen when in fact these doubters have already begun their investigation guided by the a priori that miracles are impossible." Yet when he turns to postbiblical miracles, Warfield follows precisely that "identical naturalistic a priori." Natural inexplicability is not sufficient grounds to constitute a miracle. "Warfield, like the skeptics he criticizes, simply subsumes these events, if not under the category, 'nature,' then certainly under 'not proven to be a miracle.'"[146] Thus, "Warfield's concept of miracle rests on two mutually incompatible foundations: on the one hand, that a miracle is an event which can be shown as such to any observer, naturalist or theist, simply by viewing the evidence, and on the other, that naturalists and theists necessarily determine the nature of an event from their respective a prioris."[147]

Warfield challenges skeptics' disbelief in biblical miracles by highlighting their skeptical presuppositions. "The question of miracles," he insists, "is just a question of evidence," by which he means trustworthy testimony. So biblical miracles are trustworthy because we may accept the biblical witness (yet not any postbiblical testimony). Then, circularly, miracles confirm the witness of the apostolic authors of Scripture so we may trust their testimony. The circular character of the argument undermines its evidential value for those who do not start with his presuppositions.[148] Such an overwhelmingly presuppositional apologetic might suffice for someone whose peer group shares its plausibility structures; it may produce tragic consequences in some of their children when they come of age and dare to question it.

#### DISMISSING HISTORICAL CASES

A case that illustrates Ruthven's critique of Warfield is the report of the healing of Catholic Pierre de Rudder, attested by twenty-eight physicians as miraculous. After expressing disbelief, Warfield simply dismisses the case with a naturalism-of-the-gaps shrug as merely "unexplained": "Nature was made by God, not man, and there may be forces working in nature not only which have not yet been dreamed of in our philosophy, but which are beyond human comprehension altogether. . . . We do not busy ourselves, therefore,

144. Ruthven, *Cessation*, 47.
145. Ruthven, *Cessation*, 48.
146. Ruthven, *Cessation*, 52.
147. Ruthven, *Cessation*, 53.
148. Ruthven, *Cessation*, 54.

with conjecturing how Pierre de Rudder's cure may have happened. . . . We are content to know that in no case was it a miracle."[149] Since he will accept *no* evidence, why bother pretending to investigate it?

In a classic illustration of a historiographic double standard, Warfield abandons in postapostolic history the very criteria he used to defend Scripture from skeptics, and then adopts the skeptics' arguments to discredit postbiblical miracles even when they look very much like the biblical models.[150] With utter lack of self-reflection about his own worldview, he discredits Christian witnesses through church history based on their primitive worldview, influenced by "heathen imagination."[151]

Thus even the otherwise theologically reliable Augustine, when reporting miracles, becomes "quite unreliable" and "a child of his times."[152] Never mind the affidavits of healings Augustine's diocese collected in two years, including healings of blindness and raisings from the dead and events that Augustine himself witnessed. These seventy cases reflect an average of a miracle report every week and a half.[153] How much more credible could Augustine have made his case?

As for martyrs and the deeply devoted, emotion must have clouded their thinking, Warfield insists. He complains repeatedly that such conditions as "blinding excitement," "brutal persecution," or being "inflamed by enthusiasm" distort their testimony.[154] Enlightenment critics originally applied "enthusiasm" to contemporary groups such as Methodists;[155] similarly, "hysteria," sometimes applied to miracle testimony,[156] was a presumed medical condition then thought to afflict particuarly women.[157] Just as early critics of Christianity complained about feminine involvement, many early modern critics of "faith healing" regarded it as a "feminine superstition."[158]

149. Warfield, *Counterfeit Miracles*, 119–20; Ruthven, *Cessation*, 57.

150. Ruthven, *Cessation*, 68; Turner, *Gifts*, 299.

151. Ruthven, *Cessation*, 69. Moreover, the pagan world was *not* wholly gullible about miracles or natural laws; cf. Grant, *Miracle*.

152. Ruthven, *Cessation*, 70. Warfield, *Counterfeit Miracles*, challenges Augustine on 42–45.

153. Augustine, *City of God* 22.8.

154. Ruthven, *Cessation*, 71.

155. Cf., e.g., Daston, "Facts," 118, 121; Kidd, "Healing," 161; Kidd, *Awakening*, 163; Wigger, *Saint*, 58–59, 78, 81–83, 166–67, 170, 307, 311–12, 320, 322; Oliver, *Reformations*, 119.

156. Frequently in Warfield, *Counterfeit Miracles*, e.g., 111, 149, 153, 187; Opp, *Lord for Body*, 80, 168, 186; Duffin, *Miracles*, 134–35.

157. Van Buskirk, *Healing*, 35–36; Capps, *Village Psychiatrist*, 15–22, 111–12. Cf., e.g., Warfield, *Counterfeit Miracles*, 149, on a glossolalic "hysterical madwoman"; or 153, speaking of "the crowd of hysterical women which surrounded" Irving.

158. Opp, *Lord for Body*, 76. Healing testimonies did tend to predominate among women (e.g., Opp, *Lord for Body*, 160; Espinosa, "Healing in Borderlands," 141), perhaps due to lesser social respectability restraints and expectations (Opp, *Lord for Body*, 48, 168; Curtis, *Faith*, 38–50).

#### CONSEQUENCES FOR BIBLICAL MIRACLES

Warfield's methods, employed on the Gospels, would undercut their authority. As already noted, while Warfield rejects naturalistic explanations of Jesus's exorcisms, he adopts Harnack's rationalistic treatment of all post-apostolic exorcisms as "essentially objectifications of superstitious minds."[159] Never mind that, along with healing, exorcism was the leading cause of conversion to Christianity in the 300s![160] Although "some of these cases, according to Warfield's own criteria of historical credibility, clearly demand . . . his careful examination,"[161] he simply demythologizes them as Bultmann would soon do in Germany.[162] His "rejection of this category of 'miracle' is necessary for his cessationist polemic, but represents a fatal contradiction in his historical method."[163] So for Warfield, had demons passed away? Or just the God-given power to expel them when needed?[164] Despite Bultmann's influence in Germany, even there Karl Barth, Jürgen Moltmann, and others recognized the reality of Blumhardt's successful exorcism in the 1800s that broke ground for the kingdom and a further ministry of healing and deliverance.[165]

Following Aquinas and Middleton before him, Warfield discards from the miracle category any healing that is not instant.[166] Yet Mark, though normally focused on the most dramatic examples, includes cases where Jesus's miracles occurred in two stages (Mark 8:23–25; 9:25–27; 11:14, 20–21). Even if Jesus had special reasons for these cases, they illustrate that God is not limited to following Warfield's limitation.

Moreover, for Warfield, even if the cure is dramatic and instant after prayer, if the cure ever occurs in any natural context, it doesn't count; one must also be able to prove that nothing "natural" could have happened.[167] Since most

159. Ruthven, *Cessation*, 73.

160. MacMullen, *Christianizing*, 61–62; cf. Frend, *Rise*, 566–67.

161. Ruthven, *Cessation*, 73.

162. By contrast, even David Friedrich Strauss, who treated most miracle stories in the Gospels as legends or myths, took seriously at least Jesus's exorcisms (Fabisiak, *Nocturnal Side*). For Bultmann, whatever involves supernatural forces is "myth" ("Demythologizing," 95), and myth often demands an existential interpretation (Bultmann, "Mythology," 9). Similarly, charismatic experiences of healing have challenged many members (and former members) of liberal denominations today to reject the demythologizing skepticism of their seminary professors (De Arteaga, "Parody," 25, from his observations as an Anglican priest).

163. Ruthven, *Cessation*, 73–74.

164. Ironically, many early cessationist Protestants still believed in witchcraft and *demonic* acts of power (Lecky, *History*, 1:148). Wesley's father, Samuel, like many of his contemporaries, believed in ghosts (Handley, "Ghosts," esp. 345, 355); preachers employed these stories moralistically (Handley, "Ghosts," 348–49). For Wesley's views about the demonic world in their eighteenth-century context, see Webster, "Terrors."

165. Barth, *Dogmatics*, 165ff. (noted in Kauffman, "Introduction," 7–8); Moltmann, "Blessing," 149; cf. Ising, *Blumhardt*, 413.

166. Ruthven, *Cessation*, 74.

167. Ruthven, *Cessation*, 74–75.

sorts of healings in the Gospels are reported somewhere in ancient stories or subsequent medical annals, including occasional restoration of sight or mobility, consistency with this principle would necessarily exclude Jesus's healings of blindness, walking disability, and the like (as is common among full skeptics). Once one excludes all parallels or anything that has potential medical cures, one is left with few miracles even of Jesus. This process fails to account for the sheer cluster of miracles around Jesus, but since such clusters can occur around some people of prayer today (including one of this book's authors), the consistent skeptic must reject even these.

Finally, Warfield insists that one must have a precise diagnosis,[168] a rule that would again, by modern standards, exclude most miracles in the Gospels. We could not count conditions such as fever (Mark 1:30–31; John 4:52; Acts 28:8; probably malaria[169] but described only by the key symptom) or generic skin conditions (Mark 1:40, 42; ancient *lepra*, translated "leprosy," included a variety of skin conditions).[170]

Colin Brown's assessment of Warfield's *Counterfeit Miracles* is that he compiled "an incomparable inventory of objections to the supernatural."[171] Hard cessationists claim faith in the literal truth of the Bible, the greatest collection of supernatural stories ever assembled, and then flatly deny modern miracles on rationalist grounds. That should create severe cognitive dissonance, as well as severe problems for any evidentialist apologetic!

### Conspicuous Problems in Warfield's Methodology

Various problems make Warfield's approach untenable. For example:

1. Warfield distinguishes "ordinary" spiritual gifts from "extraordinary," "miraculous" ones (a distinction we challenged as arbitrary and extrabiblical in chap. 6).
2. He limits the exercise of miraculous gifts to the apostles and people on whom they laid hands.[172] (He had to allow some credibility for the later persons on whom they laid hands, perhaps because he needed the earliest second-century fathers for their testimony to first-century apostolic Scripture.) Yet Ananias, a nonapostle, laid hands on Saul of Tarsus, who became an apostle. This was how God healed Saul and filled him with the Holy Spirit (Acts 9:17).

168. Ruthven, *Cessation*, 75.

169. It was pervasive (Touwaide, "Disease," 550; Grmek, *Diseases*, 93, 275, 282), and its incidence coincided with seasonal mortality spikes (Fiensy, *Archaeology*, 220).

170. See Keener, "*Lepra*"; other discussions in, e.g., Hulse, "Leprosy"; Matthews and Benjamin, "Leper"; Mull and Mull, "Leprosy."

171. Brown, *Miracles*, 199.

172. Deere, *Still Surprised*, 87. Deere addresses Warfield more extensively on 86–96.

3. Warfield also ties the *charismata* to the apostles, although the term appears only in the epistles and in the context of especially local church practice.[173] Believers in Rome experienced gifts such as prophecy (Rom. 12:6) before Paul or (on the usual chronology) any of the Twelve visited. Elders (1 Tim. 4:14) as well as apostles (Rom. 1:11; 2 Tim. 1:6) could impart spiritual gifts.[174]
4. Warfield builds arguments on faulty premises. For example, he rejects reports of partial healings on the basis that "it must remain astonishing, in any event, that miracles should be frequently incomplete. We should *a priori* expect miraculous cures to be regularly radical."[175] This remains a common objection, even today, when cessationists see miracles that they feel are not good enough. But since when does anyone's a priori expectations constitute a valid premise for determining what is or is not an authentic divine act? Our subjective opinions are notoriously unreliable and, in the context of spiritual things, completely irrelevant (1 Cor. 2:13–14). See chapter 11, above.

   Sometimes critics will even mock the healing of ills they deem unimportant, such as migraines or other aches and pains. I (Daniel) think such cynical judgments reflect a deep lack of gratitude and humility that must grieve the heart of God. In Africa we have found that these seemingly insignificant problems can be anything from less serious aches and pains to cancer or other life-threatening diseases. Moreover, what might seem like an insignificant problem to the critics might not be so insignificant if they were the ones with these problems—especially if they lived in a culture without the resources and medical care that we take for granted.

   The Bible says that Jesus healed *all* kinds of illnesses (Mark 1:34), which surely includes complaints invisible to others as well as the visible ones. Moreover, the idea that these are the only healing claims today is mistaken. Many dramatic postbiblical cases exist as well (see, e.g., some of them in chaps. 22–23). Why should Jesus heal less than he did in the Gospels now that he sits at the Father's side as exalted Lord of the universe?
5. When Warfield encounters a claim for which there is no apparent explanation, he simply dodges it by appealing to unknown natural causes—a sort of naturalism-of-the-gaps. Recall the already-mentioned case of Pierre de Rudder, whose amputated leg grew back one night. "We are only beginning to learn the marvellous behavior of which living tissue is

173. Deere, *Still Surprised*, 88.
174. Deere, *Still Surprised*, 89–90.
175. Warfield, *Counterfeit Miracles*, 109.

capable. . . . We are content to know that in no case was it a miracle."[176] Again, if you're going to just glibly dismiss examples that contradict your thesis, why bother to build a case on evidence at all? Wouldn't it be simpler to just say, "I refuse to believe in miracles no matter what"?

6. Warfield dismisses miracle occurrences he cannot explain with explanations common in his day such as "mind cure," "hysteria," the "power of suggestion," "religious excitement," or the psychosomatic effects of "brutal persecution" or "widespread oppression."[177] No evidence is ever offered to justify these dismissals. By exposing Warfield's conspicuous bias, his explanations of this sort do more to undermine his case than to support it.
7. Warfield's measures are often questionable, subjective, and ad hoc. For example, he will dismiss miracle claims "from the outset" if he feels immorality, irreligion, or superstition may have been involved.[178] But these judgments are often highly subjective and raise deeper theological questions, such as whether immorality, for example, should invalidate otherwise authentic miracle claims. Samson supernaturally carried away the gates of Gaza after sleeping with a prostitute (Judg. 16:1–3). Warfield's method could allow him to dismiss that biblical miracle as "counterfeit." And that leads us to the next problem.
8. As already emphasized, Warfield's method for critiquing postapostolic miracle claims would, if applied consistently, lead him to reject biblical miracles themselves.

Again, our purpose is not merely to critique Warfield and his book. Rather, we hope that hard cessationists might see in Warfield a kind of mirror for their own untenable approach to miracles and the supernatural. Warfield reflects the common tendencies of downplaying, dodging, or rejecting unwelcome evidence of the supernatural. This approach subjects history to his theological presuppositions, rather than vice versa, thus evaluating facts with unequal weights and inconsistent judgments.

Warfield predetermined that "had any miracles perchance occurred beyond the Apostolic age they would be without significance; mere occurrences with no universal meaning."[179] In other words, even if someone can point to miracles outside the "apostolic era," Warfield will be obliged to dismiss them or explain them away since they don't support his thesis. And this is exactly what Warfield and other full cessationists do with modern miracle claims. Rather than accepting them at face value, they feel obligated to poke at the

176. Warfield, *Counterfeit Miracles*, 119.
177. Ruthven, *Cessation*, 71.
178. Ruthven, *Cessation*, 55–56.
179. Warfield, *Counterfeit Miracles*, 27–28.

testimonies cynically until they figure out a way to discredit them. If at the end of the day they cannot find a legitimate reason to dismiss a miracle as fraudulent, they can always fall back on the "psychosomatic" explanation or write it off as the "placebo effect." This is exactly the way atheists and unbelievers approach the supernatural.[180]

Given his conspicuous bias against anything supernatural beyond the "apostolic age," one should take Warfield's critique of miracles in history (the primary purpose of his book) with a grain or two of salt. His book is simply propaganda for his position. Many of his methods come right out of the skeptical playbook used by his opponents—materialist critics and deists—to condemn biblical miracles themselves. This skepticism is nothing new. Jesus's challengers did not accept the message of his miracles (Mark 3:22; John 11:46–48) or believe even when Jesus rose from the dead (cf. Luke 16:30–31; Acts 4:2, 16–17). The spirit behind full cessationism is the same unbelief that underlies skepticism toward biblical miracles. It does not nurture biblical faith.

### *Counterevidence That Undermines Warfield's Approach to History*

The evangelical healing movement of the late 1800s was only several decades old when Warfield wrote. *Counterfeit Miracles* was published only about nine years after the Azusa Street Revival had ended, so the Pentecostal movement was still in its infancy.[181] Moreover, more elite religious circles generally despised Pentecostals. Early Pentecostal sympathizers were often "removed from their pulpits or dismissed by their mission boards,"[182] as well as being jailed, having homes and churches burned, and the like.[183] Warfield did not have the benefit of hindsight, so he addressed the revival only in passing.[184] He lacked access to the massive collection of data available to us today. That's not to say that he would have been sympathetic to Pentecostal theology or experience. But perhaps one can be excused for being a full cessationist on the basis of published experience in Warfield's time.

Today, however, the evidence is overwhelming, especially if one accepts biblical standards for testing miracles. And since the theological argument never had a leg to stand on, total cessationists (those that deny all postbiblical miracles) are becoming an endangered species. Most who argue for cessationism from a systematic-theological position today are not as rigid as Warfield in theory, even if they remain completely cessationist in practice. And in some

180. This is not to deny the occurrence of psychosomatic illnesses or placebo cures (see Keener, *Miracles*, 2:630–44), but rather to deny that they can cover anything like all cases—not least regarding nature miracles or resucitations from death (1:536–99; 2:712–59).

181. Oppenheimer, "Azusa St."

182. Ward, "Argument," 75, quoting Nichol, *Pentecostalism*, 70.

183. Ward, "Argument," 76, citing Campbell, *Church*, 206; Conn, *Army*, 35.

184. Warfield, *Perfectionism*, 326–30.

cases, they even, as Calvin did, allow for miracles on the mission field where the gospel is making new inroads.

I (Daniel) would like to press this point. As far as I am concerned, the whole of cessationism fails right here. Cessationism in its more rigid form is essentially a categorical proposition that can be falsified by one contradictory occurrence. In other words, if anyone has operated in any "miraculous" or "revelatory" gift of the Spirit at any time since the apostolic age, then such gifts have not ceased in any absolute sense.

Moreover, if cessationism were true, that would mean that every man and woman of God throughout church history who has claimed to operate in such a gift of the Spirit either lied or was deceived. This includes many thousands of godly, faithful men and women who defended the faith and even died for their witness.[185] It would require rejecting the claims of ministers such as John Wesley, Charles Spurgeon, and many more.

## How Much Evidence Is Enough?

Unfortunately, others have made Warfield's unjustified conclusion their premise. Renowned cessationist theologian Sinclair Ferguson even has the audacity to turn the question back on continuationists, claiming, "Restorationism [in which he includes continuationism] provides no generally convincing theological explanation for the disappearance of certain gifts during the greater part of the church's existence."[186] Ferguson is actually correct here. We have no convincing theological explanation for the cessationism of certain gifts, but that is because cessationism is his premise, not ours. We're continuationists, remember? We don't need to explain the disappearance of gifts that have not disappeared.

Still, we can easily account for what cessationists misinterpret as a "disappearance of certain gifts." Gifts and evidences for them have fluctuated in history, for rationally consistent reasons that do not require us to change, ignore, or reject clear New Testament teaching. Such reasons include the following:

1. In keeping with our contention throughout this book, the gifts of the Spirit have never ceased. They have always been active in the church, even if sometimes to a greater or lesser degree. As Carson writes, "There is enough evidence that some form of 'charismatic' gifts continued sporadically across the centuries of church history that it is futile to insist on doctrinaire grounds that every report is spurious or the fruit of demonic activity or psychological aberration."[187]

185. Note, for example, the hundreds or thousands of early Anabaptist martyrs (Kraybill, "Guide"), many of whom were effectively charismatic.

186. Ferguson, *Holy Spirit*, 223.

187. Carson, *Showing Spirit*, 166.

2. There is no reason to assume that, just because our ancient documentation of miracles or the charismata is limited, that they were always missing in the lives of ordinary believers. Up until relatively recently, documenting history was a rare luxury reserved for those who were important, wealthy, educated, and literate—which excluded the vast, overwhelming majority of people that have ever lived. Writing supplies were expensive and often difficult to get. And even if someone had writing materials and was educated enough to write something down and considered the subject worth the time and effort, there would only be one copy of the record in existence unless others felt it worth the while to painstakingly copy it by hand. These factors challenge the assumption that if the charismata were happening, we would have tons of documentation confirming it. Given sufficient evidence for them that *has* survived from most periods, arguing from partial silence makes little sense. Nevertheless, besides the church fathers, some evidence from ordinary believers survives. On a popular level, for example, Coptic texts report a range of Christian cures in Egypt.[188]
3. As most observers, whether Catholic, Protestant, or Orthodox, recognize, the institutional church went through seasons of such severe corruption that we can genuinely question whether some of its leaders were even genuine followers of Christ. (Certainly the ancient church found reasons to excommunicate some of its bishops.) So we would not expect to see gifts of the Spirit celebrated publicly when the church was controlled by the arm of the flesh. Those outside the establishment were usually condemned (sometimes but not always rightly) as heretics and thus were persecuted and oppressed. Their opponents destroyed their writings and wrote the only remaining records for many of them.

   I (Daniel) recently heard a well-known Reformed cessationist teacher mockingly comment that, through most of church history, the only people reporting supernatural experiences were "wack jobs." This is an ironic perspective coming from a Reformed Protestant. After all, many in his part of the Reformed tradition despise most of the medieval Catholic tradition (indeed, most pre-Reformation Christians) as aberrant and heretical. Medieval Catholics would have viewed those in his own tradition as "wack jobs." Who decides? If the answer is Scripture, we believe that we have already shown that it supports continuationism.
4. The Bible itself ascribes seasons of spiritual drought to the sin, rebellion, and unbelief of God's people (e.g., 1 Sam. 3:1; Ps. 74:9; Ezek. 7:26; Amos 8:11–12; Mark 6:1–6). This was the explanation given by most

188. Godron, "Healings," 1212–13. From fourth-century letters, see Barrett-Lennard, *Healing*, 44–86.

of the church fathers cited by cessationists as supporting cessationism. Wesley agreed with this perspective as well, arguing, "A general corruption both of faith and morals infected the Christian church: which by that revolution, as St. Jerome says, 'lost as much of its virtue, as it had gained of wealth and power.' . . . And this very reason St. Chrysostom himself gave in the words . . . , 'There are some who ask, why are not miracles performed still? Why are there no persons who raise the dead, and cure diseases?' To which he replies, 'That it was owing to the want of faith, and virtue, and piety in those times.'"[189]

5. Cessationism is a self-fulfilling prophecy. Wherever people don't believe in particular gifts of the Spirit, they won't operate in them—at least not consciously or willingly. But if they believe that the Word of God promises these gifts, they will experience some of them. This principle holds true irrespective of denomination. At our Gospel Campaigns in Africa, we have top bishops and leaders from every denomination sitting on our platform—for example, Anglican, Baptist, Lutheran, Methodist, Pentecostal, Presbyterian. And they all experience miracles, healings, and the gifts of the Spirit in their congregations.

   Everything in the kingdom operates by faith, and teaching people to reject miracles undermines faith for them. Jesus himself ran into this problem. He did not do many miracles in Nazareth "because of their unbelief" (Matt. 13:58). And when his disciples asked why they could not drive out a demon, Jesus responded simply: "Because you have so little faith" (Matt. 17:20). While faith does not guarantee that God will grant all requests, faith that God will *not* empower particular gifts is hardly conducive to their manifestation.

6. Despite the above point, many times people *do*, by God's grace, operate in the Spirit's gifts without realizing it. They might even call them by different names or miss their supernatural nature because they feel so natural (gifts flow easily and often seem unremarkable to the person operating in them). I (Daniel) recently heard a cessationist pastor describe how, while reading the Bible one day, he suddenly became aware of a specific issue in the life of one of his parishioners—an issue previously unknown to him. When he brought it to her attention, his quiet "revelation" hit the bull's-eye, which resulted in a breakthrough for her. Whether he realized it or not, he operated in a gift of the Spirit.

189. Wesley, "Letter to Middleton" (January 4, 1749), in Wesley, *Works*, 10:1. Amy Carmichael, the renowned mid-twentieth-century missionary to India, also shared these sentiments: "We profess to be strangers and pilgrims, seeking after a country of our own, yet we settle down in the most un-stranger-like fashion, exactly as if we were quite at home and meant to stay as long as we could. I don't wonder apostolic miracles have died. Apostolic living certainly has" (as quoted in Kim, *Obsession*, 76; cf. also Hayes, *Sub-Merge*, 115).

This probably happens often in the cessationist community, just as we illustrated in chapter 12 for the case of Spurgeon.

Many cessationists still experience the blacklisted gifts of the Spirit without realizing it. And many once opposed to these gifts' continuation changed their theology when they experienced the Spirit's power in such a way. Such cases challenge accusations of counterfeit miracles, imitations, or contrived manifestations.

7. Sometimes the simplest approach is best. (In logic, this principle is called Ockham's razor.) Many cessationists look around and notice fewer miracles than what they find in Scripture. That may be a perfectly valid observation. But to jump immediately to a categorical position—one that is extreme, binary, staunch, and dogmatic—is inappropriate both theologically and logically. We do not accept such hasty thinking in daily life. Why should we apply it to ultimate issues? If my car runs out of gas, I do not permanently abandon my car as beyond repair. Recently I woke up in the morning and noticed it was still dark outside, which seemed unusual for that time. My first thought, however, was not that the earth stopped rotating and I would never see the sun again. There were more reasonable explanations for this apparent anomaly. Maybe my curtains were closed. Maybe there was a time change I missed. If there are times of less supernatural activity (as in Judg. 6:13; Pss. 74:9; 77:10–11), we should not assume, against Scripture, that the character, nature, and promises of God have mysteriously changed without warning.
8. Finally, even if we had no record of anyone since Paul who performed a miracle, spoke in tongues, prophesied, or healed, that would still only be an argument from experience. Such historical silence would be troubling but not compelling. As cessationists often remind us, we do not determine our theology by experience or tradition, but *sola scriptura*. The Bible alone sits as the final court of appeal for accepting the gifts of the Spirit today. Again, I think that any honest cessationist will concede that Scripture contains no explicit support for cessationism.

And indeed, Scripture invites us to believe that we are in the era of the outpoured Spirit (Acts 2:17–18). We should appreciate the motto "Reformed and always reforming."

## Conclusion

Warfield's polemic against miracles, if exploited by skeptics to be consistent, makes it impossible for any New Testament scholar to defend Jesus's miracles or those in Acts. That is, his skeptical epistemology regarding miracles in subsequent history, if applied consistently to biblical texts, destroys any possibility of an apologetic for biblical miracles and makes it impossible to be a conservative biblical scholar. This is surely the opposite of what Warfield would have wanted.

# 22

# Miracles in History

We briefly addressed historical examples of prophecy and tongues in chapters 12 and 16; here we turn to miracles and healings. Any survey of miracles in history necessarily refutes full cessationism. Moderate cessationists agree with continuationists that God still does miracles; the only disagreement here is whether *gifts* of healings and miracles continue. In some cases, a sufficient cluster of such occurrences around individual ministries suggests that these do continue; at the same time, all of us agree that no one today always sees everyone healed (the authors do not believe that even the first-century apostles saw everyone always healed).

## Examining the Argument That Gifts Ceased[1]

The argument that spiritual gifts ceased in history would not be a very good argument against spiritual gifts today even if it were true. That gifts *should* cease is not a logical corollary of the assertion that they did cease. First, signs and wonders waxed and waned from one period to another (though they were never absent; see chap. 9 above) even in the Bible; they were especially prevalent in times of revival. Could they not become common again in times of revival today?

Moreover, if they are sometimes quite rare, we are still free to ask why. Certainly God may view them as more necessary in some settings than others, but other factors may also play into his choice here. Writing from a Reformed Protestant perspective on history, Sam Storms points out:

> If we concede that certain spiritual gifts were less prevalent than others in the history of the church, their absence may well be due to unbelief, apostasy, and

1. Here I (Craig) follow Keener, *Gift & Giver*, 92, 98.

> other sins that serve only to quench and grieve the Holy Spirit. We should not be surprised at the infrequency of miraculous gifts in periods of church history marked by theological ignorance and personal immorality. No one concludes from the corruption of soteriological truth in the first 1,400 years of church history that it was God's intention for the Holy Spirit to cease teaching and illuminating people concerning this vital doctrine. The same might be said of the concept of the priesthood of all believers.[2]

Second, the argument that gifts ceased and therefore should cease is an argument based on one kind of experience. Yet those who make this argument simply dismiss the experience of hundreds of millions of other Christians today. Some people's claims of spiritual experiences are inauthentic, but if Scripture does not require the gifts' cessation, on what basis can someone dismiss all these claimed experiences a priori?

In response to the hardships of their time, the earliest Christians sought continuing empowerment for evangelistic signs and wonders through prayer (Acts 4:29–31). If the church today often lacks such power, it may be in part because we have not sought it or because we have sought it only for our self-aggrandizement rather than for the evangelization of the world. Again, this is not to claim all gifts for every individual but to declare that, as a whole, the church should welcome the full range of gifts that Paul says are needed to build up Christ's body.

Here is one more reason that we should not use the cessation of gifts in church history to argue that they should have ceased. They didn't.

## Gifts and Miracles in the Early Church

Contrary to what full cessationism teaches, spiritual gifts and miraculous signs continued, in various intensities in various locations and times, throughout church history. Historians have thoroughly documented this point,[3] and continuationists have been quick to cite many of the primary sources.[4] Studies of healing in Christian history often treat not only healings but also specifically those known for gifts of healings.[5]

2. Storms, "View," 203.

3. See, e.g., Hurtado, "Function"; Shogren, "Perfect Would Come"; Shogren, "Prophecy and Canon"; Kydd, *Gifts*; Burgess, *Dictionary*, 730–69; McDonnell and Montague, *Initiation*; Burgess, "Proclaiming the Gospel"; Burgess, *Holy Spirit*; Burgess, *Spirit and Church*; Thigpen, "Power"; Riss, "Tongues"; Hyatt, *Years*; note also the fuller bibliography in, e.g., Hernando, "Continuationism," 264.

4. E.g., Schatzmann, *Charismata*, 82n40; Wimber, *Power Evangelism*, appendix A, 157–74; Dunn, *Jesus and Spirit*, 192; Storms, "View," 201n32; Allison and Köstenberger, *Holy Spirit*, 432.

5. See, e.g., recently, Opp, *Lord for Body*; Warner, *Evangelist*; Warner, *Kuhlman*; more generally but with multiple examples, Porterfield, *Healing*; Robinson, *Formative Years*; Robinson, *Years of Expansion*.

Gary Shogren, Ronald Kydd, Andrew Wilson, and many others (including one of us, Craig) trace accounts of miracles and spiritual gifts in the early church.[6] Because we have provided more detailed treatment elsewhere, here we provide merely some *samples* from Christian history.

### *Second Through Fourth Centuries*

Early Christian history provides numerous examples. Rabbinic sources associated some Christian contemporaries with healing miracles.[7] Most rabbis, however, felt free to reject their testimony by insisting that rabbinic interpretive tradition was more authoritative than arguments from experience based on miracles.[8]

Meanwhile, far from being merely incredulous about a distant and unverifiable past, various church fathers noted that miracles and healings continued in their own day.[9] In the mid-second century, for example, Justin Martyr insists that Christians continue to heal, as well as casting out demons.[10] Second- and third-century Christian apologists depict not only apostolic leaders but also ordinary Christians as miracle workers.[11]

Around the year 180, Irenaeus offers the fullest list of signs, providing almost the same range that appears in Acts, and noting that such signs were

6. Here we follow esp. the summaries in Wilson, *Spirit and Sacrament*, 103–7; Keener, *Acts*, 1:372–74.

7. Christians healed in the name of Yeshu (*t. Hul.* 2:22–23; see also Urbach, *Sages*, 1:116; Herford, *Christianity*, 103–11; Klausner, *Jesus*, 40; Pritz, *Nazarene Christianity*, 96–97), though the rabbis often associated their powers with magic or fakery (e.g., *y. ʿAbod. Zar.* 2:2, §3; Urbach, *Sages*, 1:115–16; Herford, *Christianity*, 115–17; Lachs, *Commentary*, 178; cf. Deut. 13:1–5). In some apocryphal stories, holy rabbis destroyed miracle-working Christians with greater magic (see Herford, *Christianity*, 112–15).

8. E.g., *t. Yebam.* 14:6; cf. *y. Sanh.* 11:4, §1; Vermes, *Jesus the Jew*, 80–81. Some Jewish teachers reportedly performed miracles to validate their halakah (*b. B. Meṣ.* 59b; *y. Sanh.* 6:6, §2; cf. Baumgarten, "Miracles"), though others may have often told stories about such signs simply to praise the teacher's holiness (cf. Dibelius, *Tradition*, 145–46; Urbach, *Sages*, 1:108–9).

9. Woolley, *Exorcism*, 13–25 (here esp. 13); see evidence arranged topically in Frost, *Healing*, 71–110; Kelsey, *Healing*, 149 (citing Quadratus, *Apol.* frg.; Justin, *2 Apol.* 6; *Dial.* 30, 39, 76, 85; Theophilus, 1.13; 2.8; Tertullian, *Scap.* 4; *Soul's Testimony* 3; *Spect.* 26, 29; *Apol.* 23, 27; *An.* 57; Tatian, *To the Greeks* 17–18, 20). Kelsey, *Healing*, 135–99, addresses claims of healing in the early fathers through Gregory the Great; on related matters, see Kydd, *Gifts*. More briefly, De Wet, "Signs," 62–70, addresses sources in the period AD 100–400; also Wimber, *Power Evangelism*, 157–65; bibliography in Ruthven, *Cessation*, 18–19; more generally Porterfield, *Healing*, 43–65.

10. Justin, *2 Apol.* 6.

11. See discussion in Kelhoffer, "Miracle Workers." On the patristic church's ministry in healings and exorcisms, and growth thereby, cf. also Burgess, "Proclaiming the Gospel"; Cho, "Foundation," 31–35; Womack, "Healing," 395–97; more popularly, MacNutt, *Crime*, 82–88. Minucius Felix, *Oct.* 27, also notes Christians casting out demons.

converting pagans.[12] He contrasts mainstream Christians in this regard with gnostics.

> Therefore, also, those who are in truth His disciples, receiving grace from Him, do in His name perform [miracles], so as to promote the welfare of other men, according to the gift which each one has received from Him. For some do certainly and truly drive out devils, so that those who have thus been cleansed from evil spirits frequently both believe [in Christ], and join themselves to the Church. Others have foreknowledge of things to come: they see visions, and utter prophetic expressions. Others still, heal the sick by laying their hands upon them, and they are made whole. Yes, moreover, as I have said, the dead even have been raised up, and remained among us for many years. And what shall I more say? It is not possible to name the number of the gifts which the Church, [scattered] throughout the whole world, has received from God, in the name of Jesus Christ.[13]

B. B. Warfield dismisses Irenaeus's testimony regarding the dead being raised because it is isolated and Irenaeus does not explicitly claim to be an eyewitness himself.[14] Warfield does so despite other examples of raisings in this period.[15]

In late second- or early third-century North Africa, Latin-speaking apologist Tertullian contrasts mainstream Christians with Marcionites: "Let Marcion then exhibit, as gifts of his god, some prophets . . . ; let him produce a psalm, a vision, a prayer—only let it be by the Spirit, in an ecstasy, that is, in a rapture, whenever an interpretation of tongues has occurred to him. . . . Now all these signs (of spiritual gifts) are forthcoming from my side without any difficulty."[16] Eusebius complains that because God was still graciously performing miracles in Phrygian churches, some gave false credence to Montanist prophecies.[17] Cyprian complained that the church's worldliness had sapped its spiritual power in his day,[18] but elsewhere he, too, affirmed

12. Kelsey, *Healing*, 150–51 (citing Irenaeus, *Haer*. 2.6.2; 2.10.4; 2.31.2; 2.32.4–5; 3.5.2); cf. also Woolley, *Exorcism*, 14–15; much more fully, Barrett-Lennard, *Healing*, 89–135 (on possession and exorcism in Irenaeus, see 137–65). The *Apostolic Constitutions* includes prayers that presbyters be filled with both healing and teaching gifts (8.16; Dawson, *Healing*, 147).

13. Irenaeus, *Haer*. 2.32.4 (*ANF*, 1:409).

14. Warfield, *Counterfeit Miracles*, 11.

15. Warfield, *Counterfeit Miracles*, 39–40. See further Quadratus, frg. 2 (early second century); according to a report attributed to a written second-century source, the first bishop of Arbil in Mesopotamia was converted through witnessing a Syrian evangelist raising someone from the dead in AD 99 (see Young, "Miracles in History," 110).

16. Tertullian, *Marc*. 5.8 (Forbes, *Prophecy*, 79–80; Wilson, *Spirit and Sacrament*, 104; Burgess, *Spirit and Church*, 65–68). See also Tertullian, *Spect*. 26; also Tertullian, *Scap*. 4, in Kelsey, *Healing*, 136–37; further on exorcism in Tertullian, see Woolley, *Exorcism*, 20–21.

17. Eusebius, *Hist. eccl*. 5.3.4.

18. Kelsey, *Healing*, 151, citing Cyprian, *Laps*. 6–7. By Cyprian's day, exorcism had shifted from a charism to being part of an order (Woolley, *Exorcism*, 27).

continuing healings.[19] Cyprian of Carthage (200–258) notes that Christians were sometimes cured by baptism.[20]

Meanwhile, in Greek-speaking Alexandria, Origen celebrates "signs and wonders which we must believe to have been performed" and "that traces of them are still preserved among those who regulate their lives by the precepts of the Gospel. . . . And there are still preserved among Christians traces of that Holy Spirit. . . . They expel evil spirits, and perform many cures, and foresee certain events. . . . And the name of Jesus can still remove distractions from the minds of men, and expel demons, and also take away diseases." The apostles are the foundations, but signs "increased in magnitude also in the succeeding ages, in which not a few cures are wrought in the name of Jesus."[21] Origen clearly believed that some individuals were particularly gifted for healings: "Some give evidence of their having received through this faith a marvellous power by the cures which they perform," claiming to have witnessed such cures.[22]

Exorcisms[23] proved to be a major factor in the spread of Christianity even before the 300s;[24] in the 300s, exorcisms and miracles are the most explicit causes of conversion to Christianity mentioned in early Christian sources.[25] Christians appealed to them for evidential value in public discourse. Thus Tertullian named prominent pagans who had been cured from evil spirits and became grateful to Christians.[26] Origen, arguing against Celsus and addressing pagans, in the first half of the third century claimed that Christians were still expelling evil spirits and performing cures, and that he had witnessed some

19. Kelsey, *Healing*, 151 (citing Cyprian, *On the Vanity of Idols* 7; *Ep*. 75.12–13, 15–16), also citing on continuing healings Hippolytus, *Scholia on Daniel* 10.16; Dionysius of Alexandria, *Ep*. 12, *To the Alexandrians* 4; Clement of Alexandria, *Quis div*. 34; Origen, *Cels*. 1.6, 25, 46–47, 67; 2.8, 33; 3.24, 28, 36; 7.35, 67; 8.58.

20. Cyprian, *Ep*. 75.15 (Woolley, *Exorcism*, 29–30, cites this as Cyprian, *Ep*. 69.15); on Cyprian's healing reports further see Kelsey, *Healing*, 151.

21. Origen, *Cels*. 1.2, 46, 67; 3.24, 28 (Wilson, *Spirit and Sacrament*, 105–6; Kelsey, *Healing*, 136); further on Origen, see Woolley, *Exorcism*, 20–23 (citing *Cels*. 1.22; 4.33; 7.4, 67; *Hom. Jos*. 24; *Comm. Matt*. 110).

22. Origen, *Cels*. 3.24.

23. I take this paragraph esp. from Keener, *Acts*, 1:372–74.

24. MacMullen, *Christianizing*, 40–41, 60–61. Cf. also Brown, *Late Antiquity*, 55, as cited in Jenkins, *Next Christendom*; "Miracles, Miracle-Workers," 54.

25. MacMullen, *Christianizing*, 61–62. On the patristic church's ministry in healings and exorcisms, and growth thereby, cf. also Burgess, "Proclaiming the Gospel"; MacNutt, *Crime*, 82–88; Cho, "Foundation," 31–35. Even in Justin, *Dial*. 35.8, signs perform an authenticating function. Culture apparently influenced to a degree the form taken by such signs (as also more recently; see, e.g., McGee, "Miracles and Mission"). Miracle reports grew from the mid-third century, in conjunction with saint veneration ("Miracles, Miracle-Workers," 54; cf. analogous pagan hero veneration in the same period).

26. Tertullian, *Scap*. 4; Kelsey, *Healing*, 136–37. Cf. also Minucius Felix, *Oct*. 27.

of these incidents personally.[27] Reports continued among church fathers like Basil and Gregory of Nazianzus,[28] Gregory of Nyssa,[29] John Chrysostom,[30] and also among the desert monks.[31] Four different church fathers, including some directly influenced by Gregory Thaumaturgos, testify of his effective ministry of evangelism through miracles.[32] Ephrem the Syrian (d. 373) attributes miracles to Basil.[33]

Regarding the continuing diversity of gifts, Basil of Cappadocia in Asia Minor (330–79) declared, "Through the rebirth from above . . . the Spirit enlightens all, inspires prophets, . . . is active in gifts of healing."[34] Around 350, Cyril of Jerusalem instructed believers that God works differently among different believers; "for He employs the tongue of one man for wisdom; the soul of another He enlightens by Prophecy; to another He gives power to drive away devils; to another He gives to interpret the divine Scriptures."[35]

On matters such as the Trinity and canon, Athanasius (d. 373) is a hero for modern evangelical theology. Yet the same Athanasius wrote a book praising Anthony's miracles and spiritual warfare.[36] (Most of us today, including

27. Origen, *Cels.* 1.46, 67; Kelsey, *Healing*, 136; further on Origen, see Woolley, *Exorcism*, 20–23. Kelsey notes (*Healing*, 137–38) that Origen added "that there were many instances he could set down from his own experience" (*Cels.* 1.46).

28. Woolley, *Exorcism*, 45; Kelsey, *Healing*, 167–71.

29. Kelsey, *Healing*, 171–75.

30. Kelsey, *Healing*, 175–77; Floris, "Chrysostom," 378. A number of healing reports historically came through sacraments (Dawson, *Healing*, 146–59; in recent times, Kerin, *Touch*, 8; Oursler, *Power*, 125 [Episcopal]; MacNutt, *Healing*, 163–64; Neal, *Power*, 33–34), and through bishops and elders visiting the sick to anoint them and pray for them (147). For anointing in the patristic era, see Rogge, "Relationship," 179–227; for its different meaning later, see Rogge, "Relationship," 228–42 (in the Carolingian era), 242–66 (in the scholastic era); and for the revised rite (e.g., Vatican II), see 333–70.

31. Woolley, *Exorcism*, 45–47 (note stories of Pachomius and Hilarion; though these are not eyewitness claims, stories about Hilarion appear within living memory in Jerome, *Life of Hilarion*); Kelsey, *Healing*, 163–67 (including, on 166–67, Athanasius's *Life of St. Antony*); Lietzmann, *History*, 4:160–62 (emphasizing hagiography); cf. Frend, *Rise*, 575; Ellingsen, *Roots*, 1:96. For mid-fourth-century Egyptian monks, see also Porterfield, *Healing*, 48.

32. Burgess, "Proclamation," 358–60, citing Gregory of Nyssa, *Life of Gregory Thaumaturgos* (PG 46:893–958); Basil of Cappadocia, *On the Spirit* 74; Socrates, *Ecclesiastical History* 27; Jerome, *Lives of Illustrious Men* 65. McGee, *Miracles*, 5, also cites Basil, *On the Spirit* 29.74.

33. Boys, *Evidence*, 44–45.

34. Basil, *Homily* 3 (Wilson, *Spirit and Sacrament*, 106; Basil, *On the Holy Spirit* 26.61 in Oliver, *Movements*, 87). Basil emphasized charismatic gifts, including teaching, healing, and predicting the future (Burgess, "Proclamation," 360–61; Floris, "Charismata," 372).

35. Cyril of Jerusalem, *Catechetical Lectures* 16.12 (Floris, "Charismata," 371, noting also 18.27; Wilson, *Spirit and Sacrament*, 106). For the testimony of Cyril of Alexandria, Epiphanius of Salamis, Didymus the Blind, and other figures to continuing miracles, see Floris, "Chrysostom," 383.

36. See Athanasius, *Life of Anthony*. Cf. here Wilson, *Spirit and Sacrament*, 98. By contrast, Warfield, *Counterfeit Miracles*, 62–63, treats the work as a pious fiction accommodating a superstitious culture.

mainstream charismatics, would actually think of Anthony as a bit hyper-charismatic and too demon-obsessed.) Athanasius recounts a pattern or cluster of miracles surrounding Anthony. Why treat Athanasius as credible on the one topic yet dismiss out of hand not just particular stories about Anthony but even the overall impression of him as one gifted for miracles? How much is left if one guts the account of anything miraculous?

Athanasius (in the 350s), in his *Life of St. Anthony*, portrays Anthony as confronting skeptics by challenging them either to cure certain demoniacs with their ideas and idols, or to just observe Christ's power; then Anthony himself cured them.[37] Yet Athanasius did not relegate miracles only to hermits, recognizing that even some bishops, who usually lived far more comfortably than monks and hermits, worked miracles too.[38] Like Irenaeus, Athanasius used claims of healings and exorcisms apologetically to defend the orthodox as God's movement.[39] Likewise, Athanasius invites skeptics to come and witness the efficacy of exorcism for themselves.[40]

### *Later Antiquity and Medieval Times*

In *City of God* 22.8, Augustine notes that his diocese had established a depository of documents recording miracles in Hippo only two years earlier, and already they had over seventy published documents. That is nearly one per week and a half, and Augustine knew of many miracles not recorded among these. Another shrine in the area, having kept records longer, had a much larger collection. Augustine recounts numerous healings, including some where he was an eyewitness.[41] Others include raisings from the dead and healings of blindness. One example was two siblings known for shaking with palsy. As one of them prayed in Hippo's church on Easter morning, his shaking stopped, and as the people praised God Augustine elaborated eloquently on God's work. As the service ended, his sister was healed equally suddenly, and the crowd's praises rose to God.

37. Athanasius, *Life of St. Anthony* 80; MacMullen, *Christianizing*, 112. On illness and healing in Athanasius, see Barrett-Lennard, *Healing*, 167–96.

38. Athanasius, *Letters* 49.9, to Dracontius (ca. 354–55; noted in Hyatt, *Years*, 41).

39. See Barrett-Lennard, *Healing*, 329. Apologetic use of miracles won important converts such as Arnobius (Lietzmann, *History*, 3:174). Athanasius regards Arius's timely death as miraculous (Boys, *Evidence*, 42–43).

40. Woolley, *Exorcism*, 47 (citing Athanasius, *Inc.* 48.3). Lietzmann, *History*, 4:135–36, complains about Athanasius's miracle stories; in 3:136, he suspects Athanasius's interpretation of Arius's death as judgment, remarking that "the more critical reader" will judge him as poisoned.

41. Kelsey, *Healing*, 185; Ruthven, *Cessation*, 30; cf. Gardner, *Healing Miracles*, 136; MacMullen, *Second Church*, 65; Herum, "Theology"; Sharp, "Charismata," 387; for a translation, see, e.g., that of Bettenson and Knowles: Augustine, *City of God*, 1043. In 22.8 he also claims to have been an eyewitness to many of these supernatural healings.

Previously more skeptical, Augustine had grown in his appreciation for continuing healings.[42]

Gregory the Great, pope in the Latin West in 590, recognized that miracles often accompanied evangelization, but he noted that many remained to be evangelized in his day, both pagans and schismatics. While he granted that, unlike visions, they were less common than in the original apostolic generation, he considered miracles a continuing "constant of Christian experience."[43] In his *Dialogues*, he usually cites eyewitnesses for the roughly two hundred miracles he cites, which include even raisings from the dead.[44] His *Homilies on Ezechiel* take continuing miracles and charismata for granted: "Now, generally, we see holy men do wonderful things, perform many miracles, cleanse lepers, cast out demons, dispel bodily sicknesses by touch, predict things to come by the spirit of prophecy."[45] Miracles like those of the apostles have followed the effective missionary preaching of Augustine of Canterbury and his associates in England.[46]

If God intended miracles and spiritual gifts to stop after the death of the apostles' associates, someone forgot to inform most of the church fathers.

Although the nature of hagiography diminished the reliability of most of our sources from late antiquity and the medieval period, clearly no one believed that miracles had become impossible. Healings were said to follow Martin of Tours (d. 397),[47] Paulinus of Nola (d. 431),[48] Macrius of Egypt (d. 391),[49] the Northumbrian saints,[50] Benedict,[51] and others. Some living healers were more obscure; Gregory of Tours speaks of an ascetic rural Christian

42. Kelsey, *Healing*, 186–88; Gardner, *Healing Miracles*, 135–37; earlier, see Murray, *Healing*, 174–76.

43. Burgess, "Proclamation," 363, citing Gregory the Great, *Homiliae in Evangelia* (PL 76:1091), with examples in PL 76:1075–312.

44. Burgess, "Proclamation," 363–64, highlighting multiple accounts surrounding Benedict of Nursia.

45. Burgess, "Proclamation," 365, quoting Gregory.

46. Burgess, "Proclamation," 365, citing Gregory, *Letters* 3.61; 8.29. Gregory celebrates their effective evangelism and accompanying miracles again in *Moralia in Job*.

47. See Woolley, *Exorcism*, 48; Kelsey, *Healing*, 189–91; Gardner, *Healing Miracles*, 67–72; briefly Frend, *Rise*, 709; Rapp, "Saints," 553; Burgess, "Proclamation," 366 (citing Sulpicius Severus, *Dialogi* 2.5; 3.10).

48. Burgess, "Proclamation," 366, citing Gregory the Great, *Dialogues* 3.prologue.

49. Burgess, "Proclamation," 366, citing multiple sources.

50. Gardner, *Healing Miracles*, 72–78; see esp. Gardner, "Miracles" (the revised version of his presidential address to the Newcastle and Northern Counties Medical Society, October 1982). His focus is Celtic Christianity there, which continued to flourish even after 664. Anglo-Saxon miracle accounts focus on "the promise of salvation conveyed by" divine miracles (Fadda, "Miraculous," 65).

51. In Gregory the Great, *Dial.* 2, on which see, e.g., Cavadini, "Note." Gregory recounts supernatural stories even in gardens (e.g., the demon on the lettuce in *Dial.* 1.4.7; see Müller, "Power," 47–48).

healer. This healer roughly applied consecrated oil to a fevered young man, whom the fever had made deaf and mute, and the young man was healed.[52] The fifth-century Syrian bishop Philoxenus believed that God still granted the charism of healing to some ascetics;[53] healings and exorcisms are also associated with Symeon the Stylite, an ascetic Syrian monk,[54] and Theodore of Sykeon (d. 613).[55] In the seventh century, Isidore of Seville appears to accept the continuation of miracles,[56] and multiple contemporary eyewitnesses attest a group of miracles impossible in naturalistic terms.[57]

Nevertheless, late antiquity witnessed a general transition away from emphasis on current miracles by living intercessors, especially on the official level.[58] This diminution of reports perhaps not surprisingly also coincided geographically with regions where new evangelism was less emphasized.[59] Signs claims do appear most commonly in history in the context of groundbreaking evangelism;[60] this pattern has persisted through history, for example,

52. Porterfield, *Healing*, 67–69 (citing Gregory of Tours, *History of the Franks*, ca. 592). For a proposed source for a healing miracle by Eugenius in Gregory, see Cain, "Miracles."

53. McDonnell and Montague, *Initiation*, 289.

54. Rapp, "Saints," 555; cf. Billman, *Thread*, 26. For suggestions about Symeon's ironic inversion of the new ascetic ideal, see Blowers, "Interpreting," 623.

55. See Horden, "Saints."

56. Boys, *Evidence*, 30.

57. Boys, *Evidence*, 31–33.

58. Kelsey, *Healing*, 191–217. Gregory the Great's interest differed here from many others (Müller, "Power," 49), but Dal Santo, "Gregory," argues that he was defending the cult of the saints. Emphasizing the beginning of the fifth century as a major transition and suggesting that the emphasis on the divine presence in the sacrament largely displaced the emphasis on exorcism, see Woolley, *Exorcism*, 54–68 (noting, e.g., the transition from the exorcist to the bishop, 63). See also Gardner, "Miracles," 1932 (noting from Bede, *HEGA* 1.31 that Gregory the Great seems not to have encouraged events such as the missionary Augustine's healing of a blind girl). But prayer was still made using oil (following James 5:14–15); see Woolley, *Exorcism*, 63–64. On views that gifts dominated in earlier times, see, e.g., Theodoret of Cyrrhus, *Comm. 1 Cor.* 240 (Bray, *Corinthians*, 117). On the decline in the medieval period (of the gift through living intercessors), see also MacNutt, *Crime*, 117–37; somewhat earlier, Frost, *Healing*, 180–83, 235; also the further decline during the Reformation (MacNutt, *Crime*, 139–44) and especially the Enlightenment and Christian cessationism (145–52; see further Ruthven, *Cessation*). The decline was not always viewed as an ideal state, some speaking wistfully of the past (see Theodoret of Cyrrhus, *Comm. 1 Cor.* 240, in Bray, *Corinthians*, 117; Chrysostom, *Hom. Cor.* 36.7, in Bray, *Corinthians*, 146; cf. Theodoret of Cyrrhus, *Comm. Rom.* 8:15, in *Early Commentaries*); some interpreters, such as Bengel and Christlieb, viewed periods of decline as merely "temporary" for "periods of dulled faith" (Dod, "Healer," 173; McGee, *Miracles*, 42; cf. Boys, *Evidence*, 255).

59. Medieval Europe saw itself as evangelized (Ward, "Monks," 134). Associating signs with evangelism, Severus of Antioch, *Catena on Acts* 10.44 (Martin, *Acts*, 140) averred that signs were no longer necessary, the gospel having been widely spread.

60. Ammonius, *Catena on Acts* 28.9 (Martin, *Acts*, 314), notes that "miracles are mostly performed among and for unbelievers" (cf. Bede, *Comm. Acts* 28.8; Martin, *Acts*, 314). Such an approach today would expect signs to predominate in less evangelized regions. Sociologically, signs and wonders tend to characterize a revivalist movement's initial phase but decline as the

in the cases of earlier Christian missionaries like Patrick, to Ireland;[61] Augustine of Canterbury, evangelist to the Anglo-Saxons;[62] Columba, missionary to Scotland;[63] Willibrord, missionary to the Frisians and Denmark;[64] Boniface, missionary to Germany;[65] missionaries in the early twentieth century;[66] those more recently;[67] and even in some in relatively neglected nineteenth-century reports.[68] While the early medieval West was not fully schooled in Christian faith, many treated it as Christianized.[69] The emphasis generally shifted from healings and concern to improve health toward exalting affliction "as a discipline from the hand of God."[70]

Even so, reports of healings continued to occur.[71] For example, Gregory the Great (d. 604) says he was himself healed[72] and believed that such signs would continue until the rise of the antichrist.[73] Venerable Bede (d. 735) reports "a

---

institutionalization necessary for functioning denominations progresses (see Tomlinson, "Magic Methodists," 389, 398), though oversimplified contrasts between charismatic and institutional reflect a misappropriation of Max Weber (see Kee, *Miracle*, 52–54).

61. For what Patrick apparently construed as a nature miracle, see *Confession* 19. See also *Confession* 45: "Nor will I hide the signs and wonders which the Lord has shown me even many years before they came about" (unless he means this figuratively for his visions of many converts; cf. the "wonders" of which he testifies in 3). Cf. Billman, *Thread*, 25.

62. Young, "Miracles in History," 115, citing in Bede, *HEGA* 1.31 a letter of 601 from Pope Gregory the Great to Augustine, warning him not to be proud of evangelistic success due to miracles, since they do not accompany all believers (cf. also Gardner, "Miracles," 1932; Riss, *Survey*, 8; Billman, *Thread*, 26).

63. See Latourette, *History of Christianity*, 1:344; Tucker, *Jerusalem*, 41. Some scholars use modern miracles to challenge skepticism about all miracles attributed to Columba (Finlay, *Columba*, 173; followed also by Gardner, "Miracles," 1929). Finlay does, however, recognize the elaborations of hagiography (*Columba*, 171–72, 184–85; cf. also Wilson, "Miracles," 23–24).

64. Kelsey, *Healing*, 230.

65. Kelsey, *Healing*, 230. Among those lesser known in the West, Georgia's conversion is attributed to a foreign slave girl who prayed for the healing of the nation's queen mother (McGee, *Miracles*, 5–6, following Lang, *Lives*, 13–19).

66. See, e.g., Warner, *Evangelist*, 161. In Hickson's 1921 meetings in Africa and Asia, healings were far more frequent among non-Christians, including many cures of blindness (Hickson, *Heal*, 76, 141).

67. E.g., Pullinger, *Dragon*, 123, 142; Kolenda, *Impact Africa*.

68. See McGee, "Miracles and Mission" (e.g., 146, noting Mason, *Ko Thah Byu*, 160). See, e.g., Gordon, *Ministry of Healing*, 196–97, citing reports for the Indigenous people of Greenland (for the early eighteenth century; see also Garnett, *Mountains*, 120–21, cited by McGee, *Miracles*, 9) and local believers in southern Africa in a report of 1866, and the supernatural protection of a missionary in a report of 1873; also Gordon, *Ministry of Healing*, 198–99, for healings in Burma (now Myanmar). An apparently dying missionary in India was immediately healed after prayer in 1879 (199–200).

69. Again, Ward, "Monks," 134.

70. Ludwig, *Order Restored*, 140, attributing this shift away from a wholistic perspective to the Platonic and Gnostic emphasis on the soul (from Augustine's era and later).

71. Kelsey, *Healing*, 225–30.

72. Kelsey, *Healing*, 228.

73. Bredero, *Christendom*, 69.

number of eyewitness accounts of healings by John of Beverly [d. 721], who was Bishop of York" in the late seventh century.[74] Bede's works reflect a tension between doubting that miracles continue in his own day at a biblical level and his reports of such.[75]

Healings remained prominent in the medieval Western church.[76] For example, Tainard, an oblate in northern France, experienced a debilitating paralysis in 1085 but is said to have recovered abruptly after a vision in 1088.[77] Bernard of Clairvaux (1091–1153) wrote about Malachy (1094–1148), whom he knew and whose coworkers he consulted, recounting twelve healings attributed to him.[78] Healings accompanied one revival in Normandy in 1145.[79] Traditions have often attributed miracles to Saint Francis (1182–1226),[80] such as the immediate cure of a leper's flesh.[81] Sometimes descriptions of the conditions healed are detailed enough to allow tentative diagnoses by modern specialists.[82]

The Eastern churches also continued to report healings, for example, in Constantinople[83] and Ethiopia.[84] When Thomas of Marga, a ninth-century Eastern writer, recounts the activity of four missionaries active in Asia in the prior generation, he notes healings and some exorcisms reported concerning

74. Kelsey, *Healing*, 229; see further Young, "Miracles in History," 114, noting witnesses in Bede, *HEGA* 5.3 and that John was "an older contemporary" apparently having "a gift of healing"; details and nuanced presentation in McCready, *Miracles*, 40–43.

75. See McCready, *Miracles*, esp. 230–31; McFadden, "Elements," 443–50, argues that Bede and his sources were more concerned with community faith than with verifiability of details (with McCready, *Miracles*, 199–202, 214). Gardner, "Miracles," however, argues that many of Bede's miracle accounts are in fact historically plausible in light of subsequent, medically documented analogies. In some locations Bede reports no miracles, and miracles are missing in these locations also in other sources from the era (Gardner, "Miracles," 1932). While some of Bede's accounts may be legends and others natural events, Young, "Miracles in History," 113–14, contends that at minimum some seem reliable healing reports.

76. See Porterfield, *Healing*, 67–91; cf. Cho, "Foundation," 35–37. Narrations often involved the church's monastic emphasis; see, e.g., vindication stories about nuns (see Pilsworth, "Miracles") and claims of monastic miracles (1040–140; Loud, "Miracles").

77. Karnofsky, "Vision," 15–16 (on a work composed three years after the event).

78. Darling, *Healing*, 144–48.

79. Ensley, *Sounds*, 66–67, followed in Oliver, *Movements*, 211.

80. Often recalled by writers on miracles on various levels today; see, e.g., Young, "Miracles in History," 115; Synan, *Voices*, 61; Cho, "Foundation," 36–37; Darling, *Healing*, 149–55.

81. Jörgensen, *Francis*, 253, recounting a story in the *Fioretti*, chap. 25. It is not beyond possibility that it would have been preserved, if based on authentic tradition, by some of the brothers who had, according to the account, been caring for the leper.

82. Thus the neurological approach in Moog and Karenberg, "Francis"; cf. accounts in Gardner, "Miracles."

83. See Talbot, *Healing in Byzantium*, e.g., 83–85. For healing forms in the East involving anointing the sick, see also Woolley, *Exorcism*, 69–76.

84. See, e.g, Michael, "Gäbrä-Seyon"; Menberu, "Estifanos."

one.[85] Some have also cited healing claims for reforming groups before Martin Luther, such as the Waldensians and Hussites.[86]

## More Recent Centuries

Christians in the medieval and modern periods continued to embrace these activities of the Spirit.[87] For example, Lidwina of Schiedam (1380–1433), though herself a very sick and disabled woman,[88] spent years on her sickbed praying and fasting.[89] God used her to bring miraculous physical healing to others, even though she herself remained sick.[90]

Documentation is more abundant in recent centuries. In the seventeenth century, for example, Presbyterian Richard Baxter (1615–91) claims his own healing from a sizeable tumor, as well as knowledge of others' healings.[91] Johann Albrecht Bengel (1687–1752) recounts a disabled woman healed suddenly in church in 1644 while the Lutheran pastor expounded the miraculous power of Jesus's name.[92] Hearing reports of Huguenot miracles such as the healing of Mary Maillard in 1693,[93] Cotton Mather in 1696 speculated that miracles, once restrained because of "Apostasy," might now be being renewed in a new "age of miracles."[94] George Fox (1624–91) reports numerous healings, exorcisms, and other divine activity through his

85. Young, "Miracles in History," 112. Thomas wrote the *Book of Governors* ca. 840, concerning the patriarchate of Timothy I (780–823).

86. Boys, *Evidence*, 56–62, 81–85 (for prophetic experiences among Hussites, 77–78); Norman, "Healing"; Young, "Miracles in History," 115–16.

87. Burgess, "Evidence" (esp. 20–26). For hundreds of miracles at the shrine of St. Thomas Becket in Canterbury in the late twelfth century, see Shaw, *Miracles*, 21 (as cited in Billman, *Thread*, 44).

88. Bynum, *Feast*, 124. Lidwina was already ill before she had a serious skating accident, from which she never recovered (125). The accident rendered her paralyzed, except her left hand. She suffered from fever, vomiting, and putrefaction so bad that pieces of her mouth, ears and nose fell off (125).

89. Bynum, *Feast*, 124. According to Bynum, eating was so painful for Lidwina that she stopped eating entirely and lived out her life on a perennial, supernatural fast. Philip of Burgundy sent a guard, who verified her claims of supernatural fasting.

90. One man's leg was healed when he sent for water that was used to wash Lidwina's hands (Bynum, *Feast* 126).

91. Gordon, *Ministry of Healing*, 181–83; Baxter, *Healing*, 86–88; Gardner, *Healing Miracles*, 89–90; briefly, Dod, "Healer," 174; Miller, *Miracle of Healing*, 78–79. Cf. his claims of miracles in Boys, *Evidence*, 241–46.

92. Boys, *Evidence*, 256.

93. Kidd, "Healing," 162; Walsham, "Miracles," 303. On Maillard and other women healed while reading Scripture, see further Shaw, *Miracles*, 119–25 (as noted in Billman, *Thread*, 46).

94. Kidd, "Healing," 162; for some eighteenth-century radical evangelicals who continued to expect a restoration of miracles, see 170.

ministry.[95] Catholic mystic Jeanne Guyon (1648–1717) became known for a gift of healing and began to influence key Protestant thinkers even in her lifetime.[96] Early Moravians reported miraculous healings.[97] English Baptist William Rawlings reported the instant healing of disabled Anne Munnings during prayer in 1705.[98]

John Wesley (in both 1750 and 1762) regarded the evidence of the earlier (as opposed to some later) Jansenist healings as compelling and indeed undeniable "without invalidating all human testimony."[99] Despite the radical Enlightenment's influence on both deism and cessationism in that era,[100] healing claims continued to abound, for example, surrounding Valentine Greatrakes (1628–83)[101] and the Wesleyan revival in Britain and North America;[102] and later Dorothea Trudel in Switzerland (1813–62);[103] and Johann Christoph Blumhardt in Germany (1805–80).[104]

Anabaptists, Quakers, and Pietists all claimed healings.[105] English Baptists cited a dramatic deathbed recovery from this period.[106] Eighteenth-century Moravians also reported miraculous healings;[107] instantaneous miracle cures

95. See Fox, *Works*. For an account that the witnesses understood as a raising, see Fox, *Journal*, 2:227, as cited in Oliver, *Reformations*, 75. On this information's suppression for a time, see Shaw, *Miracles*, 52 (Billman, *Thread*, 41–42).

96. Oliver, *Reformations*, 84–86.

97. Boys, *Evidence*, 301.

98. Shaw, *Miracles*, 46–49 (Billman, *Thread*, 45).

99. Kreiser, *Miracles*, 398 (noting Wesley's anti-Catholic use of the claims, in contrast to the Jansenists themselves, who were French Catholics).

100. See, e.g., Ruthven, *Cessation*, 35–40, 71; cf. MacNutt, *Crime*, 145–52; Noll, *History*, 166.

101. Rose, *Faith Healing*, 41–42; Robertson, "Epidauros to Lourdes," 187–88; he was "rediscovered" by late nineteenth-century healing advocates (Mullin, *Miracles*, 284n30).

102. Rack, "Healing," 145–50; Wesley, *Journal*, September 28, 1739; March 21, 1741; May 10, 1741; March 31, 1742; December 25, 1742; March 17, 1746; November 12, 1746; April 8, 1750; October 12, 1754; September 22, 1956; October 3, 1756; December 26, 1761; October 16, 1778; September 2, 1781; May 23, 1783; May 31, 1785 (Billman, *Thread*, 79–81); Tomkins, *Wesley*, 60, 72, 98, 106; Kelsey, *Healing*, 235; Wigger, *Heaven*, 108; Bowens, *Readings*, 91–92; cf. Mullin, *Miracles*, 89. For the late seventeenth and early eighteenth century, see also Kidd, "Healing" (esp. 162).

103. Mullin, *Miracles*, 89; Kydd, *Healing*, 142–53; Curtis, "Character," 31–32; Hardesty, *Faith Cure*, 17–19.

104. See extensive eyewitness accounts in Ising, *Blumhardt*. Karl Barth criticized Bultmann for uncritically rejecting Blumhardt's stories (Kelsey, *Healing*, 236–37), describing Blumhardt as one of his mentors (Barth, *Letters*, 251); some other German theologians also cite Blumhardt's influence favorably (Moltmann, "Blessing," 149; Heim, *Transformation*, 173–74). For the nineteenth-century healing movement generally, see Alexander, *Healing*, 8–63.

105. Anderson, *Pentecostalism*, 30.

106. See Crosby, *History*, 4:307–9 (referred to me by New Orleans Baptist Theological Seminary professor Lloyd Harsch).

107. So, e.g., Baxter, *Healing*, 77–78. These included healings through prayer of what were believed incurable cancers and tuberculosis (Miller, *Miracle of Healing*, 40).

are especially reported in 1731, several years into the famous revival at Herrnhut. Count Nicolaus Ludwig Zinzendorf accepted such experiences but insisted that they be treated no differently than other gifts occurring among the Moravians.[108] Zinzendorf declared, "At this juncture, various supernatural gifts were manifested in the church, and miraculous cures were wrought. The Brethren and the Sisters believed, in a childlike spirit, what the Savior had said respecting the efficacy of prayer; . . . it was done unto them according to their faith."[109] A general description of the Brethren churches in 1740 says, "There are occasionally observed Apostolic graces, miracles, gifts of seers, etc. They are received in a child-like spirit."[110]

Critics of the First Great Awakening rejected instantaneous healings like those of previously bedridden Mercy Wheeler as Catholic-like superstition.[111] In response, the *Boston Gazette* noted that her healing was "well known and attested."[112] The critic then conceded that the cure was genuine but protested the application of the biblical label "miracle,"[113] despite the obvious similarity to biblical accounts of paralytics' healings (e.g., Mark 2:10–12; Acts 9:33–34). As historian Thomas Kidd observes, "Cessationism was so deeply rooted that evangelicals struggled with how not to call such astonishing experiences miracles."[114]

Wesley supported "gifts of the Spirit" in his day,[115] including healing,[116] miracles, and prophecy.[117] Against the dominant approach of many of his Anglican contemporaries, Wesley complained that he found no biblical warrant for cessationism.[118] Only the church's pursuit of worldly power rather than the gospel and mission, he opined, robbed the church of such blessings.[119] Returning to wholehearted consecration to God would restore the practice of the gifts more widely.[120]

In Wesley's own meetings, people were healed, in one case convincing a skeptical physician who knew the patient in question.[121] Such healings included

108. Snyder, *Signs*, 133.

109. Boys, *Evidence*, 263; "Spiritualism in Church," 7.

110. See "Spiritualism in Church," 6–7; Boys, *Evidence*, 261.

111. Kidd, "Healing," 161; Kidd, *Awakening*, 163.

112. Kidd, "Healing," 162.

113. Kidd, "Healing," 163.

114. Kidd, "Healing," 164. Many considered miracles' only purpose confirming the gospel (initially) rather than considering their benefit (as miracles) to those who were suffering (165).

115. Xhemajli, *Supernatural*, 31, citing Wesley, *Letter to Bishop of Gloucester*, 55.

116. Xhemajli, *Supernatural*, 43, citing Wesley, *Works* (AM), 5:733–34.

117. Xhemajli, *Supernatural*, 43, citing Wesley, *Works* (AM), 5:465, 469, 470.

118. Lawton, *Miracles*, 60–61; Mullin, "Bushnell," 462; Xhemajli, *Supernatural*, 43–44, citing Wesley, *Works* (AM), 5:328, 465–76; Hyatt, *Years*, 103, citing Wesley, *Works*, 8:465.

119. Xhemajli, *Supernatural*, 44, citing Wesley, *Works* (AM), 7:75. He attributed the dearth of "extraordinary gifts of the Spirit" in his day especially to "the fallen state of the church," expecting that renewal would ideally restore such manifestations (Snyder, *Signs*, 216).

120. Xhemajli, *Supernatural*, 45, citing Wesley, *Works* (AM), 5:465, 474.

121. Xhemajli, *Supernatural*, 49, citing Wesley, *Works* (AM), 3:130.

the restoration of sight, healing a cancer, restoring ability to walk,[122] and even an apparent raising from the dead.[123] Wesley affirmed supernatural causation, against his critics, for the often instantaneous healings that occurred in his meetings, emphasizing that many witnesses were available.[124] Wesley also was involved in exorcisms.[125] He further reports nature miracles.[126] His ministry model impacted the circuit riders, who witnessed healings[127] including raisings from the dead,[128] exorcisms,[129] and nature miracles.[130]

Healing claims proliferated still more abundantly in evangelical Holiness and interdenominational circles in the late nineteenth-century United States.[131] Such signs also appeared in Christian movements outside the West in the late nineteenth and early twentieth centuries.[132] For all his skepticism of modern miracles, including "faith healing," even Warfield treats respectfully moderate continuationism advocates Blumhardt, A. J. Gordon, and A. B. Simpson.[133] (For Blumhardt, see the previous chapter.) Besides Baptist minister[134] Gordon, for whom Gordon College and Gordon-Conwell Theological Seminary are

122. Xhemajli, *Supernatural*, 50, citing Wesley, *Journal*, 2:112; *Journal (1773–1790)*, 270; Wesley, *Explanatory Notes*, 138; see also Kelsey, *Healing*, 235; Miller, *Miracle of Healing*, 40–41; Rack, "Healing," 146–47, 149–50; cf. Mullin, *Miracles*, 89.

123. Kidd, "Healing," 159. See Wesley, *Journal*, December 25, 1742; Tomkins, *Wesley*, 106.

124. Hyatt, *Years*, 193, citing Wesley, *Works*, 8:457.

125. Xhemajli, *Supernatural*, 50–51, citing Wesley, *Works* (AM), 3:162, 278, 532, 556; Jennings, *Supernatural Occurrences*, 4–47; Tomkins, *Wesley*, 72.

126. Xhemajli, *Supernatural*, 51, citing Wesley, *Works* (AM), 3:494.

127. Xhemajli, *Supernatural*, 177–82.

128. See Xhemajli, *Supernatural*, 182–84.

129. Rack, "Healing," 147–49.

130. Xhemajli, *Supernatural*, 185–87; Rack, "Healing," 146; cf. Francis Asbury in Wigger, *Saint*, 193.

131. See Chappell, "Healing Movement," 1–86 (esp. 58–86), 192–283; Hardesty, *Faith Cure*, 27–50; Alexander, *Healing*, 18–23; Curtis, *Faith*, 1–12, 64–65, 96–97; Curtis, "Lord for Body"; Curtis, "Houses of Healing"; Opp, *Lord for Body*, 46–47; cf. further Brown, "Tent Meetings"; Baer, "Bodies"; McGee, "Radical Strategy," 74, 90–91.

132. For a Ghanaian respected for healing powers who lived 1834–1917, see Jenkins, "Reindorf"; Nigerian Anglican minister Emmanuel Moses Lijadu was associated with healings, especially during the 1895 influenza epidemic in Nigeria (Kalu, "Lijadu").

133. Warfield, *Counterfeit Miracles*, 159, 195. Regarding Trudel, he notes her illness and early death (184). Not concidentally, Blumhardt, A. J. Gordon, and A. B. Simpson all had some theological training.

134. Some early Baptists seem to have experienced various charismatic gifts (e.g., in records of the Philadelphia association ca. 1743), though by the early twentieth century the majority of Baptists had accepted the arguments of cessationists (Synan, "Charismatics," 185). Kidd, *Awakening*, 246, notes that some Baptists in the mid-eighteenth century reported many signs. Gordon, who was not cessationist, was in the minority (186), though there were many other early exceptions (Free Will Baptists and even many Baptist pioneers in the early Pentecostal movement, 186–88; on some Free Will Baptists speaking in tongues more than a century ago, see also King, "Gifts," 97), and far more Baptists today (Kidd, *Awakening*, 187–92; see the especially thorough study, Weaver, *Baptists and the Spirit*).

named,[135] and Simpson, originally Presbyterian and subsequently founder of Christian & Missionary Alliance,[136] leading figures in the late nineteenth-century healing movement included Presbyterian minister William Boardman,[137] Reformed minister Andrew Murray,[138] and many Methodists.[139]

Even after the rise of the Pentecostal movement, Pentecostal and Holiness testimony did not dominate all accounts of healing in the early twentieth century. Sixteen-year-old Baptist Henrietta Mears, potentially permanently blinded by a pin jabbed into her pupil, was healed when a Presbyterian elder prayed for her. She later went on to become a leading teacher at Hollywood Presbyterian Church and influenced such leaders as Bill Bright and Billy Graham.[140] Modernism led many church leaders to offer purely naturalistic explanations for healings even while miraculous healing remained popular among rank-and-file church people.[141] But some leading Anglican figures, for example, were widely known for their gifts of healings, often including testimonies from eyewitness bishops.[142] For the purposes of this book, it is probably not necessary to recount the abundant healings reported in Pentecostal, Holiness, and charismatic circles, but simply to note that they are hardly isolated.

## Miracles Today

John MacArthur seems incredulous (in his 1992 work) about charismatic claims that "God is raising the dead," even "several times a year."[143] "Surely it is significant, then, that *not one modern occurrence of raising the dead can*

135. Pastor of a prestigious Boston church, Gordon was also a popular speaker, including at the Bible institute of D. L. Moody in Chicago (Barron, *Gospel*, 39); he was a close friend of Moody and sometimes filled in for him at his conferences (Hartley, *Evangelicals*, 23).

136. Founded in 1887, the Christian Alliance was an interdenominational network but merged with Simpson's Evangelical Missionary Alliance in 1897 and became denominational in 1926 (Curtis, "Character," 36).

137. See Dayton, *Roots*, 124–25; Gordon, *Ministry of Healing*, 239–40; Curtis, "Character," 32–33.

138. Le Roux, "Le Roux," 50 (following Sundkler, *Zulu Zion*, 17); Wilkinson, *Healing*, 278–79; Hollenweger, *Pentecostals*, 115–16; Alexander, *Healing*, 23–24; Baer, "Bodies," 129–31; Murray, *Healing*; Murray, "Healing."

139. See Curtis, *Faith*, 8–10, 64–65. For the twin emphasis on holiness and healing in the interdenominational evangelical movement of the late nineteenth century, see, e.g., Curtis, "Character," 38; Dayton, *Roots*, 133–37; Choi, *Rise*, 10, 18–20.

140. Greig, "Purpose," 315–16, citing Roe, *Dream Big*, 68, 100ff.

141. Mullin, *Miracles*, 214–16, 248–49; cf. also modernist theological deemphasis on Jesus's miracles (Mullin, *History*, 206–7, 234; contrasted with Pentecostalism in 211–12).

142. See, e.g., Mews, "Revival"; Kerin, *Touch*; Hickson, *Heal*; Gusmer, *Healing*, 12–13, 46, 112–14; Opp, *Lord for Body*, 150; Maddocks, *Ministry*, 100–101, 107; Mullin, *Miracles*, 237–41.

143. MacArthur, *Chaos*, 109.

*be verified*."[144] We recognize that fabricated or exaggerated accounts exist, but today (as opposed to 1992) there is more than sufficient verification, by any historical or journalistic standards, to recognize that raisings still happen, even if one wishes to dismiss their suspiciously frequent conjunction with prayer as mere coincidence. In chapter 11, I provide some examples that refute this false denial of modern raisings; I enumerate far more in other works.[145]

### Why Cite Nolen Rather Than Casdorph?

While MacArthur cites in detail William Nolen's fairly tendentious critique of miracles associated with Kathryn Kuhlman's ministry,[146] he (clearly tendentiously) completely ignores H. Richard Casdorph's work[147] or that of other physicians who have verified many healings surrounding her ministry.[148] Casdorph's book on healings (most surrounding Kuhlman), although on a popular level (like Nolen's), includes medical documentation, including before-and-after X-rays, unlike Nolen's.[149] That is, Nolen cites many examples of nonhealing, or nonverifiable healing, while ignoring medically verified cases of extraordinary healings. Kuhlman never claimed that everyone was healed. But the cluster of medically documented extraordinary healings around her ministry remains noteworthy.

One Christian journalist complains that Nolen "visited only one miracle service and interviewed only a handful of people who claimed healings." By contrast, Jamie Buckingham (the journalist) claims that he himself interviewed "at least two hundred medically documented cases of miraculous healings."[150] Less graciously, Lawrence Althouse complains that the research

144. MacArthur, *Chaos*, 110.

145. See, e.g., Keener, "Dead Raised"; Keener, *Miracles Today*, 137–74; Keener, *Miracles*, 1:551–79; Keener, "Dead Still Rise"; also Daniel's account in chap. 23 of the present book. For an attempted statistical evaluation of the improbability of the coincidence argument here, see Keener, *Miracles Today*, 174.

146. MacArthur, *Chaos*, 204–8. Kuhlman is lumped with the "sexually immoral" in a comment in the *Cessationist* movie (Lanphere, *Cessationist*). She married a recently divorced man, but after she discovered that his pretenses were false, she chose to live single for the rest of her life (for one academic biography of Kuhlman, see Artman, *Miracle Lady*). John G. Lake, also mentioned in the movie, was a widower who remarried; Smith Wigglesworth, further mentioned, was a widower who remained single but after being accused of flirting with a woman traveled with his daughter to avoid slander. How is the broad brush of immorality against these figures not slander? Does not the same Bible that rightly condemns adultery also rightly condemn slander?

147. Casdorph, *Miracles*.

148. See, e.g., accounts from multiple doctors noted in Spraggett, *Kuhlman*, 12–13, 58–61, 64, 84–90, 111–12, 120; Buckingham, *Daughter*, 185–89; Brown, "Healing Words," 278, 284, 288–89.

149. Some scholars have also cited the evidence in this work as credible evidence for miraculous healing (e.g., Van der Breggen, "Miracle Reports," 382).

150. Buckingham, *Daughter*, 211–12. He claims (212) that Dr. H. Richard Casdorph confronted Nolen "on the *Mike Douglas Show* in Philadelphia in 1975"; Casdorph had medical

in Nolen's widely hailed book "would hardly have been adequate for a college freshman's term paper," since it involved a single visit to one of Kuhlman's services and "a clumsy follow-up on some of the people allegedly cured at that service."[151]

Besides some of the specific accounts surveyed in my (Craig's) books,[152] I more recently learned from a friend the impact one of those healing experiences had on her family. One of the healings Kuhlman featured, though not with the medical documentation needed for my earlier books, was John LeVrier's healing from bone cancer. I add it here only because it illustrates further the long-term impact of one of the healings. LeVrier was my friend's grandfather, and the permanent healing impacted her family deeply.[153] Whatever one thinks of Kuhlman otherwise, a number of people did experience surprising healings in connection with her ministry.

### Global Statistics

So what is happening around the world today? Although the most visible growth has occurred in more recent decades, already in 1981, at one large US seminary with students from many nations, Christiaan De Wet of South Africa wrote a thesis on signs involved in church growth around the world. He surveyed more than 350 theses representing most of the world and interviewed countless missionaries. He complained, "My research has turned up so much material on signs and wonders that are happening and churches that are growing, that it is impossible to use all of it."[154] He noted that miracle claims help drive Christian growth in many parts of the world. Two decades ago, Christian philosopher J. P. Moreland noted a massive growth of evangelical Christianity around the world (possibly even a 1,000 percent increase in three decades), up to 70 percent of it "intimately connected to signs and wonders."[155]

---

records with him to verify the healing of Lisa Larios. Brown, "Healing Words," 281, notes that "Kuhlman's most adamant critics emerged from the religious, rather than the medical establishment."

151. Althouse, *Healing*, 59, complaining that "it is not scientific research" (though we are also less than impressed with some scientific research Althouse cites on other matters).

152. Keener, *Miracles*, 1:459–68; Keener, *Miracles Today*, 72–73.

153. Karen Feaver, personal correspondence, October 27, 2023; cf. Kuhlman, *LeVrier*.

154. De Wet, "Signs," 92. On healings and church growth more generally, see Kwon, "Foundations," 187–90 (based on positive responses from all 562 healing claimants among 604 respondents to his survey). For signs and wonders as a major factor in Majority World evangelism, see also Yung, "Integrity," 173–75. Wagner, "Wonders," 875, notes that signs often bring growth in areas with supernaturalist worldviews. Hausfeld, "Understanding," 74–75, notes (following J. D. Woodberry) that it is a major catalyst for members of another religious tradition deciding to follow Jesus.

155. Moreland, *Triangle*, 166–67; Moreland, "Restoration," 284.

The Pew Forum conducted a ten-country survey of Pentecostals and charismatics and in October 2006 issued a 231-page report.[156] For these ten countries alone, and for Pentecostals and Protestant charismatics in these countries alone, the estimated total of people claiming to have "witnessed divine healings" comes out to somewhere around two hundred million people. What may be more interesting to anticharismatics is the survey's control group category of "other Christians." Somewhere around 39 percent of these "other Christians" in these countries also claim to have "witnessed divine healings." That is, more than one-third of Christians worldwide who do *not* identify themselves as Pentecostal or charismatic claim to have "witnessed divine healings."

Moreover, two decades ago *Business Wire* reported a survey of 1,100 physicians. A majority affirmed their belief that biblical miracle stories are literally (37 percent) or figuratively (50 percent) true; 74 percent believe that miracles happened in the past, and 73 percent that they can happen today.[157] More surprisingly, in the context of such questions, more than half affirm they have witnessed treatment results that they consider miraculous.[158]

### *Getting Non-Christians' Attention for the Gospel*[159]

Meanwhile, experiences with extraordinary healing have convinced millions of *non*-Christians so fully that they have abandoned centuries of ancestral beliefs to follow Jesus. Obviously these converts were not motivated by Christian bias or to make Christianity look good. Certainly they did not claim extraordinary healings merely to undermine Warfield. They live in cultures with their own indigenous healing traditions, yet they regarded the Christian healings as significant enough to change some core practices in their lives and kin groups. They became followers of Jesus often at great social cost or even in the face of persecution.

#### EXAMPLES IN ASIA

For example, Bal Krishna Sharma, principal of Nepal Theological College, shared with me (Craig) that 80 percent of Christian conversions in Nepal are due to healings or deliverance from spirits. Keep in mind that in 1950 we knew of no Christians in Nepal; now there are more than half a million. In a country of fewer than thirty million people, we are therefore speaking

156. "Spirit and Power."

157. "Science or Miracle?" This updates the now defunct link in Craig's earlier works (citing the earlier announcement in *Business Wire*, December 20, 2004, no longer online).

158. "Science or Miracle?" Most doctors have seen "many cases of unusual results," but their premises will determine whether they view these as miracles or as natural anomalies or the like (Gorsuch, "Limits," 296); thus the actual number who have seen what most *believers* in miracles would call miracles would be higher than the self-reporting number.

159. I borrow material here from Keener, *Miracles Today*, 32–33, 135–36.

about a lot of conversions. Sharma himself has some good reason to believe in miracles, since his wife was healed in 1997 of inoperable tuberculosis of the brain, with no lasting effects. Her Hindu doctor remarked, "Your Jesus has healed you."[160]

In China, one source from within the state-authorized church suggests that half of all Christian conversions over a period of two decades in the late twentieth century were due to "faith healing experiences."[161] One rural house church estimate comes closer to 90 percent.[162] Whatever the exact percentage, in China alone we may be talking about *millions* of people becoming Jesus's followers due to healings in his name.

The mass conversion of the Nishi tribal people in northeast India is well documented. One dissertation explains how this movement originally began.[163] A government official's son died. Neither medicine nor sacrifices had helped the boy, but a pharmacist had suggested prayer to Jesus, the Christian God, who had once raised Lazarus. The official laid his hand on his boy's head and promised to worship this Christian God if he would heal his son. The child's eyes opened and he recovered, sparking in this region what eventually became a mass movement toward Jesus.

### SOUTH AMERICA

When I met with Douglass Norwood in 2006, he shared with me his eyewitness experience from twelve years before, also recounted in his dissertation.[164] As he was ministering in then mostly unreached Nickerie, Suriname, many non-Christians gathered at the church—a few of them hostile. One hostile visitor, perhaps in his seventies, had been paralyzed on his right side virtually all his life. Because he could not walk, his friends had brought him on a blanket or rug and plopped him down on the ground in front of Norwood.

"Your religion is garbage!" the angry man shouted. "My religion is garbage too! I've prayed to Shiva, and to Vishnu, and to my other gods, and nothing happens. Now you want me to pray to *Jesus*?"

As he uttered the name Jesus, his paralyzed arm suddenly shot up into the air. He stared at his own arm, shocked. No one had prayed for him, but when he mentioned Jesus, God healed his paralysis. Norwood reports, "At that instant, he jumped up, grabbed my mike, and began screaming, 'Look

160. Bal Krishna Sharma, interview, Bangalore, India, January 13, 2016.

161. Währisch-Oblau, "Make Healthy," 92–93; Oblau, "Healing," 313.

162. Tang, "Yellers," 481; cf. Oblau, "Healing," 313; Aikman, *Jesus in Beijing*, 76, 85, 273–74; Brown, "Introduction," 14; more generally, Oblau, "Pentecostal," 414.

163. Cunville, "Evangelization," 156–57, as cited in De Wet, "Signs," 110–11. For some other more random examples in India, see Iyadurai, *Experience*, 85–100.

164. Norwood, "Colloquium," 24–26; interview, Philadelphia, June 6, 2006; interview, Wynnewood, Pennsylvania, January 14, 2009; further details, personal correspondence, July 15, 19, 20, 22, 2016.

what Jesus did for me!' as he danced around, waving his now-healed arm in the air." The other visitors were converted almost as quickly as he was.

This was the beginning of a movement that, over the next few years, brought tens of thousands of people to faith in Christ, most of whom had previously had little exposure to him. The massive growth of the Christian movement there in recent decades is well known.

### AFRICA

Today thousands of people report being healed of blindness and deafness in Mozambique.[165] Most of these people come from non-Christian backgrounds. Their villages lacked churches, and they knew little about Jesus. Yet they and often their villages became followers of Jesus as they experienced and witnessed these miraculous healings. One missionary told me that she visited this ministry in Mozambique. She was simply preaching in an unchurched village when blind and deaf people began to be healed spontaneously before anyone had prayed for them.[166]

Hearing such reports, a team of American investigators, including both Candy Gunther Brown (a professor at Indiana University) and medical experts, traveled to Mozambique and tested many people in one of these new settings before and after prayer. Their report, published in the September 2010 issue of *Southern Medical Journal*, confirms that people were being healed of blindness and deafness. The results were far beyond any effects documented for psychosomatic cures or hypnotism.[167] Heidi Baker, who holds a British PhD in theology, led the prayers here and in many other villages where healings were reported.

Professor Brown summarizes some of the results also in a provocative online article for the *Huffington Post*.[168] "Two of 11 hearing subjects had thresholds reduced by over 50 dBHL." Another person, reported "as deaf and mute since birth," initially "made no responses to sounds at 100 dBHL." After prayer, however, this person "responded to 60 dBHL tones, imitating sounds in a hoarse, raspy voice. Three of 11 vision subjects improved from 20/400 or worse [legally blind] to 20/80 or better"; one moved from something like 20/8000 to 20/125 after prayer. Again, some critics don't count improvements

165. For deafness, see, e.g., Baker and Baker, *Enough*, 157, 169, 173; Baker and Baker, *Miracles*, 7–8, 39, 43, 78, 108, 114, 163, 172, 180, 183, 192–93; Chevreau, *Turnings*, 142; for blindness, Baker and Baker, *Enough*, 145, 169, 174, 182 (with further accounts of eyes white with blindness changing color as they were being healed, 76, 171–72, 173; Baker and Baker, *Miracles*, 189); Baker and Baker, *Miracles*, 8, 39–40, 68, 78 (often), 108, 113, 159, 160, 192; Chevreau, *Turnings*, 19, 166–67 (partial damage). For the healings of persons both deaf and blind, see Chevreau, *Turnings*, 145, 174, 182.

166. Shelley Hollis, phone interview, January 10, 2009.

167. Brown et al., "Study."

168. Brown, "Testing Prayer." See also Brown, *Testing Prayer*, 207, 219.

as miracles if vision doesn't achieve 20/20 standards. But if it's not a miracle in the sense of special divine action, then try replicating that at home.

Brown provided further evidence in a chapter in her even-handed book *Testing Prayer*, published by Harvard University Press.[169] Her account clearly shows people moving immediately from significant blindness or deafness to significant sight or hearing, immediately after prayer. Such healings have garnered attention for the gospel in village after village, leading to tens of thousands of new believers.

## Conclusion

While individual accounts could be multiplied hundreds of times over, these appear in hundreds of pages in some of our other books, as well as books by Lee Strobel and others.[170] Suffice it to say here that healings, even dramatic ones, continue today. By itself, this observation refutes only hard (Warfieldian) cessationism. Most cessationists today do allow that God often works in dramatic ways for the sake of spreading good news about his Son. Indeed, God does not discriminate against cessationists: God heals people in cessationist churches in response to prayer too.

In some of the above cases, however, we see a pattern of healings or miracles more often around particular persons of prayer, both in history and today. And why not? If God is able to do miracles today, why could he not choose to do them more often around those he has gifted with special faith in this area? Why should gifts like this have stopped in Christ's body?

If you have believed that such gifts have passed, are you sufficiently certain of the strictly exegetical foundation of your view to doubt such accounts? (And based on the exegesis of what passages?) We'll simply leave the question there.

169. See Brown, *Testing Prayer*, 207–9, 214–20, 223–30.

170. E.g., Strobel, *Case for Miracles*; Strobel, *Supernatural*; Garlow and Wall, *Miracles for Real*; Garlow and Wall, *Real Miracles*; Fazzina, *Divine Intervention*; Metaxas, *Miracles*.

# 23

# God of Miracles

As I (Daniel) write this chapter, I sit in a quiet hotel room in the mountainous city of Hosanna, Ethiopia. The room is small and quaint, dimly lit. A cold draft slips through the slightly cracked window, carrying the sounds of the downtown street below—still bustling, even though it's nearly 10 p.m. I sit quietly with a hot drink in hand, reflecting on the wonders I've witnessed this week.

We are here for nine massive evangelistic events, each drawing tens of thousands of people. For two weeks now, I've stood on a platform night after night, proclaiming the gospel, and without fail, God has met us with his healing power. It's not just Ethiopia. In over twenty years of campaigns, I can't recall a single night where someone wasn't healed. This means there is always a fresh testimony to share. In this chapter, I'll recount some of my favorite miracle stories from over the years, but first, let me tell you about one that just happened.

Barely an hour ago, as I was praying for the sick, my eyes were drawn to an elderly woman in the crowd about a hundred meters back. Her head was wrapped in a blue-and-white shawl, her hands pressed firmly to her ears as she prayed earnestly. Moved by the Holy Spirit, I pointed toward her, called her out in front of the thousands gathered, and commanded her ears to open in the name of Jesus. Instantly, she began waving her arms, her face alight with joy.

She pushed through the crowd toward the stage. I went down to meet her, took her by the hand and led her onto the platform. Tears welled in my eyes as her story poured out. For seven long years, she had been deaf in both ears. She had traveled from a remote village just to attend the crusade. When I called out to her, she said her ears immediately popped open. She could hear!

Her joy couldn't be contained. She danced and leaped across the platform, praising God for what he had done.

But she wasn't the only one. Two others were also healed of deafness tonight. One was a former soldier, medically discharged after losing his hearing. He had come to town for banking and saw the crusade advertised. During prayer, his ears opened. Overwhelmed, he made his way to the platform, fell to his knees, and clung to my legs, shaking and weeping. I helped him up and gently reminded him, "It wasn't me. It was Jesus." Many more miracles took place tonight—so many they could easily fill a chapter by themselves.

Each testimony is a gift, a life changed by the power of God. We intentionally cultivate a deep sense of gratitude for each and every one. We never want to take anything God is doing for granted—no matter how big or small it seems to us. And yet there are certain testimonies that stick with you—moments and people you can never forget.

In this chapter, I'll share just a few of those unforgettable moments.[1] Each one is a reminder that we serve a God who sees, who heals, and who loves without limits. My prayer is that these stories will stir your faith and leave you in awe of the God of miracles.

## The First Experience

I want to begin this chapter by sharing a miracle that's forever etched in my heart—special because it was the first time I remember seeing someone obviously healed before my own eyes.

It was July 2007, at one of my first evangelistic crusades. Madurai—"the city of temples"—felt like the Hindu heart of India, with its countless shrines and devotion to stone-carved gods. I lifted up the name of Jesus, night after night, against that backdrop of idolatry, trusting the God of miracles to show himself mighty.

On the second or third night of the crusade, after preaching the gospel, I prayed over the whole crowd for healing. Then I invited those still in need to come forward, and I laid hands on them, one by one.

As I sat on the steps, praying over each person, a man approached with his daughter, a young woman of about sixteen. I recognized her from earlier that night in the crowd—hands raised, voice lifted during the prayer for the sick. I'd heard her cries, guttural and monotone—the unmistakable sound of someone deaf trying to vocalize. Now, she stood before me with a look of desperation.

Without warning, she dropped to the ground, clutching my ankles, sobbing uncontrollably. I gently took her hand. She stood. Both she and her father

1. For some more, see Kolenda, *Impact Africa*.

had small dots on their foreheads, prompting me to ask her father through the interpreter if they were Hindu. He nodded. I explained I would pray for his daughter in the name of Jesus, and he agreed.

I placed my hands on her ears and prayed, then shouted "JESUS!" loudly into one ear. Nothing. Her eyes met mine, wide and filled with a desperation deeper than words. It broke my heart. I felt an overwhelming surge of divine love and compassion.

I prayed again, more earnestly, my hands pressed firmly on her ears. I remember lifting my head and whispering to heaven, "Lord, if you only heal one person tonight, let it be this one."

Then leaning in close, just inches from her left ear, I shouted again, "JESUS!" Her eyes flew open, shock rippling across her face. She turned to her father, communicating in a flurry of sign language. He looked at me, eyes wide with astonishment. Something was happening. He tested her over and over, and with each moment, her hearing seemed to grow stronger. Finally, she broke down, tears streaming. Her father, also weeping, turned to me with a trembling voice and said, "She can hear!"

By this point, much of the crowd had dispersed, so I asked the father and daughter to return the next night to share their testimony.

They came back—not just the two of them, but the mother as well. None bore the traditional marks on their foreheads; the dots were gone. They stood before the crowd and testified that they had been devout Hindus, but now the entire family declared their faith in Christ alone.

## Jean Neil

Whenever I visit the United Kingdom, I look for Jean Neil, bounding toward me with infectious joy and a smile that lights up the room. Despite her age, Jean's Holy Spirit–fueled energy feels supernatural—a testament to God's miraculous power. By all accounts, she should have been confined to a wheelchair for decades, if not for a miracle.

Jean suffered spinal issues after a fall in 1964. Multiple surgeries, including the removal of her coccyx and two laminectomies, failed to relieve her pain. A car accident in 1981 worsened her condition—one leg shortened by two inches, and her hips permanently dislocated.

In 1986, after another injury, Jean was mostly confined to a wheelchair. She endured back pain, heart attacks, angina, bronchitis, and partial blindness from heart medication. The pain sometimes caused her to lose consciousness.

In early 1988, Jean had two vivid dreams. In the first, she died during spinal surgery. The second was different—a man with a foreign accent prayed for people in wheelchairs. When he laid hands on her, she stood up and ran. That dream gave her hope.

The first dream reflected the severity of Jean's situation, as she faced a high-risk spinal surgery that potentially could end her life. The second dream, in contrast, offered hope, showing in her case that her healing would come through a miraculous touch rather than human hands.

On March 12, 1988, Jean attended the Assemblies of God National Youth Rally in Birmingham, UK, where Reinhard Bonnke was the guest speaker. Though she had never seen him, she recognized his voice from her dream. Her husband arranged for her to be transported to the event by ambulance. She sat in her wheelchair on the ground floor.

When Reinhard entered the arena, he noticed Jean, and the Holy Spirit whispered, "That woman will be healed tonight." At the end of the meeting, Reinhard ran to where Jean sat, took her by the hand and said, "You're going to be healed tonight." Jean, full of faith, replied, "I know, I know, I know!"

Reinhard prayed for Jean and commanded her to stand in the name of Jesus. She was standing slowly when she suddenly felt her hips snap into place. Her legs evened out, and her spine straightened. Moments later, Jean wasn't just standing—she was running. The crowd erupted as she raced around the auditorium, arms raised, tears flowing. Reinhard couldn't find her as the crowd pointed in every direction, struggling to keep up with her.

That night, Jean demonstrated her healing on stage—touching her toes, squatting, and running in place, things impossible just hours before. Her husband, John, pushed her now-empty wheelchair in stunned disbelief.

The next day, Jean walked into her doctor's office. Dr. Colin West was astonished. After years of suffering, she was fully healed, with no pain or disability. He called it "unbelievable" and informed the welfare office there was no longer any need to send disability checks.

Dr. Stephen Eisenstein, the back surgeon who had initially planned Jean's risky operation, later wrote after examining her: "This patient returned today to personally demonstrate her complete recovery following a religious evangelical experience several months ago. Upon examination, I found no limitations to her physical ability. She exhibited a full range of painless spinal movement, with no signs of neurological deficit. In front of witnesses, she ran up and down the outpatient clinic and reported no pain. Even applying local pressure to her previously tender spine caused no discomfort."

News of Jean's miraculous healing spread like wildfire, capturing the attention of local and national newspapers with headlines such as "New Life After 'Miracle' Cure," "Crippled Mum's 'Miracle,'" "Miracle Mum's Recovery Baffles Doctors," and "Cure 'Stranger Than Fiction.'" Jean's heart, lungs, and even her eyesight were fully restored. She returned to the very hospital where she had once suffered, this time as a volunteer, serving tea to those who had witnessed her darkest moments. Through it all, Jean gave all the glory to God, boldly proclaiming, "No glory goes to any man."[2]

## Delivered from Demons

It was the summer of 2003 when Nikki brought her boyfriend, CJ, for deliverance. From the moment I saw him, hunched over and barely able to walk, I knew his condition was serious. Torment was etched on his face, a lifetime of drugs, crime, and mental illness having taken its toll. Nikki explained that CJ's descent began early. Exposed to drugs and violence as a child, he spiraled deeper at fifteen after his mother forced him to shoot his beloved dogs. That, he believed, was when demons entered his life.

CJ's world unraveled. Violent episodes, hallucinations, and encounters with demons followed. He cycled in and out of prisons and mental institutions, eventually becoming entangled in organized crime. Diagnosed with schizophrenia and dissociative disorder, he lived in constant fear. One of his many "personalities," Frankie, would torment him often with visions of hell.

That day, after much coaxing, CJ reluctantly came forward. As we began to pray, he manifested violently—thrashing on the floor, foaming at the mouth, hurling obscenities, and sometimes mocking with a dark sinister laugh. I took authority over the spirits and addressed CJ directly, asking if he truly wanted to be free. The internal struggle was palpable, but finally, he chose surrender. I explained the gospel, and as he prayed to accept Christ, the demons fought hard. But after I repeatedly took authority over them, CJ called on the name of Jesus—and was delivered.

In an instant, everything changed. CJ was saved, filled with the Holy Spirit, and set free from the demonic torment that had bound him for years. He described it as being as if scales had fallen from his eyes. For the first time in weeks, he felt hungry. He was miraculously delivered not only from demons but from a crippling addiction to drugs—amphetamines, hallucinogens, cocaine, and more. He was freed from the heavy prescription medications for his mental health, including Thorazine, Zyprexa, and others. His schizophrenia, dissociative disorder, violent psychotic episodes, and seizures all ceased. (We do not believe that these conditions always stem from demons. But they apparently did in his case.)

His deliverance was immediate, but his walk with Christ took time. Over the years, I watched as CJ transformed. I officiated his wedding to Nikki and saw him quit smoking; eventually, he became a pastor. Twenty-two years later, as of this writing, CJ remains delivered, drug-free, and a devoted husband, father, and grandfather.

2. International School of Ministry, "Shout" (at 11:03); Bonnke, *Life of Fire*, chap. 29.

## The Truth Shall Set You Free

Independence Square in Accra, Ghana, known for hosting the nation's major events, was packed. Yet on this night, the crowd had come not for politics but to hear the gospel and witness God's power in action.

In the crowd stood a man named Muhammad. As you might guess from his name, he did not come from a Christian background and he would have had no interest in a gospel crusade. His presence was accidental. He'd missed his train home and, with time to kill, wandered into the square, drawn by the lights and the crowd—but he couldn't hear a word. Muhammad was deaf.

He found an isolated spot in the bleachers and lay down to rest. Suddenly, an explosion of sound. He shot up, disoriented, as the world filled with noise—the roar of the crowd, my voice proclaiming the name of Jesus.

He stumbled to his feet, trembling with awe and confusion, and moved toward the stage. After hearing his story, my team brought him up to me. There he stood, before the massive crowd, shaking, his voice trembling as he tried to explain the unexplainable.

"I was deaf before," he said, his words halting with emotion. "When somebody called me, I had to be hit because I couldn't hear. I spent a lot of money on medicine for my ears. Saturday morning, I came to Accra to visit my brothers. After visiting them, I was heading back to Tema, but it was late, and the train left, so I just went and slept at this place."

With a look of shock he continued. "I did not even pray. I didn't do anything. I just woke up, and I could hear."

The crowd erupted in awe, witnessing the transformation of a man stepping from darkness into light. Muhammad, with new clarity in his voice, declared, "I am standing here. I can hear, I can speak again. I think Jesus is . . . I think Jesus is God."

I looked him in the eyes, seeing the wonder etched into his expression. "Do you know who has healed you?" I asked.

"It's the messenger of the Lord, Almighty God," he said, still grappling with what he had just experienced.

"What's his name?" I pressed, knowing the answer would shift his life forever.

"Jesus," he replied, his voice steady with conviction.

Seizing the moment, I interjected, "No one else opens the ears of the deaf—only Jesus! He is not just a messenger. He is the Son of the living God. He is the way, the truth, and the life!"

Facing the cameras broadcasting live across the nation, Muhammad, with newfound boldness, pleaded: "If anyone recognizes me, please go and tell my wife that Jesus is the Son of God."

Later, with steady resolve, Muhammad declared, "I am now a Christian. I believe that Jesus is the only one person that man is supposed to worship.

If I have the opportunity, I could become a pastor, or I'll be preaching in the street. When you know the truth, the truth shall set you free."

## Raised from the Dead

On the first Sunday of December 2001, tension filled the city of Onitsha. Inside Grace Cathedral, thousands gathered to hear Bonnke preach, unaware that something miraculous was unfolding just below their feet.

Two days earlier, on November 30, Daniel Ekechukwu had been declared dead after a horrific car accident crushed his chest. His body had even been partially embalmed at Ikeduru General Hospital. But Daniel's wife, Nneka, refused to accept this finality. Her faith defied reason—and death itself.

Convinced that if she could get Daniel's body to Reinhard, her husband would live again, Nneka set out to make the impossible happen. That weekend, Reinhard was in Onitsha for the dedication of Grace Cathedral, and Nneka believed this was the place for her miracle.

When the ambulance arrived at the church, guards at the gate were skeptical. A dead body? In a church? The story sounded absurd, but Nneka wouldn't give up. Clinging to the promise of Hebrews 11:35—"Women received their dead raised to life again"—she pressed forward.

Reluctantly, the guards allowed the coffin inside, but only to the basement. Below the sanctuary, where Reinhard preached above, Daniel's body was laid out on two wooden tables.

The prayers began quietly. A few believers gathered around Daniel's cold, lifeless body, their hands trembling as they prayed. The minutes dragged on, the prayers grew louder—more desperate. And then, a flicker of movement. A twitch, a tremor.

Daniel's chest rose, slowly, then fell again. Silence filled the room. He breathed again. Whispers of "He's breathing" spread like wildfire. Even the guards, who had stood back with disbelief, rushed in. One of them, a Muslim security chief, leaned in close. He felt it—the faint exhale of breath from the man who had been dead for two days.

Above, Reinhard finished his sermon, unaware of what had just occurred beneath him. Later, in the pastor's office, Pastor Paul entered, pale and shaken. "The man who was dead . . . is now breathing," he said.

By the next morning, the news spread like wildfire across Nigeria. Headlines screamed, "Bonnke Raises Man from the Dead!" It wasn't accurate—Reinhard hadn't even prayed for the man—but the impact was undeniable.

Later that day, at the airport, the police chief approached Reinhard, still visibly shaken. "Sir, I am a Muslim," he confessed. "I have never seen such a thing. When they brought the corpse to the church, I made them take it out of the coffin to inspect for explosives. The body was stiff with rigor mortis. I pulled wads of cotton from the man's nostrils myself. Now, he is breathing."

Reinhard, stunned, called our film producer, Robert Murphree, and asked him to investigate every angle of the story. The result was the documentary *Raised from the Dead*, capturing the astonishing testimony.[3]

## Faith by Hearing

For twenty-five long years, Amina endured relentless pain that consumed her life. The pain radiated through her legs and back. Once a proud restaurant owner, her illness forced her to give up everything. As the pain worsened, her family tried to help but eventually abandoned her, leaving her isolated and hopeless. "I lost everything," she said. "My husband took me to countless doctors, but none could help. We spent all our money searching for answers, but nothing worked." She described her life as living under a curse.

Desperate for relief, Amina searched for help wherever she could. She tried different religions and sought healing from pastors, priests, doctors, and even Muslim leaders. Nothing worked. Her search took her to a dark place when she encountered a witch doctor, who performed bizarre rituals and smeared her with mud, all to no avail. But during one of these strange encounters, something unexpected happened. A man dressed in white appeared to her in a vision and spoke words she would never forget: "No one can heal you but me." He introduced himself as Jesus. At the time, she barely knew who Jesus was. A friend who was a believer invited her to a prayer meeting at church, and although Amina felt something different, the pain never left her. She was still lost, still confused.

That all changed one evening, during our crusade. The entire service was being broadcast over the radio, and by chance—or more accurately, by divine appointment—Amina turned it on that night. As I began to pray, I invited everyone listening to place their hands on the part of their body where they needed healing. Amina, alone in her home, reached out in faith. She placed one hand on her leg and the other on the radio.

Then it happened.

She later described the moment to me: "I remember the exact feeling that went through my body when you prayed. It was something I'd never experienced before—it was real." For the first time in twenty-five years, Amina stood up without pain. She was healed, walking around completely free from the agony that had gripped her for so long. "I knew in that moment," she said, "that Jesus must be real. The pain was completely gone."

3. Bonnke, *Raised*.

When we interviewed Amina, she admitted that, although she believed Jesus had healed her, she hadn't yet accepted him as her Savior. That day, we had the honor of leading her in a prayer of salvation. "I've tried many different religions," she said, "but nothing is as real as Jesus Christ. I am so happy. I'm no longer lost but I am found."[4]

## A "Great" Miracle

It was the fourth night of our crusade in Sapele, Nigeria, in December 2009. Over two hundred thousand people had gathered beneath the open African sky. Somewhere in the vast crowd, a mother held the hand of her three-year-old son named Great, clinging to hope for a miracle.

As worship filled the air, a desperate cry rang out: "Great, Great!" Her son had collapsed, his small body limp and still. His mother fell to her knees, frantic, shaking him, calling his name—but there was no breath, no pulse. Horror set in as she realized the worst. Her son was gone.

With trembling hands and faith that defied fear, she gathered her son's lifeless body and pushed through the crowd. Her only hope was Jesus. She moved toward the platform, hoping for prayer. But the well-meaning security team, unaware of the gravity of the situation, directed her toward the medical tent on site. There, the doctors confirmed her nightmare—her son was dead.

But this mother's faith didn't falter. Instead of turning away, she held her son tighter and made her way back to the stage, every step a prayer, every breath a cry to Jesus, the only one who could do the impossible.

A local pastor, part of the usher team, heard her desperate cries. Moved by her anguish, he checked the child himself—no signs of life. With a heavy heart, he did what he could. He led her behind the barriers, placing her near the stairs, hoping I would see her after the service.

As the service ended and I made my way to the car, I noticed her—eyes swollen from tears, holding a small, lifeless child in her arms. Though I didn't know the details, it was clear she was desperate and her child needed prayer.

I pushed through the guards and placed my hand on the boy. The scene was chaotic. I could barely hear the mother's tearful plea, but I didn't need to. I prayed to the one who knows everything. As I touched him, I sensed how dire the situation was. His body was limp and unresponsive. My prayer was brief, no more than thirty seconds. I said goodbye to the mother and left, not realizing the gravity of what had happened. It wasn't until the next morning that I learned more—that the boy had been declared dead by the medical team and local pastors. But there was still no word on the outcome.

4. Kolenda, "Instantly," at 2:30.

That evening, as I arrived at the field, John Darku, our event organizer, approached with a sparkle in his eye. "Daniel, I have a surprise for you. Remember the boy you prayed for last night?" He led me behind the platform, and there he was—Great was alive and well, running around, full of life. Not only had he come back to life, but the illness that had taken him was gone.

A few moments later, I stood on stage with the boy, his mother, and a pastor who had witnessed everything. The mother, voice trembling, recounted her agony and how she had cried out to Jesus. She spoke of her son's miraculous resurrection after that simple prayer.

The crowd erupted. Whispers of the miracle had already begun circulating through the city—people had been talking all day, but now, hearing it firsthand, they went wild. The atmosphere was electric.

I turned to the mother and asked, "Who raised your son from the dead?" Her answer was immediate and full of faith: "Jesus Christ." Her declaration rippled through the crowd like a wave.

"What's his name?" I shouted to the crowd. They responded in unison like thunder, "Jesus!"

## A Heavenly Blood Transfusion

Kafanchan, Nigeria, is a city that stays with me—not because of the relentless rain but because of the people's hunger for God. Despite the weather, they stood firm, refusing to leave. One night, after praying for the sick, I was on the platform interviewing those who had received healing when I felt an irresistible prompting from the Holy Spirit. It was clear: I needed to pray again—specifically for those suffering from HIV/AIDS.

I stopped the interviews and turned back to the crowd, telling them what I sensed from the Lord. I began to pray, commanding HIV-positive to turn into HIV-negative in the name of Jesus.

In the crowd, a young man stood with hope rising in his heart. He was in the final stages of AIDS, with doctors giving him only a short time to live. As I prayed, the power of God struck him, and he collapsed to the ground, unconscious. When the service ended, he got up and went home.

That night, he had an extraordinary dream. Jesus appeared to him, telling him he was healed. The next morning, filled with hope from the dream, the young man went to his doctor and requested a new blood test.

Later that evening, he returned to the crusade, holding his doctor's report high above his head. I took the paper from him and read it aloud to the crowd of over 220,000 people. The words were unmistakable: HIV-negative! The young man had been miraculously healed.

## David Attah

If you met my friend David Attah, you could never imagine what he's been through. David, a former Muslim, was struck by a drunk driver while walking to class at Nigeria State University, suffering severe injuries that left him unconscious for days. When he awoke, he was confined to a hospital bed, his body shattered. Diagnosed with aphasia, he was now mute. His once bright future seemed to crumble before him. The friends who had once crowded around him disappeared.

Days turned into weeks, and his medical bills piled up. With no family to support him and no friends to count on, David was left destitute. He received a permit from the government to beg for a living. He sold what little he owned, but even that wasn't enough. Despair settled in, and the weight of his isolation became unbearable. One night, David decided he had endured enough. Writing a final note, he explained his decision and prepared to take his own life with a lethal dose of poison.

But before he could follow through, an unexpected visitor interrupted his plans. Rita, a nursing student, had seen David's story on television and felt compelled to meet him. She entered his hospital room, her gentle demeanor and kind eyes instantly drawing David's attention. She saw the note he had written and read it, her face filling with alarm. "You must never do this," she told him firmly, her voice filled with conviction. She spoke to him about the value of life, pleading with him to reconsider. Then, with astonishing boldness, she made him a promise: If he vowed not to take his life, she would stand by him as a true friend, no matter what. David agreed.

Eight long years later, Christ for all Nations came to Makurdi, Nigeria. With Rita's encouragement, David decided to attend, though his faith was hanging by a thread. This was his last attempt at seeking a miracle, his final hope for healing.

On the second night of the crusade, David stood on the outskirts of a crowd of hundreds of thousands feeling invisible among the masses. When Reinhard Bonnke prayed for the sick, David felt a powerful light surround him, and a hand touched the back of his head. In an instant, he collapsed to the ground. When he stood up, the words he had longed to speak for eight years finally broke free: "Jesus." Over and over, David repeated the name, tears streaming down his face. His voice, once silenced by injury, was restored by the power of God.

David's healing marked the beginning of a new chapter. Reinhard personally supported him through university where he earned a degree in communication. He and Rita, who had stood by him through it all, became engaged. Together, they now travel, sharing their incredible story of faith, healing, and the unfailing love of God. David's voice, once lost, is now a powerful testimony to the God of miracles.[5]

5. Bonnke, *Life of Fire*, chap. 38.

## My Favorite Modern Miracle

This final story stands apart from the others. It carries deep personal significance, and you'll soon understand why.

Paul was born in Germany in 1892, gravely ill from the start. His head was large and misshapen, baffling doctors and causing deep distress for his parents, Ludwig and Emilie. What we now call hydranencephaly, a rare condition where fluid replaces brain tissue, was then a mystery with a grim prognosis. Doctors had little hope for Paul's survival and warned that, even if he lived, his life would be marked by severe limitations.

At just two years old, Paul faced another life-threatening battle—typhoid. His small body burned with fever and convulsed violently. He grew so frail, he was carried on a pillow, too weak to cry. The doctors offered Emilie cold comfort: "Let him go. You're young—you can have more children." Family gathered to say their goodbyes, convinced the end was near.

Ludwig felt a deep stirring, an unshakable belief that Paul's story wasn't over. He retreated to his room and knelt in fervent prayer. "Lord, I asked you for this boy," he cried. "You gave him to me. If you must take him, speak to me."

As he poured out his heart, a knock came at the door. Paul's grandmother brought the dreaded news: Paul had died. Ludwig's heart broke, but his faith held firm. "I will not leave this room until I hear from heaven," he declared, unmoved by the pleas of his family, determined to hear from God.

In the next room, Paul's body lay still, prepared for burial, a sheet over his face. Then, something incredible happened. Ludwig, filled with fresh determination, entered the room, eyes ablaze with faith. He laid his hand on Paul's cold forehead and prayed with fierce conviction, thanking God for hearing him.

Suddenly, Paul's grandmother, standing nearby, placed her hand on Paul's knees and exclaimed, "He's getting warm!" The family rushed in, massaging warmth back into his lifeless limbs. Slowly, the coldness retreated—first from his legs, then his chest, and finally his arms. Paul's eyes flickered open, and in a faint voice, he whispered, "Momma, I'm hungry."

The room erupted in joy and disbelief. But the miracle didn't stop there. The typhoid fever disappeared without a trace, and Paul's misshapen head began to return to normal. His strength came back quickly, and within weeks, the boy who had been given no hope made a full recovery.

Paul lived a long, healthy life. He became the father of ten sons who became preachers. Over one hundred of Paul's children, grandchildren, and great-grandchildren went on to become missionaries, pastors, and evangelists—and I am one of them. Paul is my great-grandfather.

As I mentioned, Paul's resurrection holds deep personal significance. If Jesus hadn't raised him from the dead, I wouldn't be here to share any of these stories.

Paul's resurrection wasn't just about saving one life; it birthed an entire legacy. Through him, countless lives were impacted. It's a powerful reminder that when the God of miracles intervenes, it ripples through time and eternity.

# Conclusion

Why have we devoted so much precious time and effort to address cessationism? It is not because cessationism, as a theological position, is a force to be reckoned with. On the contrary, as I (Daniel) travel around the world, I rarely encounter cessationists. Cessationism is a totally failed and falsified theory. It never had a biblical leg to stand on. Now, given the massive modern outpouring of the Holy Spirit around the world, even its feeble empirical argument, like that championed by B. B. Warfield, has been widely discredited. It is in many ways a powerful illustration of why we must base our theology on the Word of God, not our experience.

In his book about cessationism, Samuel Waldron says, "To my continuationist friends who read this book, let me admit that I fear you have already defeated us cessationists in the propaganda battle."[1] Waldron seems to realize the obvious: He is on the losing side of the argument. But it has absolutely nothing to do with propaganda. Charismatics are not an organized movement working in lockstep to peddle a continuationist agenda around the world. We are just a bunch of normal Christians, from all different denominations, backgrounds, races, nations, and languages, who have read the Bible, believed what it said, and experienced its promises. There is no conspiracy; only an organic connection. And this is actually a powerful testimony to the divine origins of charismatic experience. Without any earthly leader, headquarters, organization, unified doctrinal position, or agenda, the Christian movement that has welcomed spiritual gifts has so far eclipsed every other movement in the history of religion. Everywhere Christianity is thriving around the world, you will find Spirit-filled people, experiencing the gifts and power of the Holy Spirit. "*This is that* which was spoken by the prophet Joel . . ." (Acts 2:16).

1. Waldron, *Continued*, 14.

## An Appeal

This is not to say that today's charismatic movement does not need help. That Scripture teaches that gifts should remain today does not endorse the way everyone practices them. False teaching and imbalanced emphases have distorted some segments of the movement, especially where the gospel has not remained central. Solid teaching has trouble keeping up with evangelism, a problem further exacerbated by rapid population growth around the world.[2] R. T. Kendall and others rightly point out that we need to bring together the Spirit with the Word that the Spirit has already and definitively inspired. Kendall looks beyond the current state of the charismatic movement for a more balanced outpouring that brings both together.[3]

Because cessationists often focus on Scripture exposition of the texts that they do allow are for today, they can make valuable contributions to charismatics regarding those parts of Scripture. After all, the early Pentecostal figure Smith Wigglesworth is said to have prophesied a future revival that would bring together Word and Spirit.[4] With enough persevering mutual service, and humbly learning from one another in our respective areas of strength, perhaps we can yet witness Pentecostal emphasis on the Spirit combine with evangelical emphasis on the Word.[5]

There are some people who will not change their predetermined positions no matter how much evidence they see. I know that nothing I (Daniel) say will matter to these individuals. But I have taken time to write these apologetic chapters for those who are sincere and open yet still have honest questions. Maybe they were born into a denomination that taught against the continuation of particular gifts. Maybe some of their favorite theologians and Bible teachers are cessationist. Maybe they have seen and heard strange things in the charismatic movement that they didn't understand (or that they recognize as errors). Maybe they have been burned by someone's misuse of spiritual gifts. Or maybe they've just developed a disdain for the less cerebral, more emotional side of the charismatic world.

And yet, despite their reservations, they are hungry for more. They know that God has more to offer than services, sermons, liturgy, and beautiful

2. Many cessationist critics do not have the problem of teaching being unable to keep up with evangelism because they are not evangelizing millions of people. The Pentecostal denomination Assemblies of God alone reportedly starts an average of fifty new churches in Africa *every day* ("Africa Claims Share"). Still, it also hosts nearly three thousand Bible schools and seminaries worldwide (Assemblies of God World Missions, "Vital Stats").

3. Kendall, *Receiving Promise*.

4. See Stormont, *Wigglesworth*, 114. Stormont personally knew Wigglesworth, who himself read only the Bible (a Bible now held by Canon Andrew White).

5. Classical Pentecostals shared conservative Protestants' "high view of Scripture," offering natural connections (Oliverio, *Hermeneutics*, 83); they also emerged from a Holiness-evangelical matrix (as is often emphasized, esp. since Synan, *Movement*).

buildings. They have a longing for more than philosophies, theories, and doctrines. They want to know God by direct experience. These are the ones for whom I have written in this book. The Scriptures are clear, the historical record is clear, and even common sense dictates that the Holy Spirit—with all of his wonderful gifts, mighty power, and mysterious ways—has not changed. All of his wonders are for all of us today.

## Continuationism as Heresy

As this book opened with a tongue-in-cheek presentation of a heretical version of cessationism, we close with a tongue-in-cheek presentation of a heretical version of continuationism.

- It is surely heretical to say that Jesus continues to die and rise.
- It is surely heretical (even if we could persuade Bible publishers, despite their cost considerations) to say that we have new revelatory books to add to the Bible.
- It is surely heretical, or at least biologically dubious and morally dangerous, to suggest that virgin births continue.
- It is surely heretical, or at least very weird, to say that the twelve original apostles continue in apostolic ministry today. Dependent as we are on their legacy, those twelve apostles are dead. Sorry to say it, but for now, on earth, the original Twelve have *ceased*.

Jesus came once, and that is the centerpiece of history, the climax of God's saving acts that we proclaim. His work, however, goes on, so long as this world remains. That is, we are genuinely *all* cessationists on some points, such as the incarnation and virgin birth. But those involve Jesus's once-for-all saving event in history, not the continuing church or its ongoing mission in the world.

Beyond tongue-in-cheek, however, there are plenty of charismatic errors just as there are plenty of cessationist ones. These come through false teachings (i.e., false doctrines) as well as through false prophecies (i.e., usually false guidance or encouragement). Some charismatic speakers, especially those needing to market themselves as distinctive, always strive to have something new to say, and instead of basing it on solid understanding of Scripture, they risk introducing new doctrines based on "revelations." Scripture, understood in its original context the way God gave it, provides our basis for doctrine. The Spirit guides us in how to apply that message and serve people's needs. Although one might need to always say something "new" (cf. Acts 17:21) to survive, or thrive, online or even in academia, we should be driven instead by speaking God's truth.

Some charismatics also risk missing the forest for the trees. The Spirit's activity pervades our lives, but this is not only in the area of *charismata*. The Spirit gives us gifts to minister to one another, but the Spirit also produces in us moral fruit (Gal. 5:16–23). The Spirit empowers us for evangelism. It is possible to turn our eyes from the giver to the gift, and when that happens, we miss the most important point. This book focuses on the continuation of spiritual gifts because we respond to critics who challenge their continuation. But as Christians, all of us should welcome all the Spirit's work, empowering us for new life, for evangelism, and for our ministry to one another's needs.

The gracious cessationist scholar Tom Schreiner ends his book on spiritual gifts this way, echoing 1 Corinthians 13:1–3: "If I have the right view of spiritual gifts, but I don't have love, then I am nothing."[6] Should a pair of charismatics affirm any less? May we always love our brothers and sisters in Christ, regardless of theological differences. God's power and gifts are for today, and so is his fruit. May we always learn better and better how to walk in them.

## In Practice

Recognizing that all the gifts are for today does not imply that we force them on churches that don't feel ready for some of them; gifts are meant to build up Christ's body, not to tear it down. I (Craig) served for many years as an associate minister in several African American Baptist churches that were not accustomed to gifts such as prophecy or tongues in their services. The senior pastors were all continuationists, however; again, people do not become cessationists simply by studying the Bible. I taught the Bible regularly and taught about such spiritual gifts only rarely (probably less than 1 percent of the time), given the many other issues confronting these churches. Nevertheless, we were clear on what the Bible said when we did discuss it, and over time people became more open to such gifts.

While the gifts have not ceased, culture and resources have changed. Whereas "you can all prophesy one by one" (1 Cor. 14:31) in a first-century house church or a modern small group, this is hardly possible in a megachurch of thousands. Yet the interpersonal needs met in those early house churches remain today. The church is not a building but the body of Christ, so it involves relationships and ways that we can serve one another. That means that even a megachurch should make available home groups (Acts 2:46) where people can build relationships and reach others in their community who might not visit a church service. In such a setting we can minister to one another as we

6. Schreiner, *Spiritual Gifts*, 172.

pray for healing, for hearing what the Lord might be saying to some of his people, and as we share Scripture, songs (1 Cor. 14:26), food, and resources for concrete financial needs when we are able (Acts 2:42, 44–45). All this can stay on track, of course, only insofar as we remain submitted to Scripture and to Christ's commands to humbly love one another and make him known to the world.

Rather than adding an extrabiblical phase without spiritual gifts to the New Testament message of the new-covenant experience of the Spirit, cessationists should recognize that God continues to bless his universal church with the full range of biblical gifts. But this admonition also applies to charismatics, who sometimes settle for mere tokens (and sometimes counterfeits) of such gifts rather than embracing the full biblical picture in faith. Not only in terms of *charismata* but in everything, may the whole body of Christ pursue, in utter dependence, God's biblical invitations rather than simply justifying our current spiritual and moral conditions.

These are ideals, and not everyone will get on board with them. But a first step toward such ideals is recognizing that God still answers prayer (as all of us agree) and still grants, as he chooses, the full range of gifts to Christ's body. Paul is clear that we need gifts such as prophecy to build up Christ's body (1 Cor. 14:3–5, 12, 26; Eph. 4:11–12, 16), which suggests that those opposing such gifts risk tearing down Christ's body.

## Needing More Generous Dialogue

Different parts of Christ's body need each other. Michael Brown views cessationism as "a false and unbiblical teaching" but emphasizes that he would not use this understanding to justify calling "the countless thousands of godly cessationist leaders 'false teachers.'"[7] Brown cites as a positive example Daniel Wallace, a cessationist who nevertheless recognized his need for a deeper spiritual dependence on the Spirit like charismatics emphasize.[8] Wallace is also a valued and supportive friend of myself (Craig), of Sam Storms, and of other continuationist scholars.

Brown also issues a plea for cooperation, since "the eye can't tell the hand, 'I don't need you!' Nor can the head say to the feet, 'I don't need you!'" (1 Cor. 12:21).[9] Cessationists' propensity for questioning makes "them virtually immune to these carnal fund-raising schemes," but it can render them prey to "cynicism when wrongly used." Charismatics, conversely, "tend to be people of vibrant faith, ready to step out in obedience when they sense the Spirit at

7. Brown, *Authentic Fire*, 242.
8. Brown, *Authentic Fire*, 272, citing Wallace, *Who's Afraid*, Kindle locations 162–81.
9. Brown, *Authentic Fire*, 264.

work," but their positive readiness to trust, "when rightly used, is the same thing that allows them to be so ridiculously gullible, when wrongly used."[10]

In other words, we can help each other. If we humble ourselves instead of taking pride in our respective gifts (Rom. 12:3 with 12:4–8), we can each contribute to building up our Lord's body.

## A Future Without Cessationism?

When I (Craig) wrote two books about miracles, they challenged not moderate cessationism but antisupernaturalism and skepticism about the Bible's miracle claims. In this book, by contrast, Daniel and I have directly challenged cessationism. But when Christians in India and Indonesia have asked me to teach about miracles, I have quickly discovered that their interest was not in whether God does miracles but rather how to distinguish real miracles from fake or demonic ones.

Perhaps a day will come when a book like this one is unnecessary. This is already the case in many parts of the world. Without concern for throwing out the baby with the bathwater, we can get back to the biblical mandate of discerning the true from the false, while maintaining the biblical practice of pastoral sensitivity. Former cessationists can join with current continuationists, deploying biblical acumen to understand and use gifts most rightly. We can also get on with the biblical business of building up the church through all its gifted members (Eph. 4:11–13), together reaching the unreached with Jesus's good news, a message that God attests with signs, and continuing to look forward to the day when we won't need our present gifts anymore—because we shall see our Lord and Savior Jesus Christ face-to-face.

## Recommended Reading

Brown, Michael L. *Authentic Fire: A Response to John MacArthur's Strange Fire.* Excel, 2013.

Deere, Jack S. *Why I Am Still Surprised by the Power of the Spirit.* Zondervan Reflective, 2020.

Fee, Gordon D. *God's Empowering Presence: The Holy Spirit in the Letters of Paul.* Hendrickson, 1994.

———. *Paul, the Spirit, and the People of God.* 1996. Repackaged with a new foreword, Baker Academic, 2023.

10. Brown, *Authentic Fire*, 261–62.

Graves, Robert W., ed. *The Kingdom Case Against Cessationisn: Embracing the Power of the Kingdom*. Foundation for Pentecostal Scholarship, 2022.

———, ed. *Strangers to Fire: When Tradition Trumps Scripture*. Foundation for Pentecostal Scholarship, 2014.

Grudem, Wayne A., ed. *Are Miraculous Gifts for Today? Four Views*. Zondervan, 2011.

———. *The Gift of Prophecy in the New Testament and Today*. Crossway, 2000.

Keener, Craig S. *Gift & Giver: The Holy Spirit for Today*. Baker Academic, 2001. Repackaged with a new afterword in 2020.

Kendall, R. T. *Holy Fire*. Charisma House, 2014.

King, Paul L. *Moving Mountains: Lessons in Bold Faith from Great Evangelical Leaders*. Chosen, 2004.

Ruthven, Jon Mark. *On the Cessation of the Charismata: The Protestant Polemic on Post-Biblical Miracles*. Rev. ed. Word & Spirit Monograph 1. Word & Spirit, 2011.

Storms, Sam. *Understanding Spiritual Gifts: A Comprehensive Guide*. Zondervan Reflective, 2020.

Appendix 1

# The Value of Narrative for Theology

The case for continuationism is by no means limited to biblical narratives; it is in fact strongest in Paul's letters and in Peter's preaching in Acts 2. Nevertheless, because many cessationists do question the nature of theology in some biblical narratives where we also find continuationism, it is worth considering here.

While rabbinic Judaism required halakic arguments to rest on direct teachings of the Torah to be fully persuasive, Jesus reasoned also from biblical narratives (e.g., Mark 2:25–26).[1]

## *All* Scripture Is Inspired and Useful Today

Some critics today believe that biblical narratives teach us only about God's actions but do not provide models for our responses to God. They rightly argue that these texts teach us the history about how God saved us, but they may demur from seeing them as providing examples for our faith. They may suggest that one should find in narrative only what is plainly taught in "clearer," more "didactic" portions of Scripture. Yet in practice this understanding

---

Much of this appendix follows and adapts material from the following: Keener, *Gift & Giver*, 209–12; Keener, *Spirit Hermeneutics*, 22–24, 166–67, 311n11.

1. Cf. Cohn-Sherbok, "Analysis." Nevertheless, rabbis could cite narrative as a secondary support (see *b. Yoma* 83b, bar., using 1 Sam. 14:29, in Strack and Billerbeck, *Commentary*, 111). For the important value of narratives for precedent, see, e.g., Keener, *Spirit Hermeneutics*, 22–24, 166–67, 200, 252–55.

jeopardizes the doctrine of biblical inspiration. Did Paul not say that *all* Scripture was inspired and therefore useful for "doctrine," or teaching (2 Tim. 3:16)?

If Scripture teaches that we are in the era of the outpoured prophetic Spirit (Acts 2:17–18), should not the narratives in Acts help illustrate what this empowerment can look like in practice?

The fact that our traditional method of extracting doctrine from Scripture does not work well on narrative does not mean that Bible stories do not send clear messages. Instead, it suggests that the way we apply our traditional method of interpretation is inadequate because we are ignoring too much of God's Word. Because biblical narratives contain patterns of the ways that God worked in some circumstances, we can learn from these patterns.[2]

When Jesus's followers were writing the New Testament, everyone understood that narrative conveyed moral principles. Ancient biographers and historians expected readers to draw lessons (moral, political, or theological) from their examples, whether positive or negative.[3] In antiquity, students regularly recited stories of important persons in elementary school exercises, and in more advanced levels of education they learned how to apply these examples to drive home moral points.

Using only nonnarrative portions of the Bible to interpret narrative is not only disrespectful to the narrative portions, but it also suggests a misguided approach to nonnarrative parts of the Bible. Everyone acknowledges, for instance, that Paul's letters are "occasional" documents—that is, they address specific occasions or situations. Thus, had the Lord's Supper not been a matter of controversy in Corinth, we would know little about it except from Matthew, Mark, and Luke. If we then were to interpret the narrative portions of Scripture only by other portions, we might assume (if we lacked the one New Testament letter that addresses it) that we do not need to still observe the Lord's Supper today.

Of course, Jesus teaches his disciples about the Lord's Supper within the narrative. But since the teaching is within the narrative, we could protest, to be consistent with the way that many treat some other New Testament promises (e.g., Mark 11:22–24; John 14:12; 16:13), that he was addressing only his first disciples. A few hundred years ago Protestants explained away the Great Commission in just such a manner. Today, many similarly explain away teachings found in the Gospels and Acts about the usefulness of signs and wonders for evangelism.

2. Also noted by Klein, Blomberg, and Hubbard, *Introduction*, 350, in demurring from Fee and Stuart's earlier approach to narrative, including in Acts.

3. See, e.g., Pelling, "Adaptation," 135; Burridge, *Gospels*, 145–46, 181; Hägg, *Biography*, 239–81, esp. 274; Plutarch, *Aem. Paul.* 1.1–3; further discussion in Keener, *Christobiography*, 132–33.

Not only is the traditional "doctrinal" approach inadequate for interpreting the Gospels, but it is inappropriate for interpreting the Epistles as well. The "narrative" way of interpreting Bible stories, in fact, shows us how to read the Epistles properly. Paul never wrote just to say hello; he wrote to address specific needs of churches. While the principles Paul employs are eternal and apply to a variety of situations, Paul expresses those principles concretely to grapple with specific situations. Before we can understand his principles, we often must first understand something about the situations with which he is grappling. Paul's concrete words that deal with real situations are case studies that show us how to address analogous situations today. Paul's letters presuppose a sort of background story—he is responding to events and situations that arose among his original audience. In other words, we must learn from even much in Paul's letters as case studies that illustrate his divine message in contextualized forms.

This is how Paul read the Old Testament—drawing theology (and especially moral teaching) from its examples (1 Cor. 10:11: "[These punishments] happened to them as an example, and [were] written down to warn us"). Paul sees Abram's faith (Gen. 15:6) as a model for all believers (Rom. 4); in a different way, so does James (James 2:21–23). That is not to say that every aspect of Abram's behavior is a positive model, but Abram's behavior that God reckoned as righteousness certainly was. Likewise, James uses the experiences of the prophets and Job as models for endurance (5:10–11). He not only recognizes Elijah's common humanity with us but for this very reason also treats his faith for divine action as a model for us (James 5:17–18).

## Reading Narratives in Antiquity and Subsequent History

Most cultures in the world teach lessons through stories. Sound-bite-addicted Westerners are often the ones who are unable to follow the point of narratives in the Bible. Even here, children in Christian homes grow up loving Bible stories—until they become adults and are taught that they must now think abstractly rather than learn from concrete illustrations. When we read Bible stories, we not only learn the historical facts about what happened but also listen to the inspired writer's perspective on what happened—that is, the lessons to be drawn from the story. When the writer "preaches" to us from the stories he tells us, he often gives us clues for recognizing the lessons. For example, a Gospel writer often selected a number of stories with the same basic theme or themes that repeatedly emphasized particular lessons. We may expect even greater consistency when those narratives portray the perfect activity of God rather than the fallible behavior of his followers.

Today scholars recognize that narratives do indeed often communicate perspectives that can be theological, political, moral, or a combination of various emphases.[4] Against the dichotomy between history and theology that sometimes prevailed in mid-twentieth-century biblical criticism, ancient historians often explicitly noted this purpose in their writing.[5] Biblical writers themselves affirmed this practice (e.g., Rom. 15:4; 1 Cor. 10:11; 2 Tim. 3:16–17).

The emphasis on narrative does not guarantee that all scholars read that narrative in the same way or find all of the same keys for hearing the story. Nevertheless, narrative was already the most common genre in the Bible, and it provides the overarching structure that gives context to most other pieces of the canon.

Various renewal movements have looked to the early church in Acts as a model and sought to live out Acts in various ways.[6] Many restoration movements, from medieval monastic movements to early Anabaptists, German Pietists, Moravians, and Wesley's first followers, looked to Acts for appropriate patterns for church life. Similarly, Baptists base their case for believers' baptism by immersion on historical precedent in the New Testament, arguing from what baptism typically meant in first-century Judea. Late nineteenth-century missions movements and early Pentecostals rightly drew from Acts a model for mission. Traditionally Pentecostals, like many others,[7] approached Acts 2 as a model.[8] More importantly, Acts teaches us patterns of God's activity—even if part of the pattern is that God often pours out his Spirit in ways unexpected by his people.

4. See the many sources cited in Keener, *Acts*, 1:148–65; among evangelicals, see the seminal work Marshall, *Historian and Theologian*; also Marshall, "Luke as Theologian"; among Pentecostals, cf. Stronstad, *Charismatic Theology*.

5. Polybius 1.1.1; Dionysius of Halicarnassus, *Rom. Ant.* 1.2.1; Livy 1.pref.10; Valerius Maximus 2.pref.; Tacitus, *Agr.* 1; *Ann.* 3.65; Lucian, *Hist.* 59; cf. Diodorus Siculus 37.4.1; Herodian 3.13.3; Maximus of Tyre 22.5; for moralizing asides, see, e.g., Polybius 1.35.1–10; Diodorus Siculus 31.10.2; Dionysius of Halicarnassus, *Rom. Ant.* 7.65.2; Velleius Paterculus 2.75.2; Dio Cassius 1.5.4; Arrian, *Alex.* 4.10.8; Cornelius Nepos 16 (Pelopidas), 3.1; Tacitus, *Ann.* 16.15.

6. E.g., on Wycliffe and sharing possessions in Acts 2, see Evans, *Wycliffe*, 155, 226; on Wesley, see Jennings, *Good News*, 25, 97–117 (esp. 111–16); on early Moravians, see Williams, *Radical Reformation*, 429, cf. 229–33; on Hutterites, see McGee, "Possessions," 167–68; Williams, *Radical Reformation*, 232, 426–29, and, on many other Anabaptists (who interpret it less literally), see Finger, *Meals*, 21–22; on the more recent communitarian Jesus Family in China, see Anderson, *Pentecostalism*, 135; Zhaoming, "Chinese Denominations," 452–64; Yamamori and Chan, *Witnesses*, 54–62; on some elements in the North American Jesus Movement of the 1960s–70s, see Jackson, *Quest*, 32; Di Sabatino, "Frisbee," 395–96; Eskridge, *Family*, 88 (cf. 78–79).

7. For applications of Luke's Pentecost narrative in various cultures, see, e.g., Chempakassery, "Jerusalem Pentecost"; Bediako, "African Culture," 120; Forrester, "Pentecost" (addressing, e.g., castes); on Acts 2:17–21, Prema, "Paradigm"; Lloyd-Jones, *Christianity*; nonviolent direct action in Alexander, "Action."

8. For the early Pentecostal fondness for narrative, especially Acts, see also Archer, *Hermeneutic*, 182, 187–89; Mittelstadt, *Reading*, 1–2, 14, 19–45 (esp. 19–31). Mittelstadt, *Reading*, 81, cites Jerry Camery-Hoggatt (in personal correspondence) thus: "Pentecostals have been doing narrative theology for years although without the added dimension of critical self-reflection."

Of course, preachers from most traditions do find applications in whatever texts they preach. In miracle stories, however, some find exclusively spiritual applications, risking allegorical treatment of accounts despite their usual aversion to allegory. Some Greek philosophers allegorized old myths that they found offensive.[9] But in antiquity, nonmythical miracle accounts often circulated as invitations to trust deities to continue to act.[10] Although some people in antiquity doubted divine intervention, most sought it.

Ancient writers of historiography and biography did not normally expect their readers to allegorize their narratives, but they did expect their readers to draw lessons from them. As noted, this expectation is often explicit in their writings,[11] and we are remiss if we neglect such interests. Again, "all Scripture is God-inspired and beneficial for teaching, refuting error, correction, and training for right living" so God's servants may be fully equipped to serve him (2 Tim. 3:16–17). Ignoring the training value of narrative, the largest major genre in Scripture, leaves the church at best partly equipped.

9. E.g., Plato, *Laws* 1.636CD; 2.672BC; Cicero, *Nat. d.* 2.28.70 (the Stoic); Dio Chrysostom, *Or.* 1.62–63; 8.33; 60.8; Maximus of Tyre 4.5–8; 26.5–9; Heraclitus, *Hom. Prob.* 6.6; 8.4–5; 22.1; 26.1, 7–8; 30.1, 4; 31.1, 11; 39.2–17; 52.4–6; 53.1; 60.1; 68.8–9; 69.8–16; Proclus, *Poet.* K82.10–17; K90.8–14; K141.16–21; K153.25–29. Cf. Josephus's criticism in *Ag. Ap.* 2.255; Gentile critiques in Seneca, *Lucil.* 88.5; Lucian, *Z. Rants* 40.

10. Cf. Dibelius, *Tradition*, 170; Keener, *Miracles*, 1:62.

11. See Keener, *Acts*, 1:148–58 and sources cited there.

## Appendix 2

# Tongues as Diglossia or a Hearing Miracle?

Some grant that Luke claims that the disciples spoke genuine languages or dialects yet doubt that Luke assumes a miracle of speech unknown to the speakers. Because Hebrew was a holy language for Judeans, some propose that the disciples spoke "other" languages (Acts 2:4) as merely "profane" ones (non-Hebrew languages already known to the speakers).[1] But it is unlikely that the disciples spoke Hebrew on a regular basis,[2] and even more unlikely that they knew more than two languages beyond it. A supporter of the "profane languages" position might respond that many Palestinian Jews who spoke Greek or Aramaic in other settings probably recited traditional prayers and psalms in Hebrew, and prayer is certainly relevant to the nature of speech here (1:14). Granted, but Mark 14:36 and 15:34 suggest that not even the historical Jesus always prayed in Hebrew (though if Mark reports Jesus's actual practice,

---

This appendix, responding to a minority approach to tongues, follows Keener, Acts, 1:821–22. Other scholars have recently proposed tongues in Acts 10:46 and 19:6 as naturally learned languages (Chan, "Significance"), but the explicit connection with Acts 2:4 in 10:45–47 suggests that the tongues are supernatural, even if on this occasion no one understands them (though I do regard the praise in tongues as a hendiadys).

1. Zerhusen, "Judean *Diglossia* in Acts 2?" (cf. also Zerhusen, "Tongues in 1 Cor. 14"); Crystal, "Applied Sociolinguistics." (See further refutation of Zerhusen in Garland, *1 Corinthians*, 584n12.) Some also claim "tongues" meant simply "archaic language"; see the refutation in Forbes, *Prophecy*, 60–61.

2. See, e.g., Horsley, *Galilee*, 247–49; see extended discussion in Keener, *Excursuses*, 307–12.

Matthew may Hebraize the latter occasion, Matt. 27:46).[3] Hebrew would be no more mandatory for prophecy.[4]

Far more problematic, Luke provides no indication that diglossia (use of another language in a special context) was in view, or that one should expect the disciples to have spoken only Hebrew on this or another occasion. Luke is happy to specify an original Jewish language (Aramaic or some think Hebrew) when that is in view (Acts 21:40; 22:2; 26:14). Luke does not think of the disciples as limited to any Semitic language: They quote the Septuagint; they also clearly knew some Greek, or communication within the Jerusalem church would have become unintelligible (without tongues) by Acts 6.[5] Further, one must discount the explicitly parallel (Acts 10:46) passage where Cornelius's household cannot be expected to have *ever* spoken much Hebrew (10:1–2).[6] (This is not to mention discounting Paul's evidence, despite his similarly unusual use of the same term *glōssa*, and Paul emphasizing that the languages spoken were unknown to the speakers, 1 Cor. 14:13–14, 19, 27–28.)

Most importantly, this view renders implausible Luke's mention of *each* language in Acts 2:8 (*ekastos ... idia*), which Luke goes on to elaborate specifically in 2:9–11; such elaboration makes little sense if Luke meant only the *lingua franca* of the Eastern Mediterranean (Greek) and Middle East (Aramaic; or of Latin, the *lingua franca* of the West).[7] The use of *laleō* and *glōssa* in 2:11 explicitly recalls the same terms in 2:4. In the context of Acts, this event was a *sign* of the reception of the Spirit, which would hardly merit specific mention (especially in 10:45–47 and 19:6) if the persons inspired spoke merely their own languages as they had before the inspiration. This proposal seems an attempt to circumvent Luke's cross-cultural use of tongues in his story.

Some suggest a hearing miracle rather than the disciples speaking in various languages; this view appears even in some church fathers.[8] But some of the suggested background for this position is based on a misinterpretation of

3. The change from *elōi* to *ēli* could reflect such concerns (though the latter had also come into Aramaic); or to explain how listeners thought they heard "Elijah" (*Eliyahu*; Jeremias, *Theology*, 5n2; cf. Anderson, *Mark*, 346; Keener, *Matthew*, 682).

4. Cf., e.g., the *Sib. Or.*; or in Judea, Josephus's claims for his own; or the Aramaic portions of Daniel.

5. See discussion in Keener, *Acts*, 2:1255–57.

6. One can hardly aver that most of the gathering (Acts 10:24) was Jewish (see 11:1, 3, 18). As for the cases being parallel, Peter says so explicitly (Acts 10:47; 11:15–16). Though this need not mean that every aspect is the same, it is hardly plausible to assign a wholly new meaning to "tongues" in the context of the Spirit's outpouring in chap. 10 than what an ordinary reader would expect from the last usage, also in the context of the Spirit's outpouring, in chap. 2.

7. For this critique, see also, e.g., Witherington, *Acts*, 133. For other relevant discussion, too recent to incorporate fully, see Gresham, "Tongues."

8. E.g., Bede, *Comm. Acts* 2.6. We might compare divinely altered perception of a person (Luke 24:16), but in that case the reality is temporarily obscured, whereas here the focus of the miracle is cross-cultural empowerment (cf. Acts 1:8). NT reports of such altered perception miracles are infrequent, however, and much less frequent than claims of speaking miracles.

ancient texts.[9] More importantly, this proposal does not match what Luke himself says.[10] Luke reports them speaking "other languages" before mentioning that anyone hears them (2:4), and emphasizes that the Spirit enables them to speak this way; further, the gift recurs later as a supernatural sign with no indication that such understanding took place (10:45–46; 19:6).[11] Moreover, in his work, Luke emphasizes not so much the Spirit producing receptivity in crowds[12] but God working through those who are agents of his Spirit (4:8, 31; 6:3, 10; 10:38; 13:9–11; 21:4, 11). As Max Turner notes, Luke "would not wish to suggest that the apostolic band merely prattled incomprehensibly while God worked the yet greater miracle of interpretation of tongues in the *un*believers."[13]

9. The purported evidence for a hearing or speech miracle in the Homeric hymn to the Delian Apollo 156–64 (e.g., Burkert, *Religion*, 110) is not even clearly miraculous, but probably refers to "singing in dialect" (Forbes, *Prophecy*, 119–23; Van der Horst, "Parallels to Acts," 52–53), though ancients would have understood selective revelation (3 Macc. 6:18; cf. John 14:22; Acts 10:41) and hearing one sound in various languages (scholars cite *Tanhuma* 26c, whose tradition is of uncertain date).

10. Note, e.g., objections in Haenchen, *Acts*, 168n5; Hull, *Spirit in Acts*, 61; Bock, *Acts*, 97.

11. Faw, *Acts*, 319. It is clear in 10:46 that Luke intends the same phenomenon as on Pentecost, in view of 10:47; 11:15; and especially the *gar* providing 10:46 as the explanation for their recognition in 10:45. Witherington, *Acts,* 134, emphasizes that in 2:6, "in his language" modifies speaking, not hearing.

12. One might propose 5:32 and 7:51, but even these texts could refer to the Spirit working through agents. God opens people's hearts (Acts 13:48; 14:27; 16:14), but this is more explicitly providential than charismatic, not mentioning the Spirit working through the agents.

13. Turner, *Gifts*, 222–23.

# Bibliography

**Abraham, "Spirit."** Abraham, Shaibu. "Holy Spirit, Holiness, and Liberation: A Theology of Liberation in Pentecostal Perspective." *Doon Theological Journal* 5, no. 1 (2008): 86–106.

**Abrams, *Baptism*.** Abrams, Minnie. *The Baptism of the Holy Ghost and Fire*. 2nd ed. Pandita Ramabai Mukti Mission, 1906.

**"Abuse of Faith."** "Abuse of Faith: The Database." *Houston Chronicle*. Accessed December 17, 2024. https://www.houstonchronicle.com/news/investigations/abuse-of-faith/database/.

**Ackroyd, *Samuel*.** Ackroyd, Peter R. *The First Book of Samuel*. Cambridge Bible Commentary. Cambridge University Press, 1971.

**Adams, "Introduction."** Adams, Gwenfair Walters. "Introduction." In Adams, *Romans*, xliii-lxviii.

**Adams, *Romans*.** Adams, Gwenfair Walters, ed. *Romans 1–8*. Reformation Commentary on Scripture: New Testament 7. IVP Academic, 2019.

**Adewuya, "Spirit in 1 Corinthians."** Adewuya, J. Ayodeji. "The Spirit in 1 Corinthians: Spiritual Formation and Giftedness." In Keener and Oliverio Jr., *Canon*, 148–57.

**Adhinarta, *Doctrine*.** Adhinarta, Yuzo. *The Doctrine of the Holy Spirit in the Major Reformed Confessions and Catechisms of the Sixteenth and Seventeenth Centuries*. Langham Monographs, 2012.

**"Africa Claims Share."** "Sub-Saharan Africa Claims Growing Share of Christian Population." *Influence Magazine* (May 4, 2017). Accessed January 11, 2025. https://influencemagazine.com/Practice/Sub-Saharan-Africa-Claims-Growing-Share-of-Christian-Population.

**Ages, "Luther and Rabbis."** Ages, Arnold. "Luther and the Rabbis." *Jewish Quarterly Review* 58 (July 1967): 63–68.

**Ahn, *Interpretation*.** Ahn, Yongnan Jeon, *Interpretation of Tongues and Prophecy in 1 Corinthians 12–14, with a Pentecostal Hermeneutics*. Journal of Pentecostal Theology Supplement Series 41. Deo, 2013.

**Aiken, "Miracles."** Aiken, G. Taylor. "Miracles—Yes or No?" *Presbyterian Journal* 33, no. 16 (August 1974): 7–9.

**Aikman, *Jesus in Beijing*.** Aikman, David. *Jesus in Beijing: How Christianity Is Transforming China and Changing the Global Balance of Power*. Regnery, 2003.

**Akinade, *New Day*.** Akinade, Akintunde E. *A New Day: Essays on World Christianity in Honor of Lamin Sanneh*. Peter Lang, 2010.

**Alamino, *Footsteps*.** Alamino, Carlos. *In the Footsteps of God's Call: A Cuban Pastor's Journey*. Translated by Osmany Espinosa Hernández. Edited by David Peck and Brian Stewart. Original Media, 2008.

**Albright, *Stone Age*.** Albright, William Foxwell. *From the Stone Age to Christianity: Monotheism and the Historical Process*. Johns Hopkins University Press, 1946.

**Albright, *Yahweh*.** Albright, William Foxwell. *Yahweh and the Gods of Canaan*. Jordan Lectures, 1965. Doubleday, 1968.

**Alexander, "Action."** Alexander, Paul. "Nonviolent Direct Action in Acts 2: The Holy Spirit, the Early Church, and Martin Luther King, Jr." In Alexander, May, and Reid, *Trajectories*, 114–24.

**Alexander, *Fire*.** Alexander, Estrelda Y. *Black Fire: One Hundred Years of African American Pentecostalism*. InterVarsity, 2011.

**Alexander, *Healing*.** Alexander, Kimberly Ervin. *Pentecostal Healing: Models in Theology and Practice*. Journal of Pentecostal Theology Supplement Series 29. Deo, 2006.

**Alexander, *Signs*.** Alexander, Paul. *Signs and Wonders: Why Pentecostalism Is the World's Fastest Growing Faith*. Jossey-Bass, 2009.

**Alexander, May, and Reid, *Trajectories*.** Alexander, Paul, Jordan Daniel May, and Robert G. Reid, eds. *Trajectories in the Book of Acts: Essays in Honor of John Wesley Wyckoff*. Wipf & Stock, 2010.

**Allison and Köstenberger, *Holy Spirit*.** Allison, Gregg R., and Andreas Köstenberger. *The Holy Spirit*. B&H Academic, 2020.

**Almodovar, *Questions*.** Almodovar, Nancy A. *A Modern Ninety-Five: Questions Today's Evangelicals Need to Answer*. Wipf & Stock, 2008.

**Alt, "Cease."** Alt, Steven S. "Appendix C: Did the Authentic Fire Cease in the First Century? A Response to Tom Pennington's, 'A Case for Cessationism.'" In Brown, *Authentic Fire*, 393–414.

**Althouse, *Healing*.** Althouse, Lawrence W. *Rediscovering the Gift of Healing*. Abingdon, 1977.

**Amaru, "Mirrors."** Amaru, Betsy Halpern. "Martin Luther and Jewish Mirrors." *Jewish Social Studies* 46, no. 2 (Spring 1984): 95–102.

**Ames, "Calvin and Foreigner."** Ames, John M. "John Calvin and the Foreigner: A Rediscovery of the Sixteenth Century Reformer's Hidden Legacy with Missiological Considerations for the Local Church." PhD diss., Midwestern Baptist Theological Seminary, 2024.

**Amoafo, *Stand Up*.** Amoafo, Emmanuel Kwasi. *Stand Up for the Gospel: Getting the Church Back on Track*. Oasis, 2022.

**Anderson, *Ends of the Earth*.** Anderson, Alan Heaton. *To the Ends of the Earth: Pentecostalism and the Transformation of World Christianity*. Oxford University Press, 2013.

**Anderson, "Face."** Anderson, Allan. "The Charismatic Face of Christianity in Asia." In Anderson and Tang, *Asian and Pentecostal*, 1–12.

**Anderson, *Mark*.** Anderson, Hugh. *The Gospel of Mark*. New Century Bible Commentary. Marshall, Morgan & Scott, 1976.

**Anderson, *Miracles*.** Anderson, Joan Wester. *Where Miracles Happen: True Stories of Heavenly Encounters*. Brett Books, 1994.

**Anderson, *Pelendo*.** Anderson, Alpha E. *Pelendo: God's Prophet in the Congo*. Moody, 1964.

**Anderson, *Pentecostalism*.** Anderson, Allan. *An Introduction to Pentecostalism: Global Charismatic Christianity*. Cambridge University Press, 2004.

**Anderson, "Points."** Anderson, Allan. "To All Points of the Compass: The Azusa Street Revival and Global Pentecostalism." *Enrichment* 11, no. 2 (2006): 164–72.

**Anderson, "Signs."** Anderson, Allan. "Signs and Blunders: Pentecostal Mission Issues at 'Home and Abroad' in the Twentieth Century." *Journal of Asian Mission* 2, no. 2 (September 2000): 193–210.

**Anderson, "Varieties."** Anderson, Allan. "Varieties, Taxonomies, and Definitions." In *Studying Global Pentecostalism: Theories and Methods*, edited by Allan Anderson, Michael Bergunder, André Droogers, and Cornelis van der Laan, 13–29. University of California Press, 2010.

**Anderson and Tang, *Asian and Pentecostal*.** Anderson, Allan, and Edmond Tang, eds. *Asian and Pentecostal: The Charismatic Face of Christianity in Asia*. Regnum Studies in Mission, Asian Journal of Pentecostal Studies Series 3. Regnum; APTS, 2005.

**Andrews, *Sisters*.** Andrews, William L., ed. *Sisters of the Spirit: Three Black Women's Autobiographies of the Nineteenth Century*. Indiana University Press, 1986.

**Anonymous, "History in Indonesia."** Anonymous. "A History of the Pentecostal Movement in Indonesia." *Asian Journal of Pentecostal Studies* 4, no. 1 (2001): 131–48.

**"Anti-Semitism."** "Anti-Semitism: Martin Luther–'The Jews & Their Lies.'" Jewish Virtual Library. Accessed August 29, 2024. https://www.jewishvirtuallibrary.org/martin-luther-quot-the-jews-and-their-lies-quot.

**Archer, *Hermeneutic.*** Archer, Kenneth J. *A Pentecostal Hermeneutic: Spirit, Scripture and Community.* CPT, 2009.

**Arnal, "Luther and Peasants."** Arnal, Oscar L. "Luther and the Peasants: A Lutheran Reassessment." *Science & Society* 44, no. 4 (Winter 1980): 443–65.

**Arnold, *Samuel.*** Arnold, Bill T. *1–2 Samuel.* NIVAC. Zondervan, 2003.

**Aroolappen, *History.*** Aroolappen, John Christian. *The History and Diaries of an Indian Christian.* Edited by G. H. Lang. Thynne, 1939.

**Arrington, *Acts.*** Arrington, French L. *The Acts of the Apostles: An Introduction and Commentary.* Hendrickson, 1988.

**Artman, *Miracle Lady.*** Artman, Amy Collier. *The Miracle Lady: Kathyrn Kuhlman and the Transformation of Charismatic Christianity.* Eerdmans, 2019.

**Asamoah-Gyadu, "Leadership."** Asamoah-Gyadu, J. Kwabena. "'Touch Not the Lord's Anointed': Leadership in Ghana's New Charismatic Communities." In Akinade, *New Day*, 142–57.

**Asbury Seminary, "Equips."** Asbury Theological Seminary. "Asbury Seminary Equips 1,000 Church Planters." Accessed February 27, 2025. https://asburyseminary.edu/news/asbury-seminary-equips-1000-church-planters/.

**Asbury Seminary, "Jones School."** Asbury Theological Seminary. "E. Stanley Jones School of Mission and Ministry." Accessed February 27, 2025. https://asburyseminary.edu/academics/esj/.

**Ashley, *Numbers.*** Ashley, Timothy R. *The Book of Numbers.* NICOT. Eerdmans, 1993.

**Assemblies of God, "About."** Assemblies of God. "About the Assemblies of God." Accessed December 3, 2025. https://ag.org/About.

**Assemblies of God, "Truths."** Assemblies of God. "Statement of Fundamental Truths." Assemblies of God website. Accessed August 28, 2024. https://ag.org/Beliefs/Statement-of-Fundamental-Truths.

**Assemblies of God World Missions, "Vital Stats."** Assemblies of God World Missions, "Vital Stats." 2025, issue 2. Accessed February 2, 2026. https://agwm.org/en/resources/.

**Augustine, *City of God.*** Augustine. *Concerning the City of God Against the Pagans.* Translated by Henry Bettenson. Edited by David Knowles. Penguin Books, 1972.

**Aune, *Environment.*** Aune, David E. *The New Testament in Its Literary Environment.* LEC 8. Westminster, 1987.

**Aune, "Magic."** Aune, David E. "Magic in Early Christianity." *ANRW* 23.1:1507–57. Part 2, *Principat,* 23.1. Edited by H. Temporini and W. Haase. De Gruyter, 1980.

**Aune, *Prophecy.*** Aune, David E. *Prophecy in Early Christianity and the Ancient Mediterranean World.* Eerdmans, 1983.

**Aune, "Προφήτης."** Aune, David E. "The Use of προφήτης in Josephus." *Journal of Biblical Literature* 101, no. 3 (1982): 419–21.

**Baer, "Bodies."** Baer, Jonathan R. "Perfectly Empowered Bodies: Divine Healing in Modernizing America." PhD diss., Yale University, 2002.

**Bainton, *Here I Stand.*** Bainton, Roland. *Here I Stand: A Life of Martin Luther.* Abingdon, 1950.

**Bainton, *Reformation.*** Bainton, Roland H. *The Reformation of the Sixteenth Century.* Beacon, 1966.

**Baker, "Dissent."** Baker, J. Wayne. "Church, State, and Dissent: The Crisis of the Swiss Reformation, 1531–1536." *Church History* 57, no. 2 (June 1988): 135–52.

**Baker, *Testaments.*** Baker, David L. *Two Testaments, One Bible: A Study of the Theological Relationship Between the Old and New Testaments.* InterVarsity, 1991.

**Baker, *Visions.*** Baker, H. A. *Visions Beyond the Veil.* Whitaker House, 2006.

**Baker and Baker, *Enough.*** Baker, Rolland, and Heidi Baker. *There Is Always Enough: The Story of Rolland and Heidi Baker's Miraculous Ministry Among the Poor.* Sovereign World, 2001. Published in the United States as *Always Enough: God's Miraculous Provision Among the Poorest Children on Earth.* Chosen, 2003.

**Baker and Baker, *Miracles.*** Baker, Heidi, and Rolland Baker. *Expecting Miracles: True Stories of God's Supernatural Power and How You Can Experience It.* Chosen, 2007. Also published as *The Hungry Always Get Fed: A Year of Miracles.* New Wine Ministries, 2007.

**Bamberger, "Prophet."** Bamberger, Bernard J. "The Changing Image of the Prophet in Jewish Thought." In *Interpreting the Prophetic Tradition: The Goldman Lectures, 1955–1966*, edited by Harry M. Orlinski, 301–23. Hebrew Union College Press; Ktav, 1969.

**Barclay, *Gift.*** Barclay, John M. *Paul and the Gift.* Eerdmans, 2015.

**Barna Group, "Findings."** Barna Group. "The Year's Most Intriguing Findings, from Barna Research Studies." December 17, 2001. www.barna.com/research/the-years-most-intriguing-findings-from-barna-research-studies.

**Barnard, *Justin Martyr.*** Barnard, L. W. *Justin Martyr: His Life and Thought.* Cambridge University Press, 1967.

**Baroody, "Healing."** Baroody, Naseeb B. "Spiritual Healing in Psychosomatic Disease." In Frazier, *Faith Healing*, 87–92.

**Barrett, *Acts.*** Barrett, C. K. *A Critical and Exegetical Commentary on the Acts of the Apostles.* 2 vols. T&T Clark, 1994–98.

**Barrett, *Encyclopedia.*** Barrett, David B. *World Christian Encyclopedia.* 2nd ed. Oxford University Press, 2001.

**Barrett, "Renewal."** Barrett, David B. "The Worldwide Holy Spirit Renewal." In Synan, *Century*, 381–414.

**Barrett, "Statistics."** Barrett, David B. "Statistics, Global." In *Dictionary of Pentecostal and Charismatic Movements*, edited by Stanley M. Burgess, Gary B. McGee, and Patrick H. Alexander, 810–29. Zondervan, 1988.

**Barrett, Johnson, and Crossing, "Missiometrics 2005."** Barrett, David B., Todd M. Johnson, and Peter F. Crossing. "Missiometrics 2005: A Global Survey of World Mission." *International Bulletin of Missionary Research* 29, no. 1 (January 2005): 27–30.

**Barrett, Johnson, and Crossing, "Missiometrics 2006."** Barrett, David B., Todd M. Johnson, and Peter F. Crossing. "Missiometrics 2006: Goals, Resources, Doctrines of the 350 Christian World Communions." *International Bulletin of Missionary Research* 30, no. 1 (January 2006): 27–30.

**Barrett, Johnson, and Crossing, "Missiometrics 2007."** Barrett, David B., Todd M. Johnson, and Peter F. Crossing. "Missiometrics 2007: Creating Your Own Analysis of Global Data." *International Bulletin of Missionary Research* 31, no. 1 (January 2007): 25–32.

**Barrett, Johnson, and Crossing, "Missiometrics 2008."** Barrett, David B., Todd M. Johnson, and Peter F. Crossing. "Missiometrics 2008: Reality Checks for Christian World Communions." *International Bulletin of Missionary Research* 32, no. 1 (January 2008): 27–30.

**Barrett-Lennard, *Healing*.** Barrett-Lennard, R. J. S. *Christian Healing After the New Testament: Some Approaches to Illness in the Second, Third, and Fourth Centuries.* University Press of America, 1994.

**Barron, *Gospel*.** Barron, Bruce. *The Health and Wealth Gospel: What's Going on Today in a Movement That Has Shaped the Faith of Millions?* InterVarsity, 1987.

**Barth, *Dogmatics*.** Barth, Karl. *Church Dogmatics: The Doctrine of Reconciliation.* IV/3. T&T Clark, 1961.

**Barth, *Letters*.** Barth, Karl. *Letters, 1961–1968.* Translated and edited by Geoffrey W. Bromiley. Eerdmans, 1981.

**Bartholomew, *Hermeneutics*.** Bartholomew, Craig G. *Introducing Biblical Hermeneutics: A Comprehensive Framework for Hearing God in Scripture.* Baker Academic, 2015.

**Baumgarten, "Miracles."** Baumgarten, Albert I. "Miracles and Halakah in Rabbinic Judaism." *Jewish Quarterly Review* 73, no. 3 (January 1983): 238–53.

**Baumgartner, "Gifts."** Baumgartner, Chris. "The Gifts That Draw Us Closer to God." Posted May 8, 2025, by Iris Global, YouTube. Accessed May 11, 2025. https://www.youtube.com/watch?v=sAxoNBxEdlc.

**Baxter, *Healing*.** Baxter, J. Sidlow. *Divine Healing of the Body.* Zondervan, 1979.

**Baylor, *Reformation*.** Baylor, Michael G., ed. *The Radical Reformation*: Cambridge Texts in the History of Political Thought. Cambridge University Press, 1991.

**Bays, "Revival."** Bays, Daniel H. "Christian Revival in China, 1900–1937." In *Modern Christian Revivals*, edited by Edith Blumhofer and Randall H. Balmer, 161–79. University of Illinois Press, 1993.

**Beam, *Miracles.*** Beam, Christy Wilson. *Miracles from Heaven: A Little Girl, Her Journey to Heaven, and Her Amazing Story of Healing*. Hachette Books, 2016.

**Beaumont, "From Farts to Faith."** Beaumont, Douglas. "From Farts to Faith: Interesting, Surprising, and Amazing Quotes from Martin Luther." *Douglas Beaumont* (blog). October 19, 2011. Accessed October 9, 2024. souldevice.wordpress.com/2011/10/19/from-farts-to-faith-interesting-surprizing-and-amazing-quotes-from-martin-luther/.

**Bebbington, "Clash."** Bebbington, D. W. "Revival and the Clash of Cultures: Ferryden, Forfarshire, in 1859." In *Revival, Renewal, and the Holy Spirit*, edited by Dyfed Wyn Roberts, 65–94. SEHT. Wipf & Stock, 2009.

**Bebbington, *Dominance.*** Bebbington, David W. *The Dominance of Evangelicalism: The Age of Spurgeon and Moody*. A History of Evangelicalism: People, Movements, and Ideas in the English-Speaking World. InterVarsity, 2005.

**Becken, "Healing Communities."** Becken, Hans-Jürgen. "African Independent Churches as Healing Communities." In *Afro-Christian Religion and Healing in Southern Africa*, edited by G. C. Oosthuizen, S. D. Edwards, W. H. Wessels, and I. Hexham, 227–39. African Studies 8. Edwin Mellen, 1989.

**Becker, *Birth.*** Becker, Eve-Marie. *The Birth of Christian History: Memory and Time from Mark to Luke-Acts*. Anchor Bible Reference Library. Yale University Press, 2017.

**Bediako, "African Culture."** Bediako, Kwame. "Jesus in African Culture: A Ghanaian Perspective." In *Emerging Voices in Global Christian Theology*, edited by William A. Dyrness, 93–121. Zondervan, 1994.

**Behm, "καινός."** Behm, Johannes. "καινός, κτλ." In *Theological Dictionary of the New Testament*, translated by Geoffrey W. Bromiley, edited by Gerhard Kittel and Gerhard Friedrich, 3:449. 10 vols. Eerdmans, 1964–76.

**Belleville, "Live."** Belleville, Linda L. "How Then Shall We Live? (Romans 12:1–15:6)." In *The Letter to the Romans: Exegesis and Application*, edited by Stanley E. Porter and Francis G. H. Pang, 128–47. McMaster New Testament Studies Series, 7. Pickwick, 2018.

**Belleville, "Re-Examination."** Belleville, Linda. "Ιουνιαν . . . επισημοι εν τοις αποστολοις: A Re-Examination of Romans 16.7 in Light of Primary Source Materials." *New Testament Studies* 51, no. 2 (2005): 231–49.

**Belz, "Crimes."** Belz, Mindy. "War Crimes and Restoration in Congo." *Christianity Today*, May 2025, 74–81.

**Bennett, *Not Afraid.*** Bennett, Robert H. *I Am Not Afraid: Demon Possession and Spiritual Warfare; True Accounts from the Lutheran Church of Madagascar*. Concordia, 2013.

**Benoit, "Mystères."** Benoit, A. "Les mystères païens et le christianisme." In *Mystères et syncrétismes*, edited by F. Dunand et al., 73–92. EHRel 2. Librairie Orientaliste Paul Geuthner, 1975.

**Benson, *Healing*.** Benson, Herbert, with Marg Stark. *Timeless Healing: The Power and Biology of Belief*. Scribner, 1996.

**Bentley, *Relics*.** Bentley, James. *Restless Bones: The Story of Relics*. Constable, 1985.

**Berger, "Faces."** Berger, Peter L. "Four Faces of Global Culture." In *Globalization and the Challenges of a New Century: A Reader*, edited by Patrick O'Meara, Howard D. Mehlinger, and Matthew Krain, 419–27. Indiana University Press, 2000.

**Bergunder, "Turn."** Bergunder, Michael. "The Cultural Turn." In *Studying Global Pentecostalism: Theories and Methods*, edited by Allan Anderson, Michael Bergunder, André Droogers, and Cornelis van der Laan, 51–73. University of California Press, 2010.

**Bernard, "Miracle."** Bernard, J. H. "Miracle." In *A Dictionary of the Bible Dealing with Its Language, Literature, and Contents Including the Biblical Theology*, edited by James Hastings, 379–96. 5 vols. Charles Scribner's Sons, 1898–1909.

**Best, "Pneuma."** Best, Ernest. "The Use and Non-Use of Pneuma by Josephus." *Novum Testamentum* 3, no. 3 (1959): 218–25.

**Best, *Thessalonians*.** Best, Ernest. *A Commentary on the First and Second Epistles to the Thessalonians*. BNTC. Adam and Charles Black, 1977.

**Bhengu, "South Africa."** Bhengu, Nicholas. "Taking South Africa for God." *Pentecostal Evangel*, March 6, 1955, 3.

**Billman, *Thread*.** Billman, Frank H. *The Supernatural Thread in Methodism: Signs and Wonders Among Methodists Then and Now*. Rev. ed. Published by the author, 2021.

**Bird, *Gospel of the Lord*.** Bird, Michael F. *The Gospel of the Lord: How the Early Church Wrote the Story of Jesus*. Eerdmans, 2014.

**Blaising and Bock, *Progressive Dispensationalism*.** Blaising, Craig A., and Darrell L. Bock. *Progressive Dispensationalism*. Bridgepoint, 2000.

**Blomberg, *Believe Bible*.** Blomberg, Craig L. *Can We Still Believe the Bible?* Brazos, 2012.

**Blomberg, *Matthew*.** Blomberg, Craig L. *Matthew*. NAC 22. Broadman, 1992.

**Blomberg, *Reliability*.** Blomberg, Craig L. *The Historical Reliability of the Gospels*. 2nd ed. IVP Academic, 2007.

**Blosser and Sullivan, *Speaking in Tongues*.** Blosser, Philip E., and Charles A. Sullivan. *Speaking in Tongues: A Critical Historical Examination*. Vol. 2, *Tongues Through Church History*. Pickwick, 2023.

**Blowers, "Interpreting."** Blowers, Paul M. "Interpreting Scripture." In *The Cambridge History of Christianity*. Vol. 2, *Constantine to c. 600*, edited by Augustine Casiday and Frederick W. Norris, 618–36. 9 vols. Cambridge University Press, 2007.

**Blumhofer, "Portrait."** Blumhofer, Edith L. "Portrait of a Generation: Azusa Street Comes to Chicago." *Enrichment* 11, no. 2 (2006): 95–102.

**Bock, *Acts*.** Bock, Darrell L. *Acts*. Baker Exegetical Commentary on the New Testament. Baker Academic, 2007.

**Bock, *Mark*.** Bock, Darrell L. *Mark*. New Cambridge Bible Commentary. Cambridge University Press, 2015.

**Boehr, *Medicine*.** Boehr, Marian. *Medicine and Miracles amid the Multitudes: The Adventures of a Missionary Doctor in India*. American Baptist International Ministries, 2002.

**Boles, *Revival*.** Boles, John B. *The Great Revival: Beginnings of the Bible Belt*. University Press of Kentucky, 1972.

**Bonnke, *Life of Fire*.** Bonnke, Reinhard. *Living a Life of Fire: An Autobiography*. E-R Productions, 2010. Kindle edition.

**Bonnke, *Raised*.** Bonnke, Reinhard. *Raised from the Dead: The Miracle That Brings Promise to America*. Harvester Services, 2014. Kindle edition.

**Book, "Heel Kicking."** Book, Abram J. "Heel Kicking and Holy Jumping." *Christian History* 152 (2024): 25.

**Born, "Churches."** Born, Bryan. "Christian Churches in Southern Africa—Challenge of Rebuilding Civil Society." *Mission Focus* 17 (2009): 113–30.

**Bosc and Allier, "Guerre."** Bosc, Henri, and Jacques Allier. "La Guerre des Camisards: Son caractère. Ses conséquences." *Bulletin de la Société de l'Histoire du Protestantisme Français* 119 (July 1973): 335–55.

**Bosworth, *Arrian*.** Bosworth, A. B. *From Arrian to Alexander: Studies in Historical Interpretation*. Clarendon, 1988.

**Bosworth, *Healer*.** Bosworth, F. F. *Christ the Healer*. Chosen, 2008.

**Bouyer, "Movements."** Bouyer, Louis. "Some Charismatic Movements in the History of the Church." In *Perspectives on Charismatic Renewal*. Edited by Edward D. O'Connor. University of Notre Dame Press, 1975.

**Bovon, *Studies*.** Bovon, François. *Studies in Early Christianity*. J. C. B. Mohr; Baker Academic, 2003.

**Bovon, *Theologian*.** Bovon, François. *Luke the Theologian: Thirty-Three Years of Research (1950–1983)*. Translated by Ken McKinney. Pickwick, 1987.

**Bowens, *Readings*.** Bowens, Lisa M. *African American Readings of Paul: Reception, Resistance, and Transformation*. Eerdmans, 2020.

**Bowler, "Bodies."** Bowler, Catherine. "Blessed Bodies: Healing Within the African American Faith Movement." In Brown, *Global*, 81–105.

**Bowman, *Controversy*.** Bowman, Robert M., Jr. *The Word-Faith Controversy: Understanding the Health and Wealth Gospel*. Baker Books, 2001.

**Boyd, *Bomb*.** Boyd, Andrew. *Neither Bomb nor Bullet: Benjamin Kwashi; Archbishop on the Front Line*. Lion Hudson, 2019.

**Boys, *Evidence*.** Boys, Thomas. *Suppressed Evidence: Proofs of the Miraculous Faith and Experience of the Church of Christ in All Ages*. Hamilton, Adams, 1832.

**Brahinsky, *Tongues*.** Brahinsky, Josh. *Tongues of Fire: How Charismatic Prayer Changes Evangelical Brains and Inspires Spirit-Filled Activism*. Bloomsbury Academic, 2026.

**Brand, *Addresses*.** Brand, James. *Memorial Addresses on the Occasion of the One Hundredth Anniversary of the Birth of President Charles G. Finney*. E. J. Goodrich, 1893.

**Braun, *Jean*.** Braun, François-Marie. *Jean le théologien et son évangile dans l'Église ancienne*. Etudes Bibliques. Lecoffre, 1959.

**Bray, *Corinthians*.** Bray, Gerald, ed. *1–2 Corinthians*. Ancient Christian Commentary on Scripture: New Testament 7. InterVarsity, 1999.

**Bray, *Galatians, Ephesians*.** Bray, Gerald, ed. *Galatians, Ephesians*. Reformation Commentary on Scripture: New Testament 10. IVP Academic, 2011.

**Bray, *Romans*.** Bray, Gerald, ed. *Romans*. Ancient Christian Commentary on Scripture: New Testament 6. InterVarsity, 1998.

**Bredero, *Christendom*.** Bredero, Adriaan H. *Christendom and Christianity in the Middle Ages*. Translated by Reinder Bruinsma. Eerdmans, 1994.

**Brenz, *Epistolam*.** Brenz, Johannes. *In Epistolam, quam Apostolos Paulus ad Romanos scripset, commentariorum libri tres*. Frankfurt, 1564.

**Bright, *History*.** Bright, John. *A History of Israel*. 3rd ed. Westminster, 1981.

**Briones, "Already, Not Yet."** Briones, David. "Already, Not Yet: How to Live in the Last Days." Desiring God, August 4, 2020. https://www.desiringgod.org/articles/already-not-yet.

**Brougham, "Work."** Brougham, David R. "The Work of the Holy Spirit in Church Growth as Seen in Selected Indonesian Case Studies." DMiss diss., Fuller School of World Mission, 1988.

**Brown, *Authentic Fire*.** Brown, Michael L. *Authentic Fire: A Response to John MacArthur's Strange Fire*. Excel, 2013.

**Brown, *End*.** Brown, Michael L. *The End of the American Gospel Enterprise*. Destiny Image, 1993.

**Brown, *Global*.** Brown, Candy Gunther, ed. *Global Pentecostal and Charismatic Healing*. Oxford University Press, 2011.

**Brown, "Healing Words."** Brown, Candy Gunther. "Healing Words: Narratives of Spiritual Healing and Kathryn Kuhlman's Uses of Print Culture, 1947–1976." In *Religion and the Culture of Print in Modern America*, edited by Charles L. Cohen and Paul S. Boyer, 271–97. University of Wisconsin Press, 2008.

**Brown, *Holy Fire*.** Brown, Michael L. *Playing with Holy Fire: A Wake-Up Call to the Pentecostal-Charismatic Church*. Charisma House, 2018.

**Brown, "Introduction."** Brown, Candy Gunther. "Introduction: Pentecostalism and the Globalization of Illness and Healing." In Brown, *Global*, 3–26.

**Brown, *Kosher Jesus*.** Brown, Michael L. *The Real Kosher Jesus*. Frontline, 2012.

**Brown, *Late Antiquity*.** Brown, Peter. *The World of Late Antiquity*. Thames and Hudson, 1971.

**Brown, *Miracles*.** Brown, Colin. *Miracles and the Critical Mind*. Eerdmans, 1984.

**Brown, "Miracles and Kingdom."** Brown, Michael L. "The Miracles of Jesus and the Kingdom of God." In Graves, *Kingdom Case*, 27–45.

**Brown, *Objections*.** Brown, Michael L. *Answering Jewish Objections to Jesus*. Vol. 1, *General and Historical Objections*. Baker Books, 2000.

**Brown, *Power of God*.** Brown, Michael L. *Whatever Happened to the Power of God? Is the Charismatic Church Slain in the Spirit or Down for the Count?* Destiny Image, 1991.

**Brown, *Proving a Miracle*.** Brown, Joshua. *Proving a Miracle: Unlocking the Power of Prayer to Heal*. Harper, 2026.

**Brown, *Revival Answer Book*.** Brown, Michael L. *Revival Answer Book*. Renew Books, 2001.

**Brown, *Stained*.** Brown, Michael L. *Our Hands Are Stained with Blood: The Tragic Story of the "Church" and the Jewish People*. Destiny Image, 1992.

**Brown, "Tent Meetings."** Brown, Candy Gunther. "From Tent Meetings and Store-Front Healing Rooms to Walmarts and the Internet: Healing Spaces in the United States, the Americas, and the World, 1906–2006." *Church History* 75, no. 3 (September 2006): 631–47.

**Brown, "Testing Prayer."** Brown, Candy Gunther. "Testing Prayer: Can Science Prove the Healing Power of Prayer?" *Huffington Post*, March 2, 2012. https://www.huffpost.com/entry/testing-prayer-science-of-healing_b_1299915.

**Brown, *Testing Prayer*.** Brown, Candy Gunther. *Testing Prayer: Science and Healing*. Harvard University Press, 2012.

**Brown, *Thought*.** Brown, Colin. *Christianity and Western Thought: A History of Philosophers, Ideas and Movements*. Vol. 1, *From the Ancient World to the Age of the Enlightenment*. IVP Academic, 1990.

**Brown et al., "Study."** Brown, Candy Gunther, et al. "Study of the Therapeutic Effects of Proximal Intercessory Prayer (STEPP) on Auditory and Visual Impairments in Rural Mozambique." *Southern Medical Journal* 103, no. 9 (September 2010): 864–69.

**Bruce, *Acts: Greek*.** Bruce, F. F. *The Acts of the Apostles: The Greek Text with Introduction and Commentary*. 1st ed. Eerdmans, 1951.

**Bruce, "Holy Spirit in Acts."** Bruce, F. F. "The Holy Spirit in the Acts of the Apostles." *Interpretation* 27, no. 2 (1973): 166–83.

**Bruce, *Message*.** Bruce, F. F. *The Message of the New Testament*. Eerdmans, 1972.

**Bucer, *Comm. Rom*.** Bucer, Martin. *Metaphrases et enarrationes perpetuae Epistolarum D. Pauli Apostoli, quibus singulatim Apostoli omnia, cum argumenta. . . .* Strasbourg, 1536.

**Buckingham, *Daughter*.** Buckingham, Jamie. *Daughter of Destiny: Kathryn Kuhlman . . . Her Story*. Logos, 1976.

**Budd, *Numbers*.** Budd, Philip J. *Numbers*. Word Biblical Commentary 5. Word, 1984.

**Bultmann, "Demythologizing."** Bultmann, Rudolf. "On the Problem of Demythologizing (1952)." In *New Testament Mythology and Other Basic Writings*, edited by Schubert Ogden, 95–130. Fortress, 1984.

**Bultmann, *Kerygma and Myth*.** Bultmann, Rudolf. *Kerygma and Myth: A Theological Debate*. Edited by H. W. Bartsch. Edited, revised, and translated by R. H. Fuller. Harper & Row, 1961.

**Bultmann, "Mythology."** Bultmann, Rudolf. "New Testament and Mythology." In *New Testament Mythology and Other Basic Writings*, edited by Schubert Ogden, 1–43. Fortress, 1984.

**Burdick, *Tongues*.** Burdick, Donald W. *Tongues—To Speak or Not to Speak: A Contemporary Analysis of Glossolalia*. Moody, 1969.

**Burer and Wallace, "Junia."** Burer, Michael H., and Daniel B. Wallace, "Was Junia Really an Apostle? A Re-Examination of Rom. 16.7." *New Testament Studies* 47, no. 1 (2001): 76–91.

**Burgess, "Ancient Churches."** Burgess, Stanley M. "Evidence of the Spirit: The Ancient and Eastern Churches." In McGee, *Initial Evidence*, 3–19.

**Burgess, *Dictionary*.** Burgess, Stanley M., ed. *The New International Dictionary of Pentecostal and Charismatic Movements*. Zondervan, 2002.

**Burgess, "Evidence."** Burgess, Stanley M. "Evidence of the Spirit: The Medieval and Modern Western Churches." In McGee, *Initial Evidence*, 20–40.

**Burgess, *Holy Spirit*.** Burgess, Stanley M. *The Holy Spirit: Eastern Christian Traditions*. Hendrickson, 1989.

**Burgess, "Pandita Ramabai."** Burgess, Ruth Vassar. "Pandita Ramabai: A Woman for All Seasons: Pandita Ramabai Saraswati Mary Dongre Medhavi (1858–1922)." *Asian Journal of Pentecostal Studies* 9, no. 2 (July 2006): 183–98.

**Burgess, *Peoples*.** Burgess, Stanley M. *Christian Peoples of the Spirit: A Documentary History of Pentecostal Spirituality from the Early Church to the Present*. New York University Press, 2011.

**Burgess, "Proclaiming the Gospel."** Burgess, Stanley M. "Proclaiming the Gospel with Miraculous Gifts in the Postbiblical Early Church." In *The Kingdom and the Power: Are Healing and the Spiritual Gifts Used by Jesus and the Early Church Meant for the Church Today?*, edited by Gary S. Greig and Kevin N. Springer, 277–88. Regal, 1993.

**Burgess, "Proclamation."** Burgess, Stanley M. "The Proclamation of the Gospel with Accompanying Charismata in Post-Biblical Early Church History." In Graves, *Strangers*, 355–67.

**Burgess, *Revolution*.** Burgess, Richard. *Nigeria's Christian Revolution: The Civil War Revival and Its Pentecostal Progeny (1967–2006)*. Regnum Studies in Mission. Wipf & Stock, 2008.

**Burgess, *Spirit and Church*.** Burgess, Stanley M. *The Spirit and the Church: Antiquity*. Hendrickson, 1984.

**Burkert, *Religion*.** Burkert, Walter. *Greek Religion*. Translated by John Raffan. Harvard University Press, 1985.

**Burkholder, "Remembering Revival."** Burkholder, Jared S. "Remembering Revival: The Enduring Impact of the Moravian Story." *Christian History* 153 (2024): 10–12.

**Burns, *Debate*.** Burns, Robert M. *The Great Debate on Miracles: From Joseph Glanvill to David Hume*. Associated University Presses; Bucknell University Press, 1981.

**Burns, "Hume."** Burns, Robert M. "David Hume and Miracles in Historical Perspective." PhD diss., Princeton University, 1971.

**Burridge, *Gospels*.** Burridge, Richard A. *What Are the Gospels? A Comparison with Graeco-Roman Biography*. 2nd ed. Eerdmans, 2004.

**Bush and Pegues, *Move*.** Bush, Luis, and Beverly Pegues. *The Move of the Holy Spirit in the 10/40 Window*. Edited by Jane Rumph. YWAM, 1999.

**Bushnell, *Nature*.** Bushnell, Horace. *Nature and the Supernatural as Together Constituting the One System of God*. Scribner, 1858.

**Byaruhanga-Akiiki and Kealotswe, *Healing*.** Byaruhanga-Akiiki, A. B. T., and Obed N. O. Kealotswe. *African Theology of Healing: The Infinite Oneness*. University of Botswana Press, 1995.

**Bynum, *Feast*.** Bynum, Caroline Walker. *Holy Feast and Holy Fast: The Religious Significance of Food to Medieval Women*. University of California Press, 1987.

**Cain, "Miracles."** Cain, Andrew. "Miracles, Martyrs, and Arians: Gregory of Tours' Sources for His Account of the Vandal Kingdom." *Vigiliae Christianae* 59, no. 4 (2005): 412–37.

**Calvin, *Acts*.** Calvin, John. *Commentaries: The Acts of the Apostles, 1–13*. Translated by John W. Fraser and W. J. G. McDonald. Eerdmans, 1965.

**Calvin, *Epistles*.** Calvin, John. *Commentary on the Epistles of Paul the Apostle to the Corinthians*. Translated by John Pringle. Baker Books, 2003.

**Calvin, *1 Corinthians*.** Calvin, John. *1 Corinthians*. New Testament Commentaries 9. Eerdmans, 1996.

**Calvin, *Harmony*.** Calvin, John. *A Harmony of the Gospels: Matthew, Mark and Luke*. 3 vols. Eerdmans, 1972.

**Calvin, *Romans*.** Calvin, John. *Romans: John Calvin's Commentary*. Translated by John Owen. Beloved Publishing, 2014.

**Campbell, *Church*.** Campbell, Joseph E. *The Pentecostal Holiness Church, 1898–1948: Its Background and History*. Advocate Press, 1951.

**Capps, *Village Psychiatrist*.** Capps, Donald. *Jesus the Village Psychiatrist*. Westminster John Knox, 2008.

**Caram, *Fall*.** Caram, Dan. *The Fall and Rise of the Christian Church*. Zion Christian, 2007.

**Carey, *Enquiry*.** Carey, William. *An Enquiry into the Obligations of Christians*. Ann Ireland; J. Johnson; reproduced by Henderson & Spalding, 1792.

**Carlson, "Dream."** Carlson, Darren. "When Muslims Dream of Jesus." The Gospel Coalition, May 31, 2018. Accessed August 18, 2024. https://www.thegospelcoalition.org/article/muslims-dream-jesus/.

**Carpenter, "Recovering."** Carpenter, John B. "Recovering from Strange and Friendly Fire." *Christian Post*, November 5, 2013. Accessed September 5, 2024. https://www.christianpost.com/news/recovering-from-strange-and-friendly-fire-107976/.

**Carson, *Fallacies*.** Carson, D. A. *Exegetical Fallacies*. Baker, 1984.

**Carson, *Fallacies*$^2$.** Carson, D. A. *Exegetical Fallacies*. 2nd ed. Baker, 1996.

**Carson, *Showing Spirit*.** Carson, D. A. *Showing the Spirit: A Theological Exposition of 1 Corinthians 12–14*. Baker, 1987. Repackaged ed., 2019.

**Cartledge, *Charismatic Glossolalia*.** Cartledge, Mark J. *Charismatic Glossolalia: An Empirical-Theological Study*. Ashgate, 2002.

**Cartledge, "Glossolalia."** Cartledge, Mark J. "The Nature and Function of New Testament Glossolalia." *Evangelical Quarterly* 72, no. 2 (2000): 135–50.

**Cartledge, *Perspectives*.** Cartledge, Mark J., ed. *Speaking in Tongues: Multi-Disciplinary Perspectives*. Studies in Pentecostal and Charismatic Issues. Paternoster, 2006.

**Cartledge, "Tongues-Speech."** Cartledge, Mark J. "The Practice of Tongues-Speech as a Case Study: A Practical-Theological Perspective." In Cartledge, *Perspectives*, 206–34.

**Cartwright, *Autobiography*.** Cartwright, Peter. *Autobiography of Peter Cartwright: The Backwoods Preacher*. Carlton & Porter, 1857. Available online at https://archive.org/details/autobiographyofp00incart.

**Casdorph, *Miracles*.** Casdorph, H. Richard. *The Miracles: A Medical Doctor Says Yes to Miracles!* Logos, 1976.

**Cavadini, "Note."** Cavadini, John C. "A Note on Gregory's Use of Miracles in 'The Life and Miracles of St. Benedict.'" *American Benedictine Review* 49, no. 1 (1998): 104–20.

**César, "Life."** César, Waldo. "Daily Life and Transcendence in Pentecostalism." In *Pentecostalism and the Future of the Christian Churches: Promises, Limitations, Challenges*, by Richard Shaull and Waldo César. Eerdmans, 2000.

**Chadwick, *Reformation*.** Chadwick, Owen. *The Reformation*. Pelican History of the Church 3. Penguin, 1964.

**Challies, "Strange Fire Conference."** Challies, Tim. "Strange Fire Conference: A Case for Cessationism." *Challies* (blog), October 17, 2013. Accessed September 5, 2024. https://www.challies.com/liveblogging/strange-fire-conference-a-case-for-cessationism/.

**Chan, *Asian Theology*.** Chan, Simon. *Grassroots Asian Theology*. IVP Academic, 2014.

**Chan, "Significance."** Chan, Joshua H. M. "The Ethnolinguistic Significance of Tongues in Acts: From Xenolalia to Naturally Acquired Languages." *Journal of Biblical Literature* 145, no. 1 (2026): 133–55.

**Chaplin, "Conversations."** Chaplin, Jane D. "Conversations in History: Arrian and Herodotus, Parmenio and Alexander." *Greek, Roman, and Byzantine Studies* 51, no. 4 (2011): 613–33.

**Chappell, "Healing Movement."** Chappell, Paul Gale. "The Divine Healing Movement in America." PhD diss., Drew University Graduate School, 1983.

**Chempakassery, "Jerusalem Pentecost."** Chempakassery, Philip. "Jerusalem Pentecost: An Indian Reinterpretation and Challenges." *Jeevadhara* 34, no. 200 (2004): 108–21.

**Chesnut, *Born Again in Brazil*.** Chesnut, R. Andrew. *Born Again in Brazil: The Pentecostal Boom and the Pathogens of Poverty*. Rutgers University Press, 1997.

**Chesnut, "Exorcising."** Chesnut, Andrew. "Exorcising the Demons of Deprivation: Divine Healing and Conversion in Brazilian Pentecostalism." In Brown, *Global*, 169–85.

**Chester, *Reading Paul*.** Chester, Stephen J. *Reading Paul with the Reformers: Reconciling Old and New Perspectives*. Eerdmans, 2017.

**Chevallier, *Ancien Testament*.** Chevallier, Max-Alain. *Souffle de Dieu: Le Saint-Esprit dans le Nouveau Testament*. Vol. 1, *Ancien Testament, hellénisme et judaïsme, la tradition synoptique, l'oeuvre de Luc*. Point théologique 26. Beauchesne, 1978.

**Chevreau, *Turnings*.** Chevreau, Guy. *Turnings: The Kingdom of God and the Western World*. Sovereign World, 2004.

**ChildHope, "Home Page."** ChildHope home page. Accessed February 22, 2025. https://childhopeonline.org/.

**Cho, "Foundation."** Cho, Sung Hyun. "A Theoretical Foundation for a Healing Ministry in the Context of the Korean Evangelical Holiness Church." ThM thesis, Fuller School of World Mission, 1995.

**Cho, "Spirit and Kingdom."** Cho, Youngmo. "Spirit and Kingdom in Luke-Acts: Proclamation as the Primary Role of the Spirit in Relation to the Kingdom of God in Luke-Acts." *Asian Journal of Pentecostal Studies* 6, no. 2 (2003): 173–97.

**Cho, *Spirit and Kingdom*.** Cho, Youngmo. *Spirit and Kingdom in the Writings of Luke and Paul: An Attempt to Reconcile These Concepts*. PBMon. Paternoster, 2005.

**Choi, *Rise*.** Choi, Meesaeng Lee. *The Rise of the Korean Holiness Church in Relation to the American Holiness Movement: Wesley's "Scriptural Holiness" and the "Fourfold Gospel."* Pietist and Wesleyan Studies 28. Scarecrow, 2008.

**Christerson and Flory, *Rise of Network Christianity*.** Christerson, Brad, and Richard Flory. *The Rise of Network Christianity: How Independent Leaders Are Changing the Religious Landscape*. Oxford University Press, 2017.

**Church of God in Christ, "Office."** "Office of Public Policy." Church of God in Christ (website). Accessed February 9, 2026. https://www.cogic.org/publicpolicy/about/office-of-public-policy/.

**Ciampa and Rosner, *Corinthians*.** Ciampa, Roy E., and Brian S. Rosner. *The First Letter to the Corinthians*. PNTC. Eerdmans, 2010.

**Clark, "Strange Fire."** Clark, Randy. "*Strange Fire*: Analysis of Introduction, Appendix, and General Method." In Graves, *Strangers*, 59–68.

**Cloud, "Charity."** Cloud, David. "Charity: 1 Corinthians 13." Way of Life Literature, October 23, 2012. https://www.wayoflife.org/reports/1_corinthians_13.html.

**Cohen, "Contemporaries."** Cohen, Carl. "Martin Luther and His Jewish Contemporaries." *Jewish Social Studies* 25, no. 3 (July 1963): 195–204.

**Cohn-Sherbok, "Analysis."** Cohn-Sherbok, Daniel M. "An Analysis of Jesus' Arguments Concerning the Plucking of Grain on the Sabbath." *Journal for the Study of the New Testament* 2 (1979): 31–41.

**Cole, *Numbers*.** Cole, R. Dennis. *Numbers*. New American Commentary. Broadman & Holman, 2000.

**Coleman, "Wealth."** Coleman, Simon. "Why Health *and* Wealth? Dimensions of Prosperity Among Swedish Charismatics." In Brown, *Global*, 47–60.

**Collins, *Charismatic Christianity*.** Collins, Helen. *Charismatic Christianity: Introducing Its Theology Through the Gifts of the Spirit*. Baker Academic, 2023.

**Collins, *Corinthians*.** Collins, Raymond F. *First Corinthians*. SP 7. Liturgical Press, 1999.

**Conn, *Army*.** Conn, Charles W. *Like a Mighty Army Moves the Church of God, 1886–1955*. Church of God Publishing House, 1955.

**Convoy of Hope, "Home Page."** Convoy of Hope home page. Accessed February 20, 2025. https://convoyofhope.org/.

**Conwell, *Life*.** Conwell, Russell. *Life of Charles Haddon Spurgeon: The World's Greatest Preacher*. Edgewood Publishing Company, 1892.

**Cooper and Gregory, *Signs*.** Cooper, Kate, and Jeremy Gregory, eds. *Signs, Wonders, Miracles: Representations of Divine Power in the Life of the Church; Papers Read at the 2003 Summer Meeting and the 2004 Winter Meeting of the Ecclesiastical History Society*. Boydell & Brewer, for the Ecclesiastical History Society, 2005.

**Cooper-White, *Wisdom*.** Cooper-White, Pamela. *Shared Wisdom: Use of the Self in Pastoral Care and Counseling*. Rev. ed. Fortress, 2024.

**Cosmos, *Huguenot Prophecy*.** Cosmos, Georgia. *Huguenot Prophecy and Clandestine Worship in the Eighteenth Century: "The Sacred Theatre of the Cévennes."* Ashgate, 2005.

**Cottle, "Tongues."** Cottle, Ron. "Tongues Shall Cease." In Graves, *Strangers*, 487–92.

**Cotton, *Raised*.** Cotton, Margaret J., as told by Charlie and Florentina Mada. *Raised! An Inspirational True Story of Two Courageous Young Parents in the Midst of a Tragic Accident, and the Love, Grace, and Miracles That Saved Three Lives.* Christian Faith, 2018.

**Cotton, "Spirit in Numbers 11."** Cotton, Roger D. "The Spirit in Numbers 11: God's Pentecostal Plan." In Keener and Oliverio Jr., *Canon*, 12–15.

**Coulter, *College Life*.** Coulter, E. Merton. *College Life in the Old South*. Macmillan, 1928.

**Cox, *Fire*.** Cox, Harvey. *Fire from Heaven: The Rise of Pentecostal Spirituality and the Reshaping of Religion in the Twenty-First Century*. Addison-Wesley, 1995.

**Cox, "Foreword."** Cox, Harvey. "Foreword." In Brown, *Global*, xvii–xxi.

**Cox, "Miracles."** Cox, Harvey. "Into the Age of Miracles: Culture, Religion, and the Market Revolution." *World Policy Journal* 14, no. 1 (Spring 1997): 87–95.

**Cracknell and White, *Methodism*.** Cracknell, Kenneth, and Susan J. White. *An Introduction to World Methodism*. Cambridge University Press, 2005.

**Crandall, *Raising*.** Crandall, Chauncey W., IV. *Raising the Dead: A Doctor Encounters the Miraculous*. FaithWords, 2010.

**Cranfield, *Romans*.** Cranfield, C. E. B. *A Critical and Exegetical Commentary on the Epistle to the Romans*. ICC. T&T Clark, 1979.

**Crawford, *Miracles*.** Crawford, Don. *Miracles in Indonesia: God's Power Builds His Church!* Tyndale, 1972.

**Crawford, *Revival*.** Crawford, Mary K. *The Shantung Revival*. China Baptist Publication Society, 1933.

**Cripplegate, "Q&A 2."** Riccardi, Mike. "Strange Fire – Panel Q&A 2 – MacArthur, Mbewe, Johnson, & Busenitz." Cripplegate. Accessed August 23, 2024. http://thecripplegate.com/strange-fire-panel-qa-2-macarthur-mbewe-johnson-busenitz/.

**Crosby, *History*.** Crosby, Thomas. *The History of the English Baptists, from the Reformation to the Beginning of the Reign of King George I*. 4 vols. John Robinson, J. Hodges, and A. Ward, 1740.

**Cruz, *Mysteries*.** Cruz, Joan Carroll. *Mysteries, Marvels and Miracles: In the Lives of the Saints*. TAN Books, 1997.

**Crystal, "Applied Sociolinguistics."** Crystal, David. "Why Did the Crowd Think St Peter Was Drunk? An Exercise in Applied Sociolinguistics." *New Blackfriars* 79, no. 924 (1998): 72–76.

**Cullmann, *Worship*.** Cullmann, Oscar. *Early Christian Worship*. Westminster, 1953.

**Cunville, "Evangelization."** Cunville, R. R. "The Evangelization of Northeast India." DMiss diss., Fuller Theological Seminary, 1975.

**Curtis, "Character."** Curtis, Heather D. "The Global Character of Nineteenth-Century Divine Healing." In Brown, *Global*, 29–45.

**Curtis, *Faith*.** Curtis, Heather D. *Faith in the Great Physician: Suffering and Divine Healing in American Culture, 1860–1900*. Johns Hopkins University Press, 2007.

**Curtis, "Houses of Healing."** Curtis, Heather D. "Houses of Healing: Sacred Space, Spiritual Practice, and the Transformation of Female Suffering in the Faith Cure Movement, 1870–90." *Church History* 75, no. 3 (2006): 598–611.

**Curtis, "Lord for Body."** Curtis, Heather D. "The Lord for the Body: Pain, Suffering, and the Practice of Divine Healing in Late-Nineteenth-Century American Protestantism." ThD diss., Harvard University, 2005.

**Cutten, *Speaking with Tongues*.** Cutten, George Barton. *Speaking with Tongues: Historically and Psychologically Considered*. Yale University Press, 1927.

**Dale, "Healing."** Dale, Nigel. "Healing and Medicine—Complementary?" In *We Believe in Healing*, edited by Ann England, 107–18. Marshall, Morgan & Scott, 1982.

**Dallimore, *Whitefield*.** Dallimore, Arnold A. *George Whitefield*. Banner of Truth Trust, 1970.

**Dal Santo, "Gregory."** Dal Santo, Matthew. "Gregory the Great and Eustratius of Constantinople: The Dialogues on the Miracles of the Italian Fathers as an Apology for the Cult of Saints." *Journal of Early Christian Studies* 17, no. 3 (2009): 421–57.

**Danyun, *Lilies*.** Danyun. *Lilies Amongst Thorns*. Translated by Brother Dennis. Sovereign World, 1991.

**Darling, *Healing*.** Darling, Frank C. *Christian Healing in the Middle Ages and Beyond*. Vista, 1990.

**Das, *Galatians*.** Das, A. Andrew. *Galatians*. Concordia Commentary: A Theological Exposition of Sacred Scripture. Concordia Publishing House, 2014.

**Daston, "Facts."** Daston, Lorraine. "Marvelous Facts and Miraculous Evidence in Early Modern Europe." *Critical Inquiry* 18 (Autumn 1991): 93–124.

**Davey, *Robe*.** Davey, Cyril J. *The Yellow Robe: The Story of Sadhu Sundar Singh*. SCM, 1950.

**Davies, *Paul*.** Davies, W. D. *Paul and Rabbinic Judaism: Some Rabbinic Elements in Pauline Theology*. 4th ed. Fortress, 1980.

**Davies, *Torah*.** Davies, W. D. *Torah in the Messianic Age and/or the Age to Come*. Journal of Biblical Literature Monograph Series 7. SBL, 1952.

**Davies and Allison, *Matthew*.** Davies, W. D., and Dale C. Allison. *A Critical and Exegetical Commentary on the Gospel According to Saint Matthew*. 3 vols. ICC. T&T Clark, 1988–97.

**Davies and Conway, *Christianity*.** Davies, Noel, and Martin Conway. *World Christianity in the Twentieth Century*. SCM Core Text. SCM, 2008.

**Davis, "Anabaptism."** Davis, Kenneth R. "Anabaptism as a Charismatic Movement." *Mennonite Quarterly Review* 53, no. 3 (1979): 219–34.

**Davis, *War of Camisards.*** Davis, Stephen M. *The War of the Camisards (1702–1704): Huguenot Insurrection During the Reign of Louis XIV*. Wipf & Stock, 2024.

**Dawson, *Healing.*** Dawson, George Gordon. *Healing: Pagan and Christian*. SPCK; Macmillan, 1935.

**Dawson, *Reconciliation.*** Dawson, John. *What Christians Should Know About Reconciliation*. International Reconciliation Coalition, 1998.

**Dawson, *Wounds.*** Dawson, John. *Healing America's Wounds*. Regal, 1994.

**Dayton, *Roots.*** Dayton, Donald. *Theological Roots of Pentecostalism*. Scarecrow, 1987. Reprint, Hendrickson, 1994.

**De Arteaga, "Parody."** De Arteaga, William. "*Strange Fire* as a Parody of Jonathan Edwards's Theology." In Graves, *Strangers*, 15–33.

**De Arteaga, *Quenching*.** De Arteaga, William. *Quenching the Spirit: Discover the Real Spirit Behind the Charismatic Controversy*. Creation House, 1996.

**De Arteaga, "Strange Fire."** De Arteaga, William. "John MacArthur's Strange Fire as Parody of Jonathan Edwards' Theology." *The Pneuma Review*. November 8, 2013. Accessed August 29, 2024. http://pneumareview.com/john-macarthurs-strange-fire-as-parody-of-jonathan-edwards-theology-by-william-de-arteaga/17/.

**Deere, "Opinion."** Deere, Jack. "Opinion: Jack Deere Reevaluates Legacy of Mike Bickle & KC Prophets, Calls for Investigation." *Roys Report*, March 11, 2024.

**Deere, "Periods."** Deere, Jack. "Were There Only Three Periods of Miracles?" In Graves, *Strangers*, 209–24.

**Deere, "Power."** Deere, Jack. "My Desire for Power Enabled Paul Cain's Manipulation." *Divine Detours* (blog). March 13, 2024. Accessed September 28, 2024. https://stephendeere.substack.com/p/jack-deere-my-desire-for-power-enabled.

**Deere, *Still Surprised.*** Deere, Jack S. *Why I Am Still Surprised by the Power of the Spirit*. Zondervan Reflective, 2020.

**Deere, *Surprised.*** Deere, Jack S. *Surprised by the Power of the Spirit: Discovering How God Speaks and Heals Today*. Zondervan, 1993.

**Deere, *Voice.*** Deere, Jack. *Surprised by the Voice of God: How God Speaks Today Through Prophecies, Dreams, and Visions*. Zondervan, 1996.

**Deichmann, "Lessons."** Deichmann, Wendy J. "Lessons from Mozambique." *Good News*, January 2015: 20–22. https://goodnewsmag.org/2014/12/lessons-from-mozambique/.

**Deissmann, *Light.*** Deissmann, G. Adolf. *Light from the Ancient East*. Baker, 1978.

**Dempster, Klaus, and Petersen, *Called and Empowered.*** Dempster, Murray W., Byron D. Klaus, and Douglas Petersen, eds. *Called and Empowered: Global Mission in Pentecostal Perspective*. Hendrickson, 1991.

**Dempster, Klaus, and Petersen, *Globalization of Pentecostalism.*** Dempster, Murray W., Byron D. Klaus, and Douglas Petersen, eds. *The Globalization of Pentecostalism: A Religion Made to Travel.* Paternoster; Regnum, 1999.

**Dermawan, "Study."** Dermawan, Julia Theis. "A Study of the Nias Revival in Indonesia." *Asian Journal of Pentecostal Studies* 6, no. 2 (2003): 247–63.

**Derrenbacker, *Practices.*** Derrenbacker, Robert A., Jr. *Ancient Compositional Practices and the Synoptic Problem.* BETL 186. Leuven University Press, 2005.

**De Wet, "Signs."** De Wet, Christiaan Rudolph. "Signs and Wonders in Church Growth." MA thesis, Fuller School of World Mission, 1981.

**Dibelius, *Tradition.*** Dibelius, Martin. *From Tradition to Gospel.* Translated from the 2nd (1933) German ed. by Bertram Lee Woolf. James Clarke; Attic Press, 1971.

**Dihle, "Biography."** Dihle, Albrecht. "The Gospels and Greek Biography." In *The Gospel and the Gospels*, edited by Peter Stuhlmacher, 361–86. Eerdmans, 1991.

**Dillenberger, *Martin Luther.*** Dillenberger, John, ed. *Martin Luther: Selections from His Writings.* Anchor Books, 1962.

**Di Sabatino, "Frisbee."** Di Sabatino, David. "Appendix 3: Lonnie Frisbee." In *The Quest for the Radical Middle: A History of the Vineyard*, edited by Bill Jackson, 392–407. Vineyard International, 1999.

**Dod, "Healer."** Dod, Marcus. "Jesus as Healer." *The Biblical World* 15 (1900): 169–77.

**Dodwell, *Answer.*** Dodwell, William. *A Free Answer to Dr. Middleton's Free Inquiry into the Miraculous Powers of the Primitive Church.* S. Birt, 1749.

**Doles, *Miracles.*** Doles, Jeff. *Miracles and Manifestations of the Holy Spirit in the History of the Church.* Walking Barefoot Ministries, 2008.

**Dollar, "Theology of Healing."** Dollar, Harold Ellis. "A Cross-Cultural Theology of Healing." DMiss. diss., Fuller Theological Seminary School of World Mission, 1981.

**Dorries, "Controversy."** Dorries, David W. "Nineteenth Century British Christological Controversy, Centering upon Edward Irving's Doctrine of Christ's Human Nature." PhD diss., University of Aberdeen, 1988.

**Dorries, "Irving and Spirit Baptism."** Dorries, David W. "Edward Irving and the 'Standing Sign' of Spirit Baptism." In McGee, *Initial Evidence*, 41–56.

**Douglas, *Dictionary of Church.*** Douglas, J. D., ed. *The New International Dictionary of the Christian Church.* Zondervan, 1974.

**Dowd, *Prayer.*** Dowd, Sharyn Echols. *Prayer, Power, and the Problem of Suffering: Mark 11:22–25 in the Context of Markan Theology.* Society of Biblical Literature Dissertation Series 105. Scholars, 1988.

**Downen, Tedesco, and Hennes, "Need to Know."** Downen, Robert, John Tedesco, and Rebecca Hennes. "What You Need to Know About the Southern Baptist Convention and Allegations of Sexual Abuse." *Houston Chronicle*, May 23, 2022.

**Downing, *Cynics*.** Downing, F. Gerald. *Cynics, Paul and the Pauline Churches: Cynics and Christian Origins II*. Routledge, 1998.

**Doyle, *Dreams*.** Doyle, Tom, with Greg Webster. *Dreams and Visions: Is Jesus Awakening the Muslim World?* Thomas Nelson, 2012.

**Doyle, *Killing Christians*.** Doyle, Tom, with Greg Webster. *Killing Christians: Living the Faith Where It's Not Safe to Believe*. W Publishing, 2015.

**Droll, *Dreams*.** Droll, Anna M. *Dreams and Visions in African Pentecostal Spirituality: The Sub-Saharan Horizon of the Pneumatological Imagination*. Global Pentecostal and Charismatic Studies 45. Brill, 2024.

**Droogers, "Globalisation."** Droogers, André. "Globalisation and Pentecostal Success." In *Between Babel and Pentecost: Transnational Pentecostalism in Africa and Latin America*, edited by André Corten and Ruth Marshall-Fratani, 41–61. Indiana University Press, 2001.

**Dubose, "Foreword."** Dubose, Rick. "Foreword." In *Speaking in Tongues: A Multidisciplinary Defense*, edited by Timothy Laurito, ix–xi. Wipf & Stock, 2021.

**Duewel, *Revival Fire*.** Duewel, Wesley L. *Revival Fire*. Zondervan, 1995.

**Duffin, *Miracles*.** Duffin, Jacalyn. *Medical Miracles: Doctors, Saints, and Healing in the Modern World*. Oxford University Press, 2009.

**Duguid, "Kind of Prophecy."** Duguid, Iain M. "What Kind of Prophecy Continues? Defining the Difference Between Continuationism and Cessationism." In *Redeeming the Life of the Mind: Essays in Honor of Vern Poythress*, edited John M. Frame, Wayne Grudem, and John J. Hughes, 112–28. Crossway, 2017.

**Dumbrell, *Covenant*.** Dumbrell, William J. *Covenant and Creation: An Old Testament Covenantal Theology*. Paternoster, 1984.

**Dunn, *Acts*.** Dunn, James D. G. *The Acts of the Apostles*. Narrative Commentaries. Trinity Press International, 1996.

**Dunn, *Galatians*.** Dunn, James D. G. *The Epistle to the Galatians*. Black's New Testament Commentary. A&C Black; Hendrickson, 1995.

**Dunn, *Jesus and Spirit*.** Dunn, James D. G. *Jesus and the Spirit: A Study of the Religious and Charismatic Experience of Jesus and the First Christians as Reflected in the New Testament*. SCM, 1975.

**Dunn, "Kingdom."** Dunn, James D. G. "Spirit and Kingdom." *Expository Times* 82, no. 2 (1970): 36–40.

***Early Commentaries*.** *Early Commentaries on Romans: Augustine of Hippo and Theodoret of Cyrus*. Litteral Truth Publishing, n.d.

**Earman, "Bayes."** Earman, John. "Bayes, Hume, and Miracles." *Faith and Philosophy* 10, no. 3 (1993): 293–310.

**Earman, *Failure*.** Earman, John. *Hume's Abject Failure: The Argument Against Miracles*. Oxford University Press, 2000.

**Earman, "Hume."** Earman, John. "Bayes, Hume, Price, and Miracles." In *Bayes's Theorem*, edited by Richard Swinburne, 91–109. Oxford University Press, 2005.

**Eckardt, "Reformation."** Eckardt, Alice L. "The Reformation and the Jews." *Shofar* 7, no. 4 (Summer 1989): 23–47.

**Edgar, *Satisfied*.** Edgar, Thomas. *Satisfied by the Promise of the Spirit*. Kregel Resources, 1996.

**Edwards, "Account of Revival."** Edwards, Jonathan. "An Account of the Revival in Northampton in 1740–42 in a Letter to a Minister of Boston." In Edwards, *Revival*.

**Edwards, "Distinguishing Marks."** Edwards, Jonathan. "The Distinguishing Marks of a Work of the Spirit of God." In Edwards, *Revival*.

**Edwards, "Distinguishing Marks of Work."** Edwards, Jonathan. "The Distinguishing Marks of a Work of the Spirit of God." In *The Works of Jonathan Edwards*. Vol. 4, *The Great Awakening*. Edited by C. C. Goen. Yale University Press, 1972.

**Edwards, "Letter to Prince."** Edwards, Jonathan. "Letter to Rev. Thomas Prince of Boston." Dated December 12, 1743. Pressbooks. Accessed February 5, 2026. https://minnstate.pressbooks.pub/ushistory1/chapter/edwards-account-of-revival-1743/.

**Edwards, "Luther and Jews."** Edwards, Mark U., Jr. "Martin Luther and the Jews: Is There a Holocaust Connection?" *Shofar* 1, no. 4 (Summer 1983): 14–16.

**Edwards, *Mark*.** Edwards, James R. *The Gospel According to Mark*. Pillar New Testament Commentary. Eerdmans, 2002.

**Edwards, *Printing*.** Edwards, Mark U., Jr. *Printing, Propaganda, and Martin Luther*. University of California Press, 1994.

**Edwards, *Revival*.** Edwards, Jonathan. *Jonathan Edwards on Revival*. Banner of Truth, 1984.

**Eire, *Flew*.** Eire, Carlos M. N. *They Flew: A History of the Impossible*. Yale University Press, 2023.

**Ekechi, "Medical Factor."** Ekechi, Felix K. "The Medical Factor in Christian Conversion in Africa: Observations from Southeastern Nigeria." *Missiology* 21, no. 3 (1993): 289–309.

**Elbert, "Exegesis."** Elbert, Paul. "Face to Face: Then or Now? An Exegesis of First Corinthians 13:8–13." In Graves, *Strangers*, 493–520.

**Elbert, "Face to Face."** Elbert, Paul. "Face to Face: Then or Now?" Paper presented to the seventh annual meeting of the Society for Pentecostal Studies, Springfield, MO, December 1–3, 1977.

**Eliade, *Rites*.** Eliade, Mircea. *Rites and Symbols of Initiation: The Mysteries of Birth and Rebirth*. Translated by Willard R. Trask. Harper & Row, 1958.

**Ellens, *Miracles*.** Ellens, J. Harold, ed. *Miracles: God, Science, and Psychology in the Paranormal*. Vol. 1, *Religious and Spiritual Events*. Praeger, 2008.

**Ellingsen, *Roots*.** Ellingsen, Mark. *Reclaiming Our Roots: An Inclusive Introduction to Church History*. Vol. 2, *Martin Luther to Martin Luther King Jr.* Trinity Press International, 1999.

**Ellis, "Tongues."** Ellis, W. T. "Have Gift of Tongues." *Chicago Daily News*, January 14, 1908.

**Ensley, *Sounds*.** Ensley, Eddie. *Sounds of Wonder: Speaking in Tongues in the Catholic Tradition*. Paulist Press, 1977.

**Escobar, *Tides*.** Escobar, Samuel. *Changing Tides: Latin America and World Mission Today*. American Society of Missiology Monograph Series 31. Orbis Books, 2002.

**Eskridge, *Family*.** Eskridge, Larry. *God's Forever Family: The Jesus People Movement in America*. Oxford University Press, 2013.

**Espinosa, "Healing in Borderlands."** Espinosa, Gastón. "Latino Pentecostal Healing in the North American Borderlands." In Brown, *Global*, 129–49.

**Evangel University, "Confirmed."** Evangel University. "A Calling Confirmed: Chidimma Nwaedi's Journey to Evangel University." *Evangel* 7, no. 1 (2025): 26–27. https://view.publitas.com/evangel-university/evangel-magazine-winter-2025/page/26-27.

**Evans, "Pursuit."** Evans, William B. "Pursuit of 'the Common and the Constant': Mercerburg's Clash with Revivalism." *Christian History* 155 (2025): 26–29.

**Evans, *Wycliffe*.** Evans, G. R. *John Wycliffe: Myth and Reality*. IVP Academic, 2005.

**Evener, "Reception."** Evener, Vincent M. "Jewishness as an Explanation for Rejection of the Word: Caspar Güttel's Reception of Martin Luther's Anti-Judaism." *Church History and Religious Culture* 95, nos. 2–3 (2015): 203–21.

**Fabisiak, *Nocturnal Side*.** Fabisiak, Thomas. *The "Nocturnal Side of Science" in David Friedrich Strauss's* Life of Jesus Critically Examined. Emory Studies in Early Christianity. SBL, 2015.

**Fadda, "Miraculous."** Fadda, Anna Maria Luiselli. "*Constat Ergo Inter Nos Verba Signa Esse*: The Understanding of the Miraculous in Anglo-Saxon Society." In Cooper and Gregory, *Signs*, 56–66.

**Farah, *Pinnacle*.** Farah, Charles, Jr. *From the Pinnacle of the Temple: Faith or Presumption?* Logos, 1979.

**Farges, *Phenomena*.** Farges, Albert. *Mystical Phenomena Compared with Their Human and Diabolical Counterfeits*. Translated S. P. Jacques. Burns Oats & Washbourne, 1925.

**Faupel, "Speaking in Tongues."** Faupel, D. William. "Speaking in Tongues (Glossolalia)." In McClymond, *Revivals*, 1:410–12.

**Faw, *Acts*.** Faw, Charles E. *Acts: Believers Church Bible Commentary*. Herald, 1993.

**Fazzina, *Divine Intervention*.** Fazzina, Daniel. *Divine Intervention: 50 True Stories of God's Miracles Today*. Charisma House, 2014.

**Fee, *Corinthians*.** Fee, Gordon D. *The First Epistle to the Corinthians*. New International Commentary on the New Testament. Eerdmans, 1987.

**Fee, *Corinthians*[2].** Fee, Gordon D. *The First Epistle to the Corinthians*. Rev. ed. New International Commentary on the New Testament. Eerdmans, 2014.

**Fee, *Disease*.** Fee, Gordon D. *The Disease of the Health and Wealth Gospels*. The Word for Today, 1979.

**Fee, *Gospel*.** Fee, Gordon D. *Gospel and Spirit: Issues in New Testament Hermeneutics*. Hendrickson, 1991.

**Fee, *Listening*.** Fee, Gordon D. *Listening to the Spirit in the Text*. Eerdmans, 2000.

**Fee, *Presence*.** Fee, Gordon D. *God's Empowering Presence: The Holy Spirit in the Letters of Paul*. Hendrickson, 1994.

**Fee and Stuart, *How to Read*.** Fee, Gordon D., and Douglas Stuart. *How to Read the Bible for All Its Worth*. Zondervan, 1982.

**Fenner, "Garden."** Fenner, Chris. "In the Garden." *Hymnology Archive* (website), September 18, 2019. Accessed January 4, 2026. https://www.hymnologyarchive.com/in-the-garden.

**Ferguson, *Holy Spirit*.** Ferguson, Sinclair B. *The Holy Spirit*. Contours of Christian Theology. IVP Academic, 1997.

**Ferguson, *Organizing*.** Ferguson, Charles W. *Organizing to Beat the Devil: Methodists and the Making of America*. Doubleday, 1971.

**Fiddes, *Romans*.** Fiddes, Paul S. *Romans Through the Centuries*. Wiley Blackwell Bible Commentaries. Wiley Blackwell, 2026.

**Fiensy, *Archaeology*.** Fiensy, David A. *The Archaeology of Daily Life: Ordinary Persons in Late Second Temple Israel*. Cascade Books, 2020.

**Filson, "Study."** Filson, William R. "A Comparative Study of Contextualized and Pentecostal Approaches to Nominal Muslims in Indonesia." DMin diss., Asia Pacific Theological Seminary, 2006.

**Finegan, *Archeology of Religions*.** Finegan, Jack. *The Archeology of World Religions*. Princeton University Press, 1952.

**Finger, *Meals*.** Finger, Reta Halteman. *Of Widows and Meals: Communal Meals in the Book of Acts*. Eerdmans, 2007.

**Finlay, *Columba*.** Finlay, J. *Columba*. Victor Gollancz, 1979.

**"Finney: Know."** "Charles Grandison Finney: Did You Know?" Christian History Institute. Accessed November 19, 2025. https://christianhistoryinstitute.org/magazine/article/charles-grandison-finney-did-you-know.

**Finney, *Memoirs*.** Finney, Charles G. *Memoirs of Rev. Charles G. Finney*. A. S. Barnes, 1876.

**Fish, *Road*.** Fish, Ken. *On the Road with the Holy Spirit*. Charisma House, 2023.

**Fitzmyer, *Romans*.** Fitzmyer, Joseph A. *Romans: A New Translation with Introduction and Commentary*. AB 33. Doubleday, 1993.

**Floris, "Charismata."** Floris, Andrew T. "The Charismata in the Post-Apostolic Church." In Graves, *Strangers*, 369–75.

**Floris, "Chrysostom."** Floris, Andrew T. "Chrysostom and the Charismata." In Graves, *Strangers*, 377–83.

**Flowers, "MacArthur."** Flowers, Leighton. "What John MacArthur Gets Wrong About Arminius and Finney." Posted September 14, 2017, by Soteriology 101 with Leighton Flowers, YouTube. Accessed August 30, 2024. https://www.youtube.com/watch?v=7_4cyOiAzNI.

**Folarin, "State."** Folarin, George O. "Contemporary State of the Prosperity Gospel in Nigeria." *Asia Journal of Theology* 21, no. 1 (April 2007): 69–95.

**Föller, "Luther on Miracles."** Föller, O. "Martin Luther on Miracles, Healing, Prophecy, and Tongues." *Church History Society of Southern Africa* 31, no. 2 (October 2005): 333–51.

**Fontenrose, *Delphic Oracle*.** Fontenrose, Joseph E. *The Delphic Oracle: Its Response and Operations*. University of California Press, 1978.

**Forbes, *Prophecy*.** Forbes, Christopher. *Prophecy and Inspired Speech in Early Christianity and Its Hellenistic Environment*. Wissenschaftliche Untersuchungen zum Neuen Testament 2/75. J. C. B. Mohr, 1995. Reprint, Hendrickson, 1997.

**Forbes, *Studies in Technology*.** Forbes, R. J. *Studies in Ancient Technology*. Vol. 5. Brill, 1957.

**Fornara, *Nature*.** Fornara, C. W. *The Nature of History in Ancient Greece and Rome*. University of California Press, 1983.

**Forrester, "Pentecost."** Forrester, Duncan B. "The Perennial Pentecost." *Expository Times* 116, no. 7 (2005): 224–27.

**Fosl, "Hume."** Fosl, Peter S. "Hume, Skepticism, and Early American Deism." *Hume Studies* 25, nos. 1–2 (1999): 171–92.

**Fox, *Journal*.** Fox, George. *The Journal of George Fox*. Cambridge University Press, 1911.

**Fox, "Word and Power."** Fox, Douglas J. "'Word and Power': Increasing Supernatural Ministry Through a Modification of 'Disciple: Becoming Disciples through Bible Study.'" DMin diss., United Theological Seminary, 2020.

**Fox, *Works*.** Fox, George. *The Works of George Fox*. 8 vols. AMS, 1975.

**Francis, "Encounter."** Francis, Andrea. "Spirit Encounter in Catherine of Siena's Pneumatology: A Paradigm for Spirit Baptism." PhD diss., Regent University, 2024.

**Frazier, *Faith Healing*.** Frazier, Claude A., comp. *Faith Healing: Finger of God? Or, Scientific Curiosity?* Thomas Nelson, 1973.

**Frend, "Place of Miracles."** Frend, W. H. C. "The Place of Miracles in the Conversion of the Ancient World to Christianity." In *Signs, Wonders, Miracles: Representations of Divine Power in the Life of the Church*, Papers Read at the 2003 Summer Meeting and the 2004 Winter Meeting of the Ecclesiastical History Society, edited by Kate Cooper and Jeremy Gregory, 11–21. Boydell & Brewer, for the Ecclesiastical History Society, 2005.

**Frend, *Rise*.** Frend, W. H. C. *The Rise of Christianity*. Fortress, 1984.

**Frodsham, *Signs*.** Frodsham, Stanley. *With Signs Following*. Gospel Publishing House, 1928.

**Frost, *Healing*.** Frost, Evelyn. *Christian Healing: A Consideration of the Place of Spiritual Healing in the Church of Today in the Light of the Doctrine and Practice of the Ante-Nicene Church*. A. R. Mowbray, 1940.

**Frye, "Faith Healing."** Frye, Glenn R. "Faith Healing." In *Healing and Religious Faith*, edited by Claude A. Frazier, 12–18. United Church Press, 1974.

**Fuller, *Mission*.** Fuller, R. H. *The Mission and Achievement of Jesus*. Alec R. Allenson, 1954.

**Fullerton, *Spurgeon*.** Fullerton, F. Y. *Charles H. Spurgeon*. Moody, 1966.

**Gaffin, *Perspectives*.** Gaffin, Richard B., Jr. *Perspectives on Pentecost: Studies in New Testament Teaching on the Gifts of the Holy Spirit*. Presbyterian and Reformed, 1979.

**Gaffin, "Response to Saucy."** Gaffin, Richard B., Jr. "A Cessationist Response to Robert L. Saucy." In Grudem, *Gifts*, 149–55.

**Gaffin, "Response to Storms and Oss."** Gaffin, Richard B., Jr. "A Cessationist Response to C. Samuel Storms and Douglas A. Oss." In Grudem, *Gifts*, 284–97.

**Gaffin, "Spirit."** Gaffin, Richard B., Jr. "'Life-Giving Spirit': Probing the Center of Paul's Pneumatology." *Journal of the Evangelical Theological Society* 41, no. 4 (December 1998): 573–89.

**Gaffin, "Statement."** Gaffin, Richard B., Jr. "Concluding Statement (Cessationist View)." In Grudem, *Gifts*, 334–40.

**Gaffin, "View."** Gaffin, Richard B., Jr. "A Cessationist View." In Grudem, *Gifts*, 25–64.

**Galinsky, "Introduction."** Galinsky, Karl. "Introduction." In *Memory in Ancient Rome and Early Christianity*, edited by Karl Galinsky, 1–39. Oxford University Press, 2016.

**Galli, "Wouldn't Give Up."** Galli, Mark. "The Man Who Wouldn't Give Up." *Christian History* 36 (1992).

**Gane, *Leviticus, Numbers*.** Gane, Roy. *Leviticus, Numbers*. NIV Application Commentary. Zondervan, 2004.

**Gardner, *Healing Miracles*.** Gardner, Rex. *Healing Miracles: A Doctor Investigates*. Darton, Longman & Todd, 1986.

**Gardner, "Miracles."** Gardner, Rex. "Miracles of Healing in Anglo-Celtic Northumbria as Recorded by the Venerable Bede and His Contemporaries: A Reappraisal in the Light of Twentieth-Century Experience." *British Medical Journal* 287 (December 24–31, 1983): 1927–33.

**Garland, *1 Corinthians.*** Garland, David E. *1 Corinthians*. Baker Exegetical Commentary on the New Testament. Baker Academic, 2003.

**Garlow and Wall, *Miracles for Real.*** Garlow, James L., and Keith Wall. *Miracles Are for Real: What Happens When Heaven Touches Earth*. Bethany House, 2011.

**Garlow and Wall, *Real Miracles.*** Garlow, James L., and Keith Wall. *Real Life, Real Miracles: True Stories That Will Help You Believe*. Bethany House, 2012.

**Garnett, *Mountains.*** Garnett, Eve. *To Greenland's Icy Mountains: The Story of Hans Egede, Explorer, Coloniser, Missionary*. Heinemann, 1968.

**Gee, *Gifts.*** Gee, Donald. *Concerning Spiritual Gifts*. Gospel Publishing House, 1949.

**Geivett and Pivec, *Reformation.*** Geivett, R. Douglas, and Holly Pivec. *A New Apostolic Reformation? A Biblical Response to a Worldwide Movement*. Weaver, 2014.

**George, "Introduction."** George, Timothy. "General Introduction." In Bray, *Galatians, Ephesians*, ix–xxxiv.

**George, "Miracle Story."** George, Sean. "The Miracle Story of Dr. Sean George." Website. Accessed January 13, 2026. https://seangeorge.com.au/.

**George, "Revival."** George, Timothy. "Evangelical Revival and the Missionary Awakening." In *The Great Commission: Evangelicals and the History of World Missions*, edited by Martin I. Klauber and Scott M. Manetsch, 45–65. B&H, 2008.

**George, "Spirit in Galatians."** George, Roji T. "Spirit in Galatians." In Keener and Oliverio Jr., *Canon*, 163–68.

**George, "Spirit in Thessalonians."** George, Roji T. "Spirit in Thessalonians." In Keener and Oliverio Jr., *Canon*, 183–89.

**George, "Strange."** George, Timothy. "Strange Friendly Fire." *First Things*, November 4, 2013. Accessed August 29, 2024. http://www.firstthings.com/onthesquare/2013/11/strange-friendly-fire/timothy-george.

**Gibson, *Observations.*** Gibson, Edmund. *Observations upon the Conduct and Behaviour of a Certain Sect: Usually Distinguished by the Name of Methodists*. n.p.: 1740. Available online at https://books.google.com/books?id=m5xbAAAAQAAJ.

**Gibson, "Refusal."** Gibson, Jeffrey. "Jesus' Refusal to Produce a 'Sign' (Mk 8.11–13)." *Journal for the Study of the New Testament* 38 (1990): 37–66.

**Gifford, "Developments."** Gifford, Paul. "Some Recent Developments in African Christianity." *African Affairs* 93 (1994): 513–34.

**Gifford, "Healing."** Gifford, Paul. "Healing in African Pentecostalism: The 'Victorious Living' of David Oyedepo." In Brown, *Global*, 251–66.

**Gifford, "Miracles."** Gifford, Paul. "Expecting Miracles." *Christian Century* 124, no. 14 (July 10, 2007): 20–24.

**Gifford, *Pentecostalism.*** Gifford, Paul. *Ghana's New Christianity: Pentecostalism in a Globalizing African Economy*. Indiana University Press, 2004.

**Gilbert, "Charismata."** Gilbert, Daniel Briggs. "The Pneumatic Charismata in the Theology of John Calvin: A Study of Calvin's Pneumatology, Focusing on His

Concepts and Interpretation of the Pneumatic Charismata in His Life and Works." PhD diss., University of Aberdeen, 2005.

**Gladd, *Handbook*.** Gladd, Benjamin L. *Handbook on the Gospels*. Baker Academic, 2021.

**Gladstone, "Sign Language."** Gladstone, Robert J. "Sign Language in the Assembly: How Are Tongues a Sign to the Unbeliever in 1 Cor. 14:20–25?" *Asian Journal of Pentecostal Studies* 2, no. 2 (1999): 177–93.

**Global Teen Challenge, "Home Page."** Global Teen Challenge home page. Accessed December 3, 2025. https://www.globaltc.org/.

**Godron, "Healings."** Godron, Gérard. "Healings in Coptic Literature." In *The Coptic Encyclopedia*, edited by Aziz S. Atiya, 4:1212–14. 8 vols. Macmillan, 1991.

**Goff, *Fields*.** Goff, James R., Jr. *Fields White unto Harvest: Charles F. Parham and the Missionary Origins of Pentecostalism*. University of Arkansas Press, 1988.

**Goff, "Theology."** Goff, James R., Jr. "Initial Tongues in the Theology of Charles Fox Parham." In McGee, *Initial Evidence*, 57–71.

**Goforth, *Goforth*.** Goforth, Rosalind. *Goforth of China*. Zondervan, 1937. Reprint, Wipf & Stock, 2014.

**González, *Story*.** González, Justo L. *The Story of Christianity: The Early Church to the Present Day*. 2 vols. Hendrickson, 1999.

**Goodman, *State*.** Goodman, Martin. *State and Society in Roman Galilee, A.D. 132–212*. Oxford Centre for Postgraduate Hebrew Studies. Rowman & Allanheld, 1983.

**Gordon, *Civilizations*.** Gordon, Cyrus H. *The Common Background of Greek and Hebrew Civilizations*. Norton, 1965.

**Gordon, *Ministry of Healing*.** Gordon, A. J. *The Ministry of Healing*. Christian Publications, 1961.

**Gordon, *Ministry of Spirit*.** Gordon, A. J. *The Ministry of the Holy Spirit*. Revell, 1895.

**Gorsuch, "Limits."** Gorsuch, Richard L. "On the Limits of Scientific Investigation: Miracles and Intercessory Prayer." In Ellens, *Miracles*, 1:280–99.

**Goulder, *Type and History*.** Goulder, Michael D. *Type and History in Acts*. SPCK, 1964.

**Gowing, "Memory."** Gowing, Alain M. "Memory as Motive in Tacitus." In *Memory in Ancient Rome and Early Christianity*, edited by Karl Galinsky, 43–64. Oxford University Press, 2016.

**Grace to You, "Explaining 1."** Grace to You, "Explaining the Heresy of the Catholic Mass, Part 1 (Selected Scriptures)." Posted May 21, 2025, by Grace to You, YouTube. Accessed February 6, 2026. https://www.youtube.com/watch?v=1Hyb6vgSCT8.

**Grace to You, "Explaining 2."** Grace to You, "Explaining the Heresy of the Catholic Mass, Part 2 (Selected Scriptures)." Posted May 21, 2025, by Grace to You, YouTube. Accessed February 6, 2026. https://www.youtube.com/watch?v=7wQv17aTeoc.

**Grace to You, "Roman Catholicism."** Grace to You, "Roman Catholicism." Accessed July 31, 2025. https://www.gty.org/articles/DD09/roman-catholicism.

**Graf, *Healing*.** Graf, Jonathan L., comp. and ed. *Healing: The Three Great Classics on Divine Healing*. Christian Publications, 1992.

**Graf, "Prayer."** Graf, Fritz. "Prayer. III. Greece and Rome." In *Brill's New Pauly: Encyclopaedia of the Ancient World*, edited by Hubert Cancik and Helmuth Schneider, 11:791–94. 20 vols. English ed. Christine F. Salazar. Brill, 2010.

**Graham, *Holy Spirit*.** Graham, Billy. *The Holy Spirit: Activating God's Power in Your Life*. Thomas Nelson, 2011.

**Grant, *Miracle*.** Grant, Robert M. *Miracle and Natural Law in Graeco-Roman and Early Christian Thought*. North-Holland, 1952.

**Graves, "Cessationism."** Graves, Robert W. "Cessationism and the Kingdom of God." In Graves, *Kingdom Case*, 47–57.

**Graves, "Focus."** Graves, Robert W. "The Focus of the Charismatic Experience: Tongues, the Holy Spirit, or Christ?" In Graves, *Strangers*, 93–104.

**Graves, *Kingdom Case*.** Graves, Robert W., ed. *The Kingdom Case Against Cessationism: Embracing the Power of the Kingdom*. Foundation for Pentecostal Scholarship, 2022.

**Graves, "Nature."** Graves, Robert W. "What Is the Nature of Glossolalia?" In Graves, *Strangers*, 105–16.

**Graves, *Praying in the Spirit*.** Graves, Robert W. *Praying in the Spirit*. Empowered Life Academic, 2016.

**Graves, *Strangers*.** Graves, Robert W., ed. *Strangers to Fire: When Tradition Trumps Scripture*. Foundation for Pentecostal Scholarship, 2014.

**Graves and Greig, "Cessationism."** Graves, Robert W., and Gary S. Greig. "Cessationism and the Struggle for the Promises and Commands of Jesus." In Graves, *Kingdom Case*, 81–101.

**Green, *Asian Tigers*.** Green, Michael. *Asian Tigers for Christ: The Dynamic Growth of the Church in South East Asia*. SPCK, 2001.

**Green, *Publications*.** Green, Richard. *Anti-Methodist Publications: Issues During the Eighteenth Century*. C. H. Kelly, 1902.

**Green, *Thessalonians*.** Green, Gene. *The Letters to the Thessalonians*, Pillar New Testament Commentary. Eerdmans, 2002.

**Green, *Works*.** Green, Richard. *The Works of John and Charles Wesley: A Bibliography*. C. H. Kelly, 1869.

**Greenfield, *Power*.** Greenfield, John. *Power from on High*. CTM, 2018. Rev. from *Power from on High, or, The Two Hundredth Anniversary of the Great Moravian Revival, 1727–1927*. Moravian Church in America, 1928.

**Greenspahn, "Prophecy."** Greenspahn, Frederick E. "Why Prophecy Ceased." *Journal of Biblical Literature* 108, no. 1 (1989): 37–49.

**Greig, "Purpose."** Greig, Gary S. "The Purpose of Signs and Wonders in the New Testament." In Graves, *Strangers*, 315–53.

**Greig, "Sufficiency."** Greig, Gary S. "The Sufficiency of Scripture and Distortion of What Scripture Teaches About Itself." In Graves, *Strangers*, 463–67.

**Grenholm, *Dokumenterade Språkmirakler*.** Grenholm, Micael. *Dokumenterade Språkmirakler: När Gud ger människor språk de aldrig har lärt sig*. Sjöbergs Förlag, 2022. Microsoft Word manuscript.

**Gresham, "Tongues."** Gresham, John. "Tongues as Glossolalic Prayer—a Pentecostal Invention? A Reply to Blosser and Sullivan." *Journal of Pentecostal Theology* 34, no. 2 (2025): 269–89. https://doi.org/10.1163/17455251-bja10073.

**Grisar, *Luther*.** Grisar, Hartmann. *Luther*. Vol. 4. Translated by E. M. Lamond. Edited by Luigi Cappadelta. Megan Paul, Trench, Trübner, 1915.

**Grmek, *Diseases*.** Grmek, Mirko D. *Diseases in the Ancient Greek World*. Translated by Mireille Muellner and Leonard Muellner. Johns Hopkins University Press, 1989.

**Grudem, "Conclusion."** Grudem, Wayne A. "Conclusion." In Grudem, *Gifts*, 341–49.

**Grudem, "Expect."** Grudem, Wayne A. "Should Christians Expect Miracles Today? Objections and Answers from the Bible." In Graves, *Strangers*, 225–60.

**Grudem, *Gifts*.** Grudem, Wayne A., ed. *Are Miraculous Gifts for Today? Four Views*. Zondervan, 1996.

**Grudem, "Preface."** Grudem, Wayne A. "Preface." In Grudem, *Gifts*, 9–20.

**Grudem, *Prophecy*.** Grudem, Wayne A. *The Gift of Prophecy in 1 Corinthians*. University Press of America, 1982.

**Grudem, *Prophecy Today*.** Grudem, Wayne. *The Gift of Prophecy in the New Testament and Today*. Crossway, 1988.

**Gueizo, "Making."** Gueizo, Allen C. "The Making of a Revivalist." *Christian History* 20 (1988). https://christianhistoryinstitute.org/magazine/article/finney-making-of-a-revivalist.

**Gundry, "Ecstatic Utterance?"** Gundry, Robert H. "'Ecstatic Utterance' (N.E.B.)?" *Journal of Theological Studies* 17, no. 2 (1966): 299–307.

**Gupta, *Language of Faith*.** Gupta, Nijay K. *Paul and the Language of Faith*. Eerdmans, 2019.

**Gurney, *Hittites*.** Gurney, O. R. *The Hittites*. Penguin, 1972.

**Gusmer, *Healing*.** Gusmer, Charles W. *The Ministry of Healing in the Church of England: An Ecumenical-Liturgical Study*. Alcuin Club Collections 56. Alcuin Club, Mayhew-McCrimmon, 1974.

**Guthrie, "Breakthrough."** Guthrie, Stan. "Muslim Mission Breakthrough." *Christianity Today*, December 13, 1993, 20–26.

**Gutierrez, *Mujer de Milagros*.** Gutierrez, Angel Luis. *Mujer de Milagros*. Editorial Chari, 1991.

**Haenchen, *Acts*.** Haenchen, Ernst. *The Acts of the Apostles: A Commentary*. Westminster, 1971.

**Hägg, *Biography*.** Hägg, Tomas. *The Art of Biography in Antiquity*. Cambridge University Press, 2012.

**Hall, *Worship*.** Hall, Francis B. *Quaker Worship in North America: A Faith and Life Study Book*. Friends United Press, 1978.

**Hamilton, "Signs."** Hamilton, Bernard. "'God Wills It': Signs of Divine Approval in the Crusade Movement." In Cooper and Gregory, *Signs*, 88–98.

**Hammond, "Heroes."** Hammond, Leslie. "Heroes of the Faith: Lillian Trasher." *Christians for Social Action*. May 17, 2015. Accessed June 4, 2024. https://christiansforsocialaction.org/resource/heroes-of-the-faith-lillian-trasher/.

**Hanciles, *Beyond Christendom*.** Hanciles, Jehu J. *Beyond Christendom: Globalization, African Migration, and the Transformation of the West*. Orbis Books, 2008.

**Handley, "Ghosts."** Handley, Sasha. "Reclaiming Ghosts in 1690s England." In Cooper and Gregory, *Signs*, 345–55.

**Hannig, Hauritz, and Grove, "Autoresuscitation."** Hannig, Kjartan Eskjaer, Rasmus Wulff Hauritz, and Erik Lerkevang Grove. "Autoresuscitation: A Case and Discussion of the Lazarus Phenomenon." *Case Reports in Medicine*, June 8, 2015. https://doi.org/10.1155/2015/724174.

**Haran, "Continuity and Change."** Haran, Menahem. "From Early to Classical Prophecy: Continuity and Change." *Vetus Testamentum* 27 (October 1977): 385–97.

**Harder, "Reaction."** Harder, Leland. "Zwingli's Reaction to the Schleitheim Confession of Faith of the Anabaptists." *Sixteenth Century Journal* 11, no. 4 (Winter 1980): 51–66.

**Hardesty, *Faith Cure*.** Hardesty, Nancy A. *Faith Cure: Divine Healing in the Holiness and Pentecostal Movements*. Hendrickson, 2003.

**Harris, *Acts Today*.** Harris, Ralph W. *Acts Today: Signs and Wonders of the Holy Spirit*. Gospel, 1995.

**Harrison, "Miracles."** Harrison, Peter. "Miracles, Early Modern Science, and Rational Religion." *Church History* 75, no. 3 (2006): 493–510.

**Hartley, "Deception."** Hartley, Jed. "Our Stories—IHOPKC Deception in the Leadership—with Jed Hartley—Episode 190 Branham Podcast." *William Branham Historical Research Podcast*. Posted September 20, 2024, by Leaving the Message, YouTube. Accessed September 28, 2024. https://www.youtube.com/watch?v=ylcDpVen6Zo.

**Hartley, *Evangelicals*.** Hartley, Benjamin L. *Evangelicals at a Crossroads: Revivalism and Social Reform in Boston, 1860–1910*. RNENR. University of New Hampshire Press; published by University Press of New England, 2011.

**Harvey, "Agony."** Harvey, John. "The Agony in the Garden: Visions of the 1904 Revival." In *Revival, Renewal, and the Holy Spirit*, edited by Dyfed Wyn Roberts, 129–38. SEHT. Wipf & Stock, 2009.

**Hausfeld, "Understanding."** Hausfeld, Mark. "Islam in America: Understanding and Engaging Diaspora Muslims Through the Local Church." Assemblies of God Theological Seminary, 2007.

**Hayes, *Sub-Merge*.** Hayes, John B. *Sub-Merge: Living Deep in a Shallow World. Service, Justice and Contemplation Among the World's Poor*. Regal Books, 2006.

**Haykin and Robinson, *Ends of the Earth*.** Haykin, Michael A. G., and Charles Jeffrey Robinson Sr. *To the Ends of the Earth: Calvin's Missional Vision and Legacy*. Crossway, 2014.

**Hays, *First Corinthians*.** Hays, Richard B. *First Corinthians*. Interpretation. John Knox, 1997.

**Heath, "Little Prophets."** Heath, Richard. "The Little Prophets of the Cevennes." *The Contemporary Review* 49 (January 1886): 117–31.

**Hebert, *Raised*.** Hebert, Albert J. *Raised from the Dead: True Stories of 400 Resurrection Miracles*. TAN Books, 1986.

**Heil, *Role*.** Heil, John Paul. *The Rhetorical Role of Scripture in 1 Corinthians*. Society of Biblical Literature, 2005.

**Heim, *Transformation*.** Heim, Karl. *The Transformation of the Scientific World View*. Harper & Brothers, 1953.

**Heim, "Women."** Heim, Erin. "Paul and the Women He Greeted." In *The Biblical World of Gender: The Daily Lives of Ancient Women and Men*, edited by Celina Durgin and Dru Johnson, 116–24. Cascade Books, 2022.

**Heimann, "Enlightenment."** Heimann, Mary. "Christianity in Western Europe from the Enlightenment." In *A World History of Christianity*, edited by Adrian Hastings, 458–507. Eerdmans, 1999.

**Hejzlar, "Calvin and Cessation."** Hejzlar, Pavel. "John Calvin and the Cessation of Miraculous Healing." *Communio Viatorum* 49, no. 1 (2007): 31–77.

**Hendrix, *Martin Luther*.** Hendrix, Scott H. *Martin Luther: A Very Short Introduction*. Oxford University Press, 2010.

**Herford, *Christianity*.** Herford, R. Travers. *Christianity in Talmud and Midrash*. Library of Philosophical and Religious Thought. Reference Book Publishers, 1966.

**Hernando, "Continuationism."** Hernando, James D. "Continuationism—A Redemptive-Historical Perspective." In Graves, *Kingdom Case*, 103–22.

**Hertig, "Mystery Tour."** Hertig, Paul. "The Magical Mystery Tour: Philip Encounters Magic and Materialism in Samaria, Acts 8:4–25." In *Mission in Acts: Ancient Narratives in Contemporary Context*, edited by Robert L. Gallagher and Paul Hertig, 103–13. American Society of Missiology Series 34. Orbis Books, 2004.

**Hertzberg, *Samuel*.** Hertzberg, Hans Wilhelm. *I & II Samuel*. Old Testament Library. Westminster, 1964.

**Herum, "Theology."** Herum, Nathan M. "Augustine's Theology of the Miraculous." MDiv thesis, Beeson Divinity School, 2009.

**Hickson, *Heal*.** Hickson, James Moore. *Heal the Sick*. 2nd ed. Methuen, 1924.

**Hilber, "Diversity."** Hilber, John W. "Diversity of Old Testament Prophetic Phenomena and New Testament Prophecy." *Westminster Theological Journal* 56, no. 2 (1994): 243–58.

**Hilborn, "Glossolalia."** Hilborn, David. "Glossolalia as Communication: A Linguistic-Pragmatic Perspective." In Cartledge, *Perspectives*, 111–46.

**Hill, *Prophecy*.** Hill, David. *New Testament Prophecy*. New Foundations Theological Library. John Knox, 1979.

**Hillgarth, *Paganism*.** Hillgarth, J. N. *Christianity and Paganism, 350–750: The Conversion of Western Europe*. Rev. ed. University of Pennsylvania Press, 1986.

**Hine, "Glossolalia."** Hine, Virginia H. "Pentecostal Glossolalia: Toward a Functional Interpretation." *Journal for the Scientific Study of Religion* 8, no. 2 (1969): 211–36.

**Hinksman, "Transference."** Hinksman, Barrie. "Transference and Countertransference in Pastoral Settings." In *Clinical Counselling in Pastoral Settings*, edited by Gordon Lynch, 75–85. Routledge, 1999.

**Hodge, *Systematic Theology*.** Hodge, Charles. *Systematic Theology*. 3 vols. Charles Scribner, 1872–73.

**Hodges, "Authority."** Hodges, Melvin L. "The Authority of Prophetic Gifts." In Graves, *Strangers*, 459–61.

**Hodges, "Tongues."** Hodges, Zane C. "The Purpose of Tongues." *Bibliotheca Sacra* 120, no. 479 (1963): 226–33.

**Hoehner, *Ephesians*.** Hoehner, Harold W. *Ephesians: An Exegetical Commentary*. Baker Academic, 2002.

**Hoffman, *Luther*.** Hoffman, Bengt. *Luther and the Mystics*. Augsburg, 1976.

**Holladay, "Statecraft."** Holladay, John S. "Assyrian Statecraft and the Prophets of Israel." *Harvard Theological Review* 63 (January 1970): 29–51.

**Holland, *Dominion*.** Holland, Tom. *Dominion: How the Christian Revolution Remade the World*. Basic Books, 2019.

**Hollander, "Seeing God."** Hollander, Harm W. "Seeing God 'in a Riddle' or 'Face to Face': An Analysis of 1 Corinthians 13.12." *Journal for the Study of the New Testament* 32, no. 4 (2010): 395–403.

**Hollenweger, "Azusa Street."** Hollenweger, Walter J. "From Azusa Street to the Toronto Phenomenon: Historical Roots of the Pentecostal Movement." In *Pentecostal Movements as an Ecumenical Challenge*, edited by Jürgen Moltmann and Karl-Josef Kuschel. Concilium 3. SCM; Orbis Books, 1996.

**Hollenweger, "Handbuch."** Hollenweger, Walter J. "Handbuch Der Pfingstbewegung." PhD diss., University of Zurich, 1965.

**Hollenweger, *Pentecostals*.** Hollenweger, Walter J. *The Pentecostals*. SCM, 1972. Reprint, Hendrickson, 1988.

**Hong, "Mission."** Hong, Young-Gi. "Church and Mission: A Pentecostal Perspective." *International Review of Mission* 90, no. 358 (July 2001): 289–308.

**Horden, "Saints."** Horden, Peregrine. "Saints and Doctors in the Early Byzantine Empire: The Case of Theodore of Sykeon." In Sheils, *Papers*, 1–13.

**Horsch, "Faith."** Horsch, John. "The Faith of the Swiss Brethren, II." *Mennonite Quarterly Review* 5, no. 1 (1931): 7–27.

**Horsch, *Mennonites*.** Horsch, John. *Mennonites in Europe*. 2nd ed. Mennonite Publishing House, 1950. Reprint, 1995.

**Horsley, *Corinthians*.** Horsley, Richard A. *1 Corinthians*. ANTC. Abingdon, 1998.

**Horsley, *Galilee*.** Horsley, Richard A. *Galilee: History, Politics, People*. Trinity Press International, 1995.

**Horton, *Corinthians*.** Horton, Stanley M. *I and II Corinthians: A Logion Press Commentary*. Gospel, 1999.

**Horton, *Spirit*.** Horton, Stanley M. *What the Bible Says About the Holy Spirit*. Gospel Publishing House, 1976.

**Houghton, "Reexamination."** Houghton, Myron J. "A Reexamination of 1 Corinthians 13:8–13." *Bibliotheca Sacra* 153, no. 611 (1996): 344–56.

**Houston, *Miracles*.** Houston, J. *Reported Miracles: A Critique of Hume*. Cambridge University Press, 1994.

**Howie, *Scots Worthies*.** Howie, John. *Biographia Scoticana (Scots Worthies): A Brief Historical Account of the Lives, Characters, and Memorable Transactions of the Most Eminent Scots Worthies*. 2nd ed. John Bryce, 1781. Kindle Edition.

**Hudson, "Strange Words."** Hudson, Neil. "Strange Words and Their Impact on Early Pentecostals: A Historical Perspective." In Cartledge, *Perspectives*, 52–80.

**Huffmon, "Prophecy."** Huffmon, Herbert B. "Prophecy in the Mari Letters." *Biblical Archaeologist* 31 (December 1968): 101–24.

**Hull, *Spirit in Acts*.** Hull, J. H. E. *The Holy Spirit in the Acts of the Apostles*. Lutterworth, 1967; World, 1968.

**Hulse, "Leprosy."** Hulse, E. V. "The Nature of Biblical 'Leprosy' and the Use of Alternative Medical Terms in Modern Translations of the Bible." *Palestine Exploration Quarterly* 107 (1975): 87–105.

**Hultgren, *Romans*.** Hultgren, Arland J. *Paul's Letter to the Romans: A Commentary*. Eerdmans, 2011.

**Hume, *Miracles*.** Hume, David. *Of Miracles*. Introduction by Antony Flew. Open Court, 1985.

**Hunter, *Spirit Baptism*.** Hunter, Harold D. *Spirit Baptism: A Pentecostal Alternative*. Wipf & Stock, 2009.

**Hunter, "Tongues-Speech."** Hunter, Harold. "Tongues-Speech: A Patristic Analysis." *Journal of the Evangelical Theological Society* 23, no. 2 (June 1980): 125–37.

**Hurtado, "Function."** Hurtado, Larry W. "The Function and Pattern of Signs and Wonders in the Apostolic and Sub-Apostolic Period." MA thesis, Trinity Evangelical Divinity School, 1967.

**Hutton, *History*.** Hutton, Joseph Edmund. *A History of the Moravian Church*. 2nd ed. Moravian Publication Office, 1909.

**Huyssen and Huyssen, *Saw*.** Huyssen, Chester, and Lucille Huyssen. *I Saw the Lord*. Chosen Books, 1992.

**Hyatt, *Years*.** Hyatt, Eddie L. *2000 Years of Charismatic Christianity*. Charisma House, 2002.

**"Important Letter."** "An Important Letter from Bill, Kris, and Dann on Behalf of Bethel Leadership." Bethel Church of Redding (website). Accessed January 30, 2026. https://www.bethel.com/news/an-important-letter-from-bill-kris-and-dann-on-behalf-of-bethel-leadership.

**Ingle, *Friends*.** Ingle, H. Larry. *First Among Friends: George Fox and the Creation of Quakerism*. Oxford University Press, 1994.

**International School of Ministry, "Shout."** International School of Ministry. "Richard Bonnke Legacy Collection—Something to Shout About." Posted April 8, 2020, by Ministry Degree, YouTube. https://www.youtube.com/watch?v=FazIGK3vL1E.

**Iris Global, "What We Do."** Iris Global. "What We Do." Accessed August 23, 2024. https://www.irisglobal.org/about/what-we-do.

**Irvin and Sunquist, *History*.** Irvin, Dale T., and Scott W. Sunquist. *History of the World Christian Movement*. Vol. 2, *Modern Christianity from 1454–1800*. Orbis Books, 2012.

**Isaacs, *Spirit*.** Isaacs, Marie E. *The Concept of Spirit: A Study of Pneuma in Hellenistic Judaism and Its Bearing on the New Testament*. HeyM 1. Heythrop College Press, 1976.

**Ising, *Blumhardt*.** Ising, Dieter. *Johann Christoph Blumhardt, Life and Work: A New Biography*. Translated by Monty Ledford. Cascade Books, 2009. Translated from *Johann Christoph Blumhardt: Leben und Werk*. Vandenhoeck & Ruprecht, 2002.

**"Islam and Christianity."** "Tolerance and Tension: Islam and Christianity in Sub-Saharan Africa." Pew Forum on Religion and Public Life. April 2010. Accessed February 28, 2025. https://www.pewresearch.org/wp-content/uploads/sites/7/2010/04/sub-saharan-africa-full-report.pdf.

**Iyadurai, *Experience*.** Iyadurai, Joshua. *Transformative Religious Experience: A Phenomenological Understanding of Religious Conversion*. Pickwick, 2015.

**Jackson, *Quest*.** Jackson, Bill. *The Quest for the Radical Middle: A History of the Vineyard*. Vineyard International, 1999.

**Jacobsen, *Thinking in Spirit*.** Jacobsen, Douglas. *Thinking in the Spirit: Theologies of the Early Pentecostal Movement*. Indiana University Press, 2003.

**Jaki, *Miracles and Physics*.** Jaki, Stanley. *Miracles and Physics*. Christendom, 1989.

**James, "Introduction."** James, William. Introduction to "A Case of Psychic Automatism, Including 'Speaking with Tongues,'" by Albert Le Baron. *Proceedings of the Society for Psychical Research* 12 (1896–97): 277–97.

**Jeffers, *World*.** Jeffers, James S. *The Greco-Roman World of the New Testament Era: Exploring the Background of Early Christianity*. InterVarsity, 1999.

**Jenkins, *New Faces*.** Jenkins, Philip. *The New Faces of Christianity: Believing the Bible in the Global South*. Oxford University Press, 2006.

**Jenkins, *Next Christendom*.** Jenkins, Philip. *The Next Christendom: The Coming of Global Christianity*. Oxford University Press, 2002.

**Jenkins, "Reindorf."** Jenkins, Paul. "Reindorf, Carl Christian." Dictionary of African Christian Biography. Accessed November 20, 2025. https://dacb.org/stories/ghana/reindorf2-carl/.

**Jennings, *Good News*.** Jennings, Theodore W., Jr. *Good News to the Poor: John Wesley's Evangelical Economics*. Abingdon, 1990.

**Jennings, *Supernatural Occurrences*.** Jennings, Daniel R. *The Supernatural Occurrences of John Wesley*. CreateSpace, 2012.

**Jeremias, *Theology*.** Jeremias, Joachim. *New Testament Theology*. Scribner's, 1971.

**Jewett, *Romans*.** Jewett, Robert, assisted by Roy D. Kotansky. *Romans: A Commentary*. Edited by Eldon Jay Epp. Hermeneia. Fortress, 2007.

**Johanson, "Tongues."** Johanson, Bruce C. "Tongues, a Sign for Unbelievers? A Structural and Exegetical Study of I Corinthians XIV.20–25." *New Testament Studies* 25, no. 2 (January 1979): 180–203.

**Johnson, *Blood Libel*.** Johnson, Hannah R. *Blood Libel: The Ritual Murder Accusation at the Limit of Jewish History*. University of Michigan Press, 2012.

**Johnson, *Camp Meeting*.** Johnson, Charles A. *The Frontier Camp Meeting*. SMU, 1955.

**Johnson, "Camp Meeting."** Johnson, Guion Griffis. "The Camp Meeting in Antebellum North Carolina." *North Carolina Historical Review* 10, no. 2 (April 1933): 95–110.

**Johnson, *Hume*.** Johnson, David. *Hume, Holism, and Miracles*. CSPhilRel. Cornell University Press, 1999.

**Johnson, "John Knox."** Johnson, Dale. "John Knox: Reformation Historian and Prophet." MA thesis, Covenant Theological Seminary, 1983.

**Johnson, "Tongues."** Johnson, S. L. "The Gift of Tongues and the Book of Acts." *Bibliotheca Sacra* 120, no. 480 (1963): 309–11.

**Johnson, "Wolf."** Johnson, Phillip. "A Wolf in Sheep's Clothing: How Charles Finney's Theology Ravaged the Evangelical Movement." Accessed August 30, 2024. http://www.romans45.org/articles/finney.htm.

**Johnson, Barrett, and Crossing, "Christianity 2010."** Johnson, Todd M., David B. Barrett, and Peter F. Crossing. "Christianity 2010: A View from the *New Atlas* *of Global Christianity.*" *International Bulletin of Mission Research* 34, no. 1 (January 2010): 29–36.

**Johnson and Ross, *Atlas*.** Johnson, Todd M., and Kenneth R. Ross, eds. *Atlas of Global Christianity, 1910–2010*. Managing editor, Sandra S. K. Lee. Center for the Study of Global Christianity, 2009.

**Johnston, "Ordination."** Johnston, Flo. "Ordination Will Cross Racial Lines." *The Chicago Tribune*, August 9, 1991, NS 2, p. 9.

**Johnston, "Speaking in Tongues."** Johnston, Kenny. "Speaking in Tongues as Sacramental." *Journal of the Evangelical Theological Society* 67, no. 4 (2024): 761–79.

**Jones, *Filled*.** Jones, Doyle. *Be Filled with the Spirit*. Tate, 2006.

**Jones, "Fire."** Jones, Arun. "Playing with Fire." In Akinade, *New Day*, 209–24.

**Jones, *Wonders*.** Jones, Philip Hanson. *Wonders, Signs, Miracles . . . Why Not? Tales of a Missionary in China*. Exposition, 1966.

**Jörgensen, *Francis*.** Jörgensen, Johannes. *St. Francis of Assisi: A Biography*. Translated by T. O'Conor Sloane. Image Books, 1955.

**Judge, *First Christians*.** Judge, Edwin A. *The First Christians in the Roman World: Augustan and New Testament Essays*. Edited by James R. Harrison. Wissenschaftliche Untersuchungen zum Neuen Testament 229. Mohr Siebeck, 2008.

**Jurgensmeier, *Miracle Working*.** Jurgensmeier, Kurt. *Human Miracle Working: Is God Still Doing Miracles Today?* Kurt Jurgensmeier, 2012.

**Kaiser, "Pantheon."** Kaiser, Walter C., Jr. "The Ugaritic Pantheon." PhD diss., Brandeis University, 1973.

**Kallas, *Significance*.** Kallas, James. *The Significance of the Synoptic Miracles: Taking the Worldview of Jesus Seriously*. SPCK, 1961.

**Kalu, *African Pentecostalism*.** Kalu, Ogbu. *African Pentecostalism: An Introduction*. Oxford University Press, 2008.

**Kalu, "Lijadu."** Kalu, Ogbu U. "Lijadu, Emmanuel Moses." Dictionary of African Christian Biography. Accessed November 20, 2025. https://dacb.org/stories/nigeria/lijadu2-emmanuel/.

**Kalu, "Mission."** Kalu, Ogbu U. "Pentecostalism and Mission in Africa, 1970–2000." *Mission Studies* 24 (2007): 9–45.

**Kanana, *Dying in Islam*.** Kanana, Cedric, with Benjamin Fischer. *Dying in Islam, Rising with Christ: Encountering Jesus Beyond the Grave*. Pembroke Street Press, 2018.

**Kanana, *Once Dead*.** Kanana, Cedric. *I Was Once Dead*. Oasis, 2022.

**Kang, "World."** Kang, Namsoon. "*Whose/Which* World in *World Christianity?* Toward *World Christianity* as Christianity of *Worldly-Responsibility*." In Akinade, *New Day*, 31–48.

**Kantowicz, *Rage*.** Kantowicz, Edward R. *The World in the 20th Century*. Vol. 1, *The Rage of the Nations*. 2 vols. Eerdmans, 1999.

**Karnofsky, "Vision."** Karnofsky, E. S. "The Vision of Tainard, *miraculum de quodam canonico Guatenensi per Sanctum Donatianum curato*." In Sheils, *Papers*, 15–24.

**Kauffman, "Introduction."** Kauffman, Richard A. "Introduction." In *Essays on Spiritual Bondage and Deliverance*, edited by Willard M. Swartley, 6–9. Occasional Papers 11. Institute of Mennonite Studies, 1988.

**Kay, "Glossolalia."** Kay, William K. "The Mind, Behaviour, and Glossolalia: A Psychological Perspective." In Cartledge, *Perspectives*, 174–205.

**Kay, "Perspectives."** Kay, William K. "Perspectives on Prophecy." In Graves, *Strangers*, 445–52.

**Kee, *Every Nation*.** Kee, Howard Clark. *To Every Nation Under Heaven: The Acts of the Apostles*. Trinity Press International, 1997.

**Kee, *Miracle*.** Kee, Howard Clark. *Miracle in the Early Christian World: A Study in Sociohistorical Method*. Yale University Press, 1983.

**Keener, *Acts*.** Keener, Craig S. *Acts: An Exegetical Commentary*. 4 vols. Baker Academic, 2012–15.

**Keener, *Acts* (Cambridge).** Keener, Craig S. *Acts*. New Cambridge Bible Commentary. Cambridge University Press, 2020.

**Keener, *Background Commentary*.** Keener, Craig S. *The IVP Bible Background Commentary: New Testament*. 2nd ed. InterVarsity, 2014.

**Keener, "Casting Mountains."** Keener, Craig S. "Casting Out Mountains—Mark 11:23." *Journal of Gospels and Acts Research* 5 (September 2021): 47–65.

**Keener, *Christobiography*.** Keener, Craig S. *Christobiography: Memories, History, and the Reliability of the Gospels*. Eerdmans, 2019.

**Keener, "Colt."** Keener, Craig S. "The Unridden Donkey Colt—Mark 11:2 in Light of Equine Development and Pedagogy." *Bulletin for Biblical Research* 32, no. 1 (2022): 17–40.

**Keener, *Corinthians*.** Keener, Craig S. *1 and 2 Corinthians*. New Cambridge Bible Commentary. Cambridge University Press, 2005.

**Keener, "Dead Raised."** Keener, Craig S. "'The Dead Are Raised' (Matthew 11:5// Luke 7:22): Resuscitation Accounts in the Gospels and Eyewitness Testimony." *Bulletin for Biblical Research* 25, no. 1 (2015): 55–79.

**Keener, "Dead Still Rise."** Keener, Craig S. "Do the Dead Still Rise?" *Christianity Today*, June 2019, 46–50.

**Keener, *Excursuses*.** Keener, Craig S. *Mark's Gospel: Critical Excursuses*. International Critical Commentary. T&T Clark, 2026.

**Keener, "False Apostles."** Keener, Craig S. "Recognizing False Apostles." *The Christian Post*, April 23, 2019. https://www.christianpost.com/voices/recognizing-false-apostles.html.

**Keener, *1–2 Peter, Jude*.** Keener, Craig S. *1–2 Peter, Jude*. Word and Spirit Commentary on the New Testament. Baker Academic, 2025.

**Keener, "Fruit."** Keener, Craig S. "A Comparison of the Fruit of the Spirit in Galatians 5:22–23 with Ancient Thought on Ethics and Emotion." In *The Language and Literature of the New Testament: Essays in Honor of Stanley E. Porter's 60th Birthday*, edited by Lois K. Fuller Dow, Craig A. Evans, and Andrew W. Pitts, 574–98. Brill, 2016.

**Keener, "Function of Pneumatology."** Keener, Craig S. "The Function of Johannine Pneumatology in the Context of Late First-Century Judaism." PhD diss., Duke University, 1991.

**Keener, *Galatians*.** Keener, Craig S. *Galatians: A Commentary*. Baker Academic, 2019.

**Keener, "Get the Bible."** Keener, Craig S. "How Did We Get the Bible? A Scholar Explains the History and Canonization of the Bible We Have Today—in Layman's Terms." *Charisma*, January 2011, 56–60.

**Keener, *Gift & Giver*.** Keener, Craig S. *Gift & Giver: The Holy Spirit for Today*. Baker Academic, 2001. Repackaged with a new afterword in 2020.

**Keener, "Gifts."** Keener, Craig S. "Gifts (Spiritual)." In *The Westminster Theological Wordbook of the Bible*, edited by Donald E. Gowan, 155–61. Westminster John Knox, 2003.

**Keener, "Gospel and Reconciliation."** Keener, Craig S. "The Gospel and Racial Reconciliation." In *The Gospel in Black & White: Theological Resources for Racial Reconciliation*, edited by Dennis L. Ockholm, 117–30. InterVarsity, 1997.

**Keener, "Head Coverings."** Keener, Craig S. "Head Coverings." In *Dictionary of New Testament Background*, edited by Craig A. Evans and Stanley E. Porter, 442–47. InterVarsity, 2000.

**Keener, "Inspiration."** Keener, Craig S. "Greek Versus Jewish Conceptions of Inspiration and 2 Timothy 3:16." *Journal of the Evangelical Theological Society* 63, no. 2 (2020): 217–31.

**Keener, "Invitations."** Keener, Craig S. "Some New Testament Invitations to Ethnic Reconciliation." *Evangelical Quarterly* 75, no. 3 (July 2003): 195–213.

**Keener, "Invitations to Reconciliation."** Keener, Craig S. "Some New Testament Invitations to Ethnic Reconciliation: John 4:42; Luke 10:29–37; Romans; Ephesians 2:11–22." In *Forgiveness, Peacemaking, and Reconciliation*, edited by David K. Ngaruiya and Rodney L. Reed, 207–30. Africa Society of Evangelical Theology. Langham Global Library, 2020.

**Keener, *John*.** Keener, Craig S. *The Gospel of John: A Commentary*. 2 vols. Baker Academic, 2003.

**Keener, "Learning."** Keener, Craig S. "Learning in the Assemblies: 1 Corinthians 14:34–35." In *Discovering Biblical Equality: Biblical, Theological, Cultural & Practical Perspectives*, edited by Ronald W. Pierce, Cynthia Long Westfall, with Christa L. McKirkland, 146–58. 3rd ed. InterVarsity, 2021.

**Keener, "*Lepra*."** Keener, Craig S. "*Lepra* or Leprosy in Luke's Gospel." In *The Pneumatological Imagination: A Theological Concert in Honor of Amos Yong*, edited by Christopher A. Stephenson and L. William Oliverio Jr., 98–113. Global Pentecostal and Charismatic Studies 52. Brill, 2026.

**Keener, "Madness."** Keener, Craig S. "Paul's Positive Madness in Acts 26:24–25." In *Goldene Anfänge und Aufbrüche: Johann Jakob Wettstein und die Apostelgeschichte*, edited by Manfred Lang and Joseph Verheyden, 311–20. Arbeiten zur Bibel und Ihrer Geschichte. Evangelische Verlagsanstalt, 2016.

**Keener, *Matthew*.** Keener, Craig S. *The Gospel of Matthew: A Socio-Rhetorical Commentary*. Eerdmans, 2009. Rev. version of *A Commentary on the Gospel of Matthew*. Eerdmans, 1999.

**Keener, *Matthew* (1997).** Keener, Craig S. *Matthew*. IVPNTC. InterVarsity, 1997.

**Keener, *Mind*.** Keener, Craig S. *The Mind of the Spirit: Paul's Approach to Transformed Thinking*. Baker Academic, 2016.

**Keener, "Miracle Reports."** Keener, Craig S. "Miracle Reports and the Argument from Analogy." Plenary annual lecture for the Institute for Biblical Research. San Diego, CA, November 21, 2014.

**Keener, "Miracle Reports and Argument."** Keener, Craig S. "Miracle Reports and the Argument from Analogy." *Bulletin for Biblical Research* 25, no. 4 (2015): 475–95.

**Keener, *Miracles*.** Keener, Craig S. *Miracles: The Credibility of the New Testament Accounts*. 2 vols. Baker Academic, 2011.

**Keener, *Miracles Today*.** Keener, Craig S. *Miracles Today*. Baker Academic, 2021.

**Keener, "Ndoundou."** Keener, Médine Moussounga. "Ndoundou, Daniel." Dictionary of African Christian Biography. Accessed March 3, 2025. https://dacb.org/stories/congo/ndoundou-daniel/.

**Keener, "Note."** Keener, Craig S. "Three Notes on Figurative Language: Inverted Guilt in Acts 7:55–60, Paul's Figurative Vote in Acts 26:10, Figurative Eyes in Galatians 4:15." *Journal of Greco-Roman Christianity and Judaism* 5 (2008): 41–49.

**Keener, "Ongoing Evidence."** Keener, Craig S. "Appendix A: The Ongoing Evidence of Miracles, with Thoughts on African Charismatic Christianity." In Brown, *Authentic Fire*, 335–76.

**Keener, *Paul*.** Keener, Craig S. *Paul, Women & Wives: Marriage & Women's Ministry in the Letters of Paul*. Baker Academic, 2004.

**Keener, "People Met Jesus."** Keener, Craig S. "People Met Jesus Deeply Here: Craig Keener on the Asbury Outpouring." *Pneuma Review*, March 13, 2023.

**Keener, *Peter*.** Keener, Craig S. *1 Peter: A Commentary*. Baker Academic, 2021.

**Keener, "Political Prophecies."** Keener, Craig S. "When Political Prophecies Don't Come to Pass." *Christianity Today*, November 11, 2020.

**Keener, "Power for Mission."** Keener, Craig S. "God's Power for Mission in Acts 1–2." *Journal of Spiritual Formation and Soul Care* 17, no. 2 (November 2024): 227–38.

**Keener, "Recognizing False Apostles."** Keener, Craig S. "Leading New Testament Scholar Reveals How to Recognize False Apostles." *Charisma*, April 22, 2019.

https://mycharisma.com/spiritled-living/leading-new-testament-scholar-reveals-how-to-recognize-false-apostles/.

**Keener, "Reconciliation."** Keener, Craig S. "The Gospel and Racial Reconciliation." In *The Holy Spirit and Social Justice: Interdisciplinary Global Perspectives: Scripture & Theology*, edited by Antipas Harris and Michael D. Palmer, 104–27. Seymour, 2019.

**Keener, "Review."** Keener, Craig S. "A Review of MacArthur's *Strange Fire*." In Graves, *Strangers*, 35–58.

**Keener, *Romans*.** Keener, Craig S. *Romans*. New Covenant Commentary 6. Cascade Books, 2009.

**Keener, "Spirit."** Keener, Craig S. "The Holy Spirit." In *The Oxford Handbook of Evangelical Theology*, edited by Gerald R. McDermott, 159–73. Oxford University Press, 2010.

**Keener, "Spirit and Mission."** Keener, Craig S. "The Spirit and the Mission of the Church in Acts 1–2." *Journal of the Evangelical Theological Society* 62, no. 1 (March 2019): 25–45.

**Keener, *Spirit Hermeneutics*.** Keener, Craig S. *Spirit Hermeneutics: Reading Scripture in Light of Pentecost*. Eerdmans, 2016.

**Keener, "Strike."** Keener, Craig S. "One-Strike-You're-Out on the Gift of Prophecy?—Deut 18:22." *Craig Keener* (blog). March 1, 2021. Accessed August 24, 2024. https://craigkeener.com/one-strike-youre-out-on-the-gift-of-prophecy-deuteronomy-1822/.

**Keener, *Suffering*.** Keener, Craig S. *Suffering: Its Meaning for the Spirit-Filled Life*. Baker Academic, 2025.

**Keener, "Teaching Ministry."** Keener, Craig S. "A Spirit-Filled Teaching Ministry in Acts 19:9." In Alexander, May, and Reid, *Trajectories*, 46–58.

**Keener, "Tongues."** Keener, Craig S. "Why Does Luke Use Tongues as a Sign of the Spirit's Empowerment?" *Journal of Pentecostal Theology* 15, no. 2 (2007): 177–84.

**Keener, "Trump Prophecies."** Keener, Craig S. "Failed Trump Prophecies Offer a Lesson in Humility." *Christianity Today*, January 20, 2021.

**Keener and Keener, *Impossible Love*.** Keener, Craig S., and Médine Moussounga Keener. *Impossible Love: The True Story of an African Civil War, Miracles, and Love Against All Odds*. Chosen Books, 2016.

**Keener and Keener, *Reconciliation*.** Keener, Craig S., and Médine Moussounga Keener. *Reconciliation for Africa: Resources for Ethnic Reconciliation from the Bible and History*. Africa Christian Textbooks/Oasis, 2007; First Fruits, 2023.

**Keener and Keener, "Temple."** Keener, Craig S., and Médine Moussounga Keener. "One New Temple in Christ." In *Moral Pedagogies for Africa: From Ethnic Enmity to Responsible Cohabitation*, edited by Theodros A. Teklu, 95–112. Studies in World Christianity and Interreligious Relations. Routledge, 2022.

**Keener and Oliverio Jr., *Canon*.** Keener, Craig S., and L. William Oliverio Jr., eds. *The Spirit Throughout the Canon: Pentecostal Pneumatology*. Journal of Pentecostal Studies Supplement 48. Brill, 2022.

**Keener and Usry,** Faith. Keener, Craig S., and Glenn J. Usry. *Defending Black Faith: Answers to Tough Questions About African-American Christianity*. InterVarsity, 1997.

**Keener and Vaughan, *Demons*.** Keener, Craig S., and Joy L. Vaughan. *Demons in the Ancient and Modern Worlds: Essential Background for the Study of the New Testament*. Baker Academic, forthcoming.

**Keener and Vaughan, "Tongues."** Keener, Craig S., and Joy L. Vaughan. "Tongues." In *Dictionary of Paul and His Letters*. 2nd ed., edited by Scot McKnight, 1059–63. IVP Academic, 2023.

**Kelhoffer, "Maccabees at Prayer."** Kelhoffer, James A. "The Maccabees at Prayer: Pro- and Anti-Hasmonean Tendencies in the Prayers of First and Second Maccabees." *Early Christianity* 2, no. 2 (2011): 198–218.

**Kelhoffer, "Miracle Workers."** Kelhoffer, James A. "Ordinary Christians as Miracle Workers in the New Testament and the Second and Third Century Christian Apologists." *Biblical Research* 44 (1999): 23–34.

**Kelsey, *Healing*.** Kelsey, Morton T. *Healing and Christianity in Ancient Thought and Modern Times*. Harper & Row, 1973.

**Kelsey, *Tongue Speaking*.** Kelsey, Morton. *Tongue Speaking: The History and Meaning of Charismatic Experience*. Crossroad, 1981.

**Kendall, *Holy Fire*.** Kendall, R. T. *Holy Fire*. Charisma House, 2014.

**Kendall, *Prophetic Integrity*.** Kendall, R. T. *Prophetic Integrity: Aligning Our Words with God's Word*. Thomas Nelson, 2022.

**Kendall, *Receiving Promise*.** Kendall, R. T. *Receiving the Isaac Promise: Position Yourself for the Fullness of God's End-Time Outpouring*. Destiny Image, 2023.

**Kennedy, "Survey."** Kennedy, George A. "Historical Survey of Rhetoric." In *Handbook of Classical Rhetoric in the Hellenistic Period, 330 B.C.–A.D. 400*, edited by Stanley E. Porter, 3–41. Brill, 1997.

**Kent and Waite, *Beyond*.** Kent, Richard, and David Waite. *Beyond the Final Frontier*. Marshall Pickering; HarperCollins, 2000.

**Kerin, *Touch*.** Kerin, Dorothy. *The Living Touch*. Courier, 1914.

**Khai, "Pentecostalism."** Khai, Chin Khua. "The Assemblies of God and Pentecostalism in Myanmar." In Anderson and Tang, *Asian and Pentecostal*, 261–80.

**Kidd, *Awakening*.** Kidd, Thomas S. *The Great Awakening: The Roots of Evangelical Christianity in Colonial America*. Yale University Press, 2007.

**Kidd, "Healing."** Kidd, Thomas S. "The Healing of Mercy Wheeler: Illness and Miracles Among Early American Evangelicals." *William and Mary Quarterly* 63, no. 1 (January 2006): 149–70.

**Kidd and Hankins, *Baptists*.** Kidd, Thomas S., and Barry Hankins. *Baptists in America: A History*. Oxford University Press, 2015.

**Kim, "Healing."** Kim, Sean C. "Reenchanted: Divine Healing in Korean Protestantism." In Brown, *Global*, 267–85.

**Kim, *If I Perish*.** Kim, Esther Ahn. *If I Perish: Facing Imprisonment, Persecution, and Death, a Young Korean Christian Defies the Japanese Warlords*. 2nd ed. Moody, 2001.

**Kim, "Montanism."** Kim, Lucien Jinkwang. "Is Montanism a Heretical Sect or Pentecostal Antecedent?" *Asian Journal of Pentecostal Studies* 12, no. 1 (2009): 113–24.

**Kim, *Obsession*.** Kim, Brian. *Magnificent Obsession*. Charisma House, 2015.

**Kim, "Pentecostalism."** Kim, Sung-Gun. "Pentecostalism, Shamanism, and Capitalism Within Contemporary Korean Society." In *Spirits of Globalization: The Growth of Pentecostalism and Experiential Spiritualities in a Global Age*, edited by Sturla J. Stålsett, 23–38. SCM, 2006.

**King, *Applying Principles*.** King, Paul L., *Is It of God? A Biblical Guidebook for Spiritual Discernment*. Vol. 2, *Applying Biblical Principles of Spiritual Discernment*. Paul King Ministries, 2021.

**King, "Gifts."** King, Paul L. "Charismatic Gifts." In McClymond, *Revivals*, 1:95–99.

**King, *Guidebook*.** King, Paul L. *Is It of God? A Biblical Guidebook for Spiritual Discernment*. Vol. 1. Bridge-Logos, 2019.

**King, *Moving Mountains*.** King, Paul L. *Moving Mountains: Lessons in Bold Faith from Great Evangelical Leaders*. Chosen, 2004.

**Kirby, "Recovery."** Kirby, Jeff. "The Recovery of Healing Gifts." In *Those Controversial Gifts: Prophecy, Dreams, Visions, Tongues, Interpretation, Healing*, edited by George Mallone, 101–20. InterVarsity, 1983.

**Kirk, "Tradition."** Kirk, Alan. "Jesus Tradition and Memory." In *The Dictionary of the Bible and Ancient Media*, edited by Tom Thatcher, Chris Keith, Raymond F. Person Jr., and Elsie R. Stern, 196–97. Bloomsbury T&T Clark, 2017.

**Kiszonas, "Tongues Cease."** Kiszonas, Dennis. "When Did the Gift of Tongues Cease?" Berean Bible Society, September 1, 2003. www.bereanbiblesociety.org/when-did-the-gift-of-tongues-cease/.

**Klassen and Klaassen, *Writings of Marpeck*.** Klassen, William, and Walter Klaassen, ed., trans. *The Writings of Pilgram Marpeck*. Herald, 1978.

**Klaus, "Global Culture."** Klaus, Byron D. "Pentecostalism as a Global Culture: An Introductory Overview." In Dempster, Klaus, and Petersen, *Globalization of Pentecostalism*, 127–30.

**Klausner, *Jesus*.** Klausner, Joseph. *Jesus: His Life, Times, and Teaching*. Translated by Herbert Danby. Macmillan, 1925. Reprint, Menorah, 1979.

**Klein, Blomberg, and Hubbard, *Introduction*.** Klein, William W., Craig L. Blomberg, and Robert L. Hubbard Jr. *Introduction to Biblical Interpretation*. Word, 1993.

**Kling, "Corinthians."** Kling, Christian Friedrich. "The First Epistle to the Corinthians." In *Lange's Commentary on the Holy Scriptures*. Edited by John Peter Lange. Vol. 10. Reprint, Zondervan, 1960.

**Kling, "Model."** Kling, David W. "A New Model for Missions: Voluntary Societies and Parachurch Organizations." *Christian History* 153 (2024): 14–16.

**Knapstad, "Power."** Knapstad, Bård Løkken. "Show Us the Power! A Study of the Influence of Miracles on the Conversion Process from Islam to Christianity in an Indonesian Context." ThM thesis, Norwegian Lutheran School of Theology, 2005.

**Knox, *Enthusiasm*.** Knox, R. A. *Enthusiasm: A Chapter in the History of Religion*. Clarendon, 1950.

**Koch, *Revival*.** Koch, Kurt. *The Revival in Indonesia*. Evangelization Publishers; Kregel, 1970.

**Koch, *Zulus*.** Koch, Kurt E. *God Among the Zulus*. Translated by Justin Michell and Waldemar Engelbrecht. Mission Kwa Sizabanu, 1981.

**Kolb, *Luther and Word*.** Kolb, Robert. *Martin Luther and the Enduring Word of God: The Wittenberg School and Its Scripture-Centered Proclamation*. Baker Academic, 2016.

**Kolenda, "Cessationism 1."** Kolenda, Daniel. "The Heresy of Cessationism 1 (The Scriptures)." Posted October 13, 2023, by Off the Record Podcast, YouTube. Accessed October 8, 2024. https://www.youtube.com/watch?v=ayLQaUJubU0.

**Kolenda, "Cessationism 2."** Kolenda, Daniel. "Cessationism 2 (A Cascade of Lies)." Posted October 20, 2023, by Off the Record Podcast, YouTube. Accessed October 8, 2024. https://www.youtube.com/watch?v=M8fr1ovkPeA.

**Kolenda, "Cessationism 3."** Kolenda, Daniel. "Cessationism 3 (Has Prophecy Ceased?)." Posted October 31, 2023, by Off the Record Podcast, YouTube. Accessed March 26, 2024. https://www.youtube.com/watch?v=llQjh9QpWxA.

**Kolenda, "Cessationism 4."** Kolenda, Daniel. "Cessationism 4 (Have Tongues Ceased?)." Posted November 7, 2023, by Off the Record Podcast, YouTube. Accessed March 26, 2024. https://www.youtube.com/watch?v=GlpTQtvP0FU.

**Kolenda, "Cessationism 5."** Kolenda, Daniel. "Cessationism 5 (Gifts of Healings)." Posted November 14, 2023, by Off the Record Podcast, YouTube. Accessed March 26, 2024. https://www.youtube.com/watch?v=tgTvugkuhYg.

**Kolenda, "Cessationism 6."** Kolenda, Daniel. "Cessationism 6 (Evidence of Modern Miracles)." Posted November 21, 2023, by Off the Record Podcast, YouTube. Accessed March 26, 2024. https://www.youtube.com/watch?v=8qX-CQRHnOs.

**Kolenda, "Cessationism 7."** Kolenda, Daniel. "Cessationism 7 (Miracle Workers)." Posted November 28, 2023, by Off the Record Podcast, YouTube. Accessed March 26, 2024. https://www.youtube.com/watch?v=okg0-YifH_0.

**Kolenda, "Cessationism 8."** Kolenda, Daniel. "Cessationism 8 (More Calvinist Than Calvin)." Posted January 9, 2024, by Off the Record Podcast, YouTube. Accessed March 26, 2024. https://www.youtube.com/watch?v=Z_Otye072bM.

**Kolenda, "Cessationism 9."** Kolenda, Daniel. "Cessationism 9: The Pagan Origins." Posted January 25, 2024, by Off the Record Podcast, YouTube. https://www.youtube.com/watch?v=VS64t6Rp4jE.

**Kolenda, "Cessationism 10."** Kolenda, Daniel. "Cessationism 10: The Godfather." Posted February 15, 2024, by Off the Record Podcast, YouTube. Accessed March 26, 2024. https://www.youtube.com/watch?v=8gr3zhMIE0I.

**Kolenda, "Cessationism 11."** Kolenda, Daniel. "Cessationism 11: Miracles in the Middle Ages." Posted March 19, 2024, by Off the Record Podcast, YouTube. Accessed March 26, 2024. https://www.youtube.com/watch?v=TLpNCKE88nI.

**Kolenda, "Cessationism 12."** Kolenda, Daniel. "Cessationism 12: Awakening and Revival." Posted April 2, 2024, by Off the Record Podcast, YouTube. Accessed March 26, 2024. https://www.youtube.com/watch?v=ZhvL1VsZcgY.

**Kolenda, "Cessationist Movie."** Kolenda, Daniel. "Cessationist Movie: A Scathing Review." Posted July 16, 2024, by Off the Record Podcast, YouTube. https://www.youtube.com/watch?v=ZvQO-_ffvgE.

**Kolenda, "Cessationists Disobeying."** Kolenda, Daniel. "Cessationists Disobeying Scripture: Responding to Cessationist Movie." Posted June 20, 2024, by Off the Record Podcast, YouTube. https://www.youtube.com/watch?v=CYgB9xTjGLo.

**Kolenda, "Embarrassing Story."** Kolenda, Daniel. "The Embarrassing Story Cessationists Don't Talk About: Responding to Cessationist Movie." Posted June 11, 2024, by Off the Record Podcast, YouTube. Accessed March 26, 2024. https://www.youtube.com/watch?v=OiL5406p0XQ.

**Kolenda, "False Prophecies."** Kolenda, Daniel. "Shocking False Prophecies of Martin Luther! Responding to Cessationist Movie." Posted May 14, 2024, by Off the Record Podcast, YouTube. https://www.youtube.com/watch?v=UCTCaLuM6b4.

**Kolenda, "Hebrews."** Kolenda, Daniel. "Does Hebrews Say Miracles Ceased?" Posted April 17, 2024, by Off the Record Podcast, YouTube. Accessed March 26, 2024. https://www.youtube.com/watch?v=ICSjDuEk0hQ.

**Kolenda, *Impact Africa*.** Kolenda, Daniel. *Impact Africa: Demonstrations of the Real Power of Jesus Christ Today*. Christ for All Nations, 2015.

**Kolenda, "Instantly."** Kolenda, Daniel. "Instantly Healed Listening to the Radio!" Posted October 28, 2022, by Daniel Kolenda, YouTube. Accessed January 29, 2026. https://www.youtube.com/watch?v=HtEj-yy7ztU.

**Kolenda, *Live*.** Kolenda, Daniel. *Live Before You Die: Wake Up to God's Will for Your Life*. Charisma Media, 2013.

**Kolenda, "Tongues."** Kolenda, Daniel. "Are Tongues Human, Holy, or a Hoax? Responding to Cessationist Movie." Posted June 13, 2024, by Off the Record Podcast, https://www.youtube.com/watch?v=Ui-qJAT5DW0.

**Kovacs, *1 Corinthians*.** Kovacs, Judith L., trans., ed. *1 Corinthians Interpreted by Early Christian Commentators*. Eerdmans, 2005.

**Kraft, *Worldview*.** Kraft, Charles H. *Worldview for Christian Witness*. William Carey Library, 2008.

**Krause, "Principle of Authority."** Krause, Clyde Norman. "The Principle of Authority in the Theology of B. B. Warfield, William Adams Brown and Gerald Birney Smith." PhD diss., Duke University, 1961.

**Kraybill, "Guide."** Kraybill, Charlie. "The Mennonite Society's Guide to the Anabaptist Martyrs of Europe." Quaccheri Cristiani Non Evangelici + Hutteriti in Italia, October 15, 2016. Accessed February 15, 2018. https://quaccheri.wordpress.com/anabaptist-martyrs-of-europe/.

**Kreiser, *Miracles*.** Kreiser, B. Robert. *Miracles, Convulsions, and Ecclesiastical Politics in Early Eighteenth-Century Paris*. Princeton University Press, 1978.

**Kruger, *Introduction*.** Kruger, Michael J. *A Biblical-Theological Introduction to the New Testament: The Gospel Realized*. Crossway, 2016.

**Kruse, *Romans*.** Kruse, Colin G. *Paul's Letter to the Romans*. Pillar New Testament Commentary. Eerdmans, 2012.

**Kuhlman, *LeVrier*.** Kuhlman, Kathryn. *Captain LeVrier Believes in Miracles*. Dimension Books, 1973.

**Kure, "Light."** Kure, Emmanuel Nuhu. "Bringing Light to the Muslims." In *Out of Africa: How the Spiritual Explosion Among Nigerians Is Impacting the World*, edited by C. Peter Wagner and Joseph Thompson, 172–86. Regal, 2004.

**Kurz, "Models."** Kurz, William S. "Narrative Models for Imitation in Luke-Acts." In *Greeks, Romans, and Christians: Essays in Honor of Abraham J. Malherbe*, edited by David L. Balch, Everett Ferguson, and Wayne A. Meeks, 171–89. Fortress, 1990.

**Kurz, "Nature."** Kurz, William S. "The Open-Ended Nature of Luke and Acts as Inviting Canonical Actualisation." *Neotestamentica* 31, no. 2 (1997): 289–308. https://epublications.marquette.edu/theo_fac/301/.

**Kuyper, *Work of Spirit*.** Kuyper, Abraham. *The Work of the Holy Spirit*. Eerdmans, 1956.

**Kwan, "Argument."** Kwan, Kai-Man. "The Argument from Religious Experience." In *The Blackwell Companion to Natural Theology*, edited by William Lane Craig and J. P. Moreland, 498–552. Blackwell, 2009.

**Kwon, "Foundations."** Kwon, Tack Joe. "The Theoretical Foundations of Healing Ministry and the Applications to Church Growth." DMin diss., Fuller Theological Seminary, 1985.

**Kydd, *Gifts*.** Kydd, Ronald A. N. *Charismatic Gifts in the Early Church*. Hendrickson, 1984.

**Kydd, *Healing*.** Kydd, Ronald A. N. *Healing Through the Centuries: Models for Understanding*. Hendrickson, 1998.

**Kyle, *Last Days.*** Kyle, Richard. *The Last Days Are Here Again*. Baker, 1998.

**Lachs, *Commentary.*** Lachs, Samuel Tobias. *A Rabbinic Commentary on the New Testament: The Gospels of Matthew, Mark, and Luke*. KTAV; Anti-Defamation League of B'Nai B'Rith, 1987.

**Lacy, *Cry.*** Lacy, John. *A Cry from the Desert*. n.p., 1708.

**Ladd, *Gospel of Kingdom.*** Ladd, George Eldon. *The Gospel of the Kingdom*. Eerdmans, 1959.

**Ladd, *Presence of Future.*** Ladd, George Eldon. *The Presence of the Future*. Eerdmans, 1974.

**Ladd, *Theology.*** Ladd, George Eldon. *A Theology of the New Testament*. Eerdmans, 1974.

**Lagerwerf, *Witchcraft.*** Lagerwerf, Leny. *Witchcraft, Sorcery and Spirit Possession: Pastoral Responses in Africa*. Mambo Press, 1987.

**Laistner, *Historians.*** Laistner, M. L. W. *The Greater Roman Historians*. University of California Press; Cambridge University Press, 1947.

**Lambert, *Millions.*** Lambert, Tony. *China's Christian Millions: The Costly Revival*. Monarch, 1999.

**Lampe, "Miracles."** Lampe, G. W. H. "Miracles in the Acts of the Apostles." In *Miracles: Cambridge Studies in Their Philosophy and History*, edited by C. F. D. Moule, 163–78. A. R. Mowbray; Morehouse-Barlow, 1965.

**Lane, *Hebrews 1–8.*** Lane, William. *Hebrews 1–8*. WBC. Word, 1991.

**Lang, *Lives.*** Lang, D. M., ed. *Lives and Legends of the Georgian Saints*. 2nd ed. St. Vladimir's Seminary Press, 1976.

**"Language Center."** "Language Center of the Brain Is Not Under the Control of Subjects Who 'Speak in Tongues.'" *Science Daily*, October 31, 2006.

**Lanphere, *Cessationist.*** Lanphere, Les, dir. *Cessationist*. 2023. Broken Stone Studio. Accessed September 9, 2024. https://www.amazon.com/Cessationist-Joel-Beeke/dp/B0CK64SFWS.

**Latourette, *History of Christianity.*** Latourette, Kenneth Scott. *A History of Christianity*. 2 vols. HarperSanFrancisco, 1975.

**Laurito, *Speaking in Tongues.*** Laurito, Timothy. *Speaking in Tongues: A Multidisciplinary Defense*. Wipf & Stock, 2021.

**Lauterbach, *Mekhilta.*** Lauterbach, Jacob Z., trans. *Mekilta de-Rabbi Ishmael*. 3 vols. Jewish Publication Society of America, 1933–35.

**Law, *Power.*** Law, William. *Power of the Spirit*. Edited by Dave Hunt. Christian Literature Crusade, 1971.

**Lawton, *Miracles.*** Lawton, John Stewart. *Miracles and Revelation*. Association Press, 1960.

**Le Baron, "Automatism."** Le Baron, Albert. "A Case of Psychic Automatism, Including 'Speaking with Tongues.'" In *Proceedings of the Society for Psychical Research*, 12:277–97. Kegan Paul, Trench, Trubner, 1896–97.

**Lecky, *History*.** Lecky, William Edward Hartpole. *History of the Rise and Influence of the Spirit of Rationalism in Europe*. Vol. 1. D. Appletone, 1919.

**Lee, "Future."** Lee, Moonjang. "Future of Global Christianity." In *Atlas of Global Christianity, 1910–2010*, edited by Todd M. Johnson and Kenneth R. Ross, 104–5. Center for the Study of Global Christianity, 2009.

**Lee, "Korean Pentecost."** Lee, Young-Hoon. "Korean Pentecost: The Great Revival of 1907." *Asian Journal of Pentecostal Studies* 4, no. 1 (2001): 73–83.

**Lehmann, *Struggle*.** Lehmann, David. *Struggle for the Spirit: Religious Transformation and Popular Culture in Brazil and Latin America*. Polity Press; Blackwell, 1996.

**Leiman, "Josephus and Canon."** Leiman, Sid Z. "Josephus and the Canon of the Bible." In *Josephus, the Bible, and History*, edited by Louis H. Feldman and Gohei Hata, 50–58. Wayne State University Press, 1989.

**Leivestad, "Dogma."** Leivestad, Ragnar. "Das Dogma von der prophetenlosen Zeit." *New Testament Studies* 19, no. 3 (1973): 288–99.

**Le Roux, "Le Roux."** Le Roux, Harold. "White Afrikaner Zionist Pieter Louis Le Roux (1865–1943)." *Church History Society of Southern Africa* 33, no. 2 (September 2007): 45–65.

**"Letter? I 'Ardly Know 'Er."** "Letter? I 'Ardly Know 'Er: The Unknown Language (and Letters) of Hildegard von Bingen." *Medieval Studies Research Blog: Meet Us at the Crossroads of Everything*, University of Notre Dame, posted by Joseph, October 1, 2015. https://sites.nd.edu/manuscript-studies/2015/10/01/letter-i-ardly-know-er-the-unknown-language-and-letters-of-hildegard-von-bingen/.

**Levine, *Numbers 1–20*.** Levine, Baruch A. *Numbers 1–20: A New Translation with Introduction and Commentary*. AB. Doubleday, 1993.

**Levitt, *Beef*.** Levitt, Zola. *Corned Beef, Knishes, and Christ*. Tyndale, 1975.

**Levy, *Galatians*.** Levy, Ian Christopher, trans. and ed. *The Letter to the Galatians*. The Bible in Medieval Tradition. Eerdmans, 2011.

**Levy, Krey, and Ryan, *Romans*.** Levy, Ian Christopher, Philip D. W. Krey, and Thomas Ryan. *The Letter to the Romans*. The Bible in Medieval Tradition. Eerdmans, 2013.

**Lewis, *Transposition*.** Lewis, C. S. *Transposition and Other Addresses*. Geoffrey Bles, 1949.

**Libersat, "Epilogue."** Libersat, Henry. "Epilogue." In *Miracles Do Happen*, edited by Briege McKenna with Henry Libersat, 139–42. St. Martin's Press, 1987.

**Licona, *Differences*.** Licona, Michael R. *Why Are There Differences in the Gospels? What We Can Learn from Ancient Biography*. Oxford University Press, 2017.

**Lietzmann, *History*.** Lietzmann, Hans. *A History of the Early Church*. Translated by Bertram Lee Woolf. 4 vols. Meridian Books; World, 1961.

**Lim, "Gifts."** Lim, David. "Spiritual Gifts." In *Systematic Theology: A Pentecostal Perspective*, edited by Stanley M. Horton, 457–88. Gospel Publishing House, 1994.

**Lindberg, *Sourcebook*.** Lindberg, Carter. *The European Reformations Sourcebook*. Blackwell, 2000.

**Littell, *Origins*.** Littell, Franklin H. *The Origins of Sectarian Protestantism*. Beacon, 1964.

**Livingstone, *Defenders*.** Livingstone, David N. *Darwin's Forgotten Defenders: The Encounter Between Evangelical Theology and Evolutionary Thought*. Eerdmans; Scottish Academic Press, 1987.

**Livingstone, "Princeton Apologetic."** Livingstone, William D. "The Princeton Apologetic as Exemplified by the Work of Benjamin B. Warfield and J. Gresham Machen: A Study in American Theology, 1880–1930." PhD diss., Yale University, 1948.

**Llewellyn, "Events."** Llewellyn, Russ. "Religious and Spiritual Miracle Events in Real-Life Experience." In Ellens, *Miracles*, 1:241–63.

**Llewellyn-Jones, *Tortoise*.** Llewellyn-Jones, Lloyd. *Aphrodite's Tortoise: The Veiled Woman of Ancient Greece*. Classical Press of Wales, 2003.

**Lloyd-Jones, *Christianity*.** Lloyd-Jones, Martyn. *Authentic Christianity*. Studies in the Book of Acts 1. Crossway, 2000.

**Lloyd-Jones, *Spirit*.** Lloyd-Jones, Martyn. *The Sovereign Spirit: Discerning His Gifts*. Harold Shaw, 1985.

**Löfstedt, "Silence."** Löfstedt, T. "The Silence of the Spirit: A Critique of the Cessationist View of the Canon." *Svensk Teologisk Kvartalskrift* 89, nos. 3–4 (2013): 126–38.

**Loos, *Miracles*.** Loos, Hendrik van der. *The Miracles of Jesus*. NovTSup 9. Brill, 1965.

**Loud, "Miracles."** Loud, G. A. "Monastic Miracles in Southern Italy, c. 1040–1140." In Cooper and Gregory, *Signs*, 109–22.

**Lovejoy, *Enthusiasm*.** Lovejoy, David S. *Religious Enthusiasm and the Great Awakening*. Prentice Hall, 1969.

**Lovelace, *Dynamics*.** Lovelace, Richard F. *Dynamics of Spiritual Life: An Evangelical Theology of Renewal*. Paternoster; InterVarsity, 1979.

**Ludwig, *Order Restored*.** Ludwig, Garth D. *Order Restored: A Biblical Interpretation of Health, Medicine, and Healing*. Concordia Academic Press, 1999.

**Luther, *Romans*.** Luther, Martin. *Lectures on Romans: Glosses and Scholia*. Edited by Hilton C. Oswald. Vol. 25 of *Luther's Works*. Concordia, 1972.

**Luther, *Writings*.** Luther, Martin. *The Precious and Sacred Writings of Martin Luther*. 14 vols. 1903–10. Reprint, Baker, 1983.

**Lynch-Watson, *Robe*.** Lynch-Watson, Janet. *The Saffron Robe: A Life of Sadhu Sundar Singh*. Hodder & Stoughton, 1975.

**Ma, "Challenges."** Ma, Jungja. "Pentecostal Challenges in East and South-East Asia." In Dempster, Klaus, and Petersen, *Globalization of Pentecostalism*, 183–202.

**Ma, "Eschatology."** Ma, Wonsuk. "Pentecostal Eschatology: What Happened When the Wave Hit the West End of the Ocean." *Asian Journal of Pentecostal Studies* 12, no. 1 (January 2009): 95–112.

**Ma, "Manifestations."** Ma, Julie C. "Manifestations of Supernatural Power in Luke-Acts and the Kankana-eys Tribe of the Philippines." *The Spirit & Church* 4, no. 2 (2002): 109–28.

**Ma, "Mission."** Ma, Julie C. "Pentecostalism and Asian Mission." *Missiology* 35, no. 1 (January 2007): 23–37.

**Ma, "Theology."** Ma, Wonsuk. "Asian (Classical) Pentecostal Theology in Context." In Anderson and Tang, *Asian and Pentecostal*, 59–91.

**Ma, "Vanderbout."** Ma, Julie C. "Elva Vanderbout: A Woman Pioneer of Pentecostal Mission Among Igorots." *Journal of Asian Mission* 3, no. 1 (March 2001): 121–40.

**MacArthur, "Adoption."** MacArthur, John. "The Adoption of the Believer." Grace to You, October 29, 2017. Accessed August 30, 2024. https://www.gty.org/library/sermons-library/48-19/the-adoption-of-the-believer.

**MacArthur, "Battle."** MacArthur, John. "The Believer's Lifelong Battle for Holiness." Grace to You. April 22, 2018. Accessed August 30, 2024. https://www.gty.org/library/sermons-library/48-33/the-believers-lifelong-battle-for-holiness.

**MacArthur, *Chaos*.** MacArthur, John F., Jr. *Charismatic Chaos*. Zondervan, 1992.

**MacArthur, *Charismatics*.** MacArthur, John F., Jr. *The Charismatics: A Doctrinal Perspective*. Zondervan, 1978.

**MacArthur, "Foreword."** MacArthur, John F. "Foreword." In *A Biblical Case for Cessationism: Why the Miraculous Gifts of the Spirit Have Ended*, edited by Tom Pennington, iii–vii. G3, 2023.

**MacArthur, "Living."** MacArthur, John. "Spiritually Living, Yet Still Stinking." Grace to You. March 16, 2008. Accessed August 30, 2024. https://www.gty.org/library/sermons-library/80-332/spiritually-living-yet-still-stinking.

**MacArthur, "Look at Awakening."** MacArthur, John. "A Look at the Great Awakening." Grace to You. November 7, 2018. Accessed August 30, 2024. https://www.gty.org/library/blog/B181107.

**MacArthur, "Passion."** MacArthur, John. "A Passion for the Lost." Grace to You. January 26, 1986. Accessed August 30, 2024. https://www.gty.org/library/sermons-library/90-6/a-passion-for-the-lost#!.

**MacArthur, "Revelation."** MacArthur, John. "Does God Still Give Revelation?" Grace to You. Accessed November 20, 2025. https://www.gty.org/articles/A366/does-god-still-give-revelation.

**MacArthur, "Roman Catholics."** MacArthur, John. "Roman Catholics Aren't Saved." Posted June 10, 2024, by @HEBREWMKJV, YouTube. Accessed February 6, 2026. https://www.youtube.com/shorts/BCfM_fsosz8.

**MacArthur, *Strange Fire*.** MacArthur, John. *Strange Fire: The Danger of Offending the Holy Spirit with Counterfeit Worship*. Thomas Nelson, 2013.

**Macchia, Spirituality.** Macchia, Frank D. Spirituality and Social Liberation: The Message of the Blumhardts in the Light of Wuerttemburg Pietism. Pietist and Wesleyan Studies 4. Scarecrow, 1993.

**MacDonald, "Religion."** MacDonald, Michael. "Religion, Social Change, and Psychological Healing in England, 1600–1800." In Sheils, *Papers*, 101–25.

**Maclean, "Miracles."** Maclean, A. J. "Miracles." In *Dictionary of the Apostolic Church*, edited by James Hastings, 2:39–42. 2 vols. Charles Scribner's Sons, 1915–18.

**MacMullen, *Christianizing*.** MacMullen, Ramsay. *Christianizing the Roman Empire*. Yale University Press, 1984.

**MacMullen, *Second Church*.** MacMullen, Ramsay. *The Second Church: Popular Christianity A.D. 200–400*. WGRWSup 1. Society of Biblical Literature, 2009.

**MacNutt, *Crime*.** MacNutt, Francis. *The Nearly Perfect Crime: How the Church Almost Killed the Ministry of Healing*. Chosen, 2005.

**MacNutt, *Healing*.** MacNutt, Francis. *Healing*. Ave Maria, 1974.

**Maddocks, *Ministry*.** Maddocks, Morris. *The Christian Healing Ministry*. 3rd ed. SPCK, 1995.

**Magnuson, *Salvation*.** Magnuson, Norris. *Salvation in the Slums: Evangelical Social Work 1865–1920*. Baker, 1990.

**Magruder, "Reading."** Magruder, Jeff C. "What Simon Saw but Luke Didn't Say: A Pentecostal Reading of the Samaritan Revival in Acts 8.9–24." In Alexander, May, and Reid, *Trajectories*, 290–99.

**Makarian, "Concept of Revelation."** Makarian, John J. "The Calvinistic Concept of the Biblical Revelation in the Theology of B. B. Warfield." PhD diss., Drew University, 1963.

**Malherbe, "Gentle as Nurse."** Malherbe, Abraham J. "'Gentle as a Nurse': The Cynic Background to I Thess ii." *Novum Testamentum* 12, no. 2 (1970): 203–17.

**Malina and Pilch, *Acts*.** Malina, Bruce J., and John J. Pilch. *Social-Science Commentary on the Book of Acts*. Fortress, 2008.

**Malina and Pilch, *Letters*.** Malina, Bruce J., and John J. Pilch. *Social-Science Commentary on the Letters of Paul*. Fortress, 2006.

**Manschreck, *History*.** Manschreck, Clyde L. *A History of Christianity: Readings in the History of the Church from the Reformation to the Present*. Prentice-Hall, 1964.

**Mansfield, *Pentecost*.** Mansfield, Patti Gallagher. *As by a New Pentecost: The Dramatic Beginning of the Catholic Charismatic Renewal*. Franciscan University Press, 1992.

**Marans, "Luther."** Marans, Noam E. "On Luther and His Lies." *Christian Century*, October 25, 2017. Accessed August 29, 2024. https://www.christiancentury.org/article/critical-essay/on-luther-and-lies.

**Marcille, "Think of Calvin."** Marcille, Philippe. "What Are We to Think of Calvin?" Catholic Apologetics Information website. Accessed August 29, 2024. http://www.catholicapologetics.info/apologetics/protestantism/calvin.htm

**Marcus, *Mark 1–8*.** Marcus, Joel. *Mark 1–8: A New Translation with Introduction and Commentary*. Anchor Yale Bible 27. Yale University Press, 2000.

**Marguerat, *Histoire*.** Marguerat, Daniel. *La première histoire du christianisme (les Actes des apôtres)*. LD 180. Cerf, 1999.

**Marguerat, *Historian*.** Marguerat, Daniel. *The First Christian Historian: Writing the "Acts of the Apostles."* Translated by Ken McKinney, Gregory J. Laughery, and Richard Bauckham. SNTSMS 121. Cambridge University Press, 2002.

**Markle, "Body."** Markle, George B., IV. "Body, Mind, and Faith." In Frazier, *Faith Healing*, 15–20.

**Marostica, "Learning."** Marostica, Matthew. "Learning from the Master: Carlos Annacondia and the Standardization of Pentecostal Practices in and Beyond Argentina." In Brown, *Global*, 207–27.

**Marrant, *Narrative*.** Marrant, John. *A Narrative of the Lord's Wonderful Dealings with John Marrant, a Black*. 4th ed. London, 1785.

**Marshall, *Historian and Theologian*.** Marshall, I. Howard. *Luke: Historian and Theologian*. Paternoster, 1970.

**Marshall, "Luke as Theologian."** Marshall, I. Howard. "Luke as Theologian." In *Anchor Bible Dictionary*, edited by David Noel Freeman, 4:402–3. Doubleday, 1992.

**Marshall, *Thessalonians*.** Marshall, I. Howard. *1 and 2 Thessalonians*. New Century Bible Commentary. Eerdmans, 1983.

**Marszalek, *Miracles*.** Marszalek, Therese. *Extraordinary Miracles in the Lives of Ordinary People: Inspiring Stories of Divine Intervention*. Harrison House, 2007.

**Martens, "First Corinthians 13:10."** Martens, M. P. "First Corinthians 13:10: 'When That Which Is Perfect Comes.'" *Notes on Translation* 10, no. 3 (1996): 36–40.

**Martin, *Acts*.** Martin, Francis, ed., in collaboration with Evan Smith. *Acts*. Ancient Christian Commentary on Scripture: New Testament 5. InterVarsity, 2006.

**Martin, *Catholic Church*.** Martin, Ralph. *The Catholic Church at the End of an Age: What Is the Spirit Saying?* Ignatius, 1994.

**Martin, *Judging*.** Martin, Lee Roy. *Judging the Judges: Pentecostal Theological Perspectives on the Book of Judges*. CPT Press, 2018.

**Martin, "Judging."** Martin, Lee Roy. "Judging the Judges: Searching for Value in These Problematic Characters." *Pneuma Review* 13 (Fall 2010): 54–75.

**Martin, *Pentecostalism*.** Martin, David. *Pentecostalism: The World Their Parish*. Basil Blackwell, 2001.

**Martin, "Resisting."** Martin, Dennis. "Resisting the Devil in the Patristic, Medieval, and Reformation Church." In *Essays on Spiritual Bondage and Deliverance*, edited by Willard M. Swartley, 46–71. Occasional Papers 11. Institute of Mennonite Studies, 1988.

**Martin, *Tongues*.** Martin, David. *Tongues of Fire: The Explosion of Protestantism in Latin America*. Basil Blackwell, 1990.

**Mason, *Ko Thah Byu*.** Mason, Francis. *The Karen Apostle; or, Memoir of Ko Thah Byu*. SGAU Karen Press, 1884.

**Matthews and Benjamin, "Leper."** Matthews, Victor H., and Don C. Benjamin. "The Leper." *The Bible Today* 29 (1991): 292–97.

**Mauldin, *Fullerism*.** Mauldin, A. Chadwick. *Fullerism as Opposed to Calvinism: A Historical and Theological Comparison of Andrew Fuller and John Calvin*. Wipf & Stock, 2011.

**Maxwell, *African Gifts*.** Maxwell, David. *African Gifts of the Spirit: Pentecostalism and the Rise of a Zimbabwean Transnational Religious Movement*. James Currey; Weaver Press; Ohio University Press, 2006.

**May, *Witnesses to Pentecost*.** May, Jordan Daniel. *Global Witnesses to Pentecost: The Testimony of "Other Tongues."* CPT, 2013.

**McAdams, *Redemptive Self*.** McAdams, Dan P. *The Redemptive Self: Stories Americans Live By*. Oxford University Press, 2013.

**McBane, "Bhils."** McBane, George William. "The Bhils on the Indian Subcontinent (with Emphasis for Church Growth in Pakistan)." ThM thesis, Fuller School of World Mission, 1976.

**McCall, "Reassessing."** McCall, Casey G. "Reassessing American Baptist Antimissionism." *Journal of the Evangelical Theological Society* 67, no. 2 (2024): 325–45.

**McClymond, "Characteristics."** McClymond, Michael. "Seven Characteristics of Revivals: What Do These Movements of the Spirit Have in Common?" *Christian History* 153 (2024): 6–8.

**McClymond, *Revivals*.** McClymond, Michael J., ed. *Encyclopedia of Religious Revivals in America*. Greenwood, 2007.

**McClymond and McDermott, *Theology*.** McClymond, Michael J., and Gerald R. McDermott. *The Theology of Jonathan Edwards*. Oxford University Press, 2011.

**McConnell, *Gospel*.** McConnell, D. R. *A Different Gospel: A Historical and Biblical Analysis of the Modern Faith Movement*. Hendrickson, 1988.

**McCready, *Miracles*.** McCready, William D. *Miracles and the Venerable Bede*. Pontifical Institute of Mediaeval Studies, Studies and Texts 118. Pontifical Institute of Mediaeval Studies, 1994.

**McDonnell, *Presence*.** McDonnell, Kilian. *Presence, Power, Praise: Documents of the Charismatic Renewal*. 3 vols. Liturgical Press, 1980.

**McDonnell and Montague, *Initiation*.** McDonnell, Kilian, and George T. Montague. *Christian Initiation and Baptism in the Holy Spirit: Evidence from the First Eight Centuries*. Liturgical Press, 1991.

**McFadden, "Elements."** McFadden, Brian. "The Elements of Discourse: Orality, Literacy, and Nature in the Elemental Miracles of Bede's Ecclesiastical History." *American Benedictine Review* 55, no. 4 (2004): 442–63.

**McGavran, "Healing and Growth."** McGavran, Donald. "Divine Healing and Church Growth." *Renewal Journal* 17, no. 1 (2001): 1.

**McGee, "Calcutta Revival."** McGee, Gary B. "The Calcutta Revival of 1907 and the Reformulation of Charles F. Parham's 'Bible Evidence' Doctrine." *Asian Journal of Pentecostal Studies* 6, no. 1 (2003): 123–43.

**McGee, "Hermeneutics."** McGee, Gary B. "Early Pentecostal Hermeneutics: Tongues as Evidence in the Book of Acts." In McGee, *Initial Evidence*, 96–118.

**McGee, *Initial Evidence*.** McGee, Gary B., ed. *Initial Evidence: Historical and Biblical Perspectives on the Pentecostal Doctrine of Spirit Baptism*. Hendrickson, 1991.

**McGee, "Logic."** McGee, Gary B. "Taking the Logic 'a Little Further': Late Nineteenth-Century References to the Gift of Tongues in Mission-Related Literature and Their Influence on Early Pentecostalism." *Asian Journal of Pentecostal Studies* 9, no. 1 (2006): 99–125.

**McGee, *Miracles*.** McGee, Gary B. *Miracles, Missions, & American Pentecostalism*. American Society of Missiology Series 45. Orbis Books, 2010.

**McGee, "Miracles and Mission."** McGee, Gary B. "Miracles and Mission Revisited." *International Bulletin of Mission Research* 25 (October 2001): 146–56.

**McGee, *People of Spirit*.** McGee, Gary B. *People of the Spirit: The Assemblies of God*. Gospel, 2004.

**McGee, "Possessions."** McGee, Daniel B. "Sharing Possessions: A Study in Biblical Ethics." In *With Steadfast Purpose: Essays on Acts in Honor of Henry Jackson Flanders, Jr.*, edited by Naymond H. Keathley, 163–78. Baylor University Press, 1990.

**McGee, "Radical Strategy."** McGee, Gary B. "The Radical Strategy in Modern Mission: The Linkage of Paranormal Phenomena with Evangelism." In *The Holy Spirit and Mission Dynamics*, edited by C. Douglas McConnell, 69–95. Evangelical Missiological Society Series 5. William Carey Library, 1997.

**McGee, "Shortcut."** McGee, Gary B. "Shortcut to Language Preparation? Radical Evangelicals, Missions, and the Gift of Tongues." *International Bulletin of Mission Research* 25 (July 2001): 118–23.

**McGee, "Strategies."** McGee, Gary B. "Strategies for Global Mission." In Dempster, Klaus, and Petersen, *Called and Empowered*, 203–24.

**McGee, "Strategy."** McGee, Gary B. "The Radical Strategy." In *Signs and Wonders in Ministry Today*, edited by Benny C. Aker and Gary B. McGee, 47–59. Gospel, 1996.

**Mchami, "Possession."** Mchami, R. E. K. "Demon Possession and Exorcism in Mark 1:21–28." *Africa Theological Journal* 24, no. 1 (2001): 17–37.

**McInerney, "Arrian and Romance."** McInerney, Jeremy. "Arrian and the Greek Alexander Romance." *The Classical World* 100, no. 4 (2007): 424–30.

**McIntyre, *Kenyon*.** McIntyre, Joe. *E. W. Kenyon and His Message of Faith*. Charisma House, 1997.

**McKenna, *Miracles*.** McKenna, Briege, with Henry Libersat. *Miracles Do Happen*. St. Martin's Press, 1987.

**McKenzie, "Miracles."** McKenzie, David. "Miracles Are Not Immoral: A Response to James Keller's Moral Argument Against Miracles." *Religious Studies* 35, no. 1 (1999): 73–88.

**McKeown, *Cabinet*.** McKeown, J. C. *A Cabinet of Ancient Medical Curiosities: Strange Tales and Surprising Facts from the Healing Arts of Greece and Rome*. Oxford University Press, 2017.

**Medeiros, "Commitment."** Medeiros, Elias. "The Reformers' Commitment to the Propagation of the Gospel to All Nations from 1555 to 1654." PhD diss., Reformed Theological Seminary, 2009.

**Meeks, *Urban Christians*.** Meeks, Wayne A. *The First Urban Christians: The Social World of the Apostle Paul*. Yale University Press, 1983.

**Menberu, "Estifanos."** Menberu, Dirshaye. "Abba Estifanos." Dictionary of African Christian Biography. Accessed November 20, 2025. https://dacb.org/stories/ethiopia/estifanos/.

**Menzies, *Development*.** Menzies, Robert P. *The Development of Early Christian Pneumatology with Special Reference to Luke-Acts*. JSNTSup 54. Sheffield Academic, 1991.

**Menzies, "Luke-Acts."** Menzies, Robert P. "The Spirit in Luke-Acts: Empowering Prophetic Witness." In Keener and Oliverio Jr., *Canon*, 75–105.

**Menzies, *Romans*.** Menzies, Glen W. *A Pentecostal Commentary on Romans: Introduction, Translation, and Commentary*. Pentecostal Old and New Testament Commentaries. Wipf & Stock, 2025.

**Menzies, *Speaking in Tongues*.** Menzies, Robert P. *Speaking in Tongues: Jesus and the Apostolic Church as Models for the Church Today*. CPT, 2016.

**Merrill, *Miracle Invasion*.** Merrill, Dean. *Miracle Invasion: Amazing True Stories of the Holy Spirit's Gifts at Work Today*. BroadStreet, 2018.

**Metaxas, *Miracles*.** Metaxas, Eric. *Miracles: What They Are, Why They Happen, and How They Can Change Your Life*. Penguin Books, 2014.

**Metzger, "Considerations."** Metzger, Bruce M. "Considerations of Methodology in the Study of the Mystery Religions and Early Christianity." *Harvard Theological Review* 48, no. 1 (1955): 1–20.

**Mews, "Revival."** Mews, Stuart. "The Revival of Spiritual Healing in the Church of England 1920–26." In Sheils, *Papers*, 299–331.

**Michael, "Gäbrä-Seyon."** Michael, Belaynesh. "Gäbrä-Seyon." Dictionary of African Christian Biography. Accessed November 20, 2025. https://dacb.org/stories/ethiopia/gabra-seyon/.

**Michaelsen, "Ecstasy."** Michaelsen, Peter. "Ecstasy and Possession in Ancient Israel. A Review of Some Recent Contributions." *Scandinavian Journal of the Old Testament* 2 (1989): 28–54.

**Middleton, *A Free Inquiry*.** Middleton, Conyers. *A Free Inquiry into the Miraculous Powers, Which Are Supposed to Have Subsisted in the Christian Church, from the Earliest Ages Through Several Successive Centuries: By Which Is Shewn, That We Have No Sufficient Reason to Believe, upon the Authority of the Primitive Fathers, That Any Such Powers Were Continued to the Church, After the Days of the Apostles.* R. Manby and H. S. Cox, 1749. Available online at Hathi Trust Digital Library. Accessed October 9, 2024. https://babel.hathitrust.org/cgi/pt?id=mdp.39015022664075.

**Middleton, *Works*.** Middleton, Conyers. *The Miscellaneous Works of the Late Reverend and Learned Conyers Middleton: Containing All His Writings, Except the Life of Cicero: Many of Which Were Never Before Published.* Richard Manby and H. S. Cox, 1752.

**Midelfort, *History*.** Midelfort, H. C. Erik. *A History of Madness in Sixteenth-Century Germany*. Stanford University Press, 1999.

**Miller, *Finney*.** Miller, Basil. *Charles Finney*. Bethany House, 1941.

**Miller, *Miracle of Healing*.** Miller, Basil. *The Miracle of Divine Healing*. Beacon Hill, 1951.

**Miller, *Tongues*.** Miller, Denzil R. *Missionary Tongues Revisited: More Than an Evidence: Recapturing Luke's Missiological Perspective on Speaking in Tongues*. PneumaLife, 2014.

**Miller and Yamamori, *Pentecostalism*.** Miller, Donald E., and Tetsunao Yamamori. *Global Pentecostalism: The New Face of Christian Social Engagement*. University of California Press, 2007.

**Mills, *Glossolalia: Bibliography*.** Mills, Watson E. *Glossolalia: A Bibliography*. Studies in the Bible and Early Christianity. Edwin Mellen, 1985.

**Milne, *Confession*.** Milne, Garnet Howard. *The Westminster Confession of Faith and the Cessation of Special Revelation: The Majority Puritan Viewpoint on Whether Extra-Biblical Prophecy Is Still Possible*. Paternoster; Wipf & Stock, 2007.

***Minutes of Assembly*, 1870.** General Assembly of the Presbyterian Church. *Minutes of the General Assembly of the Presbyterian Church in the United States.*

Presbyterian Board of Publication, 1870. Available at Internet Archive. Accessed March 16, 2018. www.archive.org/stream/minutesofgeneral1910pres#page/272/mode/2up/search/resurrection.

**"Miracles, Miracle-Workers."** "Miracles, Miracle-Workers: Biblical-Early Christian." In *Brill's New Pauly: Encyclopaedia of the Ancient World*, edited by Hubert Cancik and Helmuth Schneider, 9:53–56. 20 vols. English ed. Christine F. Salazar. Brill, 2010.

**Misson, *Cry*.** Misson, Maximillien. *A Cry from the Desart: or, Testimonials of the Miraculous Things Lately Come to Pass in the Cevennes, Verified upon Oath, and by Other Proofs*. Paternoster-Row, 1707.

**Mitchell, "Archaeology."** Mitchell, Stephen. "Archaeology in Asia Minor 1990–1998." *Archaeological Reports* 45 (1998–1999): 125–92.

**Mitchell, "Scholar."** Mitchell, Lynette Blair. "Charismatic Scholar Targets Racism." *Charisma*, June 1996.

**Mittelstadt, *Reading*.** Mittelstadt, Martin William. *Reading Luke-Acts in the Pentecostal Tradition*. CPT, 2010.

**Mohler, "Hell."** Mohler, Albert. "Air Conditioning Hell: How Liberalism Happens." *Albert Mohler* (blog). January 26, 2010. Accessed October 9, 2024. www.albertmohler.com/2010/01/26/air-conditioning-hell-how-liberalism-happens/.

**Moltmann, "Blessing."** Moltmann, Jürgen. "The Blessing of Hope: The Theology of Hope and the Full Gospel of Life." *Journal of Pentecostal Theology* 13, no. 2 (2005): 147–61.

**Momigliano, *Development*.** Momigliano, Arnaldo. *The Development of Greek Biography: Four Lectures*. Harvard University Press, 1971.

**Monergism, "Cessationists View."** Monergism. "Cessationists View." Accessed January 3, 2019. https://www.monergism.com/topics/spiritual-gifts/cessationists-view.

**Montague, *Holy Spirit*.** Montague, George T. *The Holy Spirit: Growth of a Biblical Tradition*. Paulist Press, 1976.

**Moody, *Spirit of God*.** Moody, Dale. *Spirit of the Living God*. Westminster, 1968.

**Moog and Karenberg, "Francis."** Moog, Ferdinand Peter, and Axel Karenberg. "St. Francis Came at Dawn—The Miraculous Recovery of a Hemiplegic Monk in the Middle Ages." *Journal of the Neurological Sciences* 213, nos. 1–2 (2003): 15–17.

**Moolenburgh, *Meetings*.** Moolenburgh, H. C. *Meetings with Angels: One Hundred and One Real-Life Encounters*. Translated by Tony Langham and Plym Peters. Barnes & Noble, 1995.

**Moran, "Prophecy."** Moran, William L. "New Evidence from Mari on the History of Prophecy." *Biblica* 50 (1969): 15–56.

**Moreland, *Guide*.** Moreland, J. P. *A Simple Guide to Experiencing Miracles: Instruction and Inspiration for Living Supernaturally in Christ*. Zondervan, 2021.

**Moreland, "Restoration."** Moreland, J. P. "Restoration of the Kingdom's Miraculous Power." In Graves, *Strangers*, 281–305.

**Moreland, *Triangle*.** Moreland, J. P. *Kingdom Triangle: Recover the Christian Mind, Renovate the Soul, Restore the Spirit's Power*. Zondervan, 2007.

**Moreland and Issler, *Faith*.** Moreland, J. P., and Klaus Issler. *In Search of a Confident Faith: Overcoming Barriers to Trusting God*. InterVarsity, 2008.

**Morgan, "Impasse."** Morgan, Timothy C. "Egypt's Identity Impasse." *Christianity Today*, April 2008.

**Morosco, "Matthew 10."** Morosco, Robert E. "Redaction Criticism and the Evangelical: Matthew 10 a Test Case." *Journal of the Evangelical Theological Society* 22 (1979): 323–31.

**Morphew, "Calvin and Kingdom."** Morphew, Derek. "Calvin and the Kingdom of God." In Graves, *Kingdom Case*, 123–30.

**Morphew, "Cessationism."** Morphew, Derek. "What Is Cessationism?" In Graves, *Kingdom Case*, 1–16.

**Morris, *Romans*.** Morris, Leon. *Epistle to the Romans*. Pillar New Testament Commentary. Eerdmans, 1988.

**Morton, "Naturalism."** Morton, Peter. "Lutheran Naturalism, Popular Magic, and the Devil." In *The Devil in Society in Premodern Europe*, edited by Richard Raiswell and Peter Dendle, 409–35. Centre for Renaissance and Reformation Studies, 2012.

**Mukwege, *Power*.** Mukwege, Denis. *The Power of Women: A Doctor's Journey of Hope and Healing*. Flatiron Books, 2022.

**Mull and Mull, "Leprosy."** Mull, Kenneth V., and Carolyn Sandquist Mull. "Biblical Leprosy—Is It Really?" *Biblical Archaeology Review* 8, no. 2 (1992): 32–39, 62.

**Müller, *Autobiography*.** Müller, George. *The Autobiography of George Müller*. Whitaker House, 1996.

**Müller, "Power."** Müller, Barbara. "The Diabolical Power of Lettuce, or Garden Miracles in Gregory the Great's *Dialogues*." In Cooper and Gregory, *Signs*, 46–55.

**Mullin, "Bushnell."** Mullin, Robert Bruce. "Horace Bushnell and the Question of Miracles." *Church History* 58, no. 4 (1989): 460–73.

**Mullin, *History*.** Mullin, Robert Bruce. *A Short World History of Christianity*. Westminster John Knox, 2008.

**Mullin, *Miracles*.** Mullin, Robert Bruce. *Miracles and the Modern Religious Imagination*. Yale University Press, 1996.

**Mullins, "Empire."** Mullins, Mark R. "The Empire Strikes Back: Korean Pentecostal Mission to Japan." In Poewe, *Charismatic Christianity*, 87–102.

**Murray, "Anabaptism."** Murray, Stuart. "Anabaptism as a Charismatic Movement." Pentecostals and Charismatics for Peace and Justice, March 21, 2017. https://pcpj.org/2017/03/21/anabaptism-as-a-charismatic-movement/. Originally published in *Anabaptism Today* 8 (February 1995).

**Murray, *Healing*.** Murray, Andrew. *Divine Healing: A Series of Addresses and a Personal Testimony*. Reprint, Logos, 1974.

**Murray, "Healing."** Murray, Andrew. "Divine Healing." In *Healing: The Three Great Classics on Divine Healing*, edited by Jonathan L. Graf, 3–117. Christian Publications, 1992.

**Murray, "Hermeneutics."** Murray, Richard. "The Literalist Hermeneutics of Luther's Increasing Violence." *Clarion: Journal for Religion, Peace & Justice*, May 24, 2017.

**Murrin, *Liberty*.** Murrin, John M., et al. *Liberty, Equality, Power: A History of the American People*. Wadsworth CENGAGE Learning, 2010.

**Mwaura, "Integrity."** Mwaura, Philomena Njeri. "Integrity of Mission in the Light of the Gospel: Bearing Witness of the Spirit Among Africa's Gospel Bearers." *Mission Studies* 24 (2007): 189–212.

**"Myth of Luther."** "The Myth of Martin Luther." Catholic Apologetics Network website. http://www.canapologetics.net/luther_said.html.

**Ndyabahika, "Attitude."** Ndyabahika, James F. "The Attitude of the Historical Churches to Poverty and Wealth: A Challenge for African Christianity." *Africa Journal of Evangelical Theology* 23, no. 2 (2004): 199–214.

**Neal, *Power*.** Neal, Emily Gardiner. *The Healing Power of Christ*. Hawthorn Books, 1972.

**Neil, *Acts*.** Neil, William. *The Acts of the Apostles*. New Century Bible Commentary. Marshall, Morgan & Scott; Eerdmans, 1973.

**Neil, *Thessalonians*.** Neil, William. *The Epistle of Paul to the Thessalonians*. Moffatt New Testament Commentary. Hodder & Stoughton, 1950.

**Neill, *History of Missions*.** Neill, Stephen. *A History of Christian Missions*. Penguin, 1964.

**Newell, "Witchcraft."** Newell, Sasha. "Pentecostal Witchcraft: Neoliberal Possession and Demonic Discourse in Ivorian Pentecostal Churches." *Journal of Religion in Africa* 37, no. 4 (2007): 461–90.

**Newman, "Discovering the Spirit."** Newman, Lara. "Discovering the Spirit at Harvard." In *To God Be the Glory: Christian Alumni of Harvard Law School Tell Their Stories*, edited by Margaret M. Cross, 45–53. Program on Biblical Law and Christian Legal Studies, 2024.

**Ngewa, *Galatians*.** Ngewa, Samuel M. *Galatians*. Africa Bible Commentary. Hippo, 2010.

**Nichol, *Pentecostalism*.** Nichol, John Thomas. *Pentecostalism*. Harper & Row, 1966.

**Nichols, *History*.** Nichols, James Hastings. *History of Christianity, 1650–1950: Secularization of the West*. Ronald, 1956.

**Noll, *History*.** Noll, Mark A. *A History of Christianity in the United States and Canada*. Eerdmans, 1992.

**Noll, *Rise*.** Noll, Mark A. *A History of Evangelicalism: People Movements and Ideas in the English-Speaking World*. Vol. 1, *The Rise of Evangelicalism: The Age of Edwards, Whitefield, and the Wesleys*. InterVarsity, 2003.

**Noll, *Shape*.** Noll, Mark A. *The New Shape of World Christianity: How American Experience Reflects Global Faith*. IVP Academic, 2009.

**Norman, "Healing."** Norman, J. G. G. "Spiritual Healing." In Douglas, *Dictionary of Church*, 927.

**Norwood, "Colloquium."** Norwood, Douglass Paul. "A Reconciliation Colloquium for Church Leaders in Suriname." DMin project, Assemblies of God Theological Seminary, 2001.

**Notre Dame, "Unknown Language."** University of Notre Dame Medieval Institute. "Letter? I 'ardly Know 'er: The Unknown Language (and Letters) of Hildegard von Bingen." *At the Crossroads of Everything* (blog), posted October 1, 2015. Accessed November 17, 2024. https://sites.nd.edu/manuscript-studies/2015/10/01/letter-i-ardly-know-er-the-unknown-language-and-letters-of-hildegard-von-bingen/.

**Numbere, *Vision*.** Numbere, Nonyem E. *A Man and a Vision: A Biography of Apostle Geoffrey D. Numbere*. Greater Evangelism Publications, 2008.

**Oblau, "Healing."** Oblau, Gotthard. "Divine Healing and the Growth of Practical Christianity in China." In Brown, *Global*, 307–27.

**Oblau, "Pentecostal."** Oblau, Gotthard. "Pentecostal by Default? Contemporary Christianity in China." In Anderson and Tang, *Asian and Pentecostal*, 411–36.

**Oconer, "Methodism in Asia."** Oconer, Luther J. "Methodism in Asia and the Pacific." In *T&T Clark Companion to Methodism*, edited by Charles Yrigoyen Jr., 152–65. T&T Clark, 2010.

**O'Hare, *Facts*.** O'Hare, Patrick F. *The Facts About Luther*. Frederick Pustet, 1916.

**Olasky, "Communism."** Olasky, Marvin. "From Communism to Christ." *Christianity Today*, January 2026, 46–49.

**Olena, *Horton*.** Olena, Lois E., with Raymond L. Gannon. *Stanley M. Horton: Shaper of Pentecostal Theology*. Gospel Publishing House, 2009.

**Oliver, *Movements*.** Oliver, Jeff. *Early Prophetic and Spiritual Gifts Movements*. Vol. 1 of *Pentecost to the Present*. Bridge-Logos, 2017.

**Oliver, *Reformations*.** Oliver, Jeff. *Reformations and Awakenings*. Vol. 2 of *Pentecost to the Present*. Bridge-Logos, 2017.

**Oliver, *Revivals*.** Oliver, Jeff. *Worldwide Revivals and Renewal*. Vol. 3 of *Pentecost to the Present*. Bridge-Logos, 2017.

**Oliverio, *Hermeneutics*.** Oliverio, L. William, Jr. *Theological Hermeneutics in the Classical Pentecostal Tradition: A Typological Account*. Global Pentecostal and Charismatic Studies 12. Brill, 2012.

**Olson, *Bruchko*.** Olson, Bruce. *Bruchko*. Rev. ed. Creation House, 1995.

**"One Spirit."** "Baptized into One Spirit, Christian History Institute website. Originally published in *Christian History* 1 (1982). https://christianhistoryinstitute.org/magazine/article/baptized-into-one-spirit.

**Opp, *Lord for Body*.** Opp, James. *The Lord for the Body: Religion, Medicine, and Protestant Faith Healing in Canada, 1880–1930*. McGill-Queen's University Press, 2005.

**Oppenheimer, "Azusa St."** Oppenheimer, Mike. "Azusa St. and Modern Pentecostalism: The 100-Year Celebration of What?" Let Us Reason Ministries. Accessed March 20, 2018. www.letusreason.org/Pent57.htm.

**Orr, *Prayer*.** Orr, J. Edwin. *The Fervent Prayer: The Worldwide Impact of the Great Awakening of 1858*. Moody, 1974.

**Osborn, *Justin*.** Osborn, Eric Francis. *Justin Martyr*. BHT 47. J. C. B. Mohr, 1973.

**Osborne, *Spiral*.** Osborne, Grant R. *The Hermeneutical Spiral: A Comprehensive Introduction to Biblical Interpretation*. InterVarsity, 1991.

**Oss, "Response to Saucy."** Oss, Douglas A. "A Pentecostal/Charismatic Response to Robert L. Saucy." In Grudem, *Gifts*, 164–71.

**Oss, "Statement."** Oss, Douglas A. "Concluding Statement (Pentecostal/Charismatic View)." In Grudem, *Gifts*, 311–17.

**Oss, "View."** Oss, Douglas A. "A Pentecostal/Charismatic View." In Grudem, *Gifts*, 239–83.

**O'Toole, "Parallels."** O'Toole, Robert F. "Parallels Between Jesus and His Disciples in Luke-Acts: A Further Study." *Biblische Zeitschrift*, n.s., 27, no. 2 (1983): 195–212.

**Oursler, *Power*.** Oursler, Will. *The Healing Power of Faith*. Hawthorn, 1957.

**Packer, *Acts*.** Packer, J. W. *Acts of the Apostles*. CBC. Cambridge University Press, 1966.

**Packer, *Keep in Step*.** Packer, J. I. *Keep in Step with the Spirit: Finding Fullness in Our Walk with God*. Revised and enlarged. Baker Books, 2005.

**Palma, "Glossolalia."** Palma, Anthony. "Glossolalia in the Light of the New Testament and Subsequent History." STB thesis, New York Theological Seminary, April 1960.

**Palma, *Spirit*.** Palma, Anthony D. *The Holy Spirit: A Pentecostal Perspective*. Logion, 2001.

**Parish, "Histories."** Parish, Helen. "'Lying Histories Fawning False Miracles': Magic, Miracles and Mediaeval History in Reformation Polemic." *Reformation and Renaissance Review* 4, no. 2 (2002): 230–40.

**Park, "Calvin."** Park, Gyeung Su. "John Calvin as an Advocate of Church Unity: A New Portrait of John Calvin." PhD diss., Claremont Graduate University, 2004.

**Park, "Dissection."** Park, Katharine. "That the Medieval Church Prohibited Human Dissection." In *Galileo Goes to Jail and Other Myths About Science and Religion*, edited by Ronald L. Numbers, 43–49. Harvard University Press, 2009.

**Parke, *Oracles*.** Parke, H. W. *The Oracles of Zeus: Dodona, Olympia, Ammon*. Blackwell, 1967.

**Parke, *Sibyls*.** Parke, H. W. *Sibyls and Sibylline Prophecy in Classical Antiquity*. Edited by B. C. McGing. Routledge, 1988.

**Parker, *Calvin*.** Parker, T. H. L. *John Calvin: A Biography*. Westminster John Knox, 2006.

**Parker, "Possession Trance."** Parker, Simon B. "Possession Trance and Prophecy in Pre-Exilic Israel." *Vetus Testamentum* 28 (July 1978): 271–85.

**Parmentier, "Zungenreden."** Parmentier, Martin. "Das Zungenreden bei den Kirchenvätern." *Bijdragen* 55, no. 4 (1994): 376–98.

**Pate, "Missions."** Pate, Larry D. "Pentecostal Missions from the Two-Thirds World." In Dempster, Klaus, and Petersen, *Called and Empowered*, 242–58.

**"Patriarch Broods."** "The Patriarch Broods over His Family's Future." *Christian History* 114 (2015): 39.

**Paul, "Prophets."** Paul, Shalom M. "Prophets and Prophecy (In the Bible)." In *Encyclopedia Judaica*, edited by Michael Berenbaum and Fred Skolnik, 13:1160–64. Macmillan, 2006.

**Peachey and Peachey, "Answer."** Peachey, Paul, and Shem Peachey, trans. "Answer of Some Who Are Called (Ana-)Baptists. Why They Do Not Attend the Churches." *Mennonite Quarterly Review* 45, no. 1 (1971): 10–11.

**Peckham, *Sounds*.** Peckham, Colin and Mary. *Sounds from Heaven: The Revival on the Isle of Lewis, 1949–1952*. Christian Focus, 2004.

**Pelley, "Response."** Pelley, Grace. "A Wesleyan-Arminian Response to Cessationism." MTh thesis, Wesley Seminary, 2026.

**Pelling, "Adaptation."** Pelling, Christopher B. R. "Plutarch's Adaptation of His Source-Material." *Journal of Hellenic Studies* 100 (1980): 127–40.

**Pennington, "Case."** Pennington, Tom. "A Case for Cessationism." Grace to You. October 17, 2013. Accessed September 25, 2024. www.gty.org/library/sermons-library/TM13-7/a-case-for-cessationism-tom-pennington.

**Pennington, *Cessationism*.** Pennington, Tom. *A Biblical Case for Cessationism: Why the Miraculous Gifts of the Spirit Have Ended*. G3, 2023.

**Penn-Lewis, "Revival."** Penn-Lewis, Jessie. "The Revival: Revival in Wales Progresses." *The Christian Patriot* (October 7, 1905): 6–7.

**Perkins, *Bosworth*.** Perkins, Eunice M. *Fred Francis Bosworth (The Joybringer). Second Edition and Continued Story of Joybringer Bosworth: His Life Story*. 2nd rev. ed. F. F. Bosworth, 1927.

**Petersen, "Latin American Pentecostalism."** Petersen, Douglas. "The Azusa Street Mission and Latin American Pentecostalism." *International Bulletin of Mission Research* 30, no. 2 (April 2006): 66–67.

**Petersen, *Might*.** Petersen, Douglas. *Not by Might nor by Power: A Pentecostal Theology of Social Concern in Latin America*. Preface by Jose Miguez Bonino. Regnum; Paternoster, 1996.

**Pettinato, *Archives*.** Pettinato, Giovanni. *The Archives of Ebla: An Empire Inscribed in the Clay*. Doubleday, 1981.

**Philip, *Life*.** Philip, Robert. *The Life and Times of the Reverend George Whitefield*. George Virtue, 1837. Available online at https://books.google.com/books?id=LEcFAAAAYAAJ&.

**Phillips, "Packer on Charismatics."** Phillips, Dan. "A Word About J. I. Packer on Charismatics." *Pyromaniacs* (blog). November 6, 2013. Accessed August 29, 2024. http://teampyro.blogspot.com/2013/11/a-word-about-j-i-packer-on-charismatics_6.html.

**Phiri and Maxwell, "Riches."** Phiri, Isaac, and Joe Maxwell. "Gospel Riches." *Christianity Today*, July 2007, 22–29.

**Pierson, *Review*.** Pierson, Arthur T., ed. *The Missionary Review*. Vol. 20. Funk & Wagnalls, 1907.

**Pilsworth, "Miracles."** Pilsworth, Clare. "Miracles, Missionaries, and Manuscripts in Eighth-Century Southern Germany." In Cooper and Gregory, *Signs*, 67–76.

**Piper, *Minutes*.** Piper, Don, with Cecil Murphey. *Ninety Minutes in Heaven: A True Story of Death and Life*. Revell, 2004.

**Piper, "Prophecy and Tongues."** Piper, John. "Are Prophecy and Tongues Alive Today?" Desiring God. January 17, 2013. https://www.desiringgod.org/articles/are-prophecy-and-tongues-alive-today.

**Piper, *Reading Supernaturally*.** Piper, John. *Reading the Bible Supernaturally: Seeing and Savoring the Glory of God in Scripture*. Crossway, 2017.

**Plantinga, "Reformed Epistemology."** Plantinga, Alvin. "On Reformed Epistemology." *Reformed Journal* 32 (January 1982): 13–17.

**Plummer, *Matthew*.** Plummer, Alfred. *An Exegetical Commentary on the Gospel According to S. Matthew*. Elliot Stock, 1910.

**Pocock, Van Rheenen, and McConnell, *Face*.** Pocock, Michael, Gailyn Van Rheenen, and Douglas McConnell. *The Changing Face of World Missions: Engaging Contemporary Issues and Trends*. Baker Academic, 2005.

**Poewe, *Charismatic Christianity*.** Poewe, Karla, ed. *Charismatic Christianity as a Global Culture*. SCR. University of South Carolina Press, 1994.

**Poewe, "Nature."** Poewe, Karla. "The Nature, Globality, and History of Charismatic Christianity." In Poewe, *Charismatic Christianity*, 1–29.

**Poewe, *Religions*.** Poewe, Karla. *New Religions and the Nazis*. Routledge, 2006.

**Poewe, "Rethinking."** Poewe, Karla. "Rethinking the Relationship of Anthropology to Science and Religion." In Poewe, *Charismatic Christianity*, 234–58.

**Pogoloff, *Logos*.** Pogoloff, Stephen M. *Logos and Sophia: The Rhetorical Situation of 1 Corinthians*. Society of Biblical Literature Dissertation Series 134. Scholars Press, 1992.

**Polkinghorne, *Science and Providence*.** Polkinghorne, John. *Science and Providence: God's Interaction with the World*. New Science Library, 1989.

**Pollock, *Moody*.** Pollock, John Charles. *Moody: A Biographical Portrait of the Pacesetter*. Macmillan, 1963.

**Poloma, *Assemblies.*** Poloma, Margaret M. *The Assemblies of God at the Crossroads: Charisma and Institutional Dilemmas*. University of Tennessee Press, 1989.

**Pope-Levison, *Pulpit.*** Pope-Levison, Priscilla. *Turn the Pulpit Loose: Two Centuries of American Women Evangelists*. Palgrave Macmillan, 2004.

**Porter, "Millenarianism."** Porter, J. M. "Luther and Political Millenarianism: The Case of the Peasants' War." *Journal of the History of Ideas* 42, no. 3 (July 1981): 389–406.

**Porterfield, *Healing.*** Porterfield, Amanda. *Healing in the History of Christianity*. Oxford University Press, 2005.

**"Position Paper."** Evangelical Presbyterian Church. "Position Paper: Holy Spirit." Accessed September 9, 2024. https://epc.org/wp-content/uploads/Files/1-Who-We-Are/B-About-The-EPC/Position-Papers/PositionPaper-HolySpirit.pdf.

**Pothen, "Missions."** Pothen, Abraham T. "Indigenous Cross-Cultural Missions in India and Their Contribution to Church Growth: With Special Emphasis on Pentecostal-Charismatic Missions." PhD diss., Fuller Theological Seminary, 1990.

**Poythress, "Analyses."** Poythress, Vern S. "Linguistic and Sociological Analyses of Modern Tongues-Speaking: Their Contributions and Limitations." *Westminster Theological Journal* 42, no. 2 (1980): 367–88.

**Poythress, "Nature of Glossolalia."** Poythress, Vern S. "The Nature of Corinthian Glossolalia: Possible Options." *Westminster Theological Journal* 40, no. 1 (1977): 130–35.

**Prather, *Miracles.*** Prather, Paul. *Modern-Day Miracles: How Ordinary People Experience Supernatural Acts of God*. Andrews and McMeel, 1996.

**Prema, "Paradigm."** Prema, Sr. "Acts 2:17–21: A Paradigm for a Collaborative Mission." *Jeevadhara* 34, no. 200 (2004): 122–36.

**Price, *First Corinthians.*** Price, Brad. *First Corinthians Bible Commentary*. Brad Price, 2010.

**Price, "*Signo*."** Price, Richard M. "*In Hoc Signo Vinces*: The Original Context of the Vision of Constantine." In Cooper and Gregory, *Signs*, 1–10.

**Prince, "EEG."** Prince, Raymond. "Can the EEG Be Used in the Study of Possession States?" In *Trance and Possession States*. Proceedings of the Second Annual Conference, R. M. Bucke Memorial Society, March 4–6, 1966, edited by Raymond Prince, 121–37. R. M. Bucke Memorial Society, 1968.

**"Prince of Darkness."** "The Prince of Darkness Grim: Luther's Battle Against the Devil." Christian Library. Accessed August 29, 2024. https://www.christianstudylibrary.org/article/prince-darkness-grim-luther%E2%80%99s-battle-against-devil.

**Pritz, *Nazarene Christianity.*** Pritz, Ray A. *Nazarene Jewish Christianity: From the End of the New Testament Period Until Its Disappearance in the Fourth Century*. Studia Post-Biblica. Brill, 1988.

**Probst, *Demonizing.*** Probst, Christopher J. *Demonizing the Jews: Luther and the Protestant Church in Nazi Germany*. Indiana University Press, 2012.

**Pullinger, *Dragon*.** Pullinger, Jackie, with Andrew Quicke. *Chasing the Dragon*. Hodder & Stoughton, 1980.

**Pytches, *Come*.** Pytches, David. *Come Holy Spirit: Learning How to Minister in Power*. Hodder & Stoughton, 1985.

**Rack, "Healing."** Rack, Henry D. "Doctors, Demons, and Early Methodist Healing." In Sheils, *Papers*, 137–52.

**Rackham, *Acts*.** Rackham, Richard Belward. *The Acts of the Apostles*. 14th ed. Methuen, 1951. Reprint, Baker, 1964.

**Ragaz, *Kampf*.** Ragaz, Leonhard. *Der Kampf um das Reich Gottes in Blumhardt, Vater und Sohn—und weiter!* Rotapfel Verlag, 1922.

**Ramm, *Interpretation*.** Ramm, Bernard. *Protestant Biblical Interpretation: A Textbook of Hermeneutics*. 3rd ed. Baker, 1970.

**Rankin, "Spirit."** Rankin, Lynn Boyd. "The Ecumenical Spirit of John Calvin." STD diss., Temple University School of Theology, 1944.

**Rapp, "Saints."** Rapp, Claudia. "Saints and Holy Men." In *The Cambridge History of Christianity*. Vol. 2, *Constantine to c. 600*, edited by Augustine Casiday and Frederick W. Norris, 548–66. 9 vols. Cambridge University Press, 2007.

**"Report of Assembly."** "Report of the One Hundred and Eighty Second General Assembly of the United Presbyterian Church, U.S.A. Part I: Journal." Office of the General Assembly, Presbyterian Church, USA, 1970.

**"Report of Interim Committee."** "Appendix N: Report of the AD Interim Committee to Study the Question of Spiritual Gifts." Accessed September 9, 2024. https://pcahistory.org/pca/digest/studies/1974_Pastoral_Letter_Holy_Spirit.pdf.

**Reyes, "Framework."** Reyes, Erlinda T. "A Theological Framework on Non-Healing in the Pentecostal Perspective." ThM thesis, Asia Pacific Theological Seminary, 2007.

**Richardson, *Apologetics*.** Richardson, Alan. *Christian Apologetics*. SCM, 1947.

**Richardson, *Miracle Stories*.** Richardson, Alan. *The Miracle Stories of the Gospels*. SCM, 1941.

**Richardson, *Theology*.** Richardson, Alan. *An Introduction to the Theology of the New Testament*. Harper & Brothers, 1958.

**Ridley, *John Knox*.** Ridley, Jasper. *John Knox*. Oxford University Press, 1968.

**Riggs, *Witness*.** Riggs, Marcia Y., ed. *Can I Get a Witness? Prophetic Religious Voices of African American Women: An Anthology*. With Barbara Holmes. Orbis Books, 1997.

**"Right Remembering."** "Right Remembering in Anabaptist-Lutheran Relations: Report of the Evangelical Lutheran Church in America—Mennonite Church USA Liaison Committee." Office of the Secretary and the Department for Ecumenical Affairs, Evangelical Lutheran Church in America, 2004.

**Riss, *Survey*.** Riss, Richard. *A Survey of 20th Century Revival Movements in North America*. Hendrickson, 1988.

**Riss, "Tongues."** Riss, Richard. "Tongues and Other Miraculous Gifts in the Second Through Nineteenth Centuries." *Basileia* (1985). Most readily available now at *Pneuma Review* online. Accessed September 2, 2024. http://pneumareview.com/tongues-and-other-miraculous-gifts-in-the-second-through-nineteenth-centuries/.

**Robeck, "All-Sufficiency."** Robeck, Cecil M., Jr. "The Gift of Prophecy and the All-Sufficiency of Scripture." In Graves, *Strangers*, 453–58.

**Robeck, "Charismata."** Robeck, Cecil M., Jr. "Origen's Treatment of the Charismata in 1 Corinthians 12:8–10." In *Charismatic Experiences in History*, edited by Cecil M. Robeck Jr., 111–25. Hendrickson, 1985.

**Robeck, "Charismatic Movements."** Robeck, Cecil M., Jr. "Charismatic Movements." In *Global Dictionary of Theology: A Resource for the Worldwide Church*, edited by William A. Dyrness and Veli-Matti Kärkkäinen, with Juan Francisco Martinez and Simon Chan, 145–54. InterVarsity, 2008.

**Robeck, *Mission*.** Robeck, Cecil M., Jr. *The Azusa Street Mission and Revival: The Birth of the Global Pentecostal Movement*. Thomas Nelson, 2006.

**Robeck, *Prophecy*.** Robeck, Cecil M., Jr. *Prophecy in Carthage: Perpetua, Tertullian, and Cyprian*. Pilgrim Press, 1992.

**Robeck, "Prophecy."** Robeck, Cecil M., Jr. "Prophecy, Gift of." In *Dictionary of Pentecostal and Charismatic Movements*, edited by Stanley M. Burgess and Gary B. McGee, 728–40. Zondervan, 1988.

**Robeck, "Seymour."** Robeck, Cecil M., Jr. "William J. Seymour and 'The Bible Evidence.'" In McGee, *Initial Evidence*, 72–95.

**Roberts, "Sign."** Roberts, P. "A Sign—Christian or Pagan?" *Expository Times* 90, no. 7 (1979): 199–203.

**Robertson, "Epidauros to Lourdes."** Robertson, David. "From Epidauros to Lourdes: A History of Healing by Faith." In Frazier, *Faith Healing*, 179–89.

**Robertson and Plummer, *Corinthians*.** Robertson, Archibald, and Alfred Plummer. *A Critical and Exegetical Commentary on the First Epistle of St Paul to the Corinthians*. ICC. 2nd ed. T&T Clark, 1914.

**Robinson, "Calvin and Jews."** Robinson, Jack Hughes. "John Calvin and the Jews." PhD diss., Saint Louis University, 1989.

**Robinson, *Formative Years*.** Robinson, James. *Divine Healing: The Formative Years, 1830–1890*. Pickwick, 2011.

**Robinson, *Years of Expansion*.** Robinson, James. *Divine Healing: The Years of Expansion, 1906–1930*. Pickwick, 2014.

**Roe, *Dream Big*.** Roe, E., ed. *Dream Big: The Henrietta Mears Story*. Regal, 1990.

**Rogers, "Did You Know?"** Rogers, Chris. "Did You Know? Revivals of the Nineteenth and Twentieth Centuries Had Global Reach and Impact." *Christian History* 153 (2024): i–1.

**Rogers, "Tongues."** Rogers, Cleon L. "The Gift of Tongues in the Post Apostolic Church (A.D. 100–400)." *Bibliotheca Sacra* 122, no. 486 (1965): 134–43.

**Rogge, "Relationship."** Rogge, Louis Philip. "The Relationship Between the Sacrament of Anointing the Sick and the Charism of Healing Within the Catholic Charismatic Renewal." PhD diss., Union Theological Seminary, 1984.

**Romez, "Case Report."** Romez, Clarissa, et al. "Case Report of Instantaneous Resolution of Juvenile Macular Degeneration Blindness After Proximal Intercessory Prayer." *Explore: The Journal of Science and Healing* 17, no. 1 (2021): 79–83. https://doi.org/10.1016/j.explore.2020.02.011.

**Romez, Zaritzky, and Brown, "Report."** Romez, Clarissa, David Zaritzky, and Joshua W. Brown. "Case Report of Gastroparesis Healing: 16 Years of a Chronic Syndrome Resolved After Proximal Intercessory Prayer." *Complementary Therapies in Medicine* 43 (2019): 289–94.

**Rose, *Faith Healing*.** Rose, Louis. *Faith Healing*. Edited by Bryan Morgan. Rev. ed. Penguin, 1971.

**Rosner, "Progress."** Rosner, Brian S. "The Progress of the Word." In *Witness to the Gospel: The Theology of Acts*, edited by I. Howard Marshall and David Peterson, 215–34. Eerdmans, 1998.

**Ross, "Prophecy."** Ross, James F. "Prophecy in Hamath, Israel, and Mari." *Harvard Theological Review* 63 (January 1970): 1–28.

**Rowan, "Luther, Bucer."** Rowan, Steven. "Luther, Bucer and Eck on the Jews." *Sixteenth Century Journal* 16, no. 1 (Spring 1985): 79–90.

**Rowe, "Albright."** Rowe, Kenneth E. "Jacob Albright and the Evangelical Association." In *Methodist and Pietist: Retrieving the Evangelical United Brethren Tradition*, edited by J. Steven O'Malley and Jason E. Vickers, 37–53. Kingswood Books, 2011.

**Roynesdal, "Luther and Jews."** Roynesdal, Olaf. "Martin Luther and the Jews." PhD diss., Marquette University, 1987.

**Roys, "Lawson."** Roys, Julie. "Steve Lawson Had '5-Year Relationship' with Woman in Her 20s, GCC Pastor Says." *Roys Report*. September 25, 2024. Accessed October 1, 2024. https://roysreport.com/steve-lawson-had-5-year-relationship-with-woman-in-her-20s-gcc-pastor-says/.

**Ruble, "Tongues."** Ruble, R. L. "A Scriptural Evaluation of Tongues in Contemporary Theology." ThD diss., Dallas Theological Seminary, 1964.

**Rudnick, "Hate Speech."** Rudnick, Ursula. "Early Modern Hate Speech—Martin Luther's Anti-Semitism: Responses and Reactions." *CrossCurrents* 67, no. 2 (June 2017): 421–30.

**Rüpke, "Knowledge."** Rüpke, Jörg. "Knowledge of Religion in Valerius Maximus' *Exempla*: Roman Historiography and Tiberian Memory Culture." In *Memory in Ancient Rome and Early Christianity*, edited by Karl Galinsky, 89–111. Oxford University Press, 2016.

**Rupp and Drewery, *Martin Luther*.** Rupp, E. G., and Benjamin Drewery. *Martin Luther, Documents of Modern History*. Edward Arnold, 1970.

**Ruth, *Methodist Life*.** Ruth, Lester. *Early Methodist Life and Spirituality: A Reader*. Kingswood Books, 2005.

**Rutherford, *Survey*.** Rutherford, Samuel. *A Survey of the Spirituall Antichrist. Opening the Secrets of Familisme and Antinomianisme in the Antichristian Doctrine of John Saltmarsh and Will. Del et al.* London, 1648.

**Ruthven, "Back to Future."** Ruthven, Jon Mark. "Back to the Future for Pentecostal/Charismatic Evangelicals in North America and World Wide: Radicalising Evangelical Theology and Practice." Hope, Faith, Prayer. Accessed July 5, 2018. https://www.hopefaithprayer.com/books/Back-Future-for-Pentecostal-Charismatic-Evangelicals-Ruthven.pdf.

**Ruthven, *Cessation*.** Ruthven, Jon Mark. *On the Cessation of the Charismata: The Protestant Polemic on Post-Biblical Miracles*. Rev. ed. Word & Spirit Monograph 1. Word & Spirit, 2011.

**Ruthven, "Cessation."** Ruthven, Jon. "On the Cessation of the Charismata." Hope, Faith, Prayer. Accessed October 9, 2024. https://www.hopefaithprayer.com/word-of-faith/on-the-cessation-of-the-charismata/.

**Ruthven, "Charismata 2."** Ruthven, Jon. "The Charismata and the Messianic Age: Part 2 of 3." In Graves, *Kingdom Case*, 153–76.

**Ruthven, "Charismata 3."** Ruthven, Jon. "The Charismata and the Messianic Age: Part 3 of 3." In Graves, *Kingdom Case*, 177–96.

**Ruthven, "Gifts."** Ruthven, Jon. "The 'Foundational Gifts' of Ephesians 2:20." In Graves, *Strangers*, 469–85.

**Ruthven, "Place."** Ruthven, Jon. "A Place for Prophecy." In Graves, *Strangers*, 437–44.

**Ruthven, "Response."** Ruthven, Jon. "A Brief Biblical Response to *Strange Fire*." In Graves, *Strangers*, 11–14.

**Rutland, "Cessation Theology."** Rutland, Mark. "John MacArthur, Cessation Theology, and Trainspotting for Cave Dwellers." In Graves, *Strangers*, 3–14.

**Rutland, "MacArthur."** Rutland, Mark. "John MacArthur, Cessation Theology, and Trainspotting for Cave Dwellers." *Charisma*, October 27, 2013. https://mycharisma.com/spiritled-living/john-macarthur-cessation-theology-and-trainspotting-for-cave-dwellers/.

**Ryan, "Signs and Wonders."** Ryan, Maxwell. "Signs and Wonders." *The Voice of the Army: Salvationist* (March 24, 2011): 20. http://www.salvationist.ca/2011/03/signs-and-wonders/.

**Safrai, "Education."** Safrai, Shemuel. "Education and the Study of the Torah." In *The Jewish People in the First Century*, 2:945–70. Van Gorcum, Assen, 1976.

**Sales, *Works*.** Saint Francis de Sales. *The Catholic Controversy* in H. B. Canon Mackey, OSB, *The Library of St. Francis De Sales: Works of This Doctor of the Church Translated into English*. Bk. 3. 3rd ed. Burns & Oates, Limited, 1909.

**Samarin, *Tongues*.** Samarin, William J. *Tongues of Men and Angels*. Macmillan, 1972.

**Sanders, *Paul: Life*.** Sanders, E. P. *Paul: The Apostle's Life, Letters, and Thought*. Fortress, 2015.

**Sanneh, *Disciples*.** Sanneh, Lamin. *Disciples of All Nations: Pillars of World Christianity*. Oxford University Press, 2008.

**Sanusi, *Gloria*.** Sanusi, Abidemi. *Gloria! The Archbishop's Wife*. HippoBooks, 2014.

**Satyavrata, "Globalization."** Satyavrata, Ivan. "The Globalization of Pentecostal Missions in the Twenty-First Century." J. Philip Hogan World Missions Series Monograph 4. Assemblies of God Theological Seminary, 2009.

**Satyavrata, *Pentecostals and Poor*.** Satyavrata, Ivan. *Pentecostals and the Poor: Reflections from the India Context*. APTS, 2017.

**Saucy, *Case*.** Saucy, Robert L. *The Case for Progressive Dispensationalism: The Interface Between Dispensational and Non-Dispensational Theology*. Zondervan, 1993.

**Saucy, "Response to Gaffin."** Saucy, Robert L. "An Open but Cautious Response to Richard B. Gaffin, Jr." In Grudem, *Gifts*, 65–71.

**Saucy, "Response to Storms."** Saucy, Robert L. "An Open but Cautious Response to C. Samuel Storms." In Grudem, *Gifts*, 225–34.

**Saucy, "View."** Saucy, Robert L. "An Open but Cautious View." In Grudem, *Gifts*, 97–148.

**Schatzmann, *Charismata*.** Schatzmann, Siegfried. *A Pauline Theology of Charismata*. Hendrickson, 1987.

**Scheck, "Introduction."** Scheck, Thomas P. "Introduction," in *Commentary on the Epistle to the Romans, Books 1–5*, by Origen, translated by Thomas P. Scheck, 1–48. The Fathers of the Church: A New Translation, 103. Catholic University of America Press, 2001.

**"Schleitheim Confession."** "The Schleitheim Confession." *Baptist Studies Online*. http://baptiststudiesonline.com/wp-content/uploads/2007/02/the-schleitheim-confession-2.pdf.

**Schmid, "Geistwirkungen."** Schmid, H. H. "Ekstatische und charismatische Geistwirkungen im Alten Testament." In *Erfahrung und Theologie des Heiligen Geistes*, edited by Claus Heitmann and Heribert Mühlen, 83–99. Agentur des Rauhen Hauses, 1974.

**Schmidt, *Fairs*.** Schmidt, Leigh Eric. *Holy Fairs: Scotland and the Making of American Revivalism*. 2nd ed. Eerdmans, 2001.

**Schmitt, *Floods*.** Schmitt, Charles P. *Floods upon the Dry Ground*. Destiny Image, 1998.

**Schnabel, *Acts*.** Schnabel, Eckhard J. *Acts*. ZECNT. Zondervan, 2012.

**Schnabel, *Jesus in Jerusalem*.** Schnabel, Eckhard J. *Jesus in Jerusalem in the Last Days*. Eerdmans, 2018.

**Schnabel, *Mark*.** Schnabel, Eckhard. *Mark*. Tyndale NT Commentaries. InterVarsity, 2017.

**Schoville, "Dance."** Schoville, Keith N. "Dance." In *Dictionary of Daily Life in Biblical and Post-Biblical Antiquity*, edited by Edwin M. Yamauchi and Marvin R. Wilson, 1:374–88. Hendrickson, 2014.

**Schreiner, *Apostle of Glory*.** Schreiner, Thomas R. *Paul, Apostle of God's Glory in Christ: A Pauline Theology*. 2nd rev. ed. IVP Academic, 2020.

**Schreiner, "Cessationist."** Schreiner, Thomas R. "Why I Am a Cessationist." The Gospel Coalition, January 22, 2014. www.thegospelcoalition.org/article/why-i-am-a-cessationist/.

**Schreiner, *Galatians*.** Schreiner, Thomas R. *Galatians*. Zondervan Exegetical Commentary on the New Testament. Zondervan, 2010.

**Schreiner, *Romans*.** Schreiner, Thomas R. *Romans*. Baker Exegetical Commentary on the New Testament. Baker Academic, 1998.

**Schreiner, *Spiritual Gifts*.** Schreiner, Thomas R. *Spiritual Gifts: What They Are & Why They Matter*. B&H, 2018.

**Schwartz, *French Prophets*.** Schwartz, Hillel. *The French Prophets: The History of a Millenarian Group in Eighteenth-Century England*. University of California Press, 1980.

**"Science or Miracle?"** "Science or Miracle? Holiday Season Survey Reveals Physicians' Views of Faith, Prayer and Miracles." WorldHealth.net. Accessed on March 25, 2025. https://worldhealth.net/news/science_or_miracle_holiday_season_survey/.

**Scott, *Blundered*.** Scott, Bob. *Some Said They Blundered: Breaking My Decades of Silence on Mike Bickle, the Kansas City Prophets and International House of Prayer-Kansas City*. Joseph Company Global, 2024.

**Sears, "View."** Sears, Robert T. "A Catholic View of Exorcism and Deliverance." In *Essays on Spiritual Bondage and Deliverance*, edited by Willard M. Swartley, 100–114. Occasional Papers 11. Institute of Mennonite Studies, 1988.

**Sessions, "War."** Sessions, Kyle C. "The War over Luther and the Peasants: Old Campaigns and New Strategies." *Sixteenth Century Journal* 3, no. 2 (October 1972): 25–44.

**Sharp, "Charismata."** Sharp, Omer Jaye. "Did Charismata Cease with the Apostles' Deaths?" In Graves, *Strangers*, 385–89.

**Shauf, *Divine*.** Shauf, Scott. *The Divine in Acts and in Ancient Historiography*. Fortress, 2015.

**Shaull, "Reconstruction."** Shaull, Richard. "The Reconstruction of Life in the Power of the Spirit." In Richard Shaull and Waldo César, *Pentecostalism and the Future of the Christian Churches: Promises, Limitations, Challenges*. Eerdmans, 2000.

**Shaw, *Awakening*.** Shaw, Mark. *Global Awakening: How 20th-Century Revivals Triggered a Christian Revolution*. IVP Academic, 2010.

**Shaw, *Incidents*.** Shaw, Solomon B. *Touching Incidents and Remarkable Answers to Prayer*. Lansing, Michigan, 1893. Reprint, General-Books.net, 2009.

**Shaw, *Miracles*.** Shaw, Jane. *Miracles in Enlightenment England*. Yale University Press, 2006.

**Sheikh, *Call Him Father*.** Sheikh, Bilquis, with Richard H. Schneider. *I Dared to Call Him Father: The Miraculous Story of a Muslim Woman's Encounter with God*. Chosen, 2023.

**Sheils, *Papers*.** Sheils, W. J., ed. *The Church and Healing: Papers Read at the Twentieth Summer Meeting and the Twenty-First Winter Meeting of the Ecclesiastical History Society*. Studies in Christian History 19. Basil Blackwell, 1982.

**Shellnut, "Founder."** Shellnut, Kate. "G3 Ministries: Founder Used Fake Profiles to Slam Fellow Christians." *Christianity Today*, May 17, 2025. Accessed May 17, 2025. https://www.christianitytoday.com/2025/05/josh-buice-g3-conference-fake-social-media-accounts/.

**Shellnut, "Hundreds."** Shellnut, Kate. "Hundreds Accuse Independent Baptist Pastors of Abuse." *Christianity Today*, December 12, 2018. Accessed December 17, 2024. https://www.christianitytoday.com/2018/12/independent-fundamentalist-baptist-church-abuse-scandal/.

**Sherrill, *Tongues*.** Sherrill, John L. *They Speak with Other Tongues*. Fleming H. Revell, 1965.

**Shiell, *Reading Acts*.** Shiell, William David. *Reading Acts: The Lector and the Early Christian Audience*. BIS 70. Brill Academic, 2004.

**Shogren, "Gift of Tongues."** Shogren, Gary S. "The Gift of Tongues in the Post-Apostolic Church: A Rejoinder to Cleon Rogers." In Graves, *Strangers*, 399–410.

**Shogren, "Perfect Would Come."** Shogren, Gary. "How Did They Suppose 'The Perfect' Would Come? 1 Corinthians 13.8–12 in Patristic Exegesis." *Journal of Pentecostal Theology* 15 (October 1999): 99–121.

**Shogren, "Prophecy."** Shogren, Gary. "Christian Prophecy and Canon in the Second Century: A Response to B. B. Warfield." In Graves, *Strangers*, 411–36.

**Shogren, "Prophecy and Canon."** Shogren, Gary. "Christian Prophecy and Canon in the Second Century: A Response to B. B. Warfield." *Journal of the Evangelical Theological Society* 40 (December 1997): 609–26.

**Sigg, *Revival*.** Sigg, Michèle Miller. *Birthing Revival: Women and Mission in Nineteenth-Century France*. Baylor University Press, 2022.

**Sithole, "Supernaturally Learning."** Sithole, Surprise. "Surprise Sithole: Supernaturally Learning Languages, Witchcraft, and Fasting." Interview by Will Hart. *Green Room* podcast on Iris Global YouTube site, posted September 26, 2024. Accessed October 24, 2024. https://www.youtube.com/watch?v=x2ikchgd3nk.

**Sithole, *Voice*.** Sithole, Surprise, with David Wimbish. *Voice in the Night. The True Story of a Man and the Miracles That Are Changing Africa*. Chosen, 2012.

**Smart, *Experience*.** Smart, Ninian. *The Religious Experience of Mankind*. Charles Scribner's Sons, 1969.

**Smith, *Impossible*.** Smith, Joyce, with Ginger Kolbaba. *The Impossible: The Miraculous Story of a Mother's Faith and Her Child's Resurrection*. FaithWords, 2017.

**Smith, "Resistance Discourse."** Smith, James K. A. "Tongues as 'Resistance Discourse': A Philosophical Perspective." In Cartledge, *Perspectives*, 81–110.

**Smith, *Revivalism*.** Smith, Timothy L. *Revivalism and Social Reform: American Protestantism on the Eve of the Civil War*. Harper & Row, 1965.

**Smith, *Soul Searching*.** Smith, Christian. *Soul Searching: The Religious and Spiritual Lives of American Teenagers*. With Melinda Lundquist Denton. Oxford University Press, 2005.

**Smith, *Thinking*.** Smith, James K. A. *Thinking in Tongues: Outline of a Pentecostal Philosophy*. Eerdmans, 2010.

**Snoeberger, "Tongues."** Snoeberger, Mark A. "Tongues—Are They for Today?" *Detroit Baptist Seminary Journal* 14 (2009): 3–21.

**Snyder, *Signs*.** Snyder, Howard A. *Signs of the Spirit: How God Reshapes the Church*. Academie Books, 1989.

**Soergel, "Legends."** Soergel, Philip M. "From Legends to Lies: Protestant Attacks on Catholic Miracles in Late Reformation Germany." *Fides et Historia* 21, no. 2 (1989): 21–29.

**Soergel, *Miracles*.** Soergel, Philip M. *Miracles and the Protestant Imagination: The Evangelical Wonder Book in Reformation Germany*. Oxford Studies in Historical Theology. Oxford University Press, 2012.

**Sourvinou-Inwood, "Delphic Oracle."** Sourvinou-Inwood, Christiane. "Delphic Oracle." In *Oxford Classical Dictionary*, edited by S. Hornblower and A. Spawforth, 445–46. 3rd ed. Oxford University Press, 1996.

**Soyer, *Blood Libel*.** Soyer, François. *The Blood Libel in Medieval Antisemitism*. Arc Humanities Press, 2025.

**Spalding, "Protestantism."** Spalding, James C. "Protestantism: The Reformation in England and Scotland." Encyclopaedia Brittanica Online. Accessed December 11, 2018. https://www.britannica.com/topic/Protestantism/The-expansion-of-the-Reformation-in-Europe.

**"Spirit and Power."** "Spirit and Power: A 10–Country Survey of Pentecostals." Pew Forum Survey, October 2006. Accessed March 25, 2025. https://www.pewresearch.org/religion/2006/10/05/spirit-and-power/.

**"Spiritual Gifts."** "Spiritual Gifts." *Desiring God*. Accessed August 29, 2024. https://www.desiringgod.org/topics/spiritual-gifts.

**"Spiritualism in Church."** "Spiritualism in the Church of the United Brethren." *The Spiritual Magazine* 1, no. 1 (January 1860): 5–10.

**Spraggett, *Kuhlman*.** Spraggett, Allen. *Kathryn Kuhlman: The Woman Who Believes in Miracles*. World, 1970.

**Sproul, "Warfield."** Sproul, R. C. "B. B. Warfield: Defender of the Faith." Ligonier Ministries, April 1, 2005. Accessed October 9, 2024. www.ligonier.org/learn/articles/bb-warfield-defender-faith.

**Spurgeon, *Autobiography*.** Spurgeon, Charles. *The Autobiography of Charles H. Spurgeon, Compiled from His Diary, Letters, and Records, by His Wife and His Private Secretary*. Vol. 2, *1854–1860*. Curts & Jennings, 1899. Vol. 3, *1856–1878*. American Baptist Publication Society, n.d.

**Spurgeon, *Lectures*.** Spurgeon, Charles H. *Lectures to My Students*. Vol. 3. AGES Software, 1996. Originally published in 1875. Available online at https://www.mat.univie.ac.at/~neum/sciandf/spurgeon/spurgeon3.pdf.

**Spurgeon, "Receiving."** Spurgeon, Charles H. "Receiving the Holy Spirit." Sermon dated July 13, 1884. Christian Classics Ethereal Library. http://www.ccel.org/ccel/spurgeon/sermons30.xxxiv.html

**Spurgeon, *Sermons*.** Spurgeon, Charles H. *Sermons of the Rev. C. H. Spurgeon, of London*. 4th ser. Sheldon, Blakeman, 1858.

**Spurgeon, *Spurgeon's Sermons*.** Spurgeon, Charles. *Spurgeon's Sermons*. 1857. Reprint, Zondervan, n.d.

**Squires, *Plan*.** Squires, John T. *The Plan of God in Luke-Acts*. Society for New Testament Studies Monograph Series 76. Cambridge University Press, 1993.

**Squires, "Plan."** Squires, John T. "The Plan of God." In *Witness to the Gospel: The Theology of Acts*, edited by I. Howard Marshall and David Peterson, 19–39. Eerdmans, 1998.

**St. Stephen's Society, "About Us."** St. Stephen's Society. "About Us." Accessed August 23, 2024. https://www.ststephenssociety.com/about-us.

**Stafford, *Miracles*.** Stafford, Tim. *Miracles: A Journalist Looks at Modern Day Experiences of God's Power*. Bethany House, 2012.

**Stafford, "Miracles."** Stafford, Tim. "Miracles in Mozambique: How Mama Heidi Reaches the Abandoned." *Christianity Today*, May 2012. Accessed February 6, 2026. https://www.christianitytoday.com/2012/05/miracles-in-mozambique/.

**Stamps, "Children."** Stamps, D. L. "Children in Late Antiquity." In *Dictionary of New Testament Background*, edited by Craig A. Evans and Stanley E. Porter, 197–201. InterVarsity, 2000.

**Starling, "Analogy of Faith."** Starling, David. "The Analogy of Faith in the Theology of Luther and Calvin." *Reformed Theological Review* 72, no. 1 (April 2013): 5–19.

**Starner, "Co-Laborers."** Starner, Rob. "Luke and Paul: Co-Laborers . . . and Collaborators?" In Alexander, May, and Reid, *Trajectories*, 194–240.

**Stearns and Stearns, *Vision*.** Stearns, Bill, and Amy Stearns. *2020 Vision*. Bethany House, 2005.

**Stein, *Mark*.** Stein, Robert H. *Mark*. Baker Exegetical Commentary on the New Testament. Baker Academic, 2008.

**Stevens, *History*.** Stevens, Abel. *The History of the Religious Movement of the Eighteenth Century Called Methodism*. 3 vols. New York, 1858.

**Stevens, "Idea of Mission."** Stevens, Carl David. "Calvin's Corporate Idea of Mission." PhD diss., Westminster Theological Seminary, 1992.

**Stibbe, *Prophetic Evangelism*.** Stibbe, Mark W. G. *Prophetic Evangelism: When God Speaks to Those Who Don't Know Him*. Authentic Media, 2004.

**Stonehouse, *Areopagus*.** Stonehouse, N. B. *Paul Before the Areopagus and Other New Testament Studies*. Eerdmans, 1957.

**Stormont, *Wigglesworth*.** Stormont, George. *Wigglesworth: A Man Who Walked with God*. Harrison House, 1989.

**Storms, "Cessationist Prophesies."** Storms, Sam. "When a Cessationist Prophesies, or, What Are We to Make of Charles Spurgeon?" *Sam Storms: Enjoying God* (blog), October 25, 2013. https://www.samstorms.org/enjoying-god-blog/post/when-a-cessationist-prophesies--or--what-are-we-to-make-of-charles-spurgeon.

**Storms, *Convergence*.** Storms, Sam. *Convergence: Spiritual Journeys of a Charismatic Calvinist*. Enjoying God Ministries, 2005.

**Storms, "Ephesians 2:20."** Storms, Sam. "Ephesians 2:20—the Cessationist's 'Go-To' Text." In Graves, *Strangers*, 69–72.

**Storms, "Gifts."** Storms, Sam. "Revelatory Gifts of the Spirit and the Sufficiency of Scripture: Are They Compatible?" In *Scripture and the People of God: Essays in Honor of Wayne Grudem*, edited by John DelHousaye, John J. Hughes, and Jeff T. Purswell, 79–97. Crossway, 2018.

**Storms, *Guide*.** Storms, Sam. *The Beginner's Guide to Spiritual Gifts*. Regal, 2002.

**Storms, *Language*.** Storms, Sam. *The Language of Heaven: Crucial Questions About Speaking in Tongues*. Charisma House, 2019.

**Storms, "Response to Gaffin."** Storms, C. Samuel. "A Third Wave Response to Richard B. Gaffin, Jr." In Grudem, *Gifts*, 72–85.

**Storms, "Response to Saucy."** Storms, C. Samuel. "A Third Wave Response to Robert L. Saucy." In Grudem, *Gifts*, 156–63.

**Storms, "Revelatory Words."** Storms, Sam. "Appendix B: Why NT Prophecy Does NOT Result in 'Scripture-Quality' Revelatory Words." In Brown, *Authentic Fire*, 377–92.

**Storms, *Rise and Fall*.** Storms, Sam. *The Rise and Fall of the Kansas City Prophets*. Cascade Books, 2026.

**Storms, "Statement."** Storms, C. Samuel. "Concluding Statement (Third Wave View)." In Grudem, *Gifts*, 318–26.

**Storms, "View."** Storms, C. Samuel. "A Third Wave View." In Grudem, *Gifts*, 175–223.

**Stout, *Dramatist*.** Stout, Harry S. *The Divine Dramatist: George Whitefield and the Rise of Modern Evangelicalism*. Eerdmans, 1991.

**Strachan, *Theology of Irving*.** Strachan, Gordon. *The Pentecostal Theology of Edward Irving*. Darton, Longman & Todd; Hendrickson, 1973.

**Strack and Billerbeck, *Commentary*.** Strack, Hermann L., and Paul Billerbeck. *A Commentary on the New Testament from the Talmud and Midrash*. Vol. 1. Translated by Jacob N. Cerone. Lexham, 2022.

**Strobel, *Case for Miracles*.** Strobel, Lee. *The Case for Miracles: A Journalist Investigates Evidence for the Supernatural*. Zondervan, 2018.

**Strobel, *Supernatural*.** Strobel, Lee, *Seeing the Supernatural: Investigating Angels, Demons, Mystical Dreams, Near-Death Encounters, and Other Mysteries of the Unseen World*. Zondervan, 2025.

**Stronstad, "Baptized."** Stronstad, Roger. "On Being Baptized in the Holy Spirit: A Lukan Emphasis." In Alexander, May, and Reid, *Trajectories*, 160–93.

**Stronstad, *Charismatic Theology*.** Stronstad, Roger. *The Charismatic Theology of St. Luke*. Hendrickson, 1984.

**Sullivan, "Speaking in Tongues."** Sullivan, Francis A. "Speaking in Tongues." *Lumen Vitae* 31 (1976): 145–70.

**Sundkler, *Zulu Zion*.** Sundkler, Bengt. *Zulu Zion and Some Swazi Prophets*. Oxford University Press, 1976.

**Sunshine, "Missions."** Sunshine, Glenn S. "Protestant Missions in the Sixteenth Century." In *The Great Commission: Evangelicals and the History of World Missions*, edited by Martin I. Klauber and Scott M. Manetsch, 12–22. B&H, 2008.

**Sweeney, "John Knox."** Sweeney, Jacob. "John Knox Among the Prophets: Restoring the Prophetic Roots of Presbyterianism." DMin paper, Fuller Theological Seminary, 2018. Accessed September 1, 2024. https://www.academia.edu/37170124/John_Knox_Presbyterian_Prophet_docx.

**Sweeney, *Story*.** Sweeney, Douglas A. *The American Evangelical Story: A History of the Movement*. Baker Academic, 2005.

**Sweet, "Sign."** Sweet, J. P. M. "A Sign for Unbelievers: Paul's Attitude to Glossolalia." *New Testament Studies* 13, no. 3 (April 1967): 240–57.

**Synan, *Century*.** Synan, Vinson, ed. *The Century of the Holy Spirit: One Hundred Years of Pentecostal and Charismatic Renewal, 1901–2001*. Thomas Nelson, 2001.

**Synan, "Charismatics."** Synan, Vinson. "The 'Charismatics': Renewal in Major Protestant Denominations." In Synan, *Century*, 177–208.

**Synan, *Grow*.** Synan, Vinson. *The Spirit Said "Grow": The Astounding Worldwide Expansion of Pentecostal and Charismatic Churches*. Innovations in Missions. MARC; World Vision, 1992.

**Synan, *Movement*.** Synan, Vinson. *The Holiness-Pentecostal Movement in the United States*. Eerdmans, 1971.

**Synan, "Streams."** Synan, Vinson. "Streams of Renewal at the End of the Century." In Synan, *Century*, 349–80.

**Synan, *Tradition*.** Synan, Vinson. *The Holiness-Pentecostal Tradition: Charismatic Movements in the Twentieth Century*. Eerdmans, 1997.

**Synan, *Voices*.** Synan, Vinson. *Voices of Pentecost: Testimonies of Lives Touched by the Holy Spirit*. Servant, 2003.

**Talbert, *Patterns*.** Talbert, Charles H. *Literary Patterns, Theological Themes, and the Genre of Luke-Acts*. SBL Monograph Series 20. Scholars Press, 1974.

**Talbot, *Healing in Byzantium*.** Talbot, Alice-Mary M. *Faith Healing in Late Byzantium: The Posthumous Miracles of the Patriarch Athanasios I of Constantinople by Theoktistos the Stoudite*. The Archbishop Iakovos Library of Ecclesiastical and Historical Sources 8. Hellenic College Press, 1983.

**Talbot, *Universe*.** Talbot, Michael. *The Holographic Universe*. HarperCollins, 1991.

**Talbot, "Vision."** Talbot, Susan Gabriel. "Dream/Vision: A Language of the Soul." In *Revival, Renewal, and the Holy Spirit*, edited by Dyfed Wyn Roberts, 274–82. SEHT. Wipf & Stock, 2009.

**Tallman, *Shakarian*.** Tallman, Matthew W. *Demos Shakarian: The Life, Legacy, and Vision of a Full Gospel Business Man*. Asbury Theological Seminary Series in World Christian Revitalization Movements in Pentecostal/Charismatic Studies 2. Emeth, 2010.

**Tang, "Yellers."** Tang, Edmond. "'Yellers' and Healers—Pentecostalism and the Study of Grassroots Christianity in China." In Anderson and Tang, *Asian and Pentecostal*, 467–86.

**Tannehill, *Unity*.** Tannehill, Robert C. *The Narrative Unity of Luke-Acts: A Literary Interpretation*. 2 vols. Fortress, 1990.

**Tari, *Breeze*.** Tari, Mel and Nona. *The Gentle Breeze of Jesus*. New Leaf Press, 1974.

**Tari, *Wind*.** Tari, Mel, with Cliff Dudley. *Like a Mighty Wind*. Creation House, 1971.

**Tarr, *Foolishness*.** Tarr, Del. *The Foolishness of God: A Linguist Looks at the Mystery of Tongues*. Access, 2010.

**Taves, *Fits*.** Taves, Ann. *Fits, Trances, and Visions: Experiencing Religion and Explaining Experience from Wesley to James*. Princeton University Press, 1999.

**Taylor and Taylor, *Early Years*.** Taylor, Frederick Howard, and Mary Geraldine Taylor. *Hudson Taylor in Early Years: The Growth of a Soul*. Morgan & Scott; China Inland Mission, 1943.

**Taylor and Taylor, *Secret*.** Taylor, Howard, and Geraldine Taylor. *Hudson Taylor's Spiritual Secret*. Moody, 2009.

**Ten Boom, *Hiding Place*.** Ten Boom, Corrie, with John and Elizabeth Sherrill. *The Hiding Place*. Bantam, 1974.

**Ten Boom, *Tramp*.** Ten Boom, Corrie, with Jamie Buckingham. *Tramp for the Lord*. Fleming H. Revell, 1974.

**Tennant, *Miracle*.** Tennant, F. R. *Miracle and Its Philosophical Presuppositions: Three Lectures Delivered in the University of London 1924*. Cambridge University Press, 1925.

**Teresa of Avila, *Castle*.** Teresa of Avila. *The Interior Castle: A New Translation and Introduction by Mirabai Starr*. Berkley, 2003.

**Teresa of Avila, *Castle or Mansions*.** Teresa of Avila. *The Interior Castle or The Mansions*. Translated by Benedictines of Stanbrook. 2nd ed. Benziger Brothers, 1906.

**Teter, *Blood Libel*.** Teter, Magda. *Blood Libel: On the Trail of an Antisemitic Myth*. Harvard University Press, 2020.

**Theissen, *Aspects*.** Theissen, Gerd. *Psychological Aspects of Pauline Theology*. T&T Clark, 1987.

**Thigpen, "Power."** Thigpen, Paul. "Did the Power of the Spirit Ever Leave the Church?" *Charisma*, September 1992, 20–29.

**Thiselton, *Corinthians*.** Thiselton, Anthony C. *The First Epistle to the Corinthians: A Commentary on the Greek Text*. Eerdmans; Paternoster, 2000.

**Thiselton, "Interpretation."** Thiselton, Anthony C. "The 'Interpretation' of Tongues: A New Suggestion in the Light of Greek Usage in Philo and Josephus." *Journal of Theological Studies* 30, no. 1 (1979): 15–36.

**Thiselton, *Spirit*.** Thiselton, Anthony C. *The Holy Spirit—In Biblical Teaching, Through the Centuries, and Today*. Eerdmans, 2013.

**Thollander, *Mathews*.** Thollander, Jon. *He Saw a Man Named Mathews: A Brief Testimony of Thomas and Mary Mathews, Pioneer Missionaries to Rajasthan*. Native Missionary Movement, Cross & Crown, 2000.

**Thomas, *Religion*.** Thomas, Keith. *Religion and the Decline of Magic*. Scribner, 1971.

**Thomas, "Tongues."** Thomas, R. L. "Tongues . . . Will Cease." *Journal of the Evangelical Theological Society* 17 (1974): 81–89.

**Thomas, *Works*.** Thomas, Mathew J. *Paul's "Works of the Law" in the Perspective of Second-Century Reception*. InterVarsity, 2020.

**Thompson, *Sure Ground*.** Thompson, Mark D. *A Sure Ground on Which to Stand: The Relation of Authority and Interpretive Method in Luther's Approach to Scripture*. Wipf & Stock, 2007.

**Thrall, *First and Second Corinthians*.** Thrall, Margaret E. *The First and Second Letters of Paul to the Corinthians*. Cambridge Bible Commentary. Cambridge University Press, 1965.

**Tillotson, *Works*.** Tillotson, John. *The Works of the Most Reverend Dr. John Tillotson, Late Lord Archbishop of Canterbury Containing Fifty-Four Sermons and Discourses on Several Occasions. Together with the Rule of Faith, Being All That Were Published by His Grace Himself, and Now Collected into One Volume. To Which Is Added, an Alphabetical Table of the Principal Matters*. 4th ed. B. Aylmer and W. Rogers, 1704.

**Tomkins, *History*.** Tomkins, Stephen. *A Short History of Christianity*. Eerdmans, 2005.

**Tomkins, *Wesley*.** Tomkins, Stephen. *John Wesley: A Biography*. Eerdmans, 2003.

**Tomlinson, "Magic Methodists."** Tomlinson, John W. B. "The Magic Methodists and Their Influence on the Early Primitive Methodist Movement." In Cooper and Gregory, *Signs*, 389–99.

**Toon, "Waldenses."** Toon, Peter. "Waldenses." In Douglas, *Dictionary of Church*, 1025–26.

**Torrey, *God Used Moody*.** Torrey, R. A. *Why God Used D. L. Moody*. Fleming H. Revell, 1923.

**Toussain, *Synopsis*.** Toussain, Daniel. *Synopsis Doctrinae Apostoli Pauli de Iustificatione ex Primis Capitibus Epistolae ad Romanos Desumpta, et certis Thesibus comprehensa*. Heidelberg, 1588.

**Toussaint, "Tongues."** Toussaint, Stanley D. "First Corinthians Thirteen and the Tongues Question." *Bibliotheca Sacra* 120, no. 480 (1963): 311–16.

**Touwaide, "Disease."** Touwaide, Alain. "Disease." In *Brill's New Pauly: Encyclopaedia of the Ancient World*, edited by Hubert Cancik and Helmuth Schneider, 4:543–54. 20 vols. English ed. Christine F. Salazar. Brill, 2010.

**Trousdale, *Movements*.** Trousdale, Jerry. *Miraculous Movements. How Hundreds of Thousands of Muslims Are Falling in Love with Jesus*. Thomas Nelson, 2012.

**Tsivoery, "History."** Tsivoery, Zakaria. "The History of the Ankaramalaza Revival (1941–1970)." In *Nenilava, Prophetess of Madagascar: Her Life and the Ongoing Revival She Inspired*, edited by James B. Vigen and Sarah Hinlicky Wilson, 6–71. Pickwick, 2021.

**Tucker, *Jerusalem*.** Tucker, Ruth. *From Jerusalem to Irian Jaya: A Biographical History of Christian Missions*. Zondervan, 1983.

**Turaki, "Missiology."** Turaki, Yusufu. "Evangelical Missiology from Africa: Strengths and Weaknesses." In *Global Missiology for the 21st Century: The Iguassu Dialogue*, edited by William D. Taylor, 271–83. Baker Academic, 2000.

**Turner, *Gifts*.** Turner, Max. *The Holy Spirit and Spiritual Gifts in the New Testament Church and Today*. Rev. ed. Hendrickson, 1998.

**Turner, "Luke and Spirit."** Turner, M. M. B. "Luke and the Spirit: Studies in the Significance of Receiving the Spirit in Luke-Acts." PhD diss., Cambridge University, 1980.

**Turner, "Spiritual Gifts."** Turner, M. M. B. "Spiritual Gifts Then and Now." *Vox Evangelica* 15 (1985): 7–63.

**Tuttle, "Wesley and Gifts."** Tuttle, Robert G., Jr. "John Wesley: The Gifts of the Holy Spirit." *Good News*, May 1996, 18.

**Twelftree, "Ministry and Miraculous."** Twelftree, Graham H. "Paul's Ministry and the Miraculous." In Graves, *Kingdom Case*, 131–46.

**Twelftree, *Miracle Worker.*** Twelftree, Graham H. *Jesus the Miracle Worker: A Historical and Theological Study*. InterVarsity, 1999.

**Twelftree, *Name.*** Twelftree, Graham H. *In the Name of Jesus: Exorcism Among Early Christians*. Baker Academic, 2007.

**Underhill, *Jacopone.*** Underhill, Evelyn. *Jacopone da Todi, Poet and Mystic, 1228–1306: A Spiritual Biography*. Translated by Theodore Beck. E. P. Dutton, 1919.

**Urbach, *Sages.*** Urbach, Ephraim E. *The Sages: Their Concepts and Beliefs*. Translated by Israel Abrahams. 2 vols. 2nd ed. Magnes Press, Hebrew University, 1979.

**Usry and Keener, *Religion.*** Usry, Glenn J., and Craig S. Keener. *Black Man's Religion: Can Christianity be Afrocentric?* InterVarsity, 1996.

**Van Buskirk, *Healing.*** Van Buskirk, James Dale. *Religion, Healing, and Health*. Macmillan, 1953.

**Van der Breggen, "Miracle Reports."** Van der Breggen, Hendrik. "Miracle Reports, Moral Philosophy, and Contemporary Science." PhD diss., University of Waterloo, 2004.

**Van der Horst, "Parallels to Acts."** Van der Horst, Pieter W. "Hellenistic Parallels to the Acts of the Apostles." *Journal for the Study of the New Testament* 8, no. 25 (1985): 49–60.

**Vander Stelt, *Philosophy and Scripture.*** Vander Stelt, John C. *Philosophy and Scripture: A Study in Old Princeton and Westminster Theology*. Mack, 1978.

**Van Dijk, "Miracles."** Van Dijk, Mathilde. "Miracles and Visions in *Devotio Moderna* Biographies." In Cooper and Gregory, *Signs*, 239–48.

**Van Dijk, "Technologies."** Van Dijk, Rijk. "Time and Transcultural Technologies of the Self in the Ghanaian Pentecostal Diaspora." In *Between Babel and Pentecost: Transnational Pentecostalism in Africa and Latin America*, edited by André Corten and Ruth Marshall-Fratani, 216–34. Indiana University Press, 2001.

**Venter, *Healing.*** Venter, Alexander F. *Doing Healing: How to Minister God's Kingdom in the Power of the Spirit*. Vineyard International, 2008.

**Venter, *Reconciliation.*** Venter, Alexander. *Doing Reconciliation: Racism, Reconciliation, and Transformation in the Church and World*. Vineyard International, 2004.

**Vermes, *Jesus the Jew.*** Vermes, Geza. *Jesus the Jew: A Historian's Reading of the Gospels*. Fortress, 1973.

**Verres, *Luther.*** Verres, J. *Luther: An Historical Portrait*. Burns & Oates, 1884.

**Vigen, "Interpretation."** Vigen, James B. "Interpretation, Analysis, and Appreciation of Nenilava and Her Movement." In *Nenilava, Prophetess of Madagascar: Her Life and the Ongoing Revival She Inspired*, edited by James B. Vigen and Sarah Hinlicky Wilson, 83–113. Pickwick, 2021.

**Vineyard USA, "History."** Vineyard USA. "History & Legacy." Accessed September 22, 2024. https://vineyardusa.org/about/history/.

**Vivier, "Glossolalia."** Vivier, Lincoln Morse Van Eetveldt. "Glossolalia." PhD diss., University of Witwatersand, 1960.

**Voelz, *Mark 8:27–16:20*.** Voelz, James W., with Christopher W. Mitchell. *Mark 8:27–16:20*. ConC. Concordia, 2019.

**Voice of Martyrs, *Hearts of Fire 2*.** Voice of the Martyrs, *Hearts of Fire 2: Twelve Inspiring Stories of Costly Faith from Today's Persecuted Christians*. VOM Books, 2023.

**Vos, *Teaching*.** Vos, Geerhardus. *The Teaching of Jesus Concerning the Kingdom of God and the Church*. Eerdmans, 1951; Presbyterian and Reformed, 1972. Originally published in 1903.

**"Vox Inauditae."** "Vox Inauditae Linguae: The Language and Life of St. Hildegard Von Bingen." *Art Review PSU* (blog), posted by amk7977, September 20, 2023. Accessed November 17, 2024. https://sites.psu.edu/artreviewpsu/2023/09/20/vox-inauditae-linguae-the-language-and-life-of-st-hildegard-von-bingen/.

**Wacker, *Heaven*.** Wacker, Grant. *Heaven Below: Early Pentecostals and American Culture*. Harvard University Press, 2001.

**Wagner, "Laughing."** Wagner, Benjamin. "Laughing and Shouting in Revivals." In McClymond, *Revivals*, 1:241–42.

**Wagner, "Manifestations."** Wagner, Benjamin. "Bodily Manifestations in Revivals." In McClymond, *Revivals*, 1:55–58.

**Wagner, "Perspective."** Wagner, C. Peter. "A Church Growth Perspective on Pentecostal Missions." In Dempster, Klaus, and Petersen, *Called and Empowered*, 265–84.

**Wagner, "Wonders."** Wagner, Mark. "Signs and Wonders." In *Evangelical Dictionary of World Missions*, edited by A. Scott Moreau, 875–76. Baker Books, 2000.

**Währisch-Oblau, "Healing in Migrant Churches."** Währisch-Oblau, Claudia. "Material Salvation: Healing, Deliverance, and 'Breakthrough' in African Migrant Churches in Germany." In Brown, *Global*, 61–80.

**Währisch-Oblau, "Make Healthy."** Währisch-Oblau, Claudia. "God Can Make Us Healthy Through and Through: On Prayers for the Sick and the Interpretation of Healing Experiences in Christian Churches in China and African Immigrant Congregations in Germany." *International Review of Mission* 90, nos. 356/357 (January–April 2001): 87–102.

**Walchenbach, "Calvin."** Walchenbach, John Robert. "John Calvin as Biblical Commentator: An Investigation into Calvin's Use of John Chrysostom as an Exegetical Tutor." PhD diss., University of Pittsburgh, 1974.

**Waldron, *Continued*.** Waldron, Samuel E. *To Be Continued: Are the Miraculous Gifts for Today?* Calvary Press, 2005.

**Walker, "Cessation."** Walker, D. P. "The Cessation of Miracles." In *Hermeticism and the Renaissance: Intellectual History and the Occult in Early Modern Europe*, edited by I. Mekel and L. G. Debus, 111–24. Folger Books, 1988.

**Walker, *God in ICU.*** Walker, Dave. *God in the ICU: The Inspirational Biography of a Praying Doctor.* Tricycle, 2011.

**Walker, *Unclean Spirits.*** Walker, D. P. *Unclean Spirits: Possession and Exorcism in France and England in the Late Sixteenth and Early Seventeenth Centuries.* Scholar Press, 1981.

**Wallace, *Who's Afraid.*** Wallace, Daniel B., et al., eds. *Who's Afraid of the Holy Spirit?* Biblical Studies, 2005.

**Walls, *Movement.*** Walls, Andrew F. *The Missionary Movement in Christian History: Studies in the Transmission of Faith.* Orbis Books, 1996.

**Walsh, "Santidad."** Walsh, Arlene Sánchez. "Santidad, Salvación, Sanidad, Liberación: The Word of Faith Movement Among Twenty-First Century Latina/o Pentecostals." In Brown, *Global*, 151–67.

**Walsham, "Miracles."** Walsham, Alexandra. "Miracles in Post-Reformation England." In Cooper and Gregory, *Signs*, 273–306.

**Walvoord, *Holy Spirit.*** Walvoord, John F. *The Holy Spirit.* Dunham, 1958.

**Warburton, *Doctrine of Grace.*** Warburton, William. *The Doctrine of Grace, or, The Office and Operations of the Holy Spirit Vindicated from the Insults of Infidelity and the Abuses of Fanaticism.* A. Millar and J. and R. Tonson, 1762.

**Ward, "Argument."** Ward, Horace. "The Anti-Pentecostal Argument." In Graves, *Strangers*, 75–92.

**Ward, "Monks."** Ward, Benedicta. "Monks and Miracle." In *Miracles in Jewish and Christian Antiquity: Imagining Truth*, edited by John C. Cavadini, 127–37. NDST 3. University of Notre Dame Press, 1999.

**Warfield, *Counterfeit Miracles.*** Warfield, B. B. *Counterfeit Miracles.* Charles Scribner's Sons, 1918. Reprint, Banner of Truth Trust, 1972.

**Warfield, *Perfectionism.*** Warfield, Benjamin. *Perfectionism.* Oxford University Press, 1931. Reprint, Baker, 1981.

**Warfield, "Question."** Warfield, B. B. "The Question of Miracles." In *Selected Shorter Writings*, edited by John E. Meeter, 2:167–204. 2 vols. Presbyterian and Reformed, 1973. Originally published in *The Bible Student* 7 (March 1903): 121–26; (April 1903): 193–97; (May 1903): 243–50; (June 1903): 314–20.

**Warford, "Calvin Speaks."** Warford, Quent. "Calvin Speaks Unknown Tongue." *The Paper: Student Paper of Gordon-Conwell Theological Seminary* 1, no. 6 (March 24, 1975): 6.

**Warner, *Evangelist.*** Warner, Wayne E. *The Woman Evangelist: The Life and Times of Charismatic Evangelist Maria B. Woodworth-Etter.* Studies in Evangelicalism 8. Scarecrow, 1986.

**Warner, *Kuhlman.*** Warner, Wayne E. *Kathryn Kuhlman: The Woman Behind the Miracles.* Servant, 1993.

**Watters, *Peter Cartwright*.** Watters, Philip Melancthon. *Peter Cartwright*. Eaton & Mains, 1910.

**Waugh, *Fires*.** Waugh, Geoff. *Revival Fires*. Global Awakening. 2009.

**Weaver, *Baptists and the Spirit*.** Weaver, C. Douglas. *Baptists and the Holy Spirit: The Contested History with Holiness-Pentecostal-Charismatic Movements*. Baylor University Press, 2019.

**Webber, "Mystics."** Webber, Robert E., ed. "Mystics: Singers of a New Song." *The Complete Library of Christian Worship*. https://www.worshiplibrary.com/library/music-and-the-arts-in-christian-worship/music-in-worship/a-brief-history-of-jubilation/mystics-singers-of-a-new-song/.

**Webster, "Salvation."** Webster, Robert. "Seeing Salvation: The Place of Dreams and Visions in John Wesley's *Arminian Magazine*." In Cooper and Gregory, *Signs*, 376–88.

**Webster, "Terrors."** Webster, Robert. "'Those Distracting Terrors of the Enemy': Demonic Possession and Exorcism in the Thought of John Wesley." *Bulletin of the John Rylands Library* 85, no. 2 (2003): 373–85.

**Wenham, *Numbers*.** Wenham, Gordon J. *Numbers: An Introduction and Commentary*. TOTC. InterVarsity, 1981.

**Werntz, "Scandals."** Werntz, Myles. "Church Scandals Don't Negate God's Faithfulness." *Christianity Today*, January 6, 2026. Accessed January 11, 2026. https://www.christianitytoday.com/2026/01/church-scandals-dont-negate-gods-faithfulness/.

**Wesley, *Explanatory Notes*.** Wesley, John. *Explanatory Notes upon the New Testament*. 2nd ed. W. Bowyer, 1757.

**Wesley, *Journal (1773–1790)*.** Wesley, John. *Works of John Wesley*. Vol. 4, *Journal from September 13, 1773, to October 24, 1790*. 1872. Reprint, Zondervan, n.d.

**Wesley, *Journal* (Culley).** Wesley, John. *The Journal of the Rev. John Wesley*. Vol. 4. Robert Culley, 1909.

**Wesley, *Letter to Bishop of Gloucester*.** Wesley, John. *A Letter to the Right Reverend the Lord Bishop of Gloucester: Occasioned by His Tract, on the Office and Operations of the Holy Spirit*. William Pine, 1763.

**Wesley, "Letter to Middleton."** Wesley, John. "A Letter to the Rev. Dr. Conyers Middleton." In *The Works of the Reverend John Wesley*, vol. 5. Edited by John Emory. B. Waugh and T. Mason, 1835.

**Wesley, "Middleton."** Wesley, John. "To Dr. Conyers Middleton" (January 4, 1749). In *The Letters of John Wesley*. Wesley Center Online. Accessed September 1, 2018. http://wesley.nnu.edu/john-wesley/the-letters-of-john-wesley/wesleys-letters-1749/.

**Wesley, *Miscellaneous*.** Wesley, John. *The Works of the Rev. John Wesley, AM*. Vol. 6, *Miscellaneous*. Carlton & Porter, 1831.

**Wesley, *Works*.** Wesley, John. *The Works of the Rev. John Wesley*. Vols. 1, 4, 5, 7, 10, 13. John Mason; J. & J. Harper; Carlton and Porter, 1826–1941.

**Wesley, *Works* (1872 ed.).** Wesley, John. *The Works of John Wesley*. Edited by Thomas Jackson. 3rd ed. 14 Vols. London, 1872. Reprint, Baker, 1996.

**Wesley, *Works* (AM).** Wesley, John. *The Works of the Reverend John Wesley, AM*. Vols. 2, 3, 5, 7. Waugh and Mason, 1831–1835.

**Westmeier, *Pentecostalism*.** Westmeier, Karl-Wilhelm. *Protestant Pentecostalism in Latin America: A Study in the Dynamics of Missions*. Fairleigh Dickinson University Press, 1999.

**White, "Calling."** White, Gayle. "Colorblind Calling." *Atlanta Journal & Constitution*, November 3, 1991. M1, 4.

**White, "Revival."** White, Eryn. "Revival and Renewal Amongst the Eighteenth-Century Welsh Methodists." In *Revival, Renewal, and the Holy Spirit*, edited by Dyfed Wyn Roberts, 1–12. SEHT. Wipf & Stock, 2009.

**White, *Spirit*.** White, John. *When the Spirit Comes with Power: Signs and Wonders Among God's People*. InterVarsity, 1988.

**Whitefield, *Journals*.** Whitefield, George. *George Whitefield's Journals*. Sovereign Grace, 2000.

**Whitefield, *Works*.** George Whitefield, *The Works of the Reverend George Whitefield, M.A. Containing All His Sermons and Tracts Which Have Been Already Published: With a Select Collection of Letters . . . Also Some Other Pieces on Important Subjects, Never Before Printed; . . . To Which Is Prefixed, an Account of His Life, Compiled from His Original Papers*. Edward and Charles Dilly, 1771.

**Wigger, *Heaven*.** Wigger, John H. *Taking Heaven by Storm: Methodism and the Rise of Popular Christianity in America*. University of Illinois Press, 1998.

**Wigger, *Saint*.** Wigger, John. *American Saint: Francis Asbury and the Methodists*. Oxford University Press, 2009.

**Wiggs, "Cessationism."** Wiggs, Evans. "Cessationism: An Arid Theology." *Evan Wiggs* (blog). Accessed October 9, 2024. http://www.evanwiggs.com/articles/Cessationism%20an%20Arid%20Theology.htm.

**Wiggs, *Engines*.** Wiggs, Evan. *Engines of Heaven: Secrets of the Supernatural Life*. Xlibris, 2013.

**Wikipedia, "Boy Scouts."** Wikipedia. "Boy Scouts of America Sex Abuse Cases." Accessed December 13, 2025. https://en.wikipedia.org/wiki/Boy_Scouts_of_America_sex_abuse_cases.

**Wikipedia, "Convoy of Hope."** Wikipedia. "Convoy of Hope." Accessed February 20, 2025. https://en.wikipedia.org/wiki/Convoy_of_Hope.

**Wilkerson, *Cross*.** Wilkerson, David, with John Sherrill and Elizabeth Sherrill. *The Cross and the Switchblade*. Pyramid, 1962.

**Wilkinson, *Healing*.** Wilkinson, John. *The Bible and Healing: A Medical and Theological Commentary*. Handsel; Eerdmans, 1998.

**Williams, "Following Christ's Example."** Williams, Don. "Following Christ's Example: A Biblical View of Discipleship." In Graves, *Kingdom Case*, 59–80.

**Williams, "Germanicus."** Williams, Kathryn F. "Tacitus' Germanicus and the Principate." *Latomus* 68, no. 1 (2009): 117–30.

**Williams, "Glossolalia as Phenomenon."** Williams, Cyril G. "Glossolalia as a Religious Phenomenon: 'Tongues' at Corinth and Pentecost." *Religion* 5, no. 1 (1975): 16–32.

**Williams, *Justin Martyr*.** Williams, A. Lukyn, ed. and trans. *Justin Martyr: The Dialogue with Trypho*. Translations of Christian Literature. Macmillan, 1930.

**Williams, "Person."** Williams, J. R., ed. "The Person and Work of the Holy Spirit with Special Reference to "the Baptism of the Holy Spirit." Minutes of the General Assembly of the Presbyterian Church, USA, 1971.

**Williams, *Radical Reformation*.** Williams, George Huntston. *The Radical Reformation*. Westminster, 1962.

**Williams, *Renewal Theology*.** Williams, J. Rodman. *Renewal Theology*. 3 vols. Zondervan, 1990.

**Williams, *Signs*.** Williams, Don. *Signs, Wonders, and the Kingdom of God: A Biblical Guide for the Reluctant Skeptic*. Servant, 1989.

**Williams and Waldvogel, "History."** Williams, George H., and Edith Waldvogel. "A History of Speaking in Tongues and Related Gifts." In *The Charismatic Movement*, edited by Michael P. Hamilton, 61–113. Eerdmans, 1975.

**Wilson, *Armageddon Now*.** Wilson, Dwight. *Armageddon Now! The Premillenarian Response to Russia and Israel Since 1917*. Baker, 1977.

**Wilson, "Ecstasy."** Wilson, Robert R. "Prophecy and Ecstasy: A Reexamination." *Journal of Biblical Literature* 98, no. 3 (1979): 321–37.

**Wilson, "Miracle Events."** Wilson, William P. "How Religious or Spiritual Miracle Events Happen Today." In Ellens, *Miracles*, 1:264–79.

**Wilson, "Miracles."** Wilson, John. "The Miracles of the Gospels." *American Journal of Theology* 9 (1905): 10–33.

**Wilson, "Missional Church."** Wilson, S. Glenn. "John Calvin and the Missional Church: Encouragement for Partnering in the *Mission Dei*." DMin diss., University of Dubuque Theological Seminary, 2010.

**Wilson, "Seeing."** Wilson, C. Roderick. "Seeing They See Not." In *Being Changed: The Anthropology of Extraordinary Experience*, edited by David Young and Jean-Guy Goulet, 197–208. Broadview, 1994.

**Wilson, *Spirit and Sacrament*.** Wilson, Andrew. *Spirit and Sacrament: An Invitation to Eucharistic Worship*. Zondervan, 2018.

**Wimber, *Power Evangelism*.** Wimber, John, with Kevin Springer. *Power Evangelism*. Harper & Row, 1986.

**Winger, "Going Public."** Winger, Mike. "Bethel Wouldn't Stop Him So His Son and Victims Are Going Public." Posted January 12, 2026, by Mike Winger, YouTube.

Accessed January 13, 2026. https://www.youtube.com/watch?v=n27WA81T_Js&t=185s.

**Winger, "Insider."** Winger, Mike. "Bethel Insider Asks Accountability for False Prophet: Will Bethel Respond?" Posted June 26, 2025, by Mike Winger, YouTube. Accessed February 4, 2026. https://www.youtube.com/watch?v=9577FAA2FGA&t=10586s.

**Witherington, *Acts*.** Witherington, Ben, III. *The Acts of the Apostles: A Socio-Rhetorical Commentary*. Eerdmans, 1998.

**Witherington, *Conflict*.** Witherington, Ben, III. *Conflict and Community in Corinth: A Socio-Rhetorical Commentary on 1 and 2 Corinthians*. Eerdmans, 1995.

**Witherington, *2 Corinthians*.** Witherington, Ben, III. *2 Corinthians*. Word & Spirit Commentary. Baker Academic, 2025.

**Wiyono, "Timor Revival."** Wiyono, Gani. "Timor Revival: A Historical Study of the Great Twentieth-Century Revival in Indonesia." *Asian Journal of Pentecostal Studies* 4, no. 2 (2001): 269–93.

**Wolffe, *Expansion*.** Wolffe, John. *The Expansion of Evangelicalism: The Age of Wilberforce, More, Chalmers and Finney*. InterVarsity, 2007.

**Wolterstorff, "Reason."** Wolterstorff, Nicholas. "Is Reason Enough?" *Reformed Journal* 31 (April 1981): 20–24.

**Womack, "Healing."** Womack, David A. "Divine Healing in the Post-Apostolic Church." In Graves, *Strangers*, 391–97.

**Wood, *Meaning*.** Wood, Laurence W. *The Meaning of Pentecost in Early Methodism: Rediscovering John Fletcher as John Wesley's Vindicator and Designated Successor*. Scarecrow, 2002.

**Wood, *Pentecost*.** Wood, Laurence W. *Pentecost & Sanctification in the Writings of John Wesley and Charles Wesley with a Proposal for Today*. Emeth, 2018.

**Woodall, *Price*.** Woodall, Ann M. *What Price the Poor? William Booth, Karl Marx and the London Residuum*. Routledge, 2005.

**Woodard, *Faith*.** Woodard, Christopher. *A Doctor's Faith Holds Fast*. Max Parrish, 1955.

**Woodworth-Etter, *Miracles*.** Woodworth-Etter, Maria. *Miracles, Signs, and Wonders Wrought in the Life and Ministry of Mrs. Woodworth-Etter from 1844–1916*. Apostolic, 1984.

**Woolley, *Exorcism*.** Woolley, Reginald Maxwell. *Exorcism and the Healing of the Sick*. SPCK, for the Church Historical Society, 1932.

**Worthen, *Apostles*.** Worthen, Molly. *Apostles of Reason: The Crisis of Authority in American Evangelicalism*. Oxford University Press, 2014.

**Worthen, "Prove."** Worthen, Molly. "How Would You Prove That God Performed a Miracle?" *New York Times*, December 24, 2022.

**Worthen, *Spellbound*.** Worthen, Molly. *Spellbound: How Charisma Shaped American History from the Puritans to Donald Trump*. Forum Books, 2025.

**Wright, "Inscription."** Wright, Brian J. "The First-Century Inscription of Quintus Sulpicius Maximus: An Initial Catalog of Lexical Parallels with the New Testament." *Bulletin for Biblical Research* 27, no. 1 (2017): 53–63.

**Wright, "Miracles."** Wright, T. H. "Miracles." In *Dictionary of Christ and the Gospels*, edited by James Hastings, 2:186–91. 2 vols. Charles Scribner's Sons, 1906–8.

**Wyckoff, Pneuma.** Wyckoff, John W. *Pneuma and Logos: The Role of the Spirit in Biblical Hermeneutics*. Wipf & Stock, 2010.

**Xhemajli, *Supernatural*.** Xhemajli, Rimi. *The Supernatural and the Circuit Riders: The Rise of Early American Methodism*. Pickwick, 2021.

**Yamamori and Chan, *Witnesses*.** Yamamori, Tetsunao, and Kim-kwong Chan. *Witnesses to Power: Stories of God's Quiet Work in a Changing China*. Paternoster, 2000.

**Yeomans, *Healing*.** Yeomans, Lilian B. *Healing from Heaven*. Gospel, 1935.

**Yong, "Independent Pentecostalism."** Yong, Jeong Jae. "Filipino Independent Pentecostalism and Biblical Transformation." In Anderson and Tang, *Asian and Pentecostal*, 385–407.

**Yong, *Spirit Poured*.** Yong, Amos. *The Spirit Poured Out on All Flesh: Pentecostalism and the Possibility of Global Theology*. Baker Academic, 2005.

**Yonge, *Cameos*.** Yonge, Charlotte Mary. *Cameos from English History: Reformation Times*. Vol 4. Macmillan, 1886.

**Young, "Autobiography."** Young, James Louis. "Autobiography of James Louis Young." Unpublished paper in author's possession. Written 1956.

**Young, "Miracles in History."** Young, William. "Miracles in Church History." *Churchman* 102, no. 2 (1988): 102–21.

**Ytterbrink, *Gospel*.** Ytterbrink, Maria. *The Third Gospel for the First Time: Luke Within the Context of Ancient Biography*. Lund University—Centrum för teologi och religionsvetenskap, 2004.

**Yun, *Heavenly Man*.** Yun, Brother, with Paul Hattaway. *The Heavenly Man: The Remarkable True Story of Chinese Christian Brother Yun*. Monarch, 2002.

**Yung, "Integrity."** Yung, Hwa. "The Integrity of Mission in the Light of the Gospel: Bearing the Witness of the Spirit." *Mission Studies* 24 (2007): 169–88.

**Yung, "Pentecostalism."** Yung, Hwa. "Pentecostalism and the Asian Church." In Anderson and Tang, *Asian and Pentecostal*, 37–57.

**Yung, *Quest*.** Yung, Hwa. *Mangoes or Bananas? The Quest for an Authentic Asian Christian Theology*. Regnum Studies in Mission. Regnum, 1997.

**Zagrans, *Miracles*.** Zagrans, Maura Poston. *Miracles Every Day: The Story of One Physician's Inspiring Faith and the Healing Power of Prayer*. Doubleday, 2010.

**Zerhusen, "Judean *Diglossia* in Acts 2?"** Zerhusen, Bob. "An Overlooked Judean *Diglossia* in Acts 2?" *BTB* 25, no. 3 (1995): 118–30.

**Zerhusen, "Tongues in 1 Cor. 14."** Zerhusen, Bob. "The Problem Tongues in 1 Cor. 14: A Reexamination." *Biblical Theology Bulletin* 27, no. 4 (1997): 139–52.

**Zhaoming, "Chinese Denominations."** Zhaoming, Deng. "Indigenous Chinese Pentecostal Denominations." In Anderson and Tang, *Asian and Pentecostal*, 437–66.

# Index of Subjects

# Index of Scripture and Other Ancient Sources

## Romans



## 1 Corinthians

## 2 Corinthians



## Galatians

## Greek, Latin, and Other Ancient Works